A New Companion to
Victorian Literature and Culture

Blackwell Companions to Literature and Culture

This series offers comprehensive, newly written surveys of key periods and movements and certain major authors, in English literary culture and history. Extensive volumes provide new perspectives and positions on contexts and on canonical and post-canonical texts, orientating the beginning student in new fields of study and providing the experienced undergraduate and new graduate with current and new directions, as pioneered and developed by leading scholars in the field.

Published Recently

A NEW COMPANION TO

VICTORIAN LITERATURE AND CULTURE

EDITED BY

HERBERT F. TUCKER

WILEY Blackwell

This edition first published 2014
© 2014 John Wiley & Sons, Ltd

Registered Office
John Wiley & Sons Ltd, The Atrium, Southern Gate, Chichester, West Sussex, PO19 8SQ, UK

Editorial Offices
350 Main Street, Malden, MA 02148-5020, USA
9600 Garsington Road, Oxford, OX4 2DQ, UK
The Atrium, Southern Gate, Chichester, West Sussex, PO19 8SQ, UK

For details of our global editorial offices, for customer services, and for information about how
to apply for permission to reuse the copyright material in this book please see our website at
www.wiley.com/wiley-blackwell.

Library of Congress Cataloging-in-Publication Data

A new companion to Victorian literature and culture / edited by Herbert F. Tucker.
      pages cm
  Includes bibliographical references and index.
  ISBN 978-1-118-62449-4 (cloth)
  1. English literature–19th century–History and criticism.   2. Literature and society–Great
Britain–History–19th century.   I. Tucker, Herbert F., editor of compilation.
  PR463.N39 2014
  820.9′008–dc23

                              2013038869

A catalogue record for this book is available from the British Library.

Cover image: William Dyce, *Pegwell Bay, Kent – a Recollection of October 5th 1858*, oil on canvas,
63×89 cm. Tate Britain, London. Photo © DeAgostini / SuperStock .
Cover design by Richard Boxall Design Associates

Set in 11/13 pt Garamond3LTStd by Toppan Best-set Premedia Limited
Printed and bound in Malaysia by Vivar Printing Sdn Bhd

1   2014

Contents

Notes on Contributors

Edward Adams is a Professor of English, and the departmental chair, at Washington and Lee University in Lexington, Virginia. His *Liberal Epic: The Victorian Practice of History from Gibbon to Churchill* (2011) won the Perkins Prize for best book from the International Society for the Study of Narrative. He is completing a study of epic narratives of the decline and fall of civilizations, empires, nations, and cities, centered on the histories and autobiographies of Gibbon, Ruskin, Henry Adams, and H. G. Wells.

James Eli Adams, Professor of English and Comparative Literature at Columbia University, is the author of *Dandies and Desert Saints: Styles of Victorian Masculinity* (1995) and *A History of Victorian Literature* (2009) and the co-editor, with Andrew Miller, of *Sexualities in Victorian Britain* (1996).

The late **Richard D. Altick** was Regents' Professor of English, Emeritus, at Ohio State University. His many books include *The English Common Reader: A Social History of the Mass Reading Public, 1800–1900* (1957), *The Shows of London* (1978), and most recently *"Punch": The Lively Youth of a British Institution, 1841–1851* (1997), and *A Little Bit of Luck: The Making of an Adventurous Scholar* (2002).

Stephen Arata is Professor of English at the University of Virginia. His published work, including *Fictions of Loss in the Victorian Fin de Siècle* (1996), focuses primarily on nineteenth- and early twentieth-century English literature. He is also co-editor of the forthcoming *Blackwell Companion to the English Novel* and a general co-editor of the ongoing *New Edinburgh Edition of the Collected Works of Robert Louis Stevenson*.

James Buzard teaches literature at MIT and is the author of two books, *The Beaten Track: European Tourism, Literature, and the Ways to "Culture," 1800–1918* (1993) and *Disorienting Fiction: The Autoethnographic Work of Nineteenth-Century British Novels*

(2005), as well as of numerous articles in journals and books. He has also co-edited the volume *Victorian Prism: Refractions of the Crystal Palace* (with Joseph A. Childers and Eileen Gillooly, 2007). He is currently writing a sequel to *Disorienting Fiction* and a book on Dickens.

Karen Chase is Linden Kent Memorial Professor of English at the University of Virginia. She is the author of *Eros and Psyche: The Representation of Personality in the Works of Charlotte Brontë, Charles Dickens, and George Eliot* (1984); *George Eliot's Middlemarch* (1991); *The Spectacle of Intimacy: A Public Life for the Victorian Family* (co-author Michael Levenson, 2000); and *The Victorians and Old Age* (2009). Her edition *Middlemarch in the Twenty-First Century* appeared in 2005.

Julie Codell is Professor of Art History at Arizona State University and affiliate faculty in English, Gender Studies, Film and Media, and Asian Studies. She wrote *The Victorian Artist* (2003, 2012); edited *Transculturation in British Art* (2012), *Power and Resistance: The Delhi Coronation Durbars* (2012), *The Political Economy of Art* (2008), *Imperial Co-Histories* (2003); and co-edited *Encounters in the Victorian Press* (with Laurel Brake, 2004), and *Orientalism Transposed* (with Diane Sachko Macleod, 1998; Japanese translation 2014).

Christina Crosby, Professor of English and Feminist, Gender, and Sexuality Studies at Wesleyan University, is the author of *The Ends of History: Victorians and "The Woman Question"* (1991) and of essays on other Victorian and feminist topics. Her current work explores the phenomenological complexity and representational impossibility of writing about neurological injury.

Alan Fischler is Professor of English at Le Moyne College in Syracuse, New York. He is the author of *Modified Rapture: Comedy in W. S. Gilbert's Savoy Operas* (1991), numerous articles on Gilbert and other Victorian theater folk, such as Dion Boucicault, J. R. Planché, Douglas Jerrold, and Madame Vestris, and studies of the seventeenth-century poets John Donne and Robert Herrick.

Antony H. Harrison's interests include textual editing, gender studies, critical theory, nineteenth-century English poetry, and the history of the book. His newest authored book is *The Cultural Production of Matthew Arnold* (2009). Scholarly editions include *The Letters of Christina Rossetti* (4 vols., 1997–2004)) and *The Correspondence of Dante Gabriel Rossetti* (completing co-editor vols. 7–9, 2008–10). He has also published *Victorian Poets and the Politics of Culture: Discourse and Ideology* (1990), and *Victorian Poets and Romantic Poems: Intertextuality and Ideology* (1998). His other books include studies of Christina Rossetti (1988) and A. C. Swinburne (1988); edited collections of essays on Christina Rossetti (with Mary Arseneau and Lorraine Janzen Kooistra,1999) and gender issues in Victorian poetry (with Beverly Taylor, 1992); and *A Companion to Victorian Poetry* (co-edited with Richard Cronin and Alison Chapman, 2002).

Ann Heilmann is Professor of English Literature at Cardiff University, UK. The author of *New Woman Fiction: Women Writing First-Wave Feminism* (2000) and *New Woman Strategies: Sarah Grand, Olive Schreiner and Mona Caird* (2004), she has co-authored *Neo-Victorianism* (2010) with Mark Llewellyn and is the editor, also with Llewellyn, of *The Collected Stories of George Moore* (2007). Further (co-)edited work includes three essay collections and four multi-volume anthology sets. She is the general editor of Routledge's History of Feminism and Pickering and Chatto's Gender and Genre series.

Thomas William Heyck is Emeritus Professor at Northwestern University, where as Charles Deering McCormick Professor he taught modern British and Irish history. His books on late-Victorian Anglo-Irish relations, Victorian intellectual life, and the general history of the peoples of the British Isles since 1688 include *The Transformation of Intellectual Life in Victorian England* (1982).

Linda K. Hughes, Addie Levy Professor of Literature at Texas Christian University in Fort Worth, Texas, specializes in Victorian literature and culture with special interests in historical media studies (illustrated poetry, periodicals, serial fiction), gender and women's studies, and transnationality. Most recently she authored the *Cambridge Introduction to Victorian Poetry* (2010) and, with Sharon M. Harris, co-edited *A Feminist Reader: Feminist Thought from Sappho to Satrapi* (4 vols., 2013). Earlier books include *The Manyfacèd Glass: Tennyson's Dramatic Monologues* (1987), *Graham R.: Rosamund Marriott Watson, Woman of Letters* (2005), and two studies co-authored with Michael C. Lund: *The Victorian Serial* (1991) and *Victorian Publishing and Mrs. Gaskell's Work* (1999).

Michael Hunt recently retired from Sheffield Hallam University, where he was a Senior Lecturer in Public Administration. His particular research interests are in the operation of the UK Freedom of Information Act, and he has jointly edited (with Richard A. Chapman) *Open Government in a Theoretical and Practical Context* (2006) and *Freedom of Information: Local Government and Accountability* (2010).

Gerhard Joseph is Professor of English at Lehman College and the Graduate Center, City University of New York. He is the author of *Tennysonian Love: The Strange Diagonal* (1969) and *Tennyson and the Text: The Weaver's Shuttle* (1992), along with numerous articles on nineteenth-century poetry and fiction.

Christine L. Krueger is Professor of English at Marquette University. She is author of *The Reader's Repentance: Women Preachers, Women Writers and Nineteenth-Century Social Discourse* (1992) and *Reading for the Law: British Literary History and Gender Advocacy* (2010). Contributing editor of *The Function of Victorian Culture at the Present Time* (2002) and *The Encyclopedia of British Writers: Nineteenth Century* (2003), she has also written on the historian Mary Anne Everett Green.

David E. Latané, Jr is Professor of English at Virginia Commonwealth University, where he teaches British literature from the late eighteenth century to the present;

from 1996 to 2010 he was a faculty member in the VCU Artists and Writers Workshops hosted at the Glasgow School of Art. He is the author of *Browning's* Sordello *and the Aesthetics of Difficulty* (1987) and *William Maginn and the British Press: A Critical Biography* (2013), as well as articles, reviews, and chapters on Robert Browning, Blake, Augusta Webster, Samuel Rogers, and a range of nineteenth-century periodicals. For a decade he served as chief editor of the *Victorians Institute Journal*, and he continues as North American editor of *Stand Magazine* (Leeds), and as a member of the Board of Directors of the Research Society for Victorian Periodicals.

Michael Levenson is William B. Christian Professor of English at the University of Virginia, where he is the founding director of the Institute of Humanities. His books include *A Genealogy of Modernism* (1984), *Modernism and the Fate of Individuality* (1990), *The Spectacle of Intimacy* (co-author Karen Chase, 2000), and *Modernism* (2011); and he has edited the *Cambridge Companion to Modernism* (2000, 2011).

Mark Llewellyn is John Anderson Research Professor in English at the University of Strathclyde, Glasgow. Together with Ann Heilmann he is the author of *Neo-Victorianism: The Victorians in the Twenty-first Century, 1999–2009* (2010). Co-edited work includes, with Dinah Birch, *Conflict and Difference in Nineteenth-Century Literature* (2010) and, with Heilmann, *Metafiction and Metahistory in Contemporary Women's Writing* (2007).

Teresa Mangum is a Professor in the Department of Gender, Women's, and Sexuality Studies at the University of Iowa, where she directs the Obermann Center for Advanced Studies. Her work on nineteenth-century British late life, animal and human relationships, and women's literature and culture appears in *The Cultural Politics of Ageing in the Nineteenth Century: Interdisciplinary Perspectives* (2013), *Teaching Nineteenth-Century Fiction* (2010), *Other Mothers* (2008), *Animals in the Age of Empire, 1800–1920* (2007), *Victorian Animal Dreams* (2007), and several journals. She is the author of *Married, Middlebrow, and Militant: Sarah Grand and the New Woman Novel* (1998), editor of the volume *A Cultural History of Women: The Age of Empire, 1800–1920* (2013), and co-editor of the University of Iowa book series Humanities and Public Life.

Joss Marsh is Emerita Associate Professor of Victorian Studies at Indiana University, Bloomington. She is the author of *Word Crimes: Blasphemy, Culture, and Literature in 19th-Century England* (1998), the forthcoming *Starring Charles Dickens*, and numerous essays on Dickens, Chaplin, the nineteenth-century novel and film, Victorian visual culture, celebrity, film stardom, and the magic lantern. With her husband and research/performance partner, film archivist and historian David Francis, OBE, she has founded and is building the new Kent Museum of the Moving Image (Kent-MOMI), UK, the doors of which they hope to open to researchers and the public in late 2014. Together, they are also plotting a book on the "Dickensian" late-Victorian multi-media celebrity George R. Sims. Joss Marsh occasionally submits to stage and radio discipline, and is probably the only female academic in the world to have played Scrooge, in drag, in a professional theatre.

Helena Michie is Agnes Cullen Arnold Professor in Humanities and Professor of English at Rice University. She is the author of *Victorian Honeymoons: Journeys to the Conjugal* (2006); *The Flesh Made Word: Female Figures and Women's Bodies* (1987); *Sororophobia: Differences among Women in Literature and Culture* (1991); and co-author, with Naomi R. Cahn, of *Confinements: Fertility and Infertility in Contemporary United States Culture* (1997). She has published articles on feminist theory and on Victorian literature and is co-editor, with Ronald Thomas, of the essay collection *Nineteenth-Century Geographies: The Transformation of Space from the Victorian Age to the American Century* (2002). She and Robyn Warhol are finishing a book on Sir George Scharf, the first director of the National Portrait Gallery, London.

James Mussell is Associate Professor in Victorian Literature at the University of Leeds. He is the author of *Science, Time and Space in the Late Nineteenth-Century Periodical Press* (2007) and *The Nineteenth-Century Press in the Digital Age* (2012). He is one of the editors of the *Nineteenth-Century Serials Edition* (2008) and of *W. T. Stead: Newspaper Revolutionary* (2012). He also edits the Digital Forum in the *Journal of Victorian Culture*.

Claudia Nelson is a Professor of English at Texas A&M University. She is the author of *Boys Will Be Girls: The Feminine Ethic and British Children's Fiction* (1991); *Invisible Men: Fatherhood in Victorian Periodicals* (1995); *Little Strangers: Portrayals of Adoption and Foster Care in America* (2003); *Family Ties in Victorian England* (2007); and *Precocious Children and Childish Adults: Age Inversion in Victorian Literature* (2012). She has prepared critical editions of E. Nesbit's *The Story of the Treasure Seekers* and *The Wouldbegoods* (2013) and of source documents about the British family in the long nineteenth century (2013); and she has coedited four collections of essays.

Timothy Peltason teaches at Wellesley College, where he has served as Chair of the English department and Director of the Newhouse Center for the Humanities. He has written essays about Victorian poetry and prose, about Shakespeare, and about the state of the profession. His books include *Reading "In Memoriam"* (1985) and an edition of Arnold's poetry (1994). He has just completed an essay on Huckleberry Finn, and he is now at work on *Oscar in Earnest*, a study of the biographical and cultural significance of Wilde's essential play.

Simon Petch taught in the Department of English at the University of Sydney from 1973 until 2005. His publications include a book on Philip Larkin's poetry (1981), a co-edited collection of essays on the poetry of Robert Browning (1988), and several articles on the legal culture of Victorian England in relation to the literature of the period. Since 2005 his publications have been mainly on the Western film.

Linda H. Peterson is Niel Gray, Jr Professor of English at Yale University. Her books include *Victorian Autobiography* (1986), *Traditions of Victorian Women's Autobiography* (1999), and, most recently, *Becoming a Woman of Letters: Myths of Authorship and Facts of the Victorian Market* (2009). She has edited *The Autobiography and Letters of Margaret*

Oliphant (2012), Harriet Martineau's *Autobiography* (2007), and *The Life of Charlotte Brontë* by Elizabeth Gaskell (2006).

Lawrence Poston is Professor Emeritus of English at the University of Illinois at Chicago, where he has held a variety of administrative posts. Previously he taught at the University of Nebraska-Lincoln and was a Visiting Professor of English at the University of Tulsa. His interests include aspects of the Romantic-Victorian transition, on which he has published a number of interrelated articles and, more recently, studies of late Victorian musical culture and Victorian religion. His book, *The Antagonist Principle: Newman and the Paradox of Personality*, is forthcoming from the University of Virginia Press.

John R. Reed is Distinguished Professor of English at Wayne State University in Detroit. He has published substantially on nineteenth- and twentieth-century British literature in many articles and books. Among these are *Victorian Conventions* (1975) and, most recently, *Dickens's Hyperreality* (2010) and *The Army and Navy in Nineteenth-Century British Literature* (2011).

Lawrence Rothfield is Associate Professor of English and Comparative Literature at the University of Chicago, and author of *Vital Signs: Medical Realism in Nineteenth-Century Fiction* (1992).

Hilary M. Schor is Professor of English, Comparative Literature, and Law at the University of Southern California, where she co-directs the Center for Law, History and Culture. She is the author of *Curious Subjects: Women and the Trials of Realism* (2013), *Dickens and the Daughter of the House* (1999), and *Scheherezade in the Marketplace: Elizabeth Gaskell and the Victorian Novel* (1992). She has published articles on contemporary fiction, film, ghosts, bastards, and failed pyromaniacs, but she has yet to write anything about dinosaurs. She is at work on a study of Jews, women, and other Victorian legal fictions.

Jan-Melissa Schramm is a Fellow at Trinity Hall and a University Lecturer in the Faculty of English at the University of Cambridge, where she teaches Victorian literature. She is the author of *Testimony and Advocacy in Victorian Law, Literature, and Theology* (2000), and *Atonement and Self-Sacrifice in Nineteenth-Century Narrative* (2012) as well as a number of articles and book chapters on representations of the law in the works of Dickens and Eliot, Victorian satire, and first-person narration. She is also co-editor of *Fictions of Knowledge: Fact, Evidence, Doubt* (2011).

E. Warwick Slinn is Professor Emeritus of English and Honorary Research Fellow at Massey University, New Zealand. He is the author of *Browning and the Fictions of Identity* (1982), *The Discourse of Self in Victorian Poetry* (1991), *Victorian Poetry as Cultural Critique: The Politics of Performative Language* (2003), and several essays in companions to Victorian poetry published by Blackwell and Cambridge.

Herbert Sussman is Professor Emeritus in the English Department at Northeastern University, Boston. His books include *Victorians and the Machine: The Literary Response* *to Technology* (1968), *Victorian Masculinities: Manhood and Masculine Poetics in Early Victorian Literature and Art* (1995), and most recently *Victorian Technology: Invention, Innovation, and the Rise of the Machine* (2009) and *Masculine Identities: The History of Manliness* (2012).

Herbert F. Tucker, John C. Coleman Professor of English at the University of Virginia, is the author of *Browning's Beginnings* (1980), *Tennyson and the Doom of Romanticism* (1988), and *Epic: Britain's Heroic Muse 1790–1910* (2008). He has edited, besides the two editions of this *Companion*, several other anthologies: of Tennyson criticism (1993), of essays on literary-critical pedagogy (with David Sofield, 1998), and of Victorian literature (with Dorothy Mermin, 2001). He serves as an associate editor for *New Literary History* and a Victorian series editor for the University of Virginia Press.

Chris R. Vanden Bossche is Professor of English at the University of Notre Dame. He is the author of *Carlyle and the Search for Authority* (1991) and *Reform Acts: Chartism, Social Agency, and the Victorian Novel, 1832–1867* (2014); he is also editor-in-chief of the University of California Press Edition of the Writings of Thomas Carlyle, for which he has edited *Historical Essays* (2002) and co-edited *Past and Present* (with Joel Brattin and Dale Trela, 2005). He has published articles on a range of topics in Victorian literature and culture from copyright to separate spheres.

Jennifer Wicke is Professor of English and Comparative Literature at the University of Virginia; she has written widely on the relationship between nineteenth- and twentieth-century literature and modern economic and political forms. Her latest book, *Born to Shop: Modernism, Modernity, and the Global Work of Consumption* (Oxford University Press, 2014), follows an economic arc of consumer culture in relation to literature from Wilde to Woolf.

Introduction

This book aims to meet both short-term and long-range needs. To begin with, it is a reference work for consultation. The reader with a question about, say, the provisions or effects of the Forster Education Act of 1870 will be guided by the index to a number of places where these matters are discussed; then, as the need for punctual answers ripens into ampler curiosity, the context provided by our historical chapter 3 on "1870" or our chapter 14 on "Educational" careers will offer an expanded prospect. To take another example, the student of nineteenth-century poetry who has started to wonder what ideas about literature were in circulation during the Victorian era, and in which venues they ordinarily appeared, will find a conspective discussion in our chapter 28, "Literary Criticism"; then, at the end of this as of each chapter, a list of Cross-References will suggest where else to turn in the book for a further viewpoint or elaboration. Finally, the bibliographies that round off every chapter gesture beyond the covers of this book to hundreds of others recommended for further reading. Here then, in the first instance, is a *Companion* of somewhat the pocket-tool sort: several devices in one, designed for handy multiple applications.

Still, a companion is more than a consultant; and our book aims to do more than provide quick reference help. The *Victorian Literature and Culture* embraced by its title identifies a subject of vista so immense, and of crannies so multitudinous, that the student who means to confront that subject whole is likely to want, beyond mere information, the presence of an experienced guide. This long-range need has been anticipated in an overall plan gathering the book's chapters into discrete parts, which the student may read in order to grasp, respectively, the history of Victorian Britain (part one), the phases in a Victorian life (part two), the leading professions and careers that filled out the phase of mature adulthood (part three), the major Victorian literary genres (part four), and the limits Victorians recognized as defining their persons, their homes, and their national identities (part five). Within parts one, two, and five the editor has embraced as the organizing principle a linear narrative of development and expansion that is itself unabashedly Victorian; and the discerning reader will see how a like principle sustains the march of parts three and four, as they move from traditional cultural formations toward emergent and increasingly self-organizing ones.

Furthermore, because the individual chapters more often than not thread their information along historical narrative lines, our book gives considerable internal reinforcement to patterns of origin and development, progress and decline, that themselves became intellectual second-nature during the period under study. This past-and-present congruence between nineteenth-century and contemporary structures of understanding has obvious advantages but certain drawbacks too. So the reader is hereby advised that other, less aggressively linear modes of putting Victorian literature and culture into each other are also desirable, and that they are indeed made possible by our schemes of index and cross-reference. Advice on this score admittedly seems less urgent in view of the decentering effect that arises when a book mirrors, as this one does, three dozen different minds freshly at work on topics in which they take strong interest. Stylistic, procedural, and theoretical variety among our contributors will give the *Companion* an agreeably protean character, it is hoped, for that inner circle of readers who accompany us all the way from start to finish, in quest of a comprehensive yet complex perspective on the Victorian age. And, at the end of the line in this comprehensively revised new edition, a freshly commissioned chapter on the phenomenon of "Neo-Victorianism" will spur reflection about what is at stake, on either side of our slow but sure millennial turn, in the appropriation and repurposing of Victoriana up and down the contemporary cultural gamut.

Given this prefatory reassurance of ours about a marriage of comprehensiveness with convenience, the reader may want to proceed to the chapters right away. For those disposed to linger here, though, the editor offers this introductory perch as a viewing point from which to remark some unplanned benefits that have accrued en route. While contributors have been enjoined against lengthy assessment of the state and trend of scholarship – matters of compelling interest within the guild, but not companionable in the sense that matters here – the chapters below do in effect constitute a veritable cross-section of scholarly Victorianism in the early twenty-first century. A familiar canon of authors is alive and well, to judge from both the quantitative frequency and qualitative respectfulness of their citation here. Dickens and Eliot retain preeminence among the novelists, with strong support from Thackeray and even stronger from Trollope. Carlyle, Mill, and Arnold still lead the way as Victorian sages. Tennyson remains in a poetic class by himself, Robert Browning being a doughty second (unless Elizabeth Barrett Browning now shares that honor), with the Rossettis, Swinburne, and Hopkins receiving honorable if infrequent mention.

It is generally in the middle distance of renown that notable shifts occur. Collins and Gaskell are more often cited as cultural exponents and major fiction artists than they would have been a generation ago, at the expense perhaps of the now less-cited Brontës and Meredith, while in nonfiction prose such paraliterary figures as Bentham and Mayhew, Darwin and Marx have come to adjoin the aesthetic and social witness long since canonized in Ruskin and Morris, Pater and Wilde. For *Middlemarch* and *In Memoriam* as many uses have been found in our time as half a century ago when Victorian studies was finding its interdisciplinary feet, although the distinct novelty of some of these uses lets one affirm that stability in the canon has no automatic correlation, and by no means a simply inverse correlation, with diversification of critical approaches and findings. At all events the value that literary and cultural theory nowadays accord to difference, heterogeneity, and contestation brings *Vanity Fair* and *The Ring and the Book* to the fore in more than one of the following chapters, among other works sharing their dispersive qualities of irony and masquerade. To some extent these patterns of spontaneous preference may result from our joint mission to coordinate the events of literary history with the prevailing conditions and decisive changes that defined Victorian culture at large. When seeking to demonstrate the reciprocal influence of text and context, it makes sense to turn on one hand to writings that enjoyed wide circulation, and on the other hand to writings that expressly reflected a broad spectrum of contemporary concerns. Writings that did both, like the great social-issue novels of Dickens, accordingly loom large in these pages.

Something of the same kind may be observed about another of the book's collective determinations, that of periodization. Our annualist historical chapters in part one set the framing limits of the period deliberately far apart. Chapter 1 ("1832") finds its center half a decade before the young queen's ascension to the throne and glances back beyond that date into the late 1820s; chapter 4 ("1897"), from its vantage half a decade before the old queen's death, opens out into numerous issues pertinent to the Edwardian moment that was to follow. Our chronological frame thus claims as "Victorian" roughly the period 1830–1900 – threescore years and ten, and then some – and several contributors offer energetic, fertile speculation about its outer reaches; about the 1830s and 1880s, for example, two turbulent decades whose literary and cultural history remains unsettled. Within this expanded framework, however, contributors with few exceptions (and with the editor's blessing) have made centripetal choices about what texts, authors, and movements to discuss: none of us implies that Wordsworth or Mary Shelley, Conrad or H. G. Wells should be enlisted on strictly calendrical grounds as a Victorian. Moreover, by the collective choices of its contributors this book unmistakably confirms as High Victorian the core years 1850–75, a quarter-century which repeatedly focuses our chapters and from whose literary, legislative, and social achievements our chief examples are repeatedly drawn. From causes that exceed the capacity of an editor to declare – and that have called for *tours de force* in the composition of chapters 2 and 3 – these were the years when the interactivity between British literature and its ambient culture was most radiantly strong, year after year and right across the genres, from *Aurora Leigh* and Macaulay's *History of England* to "The Wreck of the *Deutschland*" and *The Way We Live Now*. No wonder our *Companion* gives special privilege to writings from this core period: they ring still with that textual–contextual synergy which made literature and culture such boon companions for one another at the Victorian noontide.

   While certain topics traditionally prominent or recently urgent in Victorian studies do not receive frontal treatment here, their omission is in most cases merely apparent. Neither utilitarianism nor socialism gets a chapter to itself; the evangelical and the aesthete are alike passed over; for essays dedicated to the contest of science with religion, or to the dilemma of the woman writer, the reader will scan our table of contents in vain. But that is because these topics are the very reverse of negligible: so insistently do they require our notice that they appear (witness the index) as ingredient themes throughout the book, rather than in isolation as token or special interests. The reason the *Companion* lacks a chapter on the working class is that the contributors have been urged to build a working-class perspective into each account they write. On the record, the literary documentation of Victorian experience remains overwhelmingly middle-class; but Victorian writers would never have left the record they did had the middle classes been less acutely aware of the political insistence of those whose "inferior," or for that matter "superior," social and economic position defined what ranked as a comfortable bourgeois norm. This feature of cultural history – like others respecting sexuality, ethnicity, denominational faith – is best conveyed by means of saturation. Our reader will therefore find, say, the 1864 Contagious Diseases Act discussed not in quarantine but all over the book, because the institutional and ideological bearings that regulated Victorian sexuality were all over the culture that the book is about.

   By now a brace of conspicuously changeful scholarly generations have passed since three independent *Guides to Research* took survey of the environs and prospects for Victorianist study of fiction (ed. Lionel Stevenson 1964, revised 1980), of poetry (ed. Frederic Faverty 1956, revised 1968), and of prose (ed. David De Laura 1973). Those authoritative volumes address a more advanced scholarly audience than ours does, an audience that has indeed included most of our contributors at one or another stage in their professional development. While this *Companion* has never been intended to supersede the *Guides*, the bibliographies it contains acknowledge enough new scholarship – sufficiently various in kind, diversified in scope, and innovative in method – to warrant their revision and probably reconception, along fresh lines that depart from the author-centered programs of study that held sway forty years ago. Until the *Guides* are superseded, though, it is to them that readers of this book who go on to undertake independent research should turn in the pursuit of detailed information about principal nineteenth- and twentieth-century repositories of information and channels for intellectual exchange. Also recommended here are a trio of more recent literary-historical synopses, to whose steady single-point perspective on intellectual and cultural contexts our omnibus *Companion* offers a more kaleidoscopic complement: Robin Gilmour's *The Victorian Period* (1993), *The Victorians* by Philip Davis (2002), and our contributor James Eli Adams's *A History of Victorian Literature* (2009). To these should be added two very recent group endeavors more like our own: *The Cambridge History of Victorian Literature*, edited by Kate Flint (2012), and the experiment in pointillist collective historiography that Dino Franco Felluga has conducted as *BRANCH: Britain, Representation, and Nineteenth-Century History* (http://www.branchcollective

.org). Decades hence the century-straddling efforts of every one of us are likely to be noticed, if at all, for their quaint adherence to narrative explanation, to the expository paragraph, and above all to the medium of print. But it is a safe bet that the hunger to understand our antecedents will survive us, together with the desire to appreciate those literary achievements which remain the Victorians' most subtly demanding legacy to a posterity no less vexed and inquisitive than they.

The editor thanks Andrew McNeillie for initially envisioning the first edition, and Emma Bennett and Ben Thatcher for patiently fomenting this new one. Thanks again to all our returning contributors, who in many cases have substantially revised their original chapters, and especially to the authors who join us here for the first time: Edward Adams, Julie Codell, Ann Heilmann, and Mark Llewellyn for their work on chapters entirely new; Michael Hunt, James Mussell, and Jan-Melissa Schramm for their tactful incorporation and deft supplementation of existing ones. Between editions our company has sustained only one loss, but it is a signal one: the late Richard Altick's scholarship abides as an influence, not only on the chapter he initially composed in his eighties, but on many another chapter here as well.

Part One
History in Focus

1

1832

Lawrence Poston

Finding the Beginning

When did the Victorian age begin? While the senescence of Victorian England has been located anywhere from the Queen's Golden Jubilee in 1887 to the Battle of the Somme in 1916, its beginning – the "Victorian prelude" (Quinlan) – has been placed at least as far back as the 1780s, which saw the moral reaction in English manners portended by the Wesleyans and the Evangelical revival. Here "Victorianism" is simplistically equated with a social conservatism that both antedates and postdates the queen herself; Mrs Grundy, it seems, was on the throne longer still. A literal reading of the term implies that the Victorian era begins with the accession of Victoria to the throne in 1837 and ends with her own demise in 1901. Yet the first generation of authors we now know as "Victorian" was born at the end of the eighteenth century and in the first two decades of the nineteenth. Carlyle, Mill, Macaulay, Newman were all publishing in the 1820s; Tennyson and Browning in the early 1830s. Strict adherence to the dates of reign ignores these larger continuities.

The *Wellesley Index to Victorian Periodicals* has canonized another date: 1824, the year of Byron's death and of the founding of the *Westminster Review* as a party organ for the Benthamites, designed to add a Radical voice to the select upper-middle-class reading scene dominated by the Tory *Quarterly Review* and the Whig *Edinburgh Review*. More recently, Richard Cronin has chosen the year 1824 to identify a generation of "Romantic Victorians" like George Darley, whose careers fall mostly outside what has generally been taken to be mid- or "high" Victorianism. Byron's own contemporaries saw his

A New Companion to Victorian Literature and Culture, First Edition. Edited by Herbert F. Tucker.
© 2014 John Wiley & Sons, Ltd. Published 2014 by John Wiley & Sons, Ltd.

death in symbolically charged terms. As Edward Bulwer (later the much-maligned Bulwer-Lytton) put it in his study of English society, politics, arts, and manners, *England and the English* (1833), "When Byron passed away, the feeling he had represented craved utterance no more. With a sigh we turned to the actual and practical career of life; we awoke from the morbid, the passionate, the dreaming" (286). For Bulwer, the utilitarian Bentham had succeeded the romantic egoist Byron as the cultural symbol of his day. The very strength of the recoil from Byron was a tribute to the sway his passionate and sometimes morbid nature had exercised over the reading public. Yet even Byron had prepared the way for Bentham, to the extent that the poet's own assaults on national prejudices had engendered a more skeptical climate receptive to Bentham's interrogation of national institutions.

Byron and Bentham as twin cultural symbols have a powerful resonance for the student of the period. But between them they do not begin to account either for the multitude of voices counseling different things in the years immediately preceding Victoria, or for a rapidly changing political climate. While it may be more suspicious than auspicious to proclaim the emergence of a distinctive self-awareness at a particular moment in history, most of us do so at the beginning of a new decade; we use the terms "sixties," "seventies," "eighties" to encode a cluster of political and cultural assumptions; and if we keep diaries and watch our own biological clock the onset of a new decade is likely to breed still more self-examination than a new year. One can make a case for 1830 as one of those possible Victorian beginnings. Two diarists in January 1830 saw that something was afoot, and they did not like what they saw. One of them was Charles Greville, the diarist of the reigns of George IV, William IV, and Victoria, whose sheltered position as clerk to the Privy Council gave him unparalleled access to politicians of all factions. On January 7 he wrote, "The revenue has fallen off one million and more. The accounts of distress from the country grow worse and more desponding" (Greville I, 224). Ten days later finds him in a more perturbed vein: "The country gentlemen are beginning to arrive, and they all tell the same story as to the universally prevailing distress and the certainty of things becoming much worse; of the failure of rents all over England, and the necessity of some decisive measures or the prospect of general ruin" (226). The other is one of those country gentlemen, General William Dyott, a Staffordshire magnate then 68 years old, writing on New Year's Day 1830: "I believe a year never opened with less cheering prospects to a country than the present for old England; distress attending all classes of the community . . . Meetings held in various parts of the kingdom to represent the distress of the country" (Darwin I, 248). For such disturbed but insular observers, the question was whether the Duke of Wellington and Robert Peel between them could produce any program capable of alleviating the widespread economic distress of the countryside, and thus a threat to the old order.

More shocks, some of them not altogether unwelcome, like the death of the widely discredited old rake George IV on June 26, followed throughout the year. At home, talk of reform, the antislavery agitation which Greville attributed to the bothersome Methodists, and a new Parliament in his words "full of boys and all sorts of strange men" all seemed to herald transition. So, abroad, did the overthrow of the French monarchy, in the three days of July, which in England revived radical hopes and fears; for the first time since the 1790s, the tricolor was hoisted in several English cities, and even the cautious Whigs were viewed by some of their more conservative colleagues as contemplating a doctrinaire reform in the French style. It was, again, Bulwer who sensed the impending change and embraced it openly:

> Just at the time when with George the Fourth an *old* era expired, the excitement of a popular election concurred with the three days of July in France, to give a decisive tone to the *new*. The question of Reform came on, and, to the astonishment of the nation itself, it was hailed at once by the national heart. From that moment, the intellectual spirit hitherto partially directed to, became *wholly* absorbed in, politics; and whatever lighter works have since obtained a warm and general hearing, have either developed the errors of the social system, or the vices of the legislative. (288–9)

The Reform currents given new life in England by events on the Continent had, by the time *England and the English* was published, found expression in the First Reform Act of 1832. That date itself is indeed the most convenient point around which to gather the various reforming clusters of the decade preceding Victoria's accession, and to mark an evolution from older paternalist to newer entrepreneurial ideas of the social order. Yet the latter part of Bulwer's statement suggests another aspect of the 1830s which is particularly striking to the student of literature: the displacement of works of the imagination by the all-consuming task of Reform, or their subordination to the political agendas which so preoccupied the larger public.

The paradox of the 1830s has often been described in terms of the striking contrast between the richness of their political history – Reform, the growth of political and labor unions and at the end of the decade the movement for the redress of working-class grievances, Chartism, the first stirrings of the Anti-Corn Law League, the beginning of systematic government intervention in prison conditions, education, welfare, working hours, and public order – and the apparent barrenness of the cultural scene. That prodigiously diligent later Victorian woman of letters, Margaret Oliphant, trying to account for the strange hiatus in poetry and fiction between about 1825 and 1840, wrote that "the period which witnessed Her Majesty's happy accession was not in itself a very glorious one, at least as far as literature is concerned. It was a season of lull, of silence and emptiness, such as must naturally come after the exhausting brilliance of the days just gone by" (I, 1). But Bulwer's post-Byronic characterization of a shift in sensibility from the dreaming to the practical suggests a more productive approach. It echoes in the attempt of more recent scholars to isolate a distinctive "public voice" in English literature of the 1830s and 1840s, a voice intended to "transcend the doubt which by 1830 had fatally touched the fundamental Romantic faith, while the self-consciousness of this effort found expression in the 'private' voice which qualified the work of the best writers" (Madden 97). But those writers must first of all be seen in the context of an age which itself was coming to greater self-consciousness about its aims and purposes.

Georgian or Victorian? The Political Scene

The man who succeeded George IV as king in 1830 was hardly of the stuff to give his name to an age. The choleric, well-intentioned Duke of Clarence had earlier discarded a mistress in the interests of respectability and in the hope that one of his legitimate children, should there be any, might inherit his throne. Known as Sailor Bill because of his navy career, he was also, on account of his fondness for making intemperate and embarrassing public utterances, referred to by the even less dignified sobriquet of Silly Billy. Harriet Martineau described him as "a sovereign who could not help agreeing with the last speaker, and who was always impetuous on behalf of his latest impression" (III, 42). Or, as one of Greville's colleagues observed, "What can you expect of a man with a head shaped like a pineapple?" Yet William IV, irresolute and capricious though he sometimes was, warrants some credit for restoring an aura of respectability to the monarchy after the reign of his dissolute brother. He was not, however, the best-equipped of men to preside over an age of Reform.

Reform has its origin in the 1820s, with the repeal of Test and Corporation Acts in 1828 and Catholic Emancipation in 1829, both of them measures aimed at easing the political disabilities that had hemmed in the rights of Protestant dissenters on the one hand and Roman Catholics on the other. These measures deeply divided the governing Tory party, factions of which participated in the overthrow of Wellington's Tory government in 1830. Tories were disgusted by the duke's willingness to move in the direction of free trade and by his about-face on Catholic Emancipation, and they paved the way for the Whig government of Earl Grey, whom the king summoned to office at the end of 1830 following Wellington's refusal to countenance any further change in the British constitution.

The calls for Reform were spurred on by those riots among farm laborers and that manufacturing unrest which echo in the diaries of Dyott and Greville. In March 1831 Lord John Russell introduced a bill in the House of Commons that removed parliamentary representation from many small electoral boroughs and gave such representation to the nation's growing industrial centers. The bill also attempted to regularize inconsistencies in the relationship between property-holding and the right to the franchise. It passed by a majority of only one at 3:00 a.m. on March 22, but still required a clause-by-clause reading and the approval of a hostile House of Lords. The defeat of one of the clauses led Grey to advise the king to dissolve Parliament and ask for new elections. The result was a referendum on a single issue: "the bill, the whole bill, and nothing but the bill" (Arnstein 12). Many elections in England at this time were uncontested, but in those boroughs where there was a contest, it was the reformers who were returned to power. Russell's second version of the bill commanded a substantial majority on its second reading in Commons, but ran aground in the House of Lords, where it was defeated after a five-day debate.

The opposition of the Lords seemed to call into question the very viability of the constitution. The cities were outraged; arsonists destroyed Nottingham Castle; Bristol succumbed for a few days to mob rule. That December, Grey's government went back to work and produced a third reform bill much like the second. With the bill threatened once again by a hostile House of Lords, Grey called on the king to create 50 new peers to override the opposition. William IV thought 50 a bit much; Grey found the counter-offer of 20 too few, and resigned. The Duke of Wellington, however, whom the king called back to power, was incapable of meeting the rising storm of discontent. At that juncture the king turned to Grey and reluctantly acceded to the demand to create new peers, but the House of Lords, reading the tea leaves, acquiesced in the bill rather than permit itself to be swamped with new appointees. The bill became law on June 7, 1832.

The first Reform Act is itself a transition piece, much like William's reign; it looks different from different angles. Along with the Municipal Corporations Act of 1835, the 1832 bill may well have saved England from revolution, and it certainly moved the country peacefully and without Continental-style convulsions toward democracy. Those Whigs who orchestrated Reform in the difficult first months of the decade saw the bill quite differently, as an end rather than a beginning. As one historian puts it, "the Bill had been like the legitimate heir of a loveless marriage, the child rather of necessity than of desire" (Kitson Clark 64). Though prodded by Radical colleagues on their left, with whom the Whigs had an uneasy relationship, the drafters of the bill viewed traditional social groups as providing the essential frame of reference. Grey's charge to the Committee of Four which he appointed to draft the bill is revealing. The legislation, he wrote, should be "of such a scope and description as to satisfy all reasonable demands, and remove at once, and for ever, all rational grounds for complaint from the minds of the intelligent and independent portion of the community." This in essence was Macaulay's famous advice to Parliament in his speech of 1831: "Reform, that you may preserve." Though Peel had opposed Reform, after its passage he accepted it in his Tamworth manifesto to the electors as "a final and irrevocable settlement of a great constitutional question," and his Whig opponent Lord John Russell earned the nickname "Finality Jack" for the emphasis with which he insisted, both on the floor of the House and in writing, that the authors of the bill were "peculiarly committed to finality" and that to tolerate further Reform measures "would be to confess that [the reformers] had deceived the people or themselves" (Southgate 99).

Viewed in this way, the bill looks more like Georgian farewell than Victorian halloo, just as the England of that year to many of its citizens probably seemed not so very different from the latter years of the eighteenth century. In 1833, writes a leading administrative historian, England "was not orderly, it was not planned, it was not centralized, it was not efficient, and it did little for the well-being of the citizens." Education, health, and poor relief lay beyond the purview of the national government, and the last was administered erratically by 15,000 parishes also in charge of public order (Roberts 195). Hindsight makes clearer the beginnings of slow, almost glacial changes beneath the surface of daily events. Contemporaries feel the shocks but not the trends; the earthquakes, not the subtle erosions or the drawn-out process of sedimentation. The England that James Fenimore Cooper visited in the late winter and early spring of 1828 was still the England of the great Whig houses and the breakfasts of the poet Samuel Rogers, one of the last of the Augustans, where Cooper met Coleridge, Sir Walter Scott, Thomas Campbell, John Gibson Lockhart, Thomas Moore, Earl Grey, and Lord John Russell. Cows still grazed in the heart of London. Green Park and St James's Park were "one open space" separated only by a fence, the first in Cooper's words "nothing but a large field, cropped down like velvet, irregularly dotted with trees, and without any carriage way" (28). This England survived well into the 1830s. Jeremy Bentham died in 1832 at the age of 84; as an undergraduate he had attended Blackstone's lectures on law at Oxford in the 1760s. Charles Grey, who shepherded through the first Reform Bill in 1832, was nearly 70 and, like his party, had spent almost half a century in the political wilderness; in the 1790s he had joined the Society of Friends of the People and introduced his first motion on parliamentary reform. John Scott, Lord Chancellor and first Earl Eldon, was 81 when, to his disgust, the Reform Bill became law; as Attorney General he had been identified with various of the repressive acts of the 1790s and at the turn of the century was opposing the abolition of the slave trade. But power was passing to Palmerston, Russell, and Peel, while at the further end of the age spectrum the young Gladstone at 22, listening to the Reform debates in the galleries, was still a few months from his first seat; Disraeli, six years and four defeats from his.

One striking symbol of transition is Grey's successor as the leader of the Whigs. William Lamb, second Viscount Melbourne, was the last prime minister ever to be dismissed unilaterally by a reigning monarch and the first to become prime minister as the result of a general election, against that monarch's will. Melbourne was in his mid-50s upon his appointment as prime minister in 1834 and therefore presumably at the height of his powers if he chose to use them. It was an open question whether or not he would. Elegant, languid, debonair, with a political record at best equivocal on the major issues of the day, the jotter of numerous cynical reflections on society in his commonplace book, Melbourne told his secretary, upon being offered the reins of government, that it was "a damned bore" to decide whether or not to accept. It is one of the finer ironies of the decade that this Whig aristocrat, twice cited as an adulterous co-respondent in the Brandon and Norton divorce cases (the second of these during his prime ministership), should be found in 1837 at the ear of the impressionable, rather conventional young queen as avuncular counselor and friend. Perhaps, with the changed moral atmosphere that journalists of the day were already commenting on, the transition from Regency gentleman to Victorian paterfamilias was not so difficult or arduous after all, but then Melbourne was nothing if not flexible. Much of the foregoing description is, of course, caricature; Melbourne was capable of decisive action, abandoning the dilettante's pose for a complicated mixture of deference, courtly admiration, and firmness in dealing with the 18-year-old queen (Vallone 3, 199).

Meanwhile, the Whig assumption of "finality" in political arrangements was already being battered by changes which the Reform Bill could hardly have been drafted to prevent and which made it clear that 1832 was an opening salvo, not a concluding salute. The creation of inspectors of factories (1833) and prisons (1835), the New Poor Law (1834), the new Education Committee of the Privy Council, represented stages toward the centralization which Dickens's Mr Podsnap, a quarter of a century later, was to decry as "not English." Government was becoming increasingly conscious of its own powers. It is no accident that the 1830s saw the rise of statistics-gathering, of select parliamentary commissions on matters requiring reform, of "blue books" that constituted the gathering of evidence for the purpose, and in general an almost obsessive documentation of "the condition of England question," which resonates in the novels of Disraeli, Gaskell, Charlotte Brontë, and Kingsley in the next decade. Perhaps the very *ad hoc* nature of much of this activity was responsible for what looked to foreign observers like a remarkably resilient political system. The spirit of English legislation, Alexis de Tocqueville thought when he visited the country in 1835, was "an incomprehensible mixture of the spirits of innovation and routine, which perfects the details of law without noticing their principles" (82). He saw stability in the openness of the aristocratic class to newcomers and the absence of class hatred, the presence of a relatively democratic group of reformers who respected religion and property, and the spirit of individualism that flourished under the government, along with a fair amount of administrative muddle. "In France," marveled another French visitor, the Baron d'Haussez, "a revolution is accomplished in three days. In England, the country deliberates many years before the work of reform is entered on and, once commenced, the results are without danger, for the passions . . . are already cooled" (I, 154–5).

Such assessments may have been both accurate and premonitory. Some worried Englishmen of the day would have seen them as premature. The six points of the People's Charter (1837) called for universal manhood suffrage, annual Parliaments, voting by secret ballot, equal electoral districts, the abolition of property qualifications for members of Parliament, and pay for members of Parliament. The passing of the Factory Act of 1833, limiting the working hours of children in factories, and the agitation against the seeming inhumanities of the New Poor Law (which readers now know chiefly through Dickens's vivid portrayal of the workhouse in *Oliver Twist*) are both symptoms of a broader and less focused discontent than that which clustered around the Reform Act. Reform, after all, did not bring about economic change, though it generated some utopian hopes.

Historians continue to divide on the extent to which the Act of 1832 was a genuine step forward, and if so what step it took. Influential studies by Norman Gash and D. C. Moore have suggested the danger of using the Reform Act to underplay trends and events long antedating and postdating it. A more traditional view, recently reargued, has been that the Act made possible the steps toward "an essentially modern electoral system based on rigid partisanship and clearly articulated political principle" (Phillips and Wetherell 1995: 412). For most of the reforming Whigs, the bill was intended to seal the past by increasing the total British electorate from 435,000 to 813,000 out of an adult male population of some six million, and it was drafted to guarantee that the counties would not be overbalanced by the new towns. In five general elections between 1832 and 1847 only just over half of the constituencies were contested. But it was also true that "the general election of 1841 was the first in which the government of the day, previously holding a majority in the lower House, was defeated by a disciplined opposition for electoral purposes" (Gash xii–xiii).

Nonetheless, what was not fully understood at the time turned out in the event to be a harbinger of significant if deferred change. The significance of the Reform Act was less in the measurable difference it made in the atmosphere than in the precedent it set for the Acts of 1867 and 1884: something sacred, in this case the constitution itself, had been proven nonetheless to be alterable.

The Missing Generation

On the night of October 16, 1834, the skies over London were irradiated with a glow that could be seen miles away. The Palace of Westminster had caught fire, and while the next morning's light showed that Westminster Hall had survived, the old Parliament House of St Stephen and the surrounding lawcourts were destroyed. In 1835 a Parliamentary Commission set up to consider the rebuilding of Parliament decided to hold a competition that was to require the submission of architectural designs in either the Gothic or Elizabethan modes. The winning design, submitted by a young architect named Charles Barry, constituted a clearcut identification of England's political glories with the Gothic.

In part, this has been seen as a moral revulsion against the age of the Georges, for whom the classic had been the dominant style. In part it anticipates the concurrent movement toward the Gothic as an attempt to evoke the piety as well as the pride of the medieval past, a movement emblematized in the publication in 1836 of Augustus Welby Pugin's *Contrasts*, which polemically juxtaposed pictures of fourteenth- and fifteenth-century buildings with the ugly creations of his own day. For a more recent writer, the building of the Houses of Parliament in 1834–7 marks "a cultural monument of a time neither Georgian nor Victorian," but rather "a tribute to the power of creativity between orthodoxies" (Rorabaugh 174–5). But the initial decision to exclude classical models is perhaps the most striking attribute of the competition itself. What was at stake was both a return to real or imagined national origins, and a rejection of what the immediately preceding era had come to symbolize.

The shift from "Georgian" to "Victorian" in the broader political and cultural context is almost as delusively tidy and elusively traceable as the shift from "Romantic" to "Victorian" is for the literary historian. In the visual arts, the deaths of the brilliant young painter and watercolorist Richard Parkes Bonington in 1828 and the fashionable portraitist Thomas Lawrence in 1830 can be set against the continuance of the work of Constable, Haydon, Turner, and Martin throughout the decade (Constable dying first of these, in 1837). But in poetry Keats died in 1821, Shelley in 1822, Byron in 1824. Sir Walter Scott, his life shortened by his gallant efforts to pay off creditors, died in 1832. Coleridge lingered on until 1834 and Wordsworth until 1850, but only the most ardent revisionists now contest the fact that their best creative work lay behind them. Scholars have made the most of such symbolically charged moments as Wordsworth's toast to the young Robert Browning upon the publication of *Paracelsus* in 1835, or Tennyson's highly unsatisfactory interview with the sage of Rydal Mount in 1845, during which the younger poet sought, unsuccessfully by his own account, to rouse the flagging interest of Wordsworth in natural beauty. But the fact is that there is very little to be made of such occasions as these; they heighten, rather than minimize, the effect of disjuncture. It is startling to recall that Words-worth's successor as national literary sage, Thomas Carlyle, was only a few weeks younger than Keats, but that at the time Keats died Carlyle had barely embarked on a career as a hack writer for the encyclopedias.

The 1830s do indeed see the beginnings of several brilliant, though sometimes slow-starting, careers. But they provide little evidence of an 1830s equivalent for what has been called the Auden generation of the 1930s. In both decades an atmo-sphere of impending crisis pervades the scene, but the emerging writers of the 1830s were too young, their lines of activity too disparate, and Carlyle too idiosyncratic to serve as a consistent mentor. If to be, to act, and to conceive oneself as part of a liter-ary generation require a developed self-consciousness as well as a defined corporate identity, the emerging writers of the thirties do not qualify. Yet in measurable ways all of them were products of a common historical milieu and all of them are baro-meters of what we can now define as a post-Romantic ethos. A number of these lines of development have been traced by scholars: the dwindling cult of Byron, the exhaustion of the Wordsworthian paradigm of the unity between man and nature, a growing uncertainty as to the nature of the audience for high literature, and a concern with political themes drawn from the past, often in a context – as in Browning's *Sordello* (1840) or Henry Taylor's once-popular verse drama *Philip van Artevelde* (1834) – which suggests the limits of the individual hero in an unheroic age. Even in their collectivity, however, these themes stop short of providing us with a genuinely syn-optic view of the decade.

Another way to assess that decade is less thematic than generic. One of the most interesting phenomena of the 1830s is the blurring of conventional generic distinc-tions: Tennyson's inward-turning lyrics which chart new journeys of the mind, Browning's disruption of the conventions of historical narrative in *Sordello*, Dickens's imposition of a reformist vision on the eighteenth-century picaresque novel, or Car-lyle's *Sartor Resartus* (1834), by turns autobiographical fragment, philosophical treatise, novel, and editorial doodling – possibly the biggest put-on in English literature since *Tristram Shandy*. It is tempting to make Carlyle the generic center of the decade, beginning with his splendid review-essay "Characteristics" in 1831, continuing through such works as *The French Revolution* (1837) in which history fades into a drama of lived memory, reawakened by the more recent three days of July 1830, and culmi-nating in *Heroes and Hero-Worship*, the lectures of 1840 in which Carlyle attempts to proclaim a new ethic of leadership.

Yet a work like *Sartor* requires also to be read in the context of its original place of publication, *Fraser's Magazine*, whose brilliant and eccentric editor William Maginn collected a veritable rogues' gallery of wits and satirists who left subscribers reeling. Similarly, Dickens in the latter 1830s was a young journalist whose *Sketches by Boz* (1836) can now be seen, more clearly than by Boz's first readers, as a trial run for *Pickwick Papers* (1837). The generic issue here is linked to a larger one: the need to go beyond masterpieces to explain the wonderfully diverse achievements of the 1830s. As scholars of Victorian popular culture like Patrick Brantlinger have shown us, the decade offers a remarkably pristine case for testing the familiar, recurrent process whereby literature is refreshed from below; de Tocqueville's comments on the openness of the English upper class to new influences from the emerging middle class can be replicated in the context of "high" and "low" art. Thus, behind the careers of the two major novelists of the forties and fifties, Dickens and Thackeray, lies the *Punch* circle of the late thirties – Mark Lemon, the Mayhews, Tom Hood, Douglas Jerrold and others, nearly all of whom had experienced bankruptcy and debt, who wrote reformist melodramas (Jerrold) or poetry enlivened by popular idioms (Hood), some of which is visible in the early dramatic lyrics of Browning. This middle world which at intervals feeds the high literature of the time should be expanded to include the larger world of popular tracts and stories for working-class audiences: not only the collection of Cobbett's *Rural Rides* in book form at the beginning of the decade, but Harriet Martineau's *Illustrations of Political Economy* in the form of didactic stories (1832–4), the commencement of Charles Knight's *Penny Magazine* in 1832, or the numerous pamphlets issued beginning in 1825 by the Society for the Diffusion of Useful Knowledge. And in turn beneath that world, much of which admittedly smacks of keeping a lid on working-class discontent, lie such attempts to give voice to the inchoate class consciousness as are represented by *The Poor Man's Guardian* or the Chartist *Northern Star*.

The novel of the 1830s has often been viewed as a barren stretch, enlivened perhaps only by the sea stories of Captain Marryat, and certainly it is difficult to see much that is redeeming in a time when the prolix and sometimes embarrassing Bulwer has come to stand as the chief figure, chronologically speaking, between Scott and Dickens. For nearly half a century, the rest has been relegated to the classification – a form of dismissal – of large numbers of works into "silver fork" novels (of high society) and "Newgate" novels (drawing on popular literature of crime and punishment). But in fact such fictional subgenres are much more permeable than the classifications admit. A single novel may draw on both Newgate and silver fork elements, because writers of the 1830s, as well as their audiences, were aware of increasingly fluid class boundaries: wild speculation in the early years of uncontrolled entrepreneurship, with the enhanced possibilities of making and losing entire fortunes, and the breakdown of older Tory theories of class obligation. We cannot hold fiction such as this to the test of mid-Victorian realism of George Eliot or Anthony Trollope, with its emphasis on compromise, the repatterning rather than the jettisoning of the social order, the process by which an individual consciousness comes to maturity in the context of a larger and organically evolving community. Harriet Martineau's fine (and still too seldom read) *Deerbrook* (1839) is perhaps the earliest novel in which we can even glimpse such Middlemarchian possibilities.

The thirties also offer an almost unexampled opportunity to explore public rhetoric. Civic discourse appeared along a political continuum that ranged from post-Tory prophetic radicalism à la Carlyle on the right to the leftist radicalism of James and John Stuart Mill, as well as of the less philosophically articulated but increasingly visible analysis practiced by working-class authors. Between these extremes, public rhetoric centered on the language of compromise represented by Macaulay, Russell, and Peel's Tamworth Manifesto. Brantlinger sees in the literature of the 1830s a movement from utopian, Shelleyan politics on the liberal side, or from the corporatist Tory thinking of Southey and Coleridge on the conservative side, toward gradual social improvement. For this purpose he suggests as a fitting epigraph Macaulay's famous aphorism "an acre of Middlesex is better than a principality in Utopia" – an early intimation of the mid-Victorian gospel of progress. But Macaulay is as dangerous an example as Carlyle (whose atypicality is widely proclaimed by many of his contemporaries and present-day historians alike), perhaps all the more so because the neatly balanced antitheses of Macaulay's rhetoric, with its Augustan appeal to reason and restraint in speeches that seem to have been designed more for posterity than for the passage of legislation, suggest all the rationalities of that compromise with which the liberal imagination is comfortable. Psychic as well as political terrors lurk close to the surface in this decade, and Macaulay enjoyed no exemption: the public man gives little hint of the lonely, passionate bachelor whose letters to his sisters breathe what has struck many readers as more than fraternal devotion. Since liberty and order are issues of the self as well as of politics, the history of public and private languages of the 1830s may indeed affirm both the emergence of a centrist rhetoric and the disruptive potential which it keeps at bay. Beneath these contestations, a common ground can be found for understanding the aspirations of sages, politicians, maybe even gentleman-diarists, and almost certainly the yet-nameless writers struggling to come to terms not only with the first industrial revolution but with the very meaning of reform itself.

How It Struck Some Contemporaries

For some Victorians at mid-century, the 1830s were an originary decade which was already assuming the status of myth. In *Middlemarch* (1872), but even more lovingly in the opening pages of *Felix Holt* (1867), George Eliot revisited a pastoral time in which "the glory had not yet departed from the old coach-roads" and the railroads were only barely thought of, while as late as 1911 Frederic Harrison's *Autobiographic Memoirs* evoked a green and pleasant space on Muswell Hill subsequently blanketed with suburban sprawl in his own lifetime. For John Henry Newman, this narrative of origins even had a date: July 14, 1833, when John Keble preached the Assize

Sermon in the University Pulpit at Oxford on the subject of "National Apostasy," "the start," Newman put it in his *Apologia pro Vita Sua* (1864–5), "of the religious movement of 1833" (ch. 1). The ensuing Tractarian Movement was itself a myth of origins, an attempt to lead the Church of England back to its own Catholicity and thus to offer a *via media* between Rome and Protestantism. On the eve of Keble's sermon, Newman's emotionally charged homecoming from his mysterious illness in Sicily to England takes on the character of a pilgrimage providentially guided by his rediscovery of the early Church Fathers and culminating more than a decade later at the hands of the Passionist priest who received him into the Roman Catholic flock.

But for those writing as the decade was unfolding, particularly those for whom the rediscovery of Catholic orthodoxy was no solution, there were no origins, only an end not yet discernible in the events of the day. For, perhaps more than in any preceding decade in England, writers of the 1830s were conscious of theirs as a time of transition. The popularity of such terms as "the spirit of the age," the title of an essay by William Hazlitt in 1825, was seized upon by John Stuart Mill with the remark that he did not believe it was "to be met with in any work exceeding fifty years in antiquity." Carlyle's "Signs of the Times" (1829) and "Characteristics" (1831), both published in the *Edinburgh Review*, Mill's own "The Spirit of the Age" published in the weekly *Examiner* from January through May of 1831, and Bulwer's already-mentioned *England and the English* (1833) are all evidences of the fascination – if not, indeed, the obsession – with that process by which one becomes aware of something different and as yet not fully formed in one's own times. Carlyle the transcendentalist skeptical of transitory political nostrums, Mill the rationalist discovering alternative worlds in Wordsworth and in Coleridgean political thought, Bulwer the dandy-reformer who asked Mill to write an appendix on Bentham for *England and the English* but later turned Conservative, make uneasy company; yet enough of a common temper enters these works to explain Carlyle's first hope that Mill was a "new Mystic" and Mill's exhortation to Carlyle to read Bulwer. Though Carlyle had earlier expressed the belief that Bulwer was a "poor fribble," he concluded his reading of *England and the English* with an expression of astonishment at "the contrast of the man and his enterprise."

What were the common elements of these disparate works? Even Carlyle, who in such catch-phrases as "spirit of the age" and "progress of the species" professed to find symptoms of that disease of self-consciousness which he felt had paralyzed the times, was forced to the task of anatomist he deplored. Like Carlyle, whose "Characteristics" began with the words, "The healthy know not of their health, but only the sick," Mill resorted to a medical metaphor when he attempted to describe the inconstancy of opinion in an unsettled time: "The men of the present day rather incline to an opinion than embrace it; few, except the very penetrating, or the very presumptuous, have full confidence in their own convictions. This is not a state of health, but, at the best, of convalescence." Mill's desire for greater social confidence resembles what Carlyle called "spontaneity" and "unconsciousness," the signs of a healthy organism, individual or social, working harmoniously: "Had Adam remained in Paradise," the sage of Chelsea succinctly observed, "there had been no Anatomy and no Metaphysics."

Of the three, Bulwer was perhaps unexpectedly the most eloquent. Like Carlyle he saw the uncertainties of an era marked by the eclipse if not extinction of earlier verities as a necessary if painful preface to reconstruction. "We live," Bulwer wrote,

> in an age of visible transition – an age of disquietude and doubt – of the removal of time-worn landmarks, and the breaking up of the hereditary elements of society – old opinions, feelings – ancestral customs and institutions are crumbling away, and both the spiritual and temporal worlds are darkened by the shadows of change. The commencement of one of these epochs – periodical in the history of mankind – is hailed by the sanguine as the coming of a new Millennium – a great iconoclastic reformation, by which all false gods shall be overthrown. To me such epochs appear but as the dark passages in the appointed progress of mankind – the times of greatest unhappiness to our species – passages into which we have no reason to rejoice at our entrance, save from the hope of being sooner landed on the opposite side. (318–19)

While Bulwer here refers to the millennialism of the latter-day *philosophes*, James Mill and Bentham, and thus exhibits one of those curious and characteristic recoils from those he professes to admire, Mill and Carlyle read disquieting signs of the thirties in the prophecies of Edward Irving and other preachers predicting the approaching Second Coming. In "Signs of the Times," Carlyle had distanced himself from Millites and Millenarians alike as false prophets, and in "The Spirit of the Age" Mill comments with subdued amazement on how "even the religious world teems with new interpretations of the prophecies." Though Mill and Carlyle differ on the role of a new religion, they are not far apart in seeing the crisis as, finally, one of faith. For Carlyle, the "noblest class" of would-be believers are neither those who "take up with worn-out Symbols of the Godlike" nor those who, denying all forms of faith, seek only pleasure, but rather those who "have dared to say No, and cannot yet say Yea." This is not so far from Mill's pronouncement that "at present, we are in a mixed state; some fight fiercely under their several banners, and these chiefly the least instructed; while the others (those few excepted who have strength to stand by themselves) are blown about by every breath, having no steady opinion – or at least no deep-rooted conviction that their opinion is true."

More wedded than Carlyle to a specific political program, Bulwer and Mill stood together in seeing the displacement of an aristocratic class from political power as a necessary step toward the restoration of stability; their concern was that the transition be peaceful, and that power be relocated in the hands of the most competent, which the upper class, what Mill called the "stationary part of mankind," manifestly was not. Carlyle, though he did not tackle this issue in "Characteristics," would have agreed to the extent that in his view outward trappings in church, state, or society were merely a hollow shell of pretense, the "old clothes" he denounced in *Sartor*. Bulwer's denunciation of the materialist tenor of English philosophy, which he regarded as having been essentially at a standstill since Locke, is likewise not far from Carlyle's lament at the ascendancy of "mechanism" over "organism" in English society.

Finally, all three men were concerned with an issue of fundamental importance in the politics of the decade: how stability and change might be mutually accommodated. In particular, Carlyle and Mill took full account of, and gave due credit to, those with whom they might have been expected to have little in common. Surveying an apparently widening gap between rich and poor, Carlyle confessed that "the ancient methods of administration will no longer suffice," that in change there was "nothing terrible, nothing supernatural," and that "if Memory have its force and worth, so also has hope." On the other hand, it is not a little curious to see the son of James Mill affirming that old prejudices were preferable to new impressions, that free discussion might weaken error without insuring its replacement by informed opinion, that wise men and not merely an enlarged electorate were demanded by the times, and that the object of an age of transition, rightly guided, was to call forth a new "natural state" in which "worldly power, and moral influence, are habitually and indisputably exercised by the fittest persons." When the younger Mill declares that "every age contains in itself the germ of all future ages as surely as the acorn contains the future forest," utilitarian rhetoric has at least been brushed by Romantic organicism.

A curiously paradoxical decade, then, in that while in politics and social life the sense of division must have seemed deeper than ever, this was also arguably the last decade in which such fundamentally different persons as Bulwer, Mill, and Carlyle could agree on something resembling a common diagnosis of social ills and their remedies. Conversely, as England experienced the crises of the Hungry Forties that followed, they took diverse paths. Carlyle's earlier generosity of spirit seems to evaporate in the increasingly shrill harangues that culminate years later in *Latter-Day Pamphlets* (1850) and "Shooting Niagara" (1867), while for his part, Mill spent much of the remainder of the decade as a publicist for the increasingly chimerical goal of forming an effective Radical party in Parliament, an object for which Carlyle had no sympathy and for which Mill's own hopes were to be finally and effectively dashed by the election of 1841. Bulwer, longing for the life and status of a landed gentleman and never fundamentally at ease with many of his Radical colleagues, ended his political journey by making his peace with the Conservatives and briefly holding a cabinet post under Derby at mid-century, while energetically pursuing his own career as a popular novelist.

Literature courses that focus on such mid-Victorian sages as Carlyle, Mill, Arnold, Newman, and Ruskin tend to overemphasize their representativeness. Most of these prophets reposed on the far side of a gulf which was widening between them and the larger public, and as is all too often apparent from the reviews, they tended to be regarded as at best idiosyncratic and at worst irrelevant. One may view the 1830s either with regret as marking the recession of hopes for a shared cultural consensus or with interested curiosity as inaugurating an invigorating interchange between "high" and "low" forms of art. The first is perhaps an especially dangerous oversimplification because it represents a particularly egregious form of cultural elitism; by any reasonable modern standard, there was nothing resembling a mass audience for their diagnoses. Yet in their own ways Carlyle, Mill, and Bulwer all read the signs of the times with considerable accuracy. Through their voices resonate those larger symptoms of cultural uncertainty that give the 1830s their peculiar character. Such thinkers knew more clearly than the generation of political leaders reaching the end of their careers that the thirties were not Georgian aftermath but the seedtime of a new era.

See also Administrative; Fiction, Sage Writing, Historiography; Shores

References

Arnstein, W. (1996) *Britain Yesterday and Today: 1830 to the Present*, 7th edn. Lexington: Heath.

Brantlinger, P. (1977) *The Spirit of Reform: British Literature and Politics, 1832–1867*. Cambridge MA and London: Harvard University Press.

Bulwer-Lytton, E. (1833) *England and the English*, ed. S. Meacham. Chicago: University of Chicago Press, 1970.

Cooper, J. F. (1837) *Gleanings in Europe: England*, ed. D. A. Ringe and K. W. Staggs. Albany: State University Press of New York, 1982.

Cronin, R. (2002) *Romantic Victorians: English Literature, 1824–1840*. Basingstoke: Palgrave.

Darwin, B. (1951) "Country Life and Sport." In *Early Victorian England, 1830–1865*, ed. G. M. Young, 2 vols. Oxford: Oxford University Press.

Gash, N. (1953) *Politics in the Age of Peel: A Study in the Technique of Parliamentary Representation, 1830–1850*. New York: W. W. Norton.

Greville, C. C. F. (1875) *A Journal of the Reigns of King George IV and King William IV*, ed. H. Reeve, 2 vols. New York: Appleton.

d'Haussez, C. le Mercher de Longpré, Baron (1833) *Great Britain in 1833*, 2 vols. London: Richard Bentley.

Kitson Clark, G. (1964) *Peel and the Conservative Party: A Study in Party Politics, 1832–1841*, 2nd edn. London: Cass.

Madden, W. (1963) "The Victorian Sensibility." *Victorian Studies* 7, 67–97.

Martineau, H. (1877) *A History of the Thirty Years' Peace*, A.D. *1816–1846*, 4 vols. London: George Bell.

Mill, J. S. (1831) "The Spirit of the Age." In *Collected Edition of the Works of John Stuart Mill*, ed. A. P. Robson and J. M. Robson, vol. 22. Toronto: University of Toronto Press, 1986.

Oliphant, M., and F. R. Oliphant (1892) *The Victorian Age of English Literature*, 2 vols. London: Perceval.

Phillips, J. A., and C. Wetherell (1995) "The Great Reform Act of 1832 and the Political Modernization of England." *American Historical Review* 100, 411–36.

Quinlan, M. J. (1941) *Victorian Prelude: A History of English Manners, 1700–1839*. New York: Columbia University Press.

Roberts, D. (1959) "Jeremy Bentham and the Victorian Administrative State." *Victorian Studies* 2, 193–210.

Rorabaugh, W. J. (1973) "Politics and the Architectural Competition for the Houses of Parliament, 1834–1837." *Victorian Studies* 17, 155–75.

Southgate, D. (1962) *The Passing of the Whigs, 1832–1886*. London: Macmillan.

Tocqueville, A. de (1835) *Journeys to England and Ireland*, trans. G. Lawrence and K. P. Mayer, ed. J. P. Mayer. London: Faber and Faber, 1958.

Vallone, L. (2001) *Becoming Victoria*. New Haven: Yale University Press.

FURTHER READING

Armstrong, I. (1993) *Victorian Poetry: Poetry, Poetics and Politics*. London and New York: Routledge.

Elfenbein, A. (1995) *Byron and the Victorians*. Cambridge: Cambridge University Press.

Harrison, J. F. C. (1971) *The Early Victorians, 1832–1851*. London: Weidenfeld and Nicolson.

Hollingsworth, K. (1963) *The Newgate Novel, 1830–1847: Bulwer, Ainsworth, Dickens, and Thackeray*. Detroit: Wayne State University Press.

Jordan, R. F. (1966) *Victorian Architecture*. Harmondsworth and Baltimore: Penguin.

Stein, R. (1987) *Victoria's Year: English Literature and Culture, 1837–1838*. New York and Oxford: Oxford University Press.

Vicinus, M. (1974) *The Industrial Muse: A Study of Nineteenth Century British Working-Class Literature*. New York: Barnes and Noble.

2
1851

Antony H. Harrison

Revolution and Reform

Matthew Arnold's "Dover Beach" (ca. 1851) concludes with his speaker looking away from the chalk cliffs of England toward continental Europe and lamenting that

> . . . the world, which seems
> To lie before us like a land of dreams,
> So various, so beautiful, so new,
> Hath really neither joy, nor love, nor light,
> Nor certitude, nor peace, nor help for pain;
> And we are here as on a darkling plain
> Swept with confused alarms of struggle and flight,
> Where ignorant armies clash by night. (ll. 30–7)

The disturbing worldview presented here originated with tumultuous historical events that shattered the relative calm of Europe at mid-century. In the autumn of 1848 (some eight months after Marx's *Communist Manifesto* was issued in England), Arnold traveled to the Continent and witnessed the aftershocks of unprecedented political chaos. Revolutionary activity had rocked Sicily in January, Paris in late February, Germany and Italy in March. The fall of Austria's once powerful chancellor, Clemens Metternich, on March 13 had signaled political disintegration. In April, hostilities had erupted between Germany and Poland. At the same time, Russia had prepared for war to preserve its hold on Poland.

A New Companion to Victorian Literature and Culture, First Edition. Edited by Herbert F. Tucker.
© 2014 John Wiley & Sons, Ltd. Published 2014 by John Wiley & Sons, Ltd.

By the spring of the following year, when Arnold once again traveled to Europe, matters had not improved. In March of 1849 Sardinia renewed its war against Austria, begun the previous year. On April 30, French forces clashed with Garibaldi's republican troops in Italy. In April, as well, Austrian and Hungarian forces became embattled, and in July Russian troops quashed revolutionary stirrings in Moldavia and Wallachia (Taylor 4–34). During the years immediately after the European countries shaken by revolutionary turmoil became stabilized, the standoff between major powers, all eager to usurp territory or protect what they already possessed, dominated political discourse in Europe. The German provinces were at issue between Austria and Prussia; France desired more land along the Rhine; Italy rankled under the protection of Austria; and a conflict between Russia and Turkey in the Near East seemed inevitable. Eventually, after a series of stopgap treaties and protocols had failed, Britain and France declared war on Russia in February of 1854 and inaugurated the Crimean debacle (Taylor 24–70; McCord 244–9). These events are the political subtexts of "Dover Beach."

In England, too, throughout the 1840s (but especially during the early, economically depressed years known as the Hungry Forties), insurrection was feared by the middle and upper classes, and writers often expressed their apprehensions iconoclastically. The "condition of England" question, responses to which normally focused on the social effects of laissez-faire capitalism and on class conflict, dominated novels of the period such as Benjamin Disraeli's *Sybil; or The Two Nations* (1845), Charles Kingsley's *Yeast* (1848) and *Alton Locke* (1850), and Elizabeth Gaskell's *Mary Barton* (1848), as well as the work of popular poets and essayists. In "The Cry of the Human" (1842) Elizabeth Barrett decried "the plague of gold" that "strikes far and near" and its effects upon the human heart:

> Our thoughts grow blank, our words grow strange,
>   We cheer the pale gold-diggers,
> Each soul is worth so much on Change,
>   And marked, like sheep, with figures.

Thomas Carlyle was also concerned with the dehumanizing effects of industrial capitalism. Anticipating Arnold's strategy in "Dover Beach," in *Past and Present* (1843) he compared the Middle Ages, idealized as a period of political, social, and religious stability, to industrialized England and prophetically concluded:

> I well venture to believe that in no time, since the beginnings of Society, was the lot of [the] dumb millions of toilers so entirely unbearable as it is even in the days now passing over us. It is not to die, or even to die of hunger, that makes a man wretched; many men have died, all men must die . . . But it is to live miserable we know not why; to work sore and yet gain nothing; to be heartworn, weary, yet isolated, unrelated, girt-in with a cold universal Laissez-faire: it is to die slowly all our life long, imprisoned in a deaf, dead, Infinite Injustice . . . This is and remains for ever intolerable to all men

whom God has made. Do we wonder at French Revolutions, Chartisms, Revolts of Three Days? The times, if we will consider them, are really unexampled. (book 3, ch. 8)

Carlyle collapsed the manifold threats to the survival of the English nation into two essential and momentous problems: a lack of spiritual unity or brotherhood among men, and the invisibility of great leaders who were desperately needed to reform British society.

In her preface to *Mary Barton* (dated October, 1848) Mrs Gaskell expressed the conflicted feelings of sympathy and fear that often characterized the middle-class response to the condition of the working classes:

> If it be an error, that the woes, which come with ever-returning tide-like flood to over-whelm the workmen in our manufacturing towns, pass unregarded by all but the sufferers, it is at any rate an error so bitter in its consequences to all parties, that whatever public effort can do in the way of legislation, or private effort in the way of merciful deeds, or helpless love in the way of widow's mites, should be done, and that speedily, to disabuse the work-people of so miserable a misapprehension. At present they seem to me to be left in a state, wherein lamentations and tears are thrown aside as useless, but in which the lips are compressed for curses, and the hands clenched and ready to smite.

The general subject of Gaskell's novel is the rift between rich and poor, perhaps nowhere in England more apparent during the 1840s than in Manchester, where *Mary Barton* is set. Like many other social novels of the forties, this one attempts to raise middle-class consciousness that political insurrection resulting from social and economic conditions was a very real danger in England. To her publisher Gaskell acknowledged that her book was "such as to excite attention at the present time of the struggle on the part of work people to obtain what they esteem their rights" (March 21, 1848).

The living and working conditions of the lower classes, who at mid-century constituted some 70 percent of the British population (McCord 214–19), were examined not only by novelists and poets, but also in parliamentary blue books and by numerous essayists. Perhaps the most excruciating chronicles of working-class life emerged in Friedrich Engels's *The Condition of the Working Classes in England* (first published in Germany in 1845) and Henry Mayhew's *London Labour and the London Poor* (issued serially in 1851–2). Engels presents the first major study of the effects of industrialization on workers: the occupational diseases that afflicted them, the inadequacy of their diets, clothing, medical care, and education, the dangers of their work in mines, mills, and factories, their victimization by the cycles of the marketplace, and the horrors of their living conditions. Typical are his descriptions of the working-class districts of north-eastern Manchester, an area where the "coal-black, stagnant, stinking" Medlock river divided two "disgusting" neighborhoods of 4,000 people inhabiting 400 dilapidated one-room cottages, these surrounded by "heaps of refuse, offal and sickening filth." Engels describes a neighborhood polluted by stench and thick factory smoke, an area where hordes of "ragged women and children swarm about the streets

. . . just as dirty as the pigs which wallow" nearby. He concludes that this population has "sunk to the lowest level of humanity" imaginable and suggests that its members would have little to lose in an uprising against their oppressors (Engels 71). Mayhew's survey is less polemical and more systematic than Engels's. He lays "before the reader a catalogue of such occupations in London as yield a bare subsistence to the parties engaged in them," along with descriptions of "the dwellings of the unrelieved poor." In the process he exposes "not only on how little they subsist, but [also] . . . the rent they are charged for their waterless, drainless, floorless, and almost roofless tenements" and "calculate[s] the interest that the petty capitalist reaps from their necessities" (Mayhew xix). Despite his awareness that his subjects are victimized by the hegemony of laissez-faire economic values, Mayhew, unlike Engels, prescribes no course of political action for this "proletariat."

The condition of the working classes in England did result in numerous incidents of localized violence during the 1840s, but the extraordinary historical fact is that no large-scale revolutionary movement emerged. No single event underscores that fact so much as the opening, in May, 1851, of Joseph Paxton's dazzling Crystal Palace in Hyde Park, which housed the Great Exhibition of the Works of Industry of All Nations. Indeed, despite the apprehensions of many in the middle and upper classes, others in the late forties expressed confidence that all would be well. About the time of his second novel, *The Kellys and the O'Kellys*, published in 1848, Anthony Trollope insisted "that there is no ground to fear any general rising . . . I think there is too much intelligence in England for any large body of men to look for any sudden improvement" (II, 17). Historians have offered various explanations for England's relative quiescence. G. M. Young's landmark conclusion is typical:

> The storm which swept away half the Governments of Europe passed harmlessly over the islands, and the words which Macaulay wrote at the beginning of his [*History of England from the Accession of James II*, 1848], that his checkered narrative would excite thankfulness in all religious minds and hope in the breast of all patriots, had a deep significance for his first readers, watching the nations of Europe sink one by one from convulsive anarchy back into despotism, and seeing, in the recovered unity, as much as in the prosperity of England, a triumphant vindication of the historic English way. (78)

"The historic English way" was, at the private level, the way of the stiff upper lip and muddling through; at the public level it was the way of constitutional monarchy. Well before 1848 clear evidence of legislative progress toward the amelioration of political, social, and economic ills afflicting "the lower orders" was visible. Moreover, attempts to organize workers and their supporters into a force that would have proved threatening to England's political and social stability had, by the close of 1848, proven ineffectual. The most prominent among these were the Chartist movement and the efforts of the Anti-Corn Law League.

In 1836 the radical William Lovett founded the London Working Men's Association, made up largely of self-educated artisans. Two years later he and the reformer

Francis Place drew up a program for massive political reform detailed in the "People's Charter," a document ultimately submitted as a petition for parliamentary action three times: in 1839, 1842, and 1848. Based in many respects on Benthamite reformist ideals, it supported "Six Points" of radical change: universal male suffrage, equal electoral districts, removal of property qualifications for members of Parliament, payment for MPs, a secret ballot, and annual general elections. The Chartists in 1838 established bases of operation in three major industrial cities (London, Birmingham, and Leeds) and organized large meetings of working people who were addressed by zealous speakers. The movement grew with impressive speed, and by the spring of 1839 at their National Convention the Chartists presented to Parliament a great petition with hundreds of thousands of signatures. The convention moved to Birmingham in May, but in July the House of Commons, despite localized strikes and riots, rejected the petition now boasting well over a million signatures. It did so for a second time in 1842 when the Charter was taken to Westminster from a preliminary mass meeting in Lincoln's Inn Fields. By the time of the Chartists' third (and final) attempt to move Parliament to action in April of 1848, tensions surrounding England's deep class divisions had reached an extraordinary pitch, especially in light of events on the Continent. Although the Whig government under the leadership of Lord John Russell was prepared for widespread insurrection and had banned mass demonstrations, some 50,000 Chartist supporters and observers gathered on Kensington Common. But 8,000 troops had been ordered up, in addition to more than 4,000 London policemen and a massive reserve force of special constables (which some commentators estimate at over 100,000). Thirty guns were held ready at the Tower of London, with steamers prepared to transport them to Parliament. The Chartists clearly faced overwhelming opposition, and once again Parliament could afford to be unresponsive. This was the case, however, in part because widespread support for the movement surfaced typically in times of economic hardship, and by 1848 England's economy was expanding toward prosperity.

In addition, many of the issues Chartists wanted addressed through direct and dramatic political change had already been dealt with through legislation enacted after the First Reform Act of 1832 had expanded the franchise. The list of subsequent measures designed to improve the working and living conditions of the "lower orders" is extensive. It includes the Poor Law Amendment Act of 1834 and later revisions of it; the reduction of tariffs on imported items (1842); Factory Acts of 1844 and 1848 that limited the number of hours women and children could work; the Town Improvement Clauses Act of 1847, which expedited implementation of measures for paving, draining, and lighting streets in British cities; the Public Health Act of 1848; and, as important as any of these pieces of legislation, the repeal of the Corn Laws in 1846.

Four years earlier, Elizabeth Barrett had lamented "The curse of gold upon the land" which "The lack of bread enforces." The people of England had suffered for decades from artificially high prices induced by laws which limited the quantities of grain that could be imported and which imposed high tariffs on such imports. No longer an agrarian green and pleasant land, England was a nation, according to Barrett, in which

> The rail-cars snort from strand to strand,
>   Like more of Death's White Horses.
> The rich preach "rights" and "future days,"
>   And hear no angel scoffing;
> The poor die mute, with starving gaze
>   On corn-ships in the offing. ("The Cry of the Human," 1842)

In the same year that Chartism emerged, the Anti-Corn Law League was formed. A wide and varied, politically savvy and well-funded constituency was soon brought together in a crusade against the protection of agricultural interests, most of them wealthy landowners. Despite the power of this landed opposition, the League was able to rout it within eight years.

Thus, by the time of the last Chartist demonstrations in 1848, bread was relatively cheap in England, working and living conditions for the poor were improving measurably, demand for English goods in foreign markets and at home was high, and wages were increasing accordingly. Britain was producing more than half the world's pig iron (and would treble her output during the next 30 years); her commercial steamships (and her navy) dominated the world's seas; within 20 years her foreign trade would be more than that of France, Germany, and Italy combined, and nearly four times that of the United States. England was heading toward a period of prosperity that was sustained for two decades and that was signaled by the opening on May 1, 1851 of the famous Crystal Palace international exhibition of new consumer goods and cutting-edge technologies, hailed by *The Times* as "a sight the like of which has never happened before, and which, in the nature of things, can never be repeated . . . Some were most reminded of that day when all ages and climes shall be gathered round the throne of their Maker." The Exhibition was commemorated at all levels of British culture and society, and in most imaginable venues: from the press to engravings, sketches, paintings, musical arrangements, architectural imitations, and economic analyses incontrovertibly forecasting decades of national prosperity, to publications such as Henry Mayhew's (to some viewers of the cultural scene) surprisingly celebratory novel *1851*. Prince Albert's opening speech declared that "The Exhibition of 1851 is to give us a true test and living picture of the point of development at which the whole of mankind has arrived . . . and a new starting point from which all nations will be able to direct their future exertions," with Britain presenting "itself as the measure against which 'all [other] nations' were to compare themselves" (Gillooly in Buzard et al. 26).

In the almost 773,000 square-foot glass and steel Palace, exhibits from around the world were classified into four "progressive" categories: Raw Materials, Machinery, Manufactures, and the Fine Arts, where "industry and manufacture were naturalized as activities contiguous with the world of nature itself, and the fine arts were the fruit of human work upon natural materials" (Teukolsky in Buzard et al. 86). Similarly, the amazing spectacle effaced profound conflicts within the nation: a self-consciously sublime and ostensibly transparent symbol of heterogeneous collaboration (among materials, workers, classes, and nations), the project transcended social, political, and cultural difference. "What was called into being, there in the spring of 1851, was a convulsive act of consensus, a full-dress staging of national concord" in which "'all' and 'every' became the consensual language of exhibition," and "the whole world, the entire nation, every borough" found plenitude as "the product of collective will" (Chase and Levenson in Buzard et al. 124–5).

The idea of the Great Exhibition could never have come to fruition if England had, like the rest of Europe during the 1840s, undergone cataclysmic revolution. Instead, England experienced a gradual movement toward higher standards of living sustained in subsequent decades and impelled by the ineluctable forces of industrial capitalism and legislative reform. "Progress" became the byword of the day (though the fact of it was often unperceived by many of the still-impoverished lower classes). Between 1851 and 1883 the national income was to double; real income per head to rise nearly 30 percent; and exports to increase 229 percent (Burn 16). Mid-century was a period of phenomenal growth based on technological advances and greater industrial efficiency. The pace of building – railroads, canals, bridges, factories, centers of government administration, warehouses, churches, and middle-class suburbs – was frenetic. Across the seas, Britain found ready markets for its goods, some of them in the expanding Empire. The policy of liberal imperialism established by Lord Durham's "Report on Canada" in 1839 was extended, as emigrants were directed to the most fertile of England's colonies. With the annexation of the Punjab in 1849, the dominion of the British over the vast riches and population of India was completed. In 1851, the discovery of gold at Ballarat in Australia resulted in large-scale immigration. And in 1854 New Zealand was granted self-government based on the Canadian model; its population grew to a quarter of a million by 1870 (Thompson 168). These outposts of the Empire were unified by the inheritance of British political traditions and capitalist values.

Such values were registered in the predominantly realistic fiction produced by High Victorian novelists like Thackeray, Trollope, George Eliot, Hardy, and George Meredith, in which money and financial problems are dominant issues that often provide the basis for plots. The work of these writers was readily embraced by bourgeois audiences, whose interest in their own progress toward financial prosperity and enhanced social status was boundless. The approach of such readers to getting on in the world emerges toward the end of *David Copperfield* (1850). Dickens's hero attributes his successes to a set of "golden rules" that Oscar Wilde at the close of the century would lampoon as quintessentially Victorian. David explains that "whatever I have tried to do in life, I have tried with all my heart to do well . . . whatever I have devoted myself to, I have devoted myself to completely . . . [T]here is no substitute for thorough-going, ardent, and sincere earnestness" (ch. 42).

Matthew Arnold, an indisputably earnest Victorian, writing to his close friend Arthur Hugh Clough in September of 1849, showed less concern with the situation of the working classes in England than with the plight of middle-class men like himself, living in a "modern" society defined by ambition, greed, "sick hurry," and "divided aims." "These are damned times," he sputtered,

> everything is against one – the height to which knowledge is come, the spread of luxury, our physical enervation, the absence of great *natures*, the unavoidable contact with millions of small ones, newspapers, cities, light profligate friends, moral desperadoes like Carlyle, our own selves, and the sickening consciousness of our difficulties. (September 23, 1849)

The destabilizing "difficulties" that afflicted middle-class consciousness at mid-century were not exclusively social and political: they involved moral, religious, aesthetic, and gender issues as well. In public fora and in their own hearts, mid-Victorians were often preoccupied with questions surrounding religious faith, men's and women's roles in and outside of the home, and the moral and social ramifications of aesthetic values.

Religion

Although what may have been the most important book of the century, Darwin's *The Origin of Species*, did not appear until 1859, the unparalleled controversy that its publication provoked was merely an extension of heated public and private debates about religious values and practices that had preoccupied Victorians since the 1830s. Charles Lyell's 1,600-page tome *The Principles of Geology* (1833) anticipated the theories of Darwin and inspired many thinking men and women, including Alfred Tennyson, to examine evolution as a serious challenge to the biblical story of creation and therefore as a threat to religious orthodoxies grounded in a literal acceptance of the Bible. New scientific theories and discoveries, along with the breathtaking velocity of technological advance, appeared to many observers evidence of an increasing cultural emphasis on secular matters that threatened traditional religious belief. The expanding dominion of scientific inquiry was demonstrated by the opening of honours schools in natural science at Cambridge in 1848 and at Oxford four years later, while the marvels of new technology were both exhibited and embodied in the Great Exhibition.

Some felt that religious faith was endangered not just by such developments in science and in the world of getting and spending. Eighteen years before the Great Exhibition, a group of conservative Oxford clerics and teachers identified fundamental threats to religious orthodoxy that had emerged within the Anglican Church itself, which they believed had strayed from firm belief, adherence to traditional rituals, and its true origins in Catholicism. In 1833 John Henry Newman joined forces with Richard Hurrell Froude and John Keble in a profoundly controversial attempt to reform the Church that soon came to be known as the Oxford Movement. Later joined by Edward Pusey, these educators over the course of eight years published a series of *Tracts for the Times* that attacked rationalism and liberal theology, asserted the necessity of the visible Church as the vehicle of invisible grace, and reemphasized the importance of the sacraments and Church ritual. According to the liberal-minded Thomas Arnold (the poet's father), these men's "intense love for the forms of the Church . . . absolutely engrossed their whole nature" (Arnold 82). When Newman converted to Catholicism in 1845, the public debate spawned by Tractarian teachings and writings intensified in some quarters, and it remained widespread and enduring. But by the 1840s "what was at issue was no longer the validity of Anglican orders, but for an increasing number of thinking people the validity of Christianity itself" (Gilmour 86). Discussion of religious issues continued in a variety of fora, including the novel. Newman's own *Loss and Gain* appeared in 1848, while James Anthony Froude's *The Nemesis of Faith*, in which his religious uncertainties and anti-Tractarian bias surfaced, was published the following year. Even during the 1850s controversy over vitriolic sermons delivered by conservative clergymen who were scions of the Oxford Movement caused riots outside London churches. At the other end of the spectrum, the publication in 1860 of *Essays and Reviews*, written by six Broad Church clergymen and one layman on a variety of sensitive religious topics, ignited a furor nearly as explosive as that caused by the Tractarians. (Two of the contributors were prosecuted for heresy.) The volume attacked biblical literalism in light of recent scientific discoveries, while it questioned the divine inspiration of the scriptures and the validity of events described as miracles in the New Testament. Its authors also insisted that the true bond among members of the Church as a national institution was morality rather than dogma. They demanded that scripture and dogma both be understood relativistically, in terms of the historical contexts out of which they emerged.

The controversies surrounding Tractarianism and the publication of *Essays and Reviews*, like the debate over evolution, were explosive because the questions they raised left little cover for an uneasiness about religious faith already deeply felt by many educated people groping for direction in a world destabilized by the vertiginous effects of industrialism and the new science on social and moral values. The poet Arthur Hugh Clough situates himself at the skeptical end of the spectrum in works like "The New Sinai" (1844):

> Lo, here is God, and there is God!
>   Believe it not, O Man;
> In such vain sort to this and that
>   The ancient heathen ran:
> Though Old Religion shake her head,
>   And say in bitter grief,
> The day behold, at first foretold,
>   Of atheist unbelief:
> Take better part, with manly heart,
>   Thine adult spirit can;
> Receive it not, believe it not,
>   Believe it not, O Man!

Clough's attacks on orthodoxy were relentless. In "Easter Day: Naples, 1849," he attempts once more to expose the hollowness of faith on the most sacred of Christian holidays:

> My heart was hot within me; till at last
> My brain was lightened when my tongue had said –
>   Christ is not risen!
>   Christ is not risen, no –
> He lies and moulders low.

(Presumably, the pun on "lies" is deliberate.) Clough's friend Matthew Arnold appears equally unorthodox. Though not an atheist, in poems like "To Marguerite – Continued" written around 1848, Arnold scoffs at the Christian illusion of a benevolent deity. In his view, a contrast to John Donne's, all individuals are, metaphorically, islands afflicted by a futile craving for reunion with their fellows in a continental humanity.

> Who order'd that their longing's fire
> Should be, as soon as kindled, cool'd?
> Who renders vain their deep desire? –
>   A God, a God their severance rul'd;
>   And bade betwixt their shores to be
>   The unplumb'd, salt, estranging sea.

This malevolent God designed human life as an exercise in sadism:

>   For, alas! he left us each retaining
> Shreds of gifts which he refus'd in full.
> Still these waste us with their hopeless straining –
> Still the attempt to use them proves them null. ("Self-Deception," 1852)

The profoundly frustrating result, for Arnold, is that "on earth we wander, groping, reeling."

Alfred Tennyson appears similarly disoriented in his search for a solid ground of faith in the early stanzas of his great poem *In Memoriam* (1850), a spiritual autobiography occasioned by the death of his intimate friend, Arthur Henry Hallam. This extraordinary elegy is composed of 131 lyrics of varying lengths written between 1833 and 1849. After enduring a period of virtual nihilism chronicled in the first quarter of the work, Tennyson describes his attempts to embrace traditional, consolatory Christian notions of resurrection and the afterlife, but these repeatedly fail him. Acknowledging the evidence of what Darwin was later to term natural selection ("finding that of fifty seeds," nature "often brings but one to bear"), Tennyson laments in poem 55,

> I falter where I firmly trod,
>> And falling with my weight of cares
>> Upon the great world's altar-stairs
> That slope thro' darkness up to God,
>
> I stretch lame hands of faith, and grope,
>> And gather dust and chaff.

Allusions to pre-Darwinian theories of evolution derived from geological treatises (Lyell's in particular) constitute the metaphorical strata of this poem. By its conclusion, however, a unique variety of faith has indeed evolved from the extensive process of epistemological and teleological interrogation enacted in the work. In poem 124, Tennyson can confidently announce his discovery of the *telos*,

> That which we dare invoke to bless;
>> Our dearest faith, our ghastliest doubt;
>> He, They, One, All, within, without;
> The Power in darkness whom we guess.

And with this discovery emerges a perfectibilian view of the future of mankind grounded in his agonized spiritual experience, the dark night of the soul which his friend Hallam's death has precipitated: "I dream a dream of good, / And mingle all the world with thee" (poem 128). The final lines of *In Memoriam* direct readers, with assured, apocalyptic optimism, to

> That God, which ever lives and loves,
>> One God, one law, one element,
>> And one far-off divine event,
> To which the whole creation moves.

Balanced against the outright skepticism of the Cloughs and Arnolds of mid-Victorian England, and the waverings of the Froudes and Tennysons, is the fervor of religious conviction in works written by the literary heirs of the Oxford Movement. In 1847 Charlotte Mary Yonge, who was tutored in Anglican history and theology by John Keble, published *Scenes and Characters*, an early novel that depicts life in a scrupulously Anglican household. In the same year Christina Rossetti, "the true inheritor of the Tractarian devotional mode in poetry" (Tennyson 198), began her career with the (private) printing of her first volume, simply entitled *Verses*. The intense piety of Rossetti's five subsequent books of poetry and five volumes of devotional prose typifies one important stance in the religious debates of the day. Her embrace of orthodoxy in "Sweet Death" (written in 1849) counters the *agon* of uncertainty that dominates the first half of *In Memoriam* (completed the same year). Repudiation of this world's vanities and resignation to the will of the Almighty are recurrent themes of Rossetti's work, as they are in this brief lyric, which concludes,

> . . . youth and beauty die.
>   So be it, O my God, thou God of truth:
>   Better than beauty and than youth
> Are Saints and Angels, a glad company;
>   And Thou, O Lord, our Rest and Ease,
>   Are better far than these.

Despite the apparent simplicity, in such verses, of Rossetti's ostensibly unobjectionable religious faith, her awareness of its controversial political ramifications emerges in an elegiac sonnet on John Henry Newman (who died in 1890). There she describes the leader of the Oxford Movement as a "Champion of the Cross" whose "tides were springtides, set against the neap / Of calmer souls." Unflinchingly, she asserts that his "flood rebuked their rill."

The Woman Question

Many of Christina Rossetti's nondevotional poems appear to modern readers distinctly less conservative than her religious works, intervening as they do in the mid-century controversy over women's social roles. Though she would, in the 1870s, decline an invitation from Augusta Webster to sign a petition for women's suffrage, much of Rossetti's work of the fifties and sixties in fact presents a critique of amatory relationships, the institution of marriage, or Victorian domestic values and practices and thus aligns itself with liberal and even radical commentaries on "The Woman Question" which began to emerge in the 1840s.

The Women of England: Their Social Duties and Domestic Habits, a best-seller by Sarah Stickney Ellis published in 1839, defines what is now known as the "domestic ideology," a widely accepted conservative theory of social roles and "separate spheres" of activity for Victorian middle-class men and women. According to this ideology as Ellis formulates it, "to men belongs the potent . . . consideration of worldly aggrandizement." They operate in the professions, governmental services, and the world of business and industry to acquire property, advance themselves, and improve the material condition of their wives and families. The world in which they move is seen to be dominated by "inborn selfishness," temptation, and vice. Women, by contrast ensconced in the domestic sphere, are understood to be "clothed in moral beauty" – selfless, disinterested, and spiritually pure by "nature." They are protected against worldly evils and possess a "secret [moral] influence" that can correct men's missteps. Ellis and like-minded thinkers (including the writers of ubiquitous conduct and childrearing manuals during the 1840s) assumed that a woman's goal in life was marriage and her vocation to bear and raise children. Coventry Patmore presents an idolatrous version of this cultural myth in his famous poem *The Angel in the House* (1854–62). The education of girls (satirized by Elizabeth Barrett Browning in the second book of her 1856 epic novel/poem *Aurora Leigh*) was therefore focused on "the minutiae of domestic comfort" (Ellis's phrase). In their capacity as domestic saints, English women could claim an "importance in society far beyond what their unobtrusive virtues would appear to claim." Ellis goes so far as to attribute the greatest accomplishments of the men of her nation to the "moral greatness" of its women (Ellis 70–3).

In the 1840s and 1850s this view of gender roles began to come under fire by liberal thinkers, in part because demographic realities prevented many women from living out a myth which by mid-century had ideologically subjugated the middle classes and in part because the widespread acceptance of that myth continued to deprive women of legal, economic, and political rights. Middle-class women had little choice but to aspire to marry, since work outside the domestic arena was generally considered unrespectable. The 1851 census lists only 7 percent of middle-class women as working, most of these as governesses, writers, or artists, and only 3 percent owning businesses or managing farms. But because women outnumbered men in the population at large and because older men tended to marry younger women, in that same census only 57 percent of women over 20 are listed as married. Thus, nearly half had no spouse to support them and were considered "redundant," a term first used in this context by John Ruskin (Helsinger et al. II, 134–5).

We see early reaction against the limited rights, social roles, and education of women in works from the 1840s such as Tennyson's long poem *The Princess* and Charlotte Brontë's *Jane Eyre*, both published in 1847. While Jane Eyre rankles against the limitations of female education and constrained roles for women, Princess Ida, the central character in Tennyson's poem, formulates these problems in more abstract terms, insisting that "The woman's cause is man's; they rise or sink / Together": "If she be small, slight-natured, miserable, / How shall men grow?" Ida insists that if "the parasitic forms / That seem to keep [woman] up but drag her down" are cleared away, "Then comes the statelier Eden back" (Part 7, ll. 243–77).

Until this period, married women of the middle and upper classes had been defined legally (by the doctrine of coverture) as objects rather than subjects with rights; a husband was responsible for his wife's actions, and he controlled her property. By mid-century, however, a number of Victorian men and women had begun the effort to remove obstacles to women's equality and advancement. Unmarried women of these classes were traditionally dependents (of their fathers or brothers). Caroline Norton, whose husband had unreasonably deprived her of access to her children, was instrumental in the passage of the Infants and Child Custody Bill of 1839. Writers like Norton, Harriet Martineau, Barbara Leigh Smith Bodichon, and Bessie Rayner Parkes influenced parliamentary debates throughout the 1850s. Norton and Bodichon played special roles in promoting the Matrimonial Causes Act of 1857, which empowered the courts to order payment of a maintenance to a wife separated from her husband and recovered a married woman's "rights to inherit or bequeath her own property, to enter into contracts, and to sue or be sued as if she were single." The petition to Parliament sponsored by Bodichon after her pamphlet *The Most Important Laws Concerning Women* appeared in 1854 garnered 26,000 signatures, including those of Jane Carlyle, Elizabeth Gaskell, Geraldine Jewsbury, Harriet Martineau, and Bessie Rayner

Parkes (Helsinger et al. II, 14–17). Male writers also played an important role in raising the Woman Question and bringing to the attention of middle-class readers oppressive inequities in the legal and social treatment of women. In 1849 the *Morning Chronicle* published William Acton's interviews with London seamstresses-turned-prostitutes, in an effort to dispel common stereotypes of the prostitute as an evil temptress rather than a social victim. Five years later George Drysdale countered studies of female sexuality that reinforced popular stereotypes of the "sexless" Angel in the House. In *The Elements of Social Science* he presented a thorough and systematic defense of women's sexual equality. And Acton's 1857 book on prostitution attempted to "convince doctors and administrators of the need for a more rational, 'humane' attitude" toward prostitutes (Helsinger et al. II, 57, 152–6), much like that espoused by the speaker in Dante Rossetti's poem "Jenny" (first drafted in 1848), which concludes with a commitment to "strive to clear" the "dark path" of middle-class misconceptions about these social outcasts.

Revolutionary Art

Though not truly a social revolutionary, Rossetti, a painter as well as a poet, was nonetheless instrumental in forwarding what by the end of the century could be seen as a virtual revolution in Victorian taste and aesthetic values. In 1848 he along with his brother William Michael Rossetti and fellow artists William Holman Hunt, John Everett Millais, Thomas Woolner, James Collinson, and Frederick George Stephens established the Pre-Raphaelite Brotherhood. The goal of these young men was to challenge the stodgy (that is, neoclassical and Platonic) tenets of Royal Academy painting. In 1851 John Ruskin approvingly ascribed the "schism" they caused in the art world to their "assertion that the principles on which art has been taught for these three hundred years back are essentially wrong" (Sambrook 92).

The work of the Pre-Raphaelite painters can be seen as quintessentially, and some might say paradoxically, mid-Victorian. They looked to the medieval era and early Renaissance for models of artistic "sincerity" and "naturalism" (fidelity to the details of the real world) as means to avoid the formalism and artificiality of contemporary painting. Their emphasis on the expressive value of art, on technical accuracy and on coloring inaugurated the values of aestheticism and the avant-garde that came to dominate pictorial art as well as literature by the end of the century. Their goal was not only "*épater le bourgeois*," but also ultimately to reform tastes. Thus, like Carlyle, Ruskin, and Arnold, along with members of the Oxford Movement and many novelists of the period, they sought out models of value and behavior from the past (especially the medieval past) that might serve the future. And, like the work of such commentators, their critique of the status quo helped to bring about change. In 1854, the year after the Brotherhood disbanded, Ruskin could observe that the Pre-Raphaelites had been "opposed with all the influence and all the bitterness of art and criticism." Yet their "heresy" had "gained ground, and the pictures painted on these new principles [had] obtained a most extensive popularity." The Brothers even founded a journal to propound their new dogma, *The Germ: Thoughts Toward Nature in Poetry, Literature and Art.* It survived for only four issues, all published in 1850, but is the forerunner of the many avant-garde magazines that began to proliferate in the 1890s. By the 1860s and 1870s Millais, Hunt, and Rossetti were three of the most admired and sought-after painters in England, and their works fetched huge sums. The weapons they employed in the gradual "revolution" they accomplished, with a good deal of help from prominent cultural critics like Ruskin, were ideological. This fact is underscored by the raging controversies generated by the work of poets writing during the second phase of Pre-Raphaelite activity, Rossetti, William Morris, A. C. Swinburne, and Christina Rossetti. Rossetti's *Poems* (1870) and Swinburne's *Poems and Ballads, First Series* (1866) especially were viewed by puritanical reviewers as disturbingly "fleshly" and subversive. The later socialist writings of William Morris were similarly worrisome to many commentators. But by the eighties and nineties these men were often idolized, and their style, aesthetic values, and liberalism (both moral and political) were widely emulated.

The success of Pre-Raphaelitism, a movement for reform that at first met with intense opposition but whose values and principles eventually became appropriated by the culture it challenged, might be seen as a paradigm of ideological change in mid-Victorian England. While Chartism, the Anti-Corn Law League, and legislation to improve the working and living conditions of England's poor were all hotly opposed when they emerged in the political arena, by the 1860s Britain was moving inexorably toward expansion of the franchise, toward increased intervention by government in the lives of its people, and eventually toward a welfare state. Similarly, the controversial challenges posed by the Oxford Movement thinkers on the right and proponents of extended rights for women on the left brought about greater tolerance, cultural diversity, and freedom of action for all people. The mid-century years of revolution in Europe, though not a period of widespread violent insurrection in Britain, were thus pivotal in the political and social transformation of this first industrial nation, as the chronicle of change during the second half of the century demonstrates.

See also SEXUALITIES; CLERICAL, INDUSTRIAL, COMMERCIAL, ARTISTIC; FICTION; SHORES

REFERENCES

Arnold, T. (1833) *Principles of Church Reform.* London: B. Fellowes.

Burn, W. L. (1964) *The Age of Equipoise: A Study of the Mid-Victorian Generation.* London: George Allen and Unwin.

Buzard, J., J. Childers, and E. Gillooly (eds) (2007) *Victorian Prism: Refractions of the Crystal Palace.* Charlottesville: University of Virginia Press.

Ellis, S. (1839) *The Women of England: Their Social Duties and Domestic Habits.* London: Fisher and Son.

Engels, F. (1958) *The Condition of the Working Classes in England.* Oxford: Basil Blackwell.

Gaskell, E. (1967) *The Letters of Mrs Gaskell,* ed. J. A. V. Chapple and A. Pollard. Cambridge MA: Harvard University Press.

Gilmour, R. (1993) *The Victorian Period: The Intellectual and Cultural Context of English Literature, 1830–1890.* Harlow: Longman.

Helsinger, E., R. Sheets, and W. Veeder (eds) (1989) *The Woman Question: Society and Literature in Britain and America, 1837–1883,* 3 vols. Chicago: University of Chicago Press.

Mayhew, H. (1985) *London Labour and the London Poor.* Harmondsworth: Penguin Books.

McCord, N. (1991) *British History: 1815–1906.* Oxford: Oxford University Press.

Sambrook, J. (ed.) (1974) *Pre-Raphaelitism: A Collection of Critical Essays.* Chicago: University of Chicago Press.

Taylor, A. J. P. (1954) *The Struggle for Mastery in Europe, 1848–1918.* Oxford: Oxford University Press.

Tennyson, G. B. (1981) *Victorian Devotional Poetry: The Tractarian Mode.* Cambridge MA: Harvard University Press.

Thompson, D. (1950) *England in the Nineteenth Century (1815–1914).* Harmondsworth: Penguin Books.

Trollope, A. (1983) *The Letters of Anthony Trollope,* ed. N. J. Hall, 2 vols. Stanford: Stanford University Press.

Young, G. M. (1936) *Victorian England: Portrait of an Age.* Oxford: Oxford University Press.

FURTHER READING

Armstrong, I. (1993) *Victorian Poetry: Poetry, Poetics and Politics.* London: Routledge.

Baker, J. (1932) *The Novel and the Oxford Movement.* Princeton: Princeton University Press.

Bodenheimer, R. (1988) *The Politics of Story in Victorian Social Fiction.* Ithaca: Cornell University Press.

Cockshutt, A. O. J. (ed.) (1966) *Religious Controversies of the Nineteenth Century: Selected Documents.* Lincoln: University of Nebraska Press.

Dawson, C. (1979) *Victorian Noon: English Literature in 1850.* Baltimore: Johns Hopkins University Press.

Erickson, L. (1996) *The Economy of Literary Form: English Literature and the Industrialization of Publishing, 1800–1850.* Baltimore: Johns Hopkins University Press.

Ford, B. (1989) *Victorian Britain.* Cambridge: Cambridge University Press.

Gallagher, C. (1985) *The Industrial Reformation of English Fiction, 1832–1867.* Chicago: University of Chicago Press.

Houghton, W. (1957) *The Victorian Frame of Mind.* New Haven: Yale University Press.

Mason, M. (1995) *The Making of Victorian Sexuality.* Oxford: Oxford University Press.

Morse, D. (1993) *High Victorian Culture.* New York: New York University Press.

Reardon, B. M. G. (1995) *Religious Thought in the Victorian Age: A Survey from Coleridge to Gore.* London: Longman.

Richards, B. (1988) *English Poetry of the Victorian Period, 1830–1890.* Harlow: Longman.

Schroeder, P. W. (1994) *The Transformation of European Politics, 1763–1848.* Oxford: Clarendon Press.

Tillotson, K. (1953) *Novels of the Eighteen-Forties.* Oxford: Oxford University Press.

Vicinus, M. (1974) *The Industrial Muse: A Study of Nineteenth Century British Working-Class Literature.* New York: Barnes and Noble.

Williams, R. (1958) *Culture and Society.* London: Chatto and Windus.

3
1870

Linda K. Hughes

"Our age, by virtue of its very artificiality and scientific culture," the *British Quarterly Review* pronounced in 1870, "is so far unfitted to catch the significance of life in its broadest and most individual aspects. Its self-consciousness makes it as unable to receive and accept [the] highest and most unconscious art as it is to produce it" (51, 203). The pronouncement is less compelling as criticism than as evidence of mid-Victorian legacies coexisting with an underlying shift toward modernity in 1870. If the review echoed Carlyle's attack on self-consciousness dating back to 1831 (in "Characteristics"), it also attested to the new preeminence of science and to the writer's anxiety that culture was being constructed on such new lines that its general contours could no longer be mapped.

Social historian Jose Harris in fact argues that the 1870s and 1880s, more than World War I, mark the crucial turning point between one era and another. By 1871, thanks to the Reform Bill of 1867, 33 percent of adult males were enfranchised, including substantial numbers of Irishmen living in England (Hall et al. 2000, 181). The 1870 Forster Education Act established elementary education for the masses, helping usher in an era of mass (print) media and mass leisure, both of which had profound implications for British literary production. The point is clear in George Gissing's *New Grub Street* (1891) when Whelpdale, a failed author but aspiring literary entrepreneur of the 1880s, creates a mass-circulation paper addressed to "the quarter-educated, that is to say, the great new generation that is being turned out by the Board schools" (ch. 33). Though it seems no more possible now than in 1870 to articulate a model of unified culture in that year, this chapter looks in turn at a number

A New Companion to Victorian Literature and Culture, First Edition. Edited by Herbert F. Tucker.
© 2014 John Wiley & Sons, Ltd. Published 2014 by John Wiley & Sons, Ltd.

of cultural formations that derived from early- and mid-Victorian assumptions but paradoxically helped precipitate a society that differed from earlier eras in fundamental ways.

Legislation of Social Change: 1867 and 1870

Passage of the Forster Education Act, which mandated schooling for all children five to twelve years old within their districts under the oversight of Inspectors and School Boards, was inseparable from the Second Reform Bill of 1867; MPs voting on the Education Act in 1870 were elected by those enfranchised in 1867. A reform bill had been introduced by William Gladstone, Chancellor of the Exchequer in the Liberal cabinet of Lord John Russell, in March 1866 but never won passage because the Liberal government first fell in June. The Conservative government headed by the Earl of Derby and relying on Benjamin Disraeli to orchestrate legislation in the Commons passed the 1867 bill, which admitted more than three times as many voters to the franchise as that proposed by Gladstone in 1866 (Hall et al. 2000, 2–5).

As in 1832 and 1848, political debate over reform aroused conflicting voices and public agitations. Committed to leadership by divinely inspired men, Thomas Carlyle thundered against the reform measure, which he termed "The calling in of new supplies of blockheadism, gullibility, bribeability, amenability to beer and balder-dash," in the August 1867 *Macmillan's Magazine*. Carlyle's fears of catastrophe were implicit in his title: "Shooting Niagara – And After?" In contrast, the *Annual Register* recorded demonstrations in support of the bill in Trafalgar Square (attended by 10,000), Guildhall, Manchester, Leeds, Glasgow, Edinburgh, and London. Workers' demands in part responded to progressive international events, especially the fight for Italian independence, which had also inspired poems by Elizabeth Barrett Browning earlier in the 1860s (Hall et al. 2000, 86; Chapman). But support became notorious in the so-called Hyde Park Riot on July 23, 1866, when demonstrators thwarted by police from entering the park tore down the railings. This incident became the referent for "anarchy" in Matthew Arnold's *Culture and Anarchy* (1869), which also played a crucial role in the education debates leading to the Forster Act. Arnold's title was a kind of rhetorical agitation (Dowling 1), considering that the Hyde Park Riot inspired less fear of anarchy than had the Chartist demonstrations of 1848. By mid-August 1867 the Second Reform Bill was law, Carlyle ceased to comment on English politics, and Arnold lectured on their implications for culture.

The bill enfranchised male heads of households who paid rates (taxes) directly, thus including some lodgers as well. The bill effectively doubled the number of voters in England and, when Reform Bills were enacted for Ireland and Scotland in 1868, extended the voting rolls there, if less dramatically. But legislators were not legislating democracy so much as extending prior law. As Harris remarks, "The admission to the constitution of urban male householders who paid their own rates was very deliberately designed to maintain that ancient tradition of a limited polity of independent freemen, and to exclude those deemed incapable of political and economic independence (women, lunatics, agricultural labourers, and the 'residuum' of the casual poor)" (Harris 14). But when an 1873 Act provided for "compounding," allocating the vote to those who paid rates indirectly in the form of rents owed to absentee landlords, even slum residents acquired the vote; and the traditional link between property and political power was broken, with permanent and pervasive results.

Though most English-language readers were unaware of the fact, Karl Marx's *Das Kapital* was published the same year the Second Reform Bill was adopted, Marx himself having moved to London in 1849 after being tried for treason, acquitted, then expelled from Prussia following the 1848 revolution. At the time of the Reform Bill he was living in Soho, serving as unofficial leader of the International Working-men's Association (1864–72) (Hobsbawm 110–11). His works began to be published in English in the later 1870s and 1880s, and his daughter Eleanor contributed to the pages of *Commonweal* edited by William Morris (1886–90), who with Ernest Belfort Bax also summarized Marx's doctrine in a *Commonweal* series entitled *Socialism from the Roots Up* (1886–8). In 1867 socialist organizations such as the Social Democratic Federation and the Fabian Society, both founded in 1884, were almost two decades away, but the last quarter of the century is generally identified as an era of increasing class consciousness. In 1867 and after, moreover, male workers had access (not always exercised) to direct political participation, with universal male suffrage legislated in 1918.

Workers also soon had wider access to education. In the first election held after passage of the Second Reform Bill, in late 1868, voters returned the Liberal Party to power, and Gladstone became prime minister for the first time. This Parliament ratified the Education Act named after W. E. Forster, Vice-President of the Committee of Council on Education (who then became a member of Gladstone's cabinet), in August 1870. Though the effects of this legislation would not be felt until additional schools were built and a bureaucracy established, henceforth Great Britain had in place one of the givens of late capitalist culture, a literate and universally educated populace with the requisite skills to sustain mass production, innovation, and consumption. Still, the major thrust of this reform was to educate the masses for democratic responsibility as informed citizens, an ideal based more on classical Republicanism familiar to Oxbridge-educated MPs than on systematic socioeconomic planning. Study of the Bible was admitted under the new Education Act but specifically sectarian teaching was excluded, and at the universities religious tests were abandoned after 1871 (Parry 175). Ironically, Harris suggests, these new secular dictates may have promoted a vaguely defined religious sensibility just when traditional Christian belief was under siege from the Higher Criticism and alternative cosmologies provided by science (191, 178). The legislation had literary implications as well: henceforth stories such as those of David Copperfield exiled from learning while working at the blacking factory, or of Jo the crossing sweeper in *Bleak House* (1852–3), would be less imaginable than in mid-Victorian England. In effect the Education

Act lengthened working-class childhoods by postponing employment – though the possibility of cruelty and humiliation at school, as in *Nicholas Nickleby* (1838–9), continued. In a one-room schoolhouse in the Fens, Kate Mary Edwards was forced in the 1880s to perform the work of a maid for the teachers and commented later, "Teachers in them days . . . must have despised us all as poor, ignorant creatures of a different sort from theirselves, and treated us more like animals than child'en" (Murray 250–1).

Women, Reform, and Sexuality

In the midst of debate over the Second Reform Bill, J. S. Mill, then an MP for West-minster, proposed an amendment that gave women the vote (see Mayhall 15): it was quickly rejected, though Mill's public interventions on behalf of women's rights continued with *The Subjection of Women*, published in 1869. Legislation in 1870 was more favorable to women's interests, though leaving intact fundamental gender inequities. At the time of Victoria's ascension married women had no legal rights regarding their offspring. When writer Caroline Norton left her husband on the grounds of cruelty, she lost legal access to her children, and in consequence campaigned for legislation that resulted in the Infants Custody Act of 1839. Nor did married women have rights to their own property under the principle of coverture – the absorption of the wife's identity into her husband's subsequent to marriage – unless separate property was settled on the woman at the time of marriage, a practice confined to the wealthy because of legal fees. Even in a happy marriage like that of Elizabeth and William Gaskell the novelist records in one of her letters her husband pocketing the cheque paid out for "Lizzie Leigh." For a woman like Norton the implications were severe: her public letter to the queen in 1855 revealed that the husband from whom she was alienated subpoenaed her publishers to claim her royalties and was legally entitled to her copyrights (Helsinger et al. II, 15–16). The 1857 Divorce Bill remedied this situation, giving women legally separated from their husbands sole right to subsequent earnings (though under the same bill women had to prove adultery plus desertion, cruelty, or bigamy to obtain a divorce, men merely a single act of a wife's adultery). A bill giving all married women these property rights failed in 1857.

The Married Women's Property Act of 1870 grew out of efforts by a group of Manchester feminists aided by the Social Science Association (founded in 1857) and their allies in Parliament. Though feminists hoped for legislation that gave women the same property rights enjoyed by men, the 1870 Act granted only that all wives (the poor as well as the wealthy) had rights to "separate property" comprised of their earnings, investments, and some legacies acquired after marriage. Even this bill might not have passed without the new legislative body returned after the 1867 Reform Bill. Not until the Married Women's Property Act of 1882, which Mary Shanley terms "arguably the single most important change in the legal status of women in the nineteenth century" (Shanley 103), did wives have rights to their property acquired before *and* during marriage, as well as rights and liabilities related to suits and torts. Even in 1882, however, legislation refrained from acknowledging wives' equal identity before the law.

If women's property rights were inseparable from the 1867 Reform Bill, women's social position was intimately connected to educational reform. After losing the battle for property rights in 1857, Barbara Leigh Smith Bodichon and other members of the Langham Place Circle in London focused on education and employment opportunities; Elizabeth Wolstenholme and Josephine Butler, crucial organizers for legislation affecting women in the 1870s and 1880s, helped form the North of England Council for Promoting the Higher Education of Women in 1867 (Hall et al. 2000, 134). Girton College was founded in 1869 by Bodichon and Emily Davies, Newnham College in 1871 by Henry Sidgwick and Anna Jemima Clough (sister to poet Arthur Hugh Clough). Though women could not take degrees at Cambridge, those at Girton took the same examinations as male students; both Girton and Newnham, moreover, provided a site for women's community and independent living (Vicinus 121–62). The colleges also produced such alumnae as poet Amy Levy (1861–89), the first Jewish student to attend Newnham, whose "Cambridge in the Long" (1889) looked back to this experience.

Burgeoning openings for elementary schoolteachers following the 1870 Education Act provided new employment opportunities for women; women could also vote and run for membership on the school boards established by the 1870 Act, children's education being considered part of women's assigned sphere (Harris 25, 191; Mayhall 18). In 1870 Lydia Becker, who founded the *Women's Suffrage Journal* the same year, was elected to the Manchester School Board, while Emily Davies and Elizabeth Garrett Anderson were elected to school boards in London (Hall et al. 2000, 158). Augusta Webster, whose important collection of dramatic monologues *Portraits* was published in 1870, was elected a member of the London School Board from Chelsea in 1879 (Rigg 186–95). As mention of Becker's journal indicates, suffrage was by no means a moribund issue in the 1870s even though it failed to secure parliamentary ratification. The 1869 Municipal Corporations Act restored to single rate-paying women the right they had had until 1835 to vote in local government elections (Harris 190). And an 1870 suffrage bill actually carried a majority in the House on its second reading – until Gladstone announced his opposition and the bill died (Hall et al. 2000, 156).

A last crucial focus of feminist activism in 1870 concerned the Contagious Diseases (CD) Acts (see Walkowitz). Acts passed in 1864, 1866, and 1869 mandated compulsory genital inspection for venereal disease in suspected prostitutes and detention in lock hospitals for infected women. The legislation originated in concerns with sanitation (the focus of Florence Nightingale's reforms during the Crimean War) and the spread of venereal disease among enlisted men in military garrisons and ports. But men were neither inspected nor penalized, in part because, as military leaders insisted, enforced genital inspection of men was humiliating and lowered morale. Since fallen women were already shamed, it was reasoned, no harm was done to them. An 1867 proposal to extend the CD Acts from military garrisons to civilian precincts ignited repeal efforts, first among male political liberals (who initially excluded women from the National Association for the Repeal of the Contagious Diseases Acts) and then among the Ladies' National Association (formed December 1869) under the leadership of Josephine Butler. As Anne Summers argues (190), this activism was indebted not just to current outrage but also to women's earlier participation in abolitionism, since the enslaved woman subjected to sexual abuse was likened to a prostitute (just as subjugated prostitutes were compared to slaves in Butler's campaign).

"The Ladies' Appeal and Protest Against the Contagious Diseases Acts" was published in the March 14, 1870 *Shield* (pp. 9–10), the official journal of the National Association. This declaration opposed the CD Acts on grounds that they violated women's civil rights, intruded monstrously on privacy (Butler spoke in public about "instrumental rape"), ratified the sexual double standard, and failed to eradicate venereal disease; it was signed not only by Butler but also by Harriet Martineau, Florence Nightingale, and some 250 other women. Not until 1886 were the Acts repealed, but the feminist activism of the 1870s and 1880s provided models of women's political organization, leadership, and militant activism; and later suffragists looked back to Butler "as a great founding mother of modern feminism" (Walkowitz 255). In literature the CD controversy forms the context for poems on prostitutes by D. G. Rossetti ("Jenny") and Augusta Webster ("A Castaway"), published in the same year as the "Ladies' Appeal and Protest" (see Brown). The eruption of sexually transgressive subject matter within respectable bourgeois circles represented by Butler's campaign also had its counterpart in the rise of sensation fiction in the 1860s. Novels like *Lady Audley's Secret* (1862) cracked open seemingly smooth domestic surfaces to reveal criminal intent and potential violence within – though this genre also owed its formation to the increasing role of police and divorce court proceedings in Victorian newspapers.

Sexual surveillance to control "deviancy" was not restricted to prostitutes in 1870. The same year transvestites Ernest Boulton and Frederick William Park were arrested for indecent behavior and tried in 1871 for conspiracy to commit sodomy. Not only were "Stella" and "Fanny" suspected by some observers of being female prostitutes given their male following, but the two men, like suspected prostitutes under the CD acts, were also subjected to intrusive physical examination. Boulton and Park were eventually acquitted, but their widely reported arrest and trial revealed discomfort with gender ambiguity and uncertainty about the boundaries of homosexuality (Kaplan 19–101). The death penalty for sodomy had been lifted in 1861, replaced by lengthy imprisonment, but the category of "homosexual" had not yet clearly emerged in Britain – though Foucault (1980) dates the birth of homosexuality to 1870 because of an article published that year by Carl Westphal. Only in the Labouchere Amendment to the Criminal Law Amendment Act of 1885 were British "acts of gross indecency between men" stipulated as misdemeanors carrying the penalty of two years' hard labor. Lesbian women were exempted from prosecution both because they were not deemed as socially dangerous as male homosexuals and because of their relative invisibility – though poems such as Swinburne's "Anactoria" in *Poems and Ballads* (1866) functioned along with Baudelaire's *Fleurs du Mal* (1857) to circulate the discourse of lesbianism.

The 1885 Criminal Amendment Act was another point of convergence between the CD Acts and the formation of homosexual identities. The Act raised the age of sexual consent from 13 to 16, prompted not only by general anxieties about child prostitution but also by W. T. Stead's sensational "Maiden Tribute to Modern Babylon" in the 1885 *Pall Mall Gazette*, in fact a collaboration with Butler, whose efforts Stead supported (Summers 198). Both the Act and its anti-sodomy amendment reflected antagonism toward aristocratic profligacy deemed responsible for an array of corrupt practices. The 1885 legislation also signaled a redirection of feminist politics from the early CD repeal movement to social purity campaigns designed to control male vice.

Reform and Religion

The Disestablishment of the Irish Church in 1869 led in 1870 to the Irish Land Act, which "imposed statutory rent control and compelled landlords to compensate tenants for improvements" (Harris 121). The Irish legislation pointed at once to issues of order, religion, and colonialism. Because the period 1848–70 is often characterized as one of peace and prosperity (see, for example, Hobsbawm 4–5), it is useful to be reminded that in Britain, as in other postindustrial societies not officially at war, acts of violence and disruption nonetheless occurred. In 1866–8 a series of Fenian terrorist acts in England pressured Parliament to enact reform. In December 1867, Fenians, activists aligned with the Irish Republican Brotherhood founded in the United States in the mid-1850s, attempted to blow up the House of Detention at Clerkenwell, which housed Irish prisoners; four died in the explosion and more than a hundred were injured (Hall et al. 2000, 188, 215). On March 11, 1868 in Australia, the visiting Duke of Edinburgh, Victoria's son Alfred, was shot in the back by an Irishman who claimed to be a Fenian (Alfred recovered; his assailant was executed) (Campbell 113). These events make especially notable Trollope's choice of an Irishman as hero of his parliamentary novel *Phineas Finn*, subtitled *The Irish Member*, serialized from October 1867 to May 1869. Meanwhile, violence was occurring in Ireland itself, which the government in London met by suspending habeas corpus in Ireland between 1866 and 1868.

Such violence took place amidst debate over the second Reform Bill, which underlay the disestablishment of the Irish Church, that is, the Anglican Church in Ireland, a country principally Roman Catholic. During the 1868 session Gladstone, an opposition MP, introduced a bill for disestablishment, which carried. Disraeli then called for a new election in November – the same that brought in the Liberal majority so decisive in the Forster Education and Married Women's Property Acts of 1870. But the principal issue in the election campaign was disestablishment of the Irish Church, which became law in July 1869. The dilemma of Ireland – predicated on English rule and principal ownership of land – was far from over; but at least faithful Catholics would no longer be forced to tithe to the Anglican Church.

In the wake of the first Reform Bill (1832), Parliament's proposal to eliminate ten Irish bishoprics had elicited John Keble's July 14, 1833 sermon on "National Apostasy" (so called because a secular body presumed to intervene in church governance), inaugurating the Oxford Movement. But now in 1869 the entire Irish Church was dismantled at a single blow with remarkably little protest, an indication of increasing secularism – though as Mark Knight and Emma Mason point out, "scholars from a multitude of disciplines have become increasingly sceptical about the notion that a linear and inescapable erosion of faith was at an advanced stage by the second half of the nineteenth century" (152). This secularism, marked as well by the opening of teaching fellowships at Oxford and Cambridge to non-Anglicans in 1871, did not necessarily indicate religious apathy. Intense interest in religious doctrine caused a splintering of believers into diverse denominations (Primitive Methodists, Wesleyans, Presbyterians, Baptists, Roman Catholics, etc.). Hence, governmental institutions increasingly adopted stances of neutrality, and religion became an increasingly private matter (Harris 166–8, 171). This cultural formation is mirrored by Tennyson's 1869 "Holy Grail," which amasses five different views of the grail quest ranging from fervent belief to skepticism without having King Arthur privilege a single faith.

Religious pluralism is also evident in the 1869 founding of the Metaphysical Society, devoted to discussion of philosophical and theological issues among clergymen, scientists, and men of letters whose beliefs ranged from orthodox Anglicanism and Roman Catholicism to Unitarianism and agnosticism; members included Tennyson, Thomas Henry Huxley, Leslie Stephen, Gladstone, and Cardinal Manning. Attempting to retain the paramount importance of spirituality in the face of divergent technologies of knowledge, the society failed after a decade, suggesting yet again the fragmenting of religious belief in a pluralistic society. A more forceful threat to religion came from the "Higher Criticism," first developed in classical studies, which applied historical research methods and standards of evidence to the Bible. In 1870 the head of Balliol College, Oxford was Benjamin Jowett, the distinguished Greek scholar whose influence on Swinburne and a host of other undergraduates was immense; and who had been attacked for his prominent role in *Essays and Reviews* (1860), which approached the Bible as an historical rather than divinely inspired text (LaPorte 6–10). These new secular readings of texts also had implications for literary production, since the suspension of religious justification for art made "art for art's sake" more tenable.

Reforming and Constructing Orders of Knowledge:
Victorian Science

Another important feature of Victorian England in 1870 was the expanding prominence of science. By mid-century geology's formulation of deep time and the evidence of the fossil record were exerting pressure on traditional faith, as in Tennyson's *In Memoriam* (1850). Though ideas of evolution had been circulating since the end of the prior century, Charles Darwin's *Origin of Species* (1859) gave compelling form to the argument through the mechanism of natural selection and Darwin's massive accumulation of instances, which put to scientific use the same piling of detail on detail that gave massive novels like George Eliot's *Middlemarch* (1871–2) their effect of realism (see Beer). In the *Origin* Darwin did not shrink from opposing his evolutionary model to biblical creationism, but he drew most of his evidence on evolution from animal and plant life, leaving the more controversial issue of human evolution to a later date. If the 1859 work evoked some resistance, its ready acceptance in many quarters (Knight and Mason 156) is evident in Elizabeth Gaskell's modeling the hero of her final novel, *Wives and Daughters* (1864–6), after Darwin, her distant kinsman.

In 1870 Darwin was completing *The Descent of Man, and Selection in Relation to Sex*, published in February 1871. Here Darwin carefully laid out evidence for the descent of humankind from "lower forms" and the importance of sexual selection for producing distinctive human and secondary sex characteristics not immediately connected to survival. These latter principles played an important role in subsequent naturalist fiction and works exploring the relation of the sexes (e.g. Thomas Hardy's *The Woodlanders*, 1886–7), and in feminist debate as well. If, for example, conservatives pointed to evolutionary theory to refute Mill's *Subjection* by arguing that women's subordinate position was the fit outcome of natural selection, evolution could also suggest to feminists that women were evolving into a new and higher form, as Olive Schreiner suggested in *Story of an African Farm* (1883). Indeed, Darwinian theory was accepted in part because it could readily be appropriated not only by radical thinkers opposed to orthodoxy and the social stratification it helped support, but also by conservatives (see Levine 7–8, 73). Karl Marx, for example, saw in the *Origin* "'a natural scientific basis for the class-struggle in history'" (Beer 51). Bourgeois thinkers, too, could appropriate Darwinian evolution. Herbert Spencer's "Social Darwinism" emphasized competition and survival, and *First Principles of a New System of Philosophy* (1862) applied evolution not only to social development (which moved invariably from simple to complex) but also to racial difference: "civilised [i.e. European] men depart more widely from the general type of the placental mammalia, than do the lowest men" (ch. 15). Such thinking also supported rather than critiqued class difference, since Darwinian failure offered a more comforting explanation of poverty than did a hard look at social inequities.

In *Descent* Darwin's chapter on "The Races of Man" repudiated the notion that differing races comprised separate species and acknowledged "that it is hardly possible to discover clear distinctive characters between them." But uncritical assumptions about the inherent superiority of "civilized" Europeans erupt in his text nevertheless; he expresses surprise that Fuegians and a "full-blooded negro" on board the *Beagle* shared his own mental traits and argues that "With civilised nations, the reduced size of the jaws from lessened use, the habitual play of different muscles serving to express different emotions, and the increased size of the brain from greater intellectual activity, have together produced a considerable effect on their general appearance in comparison with savages" (see also Levine 46–50, 61–6).

Victorian science, then, both reflected and helped construct in vital ways assumptions about race that also underlay the expansion of the British Empire in the last third of the century. Indeed, another principal development of Victorian science is anthropology, the interdisciplinary field that emerged from philology, travel writing, folklore, law, philosophy, and immediately out of physical anthropology and ethnology (Hobsbawm 261, 266). E. B. Tylor, preeminent among the group George Stocking terms "sociocultural evolutionists," published *Researches into the Early History of Mankind* in 1865, John Lubbock *The Origin of Civilisation* in 1870 – both cited by Darwin in *Descent*. In 1871, the Royal Anthropological Institute was founded, and Tylor published his landmark *Primitive Culture: Researches into the Development of Mythology, Philosophy, Religion, Language, Art, and Custom*. Like nineteenth-century science as a whole, comprised in earlier decades of loosely coordinated efforts among diverse practitioners, including amateurs like Revd Farebrother in *Middlemarch* or artisan naturalist Job Legh in Gaskell's *Mary Barton* (1848), anthropology was being transformed into an organized body of professionals committed to shared methodologies and sanctioned credentialing. Anthropology and other sciences were also deeply pervaded by and embedded in other social discourses. Sociocultural evolutionists argued that human spirituality and religious belief were subject to the same forces of evolution as physiological development, and that in some cases "survivals" from earlier phases of primitive development underlay advanced stages of civilization (Stocking 161–3). In this respect anthropologists blurred distinctions between British and other peoples and gestured toward shared cultural processes. But the application of such knowledge often resorted to the racial hierarchy evident in Spencer and Darwin and likewise served to validate bourgeois norms. Thus for Tylor, Lubbock, and other colleagues, religion and marriage were the two central institutions by which the rise from primitivism to higher civilization was gauged, with Victorian bourgeois marriage the hallmark of higher civilization (Stocking 197, 204). The overlap of literature and anthropology was to be clearer one to two decades later in the work of Andrew Lang or James Frazer, but Tennyson's "Lucretius," first published in *Macmillan's Magazine* in May 1868, already shows the impress of modern anthropology as well as Darwinian evolution in the scientist–philosopher's susceptibility to "the brute brain within the man's," when his physiological and moral balance is destroyed by an aphrodisiac.

Education, Imperialism, and Culture

In February of 1870 Ruskin presented his inaugural address as the first Slade Professor of Fine Art to a crowd of one thousand in the Sheldonian Theatre at Oxford. Not surprisingly, Ruskin affirmed that "The art of any country is the exponent of its social and political virtues" and urged the necessity of protecting English skies from pollution and English lives from the ills of poverty and vice. But the man whose essay "The Nature of Gothic" (1853) influenced the socialism of William Morris then veered in another direction:

> There is a destiny now possible to us – the highest ever set before a nation to be accepted or refused. We are still undegenerate in race; a race mingled of the best northern blood. . . . Within the last few years we have had the laws of natural science opened to us with a rapidity which has been blinding by its brightness; and means of transit and communication given to us, which have made but one kingdom of the habitable globe. . . . And this is what [England] must either do, or perish: she must found colonies as fast and as far as she is able, formed of her most energetic and worthiest men; – seizing every piece of fruitful waste ground she can set her foot on, and there teaching these her colonists that their first aim is to be to advance the power of England by land and sea. (*Lectures on Art*, 1870)

Art and Oxford are here indissolubly joined to British Empire. Indeed, there is a direct link between Ruskinian art criticism and the scramble for Africa, since a copy of the Inaugural Address was one of the prized possessions of Cecil Rhodes, who entered Oxford from South Africa in 1873 (Symonds 25–6, 161). Ruskin's debut as Slade Professor usefully inscribes the degree to which empire permeated every facet of Victorian England, shaping subjectivities and daily life (Hall and Rose 22–3). Even an innocuous detail like mahogany furniture in *Jane Eyre* (1847) registered imperial history and the empire's effects at home (Freedgood 3, 30–54). As Harris observes, "at a more day-to-day level, imperial visions injected a powerful stain of hierarchy, militarism, 'frontier mentality', administrative rationality, and masculine civic virtue into British political culture, at a time when domestic political forces were running in quite the opposite direction, towards egalitarianism, 'progressivism', consumerism, popular democracy, feminism and women's rights" (6). Empire was thus a means by which Britain consolidated power but also a source of struggle, conflict, and negotiation (both political and cultural) at the imperial center and in far-flung colonies (Hall and Rose 2).

In the same year the Second Reform Bill was ratified, for example, British consul C. D. Cameron and other British subjects were detained by King Theodore II in Abyssinia (as Ethiopia was then called) after two prior emissaries sent by Great Britain had been murdered by rebel troops opposed to Theodore's rule. General Robert Napier, commander of forces at Bombay, was sent to Africa and handily defeated Theodore's forces in early 1868. That available military forces in Bombay could serve at need as roving imperial troops underlines the importance of India. Yet even here, a decade earlier, British dominance had suffered a major challenge in the Indian Mutiny (1857–8), which had lasting political, cultural, and even emotional effects (see Herbert). This armed opposition to British rule (then under the aegis of the East India Company) erupted because of resentment over annexation of Indian territories, growing concerns about the westernizing of Indian culture, and British insensitivities to religious practices: indigenous soldiers came to believe that the cartridges they were ordered to handle were greased with either cow or pig fat, thus violating Hindu or Muslim observance. The rebellion began on May 10, 1857 among Bengal troops and spread throughout the northern plains, with rebels soon capturing Delhi. The single most devastating event in British eyes, however, was the massacre at Cawnpore. After negotiating the removal of the British from Cawnpore, Indian troops under the leadership of Nana Sahib opened fire when the British embarked on boats for safe passage to Allahabad, and a massacre ensued. Women and children who survived the massacre were imprisoned, hacked to death, and their bodies thrown down a well or into the Ganges (Herbert 4). The trauma such events inspired can be inferred from the poem that follows "Goblin Market" in Christina Rossetti's debut volume (1862). "In the Round Tower at Jhansi, June 8, 1857," composed September 1857, recounts how the Englishman Skene and "his pale young wife" determine on murder-suicide rather than put themselves at the mercy of attacking Indians ("The swarming howling wretches below"), and focuses on the moment of their farewells before Skene puts a gun to his wife's forehead and fires. Rossetti's note to the poem acknowledged its historical inaccuracy but defended the poem as an indication of reaction in England to news of the mutiny. The rebellion was soon subdued and governance of India transferred from the East India Company to the British Crown in August 1858, thus inaugurating British imperial rule.

The Caribbean branch of empire commanded attention in March 1867, when legal proceedings began against Governor Edward John Eyre for his role in the October 1865 Jamaican uprising. After black Jamaicans had attempted to rescue a black prisoner from the court house, encounters between rebels and the white minority escalated until white magistrates and volunteer soldiers were killed and plantation owners fled in terror. Some 20 Europeans were killed; Eyre retaliated by executing 439 black Jamaicans. Those who put a premium on maintaining order defended Eyre, including Tennyson, Carlyle, Dickens, Ruskin, and Charles Kingsley. J. S. Mill, Thomas Henry Huxley, and Herbert Spencer were incensed by Eyre's brutality and supported putting him on trial. In the end Eyre was stripped of the governorship but allowed to retire on a pension (Hall 23–5, 64).

In the wake of such events ideas about race became more problematical still. As Hall observes, "The Reform Act of 1867 . . . looked at alongside the new Canadian settlement of the same year and the Jamaica Act of the preceding year can be read as formally differentiating black Jamaicans from white British, white Canadians or white Australians . . . from brown Indians" (Hall et al. 2000, 182). Constrained notions of brotherhood inhabit Tennyson's "The Coming of Arthur" (1869), which opposes petty kings to encroaching heathens and finds resolution in an Arthur who arrives, expels heathen hordes from England, and unifies the realm. The shock of the opening installment of *The Mystery of Edwin Drood* in April 1870 – a novel left unfinished when Dickens died on June 9, 1870 – was precisely that a Chinaman, a Lascar, and an English Choir Master lie entwined on the same dirty bed in opium-induced stupor, and that the white female proprietor of the opium den resembles a Chinaman through long practice at her trade. Dickens mocks and subverts racial purity in this lurid opening scene but depends on audience assumptions of racial demarcation to create his sensation.

Succeeding years saw the defining events of imperialism, including the rapid annexation of 4,750,000 square miles of land from 1874 until 1902 (Girouard 224). Charles Dilke's *Greater Britain* (1868) also helped set the stage by forecasting a global Anglo-Saxon brotherhood united in racial superiority and compassion for inferior "natives" (Hall 436–38). As in Tennyson's 1869 *Idylls*, however, both internal and external threats motivated imperialism. According to Duncan Bell, Anglo-Saxon racial self-aggrandizement co-existed with anxiety about the competing imperial ambitions of France, Germany, and the United States; emergent socialist movements; and an increasing bifurcation between a "degenerate 'underclass'" and the "self-interested" governing elite and middle class (Bell 24).

Prussia, the United States, and the Decentering of British Hegemony

During the 1860s the modern state of Germany had begun to form under the leader-ship of Otto von Bismarck, leaving France under Napoleon III wary of the new power along its border. In 1870 the offer of a vacant Spanish throne to the cousin of the Prussian king prompted French protest, and war between Prussia and France was declared on July 19, 1870, precipitating the downfall of Napoleon III, the birth of the Third French Republic, the Paris Commune of 1871, and the emergence of Prussia as a dominant world power.

Ruskin responded to the outbreak of war in his first lecture on sculpture at Oxford in November 1870 (included in *Aratra Pentelici*, 1872). In pacific mood now, he illustrated points of sculpture by means of the plowshare deposited on his lecture table. A much wider audience was reached by another response to the Franco-Prussian war, George Tomkyns Chesney's "The Battle of Dorking" (1871), which represented the invasion of England by Prussia and stirred so much anxiety that Gladstone was obliged to dispel the fears it generated (Bell 38). Though ephemeral in literary impact, the story illustrates the looming threat a newly unified Germany posed to British minds, especially since Germany was also fully industrialized, technologically advanced, and increasingly formidable as a commercial competitor of Britain (see Hobsbawm 40–1, 256).

A significant poem was also to be inspired by events of 1870–1, though not for another 15 years. This was William Morris's *The Pilgrims of Hope*, a poem about the Paris Commune of 1871 that was serialized in the socialist paper *Commonweal* from March 1885 to July 1886. Fueled by communist resentment over French losses rati-fied by the February 1871 Franco-Prussian peace treaty and by the policies of the Third Republic, armed conflict erupted on March 18, 1871 and the Commune was declared on March 28 following election of a Communal Assembly in Paris. This early communist government lasted only two months, but Morris's poem suggests its importance in providing hope that socialist revolution was possible.

The United States was also making its impact on British life felt in 1870 as it had during the Civil War (1861–5), when the blockade of ports in the South prevented cotton from reaching textile centers in Lancashire, causing the "Cotton Famine" of 1862. In Manchester, Elizabeth Gaskell and her daughters worked to the point of exhaustion to alleviate suffering. Not surprisingly, most British newspapers and journals supported the South against the North, which was seen as the aggressor. After the Civil War ended, the American conflict still drained British coffers, for in 1868 the United States claimed compensation from the British government for commercial maritime losses due to depredations by the Confederate ship *Alabama*. In the end Britain was forced to pay more than 15 million dollars in damages under the 1871 Treaty of Washington.

The economic impact on Great Britain of events in the United States continued with the rapid postwar development of the US railroad, much of it financed by British capital. The sometime frenzy of the situation is reflected in Trollope's *The Way We Live Now* (1874–5) when an American touting a scheme for the South Central Pacific and Mexican railway, running from Salt Lake City to Vera Cruz, comes to England to bilk British capitalists. If America represented a prime investment opportunity, however, the completion of its railway network soon made the United States a powerful industrial and democratic nation that challenged British dominance (Bell 233–4).

Though many financiers fleeing Paris during the Franco-Prussian war went to London, helping transform London into the world's major center of finance (Harris 19–20), the Prussian victory was also the signal that Britain's status as unrivaled naval and commercial power was ending. Forced to compete with Prussia and the United States, which looked to world markets and territorial expansion of their own, Britain under Disraeli's second ministry launched its policy of imperialism; Queen Victoria was crowned Empress of India in 1876; and British territory grew year by year. This growth, however, was more vexed than the seemingly unlimited opportunity for progress that characterized mid-Victorian writings by Macaulay or Spencer. In this context Eliot's *Daniel Deronda* (1876) is not only a novel of empire but also one that, in having Deronda look to Jerusalem rather than London for his political career, acknowledges multiple centers of rule rather than unitary British predominance. After 1870 confident assumptions about Britain's steady "progress" and its potential for unchecked prosperity were more tenuous, more laboriously maintained. Doubt as to the desirability of the status quo became an increasingly credible position for middle-class intellectuals as well as reformers and working-class organizers.

Emergent Futures, Contingent Pasts

A number of events just prior to 1870 disclosed shifting intellectual as well as social formations in England, particularly the professionalizing of knowledge, which in turn depended on Victorian capital, Adam Smith's principle of the division of labor, and the immense prestige of scientific method (see Heyck; Colón 1–13). The *Academy*, founded by Dr Charles Appleton, and *Nature*, founded by astronomer Norman Lockyer (still an important scientific publication today), debuted in 1869. Appleton had studied Hegelian philosophy in Germany after earning his BA at Oxford and founded the *Academy* to provide an outlet for scholarly publication, promote German-style research universities in England, and feature writing that attained cultural authority through "disinterested" inquiry (see also Brake 36–50). In the 1870s Appleton also contributed to *Nature* six articles promoting "The Endowment of Research" at universities, indicating the degree to which specialist knowledge depended on association with scientific method and standards of reliability.

This emergent professionalizing of knowledge also played a role in Browning's displacing Tennyson as preeminent poet among intellectuals. By 1870 Tennyson's very popularity rendered his accessibility suspect; Browning's formerly notorious obscurity became in contrast a badge of depth and cerebration for those identified with cultural elites. Browning himself engaged epistemological impasses, and his recondite allusions and intricate syntax also called for (and thus validated) expert commentators steeped in contemporary theory and committed to rigorous exegesis. The language of expertise and scientific method, in contrast to that of amateur appreciation (associated with feminine – or effeminate – producers and consumers), is evident in the March 1869 review by John Morley of Browning's newly completed *The Ring and the Book* in the *Fortnightly Review*. Morley sneered at Tennyson's "graceful presentation of the Arthurian legend for drawing-rooms, by idylls, not robust and Theocritean, but such little pictures as might adorn a ladies' school," and praised in contrast the intellectual vigor of Browning's poem, the ending of which might serve as "no unfit epilogue to a scientific essay on history" (331, 338). The reference to "scientific . . . history" also chimes with the replacement of Charles Kingsley by John Robert Seeley as Regius Chair of Modern History at Cambridge in 1869. Reflecting the influence of German universities yet again, history was increasingly displaced from the hands of generalists such as Kingsley or Carlyle to scholars trained in rigorous research of original documents and approved protocols for presenting evidence. Such historians elevated disinterested "fact" over literary narrative, which could be informed by a rhetoricity less amenable to scientific verification or consensus. "Scientific" history also promoted study free from contemporary political conflict (Hesketh 1–10). Gender and class were additional factors in the rise of professions. Just as women were gaining a footing in Oxbridge, the institutionalization of professions raised more barriers to them. "Professions" were also carefully distinguished from trade unions – though concepts of expertise might be appropriated by feminist and working-class groups to validate their distinctive voices and social roles.

In 1870, then, even the disciplines through which we approach the study of Victorian literature today (with their unsettling historicity) were in the process of formation. Yet to those living at that moment, such developments might have been invisible. A bourgeois youth who had come of age during the Great Exhibition

(1851) would have looked upon a Great Britain still prosperous, since the great agricultural depression that would deplete rural estates in the late 1870s was off-stage. Matters in Ireland had quieted down, at least relative to 1866–8, and no other immediate threat challenged British sovereignty. Positions in Parliament and the ministry were overwhelmingly in the hands of the aristocracy, whose social prestige and collective wealth were undiminished. Married women could hold some property and work in the interests of elementary school children on school boards but could neither vote in parliamentary elections nor earn Oxbridge degrees. If labor strikes were a regular feature of British life, no socialist organization had yet been founded. Dickens had recently died, and before him Charlotte Brontë, Thackeray, and Gaskell, but Tennyson was squarely in place as poet laureate and would serve as an icon of British cultural life until his death in 1892. Nevertheless, as we have seen here, this apparent stability overlay profound social change, which moved inexorably toward a modernity that would have astonished that mid-Victorian youth and his contemporaries, and which ushered in the world that which continues to perplex their modern and postmodern heirs.

See also SEXUALITIES; EDUCATIONAL, COMMERCIAL, ARTISTIC; PARAPETS, SHORES

REFERENCES AND FURTHER READING

Beer, G. (2000) *Darwin's Plots: Evolutionary Narrative in Darwin, George Eliot and Nineteenth-Century Fiction*, 2nd edn. Cambridge: Cambridge University Press.

Bell, D. (2007) *The Idea of Greater Britain: Empire and the Future of World Order, 1860–1900*. Princeton: Princeton University Press.

Brake, L. (1994) *Subjugated Knowledges: Journalism, Gender and Literature in the Nineteenth Century*. New York: New York University Press.

Brown, S. (1991) "Economical Representations: Dante Gabriel Rossetti's 'Jenny,' Augusta Webster's 'A Castaway,' and the Campaign Against the Contagious Diseases Acts." *Victorian Review* 17, 78–95.

Campbell, M. (2007) *Ireland's New Worlds: Immigrants, Politics, and Society in the United States and Australia, 1815–1922*. Madison: University of Wisconsin Press.

Chapman, A. (2003) "'In Our Own Blood Drenched the Pen': Italy and Sensibility in Elizabeth Barrett Browning's Last Poems (1862)." *Women's Writing* 10, 269–86.

Colón, S. E. (2007) *The Professional Ideal in the Victorian Novel: The Works of Disraeli, Trollope, Gaskell, and Eliot*. Basingstoke: Palgrave Macmillan.

Dowling, L. (1996) *The Vulgarization of Art: The Victorians and Aesthetic Democracy*. Charlottesville and London: University Press of Virginia.

Foucault, M. (1980) *The History of Sexuality, Vol. 1: An Introduction*. New York: Random House.

Freedgood, E. (2006) *The Ideas in Things: Fugitive Meaning in the Victorian Novel*. Chicago: University of Chicago Press.

Girouard, M. (1981) *The Return to Camelot: Chivalry and the English Gentleman*. New Haven and London: Yale University Press.

Hall, C. (2002) *Civilising Subjects: Metropole and Colony in the English Imagination 1830–1867*. Chicago: University of Chicago Press.

Hall, C., and S. Rose (2006) "Introduction: Being at Home with the Empire." In *At Home with the Empire: Metropolitan Culture and the Imperial World*, ed. C. Hall and S. Rose. Cambridge: Cambridge University Press.

Hall, C., K. McClelland, and J. Rendall (2000) *Defining the Victorian Nation: Class, Race, Gender and the Reform Act of 1867*. Cambridge: Cambridge University Press.

Harris, J. (1994) *Private Lives, Public Spirit: Britain 1870–1914*. Harmondsworth: Penguin Books.

Helsinger, E. K., R. Sheets, and W. Veeder (eds) (1983) *The Woman Question: Society and Literature in Britain and America 1837–1883*, 3 vols. Chicago and London: University of Chicago Press.

Herbert, C. (2008) *War of No Pity: The Indian Mutiny and Victorian Trauma*. Princeton: Princeton University Press.

Hesketh, I. (2011) *The Science of History in Victorian Britain: Making the Past Speak*. London: Pickering and Chatto.

Heyck, T. W. (1982) *The Transformation of Intellectual Life in Victorian England*. New York: St Martin's Press.

Hobsbawm, E. J. (1975) *The Age of Capital 1848–1875*. New York: Charles Scribner's Sons.

Kaplan, M. B. (2005) *Sodom on the Thames: Sex, Love, and Scandal in Wilde Times*. Ithaca: Cornell University Press.

Knight, M., and E. Mason (2006) *Nineteenth-Century Religion and Literature: An Introduction*. Oxford: Oxford University Press.

LaPorte, C. (2011) *Victorian Poets and the Changing Bible*. Charlottesville: University of Virginia Press.

Levine, G. (2008) *Darwin Loves You: Natural Selection and the Re-enchantment of the World*. Princeton: Princeton University Press.

Mayhall, L. E. N. (2003) *Militant Suffrage Movement: Citizenship and Resistance in Britain, 1860–1930*. Oxford: Oxford University Press.

Murray, J. H. (ed.) (1982) *Strong Minded Women and Other Lost Voices from Nineteenth-Century England*. New York: Pantheon Books.

Parry, J. (2011) "The Decline of Institutional Reform in Nineteenth-Century Britain." In *Structures and Transformations in Modern British History*, ed. D. Feldman and J. Lawrence. Cambridge: Cambridge University Press.

Rigg, P. (2009) *Julia Augusta Webster: Victorian Aestheticism and the Woman Writer*. Madison: Fairleigh Dickinson University Press.

Shanley, M. L. (1989) *Feminism, Marriage, and the Law in Victorian England, 1850–1895*. Princeton: Princeton University Press.

Stocking, G. (1987) *Victorian Anthropology*. New York: Free Press.

Summers, A. (2011) "British Women and Cultures of Internationalism, c. 1815–1914." In *Structures and Transformations in Modern British History*, ed. D. Feldman and J. Lawrence. Cambridge: Cambridge University Press.

Symonds, R. (1986) *Oxford and Empire: The Last Lost Cause?* New York: St Martin's Press.

Vicinus, M. (1985) *Independent Women: Work and Community for Single Women 1850–1920*. Chicago and London: University of Chicago Press.

Walkowitz, J. R. (1980) *Prostitution and Victorian Society: Women, Class, and the State*. Cambridge: Cambridge University Press.

4

1897

Stephen Arata

I

Of all the verses written during the summer of 1897 to commemorate Queen Victoria's Diamond Jubilee – and there were a great many – the only ones delivered personally into sovereign hands were those of Alfred Austin, Britain's poet laureate. On a fine June morning, Austin arrived at Windsor Castle with a specially printed copy of "Victoria" for Victoria, along with some roses from his garden. There (as he wrote some years later in his *Autobiography*) he was gratified to learn "how delighted the Queen was with the Poem, which she had already seen" in her daily newspaper. Victoria received the "proffered gift," Austin recalled, with "that mixture of graciousness and dignity observed by all who approached her" (II, 261). So pleased was Her Majesty that she later asked Sir Arthur Sullivan to set "Victoria" to music so that it could be sung on public occasions. Outwardly gracious and inwardly appalled, Sullivan declined.

Indeed, though Victoria liked her poem, she was just about the only one who did. Austin's "Jubilee effusion" – Sullivan's private description – was greeted with derision by reviewers, as were most of the laureate's poetic productions. Few laureates have been held in lower esteem (though fewer still have thought more highly of themselves) than Alfred Austin. More to the point, however, was the widespread belief that his very mediocrity fitted him for the office. Shortly after Austin assumed his post, the London *Literary Digest* (February 8, 1896) quoted William Dean Howells's response to the news: "The notion of any great man seriously performing [the laureate's] duties

A New Companion to Victorian Literature and Culture, First Edition. Edited by Herbert F. Tucker.
© 2014 John Wiley & Sons, Ltd. Published 2014 by John Wiley & Sons, Ltd.

is inextinguishably comic; and the selection of a man who is not great and never can be great has the highest propriety and fitness imaginable, as far as these duties are concerned" (10). Never mind that Alfred Tennyson, Austin's predecessor and Britain's longest-serving laureate, was regarded as a great man, one who had discharged his official duties for 42 years without comicality. By the 1890s the idea of a poet laureate had come to seem faintly ludicrous. When Tennyson died in 1892, many felt that the office ought to die with him. For three years the post was left vacant, as if to acknowledge that, as William Butler Yeats put it, only "an unreadable mediocrity or fluent monger of platitudes" was likely to want the job (Beckson 99). If a poet of Tennyson's public stature were suddenly to appear on the scene, one sign of his artistic integrity would be his scorn for the very idea of the laureateship, a scorn one could not imagine Tennyson himself having felt in 1850. The only contemporary poet who came close to enjoying such stature, William Morris, unequivocally declined to be considered for the position.

II

As George Eliot wrote in another context, these things are a parable. When Victorian thinkers wanted to work through difficult intellectual problems – such as, say, how to articulate the relation of history to literature, Jubilee to Ode – they often turned to parables. The 1880s and 1890s marked the culmination of a century-long resurgence of interest in parabolic forms of narrative: folktales, fairy tales, myths, romances, ballads, sagas, allegories. The central monument in this tradition is J. G. Frazer's *The Golden Bough*, the first volume of which appeared in 1890, but many other examples could be gathered, from Andrew Lang's collections of fairy tales to Morris's translations of Norse epics to Yeats's compilations of Celtic myth and folklore. Not just the recovery of old but the creation of new forms of parabolic narrative was common practice among *fin-de-siècle* writers. The utopian fictions of Morris and Richard Jefferies, the fairy tales of Oscar Wilde, the Gothic stories of Robert Louis Stevenson and Bram Stoker, and the science fiction of H. G. Wells all fall into this category. Even narratives conceived in more traditionally realistic modes – such as Arthur Conan Doyle's Sherlock Holmes stories, Rudyard Kipling's Anglo-Indian stories, and Joseph Conrad's sea tales – often possess the feel of modern parables or myths.

Though true, the story of Alfred Austin presenting his Ode to Queen Victoria has to my mind the properties of a parable. It synthesizes a complex set of social, historical, and ideological issues into a narrative that invites multiple exegesis. On the one side there is History writ large in the form of the Jubilee, a grandiose spectacle designed to underscore the preeminence of Great Britain and its empire on the world stage. In the last two decades of the century, the empire became, as never before, a central component of Britain's collective self-definition. (We need only compare the 1897 Jubilee to the 1851 Exhibition, a comparable spectacle of national definition and self-assertion, to see the changes in the way Britain represented itself to itself.)

Imperialism and its ideological offshoots saturated nearly every aspect of *fin-de-siècle* cultural life. In 1897 the British Empire was, indeed, the largest in the history of the world. Victoria ruled one-quarter of the world's population, a fact the newspapers never tired of repeating.

Yet to many the Jubilee celebrations seemed finally to exude an autumnal chill. The event served inadvertently to underscore the frailty of the 78-year-old monarch, whose increasing debility could be taken to stand for that of the empire as a whole. Austin's first publication as laureate had been a spirited defense in verse of Leander Starr Jameson's ill-fated and unauthorized attempt to seize the Transvaal from the Boers in January 1896. The poem had pleased the queen but embarrassed the government; in the summer of 1897 a parliamentary investigation into Jameson's raid became the occasion for some anguished and angry debate over the future of the empire. As many noted, too, the emergence of Germany and the United States as industrial and imperial powers seemed to presage Britain's imminent eclipse. The Berlin Conference of 1884 had divided Africa among the European powers, though in Britain the comfort of clear colonial borders was partially offset by the realization that asserting the nation's imperial will was now a trickier matter. Two years after the Jubilee, as British losses mounted in the Boer War, the crisis of public confidence in the imperial idea would deepen, but even in 1897 there were many who saw in jingoistic extravaganzas like the Jubilee a sign of worry, not security. In this atmosphere, it is not surprising that the one Jubilee poem to win wide acclaim was Kipling's "Recessional," which, as its title suggests, is more concerned with endings than beginnings. The poem's austerely elegiac tone captured Kipling's firm commitment to the ideology of empire, but also his deep sense of historical belatedness.

And here we turn to the other half of our parable and the figure of the laureate. For many late-Victorian observers, the most obvious lesson to be drawn from what *Punch*, with its customary sneer, referred to as the Tale of Alfred the Great (Tennyson) and Alfred the Little (Austin) was that the heirs of the century's great writers were themselves far from great. Throughout the 1880s and 1890s, the passings of the Victorian literary giants – George Eliot (1880), Thomas Carlyle (1881), Dante Gabriel Rossetti (1882), Anthony Trollope (1882), Matthew Arnold (1888), Wilkie Collins (1889), Robert Browning (1889), Christina Rossetti (1894), Walter Pater (1894) – were seen as Historical Events of great import, markers of an uneasy transition in the life of the nation. Speaking at a Royal Literary Fund dinner in 1893, Arthur Balfour despairingly noted that "the great names which rendered illustrious the early years of the great Victorian epoch are, one by one, dropping away" and that there was now no one fit "to occupy the thrones thus left vacant" (Cross 214). The deaths of iconic figures like Carlyle, Eliot, and Browning were greeted with prolonged and sincere lamentation. Tennyson's funeral prompted public mourning on a scale not seen since the deaths of Wellington and Prince Albert in mid-century, and not to be seen again until Victoria herself died in January 1901.

Yet the jeers that greeted Austin were not simply the result of his poetic shortcomings. In a sense, those jeers were directed as much at the office as at the poet. Austin, as laureate, stood for a kind of writer whose cultural capital had long since been spent. The laureateship in the 1890s was a bankrupt position from which to speak; no one took you seriously. This fact in turn gestures toward a complex set of historical developments that changed the ways in which writers and readers thought of themselves and of their mutual relations. Had "Victoria" been a good poem, and it was not, it would still not have been received in the way that "Recessional" was. Kipling, like Austin, was a "public poet," though of a quite different kind. Indeed, to compare Kipling to earlier figures like Tennyson or Arnold is to begin to see how, during the last quarter of the nineteenth century, the notion of a public writer had changed. Or rather, notions: at no point earlier in the century were there so many different *ways* to be a writer. Indeed, one was no longer simply a writer, but a particular kind of writer: decadent, aesthetic, naturalist, socialist, radical, feminist, journalistic, romantic. This proliferation of modifying adjectives not only indicates the range of professional personae now available to authors, but also indirectly points toward some fundamental changes in publishing and reading practices. The last decades of the century saw wide-ranging alterations in the methods by which literature was produced, distributed, and consumed, and it was these changes that laid the ground for transformations in how writers and audiences imagined themselves and their shared relation to the history through which they were living.

III

"Recessional" first appeared in a newspaper. So did many of Kipling's poems and stories. This fact was both a defining feature of Kipling's artistic persona and an indication of the centrality of the popular press in late-Victorian culture. In 1860 there had been 31 daily papers in the whole of Britain; in 1890 there were 150, with London alone claiming more than a dozen. A number of material changes had led to this expansion, most notably the repeal of tax and paper duties in the 1850s, the steady fall of newsprint prices (itself resulting largely from the change from cotton rags to esparto and then to wood pulp in the making of paper), and the invention of the web rotary press and of mechanical typesetting machines. These changes, coupled with improvements in communication and transportation and the development of centralized news-gathering associations like Reuters, helped make late-Victorian periodicals cheaper to produce, more diverse in content, and significantly more influential than their mid-century counterparts had been.

"The newspaper is the plague, or black death of the modern world": this from Arthur Symons in 1903 (Stokes 29). He could have been writing at any time during the preceding 20 years; vitriolic denunciations of the press were a staple of *fin-de-siècle* literary discourse. In Symons's view, popular journalists had usurped the position once occupied by artists and intellectuals. Newspapers had become the primary conduit through which the majority of readers transacted with "the world." The result, many claimed, was a vulgarization of public discourse. Or perhaps "democratization" is the better word: in a May 1887 essay published in *The Nineteenth Century*, Matthew Arnold argued that what he termed the "new journalism" (the tag stuck) was the voice of "the new voters, the *democracy*, as people are fond of calling them," who had been enfranchised by the Reform Bills of 1867 and 1884. It was in the nature of a democracy to be full of "life, movement, sympathy, good instincts" but to be unable, collectively, to "think fairly and seriously" about serious issues. In a word, wrote Arnold, a democracy was "*feather-brained*," as were the journalists who spoke to and for it (638).

Arnold singled out W. T. Stead, the editor of the *Pall Mall Gazette*, as the epitome of the New Journalist. Stead was indeed unapologetic when it came to discussing the power, actual and potential, of the press. "In a democratic age, in the midst of a population which is able to read, no position is comparable for permanent influence and far-reaching power to that of an editor who understands his vocation," Stead wrote in an 1886 *Contemporary Review* essay titled "Government by Journalism." "In him are vested almost all the attributes of real sovereignty" (661). Stead believed that legislative bodies like Parliament were fast becoming irrelevant to the conduct of public business. In fact as well as in name, legislators were now the servants of a populace whose will was being expressed through the medium of the press. "The telegraph and the printing-press have converted Great Britain into a vast agora, or assembly of the whole community, in which the discussion of the affairs of State is carried on from day to day in the hearing of the whole people" (654). At the same time, an enterprising editor could shape and direct such discussion to an unprecedented extent. "The editorial pen is a sceptre of power, compared with which the sceptre of many a monarch is but a gilded lath" (661).

Hyperbole, yes, but there is no doubting the influence Stead wielded in the 1880s and 1890s. The investigative journalism he practiced under the banner of social reform was often sensationalist, underinformed, and dangerously misleading, but it also helped focus public attention on a wide variety of pressing problems. His reports on East End slum conditions were important precursors (though of course not the only ones) to the scientific studies of urban poverty compiled by Charles Booth in *Life and Labour of the People in London* (1892–7) and Seebohm Rowntree in *Poverty: A Study of Town Life* (1901). And in one instance at least Stead's ideal of "government by journalism" seemed close to realization. "The Maiden Tribute of Modern Babylon," Stead's exposé of a "white slavery" trade in underaged London girls, spurred a public outcry that led directly to the passing of the Criminal Law Amendment Act of 1885; it also inspired an enormous variety of grassroots political activities (Walkowitz 81–120). From our perspective, the 1885 Act looks, to be sure, both well-intentioned and feather-brained. Designed to advance the cause of "social purity" by raising the age of consent for girls and regulating a range of nonmarital sexual relations, in practice the Act was used primarily to harass, and sometimes to prosecute, working-class women and homosexual men. The most famous victim was Oscar Wilde, convicted in 1895 of "acts of gross indecency" with other men and sentenced to two years in prison. The conviction not only destroyed Wilde's career (he died in 1900, aged only

46) but also drove underground for at least two more generations a burgeoning gay culture in London.

Whatever its long-term effects, Stead's exposé demonstrated the newfound power of the periodical press. No high-culture writer of the late-Victorian period was able to shape public discourse in the way Stead and other New Journalists like T. P. O'Connor and H. W. Massingham did. The problem, as press accounts of the "Maiden Tribute" affair and, three years later, the Jack the Ripper murders amply showed, was the ease with which social activism slid into sensationalism when its investigative journalism turned yellow. Critics claimed that the popular press did little more than pander to, and ultimately exacerbate, the lurid tastes of its readership, and that in doing so it irreparably coarsened discussion of vital political and cultural issues. "They aim to be as vulgar as the average reader," complained *The Literary Digest* in an April 1896 essay whose title – "New Journalism versus Civilization" – indicates the form such discussions usually took. By the mid-1890s even Stead's journalism seemed restrained in comparison to that found in the papers of Alfred Harmsworth, whose *Daily Mail* was the most sensational and – with a circulation of 543,000 in 1898, twice that of its nearest competitor – the most widely read periodical in England.

Motivating much of the criticism directed at the New Journalists was the fear many felt at the expansion of the reading public. The Education Act of 1870 had made elementary education compulsory in England and Wales (Scotland had long had it). Literacy rates rose steadily as a result, though at nowhere near the rate imagined by alarmed observers, who feared the prospect of a half-educated public engaged, as Frederic Harrison put it, in "aimless, promiscuous, vapid reading" or, worse, "the poisonous inhalation of mere literary garbage and bad men's worst thoughts" (Cross 205). Coincidentally, 1870 was also the year the birth rate peaked in nineteenth-century Britain at 36 per 1,000. The generation that came of age in the 1890s was thus more numerous than any of its predecessors. Throughout the period there was a push to make education more widely available. Acts of 1892 and 1894 helped fund public libraries throughout the country; in 1895 a Royal Commission recommended a system of compulsory secondary education as well as the establishment of a national Board of Education, both of which were in place by 1902.

Yet these advances stirred anxiety at their possible consequences. Attending Tennyson's funeral in 1892, Edmund Gosse was made uneasy by the spectacle of the "unparalleled masses of the curious" crowding around Westminster Abbey. These masses, Gosse wrote later in the *New Review* (November 1892), had turned out not to honor Tennyson the poet but to ogle what remained of Tennyson the celebrity. Thanks to the vulgarizing influences of the mass media, the ancient "prestige of verse" had given way to a modern cult of personality. Few in the crowd had either the taste or the training necessary for a true appreciation of poetry, Gosse surmised, and he worried that public opinion would pressure the government to choose a new laureate based on "mere commercial success" rather than "literary merit" (516). Seeing in the old laureate's funeral "a parable of the condition of poetry in England" (514), Gosse ominously warned of "the eruption of a sort of Commune in literature," an "outbreak of rebellion against tradition" that would finally overwhelm "whatever is rare, or delicate, or abstruse" (520–1).

Gosse's choice of analogies is telling. His own candidate for laureate was Algernon Swinburne, whose ardent support for the real Commune – the one briefly established in Paris in 1871 – was of a piece with his life-long republicanism. Gosse's worries concerning a "Commune in literature," then, had little to do with political ideology or literary convention. By either criterion Swinburne was an extremist, but he never-theless retained what Gosse considered the aura of a poet. In slightly less mystified terms, this meant that his work had not been swept up into the machinery of mass culture. (At Tennyson's funeral Gosse had been distressed by the sight of street vendors hawking broadsheets of "Crossing the Bar.") The penny-paper, the mass-market periodical, the music-hall, popular theater like the variety and burlesque, and, beginning in 1896 at the Empire Theatre, the cinema – for Gosse as for many others these were signs that a radical split had opened up between genteel and popular culture. The masses, enfranchised and educated and largely uninterested in the rare or delicate or abstruse, were seeking their own forms of cultural expression. When, in George Gissing's *New Grub Street* (1891), the writer Whelpdale at last abandons his high literary aspirations, it is so that he can make his fortune by publishing a magazine aimed at "the quarter-educated, that is to say, the great new generation that is being turned out by the Board Schools" (ch. 33). Gissing's response to mass culture was invariably sour, and in this he had much company. Thanks to the Reform Bills and the Education Act, wrote an apoplectic Robert Buchanan in *A Look Round Litera-ture* (1887), the "great waters of Democracy" were "arising to swallow up and cover the last landmarks" of high Victorian culture. "After the School Board has come the Deluge" (359–60).

IV

In his still helpful study, *The Eighteen Nineties* (1913), Holbrook Jackson points out that the period was "to no small extent the battleground of . . . two types of culture – the one represented by *The Yellow Book*, the other by the Yellow Press" (61). Jackson is right to insist on the connection of these two phenomena. If the *fin-de-siècle* saw the apotheosis of the mass-market periodical, it also witnessed the emergence of that characteristically Modernist venue, the little magazine. If papers like the *Daily Mail* and the *Pall Mall Gazette* spoke to and for the average middle-class reader, short-lived publications like *The Century Guild Hobby Horse*, *The Dial*, *The Butterfly*, *The Dome*, *The Equinox*, *The Pagan Review*, and *The Savoy* were self-consciously avant-garde in their orientation. The little magazine was one sign of collapse in the Victorian cultural synthesis that had been embodied in the quarterly reviews, and of a corresponding shift toward publications addressed to smaller market segments. Yet, as *The Yellow Book* briefly proved, a coterie publication properly marketed could also be a commer-cial success. Published between 1894 and 1897 by Elkin Mathews and John Lane, the *fin-de-siècle*'s most visible purveyors of limited edition and "fine" books, *The Yellow Book* frankly presented itself as a high-culture periodical, one whose ethos was diametrically opposed to that of the vulgar masses. Its contributors were aggressively elitist in their self-representations, and so too was *The Yellow Book* as a whole. Yet, perversely, the magazine was popular, if by popular we mean that it sold well. Mathews and Lane were among the savviest marketers of their era, and *The Yellow Book* was among the most financially successful of their publications. Its readership, moreover, was almost exclusively middle class – the very class that *The Yellow Book* professed to despise.

These facts suggest that the relation between mainstream culture and the avant-garde in the *fin-de-siècle* was considerably more tangled than is usually thought. Jackson indicates one aspect of this entanglement when he writes that *The Yellow Book* and the *Daily Mail* each exemplified "the characteristic excitability and hunger for sensation" of the period. Post-Paterian aestheticism, in other words, was simply sensationalism "seen from the cultured side" (61–2). Indeed, the commercial success of *The Yellow Book* resulted largely from Lane's ability to market "culture" to the many. Like other Lane publications, *The Yellow Book* was relatively inexpensive to produce, but it did not *look* inexpensive. "Beautiful to see and convenient to handle," as its Prospectus put it, *The Yellow Book* appeared anything but mass-produced, which it was. The elegantly distinctive look of its pages – generous leading, wide margins, clean lines, slightly larger than usual typeface, ample white space – positively oozed culture, as did the sinuously sinister lines of Aubrey Beardsley's drawings. Yet this layout also called to mind the design features of such lowbrow periodicals as George Newnes's *Tit-Bits*, which relied on large type and wide margins to draw in readers who might feel daunted by the densely packed pages characteristic of Victorian journals. Like *Tit-Bits*, too, *The Yellow Book* trafficked in short, easily digestible essays, tales, and verse, pieces that could be consumed several at a sitting. And the line block technology that Beardsley favored to reproduce his drawings had originally been developed in order to print simple illustrations quickly and cheaply in popular magazines like the *Illustrated London News* or the *Graphic*. There were of course differences in artistic quality, but the underlying aesthetic was the same. *The Yellow Book* sold culture to the middle classes in the same way that *Tit-Bits* and the *Graphic* sold entertainment.

Lane's mass-market elitism opened up new opportunities for certain classes of *fin-de-siècle* writer. *The Yellow Book* marketed itself as England's definitive avant-garde periodical, and it quickly became associated in the public mind with broader literary movements, especially poetic movements such as aestheticism, symbolism, and decadence. (Indeed, contemporary poetry was one of Lane's passions, and most English poets of the 1890s eventually published in *The Yellow Book*.) What these movements shared was a pronounced distaste for bourgeois aesthetics, a distaste that manifested itself most conspicuously in a loud disregard for the common reader. Lane's triumph was to recognize and exploit the public's desire to hear itself abused. It was thus no accident that Henry Harland, *The Yellow Book*'s literary editor, asked Henry James to contribute the opening story to the first volume. As England's best-known unpopular writer, James occupied the precise market niche to which *The Yellow Book* aspired. By the 1890s, James had recognized that unpopularity possessed a certain cachet, that some kinds of failure meant success – not just aesthetic success, but financial as well. Like the more flamboyant Wilde, James knew the value of a sharply conceived and shrewdly disseminated public persona. The tale he offered to Harland, "The Death of the Lion," reads like a proleptic parody (the hero is a writer named Paraday) of *The Yellow Book* itself. In telling the story of Paraday's fatal encounter with the forces of mass culture, James stages a familiar confrontation between art and commerce, but he does so in such a way that the distinction between the two terms finally makes no sense. At the heart of the tale is a "sacred" text, Paraday's manuscript notes for an as yet unwritten novel. No one can adequately appreciate its artistry, yet – or perhaps we should say, and so – it becomes the basis of his celebrity. Precisely because the book is too beautiful to read, it acquires the aura that makes for commercial success.

V

Paraday becomes a public figure by shunning publicity; his financial success stems from a sincere disregard for money. His is a characteristically *fin-de-siècle* persona, one that would be adopted and further refined by the rising generation of Modernists. In practice, though, disdain for the marketplace could be indulged only by writers like James whose commercial sense was sufficiently shrewd. For the less shrewd, help was available after 1884 in the form of the Society of Authors. In the words of its founder and driving engine, Walter Besant, the Society's primary goal was "to spread abroad and to cultivate" among writers "the knowledge of the reality of literary property" by throwing "a flood of light upon all those matters connected with the literary trade which have hitherto been kept mysteriously dark and secret," namely, matters of economics and trade (306). Besant was tireless in his efforts to convince writers to consider their works first and foremost as property and themselves as businessmen. Through the Society and its journal, *The Author*, Besant was instrumental in further- ing what Arnold Bennett later called "the economic education of the creative artist" (quoted in Keating 66). The Society worked to standardize book contracts, to make royalty agreements more equitable, to weaken the influence of lending libraries, to promote the use of literary agents, and to strengthen international copyright laws. Besant insured the legitimacy of the Society by persuading Tennyson to be its first president; he was followed in this largely ceremonial role by George Meredith and Thomas Hardy. Despite the initial mistrust of some writers who disliked Besant's mercantile bent, Society membership grew rapidly, from 68 in 1884, to 870 in 1892, to over 2,000 after the turn of the century. Thanks in part to its efforts, international copyright laws were strengthened among European nations through the Berne Con- vention of 1886 (revised in 1896 and 1910), while in the United States the Chace Act of 1891 at last made it difficult for American publishers to pirate English literary works without paying royalties, a practice that had exasperated English writers throughout the century.

Besant's ultimate goal was twofold. Not only should writers be fairly paid, he argued, they should also be accorded the respect they deserved. The "contempt of letters" existing "deep down in the national heart" would only be erased when writers began to comport themselves as "professionals" (314–15). He hoped that the Society of Authors would "ultimately do for literature what the Inns of Court do for law and the Medical Corporations do for the medical profession" and so ensure that "literature in every branch . . . takes its place as a recognized and honourable profession" (313). In Besant's view, the writer provided a service to society as valuable and useful as that provided by the solicitor, the doctor, the clergyman, or the soldier. One sign that writers had achieved their rightful stature, he argued, would be when they, like other professionals, began to be awarded knighthoods and peerages. The notion that authors could be considered professionals does not originate in the *fin-de-siècle*, though it does then gain a certain clarity, and not only because Besant was himself made a knight in 1895 for his "services to the dignity of letters." The new professional author arose in reaction to and defined himself against a diverse array of other possible personae – the Grub Street hack, the court poet, the New Journalist, the dilettante, the high priest of art, and, yes, the poet laureate – in order to assume his rightful place in the social hierarchy.

VI

I use "him" and "his" advisedly here, since what is likely to strike us is how the professionalizing of authorship worked, in Gaye Tuchman's (1989) phrase, to "edge women out" of the field. To call authors professionals – or alternatively priests, as many aesthetes did – is subtly to define writing as a masculine activity, since the professions were primarily, and the clergy exclusively, male enclaves in this period. While the existence of organizations like the Society of Women Journalists, founded in 1894, indicates that women writers were beginning actively to appropriate the status of professionals, the last quarter of the century also saw a backlash against what many male writers considered as the feminizing of British letters. The backlash took a variety of forms. Legitimate complaints about censorship and Grundyism, for instance, were often couched in terms that laid blame solely at the door of an unduly moralistic female public. Membership in the infamous National Vigilance Association, organized in 1885 to root out public vice in every form, was largely male, though from reading some contemporary accounts one might think the reverse was true. One might also think, upon reading George Moore's influential 1885 polemic, "Literature at Nurse," that all the three-deckers purchased by circulating libraries were written by and for timid women. The dramatic collapse in the 1890s of those two bulwarks of Victorian publishing – the circulating library and the three-volume novel – was due not simply to changes in the economics of the book trade but also to a concerted effort on the part of "serious" writers, mostly male, to redefine what counted as real literature.

And what did not. During this period words like "literature" and "literary" fully take on their modern connotations. They become primarily terms of exclusion, ways to make sharp demarcations between different forms of writing and thus to delegitimate certain kinds of texts. The furor over the "New Woman" novel is a case in point. The New Woman herself – typically portrayed as self-reliant, adventuresome, outspoken, and intelligent – clearly affronted conventional notions of femininity. By contrast, the novels in which she appeared tended, formally speaking, to be quite conventional. As developed by writers like Sarah Grand, Mona Caird, Ella Hepworth Dixon, Olive Schreiner, Emma Brooke, and Gertrude Dix, the New Woman novel represents a late flowering of two highly respectable Victorian forms, the social problem novel and the novel of domestic realism. Yet these heirs to the tradition of Gaskell and Dickens were dismissed by hostile critics who labeled their works "polemical," "pedantic," and thus "unartistic." Writing in the *Westminster Review* on "The Tyranny of the Modern Novel" (April 1895), D. F. Hannigan deplored "that tendency toward pedantry which appears to beset all women of profound learning and fixed intellectual habits" (304). The novels such women produced, he suggested, were not works of art but screeds. As if in response, the artist–heroine of Grand's *The Beth Book* (1897) defiantly asserts that "manner has always been less to me than matter. When I think of all the preventable sin and misery there is in the world, I pray God give us books of good intention – never mind the style!" (ch. 47). Such a sentiment, which Dickens would undoubtedly have applauded, was now more often greeted with sneers.

To equate artistry with formal or stylistic innovation, as critics first began to do at this time, is among other things to devalue certain kinds of politically charged writing. Writers like Grand, Caird, and Schreiner consciously presented themselves as public intellectuals in the tradition of Carlyle and Arnold, though they received nothing resembling the respect their predecessors enjoyed. More generally, Judith Walkowitz has noted how "middle-class women's forceful entry into the world of publicity and politics" in the 1880s and 1890s fundamentally changed the terms of public discourse (7). Women were "visible" as never before, a situation that caused no end of uneasiness in some quarters. Activists like Josephine Butler, Florence Fenwick Miller, Frances Power Cobbe, Clementina Black, and Annie Besant were instrumental in shaping public discussion and political policy on a wide range of issues. Women's rights advanced on a number of fronts in this period, though the pace of reform remained glacial. The generations-long push to secure women's property rights culminated in the Married Women's Property Act of 1882. The iniquitous Contagious Diseases Acts of the 1860s were at last repealed in 1886. The move towards suffrage gained ground as well. Under the 1870 Education Act women could stand for election to the newly created school boards; in 1888 they gained the vote in municipal and county elections; and in 1894 the Local Government Act decreed that "no person shall be disqualified by sex or marriage from being elected" to district or parish councils. (Women continued to be barred from voting in national elections, however, despite the introduction of several full suffrage bills into Parliament during the 1890s.) Educational opportunities also widened, though women did not receive fully accredited degrees from either Cambridge or Oxford until well into the twentieth century.

For many feminists, efforts to advance women's rights inevitably formed part of a larger political struggle to reform, enlighten, and humanize the social realm as a whole. Annie Besant, for instance, was active across a range of causes whose interconnections she continually stressed. One-time spouse of an Anglican minister, she renounced both marriage and faith in 1873; over the next 20 years she became known as a leading figure in the National Secular Society, the Malthusian Society (which advocated birth control), and the socialist Fabian Society; a frequent contributor to the radical *National Reformer*, and a co-founder of the Freethought Publishing Company; and a charismatic public speaker. In the 1880s she turned more firmly toward socialist and labor causes, earning her greatest notoriety from the role she played in the Bryant and May match-girl strike in 1888. A decisive event in the history of labor unions, the strike not only focused public attention on the industry's deplorable working conditions and unfair wages but also – thanks largely to Besant's keen instincts in manipulating the press – demonstrated how public opinion could be effectively mobilized to gain political advantage.

VII

For students of the period, Annie Besant's career illuminates two facts about the *fin-de-siècle* worth keeping in mind. The first is that the 1880s and 1890s were a time of extraordinarily rich political ferment. At no time since the 1840s had the political landscape in Britain been quite so unsettled. If to our eyes a writer like Besant seems to have been bewilderingly active in causes, that is in part because there were so many causes to be active in. The match-girls' strike, for instance, was only one of the culture-altering labor actions of the period. In 1889 gas workers in Beckton successfully struck for higher wages and an eight-hour day; within a year 30,000 additional laborers had joined the newly formed National Union of Gas Workers and General Labourers. That same year 10,000 London dock workers struck for four weeks, eventually winning wage increases, overtime pay, and the end of piece work. The success of these and other strikes (most notably by miners) accelerated the nascent labor movement – in all, over 200,000 workers joined unions between 1888 and 1890 – and heightened the visibility of the burgeoning socialist movement in Britain. Some key dates in what has been called the late-Victorian socialist revival are 1884, which saw the founding of both H. M. Hyndman's moderately radical Socialist Democratic Federation and the more mainstream Fabian Society; 1892, when James Keir Hardie became the first labor candidate to win a seat in Parliament; and 1893, when the Independent Labour Party was formed under Hardie's leadership.

For many, of course, agitation on behalf of workers' rights gave cause for much wringing of hands. Tensions were especially high in London, where attempts on the part of the government to suppress or at least control an increasingly radicalized proletariat led to a number of dramatic confrontations. The "Black Sunday" riots in Trafalgar Square in February 1886 led to a ban on public meetings in the square, which in turned provoked socialist and radical groups (with the backing of Stead's *Pall Mall Gazette*) to plan an even larger demonstration for November 1887. Some 20,000 marchers – whose numbers included Stead, Hyndman, Annie Besant, William Morris, Bernard Shaw, the Scots radical R. B. Cunninghame Graham, and Karl Marx's daughter Eleanor Aveling – were met by 2,400 soldiers and policemen deployed by the chief commissioner of police. The resulting clash, memorialized as "Bloody Sunday," while not in fact very bloody, passed quickly into public mythology and inspired several subsequent generations of British radicals.

To read the letters, diaries, and memoirs of many of the period's leading literary figures – and this is the second lesson to be learned from contemplating Annie Besant's career – is to see how deeply involved they were in the political and social struggles of the day. It is also to confirm how thoroughly enwoven, for them, were aesthetics and politics. This kind of awareness was especially notable in British drama, which awoke from its long Victorian slumber to become once again a socially engaged art form. J. T. Grein's notorious 1891 production of Ibsen's *Ghosts* for the Independent Theatre of London was for many spectators the defining theatrical event of the age. Ibsen's plays, ably translated throughout the 1880s and 1890s by William Archer, in turn provided a model of socially efficacious drama that British playwrights such as Shaw, Arthur Wing Pinero, and Henry Arthur Jones sought to emulate.

At the same time, the Victorian *fin-de-siècle* is unquestionably the moment when the impulse to disentangle the public from the private begins to gather strength. To their Modernist successors and critics that inward turn away from political commitment seemed, for good or ill, the definitive gesture of the late-Victorian artist. To read the *fin-de-siècle* exclusively in this way, however, is seriously to distort and diminish its accomplishments. It is to undervalue the achievements – and they continue to be consistently undervalued – of writers like Shaw and Morris. It is also entirely to erase the work of someone like Besant, who over the course of her long career published so much writing on such diverse topics: marriage, private property, population control, land reform, socialism, prostitution, art, imperialism, labor, religion, political equality. Much of her writing is superb: rhetorically sophisticated, intellectually challenging, aesthetically engaging. None of it is much read now, at least by students of literature.

VIII

During the summer of 1897 Thomas Hardy traveled to Switzerland, partly to escape the Jubilee. Toward midnight on June 27 he found himself, by coincidence, staying at the very hotel in Lausanne where, precisely 110 years earlier and virtually on the eve of the French Revolution, Edward Gibbon had written the final words of his *Decline and Fall of the Roman Empire*. The poem Hardy wrote to commemorate this moment, "Lausanne," conspicuously avoids the temptation to use Gibbon as an occasion to comment directly on the Jubilee celebrations or the fate of empires or even on the question of history itself. Instead, he conjures up the shade of the historian in order to cast him as the prototype of the Modern writer, one who knows that to tell the truth one must tell it slant. "How fares the Truth now?" Gibbon inquires of the poet. "Do pens but slily further her advance? / May one not speed her but in phrase askance?" For Hardy in 1897, still smarting from the critical abuse heaped on *Tess of the d'Urbervilles* and *Jude the Obscure*, the askant phrase now seemed the one remaining avenue open to the writer. Any more direct speech brought only censure. In the trajectory of Hardy's career, from Victorian novelist to Modernist lyricist, we can trace the more general turn from public to private utterance characteristic of twentieth-century literature. In Hardy's hands even poems on public figures, such as his poem on Gibbon or, four years later, his strikingly cold and distanced elegy for Queen Victoria ("V.R. 1819–1901"), do not pretend to speak to or for a wider audience, nor do they offer poetic speech as a way to make sense of the flux of history or of the individual life. Indeed, "V.R." seems in part an elegy for elegy, a lament for a kind of utterance that, like Victoria herself, was now dead and laid to rest beside the century's corpse outleant.

See also ARTISTIC, PUBLISHING; POETRY, DRAMA; SHORES

REFERENCES

Austin, A. (1911) *The Autobiography of Alfred Austin, Poet Laureate, 1835–1910*, 2 vols. London: Macmillan.

Beckson, K. (1992) *London in the 1890s: A Cultural History*. New York: W. W. Norton.

Besant, W. (1970) *Essays and Historiettes*. Port Washington: Kennikat Press.

Cross, N. (1985) *The Common Writer: Life in Nineteenth-Century Grub Street*. Cambridge: Cambridge University Press.

Jackson, H. (1913) *The Eighteen Nineties: A Review of Art and Ideas at the Close of the Nineteenth Century*. London: Grant Richards.

Keating, P. (1989) *The Haunted Study: A Social History of the English Novel 1875–1914*. London: Secker and Warburg.

Stokes, J. (1989) *In the Nineties*. Hemel Hempstead: Harvester Wheatsheaf.

Tuchman, G. (1989) *Edging Women Out: Victorian Novelists, Publishers, and Social Change*. New Haven: Yale University Press.

Walkowitz, J. (1992) *City of Dreadful Delight: Narratives of Sexual Danger in Victorian London*. Chicago: University of Chicago Press.

FURTHER READING

Anderson, A., and J. Valente (eds) (2002) *Disciplinarity at the Fin de Siècle*. Princeton: Princeton University Press.

Arata, S. (1996) *Fictions of Loss in the Victorian Fin de Siècle*. Cambridge: Cambridge University Press.

Ardis, A. (1990) *New Women, New Novels: Feminism and Early Modernism*. New Brunswick: Rutgers University Press.

Ardis, A., and P. Collier (eds) (2008) *Transatlantic Print Culture, 1880–1940: Emerging Media, Emerging Modernism*. Basingstoke and New York: Palgrave Macmillan.

Brake, L. (2001) *Print in Transition, 1850–1910: Studies in Media and Book History*. Basingstoke and New York: Palgrave.

Brantlinger, P. (1988) *Rule of Darkness: British Literature and Imperialism, 1830–1914*. Ithaca: Cornell University Press.

Bristow, J. (ed.) (2005) *The Fin-de-Siècle Poem: English Literary Culture and the 1890s*. Athens: Ohio University Press.

Constable, L., D. Denisoff, and M. Potolsky (eds) (1999) *Perennial Decay: On the Aesthetics and Politics of Decadence*. Philadelphia: University of Pennsylvania Press.

Daly, N. (1999) *Modernism, Romance, and the Fin de Siècle: Popular Fiction and British Culture, 1880–1914*. Cambridge: Cambridge University Press.

Dowling, L. (1986) "Letterpress and Picture in the Victorian Periodicals." *Yearbook of English Studies* 16, 117–31.

Frankel, N. (2009) *Masking the Text: Literature & Mediation in the 1890s*. High Wycombe: Rivendale Press.

Gagnier, R. (2010) *Individualism, Decadence, and Globalization: On the Relationship of Part to Whole, 1859–1920*. Basingstoke and New York: Palgrave Macmillan.

Marshall, G. (ed.) (2007) *The Cambridge Companion to the Fin de Siècle*. Cambridge: Cambridge University Press.

Parrinder, P., and A. Gasiorek (eds) (2012) *The Reinvention of the British and Irish Novel, 1880–1940*. Oxford: Oxford University Press.

Powell, K. (ed.) (2004) *The Cambridge Companion to Victorian and Edwardian Theatre*. Cambridge: Cambridge University Press.

Schaffer, T., and K. Psomiades (eds) (1999) *Women and British Aestheticism*. Charlottesville and London: University Press of Virginia.

Showalter, E. (1990) *Sexual Anarchy: Gender and Culture at the Fin de Siècle*. Harmondsworth: Penguin Books.

Wiener, J. (ed.) (1988) *Papers for the Millions: The New Journalism in Britain, 1850s to 1914*. New York: Greenwood Press.

Part Two
Passages of Life

5

Growing Up: Childhood

Claudia Nelson

Historical stereotypes notwithstanding, the Victorian era did not "discover" childhood. The inclination to define childhood as intrinsically different from adulthood had existed for well over a millennium; Albrecht Classen, among others, notes that it was entrenched in Anglo-Saxon England, and closer to the Victorian era there was ample attention given to child psychology and the training of the young by such figures as John Locke (1632–1704), Jean-Jacques Rousseau (1712–78), and Irish educationists Richard Lovell Edgeworth (1744–1817) and his daughter Maria (1768–1849). These theorists' ideas about the developmental significance of environment and empirical experience shaped Victorian views, and indeed still resonate today. Nor can the Victorians be credited with having invented children's literature. What is often termed the first picture book for children, Johannes Amos Comenius's *Orbis Sensualium Pictus*, appeared in 1658, while the eighteenth century produced much fiction and poetry aimed at the young, and today's scholars continue to assert the importance of children's consumption of texts among early Christians, in classical Greece, even in ancient Mesopotamia.

But even while we concede that the Victorians inherited from older generations their interest in childhood, and some of their ideas about it, we may legitimately contend that Victorian conceptions of childrearing, of the state of being a child, and of the emotional importance of children to a society dominated by adults took on such weight as to represent something new in Western history. Never before had childhood become an obsession within the culture at large – yet in this case "obsession" is not too strong a word. Sociologist Charles Booth concluded from census data in 1886 that in every decade from 1851 to 1881 children under 15 made up slightly

A New Companion to Victorian Literature and Culture, First Edition. Edited by Herbert F. Tucker.

over 35 percent of the population of England and Wales, outnumbering both adult males and adult females (see Jordan). In Carolyn Steedman's phrase, "Mid-Victorian society was a society of the young," and their elders knew it (125).

Childhood, then, was omnipresent, especially since compulsory schooling only gradually removed children from adult notice during the day; the 1851 education census suggests that about 55 percent of boys and 62 percent of girls aged 3 to 15 were not in school, and Henry Mayhew estimated in the same year that some 10,000 children were scratching a living on the streets of London, very much in the public eye. But adult attitudes toward childhood varied. For some Victorians, it was a threat, a stage during which desire outstripped self-control and animal nature proved the ineffectuality of civilization. For many others, it was the arena within which a better society might be engineered, whether through adept molding of the malleable young or through the reform of men and women whose hearts were to be softened by contact with childish innocence. For a third group, it was a reminder of personal and social injustices endured in youth that continued to shape their adult lives, as Charles Dickens's enforced sojourn in a blacking warehouse at age 12 resurfaces throughout his oeuvre. And for still others, childhood was a commodity to be marketed, in forms ranging from child labor to the sentimental greeting card, giving rise to both profit and protest. In short, the range of Victorian responses to childhood is far too wide to be covered adequately here; this chapter can only summarize, emphasize, and suggest the development, boundaries, and repercussions of nineteenth-century Britain's fascination with childhood real and imagined.

Real Children I: The Privileged

While Victorian writers on domesticity stressed the wonders of the parent–child bond within the privileged classes, in practice children belonging to those classes often had minimal contact with their parents. Small children were cared for by nursemaids, older ones taught by governesses, who had some 50,000 children in their charge in 1851 (see Jordan); boys aged seven and older were increasingly likely to be boarders at preparatory or public schools. Many Victorians, then, saw childrearing as a matter for specialists – not necessarily trained professionals, as teachers and childcare workers retained a certain amateur quality until comparatively late in the century, but certainly individuals who devoted all their time to the effort. Perhaps as a result, a major genre during the period consisted of works relating to raising the young. Housekeeping manuals offered advice for supervising nursemaids, outfitting nurseries, ensuring children's health; domestic writers exalted the gentle influence of the middle-class mother, which was to permeate the schoolroom and impart morals to her offspring; scientists and philosophers, from Charles Darwin to Herbert Spencer, theorized about the mind of the infant and the training of the growing child.

Much of this outpouring of articles and treatises concerned education, especially that of boys. Beginning in 1828, when Thomas Arnold became headmaster of Rugby, the British public schools received substantial scrutiny, and the century also witnessed the founding of many new schools after the Arnoldian efforts at reform gained a foothold. Whereas eighteenth-century public schools had pursued a policy of purposeful neglect, leaving pupils outside the classroom to their own, often anarchic, devices, Arnold sought (though historians dispute the degree to which he was successful) to institute a tighter discipline and a nobler outlook among his boys, turning Rugby into an establishment where the godly middle classes would be happy to send their sons. Moving on to govern other schools in their turn, Arnold's disciples expanded on his principles, especially by using athleticism as a pivotal force in the attempt to breed manly Britons. Curricular reforms – the introduction of subjects other than mathematics and the classics as important to boys' education – were secondary to the attempt to reform identity, which became so central to the public schools' self-description that many educators claimed that even wealthy, leisured parents were incapable of raising sons well. To be sure, the schools themselves were not beyond reproach; the findings of Parliament's Public Schools Commission in 1864 were largely uncomplimentary, and commentators throughout the century continued to note educational failings, although headmasters gained significantly in the public esteem over the century. Nevertheless, attendance at a public school was increasingly an unwritten requirement for admission into England's ruling elite.

This linkage of formal education and public power helped to motivate the changes that took place in the way middle-class girls were educated during this period. The mid-century agitation for higher education for women encompassed also a drive for better secondary schooling for girls. Reformers launched a major effort to found girls' schools that would function as equivalents to the great boys' public schools and raise the status of women associated with these institutions as teachers or as graduates. The campaign was highly successful. By the time of the Bryce Commission on Secondary Education in 1894 there were at least 218 endowed and proprietary schools for girls, most of them founded since 1870 (see Pedersen). More numerous still were private schools, which differed from "public" endowed and proprietary (joint-stock) institutions in that they were the property of an individual or a family. Through them passed an estimated 70 percent of those girls enjoying a secondary education at the end of the century. Like Victorian headmasters, female educators saw themselves as training character as well as intellect; they also often congratulated themselves on enabling the continued reshaping of gender relations and of women's role in the England of the future.

Real Children II: The Poor

Working-class childhood presented a darker picture. Although working-class households often accepted middle-class morality and ideas about marriage and parenthood, many nineteenth-century commentators painted family life among the lower working classes as damaged and damaging, dominated not by loving domesticity but by brutishness or ignorance. Working-class mothers were criticized as unversed in housekeeping and child nurturance, so that their offspring grew up puny and unfit; working-class fathers were characterized as abusive drunkards incapable of normal husbandhood and fatherhood. Eighteenth-century efforts to open free clinics for the poor that would both treat sick children and educate their parents in how to care for them – information that the poor were presumed to lack – expanded in the nineteenth century; concerns about child endangerment migrated, as Monica Flegel has chronicled, from literature to the new genre of social casework reports. Such trends increasingly led to a sense that the nation should step in to care for the "children of the state." Over the course of Victoria's reign, more and more legislation was aimed at the children of the poor, especially the urban poor; these laws were designed both to protect and to control.

From the 1830s onward, then, especially in London, we notice new and vocal anxiety about "street children," a category that might include children with homes and parents as well as waifs, children who earned money by boot-blacking or flower-selling or tumbling as well as children who seemed to be running wild. Just as some writers considered even middle-class boys a more "primitive" species than adult men (the dichotomy did not typically apply to females), the children of the urban poor were often described as "savages," implicitly establishing the responsibility of the ostensibly more highly evolved to bring these children to civilization, by force if necessary. Because they were often associated not merely with poverty and ignorance but also with criminality, with their own offenses present and future and with those of their parents, creating new laws to affect them seemed a logical response.

These laws typically sought to remove children from the power of individual adults, who were presumed likely to misuse their authority, and to place them under the control of the state. Over a lifetime of philanthropic effort, Anthony Ashley Cooper, seventh Earl of Shaftesbury, paid particular attention to the young; causes to which he lent his name included legislation for the protection of the "climbing boys" apprenticed to chimney sweeps and of child acrobats, the London Society for the Prevention of Cruelty to Children (founded in 1884, the year before his death), and Thomas Barnardo's work with homeless children, in addition to an assortment of building and sanitary reforms designed to promote the well-being of the working-class family as a unit. The scope of Shaftesbury's concern mirrors the range of issues with which Parliament occupied itself over the period. Children in mines, in factories, in theaters, on farms, even in their own homes gradually came under the eye of what its opponents dubbed "grandmotherly government," just as children from wealthier families involved in custody disputes were increasingly seen as belonging not to their fathers (who would once have gained custody almost automatically) but rather, in a sense, to the judicial system, which had new power to determine their disposition.

Since Parliament was reluctant to intrude into the internal affairs of the home, legislation affecting the relationship between employer and employee was easier to enact than that affecting the relationship between parent and child. Nevertheless, child labor did not disappear during Victoria's reign. The working classes could not afford that middle-class luxury, an extended childhood; their offspring entered domestic service, agricultural labor, apprenticeships, and other employment at ages when their richer peers were deemed incapable of supporting themselves or of contributing to the family exchequer. If the regulation or the economic decline of a particular industry lessened the chance of a child's employment in it, the presence of the young in other jobs might swell. Thus, for instance, only about half as many children worked in the mines in England and Wales in 1881 as had done so in 1841, before the enactment of various pieces of legislation – but during the same period, the number of children working as servants nearly doubled (see Jordan). Numerous commentators welcomed the idea that working-class girls, in particular, would be exposed to middle-class housekeeping practices and removed from the potentially noxious influence of their own parents; domestic service could be seen, conveniently, as a missionary endeavor in which the "converts" did all the work.

In this regard certain forms of child labor might serve the same functions as more official means of separating endangered children from their parents. Consider the Victorian interest in reformatories for young delinquents, "Ragged Schools" or emigration for waifs, and group homes for children whose parents had died or proved unworthy; all these solutions were intended to redress the faults of domestic life among the lower orders by substituting discipline for a parental order presumed to have been chaotic and probably criminal. Accustomed to the idea that their own boys might be best raised in boarding schools, the privileged classes had no qualms about making this decision for their social inferiors as well. Sending a delinquent boy to a reformatory, wrote W. R. Greg in the influential *Edinburgh Review* in April 1855, shortly after the passage of the Reformatory Schools Act, "is the greatest kindness you can render him," because the reformatory is "more healthy, more kindly" than the boy's family is likely to be, "softening and training, not crushing or terrifying." Similar theories were applied to destitute children who had committed no crime; whereas until 1853 such children were usually remanded to workhouses, along with destitute adults, after 1853 they might go to "barrack schools" or "industrial schools," there to be taught the life skills and mores approved by middle-class reformers. In addition to getting intellectual and moral instruction, girls would learn to perform housewifely tasks, while boys would receive manual training. By such means, the children of the lower working classes could be used to inject bourgeois ideals into the proletariat, and (so ran the theory) future crime would diminish accordingly.

In this formula, children are both the object and the vehicle for social reform. And although most Victorians saw a wide gulf between the undeserving poor – criminals, vagrants, drunkards – and the respectably employed deserving poor, whose children were unlikely to require institutional care, we may nonetheless discern in the push for compulsory schooling a desire to colonize or convert even the latter group. At the beginning of the century, voluntary or charity schools played the leading role in the effort to educate the working-class child; especially important was the eighteenth-century institution of the Sunday school, which instilled in children sufficient literacy to permit Bible reading and emphasized character training through religion. Sunday schools expanded dramatically in the first three-quarters of the nineteenth century, at their height enrolling nearly six million, but reformers deemed their efforts inadequate. As Charles Booth argued in an unpublished article of 1873, state-supported education could exert a much-needed "humanizing influence" upon the working classes (see Himmelfarb). Parliamentary inquiries indicated that working-class children were profoundly ignorant. In slow response, a series of Education Acts from 1802 onward extended the categories of children required to attend school and the number of hours each day to be spent in the classroom, while the average number of years of schooling rose correspondingly. Until it was superseded in 1902, the Act of 1870 was the most influential. Upon its passage, 26 percent of school-age children were attending classes; ten years later that number stood at 46 percent, while the number of elementary teachers went from 13,729 in 1870 to 94,943 in 1896 (see Bergen). The point of instituting these changes was not merely to provide England with a more literate workforce, but also, as many commentators pointed out in the pages of prestigious periodicals, to redress the inadequacies of the working-class family, even among the respectable poor. Again, children were the key to social reform.

Imagined Children I: Literature for Children

One result of increasing literacy – and also of improvements in printing technologies and transportation networks for the distribution of commercial products, to name only two other factors – was to expand the market for children's reading over the course of the nineteenth century: more potential readers existed, and books and magazines might be produced and shipped more efficiently, than ever before. The boom in Victorian periodical publishing, for instance, was as evident in the nursery as in the smoking-room or boudoir; by Diana Dixon's count, the five children's magazines extant in England in 1824 had ballooned to 160 by 1900. By the end of the century, children's periodicals could afford to specialize, aiming at the urban working-class boy or girl as well as at middle-class consumers such as the public-school boy, the Tractarian young lady, even the young vegetarian or Theosophist or anti-smoking enthusiast. Other forms of children's literature proliferated as well, perhaps most notably the illustrated book. Under the stimulus of newly inexpensive and effective color printing techniques and the new right of illustrators to copyright their work, scores of elaborately bound gift books destined for the middle class appeared on the Christmas market, adorned with glowing pictures by such artists as Randolph Caldecott and Walter Crane – and later by Kate Greenaway, Arthur Rackham, Edmund Dulac, and other luminaries of this "Golden Age of Book Illustration."

If the quantity of books available and the quality of their design changed dramatically over Victoria's reign, so too did their content. Early nineteenth-century children's literature typically emphasizes either Evangelical religion or secular rationalism. Often described as the first work of Victorian children's literature, Catherine Sinclair's *Holiday House* (1838) offers a new priority, fun. To be sure, religious sentiment is not lacking, in that the virtuous older brother of feckless Harry and Laura dies a saintly death for the joint edification of his siblings and the reader, but the primary focus lies on the entertainment rather than on the serious messages hidden beneath it. When Laura cuts off her hair and Harry sets fire to the nursery, the reader is more likely to enjoy the children's attack on domestic order than to worry about whether they are doomed to perdition.

In this sense, Sinclair bridges two apparently unrelated forms, the Evangelical moral tale and Victorian nonsense writing, since the great exemplar of the latter, Lewis Carroll, likewise based *Alice's Adventures in Wonderland* (1865) and *Through the Looking-Glass* (1871) on an undermining of the nursery regimen. The antididacticism of the *Alice* books, suggested a contemporary reviewer, was the secret of their popularity. And the idea that there is pleasure to be found in identifying with the child who subverts conventional domesticity – usually characterized in these texts as rigid or otherwise inadequate – continues through a host of mischievous literary "pickles" to the end of the century, with Rudyard Kipling's wolf-boy Mowgli and E. Nesbit's energetic Bastables.

But we cannot well argue that the difference between Victorian children's literature and what preceded it is the difference between the amoral and the moral. After all, a major function of children's literature is to explain to the young the principles, ethical as well as practical, by which the society that has produced it works or should work. We might rather postulate (although such judgments are necessarily subjective) that much – not all – Victorian writing for children attacks what the author perceives to be the established order, emphasizing the ideal over the status quo. Working-class children were not the only objects of social engineering during this period; through their pleasure reading, middle-class children too could be indoctrinated with ethical and political views of which their parents might not always approve, sometimes, as Marah Gubar observes, receiving encouragement to collaborate imaginatively with a narrative's subversive agenda. Beneath the apparently innocent surface of many stories and poems for the young, critics have discerned radical statements on three overlapping principles in particular: religion, social class, and gender and sexuality.

Pre-Victorian religious tracts for children focus largely on what the child must do to achieve salvation. Examples of error abound – the eponymous Sluggard of Isaac Watts's verse, too lazy to read his Bible; Mary Martha Sherwood's Augusta Noble, interested only in the trappings of privilege, who burns to death when her frock catches fire, unprepared as she is for God's judgment. In contrast, Victorian religious works often locate error not in the child protagonist but in the surrounding adult population. Take the best-selling *Jessica's First Prayer*, written in 1867 by "Hesba Stretton" (Sarah Smith) and targeting both children and adults. Jessica is a street child, the daughter of an alcoholic actress; her religious education and her general well-being have been utterly neglected. Yet it is she who brings the main adult character to salvation, not vice versa. Her innocent trust in God both indicts middle-class society, which is more interested in respectability and in avoiding unpleasantness than in fulfilling the divine will, and establishes the waif as an object of emotional interest: Stretton's short work touched off a boom in waif fiction, some religious, some secular, all sentimental in tone and activist in implication.

Religious fiction for the young might also concern itself with the educated classes, as the work of the prolific Tractarian writer Charlotte Mary Yonge shows. A protegée of noted Anglican divine John Keble, Yonge specialized in family sagas and historical novels that brought moral and doctrinal questions into daily life. The answers to these questions, as so often in Victorian women's fiction, involve self-sacrifice and not "putting oneself forward"; at the same time, the novels insist upon the importance of the flawed individual, who plays a central role in the story. Similarly, Yonge's adored father sanctioned her writing only if it was intended as an offering to God and not as self-aggrandizement – yet this dutiful daughter wrote herself into the position of best-selling author, magazine editor, and role model for untold middle-class girls with High Church leanings.

The paradox of Charlotte Yonge, an avowed antifeminist whose works teem with strong-minded and interesting women, informs many Victorian children's novels by female authors. On the one hand, the nineteenth century saw childrearing as a primarily female duty. Since entertaining children, understanding them, and training them through gentle moral suasion were considered well suited to women's capabilities, few people would complain that a woman who wrote children's books was improper and unfeminine, which helps to explain why so many female writers talented and untalented entered this field. On the other hand, as today's feminist critics have noted, children's fiction by women often quietly subverts established gender mores. Dinah Mulock Craik's *The Little Lame Prince* (1875) is a good example, in which the feminized title character is barred by his physique from the world of male prerogative yet derives moral strength from his physical weakness. Male authors, too, might employ children's literature to suggest female superiority, as in the case of Scottish novelist George MacDonald, a supporter of women's higher education whose fantasies feature goddess figures astonishing for their wisdom, virtue, and power.

Predictably, boys' literature also has much to say about gender, and as critics such as Jenny Holt have argued, it offers an excellent way to chart changes in ideals of manliness and male citizenship over the Victorian period. The two major genres within Victorian boys' fiction are the public school story and the adventure tale; the one reached its peak after Arnold's influence established moral training as a goal of the middle- and upper-class educational system, the other after Britain became accustomed to thinking of itself as an imperial power. The school story, whose popularity was set in 1857 with the publication of Thomas Hughes's *Tom Brown's Schooldays*, a story of Arnold's Rugby, tends to describe self-mastering within a system in which one begins as an inferior (a new boy, a younger child, and so on). In contrast, the adventure tale often focuses on reaching some exterior goal – discovering pirate treasure in Robert Louis Stevenson's *Treasure Island* (1883), slaughtering three dozen gorillas in R. M. Ballantyne's *The Gorilla Hunters* (1861), triumphing over a foe in countless military or naval dramas. Even so, this outward object typically confers upon its possessor new maturity and manhood; readers understand that an inner victory has been gained as well.

Boys' stories suggest a redefinition of manliness over the second half of the nineteenth century, a movement away from emotionalism and androgynous virtue and toward a more hard-bitten, stoic, and physical ideal. Children's magazines and textbooks sought to shape young empire-builders, particularly boys, by instilling a set of attitudes toward the inhabitants of India, Africa, and China that would prepare readers for their colonial responsibilities and privileges (see Castle). Adventure serial after adventure serial in the late-Victorian years minimized introspection in favor of action and unquestioning belief in British superiority. Writers such as G. A. Henty chronicled dozens of military campaigns without wasting ink on character development, signaling to readers that history is about derring-do, not feelings. Yet even while this form dominated boys' fiction, other writers upheld an older version of manliness involving passionate same-sex friendship, doubts, tenderness, and soul-searching. If girls' stories often covertly asserted the superiority of the feminine over the masculine, directly or indirectly supporting the feminist cause, boys' stories often suggested that manliness, too, could benefit from embracing womanly ideals.

The strategy of two magazines published by the Religious Tract Society, the *Boy's Own Paper* (founded 1879) and the *Girl's Own Paper* (founded 1880), mirrored that of Victorian children's literature overall. First, both titles stressed audience appeal, quickly becoming the most popular adolescent periodicals of the late-Victorian age, with weekly sales of around 200,000 copies each; since children typically shared copies, actual readership was considerably higher (see Drotner). Second, their primary goal was neither entertainment nor profit – indeed, the more high-minded members of the Society found the magazines' financial health dismaying – but social engineering. The founders' object was to offer young readers an appealing but clean alternative to sensational literature, then as now often considered socially destructive, in order to improve the moral tone of the rising generation in the upper working class and above. But in order to sustain the entertainment value necessary to keep the attention of the desired audience, both magazines had to submerge their didactic intent. Overt religious messages are often lacking, while messages about the nature of manliness or womanliness, appropriate gender roles, imperial responsibilities, and the like derive much of their interest from their ambiguity. In this regard these periodicals serve as a synecdoche for the children's literature of their era, which often combines instruction and delight in such a way as to turn the instruction into something surprising, even potentially radical.

Imagined Children II: Children for Adult Consumption

Arguably, nineteenth-century adult literature is as morally and politically didactic as its counterpart for children. Indeed, it is sometimes hard to assign a particular work to one category or the other, especially since much fiction and poetry was intended for, and enjoyed by, a multigenerational audience. Take Christina Rossetti's "Goblin Market" (1862), a poem about adolescents that was aimed at an adult audience but that found its way into school anthologies by the end of the century; by the 1970s, it was simultaneously available in the United States in picture-book format and in *Playboy* (see Kooistra). This crossover appeal characterizes other Victorian poems of faëry for adults, such as William Allingham's "The Fairies" (1850) and Matthew Arnold's "The Forsaken Merman" (1849), and indeed the scholarly, artistic, and popular fascination with "the Little People" after the middle of the century bears a strong kinship to the simultaneous scholarly, artistic, and popular fascination with those other "little people," children. Similarly, Victorian poetry for children such as Stevenson's *A Child's Garden of Verses* (1885) has always given considerable nostalgic delight to adults, and the parodies and nonsense verse of, say, Edward Lear and Hilaire Belloc defy classification along generational lines.

Such "cross-writing" is facilitated in Victorian fiction by nineteenth-century authors' fondness for using child characters. The *Bildungsroman*, or novel about maturation, was a popular form among Victorian authors following upon Thomas Carlyle's 1824 translation of Goethe's *Wilhelm Meister's Apprenticeship* (1795–6), a novel that Steedman identifies as seminal to nineteenth-century conceptions of the child. Thus, there are many Victorian protagonists whose recorded histories end in adulthood but begin in childhood or even at birth: David Copperfield and Pip, Jane Eyre, Heathcliff, Maggie Tulliver, Henry Esmond, Ernest Pontifex, Molly Gibson of *Wives and Daughters*, Lyndall of *The Story of an African Farm* – the distinguished list continues. For many of these fictional characters, and perhaps for their creators as well, childhood is an intensely frustrating time, shaped by loneliness, boredom, abuse or neglect, and shame at their own inadequacies or misdeeds. Adulthood has its miseries, but insofar as it brings some authority over the self, it usually seems preferable to youth.

The cumulative effect of such narratives, especially when taken in tandem with such major exercises in the writing of real lives as Elizabeth Gaskell's *The Life of Charlotte Brontë* (1857) and John Stuart Mill's *Autobiography* (1873), is to produce an indictment of adult attitudes toward childhood much more scathing than is to be found in most children's literature. Victorian children's fiction about social injustice typically suggests that children can soften the hard hearts of their seniors, as Jessica does for Daniel Standring and as little Lord Fauntleroy does for his curmudgeonly grandfather; indeed, this trope seems to have had still more appeal for adults than for child readers. Victorian adult fiction may use the same plot trajectory, often in strikingly similar ways, when the protagonist is the adult and the child exists primarily as a device to explain radical character change: witness *Silas Marner* (1861), the story of a misanthropic linen-weaver redeemed by adopting a foundling. But adult fiction about injustice or the abuse of authority offers a bleaker picture when the narrative focuses closely on the feelings of the child, instead of treating that child iconically. Jane Eyre fails to stir the affections of her Aunt Reed or of Mr Brocklehurst, although both love their own children. Florence Dombey wins the hearts of all the good people she encounters, but she cannot gain her father's love until she is an adult and he a broken man; Oliver Twist makes a lengthy odyssey from workhouse to undertaker's establishment to thieves' den before finally achieving the affection and financial security that are his birthright. Maggie Tulliver, daughter of a fond father, nonetheless never manages to conform to the rules laid down for girls within her rural society. The happy endings that mark Victorian children's fiction are, at best, harder to achieve within novels for adults.

In an era fascinated by education and child development, the difficult lives of these fictional children suggest that the most serious charge leveled against the adult world is not outright sadism, which is comparatively rare, but rather neglect and an inability to fathom childish needs. Appropriately, one popular sentimental novel of 1869, by Florence Montgomery, takes as its title the single word *Misunderstood*: adult incomprehension, Montgomery charges, may prove lethal even to the children of wealthy, aristocratic, and normally conscientious adults. Given the frequency with which such literary accusations were made, it is not surprising that the later decades of the century saw a backlash in the form of sugary magazine fiction about intensely loving relationships between golden-haired moppets and older men who, like Silas Marners flattened to unidimensionality, devote their lives to surrogate fatherhood.

Such stories indicate that although the Victorians were taking steps to curtail child labor, children were still often contemplated in light of what they could do for the adult world, and not merely what the adult world could or should do for them. A major function of childhood in the mid- to late-nineteenth century was to serve, in rhetoric if not always in fact, as a kind of spiritual palate cleanser – a dose of innocence and purity protecting adult men, in particular, from the moral dubiousness of the public sphere (see Robson; Nelson). In earlier centuries, children's major value was often economic: they performed work of real monetary value to their parents or other employers, or they were used to cement alliances between two powerful families, for instance through betrothal. In the nineteenth century, raising a child within the middle or upper classes meant considerable expense, not profit. Nevertheless, children could be seen as assets not only in terms of conspicuous consumption (the parent who can afford many costly sons and daughters must be wealthy) but also because of their emotional and iconic value. So, at any rate, went the rhetoric that was current in Victorian society, which worked hard to turn children into panaceas for adult malaise.

James Kincaid has expounded what he sees as the pedophilic tendencies of Victorian society, with its emphasis on the beauty and desirability of young girls and boys. To a great extent, however, this now-disturbing imagery was intended not to open childhood to adult contamination, but to open adulthood to childish purity. In a culture greatly concerned by sexuality and its repercussions, middle-class children – often presumed to be nonsexual – were seen as pointing to a solution, not as part of the problem. Late-Victorian sex-education manuals, for instance, typically assume that the careful parent can both enlighten children's ignorance and preserve their virtue, helping to create a culture of social purity; similarly, the man who forms loving bonds with children is establishing for himself an emotional life centered on innocence, purifying his own existence retroactively. And in a culture distressed by the undesirable side effects of money-making, middle-class children, who operated outside the economy, suggested that life has other purposes than financial profit. That working-class children appeared to be implicated to a greater extent than their more affluent peers in sexuality, money, and the public sphere in general helps to explain the anxieties they aroused in reformers, and why those reformers should so often have concluded that it was vital to import such children into the bourgeois sphere of influence.

In an era of rapid change, social instability, and religious doubt, adults felt the need for faith. One kind of faith was furnished by the wave of sentimentality that washed across the century, emphasizing the healing power of emotion and promising ready access to human virtue, since to feel one's heart touched is to confirm that one still has a heart, that the harshness of the modern world has not destroyed one's finer self. And to a great extent, sentimentality invoked the image of the child. Illustrations and greeting cards, paintings and photographs, verses and novels and advertisements, offered up children for adult consumption. Such fictional – or fictionalized – children share certain important characteristics: they are depicted as infantile, with large heads or rosebud mouths or lisps, and thus as innocent; as vulnerable, in need of adult protection; as trusting, perceiving only the good in the world.

The tendency to use children as instruments for social engineering, then, worked in two ways. On the one hand, we see behind the reformist rhetoric of the era a conviction that children could be acted upon. *Tabulae rasae*, they might be shaped and molded to middle-class adult specifications to create a new society. The eugenists of the end of the century sought to approach perfection in future generations by cleansing the gene pool, encouraging the fit to breed and the unfit to remain childless; the moral reformers who busied themselves with reclaiming delinquents or with instilling ethical concepts through children's fiction sought to accomplish this utopian end by psychological rather than biological means. On the other hand, we see simultaneously a conviction that children could themselves accomplish the reformation of their elders, serving as the instrument rather than as the object of character change. If many works of art achieve their emotional power by portraying the child as unable to elicit sympathy from the surrounding adults, this power depends on the assumption that the work's adult *audience* can and will feel the understanding and concern that the adult characters do not provide; the real world is to profit morally from the flaws of the fictional one. The Victorian obsession with childhood becomes the more explicable when we consider the importance of the tasks that many in the nineteenth century hoped to use children to accomplish.

See also SEXUALITIES; EDUCATIONAL, PUBLISHING; LIFE WRITING; SKIN

REFERENCES

Bergen, B. H. (1982) "Only a Schoolmaster: Gender, Class, and the Effort to Professionalize Elementary Teaching in England, 1870–1910." *History of Education Quarterly* 22, 1–21.

Castle, K. (1996) *Britannia's Children: Reading Colonialism through Children's Books and Magazines*. Manchester: Manchester University Press.

Classen, A. (2005) "Philippe Ariès and the Consequences: History of Childhood, Family Relations, and Personal Emotions: Where Do We Stand Today?" In *Childhood in the Middle Ages and the Renaissance: The Results of a Paradigm Shift in the History of Mentality*, ed. A. Classen. Berlin: Walter de Gruyter.

Dixon, D. (1986) "From Instruction to Amusement: Attitudes of Authority in Children's Periodicals before 1914." *Victorian Periodicals Review* 19, 63–7.

Drotner, K. (1988) *English Children and Their Magazines, 1751–1945*. New Haven: Yale University Press.

Flegel, M. (2009) *Conceptualizing Cruelty to Children in Nineteenth-Century England: Literature, Representation, and the NSPCC*. Burlington: Ashgate.

Greg, W. R. (1855) "The Correction of Juvenile Offenders." *Edinburgh Review* 101, American edition 197–213.

Gubar, M. (2009) *Artful Dodgers: Reconceiving the Golden Age of Children's Literature*. New York: Oxford University Press.

Himmelfarb, G. (1991) *Poverty and Compassion: The Moral Imagination of the Late Victorians*. New York: Vintage.

Holt, J. (2008) *Public School Literature, Civic Education and the Politics of Male Adolescence*. Burlington: Ashgate.

Jordan, T. E. (1987) *Victorian Childhood: Themes and Variations*. Albany: State University of New York Press.

Kincaid, J. R. (1992) *Child-Loving: The Erotic Child and Victorian Culture*. New York: Routledge.

Kooistra, L. J. (1997) "*Goblin Market* as a Cross-Audienced Poem: Children's Fairy Tale, Adult Erotic Fantasy." *Children's Literature* 25, 181–204.

Nelson, C. (2012) *Precocious Children and Childish Adults: Age Inversion in Victorian Literature*. Baltimore: Johns Hopkins University Press.

Pedersen, J. S. (1987) *The Reform of Girls' Secondary and Higher Education in Victorian England: A Study of Elites and Social Change*. New York: Garland.

Robson, C. (2001) *Men in Wonderland: The Lost Girlhood of the Victorian Gentleman*. Princeton: Princeton University Press.

Steedman, C. (1995) *Strange Dislocations: Childhood and the Idea of Human Interiority, 1780–1930*. Cambridge MA: Harvard University Press.

FURTHER READING

Berry, L. (1999) *The Child, the State, and the Victorian Novel*. Charlottesville: University Press of Virginia.

Bratton, J. S. (1981) *The Impact of Victorian Children's Fiction*. London: Croom Helm.

Cunningham, H. (1991) *The Children of the Poor: Representations of Childhood since the Seventeenth Century*. Oxford: Blackwell.

Dyhouse, C. (1981) *Girls Growing Up in Late Victorian and Edwardian England*. London: Routledge and Kegan Paul.

Fletcher, A. (2008) *Growing Up in England: The Experience of Childhood 1600–1914*. New Haven: Yale University Press.

Nelson, C. (1991) *Boys Will Be Girls: The Feminine Ethic and British Children's Fiction, 1857–1917*. New Brunswick: Rutgers University Press.

——(2007) *Family Ties in Victorian England*. Westport: Praeger.

Reynolds, K. (1990) *Girls Only? Gender and Popular Children's Fiction in Britain, 1880–1910*. New York: Harvester Wheatsheaf.

6

Moving Out: Adolescence

Chris R. Vanden Bossche

The Victorians were very much concerned with the question when one stopped being a child and became an adult. It was during the Victorian era that the years from age 13 to 24 came to be regarded as a distinct epoch in individual development: adolescence. The word "adolescence" came into vogue in the late nineteenth century, and the first major sociological study of it, G. Stanley Hall's *Adolescence*, appeared in 1905. While adolescents came to be regarded as distinctly different from children or adults, the concept of adolescence (the word is derived from the Latin *adolescere*, "to grow up") was implicitly tied to Victorian notions of what it meant to be an adult. Consequently, it was regarded as a complex social, psychological, and moral process that was intimately linked to the Victorian ideal of the independent, mature, and cultivated adult self. Arriving at adulthood meant not just coming of age, but developing a particular kind of self. If these concerns seem familiar, it is probably because in the twentieth century the new fields of psychology and sociology were built up from a foundation in the Victorian conception of adolescence and the process of human development. Indeed, Hall's *Adolescence* both looked back at the Victorian era and pointed forward to modern concerns. The Victorian formulation of adolescence is, in fact, just one part of a larger set of concepts related to the process of coming of age that arose as the Victorians sought to come to terms with changes in the social structure and the institutions, such as marriage, through which that structure manifested itself.

The Victorians employed various rituals to mark one's symbolic entry into adulthood. In elite society, a young woman would be presented to the queen soon after her eighteenth birthday, in a ritual known as "coming out" (a term that had quite another meaning for the Victorians than for us). Further down the social ladder, a family might

A New Companion to Victorian Literature and Culture, First Edition. Edited by Herbert F. Tucker.
© 2014 John Wiley & Sons, Ltd. Published 2014 by John Wiley & Sons, Ltd.

indicate a woman's coming out by participation in a private dance or hunt ball. Outside the upper classes, a woman might indicate she had come of age by putting up her hair, wearing long skirts, joining the adults for dinner, or calling on friends with her mother. Most importantly, coming out meant that a woman was available for courtship and marriage. It is perhaps indicative of the Victorian tendency to situate men and women in separate spheres of activity that, whereas the emphasis for women was on "coming out," the important moment for men was "coming of age," reaching their majority. At age 21, heirs would take possession of their property and guardianship would end. "Coming out" and "coming of age" were rituals intended to indicate that an individual had crossed the threshold into adulthood. The change from cloistered adolescent to debutante was often compared to the butterfly's emerging from its chrysalis, and the corresponding notion of a metamorphosis from dependency to autonomy was at the heart of the Victorian idea of adolescence.

Yet merely being presented to society or passing one's twenty-first birthday did not ensure that one had reached mature adulthood. Such events were symbolic markers of what was understood to be a long and complex process that began in adolescence and in most cases was not to be concluded until about age 30. These events stood for, but did not cause, the transition. The arbitrariness of birthdays as markers of coming of age is pointed up by the paradoxical situation of Frederick in Gilbert's *The Pirates of Penzance* (1879). This virtuous young hero discovers that, although he has lived for 21 years, he has reached only his fifth birthday because he was born on February 29; technically, he has not come of age and must remain indentured to a band of pirates. Like other Victorian heroes and heroines, Frederick must undergo a series of trials before earning adult status.

The Victorians did not explicitly divide the process of maturation into specific stages, but one can recognize in social and literary history an implicit set of conditions for achieving the culminating condition of adulthood. The transformation began with the stage at which the child began to be differentiated from parents and family and ended with the achievement of a fully realized and autonomous self. Important milestones included leaving school, choice of vocation, marriage, and setting up a household. The relationship to one's family was at the heart of this process, for each stage was a point at which one achieved a degree of independence from one's family of origin and moved towards self-definition in relation to a new family of one's own. Of course, it was possible to achieve adult status without going through all of these stages, and, by the same token, passage through these stages, like passage through the rituals of coming out and coming of age, did not necessarily mean that one had become an adult. Rather, adulthood was understood as a psychological state defined by how successfully one negotiated each of these life stages.

At the core of the idea that successful achievement of adulthood meant the fulfillment of one's capacity for intellectual, emotional, and moral development was the idea of culture. In the eighteenth century, educational reformers had depicted education as the cultivation of a plant, and the term *culture* had been transferred from agri*culture* to the nurture of human beings. In the nineteenth century, the idea of culture broadened to comprehend the general process of individual development. The metaphor underlying the concept of culture suggested that this development was a gradual, "natural" process. This idea was most eloquently expressed in Matthew Arnold's *Culture and Anarchy* (1869), where he contended that human perfection consists in constant "growing and becoming." The ideal adult remained open and capable of responding positively to new experiences that would further develop his or her intellectual, emotional, and moral capacities. This concept of the continuous unfolding of the self meant that achievement of adulthood could be regarded as always tentative, for one could always move on to a higher stage of development from the perspective of which one's former self appeared immature. Thus, in his *Autobiography* (1873) John Stuart Mill depicted his life as a series of crises, each of which enabled him to move closer to self-completion and self-understanding. Correspondingly, Victorian literature often depicts heroes or heroines who have achieved a high level of self-culture by comparison with which other characters appear to remain perennially adolescent.

Closely linked to this concept of self-culture was the belief that the ideal adult ought to be independent and autonomous. This status was achieved only in part by financial independence from one's parents. Just as important was the achievement of emotional and psychological autonomy. At the heart of Mill's endless quest for more complete knowledge was his belief that one cannot depend on the thinking of others, that one must master knowledge for oneself; indeed, Mill was the era's most eloquent defender of individual liberty. The idea that each individual should seek to make his way in the world without the aid of others also provided the title and basic argument for Samuel Smiles's highly popular *Self-Help* (1859), as well as for innumerable narratives depicting the self-made man. Yet many Victorians were concerned that the desire for individual autonomy was at odds with the achievement of social harmony; if all individuals sought only to promote their own personal gain, they would inevitably come into conflict with one another. The role of culture was to enable one to achieve a perspective from which to understand one's individual needs in terms of the needs of society as a whole.

The beginning of adolescence was marked by puberty, which popular medical manuals described as a transformative moment. Because sexual difference became obvious at this stage, parents were encouraged to treat boys and girls differently. Puberty thus marked the point at which one assumed one's sexual and gender identity, and signaled the beginning of the transformation into adult men and women. But the idea of adolescence also meant that puberty did not have to be regarded as completely transforming the child into the adult; rather, the period of transformation was understood to extend beyond puberty and into the early twenties. Indeed, historians ascribe the "invention" of adolescence to the sharp increase in the practice, among the middle and upper classes, of sending children of this age to boarding schools where they led a life quite separate both from that of younger "children" and from the world of "adults." The effect of such schooling was to delay the transition to adulthood, both by keeping young people out of the work force and by keeping a rein on their development. It has even been argued that the public schools became widely favored in the later nineteenth century precisely because they could be trusted to impede the student's progress towards maturity more successfully than could parents. As one schoolmaster put it, their goal was to "keep boys boys – children children – young men young men" (Musgrove 55). Like the ideal of culture, the concept of adolescence meant that the process of growing up could be regarded as never-ending, with adulthood remaining always just beyond the horizon.

While the situation was different among the working classes, where children often went to work at the beginning of the adolescent years, working-class adolescents remained, in many ways, dependent children. In fact, the age at which young people left home rose steadily during the Victorian era because working-class adolescents could not afford to set up a household of their own. Universal schooling, instituted in 1870, also encouraged the tendency to remain at home, and the age of school-leaving rose throughout the century. The education movement in turn was prompted in part by the desire to keep adolescents off the streets and out of the work force. So while adolescence tended to be more abbreviated in the working classes, it was increasingly recognized as a transitional stage between childhood and adulthood there as well as among the middle and upper classes.

If self-culture was a continuous process, then one's education could not be confined to formal schooling, and must continue beyond the school years into early adulthood. John Henry Newman argued in *The Idea of a University* (1873) that forcing "a mass of undigested knowledge" on students will only distract and "enfeeble" them (section 8). The aim of the teacher, he went on to say, should be to inculcate a "habit of mind," rather than rote learning (section 1). Like Arnold, he contended that knowledge should be pursued for its own sake, not for practical ends; specific knowledge, techniques, and information are always finite, he concluded, while life's possibilities are infinite. The ideal of education was to develop a habit of mind that would enable one to deal wisely with any situation. Although Samuel Smiles approached the question of education quite differently – like much of the middle class he was suspicious of the classical curriculum of the ancient schools and universities – his *Self-Help* promoted an ideal of "self-culture," as opposed to formal education, that had much in common with the ideal advocated by Newman and Arnold. For Smiles, formal education could be expected to provide only the "beginnings" of an education that must be completed by experiencing "actual life" (ch. 11). In this regard, achieving adulthood meant completion of the process of self-cultivation, the attainment of complete womanhood or manhood. While these writers disagreed about which curriculum best realized the goal of self-culture, they shared the assumption that education should not be about acquiring a specific body of knowledge but about developing "character" – the cultivated self – and that, therefore, education was a process that inevitably continued long after leaving school.

This concept of culture can be seen at work in the treatment of education in Victorian narratives of self-development. Educational reformers were worried that too many schools resembled greenhouses in which teachers were attempting to force children to develop at a faster rate than they would in nature. Following their lead, Dickens describes Blimber's Academy in *Dombey and Son* (1848) as "a great hot-house in which there was a forcing apparatus incessantly at work" and "Nature [was] of no consequence at all" (ch. 11). Driven to maturity too quickly, the young scholars never really blossom but proceed into premature decline: Mr Toots's brains are addled and young Paul Dombey, whose father is trying to hurry him into adulthood, wastes away and dies. What concerns Dickens is not the school subjects themselves, but rather the fact that they are pursued single-mindedly with no attention to the children's moral and psychological development.

Not surprisingly, when literary works depict more positive school experiences, the focus is not on formal learning, but on development of character through personal relationships and extra-curricular experiences. Thus, Esther Summerson and Jane Eyre emphasize the importance of their relationships with fellow students and teachers; deprived of formal education, Maggie Tulliver and Aurora Leigh pursue intellectual development on their own, supported only by a supply of books. Thomas Hughes's fictional account of Rugby School focuses on the development of a code of honor among the boys, and treats participation in sports – Tom's first major experience at the school is playing in a football match – as an important learning experience. Completing one's formal education, even at a good school like Dr Strong's in *David Copperfield* (1850), is no guarantee that one is ready for adult life. Dickens demonstrates that David still has everything to learn about life by having him develop an absurd infatuation with the elder Miss Larkins – she shortly thereafter marries a well-to-do hop-grower – during his last weeks at school. As with many of his fictional counterparts, David's education must continue during his first years as a working man and into his married life as well.

For boys, leaving school almost inevitably meant entering on a career. Most were likely to follow in their parents' footsteps. Members of the genteel professions – the law, the Church, and medicine – almost always sought to have their sons follow their profession. The sons of manufacturers, tradesmen, or bankers were likely to obtain employment in the family business or through a family connection. In the early Victorian period this tendency was reinforced by the fact that (owing to the absence of limited liability) most firms were owned by contractual partnerships rather than stockholders; the result was that most businesses were run by a group of partners who were related to and could trust one another. For the majority of the working poor, a future of manual labor was almost certain, and opportunity for advancement limited, even after the institution of universal education in 1870. Of course there were numerous exceptions. An intelligent working-class boy might become a schoolmaster, or a couple might save enough to open a public house or shop. Among the more prosperous classes, there were sons who rebelled against their middle-class parents and refused to enter the family firm, while there were others who succeeded in rising above the fortunes of their parents. The prevalence of stories about individuals rising from a humble station to wealth and eminence – however exceptional such ascents were in actual fact – supported the ideal of self-culture, and encouraged belief in the possibility of social mobility, while also reinforcing the idea that one's character was more important than one's career.

In the middle and upper classes, the situation for girls and for boys was entirely different, since their families invariably strove to avoid circumstances that would require girls to earn an income. Most middle-class women performed a great deal of labor in the home, but they were also counseled by authors of domestic manuals to keep their labor out of the public eye. While the daughter who remained at home would help with running the household, she would not seek paid employment unless left without resources. In the latter circumstances – as when a father died without leaving a sufficient inheritance and his daughter remained unmarried – teaching was the sole respectable option. Whereas the number of employed women among the middle and upper classes was minuscule, nearly all working-class women did indeed "work" for wages at one time or another, as domestic servants, agricultural laborers, or factory laborers, and young women entered the work force at about the same time as their brothers. Indeed, about a third of manual laborers were women. Nonetheless, the ideal of keeping wives and daughters at home appears to have been adopted increasingly by the working classes, and working-class women often gave up paid labor after marrying and bearing children.

Working-class women had little choice in the matter, but many women in the upper classes, recognizing that the ideal of the cultivated self was at odds with the ideal of the nonworking woman, were not content with confining themselves to running a household. One of the most famous instances was Florence Nightingale, who, having lamented in *Cassandra* (1852) that women had nothing meaningful to do, set out to make nursing a respectable career. Middle-class moral concern with idleness made the social ideal of the nonworking wife and daughters an uncomfortably conflicted one. Nightingale's choice of nursing was a partial resolution to the conflict, as this profession could be pursued for other than monetary rewards. Nightingale's solution suggests that for women the kind of work mattered more than for men. The attention that Nightingale and others focused on the need for a greater variety of respectable employment for women led, in the last decades of the century, to new careers for women – as clerical workers, shop assistants, and so on.

In any case, going to work or choosing a career seems to have had only an indirect relationship to the transition to autonomous cultivated adulthood. To be sure, some professions did confer more status than others. But by focusing on work itself, rather than the particular profession, Victorian literature was in tune with the reality that the majority of individuals chose the career dictated by their family background. More important than the career itself was the work ethic one exhibited in pursuing that career. Thus, the ideal Victorian entrepreneur was the active manager, not the passive investor. Thomas Carlyle, who preached a gospel of "work" in *Past and Present* (1843), praised energetic entrepreneurs, designating them the "working aristocracy" in marked contrast with the "unworking aristocracy," who merely collected their rents and sat idly by while the poor starved (book 3, chs 8–11). The virtue of persistent effort was also at the core of Smiles's philosophy in *Self-Help*, which describes case after case of men who rose to prominence through their own hard work. Even Sarah Stickney Ellis's manuals on feminine behavior, which reinforced the commonplace that women should not work, insisted that it was shameful for women to avoid work when circumstances required it. Paradigmatic of the Victorian belief in the virtue of work is Mr Thornton in Gaskell's *North and South* (1855), who works tirelessly to pay off his father's debts and to raise his family back to their former status and affluence. It was not just hard work that mattered, but the moral character affiliated with it, as evinced by Thornton's perseverance, honesty, and self-sacrifice. In literature, the results of such labor were not measured by the income they produced; rather, they were regarded as moral training that prepared one both for the responsibility of supporting a family and for one's social responsibilities in the public sphere. The adult self was thus capable of comprehending the needs of others as well as harmonizing the interests of others with individual desires.

As with education, the goal of work was development of the autonomous moral self. Walter Gay, David Copperfield, Aurora Leigh, Lucy Snowe, and many others find the route to happiness through dedication to their professions, rather than in the professions themselves. Work can provide the education that school has failed to complete. Tom Tulliver's father errs in choosing a teacher who will give him the education of a gentleman rather than the practical education appropriate for his class, and Tom achieves manhood by working to pay off his father's debts. Some literary characters abandon an initial career that hampers their individual progress and adopt a new career that allows them to develop independence and moral character. Thus, Walter Hartright, in Wilkie Collins's *The Woman in White* (1860), begins as a drawing master, a career that limits him because it makes him subordinate to the families that employ him to teach their daughters. His subsequent career as an illustrator for a London newspaper might appear to be a step down the social ladder, but it makes him a free agent and requires energetic exertion, as opposed to his servantlike existence in a genteel country house. Or consider David Copperfield, who begins to take charge of his life only when he is forced to abandon the situation that has been purchased for him in a law office and begins rigorous training for becoming a court reporter, a change that leads to his eventual success as a novelist. By contrast, Richard Carstone in *Bleak House* (1853) cannot settle down to any profession because he has adopted the genteel view that he need not work at all; *his* coming of age leads not to the achievement of manhood but decline and death. If finding one's work enabled one to come of age, it seems, the failure to find it meant one would never mature at all.

If work bore a somewhat indirect relationship to coming of age, marriage was absolutely central to it. As W. G. Hamley put it, in an essay entitled "Old Maids" (1872), "to be married is, with perhaps the majority of women, the entrance into life" (126). Marriage marked the point at which young adults began to define themselves primarily in relation to each other rather than to their birth families. Marriage also coincided with two other key markers of coming of age: embarking on a career and setting up a household. Because a man could not think of marrying unless he could support a family, marriage often went hand in hand with obtaining a job, becoming a partner in a firm, or inheriting property. Among the working classes, the combined incomes of husband and wife would determine whether they could afford to marry. In the middle classes, the husband's opportunities would be decisive, but his wife's family might contribute by making him a partner in the family firm. At the same time, marriage did not necessarily mean immediate independence, for couples in all classes often lived with one of their families until such time as they had the financial resources to establish a separate household. The need to provide for the expenses of setting up house is considered the principal reason that, on average, most individuals did not marry until about age 25.

The role of marriage as a rite of coming of age was complicated by the fact that the institution had changed considerably over the previous three centuries. In the sixteenth century, when the primary consideration had been economic or social advantage, parents chose their children's spouses. By the nineteenth century, when prior personal affection, physical attraction, and romantic affinity had come to be considered legitimate grounds for marriage, it was taken for granted that children would choose their own spouses. Influences ranging from puritanism to the rise of individualism gave increasing weight to the principle that husband and wife were equals, as opposed to what was deemed an outmoded patriarchal ideal that regarded the husband as ruler of wife and children alike. These new assumptions in turn led to higher expectations of emotional compatibility in marriage. Browning could not have created the complex ironies of "My Last Duchess" (1842) – in which the Duke complains about the inadequacy of his first wife while negotiating the dowry for his second – if he had not been able to set the Victorian reader's expectations about marital relations against the Duke's Renaissance views. For Browning's audience, this effect was undoubtedly reinforced by the fact that expectations about marriage were still too much in flux to be taken for granted and remained subject to discussion throughout the century.

For the most part, the newly emergent conception of companionate marriage was widely shared across all of the classes. In spite of its disadvantages, most women preferred marriage to spinsterhood, for both emotional and more pragmatic reasons. The issues of property that concerned the upper and middle classes were not at stake for the working classes, but working-class men and women seem to have felt that their economic condition would be better if they married than if they remained single. While various folk customs such as the practice of marriage by "jumping over the broomstick" lingered into the early Victorian era, modern middle-class assumptions about marriage were widely accepted among the working classes. Variations in marriage practices and married life in the different classes ultimately had more to do with variations in their living conditions than with differences in their attitudes about marriage.

Yet while ideas about marriage had been changing, equality between husband and wife was still a new idea accepted only by a few, and the laws of England concerning marriage remained in several important respects what they had been three centuries earlier. One of the main problems was how to reconcile the ideal of equality between spouses with the assumption that men and women were fundamentally different. In the late eighteenth century, just as the principle of married equality was coming to be widely accepted, the principle of separate spheres began to emerge. The doctrine of separate male and female spheres, which was set forth in innumerable etiquette books and manuals for domestic management, dictated that men should struggle in the competitive wilderness of commerce in order to provide for their families, while women should provide a peaceful refuge in which to apply balm to the wounds men received while engaged in business. Because both spouses possessed authority in their respective spheres, the idea of separate spheres was compatible with the notion of relative equality between wife and husband. But it also implicitly supported the older assumption that women's sphere was relative and subordinate to men's. Because the husband generated the income that supported the domestic establishment, his wife was financially dependent on him. Although the work of supervising servants, raising children, and, in many cases, cooking and cleaning made an important contribution to the household economy, the authors of domestic manuals nonetheless insisted that women should not appear to work (signs of labor would ruin the peaceful aspect of the domestic sphere) and so perpetuated the myth that women were not involved in the economy proper. Like the principle that women should not work, the principle of separate spheres suggested that women should remain, in this crucial regard, adolescent. The ideal of the cultured self was at odds with both of these principles. Thus, while the idea of separate spheres was so widespread that its influence can be detected everywhere in Victorian literature, it seldom appears there as a rigid doctrine. Rather, the ambiguities built into the idea enabled writers to produce endless variations on the marriage plot, and so to reimagine marriage and the social relationships it symbolized. Especially in novels written by women, the heroine often seeks, like Florence Nightingale, to find a vocation that enables her to employ her talents and intellect, even as it accommodates her to expectations about a "woman's mission."

Prior to the last two decades of the century, the Victorians were content to reimagine marriage rather than to question its viability. When in 1851 John Stuart Mill and Harriet Taylor, two of the era's most eloquent advocates for the rights of women, contemplated marriage, they set out to reinvent the marriage contract so that they could obtain the emotional benefits of marriage without its psychological and economic constraints. Two months before their wedding, Mill put in writing a "solemn promise" never to use the powers conferred on him by British law and pledging that Harriet Taylor should "retain in all respects whatever the same absolute freedom of action and freedom of disposal of herself . . . as if no such marriage had taken place" (Mill and Taylor 45–6). The problem of how to reconcile marriage with individual autonomy was, as Mill and Taylor recognized, related to the idea of separate masculine and feminine spheres, which, in its doctrinaire form, was at odds with the cultivation of the self and achievement of mature adulthood. As Taylor argued in "The Enfranchisement of Women" (1851), the "proper sphere for all human beings is the largest and highest they are able to attain to." In other words, reform of the institution of marriage could not be limited to the legal and financial realm, but must apply to the moral and psychological domains as well.

Mill's and Taylor's attempt to create their own marriage outside of the legal institution was akin to the use of the marriage plot in Victorian literature to imagine new forms of relationship. The marriage plot is a literary device with a long history and so is not unique to the Victorian era. What distinguishes the Victorian marriage plot from the marriage plot in the comedies of Shakespeare is the kinds of questions it raises about marriage. Just to cite one instance, whereas a comedy such as *A Midsummer Night's Dream* does not concern itself with the question of what makes the lovers suitable to one another, the question of suitability is pursued almost obsessively in Victorian literature. In order to reconcile the principle of equality and mutual respect with legal institutions and the idea of sexual difference, Victorian authors sought to imagine ways to equalize the economic and psychological power equation. Even a conservative like Sarah Stickney Ellis advised her female readers to judge carefully the character of their prospective mates, precisely because they would be in their power. Novelists like Charlotte Brontë went further, attempting to imagine circumstances that would equalize the power relations between husband and wife. While individuals were now free to choose their own marriage partner, they were expected to choose someone of the same socioeconomic status, and financial or status considerations were considered just as important as romantic attraction. Nonetheless, novels like *Jane Eyre* (1847) take as a given the principle that a marriage based solely on financial or class considerations cannot be happy. The basic problem in *Jane Eyre* is that, while Jane has declared that in "spirit" she and Rochester are "equal," marriage – as a social, not merely spiritual, institution – favors Rochester, who is older, wealthier, and better connected. Brontë attempts to solve this dilemma by changing the social relations between the two: Jane inherits a fortune that gives her economic autonomy; Rochester, maimed in a fire that destroys his country house, thus loses his physical and psychological advantages. Brontë has shaped social circumstances so as to reshape the marriage relation in a new form, albeit a form that does not solve all of the problems the novel raises. But the ideal aimed at is one in which husband and wife each are able to move out together, to develop into fully mature and independent adults.

While in its more doctrinaire forms the principle of separate spheres drew a sharp line between male and female, Victorian literature frequently depicted the ideal of self-culture as involving a convergence of the two spheres. This possibility was opened up by a central tenet of the separate-spheres doctrine, namely that the male commercial sphere was amoral, if not actually immoral, and that women should therefore serve as moral guides. While in its more conventional form this tenet reinforced gender difference, it also led many Victorian authors to conclude that the ideals of the domestic sphere should be injected into the commercial realm. Thus, the problem with Dickens's Mr Dombey is that he does not recognize the value of his daughter, Florence, and cares only about his business; girls, he declares, "have nothing to do with Dombey and Son" (ch. 10). By contrast, Thornton, the hero of Gaskell's *North and South*, combines the male virtues of energy and industry with a feminine cultivation that sets him apart from his fellow mill-owners. Under the feminine moral influence of Margaret Hale, Thornton joins his employees in establishing a cooperative dining room, thus supplementing what had formerly been a purely commercial relationship with a domestic one. Dombey and Thornton are representative of many Victorian heroes whose ability to recognize the virtues of the novel's heroine entails the recognition of the value of the feminine and even the acquisition of feminine characteristics. In this regard, self-culture involves recognition and acceptance of feminine aspects of oneself as a means of achieving a balance between individual desire and social responsibility.

Corresponding to these heroes, Victorian literature depicts as strong-minded, intelligent, and active women such heroines as Jane Eyre, Shirley Keeldar, Margaret Hale, Maggie Tulliver, Dorothea Brooke, Esther Summerson, and Aurora Leigh. Typically, the heroine chooses between two suitors, one who fails to recognize her intelligence and autonomy and another who, although perhaps less attractive in other ways, not only appreciates her intellect and respects her independent spirit but also acknowledges her superiority. These heroines moreover take a leading role in courtship and in running the ménage once they marry. Margaret Hale's capital enables Thornton to re-establish himself in business, and, after the failure of his utopian project, Romney Leigh submits to Aurora Leigh's moral and domestic authority. Of course, acknowledging a woman's moral superiority could simply reinforce the idea that men and women are fundamentally different and therefore in certain respects not equal. Indeed, the device of demonstrating a woman's worth and superiority by suggesting that she deserves an equally superior husband tends to turn back against itself. For by providing a husband who matches his wife in intellect and moral character, the author assures us that the heroine will not threaten the dignity of the hero by presuming to dominate their relationship. Thus, while Dickens implies that Dombey must learn the value of the feminine and that the feeble-minded Mr Toots does well to marry the strong-minded Susan Nipper, in the same novel he depicts Captain Bunby's marriage to the domineering Mrs MacStinger as a scene of comic horror. Nonetheless, like Victorian heroes, Victorian heroines tend to achieve self-completion by combining within themselves aspects of the masculine and feminine domain and so reconciling the needs of self and other. As the Prince concludes in Tennyson's *The Princess* (1847):

> For woman is not undevelopt man,
> But diverse: could we make her as the man,
> Sweet love were slain: his dearest bond is this,
> Not like to like, but like in difference.
> Yet in the long years liker must they grow;
> The man be more of woman, she of man . . . (7, 259–64)

Underlying these plots is the principle, enunciated by Harriet Taylor, that marriage should enable, rather than preclude, individual self-development. As Frances Power

Cobbe argued in "Criminals, Idiots, Women, and Minors" (1868), the laws that denied women property and legal rights implied that all women, even those who had legally come of age, were "minors." Brontë's Shirley Keeldar and Gaskell's Margaret Thornton initially resist marriage because it would restrict their independence and the possibility of self-development, a concern justified by the experiences of married women in their social circles. Margaret's cousin Edith is not unhappy in marriage, but she fails to mature into a maternal woman; both she and her husband, who resigns his army commission shortly after they marry, lead socially useless lives that provide no opportunity for self-development. The appeal of childlike women is a recurrent theme in Dickens, yet he also recognized, as does David Copperfield, that a "child-wife" like his Dora, who never reaches adulthood, will always leave "something wanting" (ch. 48). Furthermore, David's recognition that his choice of Dora as wife was the result of an "undisciplined heart" suggests that he too has not reached maturity and that his marriage has inhibited his growth (ch. 45). Only when Dora dies and he marries the ideal domestic woman, Agnes Wickfield, is he able to complete himself.

The heroine's marriage to a man who can appreciate her unique character enables the literary work to imagine a marriage in which a woman can do what Victorian law and separate-spheres doctrine seem to have decreed impossible: come of age and reach her full potential as an autonomous individual. While it has sometimes been suggested that in their fondness for the marriage plot the Victorians assumed that women could not achieve fulfillment without marriage, the model of self-culture can enable us to see the marriage plot in a different light. Victorian literature tends to ask instead how, given that marriage was assumed to be likely for most individuals, individual development could proceed to completion within marriage. The goal of the marriage plot thus amounted to something of a paradox. What undoubtedly scandalized many of the first readers of *Jane Eyre* was that Jane sees in marriage not a social institution – she cares nothing for gaining status or money for their own sake – so much as a means of achieving individual fulfillment.

As the laws regarding marriage were debated and changed from the 1850s on, Victorian literature began to explore possibilities outside the traditional marriage plot. In "Rebecca and Rowena" (1850) Thackeray had complained that too many novels end "prematurely" with the marriage of the hero and heroine; he concluded that we need more "middle age" novels that record the vagaries of their married lives. In *Vanity Fair* (1848) he did just that, depicting a marriage in which the hero and heroine do not live happily ever after. However, the plot of *Vanity Fair* is finally not unlike that of contemporary novels, such as *Wuthering Heights* (1847) or *Middlemarch* (1872), in which the unhappy marriage depicted in the first part of the novel is used to raise problems that are solved by the marriage with which it concludes. The sensation novels of the 1860s – such as Collins's *The Woman in White* (1860) and Braddon's *Lady Audley's Secret* (1862) – brought the darker side of marriage more to the fore, but they too worked within a comic framework in which a romantic marriage succeeds a disastrous one. What set sensation novels apart from earlier examples of the marriage plot was that, while the marriages with which they concluded brought together the hero and heroine, this marriage did not depict romantic self-completion. Increasingly, then, individual development was imagined separately from marriage. The "New Woman" novels of the 1890s – such as Hardy's *Tess of the d'Urbervilles* (1891) and *Jude the Obscure* (1896), and Sarah Grand's *Heavenly Twins* (1893) and *The Beth Book* (1897) – were unrelenting in their portrayal of mismatched couples whose marriages have disastrous consequences for both parties. But although these novels sometimes explored the possibilities of self-development and romantic attachment outside marriage, they were equally skeptical about the idea of self-culture itself. Hardy's protracted adolescent Jude, adopting Smiles's ideal of self-culture, attempts to teach himself Latin so that he can study at the university, only to discover that he is shut out from advancement by fate and social prejudice. Thus, the decline of the marriage plot coincided with the rise of skepticism about the very possibility of achieving autonomy and self-completion.

What should be clear from the way coming of age is represented in Victorian literature is that it involved the acquisition of certain mental or psychological qualities in addition to physical development and changes in one's material circumstances. Florence Nightingale never married and remained financially dependent on her family, but no one would doubt that she had become fully adult, not only because she set up her own household, but because of the qualities she exhibited in the Crimea and during her subsequent career. Nightingale could break with Victorian expectations about women's roles in part because she shared with her fellow Victorians another set of expectations about self-culture and in part because she had the financial resources to do so.

The latter circumstance should help us keep in mind that, although the idea of self-culture explicitly depicted maturation as a natural process that all individuals undergo, it was to a certain degree class-bound. Several of the principal moral and psychological qualities that signaled arrival at maturity – energetic industry, selflessness, and self-discipline – were particularly valued by the middle class. Furthermore, adult laborers faced, along with women, the contradiction between the idea of coming of age and the idea that they were perennial "minors." The relationship between factory owners and workers was often described as a relationship between parent and child, and workers' inability to save money as a reserve to fall back on during hard times was regarded by some as a sign of their childish tendency to think only about the present. Other, less sympathetic, observers regarded them simply as unreasoning "brutes." Victorian literature frequently criticizes this tendency to dehumanize the laborer, but it nonetheless holds up as a standard of adult maturity the acquisition of qualities more suited to the middle class than to laborers.

At the same time, the ideal of coming of age, like the ideal of culture to which it was linked, reflected the Victorian desire to imagine the resolution of class conflict. One of the few novels to take as its hero a working-class character, Charles Kingsley's *Alton Locke, Tailor and Poet* (1850), depicts Locke achieving maturity when he leaves behind his belief in the use of "brute" force that would, the novel suggests, achieve only narrow political aims and commits himself to peaceful social reform based on broadly conceived religious principles. The fact that coming of age means Locke must abandon his political cause manifests Kingsley's middle-class bias. Yet recognition of this bias should not prevent us from understanding that, as in novels depicting the coming of age of middle-class males, the novelist is here seeking to imagine a transformation not only of the individual but also of society as a whole. At the climax of Kingsley's novel, Locke falls ill and has a long hallucinatory dream in which he recapitulates animal evolution, from madrepore (coral) to human being, followed by the evolution of human society as it moves toward utopian mutual cooperation. Kingsley is drawing on popular ideas about evolution – Darwin's *Origin of Species* would appear in 1859 – that influenced social scientists such as Herbert Spencer, whose *Principles of Sociology* (1876–96) linked the maturation of the individual and of human society. In this context, it should come as no surprise that Hall's *Adolescence* would explain the existence of an adolescent phase of human development by suggesting that each individual recapitulates the history of the human race. Perhaps the best example of this utopian impulse to link the evolution of self and society is Tennyson's *In Memoriam* (1850), which culminates with the celebration of a marriage that the poet hopes will produce a "crowning race" (Epilogue, 1. 128).

In this context, we should keep in mind that "culture" referred not only to the development of the individual, but also to the complex of beliefs and institutions that made up a social group. As the examples just cited indicate, growth and maturation were key metaphors underlying not only ideas of self-development, but also ideas of social progress. While these metaphors tended to privilege members of those groups that were regarded as more "adult" – men, the middle class, the English – those that had been traditionally regarded as "minors" – women, the working class, non-Europeans – could use the metaphor of maturation to insist on their ability, and right, to enter the adult world. Thus, while narratives of coming of age reflected class assumptions about individual development, they were also a means of imagining the coming of age of British society as a process that had always arrived yet was always, also, about to happen.

See also EDUCATIONAl, INDUSTRIAL; FICTION, LIFE WRITING; SKIN, PARAPETS

REFERENCES

Hall, G. S. (1905) *Adolescence; Its Psychology and Its Relations to Physiology, Anthropology, Sociology, Sex, Crime, Religion and Education.* New York: Appleton.

Hamley, W. G. (1986) "Old Maids." *Blackwood's Magazine* 112, 94–108. In *Women from Birth to Death: The Female Life Cycle in Britain 1830–1914,* ed. P. Jalland and J. Hooper. Atlantic Highlands: Humanities Press International.

Mill, J. S., and H. Taylor Mill (1970) *Essays on Sex Equality,* ed. A. S. Rossi. Chicago: University of Chicago Press.

Musgrove, F. (1965) *Youth and the Social Order.* Bloomington: Indiana University Press.

Further Reading

Armstrong, N. (1987) *Desire and Domestic Fiction: A Political History of the Novel*. New York: Oxford University Press.

Davidoff, L. (1973) *The Best Circles: Society, Etiquette and the Season*. London: Croom Helm.

——(1987) *Family Fortunes: Men and Women of the English Middle Class, 1780–1850*. Chicago: University of Chicago Press.

Ellis, S. S. (1839) *The Women of England*. London: Fisher, Son and Co.

Frost, G. S. (1995) *Promises Broken: Courtship, Class, and Gender in Victorian England*. Charlottesville: University Press of Virginia.

Gallagher, C. (1985) *The Industrial Reformation of English Fiction: Social Discourse and Narrative Form, 1832–1867*. Chicago: University of Chicago Press.

Gillis, J. R. (1974) *Youth and History: Tradition and Change in European Age Relations, 1770–Present*. New York: Academic Press.

——(1985) *For Better, For Worse: British Marriages, 1600 to the Present*. New York: Oxford University Press.

Holt, J. (2008) *Public School Literature, Civic Education, and the Politics of Male Adolescence*. Farnham: Ashgate.

Langland, E. (1995) *Nobody's Angels: Middle-Class Women and Domestic Ideology in Victorian Culture*. Ithaca: Cornell University Press.

Marcus, S. (2007) *Between Women: Friendship, Desire, and Marriage in Victorian England*. Princeton: Princeton University Press.

Perkin, H. J. (1969) *The Origins of Modern English Society 1780–1880*. London: Routledge.

Perkin, J. (1989) *Women and Marriage in Nineteenth-Century England*. Chicago: Lyceum.

Phegley, J. (2012) *Courtship and Marriage in Victorian England*. Santa Barbara and Oxford: Praeger.

Poovey, M. (1988) *Uneven Developments: The Ideological Work of Gender in Mid-Victorian England*. Chicago: University of Chicago Press.

Springhall, J. (1986) *Coming of Age: Adolescence in Britain, 1860–1960*. Dublin: Gill and Macmillan.

Stone, L. (1977) *The Family, Sex and Marriage in England, 1500–1800*. New York: Harper and Row.

Tosh, J. (1999) *A Man's Place: Masculinity and the Middle-Class Home in Victorian England*. New Haven: Yale University Press.

Vicinus, M. (1985) *Independent Women: Work and Community for Single Women, 1850–1920*. Chicago: University of Chicago Press.

Vickery, A. (1993) "Golden Age to Separate Spheres: A Review of the Categories and Chronology of English Women's History." *Historical Journal* 36, 383–414.

Williams, R. (1958) *Culture and Society, 1780–1950*. New York: Columbia University Press.

7

Growing Old: Age

Teresa Mangum

" 'Old Age,' " muses the anonymous author of "The Art of Growing Old" in *The Argosy* for 1866, "in theory, demands respect, veneration, and even admiration. 'Old Age,' in reality, suffers contempt, ridicule, and neglect" (39). Pulled between these extremes of expected veneration and practical neglect, Victorian writers and artists responded with diverse and often contradictory representations of old age. Even a quick survey of popular poetry provides evidence of the many ways of experiencing old age and of varied attitudes toward aging during the period. Thus, we find William Barnes's colloquial celebration of late love in "Uncle an' Aunt" (1840) and the speaker's booming invitation, "Grow old along with me! / The best is yet to be," in Robert Browning's dramatic monologue "Rabbi Ben Ezra" (1864). Matthew Arnold's "Growing Old" (1867) mourns emotional paralysis caused by old age, a stark contrast with the speaker's gathering wisdom in Alfred Tennyson's "Locksley Hall Sixty Years After" (1886) or Dollie Radford's witty portrait of healthy elderly egotism in "Soliloquy of a Maiden Aunt" (1891). The visual artists of the period were also inspired by the faces, relationships, and social circumstances particular to the elderly. Laurits Tuxen's famous family portrait of "Europe's Grandmama" (otherwise known as Queen Victoria), *The Royal Family at the Time of the Jubilee* (1887), places the aging queen squarely at the center of an enormous family gathering, while other family paintings push elderly figures to the margins, as does George Elgar Hicks's sweeping canvas of a bridal party, *Changing Homes* (1863). The consequences of being at once elderly, female, and poor are rendered with special poignancy in George Clausen's *Schoolgirls* (1880), where elegant young ladies in the foreground disdainfully turn their backs on an elderly worker struggling with heavy buckets. Even common speech reveals a

A New Companion to Victorian Literature and Culture, First Edition. Edited by Herbert F. Tucker.
© 2014 John Wiley & Sons, Ltd. Published 2014 by John Wiley & Sons, Ltd.

fascination with old people and the experience of aging. Victorian synonyms and adjectives used to describe elderly people tended to attribute particular traits and habits to aging, as suggested by phrases like "old bird," "old trout," "old crow," "tabby," "old maid," or "gay old dog" (Covey).

Of the many literary works that contemplate old age, one is particularly attentive to Victorian debates about the place of the elderly in society. At 67 and approaching his death, Anthony Trollope drew upon popular conceptions of aging in *The Fixed Period* (1882), a futurist novel set in 1979–80 on the island of Britannula, settled 40 years earlier by English colonists. In the early days of the colony when most settlers were in their thirties, they agreed to a policy called the Fixed Period. To abolish "the miseries, weakness, and *fainéant* imbecility of old age," their Parliament, having established 67 as the average age at which reason, labor, and independence fail, decreed that on that birthday men and women would voluntarily withdraw for a year of meditation, followed by euthanasia and cremation. The middle-aged narrator disingenuously acknowledges that the policy will liberate young men from the encumbering authority of powerful older men and absolve society of caring for the elderly. The novel mocks fears of a newly visible population of elderly people sparked by Charles Booth's *The Aged Poor in England and Wales* (1894) and fanned by parliamentary discussions of pension plans and by melancholy portrayals of aged pensioners and workhouse inhabitants by painters like Hubert Von Herkomer. A witty satire, *The Fixed Period* succinctly summarizes growing Victorian concern over what was falsely perceived to be an increasing "aged" population in an era obsessed with youth, energy, activity, and progress.

The Science of Defining Old Age

One of the most important changes in the nineteenth-century understanding of old age is that intuitive folk ways of defining old age, which took little note of actual birthdates, gradually gave way to quantitative systems of definition that possessed the advantage of uniformity but the disadvantage of over-generality. Accordingly, a chief difficulty in studying an issue like aging – which compounds genuine physiological changes with socially constructed beliefs and practices – is that, while popular opinions have little direct connection to scientific developments or government reports, they may have great bearing on an individual's experience of growing old and on a society's treatment of its older citizens. Victorians were far less committed to chronology when they defined aging than we are today. Before the British Pension Plan of 1908 dictated the need for a specific age at which individuals were eligible for state support, old age had been a floating, flexible identity. As sociologist Janet Roebuck explains, before the nineteenth century a person was considered old only when two things happened simultaneously: the person must exhibit behavior betraying physical and mental failure, and the person must look old. Authorities like Poor Law Guardians who decided when to give aid to the elderly did not label anyone old based on chronological age alone. Instead, a person was assumed to be aging but not actually old until he or she manifested these two conditions – behavioral infirmity and physical deterioration. Karen Chase further argues that we can place Victorian constructions of "agedness" into "signal clusters of related phenomena" in social and literary cultures; she notes the special real and imaginative power wielded by "portraits of institutions" like the workhouse, almshouse, and asylum that shaped the late lives of so many Victorians (5–7).

Nineteenth-century popular standards for deciding when old age began seem even more arbitrary if we consider Victorian arguments that women grow old before men. While government programs and medical prescriptions often treated all old people as if they were the same, and most Victorians routinely used gender-neutral terms like "the aged" or "the elderly" to refer to old people, the basis on which men and women were deemed old differed markedly. For men, age was largely determined by their ability to work. Before 1908 most working-class and working middle-class men labored until they died. Women, however, were labeled old with reference to their reproductive rather than productive capacity, and most popular medical advice texts subscribed to the traditional belief that menopause signaled the onset of old age. Literature and popular lore share an underlying assumption that men and women are fundamentally dissimilar and therefore will experience old age differently. Because of its attention to details of character, fiction often accentuated discrepancies between men's and women's experiences in later life. For instance, Elizabeth Gaskell's domestic novel *Cranford* (1853) elaborates the stratagems by which lower middle- and middle-class elderly widows and spinsters with little income piece together self-respect and a meager independence in their provincial village. The social roles available to older women – grandmother, widow, old maid – also inspired such poems as Frances Browne's "Recollections of a Faded Beauty" (1830), Tennyson's dramatic monologue "The Grandmother" (1859), and Alice Meynell's poignant "A Letter from a Girl to Her Own Old Age" (1875).

Furthermore, literature wrestled with a subtler connection between gender and old age. Often, after a male character has accepted the status of being old, he finds that status involves if not an outright loss of sexual identity then a lapse into a state akin to helpless femininity. In *Vanity Fair* (1848), Thackeray portrays the fall of Amelia Sedley's elderly father from businessman to bankrupt. Humbled, feeble, and friendless, Mr Sedley lives in seclusion with his wife, daughter, and grandson. Bowing to his sad fate, he serves as a pathetic version of the feminizing effects of old age. However, this feminization, while representing a fall from one kind of idealized man – the youthful, virile, assertive man of action – sometimes signals moral, spiritual, and domestic fulfillment. The tolerance for a gentler, more maternal masculinity in old age helps to explain the appeal of characters like Charles Dickens's reformed Scrooge in *A Christmas Carol* (1843), Job Legh (who is single-handedly raising his granddaughter) in Gaskell's *Mary Barton* (1848), Eliot's ineffectual but beloved elderly protagonist in *Silas Marner* (1861), or the Tibetan lama with his winning blend of wisdom and innocence in Rudyard Kipling's *Kim* (1901). As all of these examples suggest, clarifying when old age began was complicated by the inconsistency of the criteria – labor here, biology there – that Victorians used to determine age and by the way each individual's experience of old age was affected by being male or female, poor or prosperous, British or foreign-born.

Other popular conceptions of aging were shaped by changing understandings of life stages. "Ages of Man" paintings, which depicted life as a journey marked by childhood, maturity, parenthood, and years of decline, then death, have existed for centuries and remained popular in the first half of the Victorian period. But where early versions of these paintings tied life stages to seasonal changes and functioned allegorically to represent the life span as natural and universal, by mid-century the stages of life were represented as distinct, incremental, and scientifically measurable. It hardly seems an accident that the same American psychologist, G. Stanley Hall, who formulated the concept of adolescence in the 1880s, later staked out *Senescence* (1920) as a particular life stage. Such changes in definition justified imaginatively and literally relocating older people to workhouses, hospitals, and even chimney corners. They also encouraged middle-aged Victorians to pigeonhole old people and children as the two age groups most in need of care (Hareven). The cultural consequences of using the metaphor "second childhood" for old age abound in Victorian children's literature. Dozens of Edward Lear's *Nonsense* limericks (1846, 1872) begin, "There was an old person of . . ."; the old person then behaves like a naughty child. John Tenniel's drawings of Lewis Carroll's Queen and Duchess in *Alice's Adventures in Wonderland* (1864) render Alice a dull adult by comparison with her rowdy, puerile elders, and many of the fairies and godmothers that people the Victorian fairy tales of writers like Dickens, Anne Isabella Ritchie, Mary De Morgan, and Frances Browne are, like their child readers, diminutive, squeaky, and sentimentalized, even when they share irritation at adult authority. While quaint and amusing, these fictional embodiments of second childhood (like the metaphor itself) reinforce the view that older people are inept, unreasonable, and helpless; however, the old suffer doubly from the comparison because, unlike children, they are past the age when society accepts dependency as an appropriate or endearing quality.

One of the most enduring fantasies about old age – it survives among us even today – focuses on the supposed reverence for elderly people in an imagined past. First, it was assumed that at some earlier time in history older people were venerated for their wisdom; and, second, it was believed that in this imagined past the elderly were lovingly cared for by families. The first fantasy arises from several misconceptions: that before 1800 few people survived into old age; that before widespread literacy older people's knowledge was crucial to a group's survival; that in the past, when extended families were common, adult children believed it was their personal responsibility to care for aging parents. Proponents of this nostalgic view argued that the rise of industrialism disrupted traditional support systems for elders. This Golden Age view tends to romanticize earlier attitudes toward aging, to obscure historical continuities with the past, and to discount cultural and psychological aspects of aging by focusing exclusively on the very real impact of broad economic changes.

Twentieth-century family history and demographic studies offer statistical evidence to counter the Golden Age claim that fewer elderly people existed before 1800 and that elders were more valued by earlier societies. Demographic historians like Peter Laslett explain that although the mean age for life expectancy during the nineteenth century may have been 40.9 in 1838 and only 46 by 1900, these figures taken alone are misleading. Death rates were extremely high for children under five; those who survived infancy, however, could expect to reach adulthood, and those who reached 40 were likely to live into their sixties, even seventies. The mean life expectancy, then, reflected a high infant mortality rate rather than a scarcity of old people. There is also a difference between actual *numbers* of the elderly and the *proportion* of any age group in the total population. The number of old people actually fell slightly in the nineteenth century. Nevertheless, even though the predicted life span did not increase during the Victorian period, as the birth rate began to drop the proportion of the population over 40 rose significantly in England and Wales and more slowly in Scotland (Laslett; Tranter). In other words, although great numbers of people did not start living longer until the 1930s, the increasing proportion of elderly attracted attention in the news, the government, the medical profession, and literature long before that date, creating a general but false impression in the second half of the century that England was growing old.

Another reason fantasies of a kinder past persisted was that as village gossip, newspapers, periodicals, and novels circulated stories about the harsh conditions of workhouses at mid-century, and as government reports disclosed the sufferings of the elderly poor late in the century, upper- and middle-class Victorians grappled with the embarrassing revelation that one of the wealthiest countries in the world was allowing its old people to starve. Twentieth-century scholars have put these fantasies to the test through careful study of parish, poorhouse, and census records (see Laslett; Wall; Chase). Even an imperfect demographic record suffices to unsettle images either of families as all-embracing, intergenerational assemblies or of old people as helpless dependents. Such research reveals that the desire of older people to maintain an independent life, apart from their children as well as from paternalistic institutions, has remained consistent throughout recorded history.

As these examples suggest, the idealization of the past cast elderly Victorians as victims. While historians use empirical data to combat nostalgic excesses, literature offers a different kind of corrective. The literary profession offered a few privileged poets and philosophers perhaps the most distinguished social role available to an elderly Victorian man, that of the sage. It also provided many older women with meaningful careers (see Looser). But literary texts themselves were heavily populated with more common figures who offered alternatives to mere victimage. Though novels are hardly repositories of fact, the genre's attention to relations among characters does suggest that, faced with the trials of aging, many Victorians showed both agency and initiative. Indeed, one recurring character type hints that older people who held on too tightly to property or to power were more unnerving than those who became burdens. In contrast to the quiet lives of accommodation or yearning that mark realist fiction like Trollope's Barchester and Palliser novels or his posthumous *An Old Man's Love* (1884), popular narrative genres that permitted extravagant exaggeration of fears and social tensions – sensation fiction, Gothic fiction, fantasy, adventure, science fiction – often treated older characters who eluded death as evil predators. Many sensation novels wove plots around wealthy old men and the writing, hiding, and challenging of wills. Sheridan Le Fanu's sensation villain in *Uncle Silas* (1864) schemes to murder his niece in order to keep the family fortune, while even in the less hyperbolic sensation-style subplot that George Eliot included in *Middlemarch* (1872) Mr Featherstone maliciously toys with potential inheritors and then leaves his estate to an illegitimate son. Dickens carries the image of the rapacious old person to grotesque extremes in the Smallweed subplot of *Bleak House* (1853), where even grandchildren are described as being prematurely aged by their obsession with family money. In H. Rider Haggard's adventure novel *King Solomon's Mines* (1885) an African witch who has lived for centuries holds the destiny of her people hostage, while the heroine of *She* (1887), uncomfortably similar to Victoria, is a tyrannical queen who has prolonged life for thousands of years to grieve for a dead lover. Traveling to the future, the protagonist of H. G. Wells's science fiction novel *The Time Machine* (1895) encounters gray-haired, wizened, subterranean Morlocks, who cannibalize childlike surface dwellers. Contrary to the images of helplessness and neglect implicit in sentimental representations of late life, the rapacity of so many fictional elders bespeaks increasing anxiety among middle-class, middle-aged readers that old people might abuse rather than lose authority with the passage of time.

One final public spectacle that drew attention to old age in the nineteenth century was the queen herself: her reign from 1837 to 1901 spanned three generations of Victorians. Her subjects must have been uniquely aware of the particulars of aging as they watched their queen's protracted widowhood and determined refusal to turn the reins of government over to her son, the Prince Regent, who was himself an elderly man by 1900. In effect, she became England's most prominent and most costly elderly dependent. The aging of Queen Victoria also suggests how coincidental connections lead to sometimes intractable associations, in this case among old age, an aged queen, and an old order. By the end of the century, the term "Victorian" itself was correlated with negative stereotypes of old age; to be Victorian was to be antiquated, dowdy, prudish, burdensome: the antithesis of youth, a newborn century, and modernity.

Despite assumptions to the contrary, empirical evidence indicates that "the aged" did not emerge as a class of record-breaking numbers during the nineteenth century. What, then, prompted such a commonly expressed view and its Victorian consequences? One answer lies in the sheer proliferation of information possible in an age of mass-market publishing. Throughout the century, books and articles touted diets for longevity, debated the human life span, offered evidence of alleged centenarians, and wrangled over society's responsibilities to its longest-lived members. Whatever the facts and figures, from as early as mid-century the aged were a Victorian media event.

Consequences for Elderly Care

Perhaps the longest-running story of old age can be traced in print through periodical, newspaper, parliamentary, and parish discussions of how to provide for old people, and in practice through the resulting consequences. Financial security and care obviously varied across class and economic lines. Wealthy Victorians could afford to pay nurses, servants, and family members for whatever assistance they required; but, for the vast majority of the people, surviving into old age meant facing financial hardship. A very small number of working-class people derived retirement income by participating in occupation-based Friendly Societies or trade union subscriptions, and many elderly women received small government pensions, but most people saved only enough for emergencies or burials. The English Poor Law Reform Act of 1834 promoted the value of work and self-help, curbing so-called "outdoor relief" by giving local authorities the power to administer aid only to the "deserving poor" and by forcing beneficiaries to enter sex-segregated workhouses where they had to work in order to qualify for aid. While earlier versions of this institution had existed and later versions would persist until 1948, Victorian workhouses inspired particular abhorrence. Occupants over 50 were granted a few privileges due to age: they were exempt from restrictions on diet, alcohol, tobacco, wearing uniforms, and even sex-segregated living arrangements, since they were sometimes allowed to share quarters with married partners. Nevertheless, few chose this option. Workhouse rosters suggest that in 1851 fewer than one in eight workhouse inmates were 65; by 1891 the ratio increased to one-third in most regions; however, the increase was partially brought about when younger mentally or physically ill workhouse inmates were hospitalized, so that the proportion of the elderly increased more than actual numbers (Thomson). Institutions in industrial centers, especially London, housed far greater numbers of poor elderly people, most of them by the end of the century, women. Chase argues that these incarcerations were all the more dire as "the workhouse and the madhouse became two faces of one system" (39).

The large population of elderly poor in the cities created an indelible impression in the public imagination that workhouses largely served (and abused) older people. Public perceptions were grim, as suggested by the drunken, exploitative harridans who steal personal belongings from the dying in Dickens's *Oliver Twist* (1838) or the mournful old women in Von Herkomer's painting *Eventide: A Scene in the Westminster Union* (1878). These representations form a stark contrast to the warm relations between the parish-housed old men and the title character of Trollope's *The Warden* (1855). This novel, Gaskell's *Cranford* (1853), and innumerable village paintings through the second half of the century are all reminders that, as the young sought employment in cities or by emigrating across the empire, the average age of rural inhabitants steadily increased.

In the 1870s, changes in the law harshly cut back pensions. Families were called upon to care for older members and old people were pressured to support themselves.

As social support ebbed, labor unions and employees of the Civil Service, major banks, the mining and railroad industries, and other businesses lobbied for work-related subsidies, and Parliament deliberated on the merits of a national pension plan and mandatory retirement. Factories required workers capable of speed, adroitness, and tolerance for repetitive tasks under sometimes brutal working conditions; since older workers were stigmatized as slow, inept, and prone to accidents, retirement seemed to serve the interests of industry and individuals. Though economic changes alone did not prompt associations between the term "old" and images of inadequacy, the growing technological drive toward rapid transport and industrial production con-tributed to these stereotypes. Even so, through the end of the century "old age" resisted definition. While the Friendly Societies Act of 1875 established 50 as the age at which people could receive charitable gifts, the government waffled on pension eligibility. The Old Age Pensions Committee of 1898 first named 65 the retirement age for men. However, after considering the cost to the nation of paying from age 65, members of Parliament pushed old age up to 70 before passing the Old Age Pensions Act of 1908. When this Act established a clear and uniform onset for "old age," a quantified life span finally superseded, by eminently Victorian statistical logic, what had remained in Victorian practice a loose set of qualitative measures for age-identity.

While the workhouse and the pension plan dictated how Victorian society would care for "the aged" collectively, the aging body also attracted the attention of social scientists. In the last decades of the nineteenth century, Charles Booth conducted Royal Commission research on poverty and then on pensions. Made available to the larger reading audience as *Pauperism, a Picture; and The Endowment of Old Age, an Argu-ment* (1892), *The Aged Poor in England and Wales* (1894), and *Old Age Pensions and the Aged Poor* (1899), Booth's research revealed that poor people were often old people. Parliamentary discussion of the reports was regularly covered in newspapers and peri-odicals, heightening contemporary belief that the aged were proliferating, in need of care, and threatening to become a national burden.

The Pathologizing of Old Age

The desire to document, quantify, and classify old age swept the biological sciences as well. Prior to the nineteenth century, no clear distinction separates what we would now call medical information from philosophical speculation, as suggested by what may be the first survey in English of literature on aging, Sir John Sinclair's four-volume *Code of Health and Longevity* (1807). An eclectic collection of letters, classical quotations, and scientific explanations for aging, Sinclair's nearly 2,000 references document theories, treatments, and consolations offered by past authorities. Since old age was, inevitably, a prelude to the end of life, most of these earlier studies urged readers to accept death with stoicism once symptoms of illness or frailty appeared. We can see evidence of medical practitioners' acquiescence to the long-held belief that the elderly could not expect to be given the same treatments as younger people in doctors' willingness to pronounce the verdict "death of old age" when they filled out death certificates. An impressive medical statistical study appeared in 1889 when Sir George Humphrey published *Old Age*, a survey of nearly 900 people who had reached 80, including 74 centenarians.

Whereas many practicing Victorian doctors clung to past beliefs about old age, traditional wisdom faltered before modern science in laboratories across Europe where medical researchers, using greatly improved microscopes, launched sophisticated clinical examinations of the tissues and organs that comprised the aging body. The rise of large hospitals magnified attention to aging because charity hospitals housed so many elderly poor people. In France, the Saltpetrière, a hospital for women that at times slept 5,000, provided a grim wealth of illnesses and cadavers, leading researchers like Jean-Martin Charcot to seek in aging tissue and later in cells an explanation for physical decline and decrepitude. Charcot's 1867 treatise on the subject, translated into English in 1881 as *Clinical Lectures on the Diseases of Old Age* (1867), dramatically affected how European scientists studied aging, as a result of Charcot's emphasis on clinical investigation of the body rather than caring for old people. England lagged behind Germany, Russia, and France in clinical medicine, and the English public were deeply suspicious of European practices. Only late in the century did the Chelsea Royal Hospital, home to invalid elderly soldiers, become an important English site for research under the direction of Daniel MacLachlan.

Examining the impact of medical studies on perceptions of old age, Stephen Katz traces an emerging "discourse of senescence" in the competing Victorian medical explanations for old age. Katz argues that one effect of nineteenth-century medical researchers' careful classification of the workings of the human body was that the body became fixed in description as a set of signs. Because these signs were interpreted as indicators of health or infirmity and of normality or deviance, researchers laying the groundwork for the disciplines of gerontology and geriatrics were also imposing discipline upon the body. The old body was treated as a sign system that signaled deterioration and degeneration. These signs could be interpreted only by scientists. While sociological and political surveys of old people encouraged the Victorians to conceptualize a faceless impersonal mass of the aged, clinical studies threatened to reduce the complex psychological and social experience of aging to the study of tissue and organ damage. These clinical studies provided valuable information about the diseases and changes endemic to the aging body, but years would pass before the discoveries prompted practical medical treatments that actually improved old people's health or longevity.

The greatest achievement of nineteenth-century researchers may have been paving the way for the formal establishment of geriatrics and gerontology in the early twentieth century. Over the course of a century, medical studies of aging had moved from characterizing old age as a distinct and special time of life when an individual was best served by a bland diet, an end to illicit pleasures, and moderation in all things to viewing old age as the last of a systematically classified series of life stages in which aging was notable for distinct biological signs of deterioration. As medicine gained cultural as well as scientific authority, these medical opinions had far-reaching pragmatic consequences. One of the most immediate was that the testimony of medical experts was regularly used in courtrooms to determine when elderly people should be denied their rights to run family businesses, to write wills, to command resources, or to live independently – a stark counter-narrative to novelistic accounts of powerful misers and unyielding aging patriarchs.

For the most part, clinical medicine had a far less immediate effect upon the reading public than popular advice literature, readily available in books, periodical essays, and even in the testimonials that accompanied advertisements for tonics or medicines. Two long-held, contradictory conceptions of old age were argued with tenacity by popular medical authors. The first, the vitality model, defined old age as the gradual oozing away of a given supply of energy and ability. This theory participated in a general fear, contrary to optimists' insistence that England was the world's center of industry and activity, that the nation might just as easily be sliding into entropic and degenerate decline. Diametrically opposed to this view, the second theory contended that a "grand climacteric" marked the change of life. Proponents argued that old age emerged suddenly, causing pronounced physical collapse, a loss of sexual identity and desire, and often abrupt mental deterioration (Haber). For women the climacteric was believed to occur between 45 and 55 with the advent of menopause, while men could expect the sudden change between 50 and 75 (see Heath on these theories and their impingement on "midlife" experience). Because women were thought to have less authority and social status to lose in the first place, they supposedly weathered the dramatic change more easily than men. The climacteric was also linked to senility, a word that accrued ominous associations in the Victorian age in both clinical and popular medical contexts. Formerly, "senile" had simply meant belonging to or characteristic of old age. During the nineteenth century, however, to be senile was to be not only old but also mentally or morally incompetent; alleged symptoms of nineteenth-century senility sounded more like moral judgments than evaluations of health. Thus, diagnoses might comment on selfishness, querulousness, miserliness, or lasciviousness as though they were on a par with lung congestion or rheumatism.

Like readers today who furtively peruse magazine headlines that promise eternal youth, Victorians read both advice literature for prolonging life and accounts that claimed to document lives of 105, 120, even 150 years. Christopher Hufeland's book *The Art of Prolonging the Life of Man* (1797) remained popular in translation in England throughout the century. Thomas Bailey's *Records of Longevity: With an Introductory Discourse on Vital Statistics* (1857) included an alphabetical list of centenarians along with their places and dates of birth and death. Like its classical antecedents, Aristotle's comments on youth and aging, Galen's *De Sanitate Tuenda*, and Cicero's *De Senectute*, Bailey's volume and those of many fellow Victorian writers wove medical nostrums for the preservation of the body's energy together with philosophical arguments for resignation to the loss of that energy. Victorian writers frequently cited classical arguments to support contemporary bourgeois values such as thrift, independence, and self-denial. Thus, Bailey's prescription for long life restates ancient philosophy as moral economy: a person could "profanely consume life, by a profligate expenditure of its unappreciable powers, in riotous excess; or let its energies run to waste by a listless disregard to the performance of its important and responsible duties" or, instead, could prolong life on the "due preservation and right employment of which our creatural responsibility mainly depends" (2).

Few Victorians seem to have heeded the dangers of prolonging life without prolonging youth, even though literature of the period often warns of the potentially dire consequences. Jonathan Swift's peevish, decrepit *struldbruggs* are memorable among the foreign civilizations encountered in *Gulliver's Travels* (1726), a novel that was still popular in the nineteenth century. Tennyson's mournful poem "Tithonus" (1860) retells the classical myth in which Tithonus's immortal lover secures Zeus's promise that Tithonus will live forever but neglects to request eternal youth, leaving him to excruciating, interminable aging. The moral dangers of prolonged aging suffuse Oscar Wilde's *The Picture of Dorian Gray* (1891). When the seductively decadent Lord Henry laments the miseries of growing old and the fleeting pleasures of youth, Dorian barters his soul for perpetual youth, but his portrait records the horrors of lascivious old age. The sunny periodical essays that continued to advise moderation of diet, pleasures, and sex form a curious foil for what is perhaps the most famous of all prolongation narratives, Bram Stoker's *Dracula* (1897). Dracula's erotic appetite for life-sustaining young blood was a motif in vampire-manqué tales as well. The title character of Mary Elizabeth Braddon's "Good Lady Ducayne" (*The Strand*, 1896) hires a doctor to use the new and dangerous technology of blood transfusion to milk the veins of young women. These writers, it should be noted, were merely exaggerating experimental medical practices of the day, such as injections of crushed animal testicles, which promised to rejuvenate youth, vitality, and sexual performance, or the still extremely dangerous transfusion of blood.

The first serious challenge to claims of extraordinary life spans was William Thoms's *Human Longevity: Its Facts and Its Fictions* (1873). The Deputy Librarian to the House of Lords, Thoms set out to apply what he called scientific standards to the investigation of alleged centenarians. Noting that in the 1851 census some 111 men and 208 women were listed as being from 100 to 119 years old, Thoms painstakingly proved that lost or inaccurate records made most cases impossible to verify; he also quickly realized that many poor and illiterate claimants had no real idea of their true birthdates.

Though studies of aging like Thoms's took formal shape in the world of medicine, the social "disease" of ageism mutated into ever more resistant strains there as elsewhere. When the famous Canadian physician William Osler left his position as head of the Johns Hopkins Medical School to accept a named chair at Oxford University, his 1905 farewell speech "The Fixed Period" (a direct allusion to Trollope's novel) bemoaned the uselessness of men over 40 and jokingly advocated chloroforming those over 60. Osler's speech fomented outraged attacks from American and British doctors and newspapers alike in a contretemps that provides a snapshot of attitudes toward old age at the end of the century. Then, as now, the public imagination was capable of supporting deeply contradictory images. On one hand, the elderly were cast as children or old dears who deserved loving care and state support. On the other, older people were represented as an emerging, recalcitrant class of dependents who refused to contribute their fair share to the nation. This second view was heavily influenced by the more pessimistic among the Social Darwinists and eugenists, who believed that weaker members of society, including the infirm, the poor, and the old, were threatening the health of the nation.

Once again Victorian culture capaciously incorporated myriad extremes in varying gradations. As figures of popular culture, older characters appeared in the guise of comical spinsters in children's fiction like *Dame Wiggins of Lee and Her Seven Wonderful Cats* (1823); the gentle, loving grandmotherly character of Juliana Ewing's *Mrs Overtheway's Remembrances* (1894); or the wise supernatural ancestor of George MacDonald's *The Princess and the Goblin* (1872). Yet old age could also be cast in malevolent forms such as the demonic, ill-spirited witches, fairies, or ogres of countless Victorian fairy tales. Older figures represented in high culture also indicate contrasting opinions about old age: compare Tennyson's morose narrator of "Ulysses" (1842), champing against the constraints of an "aged wife" and the disappearance of his own youth, with the ennobled elders (Tennyson among them) in the photographic tableaux of Julia Margaret Cameron. The mass market was saturated with replicas of the elderly queen stamped on commemoration curios and splashed across newspaper and magazine pages. Her image assimilated age into national narratives of declining empire, unyielding traditionalism, and anxiety in the face of rapid cultural transformation. Perhaps most importantly, throughout a period of enormous change in attitudes toward late life, older people themselves were humans of every color, class, belief, and behavior: mothers, hard-working "grans," helpful aging neighbors, elder statesmen and political activists, artists, authors, and far, far more, many of whom remain alive to us in government documents, newspapers, photographs, autobiographies, and even, after 1895, film. Resisting attempts like Osler's to fix old age or old people in a phrase, these fleeting images challenge any simplistic account of what it meant to anticipate aging, to grow old, or to be aged a century ago.

See also MEDICAL; FICTION, SAGE WRITING; SKIN

REFERENCES

Bailey, T. (1857) *Records of Longevity; With an Introductory Discourse on Vital Statistics*. London: Darton.

Chase, K. (2009) *The Victorians and Old Age*. Oxford: Oxford University Press.

Covey, H. C. (1988) "Historical Terminology Used to Represent Older People." *Gerontologist* 28, 291–7.

Haber, C. (1983) *Beyond Sixty-Five: The Dilemma of Old Age in America's Past*. Cambridge: Cambridge University Press.

Hareven, T. K. (1986) "Historical Changes in the Social Construction of the Life Course." *Human Development* 29, 171–80.

Heath, K. (2009) *Aging by the Book: The Emergence of Midlife in Victorian Britain*. Albany: State University of New York Press.

Katz, S. (1996) *Disciplining Old Age: The Formation of Gerontological Knowledge*. Charlottesville: University Press of Virginia.

Laslett, P. (1977) *Family Life and Illicit Love in Earlier Generations*. Cambridge: Cambridge University Press.

Looser, D. (2008) *Women Writers and Old Age in Great Britain, 1750–1850*. Baltimore: Johns Hopkins University Press.

Roebuck, J. (1979) "When Does 'Old Age' Begin? The Evolution of the English Definition." *Journal of Social History* 12, 416–28.

Thomson, D. (1983) "Workhouse to Nursing Home: Residential Care of Elderly People in England Since 1840." *Ageing and Society* 3, 43–69.

Tranter, N. L. (1973) *Population Since the Industrial Revolution: The Case of England and Wales*. London: Croom Helm.

Wall, R. (1995) "Elderly Persons and Members of Their Households in England and Wales from Preindustrial Times to the Present." In *Aging in the Past: Demography, Society, and Old Age*, ed. D. I. Kertzer and P. Laslett. Berkeley: University of California Press.

FURTHER READING

Bothelho, L., and P. Thane (eds) (2001) *Women and Aging in British Society since 1550*. New York and London: Longman.

Casteras, S. (1987) *Images of Victorian Womanhood in English Art*. London: Associated University Presses.

Covey, H. C. (1991) *Images of Older People in Western Art and Society*. New York: Praeger.

Featherstone, M., and A. Wernick (eds) (1995) *Images of Aging: Cultural Representations of Later Life*. London: Routledge.

Gullette, M. M. (1994) "Male Midlife Sexuality in a Gerontocratic Economy: The Privileged Stage of the Long Midlife in Nineteenth-Century Age-Ideology." *Journal of the History of Sexuality* 5, 58–89.

Pelling, M., and R. M. Smith (eds) (1991) *Life, Death and the Elderly: Historical Perspectives*. London: Routledge.

Quadagno, J. (1982) *Aging in Early Industrial Society: Work, Family and Social Policy in Nineteenth Century England*. New York: Academic Press.

Roebuck, J., and J. Slaughter (1979) "Ladies and Pensioners: Stereotypes and Public Policy Affecting Old Women in England, 1880–1940." *Journal of Social History* 13, 105–14.

Small, H. (2007) *The Long Life*. Oxford: Oxford University Press.

Thane, P. (1993) "Geriatrics." In *Companion Encyclopedia of the History of Medicine*, ed. W. F. Bynum and R. Porter. London: Routledge.

——(ed.) (2005) *The Long History of Old Age*. London: Thames and Hudson.

Woodward, K., and M. M. Schwartz (eds) (1985) *Memory and Desire: Aging – Literature – Psychoanalysis*. Bloomington: Indiana University Press.

8
Passing On: Death

Gerhard Joseph and Herbert F. Tucker

I

The Victorians wrote about death because they couldn't help it. They didn't know any better. Like us, and like every generation since self-consciousness dawned on mortality, Victorian people could not know death at first hand. Yet they could not but know, and talk, *about* it. The one experience inescapably entailed by life, death nevertheless remains empirically inaccessible to the living: a cognitive zero, it gives rise to an unending discursive speculation that exhausts whatever imaginative options culture and history make available to the speculator. Each society, each epoch fills in the blank of mortality with what lies to hand, and what lies to hand is its own clutch of preoccupations. So what the Victorians themselves never tired of invoking as death's mystery makes our topic in this chapter an ideal register for understanding them and the cultural forms they produced. Death the Penalty, Death the Prize, Death the Wall, Death the Threshold, Death the Abyss: for the historian of literature these and other Victorian tropes all present aspects of a cultural complex. Call it Death the Portrait – if not, indeed, with the period's most celebrated framer of mortal speculations, Death the Mirror: "And on the depths of death there swims / The reflex of a human face" (Tennyson, *In Memoriam* [1850], section 108). When the Victorians coped with their unbearable yet inevitable ignorance of the topic, they were depicting themselves.

Victorian speculation on death tended, as did nineteenth-century thought generally, to assume a narrative shape. What Victorians knew about nature or culture (or thought they knew) they habitually cast in the form of a story of development; so,

A New Companion to Victorian Literature and Culture, First Edition. Edited by Herbert F. Tucker.
© 2014 John Wiley & Sons, Ltd. Published 2014 by John Wiley & Sons, Ltd.

understandably, it was story that furnished the forms in which they reassured them-selves about what they did not know. Their beliefs about death produced two master narratives with which we shall be concerned here. The first has to do with the act and fact of dying itself: its scene of choice is that favorite Victorian topos the gently lighted and lovingly attended deathbed; its conventions include the deliberate taking of leave, the face turned to the wall or else the gaze cast upward beyond this world, the passage through pain into illumination, the word or gesture expressive of a life's concentrated essence. Our second master narrative concerns not the hour of death but the days and months afterward, as experienced by the survivor in mourning. Mourn-ing, unlike dying, is a lived and to that extent a communicable experience; still, it was a notorious peculiarity of Victorian culture to shroud its mourning in as richly mystified, even eroticized, a ritual narrative as that which it accorded to dying. Within this narrative the mourner underwent a process that led, by halting steps, from the prostrating disintegrations of private grief, through beneficent touches of recognition and commemoration, to the reconstruction of a changed yet strength-ened self, healed within and ratified anew as a wiser if sadder member of the Victorian social body.

Each of these shapely narratives was in effect a manual for safe conduct along the darkest of itineraries. Small wonder, given this prescriptive function, if in their cul-tural dissemination Victorian death stories sometimes stiffened into maudlin sentiment, saccharine hypocrisy, compulsory gloom or cheer. While we latter-day moderns can scarcely avoid deflating their pomp and deriding their circumstance, we should first acknowledge the height of agonized terror, the depth of numb despair, through which the Victorian master narratives offered passage. We mock these stories of passing-on at our cost; they were, after all, equipment for living, which Victorian people valued for their practical therapeutic force and to which they clung the more fervently the less they could credit the age-old Christian *ars moriendi* or could depend on traditional networks of support among an extended family and community. Still, stories are what they were, and we cannot appreciate their fictive ideality without also coming to terms with the upsets that took place every time Victorian reality presented the unlovely form of a grotesque or pointless death, of a mourning brutally foreclosed or else drawn out into addictive grieving. Such failure to conform to the "stock story" thrust on the Victorian mind what we shall call, borrowing from another context, a "counterstory" (Harris). This counterstory about death and grief foregrounded ele-ments of absurdity and irresolution that Victorians could hardly welcome yet must have found uncannily familiar. For these refractory elements attested the cultural underside or repressed bad faith of the era's official confidence that the last word on last things should be good. That cultural master narratives thus secrete their own opposites is not only a sociological key to the understanding of complex modernity; it is also, we suggest, a core insight of the most highly imaginative literature about death. It is those fictions and poems which dialectically combine stock story with counterstory that represent their age most accurately, and that remain most compel-ling for posterity.

II

What qualities typify the stock story, the conventional narrative concerning Victorian death? "As everyone allows," says Garrett Stewart, "characters die more often, more slowly, and more vocally in the Victorian age than ever before or since" (8); and the novels and poems John Reed itemizes in *Victorian Conventions* display that period's patent consistency with compelling evidentiary force. In illustration here of what "everyone allows," we might look at a specific pathos-filled death scene originating not in Victorian fiction or poetry but in that fiction by another name, biographical anecdote. For several days before his decease in 1892, and well aware of its imminence, Tennyson took to summoning his most illustrious predecessor in the English literary pantheon. "Where is my Shakespeare? I must have my Shakespeare," his son Hallam remembers him repeatedly calling out – so that the poet could touch the volume even when he could not read it. On the evening of his death, his last meal taken, he found all reading impossible. In the moon-drenched room he opened the volume instead, to the lines from late in *Cymbeline* where Posthumus and Imogen are reconciled in exuberant joy after five long acts of division and delay. Shortly thereafter Tennyson spoke his last words of blessing to the assembled family and passed on, one finger inserted at the *Cymbeline* passage, a laurel wreath from Virgil's tomb placed at his side by his wife and son (Tennyson II, 25–9).

The salient characteristics of a textbook Victorian death are impossible to miss in this final rite of passage, lovingly recorded yet artfully wrought too, in tribute to one of the most representative of Victorian men. The composed, elaborated quality is what most strikes us: the stately pace, the allusive and premeditated weave. It is diverting but finally not surprising to know that the laurel wreath from Virgil's tomb was a gift from Alfred Austin, who had gathered its leaves years earlier in express anticipation of Tennyson's passing, and whose ambition to succeed to the laureateship was to be duly realized before long. The entire cultural text is an aestheticized "good death," and a spiritualized one too, an ideal valediction to which the priestly validation of last rites seems superfluous. This death that is manifestly designed to take national center-stage also takes place – so the cultural script ordains it – within the warmth of home, in the company of family and of the dying man's personal physician and friend, one Dr Dabbs.

Last but not least, here as so often in the stock story of Victorian death, famous last words put a culminating full stop to the life they epitomize. Whatever one thinks of the enigmatic leave taken by the dying Kurtz in *Heart of Darkness* (1899), when Marlow unswervingly receives "The horror!" as a mad sage's summary judgment on the human condition, Conrad's message could hardly be more starkly, existentially modern; and yet, in the very confidence of his construal, Marlow displays impeccably Victorian credentials. In Tennyson's case, family tradition took down from dying lips the words "I opened it." Opened his Shakespeare, one literal-mindedly supposes, though the phrase properly nurtured opens an eye on eternity in as Tennysonian a fashion as might be hoped. Not so witty as "That wallpaper has to go or I do" (irresistibly if apocryphally attributed to Oscar Wilde), but withal deeply appropriate to the laureate's life-long susceptibility both to Shakespeare and to diaphanously adumbrated longings.

For longings they had to be, not certitudes. The final clause in the stock-story script of death would be less than fully Victorian were there not something inconclusive about it. As the protagonist of a death good enough for his own (Morte d')Arthur, Tennyson virtually had to go on record saying it was finished by saying it was opened. For the Victorian good death was not to be cloistered by the confines of holy writ or ecclesiastical dogma. In *A Tale of Two Cities* (1859) Sydney Carton's culminating incantation of "I am the Resurrection and the Life" (John 11: 25) constitutes a social and secular liturgy that reflects Dickens's vigilance to canonize a modern urban martyr on the novel's terms, not the Bible's. Scripture is included, but only on condition that it be circumscribed by fiction; Carton dies for, and into, literature. That same Bible phrase from the gospel of John galvanizes the moribund St John himself, the speaker of Robert Browning's 1864 monologue "A Death in the Desert," into dictating from his deathbed hideout a postscript that is, in effect, a latter-day hermeneut's prescription for faith. The Victorian resurrection of Christianity, its rescue from the fundamentalism of the dead letter, would entail betting the true Church on the figurality of scripture, its capacity to be "opened" like poetry (or Tennyson's fingered Shakespeare) to contemporary uses. Thus, when Browning's saintly Pompilia expires a few years later in *The Ring and the Book* (1868–9), it is only after explicitly giving scripture her seal of approval, not vice versa: "Oh how right that is, how like Jesus Christ / To say that!" (book 7, ll. 1829–30). Within the Tennysonian idealization of death, the casement always "grows a glimmering square" ("Tears, Idle Tears," 1847), an aperture that outlines an otherworldly opportunity at the same time that it invites perennial lingering, Enoch Arden-like, at the sill. Where the mere intimation of immortality meant so much, there arose a distinctive tendency to immortalize the intimation, to read death's text by the glimmering twilight of a faith in doubt. Not for nothing did the Victorian spiritualist medium drive a brisk trade, or the Metaphysical Society (1869) and the Society for Psychical Research (1882) attract eminent membership rosters.

In order to explain something as overdetermined as a period's attitude towards death, historians evoke a plurality of causes. The "beautiful death" that Philippe Ariès sees as a Victorian cultural style results, he argues, from a Romantic transformation of eighteenth-century terrors into something beautiful, something to be eagerly awaited and orchestrated into the sort of deathbed finale we have been considering. Pat Jalland, on the other hand, cautions against applying to Britain what is limited and eccentric in the work done on death by Ariès and his *Annales* school of historiography. Ariès's analysis is largely based upon the records left behind by a Brontë family ravaged by tuberculosis – he elaborates as his prime example the episode of Helen Burns's death in *Jane Eyre* (1847) – and his view is furthermore Catholic rather than Protestant in emphasis. By contrast Jalland, having studied in manuscript a collection of private diaries, extensive correspondence, wills, and memorials of death covering over 50 families and almost 100 years, suggests that "if death in nineteenth-century Britain is to be characterized in terms of a single model or an ideal, then it should be the Evangelical 'good death' and not Ariès's 'beautiful death'" (8). In aid of such a death there were not only numberless evangelical tracts, but also such older works as Bishop Jeremy Taylor's *The Rule and Exercises of Holy Dying* (1651), which George Eliot's novel *Adam Bede* (1859, ch. 19) names as the standard Victorian reference guide to the good death in an Anglican home.

In death as in philosophy, of course, the beautiful and the good might prove compatible. Much Victorian devotional writing (especially women's) was devoted to illustrating just this compatibility. So was much Victorian fashion (especially men's). Men in black sustained for decades variations on a masculine aesthetic that united severe elegance with sober power, casting its shadow across a national "cult of death" that was "funereal even when feasting" (Harvey 177). Not only in *Little Dorrit* (1855) and *Middlemarch* (1873) was there something coffinlike about domestic interiors, where recreational or study space denoted masculine was especially liable to be somber-wooded and plumb-boxed. On the street and square as well, the sarcophagus bulk of state architecture and imperial monument recorded in bronze and stone the Victorian habit of sacrificing at death's cryptic altar, engarlanding public honor with the crape of commemoration. The same Tennyson who reverently hoped to see his Pilot face to face when he had crossed the bar from body into spirit had, just a few lines before, booked passage on a flood of sensuous and hypnotic beauty, "such a tide as moving seems asleep, / Too full for sound and foam" ("Crossing the Bar," 1889). Both moments in the poem flow with the Victorian mainstream, which might indeed be worse conceived than as an habitually rehearsed passage from the one moment to the other, a current from sense to soul connecting – or hoping to connect – the fleshly with the metaphysical. It was at the ideal hour of death, or at the frequent but no less ideal anticipations of death with which Victorians punctuated their lives, that beauty could be truth, truth beauty. And such beauty frequently took the form of the dying maiden, the elegiac female object enshrouded in dreamlike haze who haunts Pre-Raphaelite stanzas and canvases especially, but who is seldom far to seek in Victorian poetry and painting at large.

III

Whether Romantic or Evangelical influence furnishes the best explanation for the obsession with death in the Victorian period, material factors also have to be taken into account. For one thing, there was so much more early death – especially among the very young – than at present, when most people in the industrialized West die at a relatively mature age. Anthony Wohl calls it a "massacre of the innocents": in any given year during the High Victorian period something like 100,000 children died before their first birthday. The death rate in England and Wales for infant mortality per thousand was 154 in 1840, 148 in 1860; and a persistent if slow decline brought the rate to 100 in 1916 and below 16 in 1983. In appreciating the Victorian encounter with death, then, we must multiply tenfold our own apprehensiveness over a baby's survival, compounded by a comparable if less statistically daunting risk to the life of the baby's mother. Among us the advance of age has supplanted the fact of birth as the most probable cause for death; to reverse these proportions is to conceive what stern necessities underlay the omnipresence of death to the Victorian mind as it tried to keep in tolerable view a reality that could never be kept at bay, in any family, for long (Lerner; Dever).

Two turning points may be mentioned in the history of these accommodations to necessity (Jalland). The first centers roughly on 1870, when, in a textbook Victorian shift of priorities, scientific advance supervened on a religion in retreat. As sanitary reforms took hold, and as antiseptic and obstetric medicine progressed with the century, life and death expectancy came more predictably under human control; this matter of fact soon became (what is not the same thing) a matter of faith, and it did so the more readily with the recession of orthodox belief that marked the last quarter of the century. As moral psychology uncoupled convictions about sin from certainties of penal torment in a Hell in which fewer and fewer Victorians put real faith (Rowell), the physical pain of dying came into focus as a *summum malum*. In this connection Dr William Munk's 1887 textbook *Euthanasia; or Medical Treatment in Aid of an Easy Death*, while its title denotes not mercy killing but the tranquil passing-on spelled out in its subtitle, nevertheless marks a modern corner turned.

A second and more acute turning point confronts us in World War I, which effected a traumatically abrupt change in the national imagination of death. The horror of mass extinction in the trenches, decimating a generation of young Britons, was if anything made more horrible by contrast to the "good" and "beautiful" ideals of dying that their forebears had cherished. That this decisive historical watershed was post-Victorian is precisely our point, for in no respect did the Great War cashier Victorian conventions more dramatically than in this. What the nineteenth century had constructed as a tranquil and carefully attended rapprochement with a fore-known end yielded overnight to staccato cataclysm. Suddenly death betokened cruel caprice, absurdity, a moral anomie that was ironically embittered by the Victorians' recently won conviction that dying might become a medically manageable secular process.

In another sense, though, the pointless violence which overtook the Western imagination with the Great War merely brought to public consciousness a widely disseminated knowledge, which Victorian culture had as widely suppressed. The old counterstory about death from the nineteenth century was thus in effect promoted by shocking, immedicable news from the military front into a new stock story for the twentieth, one that pivoted in a new way on the issue of class. For the story on which we have thus far dwelt concerns preponderantly the upper-middle class; and, while it has frequently been assumed that the attitudes of the upper classes filtered down to the working classes, such an assumption is quite mistaken

(Richardson). Death for the working class, especially the indigent whose number was legion during the Victorian period, was a decidedly grimmer matter than for their social betters.

One horror in particular attached to the approach of poor people's death that was unknown among the well-to-do. This was the possibility of what the celebrated final sentence of Emily Brontë's *Wuthering Heights* (1847) calls, albeit preventively, "unquiet slumbers, for the sleepers in that quiet earth." The supply of cadavers for medical research and teaching was legally limited at the turn of the nineteenth century to the census of hanged murderers transferred into medical hands by the arm of the law, and these were relatively few. As a result, the sale of bodies illegally snatched from cemeteries, in which the graves of the poor enjoyed least protection, had become a lucrative business during the eighteenth century. Still, a persistent shortage of corpses led anatomists, surgeons, and others to press for an expansion and legitimation of the supply, which were eventually granted in the Anatomy Act of 1832. Intended to preempt the most ghoulish of black markets, the Act stipulated that government authorities should surrender for medical dissection the bodies not merely of hanged felons, but now too of paupers dying in workhouses and hospitals who lacked the funds to defray their own funerals. What generations of the poor since 1750 had feared and hated as a penalty for murder thus became in 1832 a statutory penalty for poverty itself. Thereafter body-snatching did largely disappear, enough so to dwindle into macabre comic relief in the Cruncher subplot from *A Tale of Two Cities*. But the terror of a pauper's death remained; and the Anatomy Act goes a long way towards explaining the growing prestige of the respectable funeral among Victorian poor people, and of the death-insurance and undertaking businesses that guaranteed and carried it out.

That not all Victorian deaths were the stately and ritualized affairs of stock story was, to be sure, evident to members of all classes and not merely to the poor: the egalitarian democracy of death made persons up and down the social ladder liable to violent or hideous ends. For a demonstrative supplement to the idealized death of Tennyson, we turn again to biography, this time to Tennyson's only contemporary rival in literary eminence, Charles Dickens. If one accepts the retrospective approximations of his biographers, Dickens's life did not come to a graceful close: his end broke suddenly and awkwardly, as many Victorian deaths surely did, *in medias res*. To be sure, he had been unwell during his last years, too exhausted to write much: Wilkie Collins petulantly assures us that the late *Mystery of Edwin Drood* was "Dickens's last laboured effort, the melancholy work of a worn-out brain," George Bernard Shaw that it was "the gesture by a man already threequarters dead" (Fielding 246, 242). On June 8, 1870, Dickens spent all day working alone at Gad's Hill on *Drood*. At dinner he confessed that he had been feeling ill. Then, abruptly, he rose and fell to the floor. Georgina Hogarth, his sister-in-law and the only family member present, sent away for the children and (apparently) for his mistress Ellen Ternan. While Dickens lived through the night and all the next day, he never regained consciousness and died the next evening.

No preparation, no final *bon mot*, no bracing valediction with which the family (already skewed from the norm) could console itself during the mourning period; just an anti-climactic dying fall without meaning, an apoplectic bang and then hours of whimper petering out into insignificance – such are the mortal certainties of the case, although biographers wrapping things up with the stately funeral at Westminster Abbey may dispose us to think otherwise. We concentrate here upon the bleak death of Dickens the man precisely because of its incongruity with the drawn-out, emotionally upholstered and fully articulated deaths of so many of his characters, among them Nell and her grandfather in *The Old Curiosity Shop* (1841), Paul in *Dombey and Son* (1848), Jo in *Bleak House* (1853), each presumably transported into that second of Dickens's "two cities," the "far, far better place" into which Sydney Carton also exits. Not all deaths in Dickens wear this aura of aestheticized solemnity and sentimental spirituality. There are also the violent, unredeemed drownings of Eugene Wrayburn and Gaffer Hexam in *Our Mutual Friend* (1865) and of Quilp in *The Old Curiosity Shop*, the morcellation of Carker's body by the railway locomotive that disfigures a "he" into an "it," the Byronic whelming of Steerforth in *David Copperfield* (1850).

Like the definitive extreme case from *Bleak House*, Krook's notoriously spontaneous combustion, these fast and dirty deaths were spectacular but were also exceptional. Such blunt ends got comparatively short shrift in Dickens's book – in the great mid-century genre of the novel, that is – and one reason was that they made for scant copy. (In our book too: note above how few words Dickens's death takes next to Tennyson's.) It was pre-pondered death that preponderated: the long deaths of Kingsley's Alton Locke (1850), Thackeray's Colonel Newcome (1855), Trollope's Septimus Harding (*The Last Chronicle of Barset*, 1867), Eliot's Mordecai Cohen (*Daniel Deronda*, 1876) all represent different values; but across a quarter-century they represent in common an established mode of making values tell.

The High Victorian narrative advantage went to plots of passing-on that were laid thick with foreshadowing, were prolonged with care, and above all were sequel-friendly. Styles of dying thus entrained other aspects of style that prepared or attended the Victorian mortal climax. Indeed, the end of the line for serial three-decker novels came into view when 1860s sensation fiction started weaning readers from the long fadeout and habituating them instead to the stab in the back and the shot in the dark. Even so severe a High-Church apostate from secular fashion as Gerard Manley Hopkins was spurred into sacred song, not by extreme unction, but by the quick ecstasy of an accidental disaster written up in the news ("The Wreck of the *Deutschland*," 1876). This vogue for death by surprise heralded a late-century taste for racier closures, more of them and at a swifter clip, and thus cooperated with the morbid thematics of the Decadent movement to usher in the abbreviated literary forms that typified literary production by the 1890s. In a longer work like *Jude the Obscure* (1895), one way Hardy put paid to High Victorian fiction was with the grim zest of an indecorum that dotted the novel with signally graceless deaths. The unDickensian manner of Dickens's demise seems, in retrospect, to have portended emerging lines of change within the genre over which he had presided while alive.

IV

Sigmund Freud became the twentieth century's psychic mythmaker because he had been the nineteenth century's psychic mapmaker first; and it is to his "Mourning and Melancholia" that we turn for the stock story on Victorian bereavement (Sacks). The death of a loved one brings on the painful affect of grief, which mourning works through in a gradual process that later psychologists have analyzed into "stages" on the way to recovery (Kübler-Ross). For all its attendant anguish, mourning is consolatory and restorative: once the mourner has passed through its stages he or she can proceed, if not to new objects of desire, then at least to a life relatively free of incapacitating pain. Still, mourning is made exquisitely difficult by the ferocity with which the grieving self can resist its own cure:

> People never willingly abandon a libidinal position, not even, indeed, when a substitute is already beckoning to them. This opposition can be so intense that a turning away from reality takes place and a clinging to the object through the medium of hallucinatory wishful psychosis. Normally, respect for reality gains the day. Nevertheless its orders cannot be obeyed at once. They are carried out bit by bit, at great expense of time and cathectic energy, and in the meantime the existence of the lost object is psychically prolonged. (Freud 244–5)

Freud emphasizes the "expense of time and cathectic energy" that is required of individual consciousness. But that psychic economy must be further understood in its interdependent relation with the larger cultural economy. As Esther Schor has maintained (1994), to focus exclusively on the isolated act of mourning may well be wrongheaded, since acts of mourning are diffusively conditioned by larger epistemic considerations.

Every society develops rules and rituals by and against which individuals define themselves, so that public acts of mourning – for the Duke of Wellington once upon a time, for Princess Diana more recently – both shape and are shaped by the responses to death in one's immediate ken. This dialectic, which Victorian writers grasped very well, made it possible for a literature of private grief to enjoy a mass circulation, not only in the several splendid elegies produced by the era's poets – Arnold's "Thyrsis" (1866) and Swinburne's "Ave atque Vale" (1868) among them – but also in the pronouncedly elegiac strain that suffuses much of its classic autobiographical and fictional prose. At the official level, mourning rituals were marked by extraordinary ostentation, the sumptuous obsequies of Wellington in 1852 elaborating a High Victorian ideal for state funeral pomp: a million and a half mourners along the parade route, a coffin of quadruple ply, a hearse costing £11,000, and £80,000 expended on funeral seating alone (Wolffe; Sinnema). By 1880, less showy funerals were coming to be preferred, thanks partly to efforts by the National Funeral and Mourning Reform Association (1875): witness the widespread condemnation of lavish display at the 1865 funerals of the Duke of Northumberland and Cardinal Wiseman, or the relative simplicity of Gladstone's in 1898. Clearly, however, for a long time sheer aggrandizement was reckoned desirable in both highlighting a national grief and facilitating a national therapy. The more extravagant the display, the more expeditious might be the public catharsis.

At the level of private grief we find a similar extravagance, manifest in elaborate memorial rites (fixed periods of mourning, with purpose-made stationery, jewelry, attire, and so on), as well as the establishment in suburban London of eight new cemeteries permitting the observance of those rites in monumental splendor within a garden setting (Lutz). Thus, private family burials, at least among the more prosperous members of the middle class, as a rule took their cue from the funerals of state. What these private acts of mourning might lack in ostentation, they could make up for in temporal extension. This was especially the case for women; while bourgeois men did also mourn, their need to go to work in a man's world encouraged a discourse of Victorian mourning that remained gender-marked: etiquette books, for example, tended to enunciate rules for mourning on the part of widows and mothers. During the first year of mourning over a parent, spouse, or child, women clad in jet black were expected to behave as veritable social outcasts and refuse all invitations to leave the home. But once the specified period of mourning was past, there set in a no less binding expectation that the mourner speedily reactivate her discarded social identity.

The compromise that society thus struck between an intensely elaborated commemoration, and a consolation distant yet secure, achieved its classic literary treatment with *In Memoriam*. This is so, not in spite of what can seem duplicitous about the rhythm of remembering and forgetting in Tennyson's elegy, but because of it. Duplicitous, or else profoundly paradoxical: according to Freud the ego, in its desire for self-preservation, remembers *in order* to forget, prolongs the attachment *in order* to effect a detachment on terms the ego can accept. No wonder the mourning speaker, shot through with shame at abandoning his loved object, wants at times to write himself off as a creeping "guilty thing" (*In Memoriam*, section 7). Still, the iron law demarcating mourning from melancholia – and governing the Victorian persistence of the classical elegiac genre – is that the object shall at last be put aside. Eventually even *In Memoriam* becomes street-legal, subsiding unspecifiably yet undeniably into a consolation that is crowned by the celebration of a marriage. But the reluctance of Tennyson's compliance with the law manifestly strains the limits of the stock story about mourning that it confirms. The most Victorian thing about this elegy, its inordinate length, repeatedly raises the possibility that, if a pageant of grief can last for 131 meandering lyrics and for at least three Christmases, it just might last forever.

V

This possibility did not go unrealized in fact or fiction. Exceptions were abundant to the Victorian mourner's narrative of progress through intense bereavement to muted recovery; the recent widow whose "hair has turned quite gold from grief" would not have raised the laugh she still gets in Wilde's *The Importance of Being Earnest* (1895) had real-life exemplars been wanting. Then as now some spouses, heirs, and other skeptics were fully capable of accepting the loss of intimates with quiet relief or frank indifference. Because the stock story made no place for such reactions, however, and also because such reactions were by nature not very news- or plot-worthy, they remain matter largely for inference, for example, as sources of the mourner's diffuse guilt in *In Memoriam*, or of the gentle comic thread that stitches Trollope's Barsetshire novels. More conspicuous in the Victorian newspapers, and in novels of sensation such as Mary Elizabeth Braddon's *Lady Audley's Secret* (1862), were splashier cases in which the survivor was believed to have taken an active role in helping the death along. Such cases, as well as the many instances of Victorian suicide, bore out the logic generally operative in scandal. They owed their notoriety to the norms which they scandalized – and thus served to reinforce – norms sufficiently stringent that few Victorian dissidents against compulsory mourning withheld the tribute of lip service. (Witness, again, Wilde's *Earnest*, with Jack's deadpan dumbshow of grief over the non-person Bunbury.)

The most remarkable cultural opposition to the regime of Victorian mourning was the one – melancholia – that emerged from within it, born of its very triumph. For in melancholia, where the stock story of mourning never reaches its scripted denouement, mourning ceased to be mourning precisely because it would not cease. Letters, diaries, and journals of the period provide ample evidence of a chronic grief that, far from *working*, went on permanent detour into the wilds of sorrow. Imaginative enlargements of this cultural disorder appear as the Victorian undead, caricatures of survivorship who command attention in Tennyson's "Tithonus" (1860), Haggard's *She* (1887), and Stoker's *Dracula* (1897). Trollope created in Lily Dale a character who, for all the social realism of *The Small House at Allington* (1864), stands comparison with these fantasy survivals in her steadfastness to a love that is stillborn because unrequited, absurdly disproportionate to its undeserving object – yet that her stunned heart will not surrender. As may be seen from the extraordinary record of multiple bereavement that charges Margaret Oliphant's unpublished autobiography, some Victorians never did recover from the death of a beloved spouse or child. Refusing the final therapeutic turn toward integration, they incurred the additional pain of censure at the hands of a society whose highly visible mourning customs made instances of nonconforming refusal impossible to miss and easy to interpret as antisocial vanity.

So, while as a matter of literary history the mourning of a Victorian elegist like Swinburne may have had more in common with Spenser's three centuries before him than with Wilfred Owen's atavistic, violent, and untranscendable modernist melancholia three decades after, as a cultural phenomenon full-blown "'melancholic' mourning" (Ramazani) did not have to wait for the twentieth century. The Victorian period had its share of inconsolables already; and none more amply represented the disposition of the age toward extravagant bereavement than that foremost of cultural icons, Queen Victoria herself. Victoria's elaborate mourning for Prince Albert after his death by typhus made her an archetype whose influence upon subsequent custom was crucial and pervasive. Quintessential ideal of middle-class Christian wifehood, she became in 1861 the instigator and impeccable exemplar of a cult of flamboyant widowhood, whose adherents took the staying power of grief to be the surest authentication of the marital sanctities it ratified. But then the queen's stipulated period of formal mourning doubled from two years to four, and then quadrupled to eight, becoming at length a 20-year retreat from public life into sovereign sequestration at Balmoral and Windsor Castles. Victoria's subjects became at first increasingly suspicious, and at last inevitably convinced, that there was something wrong about their monarch's prostration, something downright pathological; and a combined journalistic and parliamentary campaign said so in strong terms.

But even an empress may claim her counterstory, and even melancholia may have its uses. Victoria's response to the death of Albert surely became more complex with the years than the well-advertised, duly received story of irremediable suffering would suggest. While Victoria's mourning was indeed over-the-top, she did without question, and earlier than it appeared, recover mental equipoise and self-command. So it is sensible to suppose that the officially circulated tale served other purposes; that the queen, in keeping to herself, kept the trappings of stricken privacy in full public view with a conscious theatrical flair and evident political results (Munich). Had the "Widow at Windsor" – Kipling's 1890 poem caught a slogan that was already in the air – gotten over her sorrow in too public a fashion, it might have brought pressure on her to marry again, or might have sponsored even more fancifully intimate tales than made the rounds anyhow concerning her friendship with the devoted and beloved servant John Brown. The decorously flirtatious homage that Disraeli paid the queen during his years of parliamentary ascendancy highlights from a different side the relation Victoria's aggressively defended widowhood bore to questions of political advantage.

To these personal motives we add here a cultural one: Victorian society needed a scapegoat on which to fix the burden of its own self-delightingly morbid excess. On one hand the conventions of mourning were too prescriptively rigid to fit the varieties of emotional aftermath actually experienced by survivors guilty, complacent, or otherwise. On the other hand those conventions were pathetically inadequate to the towering passions that bereavement could release, passions whose capacity to become habit-forming many Victorians must have glimpsed in themselves as possibilities and observed more or less actualized in others. On either hand the Victorian system of mourning thus generated a surplus; and whether this surplus was apprehended as hypocrisy or as addiction, the already idealized figurehead of the queen attracted it with all the occult force that the nascent mass culture of the nineteenth century vested in celebrity. The realm at large thus converged on Victoria's endlessly grieving widowhood as both a congratulatory and a cautionary tale, fashioned by her even as she was fashioned by it, for the sake of a common welfare more felt after than planned or understood.

If we would seek the dead – and what else is this scholarly séance of ours with Victorian cultural ancestors? – we have no choice but to inquire among the living. This is so in several senses. One is that in which the literature of death perforce concerns survivors rather than predecessors. The subtle evangelical Browning knew as much when he put at the focus of "An Epistle . . . of Karshish" (1855) not the perished and resurrected Lazarus but the medical student who, having examined Lazarus as a patient, can neither understand what he has met nor stop trying. Likewise the unsubtle evangelical Edward Bickersteth, who, having put the protagonist of *Yesterday, To-Day, and For Ever* (1867) to good death in an opening episode, made him his own survivor for 11 more books of epically detailed dispatches from the afterlife. The needs of life directed Victorian death in another sense, too: the phenomena of necroculture that this chapter has considered were stabilizing devices, which the Victorians installed to counteract what they saw, with real cause, as the unprecedented chase they were leading each other. If the whole society appeared funereal, that is because it was in mourning for lost fixtures, in the world and of the spirit, which the acceleration of a coveted yet feared modernity had swept away. It was toward us, of course, and through us, that the force of that acceleration swept, and sweeps apace. Our house of mourning today is by Victorian standards spare and drafty and cold. We now treat with hasty neglect the great last fact of life that once obsessed our forebears, and part of the price we pay is the way our observance of death defaults to a threadbare, hollow repetition of theirs. Among many human necessities for which the Anglophone West still calls on Victorian help, the needs of dying and mourning may be foremost.

See also CLERICAL, MEDICAL; POETRY; PARAPETS

REFERENCES

Ariès, P. (1981) *The Hour of Our Death*, trans. H. Weaver. New York: Knopf.

Dever, C. (1998) *Death and the Mother from Dickens to Freud: Victorian Fiction and the Anxiety of Origins*. New York: Cambridge University Press.

Fielding, K. J. (1958) *Charles Dickens: A Critical Introduction*. Boston: Houghton Mifflin.

Freud, S. (1915) "Mourning and Melancholia." In *The Standard Edition of the Complete Works of Sigmund Freud*, trans. J. Strachey (1953), vol. 14. London: Hogarth Press.

Harris, J. H. (1996) *Edwardian Stories of Divorce*. New Brunswick: Rutgers University Press.

Harvey, J. (1995) *Men in Black*. Chicago: University of Chicago Press.

Jalland, P. (1997) *Death in the Victorian Family*. London: Oxford University Press.

Kübler-Ross, E. (1970) *On Death and Dying*. London: Routledge.

Lerner, L. (1997) *Angels and Absences: Child Deaths in the Nineteenth Century*. Nashville: Vanderbilt University Press.

Lutz, D. (2011) "The Dead Still Among Us: Victorian Secular Relics, Hair Jewelry, and Death Culture." *Victorian Literature and Culture*, 39, 127–42.

Munich, A. (1996) *Queen Victoria's Secrets*. New York: Columbia University Press.

Munk, W. (1887) *Euthanasia: or Medical Treatment in Aid of an Easy Death*. London: Longmans, Green, and Co.

Ramazani, J. (1994) *The Poetry of Mourning: The Modern Elegy from Hardy to Yeats*. Chicago: University of Chicago Press.

Reed, J. R. (1975) *Victorian Conventions*. Athens: Ohio University Press.

Richardson, R. (1989) *Death, Dissection, and the Destitute*. London: Penguin Books.

Rowell, G. (1974) *Hell and the Victorians: A Study of the Nineteenth-Century Theological Controversies Concerning Eternal Punishment and the Future Life.* Oxford: Oxford University Press.

Sacks, P. (1985) *The English Elegy: Studies in the Genre from Spenser to Yeats.* Baltimore: Johns Hopkins University Press.

Schor, E. (1994) *Bearing the Dead: The British Culture of Mourning from the Enlightenment to Victoria.* Princeton: Princeton University Press.

Sinnema, P. (2006) *The Wake of Wellington: Englishness in 1852.* Athens: Ohio University Press.

Stewart, G. (1984) *Death Sentences: Styles of Dying in British Fiction.* Cambridge MA: Harvard University Press.

Tennyson, H. (1897) *Alfred Lord Tennyson: A Memoir,* 2 vols. London: Macmillan.

Wohl, A. (1983) *Endangered Lives: Public Health in Victorian Britain.* Cambridge MA: Harvard University Press.

Wolffe, J. (2000) *Great Deaths: Grieving, Religion, and Nationhood in Victorian and Edwardian Britain.* Oxford: Oxford University Press.

Further Reading

Cannadine, D. (1981) "War and Death, Grief and Mourning in Modern Britain." In *Mirrors of Mortality,* ed. J. Whaley. New York: St Martin's Press.

Hotz, M. E. (2009) *Literary Remains: Representations of Death and Burial in Victorian England.* Albany: State University of New York Press.

Morley, J. (1971) *Death, Heaven, and the Victorians.* Pittsburgh: University of Pittsburgh Press.

O'Gorman, F. (2010) "The Dead." In *The Cambridge Companion to Victorian Culture,* ed. F. O'Gorman. Cambridge: Cambridge University Press.

Oppenheim, J. (1985) *The Other World: Spiritualism and Psychical Research in England 1850–1914.* Cambridge: Cambridge University Press.

Wheeler, M. (1990) *Death and the Future Life in Victorian Literature and Theology.* Cambridge: Cambridge University Press.

9
Victorian Sexualities

James Eli Adams

For the young Virginia Woolf, the world changed one spring evening in 1908, when her friend Lytton Strachey pointed at a stain on her sister's dress and inquired, "Semen?" "With that one word," she recalled,

> all barriers of reticence and reserve went down . . . Sex permeated our conversation. The word bugger was never far from our lips. We discussed copulation with the same excitement and openness that we had discussed the nature of good . . . So there was now nothing that one could not say, nothing that one could not do, at 46 Gordon Square. It was, I think, a great advance in civilisation. (*Moments of Being*, ch. 3)

This galvanizing moment in the formation of "Bloomsbury" may suggest how powerfully the Victorians, those unmentioned parents against whom Woolf and her friends were rebelling, have shaped twentieth-century understandings of sexuality – never more powerfully, perhaps, than in such moments of self-conscious rebellion.

Almost from its first wide currency in the late nineteenth century, "Victorian" has been a byword for a rigorous moralism centered on sexual repression. Long after Strachey challenged Victorian "reticence and reserve," however, its effects continued to be felt in the assumption that the most private and intimate facts about human beings have to do with sex. In the work of Sigmund Freud, himself an eminent late Victorian, sexuality became the paradigm of "deep" truth about human identity. Moreover, sexual repression as Freud described it could be both the foundation of human discipline and the archetype of human oppression. To speak the truth about sex – merely to speak *of* sex – was therefore to address the most basic structures of

---

A New Companion to Victorian Literature and Culture, First Edition. Edited by Herbert F. Tucker.
© 2014 John Wiley & Sons, Ltd. Published 2014 by John Wiley & Sons, Ltd.

knowledge and power. To pronounce the word "semen" in mixed company was not merely a breach of etiquette; it amounted to a revolution. The exhilaration Woolf recalls thus helps to explain why we have been so long entertained by anecdotes about anxious or anesthetic Victorians draping piano legs, concocting euphemistic names for chicken parts, and being told on their wedding nights to "close your eyes and think of England." We have enjoyed this image of Victorian sexuality – or rather, of the Victorian avoidance of sexuality – because it provided us with a basis for proclaiming our own liberation and enlightenment. But this self-congratulation required averting our own gaze from more complicated realities.

Received wisdom about the Victorians and sex has recently been challenged on two broad fronts. First, archival research has led to more thorough knowledge of Victorian private lives and public commentary on them. This research has uncovered much more variety of sexual experience – including erotic fulfillment – and much less unanimity in official stories about that experience. What has been called "the most notorious of Victorian statements about sex," for example, the remark of the physician William Acton that "the majority of women . . . are not very much troubled with sexual feeling of any kind," seems to have been a relatively eccentric medical opinion (Mason 195). Yet the remark continues to be cited as a representative Victorian view, nearly 50 years after it was given prominence in Steven Marcus's pioneering study *The Other Victorians* (1966) – a persistence which suggests the strength of our curiously wishful thinking about the Victorians.

Such wishful thinking has been most trenchantly criticized by the French historian Michel Foucault, who is the main voice of a second, more radical questioning of received views about Victorian sexuality. The Victorians, Foucault urges in his Introduction to *The History of Sexuality*, far from being silent about sex, were caught up in manifold and urgent imperatives to talk about it, and to translate it into "discourses" of knowledge and power. The very concept of "sexuality," we are reminded, is a nineteenth-century invention, which took shape when the traditional moral agency of the priest was subsumed and transformed by developing discourses of (among other things) medicine, biology, psychology, political economy, sanitation, criminology, and law. "The reticences of 'Victorian puritanism,'" in this view, were "a digression, a refinement, a tactical diversion in the great process of transforming sex into discourse" (Foucault 22), a process vigorously forwarded in Woolf's Gordon Square flat. And as this transformation turned sexuality into an object of knowledge and regulation, Foucault contends, it also constructed multiple, heterogeneous forms of sexual identity, in which norms were reinforced by hosts of perversions: sexuality gave way to sexualities, most notably that enduringly tendentious binary, "homosexual" and "heterosexual."

History is of course less neat than this schematic overview implies. But Foucault's suggestions have been provocative in several respects. First, they urge us to see ostensibly marginal or "deviant" forms of sexuality as central to understandings of human identity generally. The very concept of "the heterosexual," for example, is a nineteenth-century invention that follows closely – both logically and chronologically

– the construction of "the homosexual." Moreover, by approaching sexuality as a discursive configuration, Foucault's views have encouraged a fuller awareness of sexuality – the way in which we organize our understanding and experience of erotic life – as a profoundly historical phenomenon, which is responsive to social and political forces that may seem far removed from the world of instinctual drives. In provoking such reflection, finally, Foucault carries on one of the great skeptical commitments of Victorian ethics – one nobly urged by John Stuart Mill, among others: an alertness to the moral obfuscations often wrought by invocations of "nature" and "the natural."

Efforts to comprehend distinctively "Victorian" attitudes to sexuality typically begin well before the birth of the monarch herself, in the late eighteenth-century religious revival loosely known as the "Evangelical" movement. Under the leadership of William Wilberforce, the Evangelicals from roughly the 1780s sought to transform both British politics and everyday conduct by reinvigorating Christian piety, and approaching human life as an arena of constant moral struggle, of resistance to temptation and mastery of desire. For the most vigorous of Evangelicals, pleasure itself was memorably suspect: as Leslie Stephen (Virginia Woolf's father) recalled of his father, "He once smoked a cigar, and found it so delicious that he never smoked again" (Houghton 236).

Of course, the body and its pleasures had always held an uneasy place in Christian ethics, and the Church had long been the dominant sexual authority in the Christian West. In the nineteenth century, however, sex was subjected to a broader array of disciplines; its traditional place in concerns of individual and familial welfare – whether physical, emotional, or spiritual – was subsumed in large economic and political questions. We glimpse this reconfiguration in the economic tropes widely associated with Victorian attitudes to sexuality: sex is a vital force to be carefully regulated and conserved, with potentially dire consequences awaiting those who "spend" too much. There was nothing novel in the mere idea of a sexual economy, which responds to the commonplace experience of sex as a loss of self-possession, the lapse of (traditionally masculine) mastery over oneself and the world (Gay 317). What was distinctive was the vigor and pervasiveness with which Victorians elaborated the congruence of *homo sexualis* and *homo economicus*. That elaboration reflected the remarkable Victorian faith in the power of will. The Industrial Revolution represented a massive and breathtakingly successful investment in disciplining the earth and its inhabitants to human control. The emergent discourse of political economy accordingly pointed the way to success through self-mastery, the power to defer present gratification for later, greater rewards. So, for example, the capitalist's profit was understood as reward for his "abstinence," while the working man was exhorted to emulate that self-discipline as the keystone of what Samuel Smiles called, in one of the best-selling books of the period, "Self-Help" (1859).

Economic thought thus turned the energies of evangelicalism to powerful secular use in pointing a markedly ascetic path to fulfillment: the young Karl Marx wryly called political economy "the science of renunciation." This asceticism was also reinforced by emergent sciences of population, most notably the work of Thomas Malthus, who influentially placed sexuality at the very center of socioeconomic thought. In his *Essay on the Principle of Population* (1798) Malthus famously proposed that human reproduction has an inherent tendency to outstrip advances in food supply. On this view, the very future of mankind depended on a proper regulation of human sexuality – a challenge that led Carlyle to dub economics "the dismal science." Conservative as it might sound, Malthus's work in fact shocked many conservative commentators. The very framing of the problem emphasized that sex was a central feature of healthy human life, even as it confounded the biblical exhortation to be fruitful and multiply. At the same time, Malthus (who was an Anglican clergyman) believed that sex was intended solely for reproduction, which led him to refuse one obvious solution to the ostensible problem, contraception. The leading response to the challenge, Malthus urged, would be "moral restraint" – an emphasis echoed throughout the writings of early political economists, who nowhere allow for the possibility that population dynamics might be shaped by other kinds of human intervention (Folbre).

Well before Victoria came to the throne, then, self-discipline was a pervasive theme in British culture, whose prominence confounds any simple understanding of sexual politics. Malthus, for example, intended his *Essay* principally as a rebuke to the utopianism of the French Revolution and its sympathizers – most notably, the British philosophical radical William Godwin. And yet Godwin's own vision of an ideal society, set forth in *Political Justice* (1793), was itself powerfully anti-sensual: the progress of civilization, it held, would be marked by the withering away of sexual desire, to the point where reproduction would be a social duty wholly susceptible to rational control. This unexpected congruence points to a further strand in the genealogy of Victorian sexualities, which emerges most clearly in avowedly radical or dissident stances: post-Enlightenment schemes of progress often disdain sex as an "animal" function at odds with a distinctively human rationality. Thus, the early feminist Mary Wollstonecraft complained in *A Vindication of the Rights of Woman* (1792) that the education of women solely for marriage made "mere animals of them," turning them into "weak beings fit only for a seraglio." More than half a century later, John Stuart Mill – the leading mid-Victorian male advocate of women's rights – confided to his diary that "any great improvement in human life is not to be looked for so long as the animal instinct of sex occupies the absurdly disproportionate place it does therein."

As it makes for such unlikely bedfellows – conservative and radical, atheist and pious – the pervasiveness of Victorian asceticism suggests the political leverage inherent in the ideal of sexual discipline. In justifying attacks on an allegedly dissolute, profligate aristocracy for failing to live up to its inherited authority, self-restraint became a highly effective basis for claiming moral authority for the middle classes. Despite the persistent assumption that Victorian public and private realms were "separate spheres" divided along rigidly gendered lines, Victorian domestic virtues were charged with public significance (anticipating in this regard their late twentieth-century recrudescence as "family values"). This significance, arising out of Evangelical celebrations of the family, gained wide currency with George IV's divorce proceedings against his wife, Caroline, in 1820. That the notoriously dissolute, adulterous king should publicly accuse his wife of infidelity aroused widespread revulsion, and prompted a host of tributes to an imagined "quiet domestic nest" set against George's public debauchery (Davidoff and Hall 153). The ascension of a female monarch in 1837 provided occasion for locating such a refuge at the very heart of the British state.

Over much of Victoria's reign the quiet domestic nest was elaborated into a conception of "home" as an ideal repository of sympathy and tranquility centered on the middle-class wife and mother, who was apotheosized in John Ruskin's *Sesame and Lilies* (1865). In what became the most enduring icon of Victorian anti-sensualism, the domestic woman was "the angel in the house" (a phrase borrowed from Coventry Patmore), a quasi-spiritual being selflessly dispensing love and moral guidance to her family, largely untroubled by wayward personal desires – including erotic longing. What we now know about the rich sensuality of many Victorian marriages makes this peculiar ideal seem all the stranger. The most familiar explanation – that it made the home a haven from the cutthroat world of Victorian economic struggle – focuses on its appeal to men, and does not account for its anti-eroticism. But the angelic ideal did offer women a dignity absent in traditional notions of the woman as temptress, that image of unregulated sensuality against which Wollstonecraft and others had rebelled. "Passionlessness," as Nancy Cott has argued, might seem a norm worth embracing in return for this moral elevation. Nonetheless, the persistent dichotomy between dignity and desire – the absence of a middle ground between erotic enthrallment and a perfectly disinterested "influence" – tellingly reflects the enduring force of anti-sensualism in all its forms.

The angel's appeal to men seems easier to grasp: not only did she offer an image of complete subservience, but she enforced a disjunction between female morality and female power. The very unworldliness of woman's love, it was claimed, made it important that she be insulated from the coarsening influences of public life – such as the right to vote. Still, for all but the closest readers of *Paradise Lost*, sex with an angel might seem a daunting prospect. Yet many Victorian men seem to have thought that the very social order depended on the power of angelic womanhood: as Krafft-Ebing remarked in his *Psychopathia Sexualis* (9th edn, 1894), "Were it not so, the whole world would be a bordello, and marriage and the family unthinkable" (Gay 154). Even in Krafft-Ebing's cynicism, however, we glimpse a further, more subtle impulse animating the angelic ideal: a widespread Victorian unease with male sexual aggression. In political economy, evangelical religion, and radical politics over the first half of the century, the aristocratic manhood that stressed social graces and sexual prowess was challenged by a norm of "character" understood as inward fortitude, self-regulation, and a sense of duty. The ascendancy of this new ideal can be measured by the force of sexual scandals in Victorian politics. Whereas the widely known sexual adventures of Melbourne and Palmerston, two of Victoria's early prime ministers, were politely overlooked, the careers of two important late-century MPs, Charles Parnell and Sir Charles Dilke, were destroyed by extramarital affairs. In the interval, Tennyson's vastly popular *Idylls of the King* (1859–85), with its markedly passive, feminized king likening his unfaithful queen to a virulent "disease," suggested that the angel in the house could appeal to men as an emblem of freedom from – or at least the mastery of – desires that they themselves found discomforting. A similar point might be drawn from the many ritual humiliations of male characters in Victorian fiction – Charlotte Brontë's Rochester, Dickens's Eugene Wrayburn, and Thackeray's Henry Esmond, among others – who enjoy moral redemption, and the love of the heroine, only after their aggression has been thoroughly disarmed, even to the extent of physical incapacitation. While these scenarios typically conjure up the redemptive agency of a woman in gratification of a man's desires, they also place the heroes in conditions of traditionally feminine passivity – and at times evoke the less orthodox pleasures of masochism.

As they set morality in collision with sexuality, the idealizing impulses of Victorian domesticity point to the culmination of Victorian asceticism in Freud's pronouncement, "It is not possible for the claims of the sexual instinct to be reconciled with the demands of culture" (see Marcus vii). Ironically, however, by the time of Freud's assessment, culture had come to seem in many respects more sexually hospitable. Although British writers rarely displayed the sexual license invariably associated with all things French, popular novelists addressing a largely working-class audience, such as G. W. M. Reynolds, had long presented female characters in highly sensual prose that sometimes borders on soft-core pornography. And even domestic novelists aiming at a more decorous readership developed rich strategies of indirection and obliquity for representing sexuality, not only by projecting it onto stigmatized bodies – fallen women and predatory men – but also through more subtle embodiments of desire in morally compelling characters. The sheer power of repression displayed by George Eliot's heroines, for example, works as much to evoke as to regulate a richly sensual inner life, reminding us that the very austerities of "character" could be sexy. Indeed, repression itself is frequently eroticized in Victorian novels, where it is presented as a seductive index of libidinal depth, as in the contrast between Jane Eyre and her overtly sensual rivals, Blanche Ingram and Bertha Rochester – aristocracy and madness both signifying a failure of erotic discipline (Kucich). The sensuality repudiated in *Jane Eyre* became a more central and overtly disruptive presence in the "sensation" novels of the 1860s, in the wake of national debate over women's rights to property ownership and divorce. Heroines like Mary Braddon's Lady Audley, who resisted or cunningly manipulated norms of domestic femininity, invariably conjured up a troubling yet seductive sexual autonomy. Meanwhile, adventure narratives animated by an expanding consciousness of imperial rule became a popular vehicle for renewed celebration of physically aggressive masculinity. In his sermons and novels such as *Westward Ho!* (1855) Charles Kingsley became the leading voice of "muscular Christianity," which repudiated the early-Victorian austerity of Evangelicalism and the Oxford Movement. In the works of "the apostle of the flesh," as Kingsley was dubbed, sexual desire was ostensibly sublimated in athletic prowess, but critics recognized in Kingsley's glorification of the body and its instincts a recrudescence of traditional marital norms that (they objected) could be taken to license profligacy.

Kingsley's career opens a surprising link between the Victorian cult of athleticism and the rise of aestheticism, another cultural development centrally concerned with rescuing the body from ascetic morality. As "morality" in popular usage became increasingly identified with purity, conflicts over the moral dimensions of art were typically fought out in terms of its sexual content. Swinburne, at the forefront of the cultural avant-garde in the 1860s, claimed moral autonomy for his poetry through the sexual audacity of its subject matter, which included incest, necrophilia, homo-erotic desire, and a consistently sado-masochistic rendering of pleasure in terms of domination and pain. The 1850s and 1860s also saw a revival of interest in the sexual content of painting and sculpture, whether in debate over the morality of the nude as artistic subject or (more subtly) in speculation over the erotics of creativity and collecting, a recurrent preoccupation of Robert Browning's monologues. Criticism of erotic content in art predictably took a highly sexualized bent as well – although of a divided character that would prove increasingly central to late-century understand-ings of culture. The representation of women in avant-garde painting and poetry was frequently attacked as a form of traditional male promiscuity: "the fleshly school of poetry" was one critic's phrase for the work of Swinburne and D. G. Rossetti. Yet avant-garde celebrations of ancient Greece as a culture unburdened by "conscience" – and thus a model for contemporary artists – aroused another, more nervous suspicion in conservative commentators: that the forms of Greek art might cater to powerful homoerotic desires.

Mid-Victorian culture was thus marked by a newly emphatic, broad-based concern with the uses of pleasure (an emphasis congruent with the shifting focus of economic theory from production to consumption). In medicine, this concern was most point-edly registered in the issue of contraception: although still opposed by the medical establishment, it was evidently widely used by the 1860s, to gauge by the marked decline in middle-class family size from that decade. Indeed, one of the best-selling medical works of the period, *The Elements of Social Science* (1855), was an "underground" treatise by the elusive George Drysdale, which offered an account of reproductive health united with an apology for free love (and the use of contraceptives) as a remedy to both personal and social problems. The extraordinary popularity of Drysdale's book suggests that anti-sensual medical authority was often of limited influence. The well-known Victorian obsession with masturbation is the leading exception, representing as it does a remarkably widespread and psychologically traumatic fantasy. "Masturba-tion mania" remains a perplexing phenomenon, but as it focuses suspicion and discipline on the most antisocial of sexual practices, the one least amenable to regula-tion, it perfectly exemplifies Foucauldian dicta regarding the far-reaching authority of "medico-juridical" discourse. Nonetheless, Victorian medical literature on the whole displays a more diverse and, from a modern vantage, much healthier array of attitudes than most Foucauldian accounts allow. Female orgasm, for example, is ubiquitous in medical literature, not least because of widespread belief that women must experience orgasm to conceive (Mason 201ff.). Thus, the familiar image of a Victorian married woman's "joyless inhibition and ignorance," Mason suggests, may conceal another somber reality, "of women fearing and regretting sexual pleasure because they above all wished to avoid having another child." Despite all the reserve surrounding female sexuality, however, for Victorian medical writers marriage in large part *is* sex, the one arena in which sexual activity is not merely licensed but encouraged – a fact stressed more obliquely in the large families that populate so much Victorian fiction.

Reproduction became a more problematic issue in relation to what Engels famously called "the condition of the working class." For almost all commentators (few of whom were themselves working-class) the problems of the urban poor were centrally bound up with sexuality, which was typically understood as a challenge of sanitation. Victorian urban surveyors such as James Kay-Shuttleworth, Henry Mayhew, and William Booth were invariably agitated by a "promiscuous mixture of the sexes" within the crowded spaces inhabited by the urban poor. "How they lay down to rest, how they sleep, how they can preserve common decency, how unutterable horrors are avoided, is beyond all conception," one observer wrote (Mort 38). As Frank Mort points out, this discourse offered no positive representations of sexuality: it was a form of "licentiousness" quite explicitly likened to disease or contagion. It is against this backdrop of foreboding and danger that the middle-class characters of Dickens, for example, venture into the hovel of the nameless brickmaker's family in *Bleak House* (1853). Such visits, which frequently suggest a proto-anthropological contact with alien cultures, might have many different motivations; even the more disinterested accounts, however, tend to have a profound aura of fantasy, depicting as they do either exaggerated submission or complete obliviousness on the part of the poor to the strangers who have been ushered into their homes. In the mesmerized preoccupation of urban chroniclers, the sexual anxieties of Malthus, under which the reproductive body is a constant threat to social well-being, were reinforced by what seemed a demonic subversion of Victorian domesticity, in which the threat of incest is unmistakable.

The condition of the urban poor was a standing embarrassment to Victorian schemes of progress, a reminder of how many seemed to have been left behind. In this regard, as George Stocking (1987) has pointed out, Victorians confronted a "savageness" at home as well as abroad, which in both locales was associated with a dangerously unregulated sexuality. That very association provided one answer to the social problem, the loosely Malthusian view that the poor were largely responsible for their own predicament, owing to their lack of self-discipline. "Done because we are too menny," the grotesque suicide note left by "Father Time" in Hardy's *Jude the Obscure* (1895), offers a mordant comment on this logic. In middle-class representations of working-class men, this failure was typically figured as a tendency to drunkenness and violence. Among the female poor, the failure of self-control was more often identified with promiscuous sexuality. But the sympathy frequently accorded the "fallen woman" in contemporary novels and melodrama – in Gaskell's *Ruth* (1853) and Dickens's *Oliver Twist* (1838), to name just two – not only acknowledges the social pressures besetting working-class women; it also evokes a distinctly Victorian pathos, which tacitly sets a sexualized degradation against the lost redemptive possibility of domestic femininity. A less sentimental view is offered by widespread accounts of female workers sexually exploited by their employers, or by affluent strangers such as the pseudonymous Walter in *My Secret Life* (ca. 1890), for whom working-class women were virtually indistinguishable from prostitutes.

Prostitution has long seemed the most glaring example of the Victorian double standard. While commentators of every stripe celebrated the virtues of self-control and marital fidelity, prostitution became an ever more visible feature of life in the burgeoning towns and cities. In large part this prominence seems to have been a by-product of social mobility and economic insecurity. Middle-class men – and those with ambitions to be such – increasingly postponed marriage until they achieved a modicum of economic security requisite to "respectability," and in the interval – licensed by traditional norms of masculinity – seem to have found sexual gratification with prostitutes. On the other hand, for many women, predominantly but not exclusively working class, prostitution was a means of supplementing or replacing the notoriously dismal wages and working conditions of domestic service or piece work. Yet the demographics of prostitution remain elusive, not only because of the circumspection inherent in the activity, but because contemporary surveys were typically responsive to spasmodic outbreaks of something akin to moral panic in the popular press. In such panic, one glimpses a further reason for the prominence of prostitution in the Victorian imagination: the uneasy recognition later codified by Freud, that when "culture" is identified with sexual purity, many erotic drives can be satisfied only outside the bounds of respectability.

Prostitution would occasion the single most controversial state intervention into Victorian sexuality, the series of Contagious Diseases Acts passed during the 1860s. Here public anxiety was aroused by the effects of prostitution, not on respectable domesticity or urban life, but on the health of the military, where it was feared that sexually transmitted diseases would undermine Britain's imperial vigor. Under the Acts, which applied to an increasing number of naval ports and army garrison towns, women suspected of prostitution were subject to forced medical examination and detention without trial for up to three (subsequently six) months. The legislation quickly prompted what would become one of the galvanizing episodes in an emergent feminist movement, as many women protested that these regulations only reaffirmed the traditional sexual double standard, failing to require any self-restraint on the part of men while depriving women of basic civil liberties. The familiar rhetorics of early Victorian sexual discipline were thus harnessed to new political concerns: in Josephine Butler's words, the outcry was that of "women crushed under the yoke of legalized vice" (Mort 93).

But these protests had reverberations beyond feminist politics. The Acts represented a newly specific intervention of state authority in sexual conduct, which entailed not only intensified forms of police surveillance, but also increasingly precise typologies of sexual deviance (which, ironically, often proved unable to distinguish prostitutes from "respectable" women). Although the Acts were repealed in 1886, opposition to them had been subsumed in a nationwide purity campaign that in turn generated new targets of sexual regulation (and new sexual norms). In 1885, the editor of the *Pall Mall Gazette*, W. T. Stead, published a series of articles entitled "The Maiden Tribute of Modern Babylon," luridly exposing child prostitution in England. The resultant storm of protest goaded Parliament to pass the Criminal Law Amendment, "An Act to make further provision for the Protection of Women and Girls, the suppression of brothels, and other purposes." While the Act was principally concerned to formalize ages of consent and dictate harsher punishment for owners of brothels, it has become best known for a last-minute addition, the so-called Labouchere amendment (section 11), which introduced into law a new statutory category. Any man convicted of "any act of gross indecency with another male person," it stipulated, might be punished by up to two years at hard labor – the very sentence that ten years later would be passed on Oscar Wilde. The concern with regulation of male lust thus converged with a new conception of sexual identity anticipated in the rise of aestheticism: the homosexual.

This new category is the best-known outgrowth of the far-reaching "normalizing" of sexuality over the course of the nineteenth century. Sex between men has been around from time immemorial, but there is little evidence that men who enjoyed such activity therefore thought of themselves as different *in kind* from other men. At some point, however, in Foucault's influential rendering, what had been an activity was reconceived as a form of identity: "The sodomite had been a temporary aberration; the homosexual was now a species" (Foucault 43). British law included longstanding prohibitions against sodomy, but this crime traditionally had been understood as any sexual act "against nature," not just between men. What was new in the Labouchere amendment was the inclusiveness of the term "acts of gross indecency" and its specific application to relations between men as a separate category of offense – a category further solidified by the concept of the "homosexual," a term that gained currency in Britain in the 1890s following the translation of Krafft-Ebing's *Psychopathia Sexualis*. Labouchere's statute, moreover, firmly rebuked the secularizing tolerance of utilitarian reform through much of the century: Bentham himself had drafted various arguments for decriminalizing sexual relations between men, although it was a measure of the force of traditional morality that even this intrepid dissident refrained from publication.

More difficult to gauge are understandings of transgressive sexual desire outside "official" discourse. This has proved a special challenge with regard to lesbian relationships, which were more readily confined within traditionally feminine privacies, and thus amenable to greater circumspection under the guise of "romantic friendship" or spinsterhood (Vicinus). Among men, what Eve Kosofsky Sedgwick has called "the homosocial continuum" of male–male relations is not only more visible, but far more central to social power: traditionally almost every social structure – including marriage – locates power in some form of bond between men. Much recent work on

Victorian sexualities has explored the erotic investments of those bonds – such as the friendship between Tennyson and A. H. Hallam, commemorated in *In Memoriam* – particularly as they were affected by what Sedgwick calls "male homosexual panic," the fear of being perceived to be "interested in men." In this context, the figure of "the homosexual" codifies a homophobia that imposes on the homosocial continuum (and, more broadly, the field of gendered identity) a single, momentous binary of sexual object choice. Like the work of Foucault, Sedgwick's speculations thus offer an influential account of the social and political dimensions of ostensibly private desires.

More elusive than homophobia, unsurprisingly, are sympathetic constructions of unorthodox sexualities, which would attempt to transform stigma into affirmation. Half a century after Bentham's plea for tolerance, as Linda Dowling has shown, a more concerted, although still guarded, apology for male–male desire developed out of the Victorian interest in classical Greece. As the rise of aestheticism drew new attention to the place of sexuality in art, a group of writers associated with Oxford liberalism subtly emphasized the pronounced homoeroticism informing Greek art and culture. The writings of Plato and the relics of Greek sculpture, in particular, thus provided occasion to celebrate not only individual liberty, but a distinctly homoerotic cultural tradition, and with it a sense of historical and ethical community – an achievement most evocatively realized in Walter Pater's 1867 essay "Winckelmann." By the 1890s, this project had branched into a host of offshoots, including a "Uranian" poetry of pederastic desire, a "new chivalry" of male comradeship that looked to the model of Sparta, and Wilde's arch punning on "Dorian" beauty. Through such apologies, a proscribed sexual identity became associated not only with a particular historical epoch, but with rhetorical strategies that would become hallmarks of literary modernism. As homoerotic writers tacitly addressed an informed, sympathetic elite within a larger audience, they invited a form of "double reading," thereby developing strategies of obliquity and reserve that would be central to the emergence of modernist writing in the works of Henry James and others.

Such rich strategies of obliquity and indirection depended on a body of sexual knowledge that was unsettled, multiple, and often indeterminate. Writers like Pater and Wilde daringly exploited points of contact and disjunction between the often radically different modes of awareness that distinguished initiates from the culture at large. The newspaper-reading public certainly would have had glimpses of homosexual subcultures from at least 1870, which saw the widely reported prosecution of two male transvestites, Boulton and Park; in 1889, the exposure of a male brothel in Cleveland Street caused a much greater sensation, which included the rumored involvement of Prince Albert Victor. But even in such widely publicized cases, discretion typically veiled the most telling details, both sexual and social. This reticence allowed the scandals to be submerged in vaguer and more familiar tales of aristocratic profligacy or working-class corruption, which evoked in turn a public response recalling early Victorian attacks on debauchery. Only with the trials of Oscar Wilde in 1895 was a clear image of "the homosexual" firmly fixed in the public mind, along with a vivid association of literary and sexual "decadence."

In the Wilde trials, oblique and idealizing literary constructions of a new masculinity collided with the demotic world of sexual trade. For middle- and upper-class men, male–male sexuality was largely governed by the cash nexus: it was most readily available through prostitutes. This was a predicament rife with potential for extortion – the Labouchere amendment quickly was dubbed "the blackmailer's charter" – and thus for scandal, on which the popular press increasingly seized. Wilde, however, offered prosecutors and journalists a uniquely resonant occasion to denounce both the cultural avant-garde and sexual deviancy as facets of a more inclusive "degeneration" (the title of Max Nordau's 1895 best-seller). The result was an enduring popular image of both homosexual and artist. The middle-class Wilde, as Alan Sinfield points out, had appropriated a traditionally aristocratic "effeminacy" of demeanor as a means of underscoring his cultural pretensions: with his arrest and conviction, that attribute became the distinguishing mark of the homosexual. The vagaries surrounding "gross indecency" were dispelled by a damningly unequivocal image, conjured up by the anguished confession of the title character in E. M. Forster's 1912 novel *Maurice*: "I'm an unspeakable of the Oscar Wilde sort" (ch. 31).

Wilde thus became the prototype of the "homosexual role," which, as Mary McIntosh has argued, serves to carefully delimit a disturbing presence, to keep the rest of society pure, much as the labeling of delinquency helps to keep the rest of society law-abiding. The stigmatizing force of the Wilde trials helped to freeze what had been a decade of tremendous upheaval in sex and gender roles. During this tumult, which George Gissing summed up as "sexual anarchy," new possibilities and confusions were debated and enacted in virtually every realm of British life. In the midst of the purity campaigns of the 1880s, a literary avant-garde welcomed a wealth of sexually daring foreign works, most notably Zola's novels and Ibsen's dramas, both of which launched frontal assaults on conventional morality, not least through associating its effects with inherited syphilis. A more subtle but wide-ranging scrutiny of domesticity was sparked in 1888 by Mona Caird's series of columns in the *Daily Telegraph*, "Is Marriage a Failure?", which elicited a staggering 27,000 replies. As the controversy aired visions of alternatives to domesticity, it helped shape an image of the "New Woman," who refused the consolations of marriage to pursue new forms of independence and fulfillment, sometimes alone, sometimes with men outside of marriage, sometimes with other women, and sometimes in agonized indecision – the last memorably embodied in the character of Sue Bridehead in Hardy's *Jude the Obscure*. In the so-called "New Woman" fiction of Sarah Grand, George Egerton and others, writers discarded the familiar marriage plot to evoke female autonomy through narrative innovation and indeterminacy. As in most forms of Victorian reticence, however, the refusal of normative sexuality tends to be much clearer than the affirmation of an alternative. A similar indeterminacy attends the male "decadent," who is a counterpart of the New Woman in his refusal of familiar norms of gendered destiny. Although most often associated with homosexuality, the decadent as embodied in such figures as Wilde's Dorian Gray is a manifoldly "perverse" character, estranged from not only conventional sexual relations but social life generally, along with most traditional moral imperatives.

This seeming explosion of new sexual possibilities – at once exhilarating, threatening, and bewildering – confounds the familiar associations of "Victorian" with repression; indeed, it has struck many as an uncanny foreshadowing of the cultural moment we inhabit now. But the congruence between late Victorian sexualities and our own goes beyond the well-publicized and fiercely debated proliferation of sexual alternatives. The very notion of sexuality as a subject of critical study is itself an outgrowth of the "sexual anarchy" that prompted the pioneering "sexology" undertaken by Havelock Ellis and others in the 1890s. And this genealogy may confirm the larger relevance of Victorian attitudes to our own time, not as a benightedness over which we have triumphed, but as the prototype of our own powerfully divided understandings of sexuality: as both bestial and angelic, utterly banal and profoundly mysterious, a "natural" instinct and a cultural imperative, merely "animal" yet a crux of human identity, "unspeakable" and yet our enduring obsession.

See also MEDICAL, INDUSTRIAL; FICTION; SKIN, PARAPETS, SHORE

REFERENCES

Cott, N. (1978) "Passionlessness: An Interpretation of Victorian Sexual Ideology, 1790–1850." *Signs* 4, 219–36.

Davidoff, L., and C. Hall (1987) *Family Fortunes: Men and Women of the English Middle Class, 1780–1850*. Chicago: University of Chicago Press.

Dowling, L. (1995) *Hellenism and Homosexuality in Victorian Oxford*. Ithaca: Cornell University Press.

Folbre, N. (1992) "'The Improper Arts': Sex in Classical Political Economy." *Population and Development Review* 18, 105–21.

Foucault, M. (1978) *The History of Sexuality*, vol. 1: *An Introduction*, trans. R. Hurley. New York: Random House.

Gay, P. (1984) *The Bourgeois Experience: Victoria to Freud*, vol. 1: *Education of the Senses*. New York: Oxford University Press.

Houghton, W. (1957) *The Victorian Frame of Mind*. New Haven: Yale University Press.

Kucich, J. (1987) *Repression in Victorian Fiction: Charlotte Brontë, George Eliot, and Charles Dickens*. Berkeley: University of California Press.

McIntosh, M. (1968) "The Homosexual Role." *Social Problems* 16, 182–92.

Marcus, S. (1966) *The Other Victorians: A Study of Sexuality and Pornography in Mid-Nineteenth-Century England*. New York: Basic Books.

Mason, M. (1994) *The Making of Victorian Sexuality*. Oxford and New York: Oxford University Press.

Mort, F. (1987) *Dangerous Sexualities: Medico-Moral Politics in England since 1830*. London and New York: Routledge and Kegan Paul.

Sedgwick, E. K. (1985) *Between Men: English Literature and Male Homosocial Desire*. New York: Columbia University Press.

Sinfield, A. (1994) *The Wilde Century: Effeminacy, Oscar Wilde, and the Queer Moment*. New York: Columbia University Press.

Stocking, G. W., Jr (1987) *Victorian Anthropology*. New York: Free Press.

Vicinus, M. (2004) *Intimate Friends: Women who Loved Women, 1778–1928*. Chicago: University of Chicago Press.

FURTHER READING

Adams, J. E. (1995) *Dandies and Desert Saints: Styles of Victorian Masculinity*. Ithaca and London: Cornell University Press.

Cocks, H. G. (2003) *Nameless Offenses: Homosexual Desire in the Nineteenth Century*. London: I. B. Tauris.

Cohen, W. A. (1996) *Sex Scandal: The Private Parts of Victorian Fiction*. Durham NC: Duke University Press.

Craft, C. (1994) *Another Kind of Love*. Berkeley: University of California Press.

Mason, M. (1994) *The Making of Victorian Sexual Attitudes*. Oxford and New York: Oxford University Press.

Maynard, J. (1993) *Victorian Discourses of Sexuality and Religion*. Cambridge: Cambridge University Press.

Michie, H. (2006) *Victorian Honeymoons: Journeys to the Conjugal*. Cambridge: Cambridge University Press.

Miller, A. H., and J. E. Adams (eds) (1996) *Sexualities in Victorian Britain*. Bloomington: Indiana University Press.

Nead, L. (1988) *Myths of Sexuality: Representations of Women in Victorian Britain*. Oxford: Blackwell Publishers.

Rosenman, E. B. (2003) *Unauthorized Pleasures: Accounts of Victorian Erotic Experience*. Ithaca: Cornell University Press.

Sedgwick, E. K. (1992) *Epistemology of the Closet*. Berkeley: University of California Press.

Showalter, E. (1990) *Sexual Anarchy: Gender and Culture at the Fin de Siècle*. New York: Penguin Books.

Walkowitz, J. (1980) *Prostitution in Victorian Society*. Cambridge: Cambridge University Press.

Part Three
Walks of Life

10
Clerical

Christine L. Krueger

To write about the Victorian clerical walk of life is to follow in the footsteps of a Victorian, John Cordy Jeaffreson, whose breezy two-volume *Book about the Clergy* (1870) came between his popular books about doctors and lawyers. It is notable that we share with Jeaffreson's readers an interest in nineteenth-century versions of the ancient professions and inevitable that our focus, like his, must be on the Christian clergy, which was the dominant clerical presence. Jeaffreson, who discussed only clergy of the established or Anglican Church, wrote admiringly of the civilizing influence of clergymen and their wives on isolated rural parishes. His mildly satirical treatment of the clergy's social position, particularly as marriage prospects for status-seeking daughters of the *nouveaux riches*, makes for entertaining reading to this day. Unlike Jeaffreson's audience, however, readers of this volume will expect recognition of the diversity of Victorian faiths and of the wide range of religious vocations within Victorian Christianity. Protestants constituted the largest religious group by far, but membership in the Established Church declined relative to dissenting Protestant sects. Roman Catholics, who made up the majority in Ireland, were a growing minority in England. The Trinitarian Act (1812) had legalized the practice of Islam. Though their numbers were small, Muslims as well as Hindus made their mark on British society. In 1828 and 1829, legislation ended a range of religious exclusions, including that against Catholics and Jews serving in Parliament. Between 1830 and 1911, the Jewish population grew from around 30,000 to nearly 300,000 (Finestein xv).

Leaders of most of the world's principal religions were found in Victorian Britain. Rabbis were a significant presence, and the Hindu and Muslim communities also

A New Companion to Victorian Literature and Culture, First Edition. Edited by Herbert F. Tucker.
© 2014 John Wiley & Sons, Ltd. Published 2014 by John Wiley & Sons, Ltd.

boasted influential figures, if not always clergy, *per se*. The Protestant emphasis on preaching produced a distinctive Anglo-Jewish pastorate, whose rabbis increasing delivered sermons in English aimed at unifying the diverse Jewish community (Finestein 54–5). Rabbi Nathan Marcus Hakohen Adler, chief rabbi of the British Empire from 1845 until his death in 1890, founded the National Society for the Protection and Better Treatment of Children and was considered the leading Orthodox rabbi in the English-speaking world. In 1889, Western Europe's first purpose-built mosque outside of Spain, the Shah Jahan mosque, was opened in Woking. It was built by Dr Gottlieb Wilhelm Leitner, a Jewish immigrant from Hungary, who had served as Principal of the Government College in Lahore from 1864 until his return to England in 1883. The prominent Indian Hindu reformer Raja Ram Mohan Roy spent the last four years of his life in England (1829–33), during which he had an audience with William IV and left a lasting influence on British social reformers. Swami Vivekananda visited England in 1895 and 1896, giving talks on Hinduism.

Still, the story of the Victorian clergy is principally a Christian one, a story offering its own share of diversity. Indeed, varieties of religious vocation among Victorian Christians defy strict definitions of "clergy," ranging instead from priests to lay preachers to believers who experienced a calling to repent and share the gospel, among them uneducated workers and women. The term "clergy" may refer exclusively to ordained ministers – bishops, priests, and deacons – who were understood to descend in a direct line from the sacrament of holy orders instituted by Jesus. Most denominations, particularly the Anglican and Roman Catholic Churches, restricted certain sacramental and pastoral duties to ordained clergymen: they alone performed baptisms, marriages, and funerals, and conferred holy orders. Across denominations, elite clergy might acquire celebrity status, ranging from the Catholic Cardinal Manning, who was to receive the dubious distinction of a chapter in Lytton Strachey's *Eminent Victorians* (1918), to Dr John Cumming, the evangelical preacher attacked by George Eliot for ignorance and bigotry, who attracted huge crowds to his London sermons. More often than not, elite professional status and humble service were reconciled. For example, the Revd John Keble, founder of the Oxford Movement and author of *The Christian Year* (1827), one of the century's most popular poems, was known to his country parishioners not as a celebrity with an international reputation but as the parson who lived among them, conducted their services, and taught daily in the village school (Colloms 24). In St Peter's use of the term, however, *kleros* (1 Peter 5: 3) comprised the entire priesthood of believers. In many nonconforming Protestant sects, such as the Quakers and Primitive Baptists, lay persons preached, taught scripture, and led prayer. During the Victorian period, laity in the Established Church also came to share more pastoral duties with clergy. Conversely, the ordained clergy participated in secular activities as scientists, philologists, historians, and literary authors. Only Roman Catholic priests vowed celibacy; most clergy, like most Victorians in other walks of life, functioned in a network of domestic relationships, and members of their families – especially parsons' wives – were expected to share parish duties, though they had no formal status. In significant respects, the boundaries between clergy and laity were permeable, and many Victorians understood themselves to have a religious vocation whether they enjoyed institutional recognition or not, while others held a clerical title but felt no sense of vocation whatsoever.

Christians, ordained or lay, and regardless of denomination, shared one common ground, the Bible, which therefore offers an appropriate starting point for a discussion of clerical life in Victorian Britain. An appreciation of the extent of lay people's Bible literacy is key to understanding Victorian culture. The Bible was preached from pulpits, read daily by heads of households to family members and servants and by Bible readers in the homes of the poor, dispensed through domestic and foreign mission societies, and studied in Church-sponsored and nonconforming study groups, as well as by clerical biblical scholars. Victorian printing technologies enabled the realization of evangelical dreams of mass Bible distribution: for example, John Cassell's *Illustrated Family Bible* (1836–8) sold 300,000 copies a week in one-penny numbers. The Bible provided a common cultural currency for Christian clergy and laity – what Elizabeth Gaskell in *Mary Barton* (1848) called "Bible language" – and, as George Landow has shown, a widely shared typology by which to interpret history, politics, art, and individual experience. In 1828 Macaulay declared of the English Bible that, "if everything else in our language should perish, [it] would alone suffice to show the whole extent of its beauty and power."

Controversies centered on the Bible demonstrate its importance as a cohesive force in Victorian culture. Biblical scholars upset both fellow clerics and the laity when, in 1870, they appeared ready to sacrifice the beauty and power of the King James Version (KJV) to historical and linguistic accuracy with a new translation. Scholarly expertise and Church authority could not subdue personal devotion, however, and the KJV continued to sell briskly after the English Revised Version was published in 1881 (New Testament) and 1885 (Old Testament). The Revised Version was only one consequence of the principal religious controversy of the Victorian period, which pitted a majority of clerics and lay people, committed to a belief in scripture as the word of God, against historical biblical scholars. Geology and biology may have threatened biblical literalism from without, but clerics engaged in textual and philological criticism – such as B. F. Westcott, Cambridge Divinity Professor and Bishop of Durham, and his colleague the Revd Fenton J. A. Hort, who together produced a major critical text of the Greek New Testament (1881) – opened a gap between naive and critical belief within both the clergy and the laity. Faced with these challenges to belief, the best Alfred Tennyson could offer in *In Memoriam* (1850) was "faith that comes from self-control" (section 131, l. 9). And Matthew Arnold, son of the Broad Church clergyman Dr Thomas Arnold, in "Stanzas from the Grande Chartreuse" (1861) described himself as "Wandering between two worlds, one dead, / The other powerless to be born" (ll. 85–6). Yet in his spiritual autobiography *Sartor Resartus* (1833–4) Thomas Carlyle could assert an "Everlasting Yea" against skepticism, and in the same year as

In Memoriam Robert Browning's poem *Christmas-Eve* would review the options of German Higher Criticism and Roman Catholicism only to reassert the vitality of Nonconformist Protestantism. From one point of view, then, the clash between literalists and critics produced a "crisis of faith." But from another point of view, both of these movements contributed to a consequence fully consistent with the logic of Protestantism: the empowerment of individual conscience as the final authority in religious questions, realizing a "priesthood of the people."

Against this backdrop of a pervasive Bible Christianity, we can turn to the diversity of Christian clerical experience in the Victorian period. At the opening of Victoria's reign new Anglican ordinands joined a powerful but troubled institution, while the ministers of the nonconforming denominations and, eventually, Roman Catholic priests, were gaining in prestige and influence. The Established Church was actually two: the Church of England, which was episcopal (bishop-governed), and the Church of Scotland, which was presbyterian (elder-governed). This bit of illogic predicated on Scottish nationalism and English political compromise was not lost on Victorian supporters of disestablishment. Numerous nonconforming or dissenting Protestant sects existed alongside the Established Church, with their own ministers and governing organizations. Most prominent among these groups were the Methodists, Quakers, Presbyterians, Congregationalists, Unitarians, and Baptists. In 1850, the Roman Catholic hierarchy in Britain was restored by Pope Pius IX. Though its share of Christian congregants declined through the nineteenth century, the Established Church remained politically dominant, not only through such means as mandatory tithes, control of the schools and universities, and blasphemy and heresy prosecutions, but also because of the gentlemanly status of the majority of Anglican clergy and their followers. The Anglican Church was jokingly known as the Tory party at prayer.

The elaborate hierarchy of the Established Church suggests why Victorian detractors characterized the clergy as preoccupied with professional status and governance rather than pastoral duties. The Established Church was headed by Queen Victoria, who inherited from Henry VIII the title "Defender of the Faith." The government appointed the clerical leaders of the Church, the Archbishops of Canterbury, York, Durham, and Dublin. At the next level of hierarchy were bishops, also appointed by the government, who presided over dioceses administered from cathedral towns. Bishops also sat in the House of Lords, and they, or their agents, sat as judges in the Ecclesiastical Courts, which heard cases ranging from heresy to (until 1857) inheritance. The dioceses, in turn, were made up of parishes organized into deaneries and archdeaneries. Only ordained priests appointed by the bishops served in all of these roles, as deans and archdeacons, and, at the parish level, as rectors, vicars, and curates. Bishops made up the first order of the ministry, priests the second; a third order, deacons, were ordained to assist the clergy, but were not empowered to perform the sacraments themselves. The terms "rector," "vicar," and "parson" all referred to a priest who held the benefice or living of a parish, an income derived from fees on Church lands and parish tithes and who, theoretically, performed sacramental and pastoral duties for his parishioners. Too often, in practice, curates hired by incumbents did the lion's share of the labor for little pay.

The complex hierarchy suggested by even this rudimentary taxonomy of Anglican clerical roles explains why sociologists point to clerical organization as the paradigm for status mechanisms in professions generally. Anthony Trollope rose to prominence chronicling clerical politics in his six Barsetshire novels (1855–67). George Eliot's *Middlemarch* (1872) provides a succinct illustration of what gradations of clerical prestige may have meant to a parishioner in the 1830s. Eliot describes the status-conscious Peter Featherstone contemplating his funeral:

> Having a contempt for curates, whom he always called understrappers, he was resolved to be buried by a beneficed clergyman. Mr Casaubon was out of the question, not merely because he declined duty of this sort, but because Featherstone had an especial dislike to him as the rector of his own parish, who had a lien on the land in the shape of a tithe, also as the deliverer of morning sermons, which the old man, being in his pew and not at all sleepy, had been obliged to sit through with an inward snarl. He had an objection to a parson stuck up above his head preaching to him. (ch. 34)

Featherstone settles on the rector of a neighboring parish, Revd Cadwallader, because this priest has been obliged to seek permission to fish the old man's stream.

Featherstone's attitude towards the clergy, like all his values, is decidedly worldly. And though it may be exaggerated, it is one reason reform-minded Victorians would count the Anglican Church amongst the institutions targeted for change in the 1830s. To obtain holy orders, the vast majority of candidates completed a university degree or, in smaller but increasing numbers, attended a theological college. A tiny number without formal training, referred to as "literates," were ordained, generally in remote areas. A candidate presented himself, with references, to a bishop for an interview. But there were no strict requirements as to his spiritual credentials (except, perhaps, for the literates, who distinguished themselves in no other way). Many benefices were held by the younger sons of aristocratic families, "squarsons" as they were derisively called, for whom the clerical life was little more than a means of supporting their hounds and horses. While such abuses were notorious, it was also the inadequacy of many livings that restricted clerical appointments to men who could supplement their pay with private income. For example, after the Napoleonic Wars, when about 80 percent of livings produced less than £400 annually, many former officers entered the Church, bringing their half-pay army and navy pensions with them (Colloms 18–19). The failure of these funding systems in the late eighteenth century had demoralized the lowest ranks of clergy and left many parishes without a priest in residence. The diocesan reports of 1827 and 1829 indicated that fewer than 42 percent of Anglican incumbents resided in their parishes. Pluralities, or the holding of multiple benefices (out of greed or necessity), accounted for much of the nonresidence. Curates who filled these absences frequently received stipends so paltry as to give the term "perpetual curate" the ring of a life sentence rather than a permanent appointment. It is certainly true that many devout parsons soldiered on, ministering to their congregations under difficult conditions. But the success of dissenting sects in areas of rural poverty and in the growing industrial cities testified to the failure of the Established Church to demand vocational zeal from its clergy, to support them in their duties, and to send clergy where they were needed.

These problems made the Church vulnerable to critics within Parliament and its own ranks. The secular zeal that had produced the Reform Bill of 1832 could be turned, as well as religious fervor could, on traditional Church authority. The celebrated Anglican clergyman and wit Sydney Smith wrote in the early 1830s, "No man could tell to what excesses the new power conferred on the multitude would carry them. It was not safe for a clergyman to appear in the streets. I bought a blue coat, and did not despair in time of looking like a layman" (Chadwick I, 129). The first crisis came in Ireland, where Dr Richard Whately, appointed Archbishop of Dublin in 1831, complained loudly of the injustice of a bloated Protestant hierarchy ruling over a Roman Catholic majority, and talk of disestablishment was heard in Parliament. In the end, to the bitter regret of Irish members, the Church of Ireland was not disestablished, but was sufficiently reduced in size to horrify staunch supporters of the Established Church. Another crisis came in 1834, when the General Assembly of the Church of Scotland, under the influence of evangelicals who objected to Peel's reforms, sought to expand their independence from the government by ruling, in direct opposition to the law, that congregations could not be forced to accept pastors appointed against their will. The upshot of the ensuing contest between the Church of Scotland and Westminster was the Scottish Disruption of 1843. Over 200 representatives to the 1843 General Assembly, including the charismatic clergyman and reformer Dr Thomas Chalmers, withdrew in protest to form the Free Church of Scotland, taking with them 474 of the 1,200 ministers of the Church of Scotland, which was left with little support outside the aristocracy.

The predominantly Tory Anglican bishops dug in their heels against the Whig reforms of the 1830s, but soon they would be overtaken by reform movements from within the Church itself: Evangelicalism, Tractarianism (or the Oxford Movement), and the Broad Church movement. Though these groups sparred over the particulars of clerical reform, they shared a conviction that the national Church must defend itself against unsympathetic government reformers, and together they effected a revival of the Anglican clergy.

Led by the charismatic Anglican ministers John Wesley and George Whitefield, the eighteenth-century evangelical revival from which Methodism arose had produced substantial reforms in Christian practice. Evangelicalism emphasized a personal relationship between the believer and God, marked by a conversion experience in which God called the believer to a life of Bible reading, prayer, reformed habits, and, perhaps most importantly, spreading the gospel to others. By the late eighteenth century, prominent Anglicans were adopting evangelical teachings and practices. The Clapham Sect, a group of Anglican laymen founded by William Wilberforce, undertook various projects, including Sunday schools for the poor, agitation for the abolition of slavery, publication of religious tracts, and the dissemination of Bibles. This was only the most celebrated of Anglican laymen's groups joining with dissenting clergy and lay people in such evangelistic and philanthropic activities.

To the founders of the Oxford Movement, evangelicalism represented a threat to clerical authority, but not so great a threat as that offered by the government. In a series of Tracts beginning in 1833, three Oxford clergymen, John Keble, John Henry Newman, and Edward Pusey, denounced the government's actions against the Irish Church and called for a renewed commitment to the Established Church – its doctrines, services, clergy, and hierarchy. A declaration signed by 7,000 clergymen and an address of the laity with 230,000 signatures were presented to Archbishop Howley of Canterbury in 1834, acknowledging the need for reform but insisting that it come from within. Although the direct result of these actions was minimal – as Owen Chadwick notes, the declaration was a web of compromises satisfying no one and playing into the hands of Tory conservatives (I, 75–8) – the diffusive effects of the Oxford Movement were considerable, renewing devotion among clergy and laity.

The Broad Church movement or latitudinarians argued, as did Dr Thomas Arnold in *The Principles of Church Reform* (1833), that tolerance rather than sacerdotal vigilance would attract the largest number of followers to the Church of England. Samuel Taylor Coleridge maintained in his *Constitution of Church and State* (1829) that a national Church must be central to Britain's spiritual and cultural life. Only a tolerant and inclusive Church could command such loyalty. Religious reformers may have split over Liberal vs. Tory politics, pacifism, the empire, and whether to identify themselves with evangelicalism or against it; yet the effects of reform were generally evangelical in nature, permeating the Church as they had the chapels and the culture at large.

The charges Wesley had leveled against the Anglican priesthood – neglect of the faithful and lack of evangelical fervor – were addressed in the Victorian period by efforts to increase the number of men ordained and, more importantly, to enhance their training, sense of mission, and pastoral duties. Preaching at Sunday morning and evening services was supplemented by mid-week services, as well as by prayer meetings, Bible studies, and house-visitations, in imitation of such activities carried on by dissenting sects. An aggressive church building campaign was initiated as well, constructing almost 3,000 churches between 1840 and 1870. To increase the supply of clergy for the north of England, Wales, and urban parishes, the Church expanded the theological colleges and ordained more men who were not Oxbridge graduates. At the same time, the ordination of literates was limited to rare exceptions. Despite growing numbers of ordinands from the 1840s until the end of the century, however, it proved impossible to keep pace with the rapidly expanding population. In 1841 there was one clergyman for each 1,098 people in England and Wales; in 1901, the ratio was 1:1,288. Still, the clergy became a more energetic presence in the culture, in part simply because the influx of new ordinands at mid-century meant that over half of the Anglican clergy were under 45 years of age, and only one-fifth older than 55 (Haig 4). Infused with evangelical fervor or Tractarian devotion, these young clergymen sought to set an example by their own manner of living. Although the foxhunting parson did not disappear – the Revd John "Jack" Russell, the sportsman whose name is carried on by the terriers he bred, served as Perpetual Curate of Swymbridge from 1832 to 1880 – many clergy lived abstemiously, forgoing drink, sports, and dancing. Undeniably, there were sanctimonious hypocrites, the objects of Trollope's satire in the evangelical clergyman Mr Slope from the Barsetshire novels. But there were also men whose devotion, like that of Mr Tryan in George Eliot's *Scenes of Clerical Life* (1858), effected a humanitarian reform of manners in their congregations.

Members of the Broad Church movement, notably the Revd F. D. Maurice and the Revd Charles Kingsley, promoted a social consciousness amongst the clergy, urging them to support the working poor. Kingsley's novel *Alton Locke* (1850) spread his view of Christian Socialism, dramatized through the trials of its working-class hero. Many clergymen labored quietly to alleviate the suffering of the sick and unemployed, to educate, and to persuade wealthy landowners to charity. A very few lent public support to workers' organizations. Though vastly outnumbered in urban areas by the rapidly expanding population, clergymen nevertheless made their presence felt thanks to the cooperation of lay ministers and charity workers, who helped to extend their influence and spread God's word in such organizations as the London City Mission (1835) and Evangelical Alliance (1845). The Church Pastoral Aid Society (1836) sent staff to assist clergy in needy parishes. The London City Mission, a joint effort of Anglicans and Nonconformists, employed 375 laymen in 1860, whose schedules of home Bible reading reached an estimated 375,000 Londoners, more than 10 percent of the city's population. Ellen Ranyard's Bible Society, founded in 1857, sent out 137 women as visitors and 119 scripture readers.

Imperial ambitions also boosted government and popular support for the Church. Foreign mission activity of the Established Church and dissenting sects had waned by mid-century when high taxation, skepticism regarding imperial expansion, and the Crimean War discouraged contributions. David Livingstone's return in 1856 from Africa and the Indian Mutiny of 1857 lent new urgency to the missionary effort. Bishop Samuel Wilberforce took up Livingstone's cry of "Commerce and Christianity," declaring at a meeting of the Oxford and Cambridge Mission to Central Africa in 1859 that "Commerce is a mighty machinery laid down in the wants of man by the Almighty Creator of all things, to promote the intercourse and communion of one race with another, and especially of the more civilized races of the earth with the less civilized" (Stanley 75). Expanded missionary activity, particularly in India, Africa, and China, transformed the Anglican Church into a global organization, and at ten-year intervals beginning in 1867 Anglican bishops from around the world gathered in London for the Lambeth Conference. But the more missionaries went abroad, the more clergy were exposed to non-Christian religions. Among the most famous instances of this cross-fertilization was that exerted by the Zulus on Bishop Colenso of Natal. Assisting in his translation of the Bible into the Zulu language, they led him to question a literal reading of scripture. Colenso's bizarre work on the Pentateuch (1862–3), attacking literalism through arithmetic calculations, resulted in his being deposed from the see of Natal, though he continued to fight for Zulus' rights in the courts. Biblical scholars in England were embarrassed by Colenso's methods; however, more sophisticated scholarship would complicate domestic evangelism as the century wore on.

David Bebbington argues that, despite the notorious difficulty of interpreting the 1851 Census of Religious Worship (a count of attendance at churches and chapels in England and Wales on Sunday, March 30, 1851), it demonstrates the success of domestic evangelistic efforts within and outside the Established Church (107–11). Methodism, Congregationalism, and Presbyterianism had all grown in comparison to the total population. Despite a shrinking share of worshipers, the Church of England as a whole had gained members, thanks principally to growth in its evangelical parishes. Different denominations thrived in various areas of the country and with various classes of people: thus, the north of England was predominantly Methodist and Evangelical Anglican. Generally, rates of churchgoing were highest among the middle and upper classes. Skilled labor gravitated towards nonconforming sects, making up a majority of the Primitive Methodists, to cite one example. Although skilled and even nonskilled laborers played an active role in nonconforming sects, the widespread alienation of workers from organized religion remained a scandal in Victorian Britain, and a focus of evangelical activity. Yet it should be noted that organized secularism, such as the National Secular Society (1870), fared no better with this group. Instead, as Victorian folklorists demonstrated, folk religions and magical practices remained vital among the poor, especially in remote rural areas.

In sum, despite a significant revival in the Victorian Anglican Church, and the efforts of its reformed clergy, it failed to displace nonconforming sects or stem the growth of Roman Catholicism and win over a majority of Britons. Though the ordination of nongraduate clergy both increased and diversified the clergy's ranks, these parsons were denied the influence in local affairs that their gentlemanly predecessors had enjoyed. What is more, the solicitation of lay people to assist clergy in pastoral duties and philanthropic projects institutionalized a priesthood of the people and helped pave the way for the secular welfare state, which eventually moved the clergy out of their traditional roles in the community.

The popularity of dissenting clergy relative to their Anglican brethren may be difficult for us to fathom, owing to certain famous Victorian attacks upon them. Valentine Cunningham, who titled his study of dissent in the Victorian novel *Everywhere Spoken Against*, catalogues stereotypes of dissenters as vulgar, hypocritical, social-climbing, ignorant, etc. Dickens's Mr Chadband in *Bleak House* (1853), forever raising his hand before intoning some platitude, indelibly etches smug inhumanity on the imagination. Matthew Arnold in *Culture and Anarchy* (1869) rather snidely referred to the enthusiasm for division amongst dissenting sects as "the protest of Protestantism," identifying disputation as the essential activity of a religion founded on the principle of dissent. Still, it is worth noting that many divisions stemmed from the earnest convictions of small groups of people that their interpretations of scripture were true, while their leaders' preachings were prevarications or corruptions of God's word. Alongside the lengthy list of dissenting sects named by Cunningham were many informal groups without institutional identities. Witness Brooke Herford's 1867 biography of Travers Madge, a friend of Elizabeth Gaskell who gave up his Unitarian ministry in 1859 to hold meetings in a room in Hulme:

> Religious life in our great cities takes more varied forms than most people are aware of. Not even the divergent types of the Anglican church, with the varieties of Baptist and Independent Nonconformity, and the multiform sections of the great Methodist family, can satisfy the restless individuality of the human soul . . . Probably there is no large town but has, here and there in its great wilderness of absorbed busy life, some half dozen of these little sporadic churches, that, mostly in little upper rooms in back streets, are carrying on their humble work and worship, and aiming at something nearer to their ideal of what a church of Christ should be, than their members have been able to find in the larger ecclesiasticism of the religious world. (Cunningham 31)

This is not to say that clerical hierarchy was absent in dissenting sects. The Methodist Connexion, Baptist Union, and Congregational Union evidence the growing institutionalization of Victorian dissent. Nor were dissenting ministers mainly untrained amateurs. The Congregationalist divine Samuel Davidson, professor of biblical literature at the Lancashire Independent College, cited German biblical criticism in his scholarship as early as 1856. Elizabeth Gaskell's husband William, a Unitarian minister, was a noted linguist, and her friend, the Unitarian minister Revd William Turner, helped to found the Newcastle Literary and Philosophical Society. But the traditions of old dissent, notably the unprogrammed worship among Quakers and the evangelical teachings of the Methodists, Baptists, and their offshoots, encouraged lay ministries that were difficult to supervise or contain, especially in remote rural areas and cities that had been neglected by the Anglican Church.

The Anglican effort to ordain more nongraduates (Hardy's Jude pursues ordination by license) reflects the impossibility of supplying sufficient clergy from the ranks of university men, even if none of these men had been reluctant to accept appointments in unpopular places like Wales or the north of England. But that effort also suggests that the homogeneous product turned out by Oxbridge could not meet the needs of a socially diverse population. Thomas Wright defended his fellow working men against the perception that absence from church meant irreligion, writing in 1868,

> the Dissenting sects have the greatest attractions. Their services and ministers are considered simpler and more practical than those of the Church; the ministers are paid with a nearer approach to equality, and have, to a far greater extent than those of the Church,

entered into their profession from personal predilection, or as they put it, from having "experienced a call." (Moore 325)

What is more, dissenting sects allowed ministries to women, who were the group most grotesquely unrepresented by the Anglican clergy, in that they made up a majority of churchgoers.

Dinah Morris, a character in George Eliot's *Adam Bede* (1859), was once the best-known example of a female preacher, and one who submitted to the Methodist Connexion's injunction against women's preaching at that. But scholarship has restored the significance of the scores of female preachers who flourished in the nineteenth century. The census of 1901 indicates that there were 4,803 women serving as local preachers (Chadwick II, 244). Among the most notable of the nineteenth-century women preachers was Elizabeth Fry, a Quaker who began a ministry to female prisoners and founded the Ladies' British Society for Promoting Reformation of Female Prisoners (1821). She testified before a Select Committee of Parliament on prison reform, influencing legislation enacted later in the century. Fry inspired Sarah Martin, a woman from a humble background, to preach and conduct services at the Yarmouth Prison, for which she received favorable notice in a parliamentary report of 1835. Florence Nightingale embarked on her mission to train female nurses after visiting a German institution for the training of deaconesses in 1851. Having articulated her belief in women's religious vocation in her prophetic work *Cassandra* (1860), she would be immortalized as "the Lady with the Lamp" for her pioneering nursing services to British soldiers in the Crimean War. Similarly, Catherine Booth, a founder of the Salvation Army, urged an evangelical mission on all women in her "Female Ministry; or, a Woman's Right to Preach the Gospel" in *Papers on Practical Religion* (1878). Women served as officers in the Salvation Army.

Harriet Taylor Mill sneered at such female philanthropists in *The Emancipation of Women* (1851), labeling them a "sentimental priesthood." Still, Victorian feminism drew effectively on the evangelical notion of a calling to ministry. Frances Power Cobbe was born into an evangelical Anglican family in Dublin, and, though she rejected orthodox Christianity, based her *Duties of Women* (1881) on a religious conception of service. Likewise, Josephine Butler, the key campaigner against the Contagious Diseases Acts, claimed that women were "redeemed" by philanthropic work.

Women's religious ministries encouraged the founding of Anglican sisterhoods in the nineteenth century. The Sisters of Mercy, for example, were founded in 1848 by Lydia Sellon in Devonport in response to Bishop Phillpott's appeal for help in ministering to seacoast towns. Maria Rossetti, sister of Christina and Dante Gabriel, entered the Sisters of Mercy. By the end of the century there were 80 communities of Anglican sisters with a membership of 2,000–3,000. From 1862 women served as deaconesses in the Church of England, and by 1897 limited permission was granted to elect them as churchwardens, legitimating the practice of a few parishes that had previously gone unnoticed. In these ways, Anglicans followed the lead of the Quakers and other dissenting sects.

Whereas women's ministries flourished throughout the nineteenth century, the influence of the Anglican clergy progressively declined. Several factors contributed to this decline. For one, clerical reform had produced a paradoxical result. By emphasizing a vocational calling, reformers had encouraged potential clergymen to scrutinize their beliefs more closely. Since other professions, such as the civil service, were opening up to young gentlemen, they were free to choose careers that made fewer demands on their souls. Still, ordinations peaked in the 1880s and did not fall off seriously until the 1890s (Haig 4–5). Many potential clergymen and those already ordained were troubled by historical and scientific critiques of the Bible and religious belief. *Essays and Reviews*, published in 1860 by Benjamin Jowett along with other clergy and one layman, encouraged open discussion of challenges to biblical literalism and other matters, which they believed would contribute to the intellectual well-being of the Church. They ignited a tinderbox. Evangelical and Tractarian bishops alike condemned the volume, and several of the authors were prosecuted for heresy, but a judicial committee of the Privy Council overturned judgments against them. Indeed, one of the authors, Frederick Temple, went on to become Archbishop of Canterbury. These events alone would have sorely tested the simple faith of earnest clergymen, but the increasing controversies over geological discoveries, Darwin's evolutionary theory – staged most famously in Bishop Samuel Wilberforce's debate with T. H. Huxley – along with historical biblical criticism, left many reeling. Clergymen's spiritual crises retained their cultural significance through the final decades of the century, as is evident from William Hale White's novel *The Autobiography of Mark Rutherford* (1881), Mary Ward's best-seller *Robert Elsmere* (1888), and Thomas Hardy's *Jude the Obscure* (1895). The authority of dissenting clergy eventually suffered too, as Edmund Gosse recorded in *Father and Son* (1907), which recounts his disillusionment with the biblical literalism of his father, a Plymouth Brethren clergyman.

What is more, the Oxford Movement, which had sought to strengthen the Established Church by emphasizing Apostolic Succession, ritual, and doctrine, unintentionally strengthened the appeal of Roman Catholicism. When the Tractarian leader John Henry Newman converted to Roman Catholicism in 1845, many of his disciples faced the dilemma: Rome or doubt? Gerard Manley Hopkins, for one, chose Rome in 1866 and entered the Society of Jesus in 1868. The poetry he wrote privately was deeply influenced by the Scholastic philosophy of medieval Catholicism. J. A. Froude, at one time a great admirer of Newman, was among those who could not embrace Rome. His novel *The Nemesis of Faith* (1849) chronicled the doubts that led its hero to resign his living and its author to resign his fellowship. Froude's *History of England* (1856–70) occasioned the controversy between one of its reviewers, Charles Kingsley, and Newman that prompted the latter to write his spiritual autobiography *Apologia pro Vita Sua* (1864). The sensational conversion of Newman, who would become the Roman Catholic Bishop of Birmingham, alarmed devout Protestants. Indeed, Dr Nicholas Wiseman sought Tractarian support in his efforts to restore the

Roman Catholic hierarchy in Britain. Old Catholic families in England and Irish Catholics had been served by vicars since the Reformation; the influx of Irish immigrants, however, called for a more elaborate Church organization in England. In 1850 Pope Pius IX approved Wiseman's request and established 13 sees in England and named Wiseman Archbishop of Westminster. Wiseman's flamboyant announcement of the Pope's decision further alarmed British Protestants. Anglican clergy protested "papal aggression," yet more conversions followed. Among them was the prominent Anglican churchman Henry Manning, who would succeed Wiseman as Archbishop of Westminster in 1865. Manning, with his less confrontational style, did much to involve Roman Catholics in the life of the nation, supporting Irish causes, national education, and workers' rights. Newman's *Apologia* likewise encouraged rapprochement between Protestants and Catholics. Though anti-Catholic prejudice persisted, it became less vitriolic. The Irish Church was disestablished in 1871. Victoria, Defender of the Faith, welcomed a papal envoy to her jubilee in 1887.

In his novel *The Way of All Flesh* (1901) Samuel Butler, who was the son of a rector and grandson of a bishop, offers an especially savage account of the decline of the Anglican clergy. Despite his religious doubts, Ernest Pontifex takes holy orders at the insistence of his father, a tyrannical evangelical clergyman who was himself forced to enter the Church by his father. Warped by his repressive religious upbringing, Ernest sexually assaults a woman. After serving a prison sentence and enduring other misadventures, he retires to a contented existence as a secular man of letters. Butler's novel depicts the growing secularism in the final decades of the Victorian period, but it is hardly representative of Victorian religious attitudes. Even the movements for disestablishment, as Owen Chadwick argues, were signs less of secularization than of a desire on the part of fervent Christians to worship as they liked (II, 427). Although the University Tests Act of 1871 opened all degrees and offices to non-Anglicans, in the 1880s undergraduate religious societies flourished, university religious services increased in number, and students were active in evangelical and relief missions to London's poor. Of particular importance to students of literature is what Joel Christenson calls "the theologization of literary studies" by the clergymen who guided the introduction of English into university curricula. Even in the non-sectarian University of London, the first two appointments as professor of poetry were held by Anglican clergymen: Thomas Dale and F. D. Maurice. The belief that resulted in their appointments – that literature was a source of inspiration and moral guidance – profoundly influenced academic literary study in Britain and America well into the twentieth century. With scholars continuing to complicate the biblical text, earnest devotion could be transferred to literature, and professors – clerical and lay – became priests of poetry. As Matthew Arnold wrote in "The Study of Poetry" (1880):

> The future of poetry is immense, because in poetry, where it is worthy of its high destinies, our race, as time goes on, will find an ever surer and surer stay. There is not a

creed which is not shaken, not an accredited dogma which is not shown to be questionable, not a received tradition which does not threaten to dissolve . . . The strongest part of our religion today is its unconscious poetry.

See also 1832, 1851; Passing On, Sexualities; Legal, Educational; Sage Writing

References

Bebbington, D. (1989) *Evangelicalism in Modern Britain: A History from the 1730s to the 1980s.* Grand Rapids: Baker Book House.

Chadwick, O. (1966, 1970) *The Victorian Church,* 2 vols. New York: Oxford University Press.

Christenson, J. (1997) *The Theologization of English Studies.* Unpublished dissertation. Milwaukee: Marquette University.

Colloms, B. (1977) *Victorian Country Parsons.* Lincoln and London: University of Nebraska Press.

Cunningham, V. (1975) *Everywhere Spoken Against: Dissent in the Victorian Novel.* Oxford: Clarendon Press.

Finestein, I. (1999) *Anglo-Jewry in Changing Times: Studies in Diversity 1840–1914.* London and Portland: Vallentine Mitchell.

Haig, A. (1984) *The Victorian Clergy.* London and Sydney: Croom Helm.

Jeaffreson, J. C. (1870) *A Book About the Clergy.* London: Hurst and Blackett.

Landow, G. (1980) *Victorian Types, Victorian Shadows: Biblical Typology in Victorian Literature, Art, and Thought.* Boston and London: Routledge and Kegan Paul.

Moore, J. R. (ed.) (1995) *Religion in Victorian Britain,* vol. 3. Manchester: Manchester University Press.

Stanley, B. (1983) " 'Commerce and Christianity': Providence Theory, the Missionary Movement, and the Imperialism of Free Trade, 1842–1860." *The Historical Journal* 26, 71–94.

Further Reading

Brown, S. J. (2001) *The National Churches of England, Ireland, and Scotland, 1801–1846.* Oxford: Oxford University Press.

Davies, H. (1961) *Worship and Theology in England: From Watts and Wesley to Maurice, 1690–1850.* Princeton: Princeton University Press.

——(1962) *Worship and Theology in England: From Newman to Martineau, 1850–1900.* Princeton: Princeton University Press.

Jay, E. (1979) *The Religion of the Heart: Anglican Evangelicalism and the Nineteenth-Century Novel.* Oxford: Clarendon Press.

Johnson, D. A. (1983) *Women in English Religion, 1700–1925.* New York and Toronto: Edwin Mellen Press.

Knight, F. (1995) *The Nineteenth-Century Church and English Society.* Cambridge and New York: Cambridge University Press.

Knoepflmacher, U. C. (1965) *Religious Humanism and the Victorian Novel: George Eliot, Walter Pater and Samuel Butler.* Princeton: Princeton University Press.

Krueger, C. L. (1992) *The Reader's Repentance: Women Preachers, Women Writers, and Nineteenth-Century Social Discourse.* Chicago: University of Chicago Press.

Lloyd, J. M. (2009) *Women and the Shaping of British Methodism: Persistent Preachers, 1807–1907.* Manchester: Manchester University Press.

Machin, G. I. T. (1977) *Politics and the Churches in Great Britain, 1832–1868*. Oxford: Clarendon Press.

McKelvy, W. (2007) *The English Cult of Literature: Devoted Readers, 1774–1880*. Charlottesville: University of Virginia Press.

Mumm, S. (1999) *Stolen Daughters, Virgin Mothers: Anglican Sisterhoods in Victorian Britain*. London: Leicester University Press.

Norman, E. R. (1976) *Church and Society in England, 1770–1970: A Historical Study*. Oxford: Clarendon Press.

Semmel, B. (1973) *The Methodist Revolution*. New York: Basic Books.

Valenze, D. M. (1985) *Prophetic Sons and Daughters: Female Preaching and Popular Religion in Industrial England*. Princeton: Princeton University Press.

Wheeler, M. (1994) *Heaven, Hell, and the Victorians*. Cambridge: Cambridge University Press.

Wolffe, J. (1994) *God and Greater Britain: Religion and National Life in Britain and Ireland, 1843–1945*. London: Routledge.

11
Legal

Simon Petch and Jan-Melissa Schramm

Practice

The nineteenth century saw widespread reform of both the legal profession and the laws of the nation. As J. S. Mill observed in 1838 of the great utilitarian philosopher Jeremy Bentham (1748–1832), he "found the philosophy of law a chaos, he left it a science; he found the practice of the law an Augean stable, he turned the river into it which is mining and sweeping away mound after mound of its rubbish" (1980: 158). But where utilitarianism prioritized anonymity, impartiality, and the "many" above the "one" as the foundational unit of ethico-political decision-making, contemporary literature tended to privilege individuality and the particularity of lived experience. Mediating between abstract legal rules and the facts which illustrated their application were judgments on individual cases, the bedrock of the English common law. Relentless literary attention to, and interrogation of, "hard cases" which troubled the law was partly the product of newly energetic journalism, but it was also the product of an urge to understand the relation between the particular and the general – between the force of precedent and the universal principles which were understood to animate the law – at a time of rapid social change.

Nothing seized the Victorian public imagination like the trial of a notorious killer in the Central Criminal Court (as the Old Bailey was known after 1834). Eighteenth-century trials had been hasty affairs, usually conducted without the assistance of legal professionals: a trial for a capital offence habitually lasted no more than 30 minutes, there was no appellate procedure, and the accused was required to make

A New Companion to Victorian Literature and Culture, First Edition. Edited by Herbert F. Tucker.
© 2014 John Wiley & Sons, Ltd. Published 2014 by John Wiley & Sons, Ltd.

his own defense, regardless of factors like illness or illiteracy which might hamper his attempts to counter the evidence presented by the prosecution (Beattie 375–80). The nineteenth century saw the professionalization of criminal trial proceedings, an initiative driven at least partly by the desire of reformers as diverse as the radical Samuel Romilly (1757–1818) and the Christian philanthropist Elizabeth Fry (1780–1845) to render forensic process and penal conditions fairer and more humane for all parties. There was as yet no general discourse of human rights, but throughout the 1820s and early 1830s many politicians and lawyers agitated for full legal representation to be made available to those accused of felony. This was effected by the Prisoners' Counsel Act of 1836, and although its practical impact on criminal trials was initially small (only a minority of prisoners could afford defense counsel), its symbolic significance was substantial: professional men could now be employed to defend those whose alleged villainy was of the highest order, thus potentially tainting legal rhetoric with vicarious guilt and threatening to undermine the codes of professional etiquette which were formulated in the 1840s and 50s (Langbein; Cairns). The middle decades of the nineteenth century witnessed intense competition among the various public discourses which sought to interrogate and understand criminal behavior: barristers constructed elaborate fictions in support of their criminal clients, law reporters increasingly described criminal matters at great length in order to enhance circulation of newspapers, and novelists quarried the salacious details of famous trials to enhance their argument that narrative art could serve as an important public intervention in political debates about criminal etiology and punishment (Schramm 2000: 101–44).

Public memory of sensational murder trials was strong, and the same cases were revisited time and time again in different literary genres as each generation sought to understand afresh the intricacies of criminal motivation: the crimes of murderers such as Eugene Aram and John Thurtell formed the subject of numerous novels, dramas, and long narrative poems in the centuries after their deaths on the scaffold (in 1759 and 1824 respectively). This was partly because readers' taste had been formed by criminal biographies and broadsheets (the *Newgate Calendar* was first published in five volumes in 1773–4 and a number of new editions appeared in the early nineteenth century). The format of the "case study" was crucial not only to the operation of the common law but also to the types of claim which the novel could make to a knowledge of human psychology. Authors of literature were particularly attentive to the rhetoric of their story-telling counterparts in courts of law, and they were quick to put the trial itself on trial when they felt that standards of fairness were not being upheld.

A clear example of what publishing authors could learn from the theater of the criminal courts emerges from the trial of William Palmer for murder in 1856, which lasted for 12 days – at that time, the longest criminal trial in history. Each day, the galleries of the Central Criminal Court were crowded with members of the paying public, including many women and, notably, the authors Charles Dickens and Wilkie Collins. Dickens used his time in court to scrutinize the physiognomy of the accused, searching for physiological clues of his villainy: writing in *Household Words* after the trial ("The Demeanour of Murderers," June 14), he noted that Palmer's malice was evident for all to see, although authors were significantly more skilled at detecting such villainy than the legal professionals who existed only to perform what Anthony Trollope in *Orley Farm* (1862) was to call "the manumission of murderers" (ch. 10). Collins, too, reflected at length on the oral contest that he had seen unfold before his eyes in court: as John Sutherland observes, "he was struck by the way each witness rose in turn to contribute a personal fragment to the chain of evidence," and Collins recorded how "[i]t came to me then . . . that a series of events in a novel would lend themselves to an exposition like this . . . one could impart to the reader that acceptance, that sense of belief, which was produced here by the succession of testimonies" (Sutherland 244). On this basis Collins refined the form of forensic realism whereby in effect *The Woman in White* (1859–60) and *The Moonstone* (1868) appealed to his readership as if they represented a national court of public opinion (Welsh 1992: 122–40): "In this matter of the Moonstone the plan is, not to present reports, but to produce witnesses . . . Lord! What a compliment [a reader] will feel it, to be asked to take nothing on hearsay, and to be treated in all respects like a judge on the bench" (ch. 23).

In Palmer's case, the jury of 12 of his peers deliberated for only an hour and 18 minutes before finding him guilty: he was executed four days later in his native Staffordshire. The so-called "Bloody Code" (a collection of approximately 200 offences, primarily against property) was progressively dismantled throughout the early nineteenth century, and by the 1860s the only remaining capital offences were murder and treason (Gatrell 618–19). Growing agitation against the implementation of the death penalty culminated in the cessation of public executions in 1868: from then on, hanging was conducted within the privacy of prison walls. Other offences, both felonies and misdemeanors, were increasingly punished with terms of imprisonment and transportation, whose emphasis on the reformation of individual character can be mapped alongside changing theological opinion.

Partly because of the severity of the penalty that might be incurred, contentious criminal trials tended to attract the greatest publicity. Civil trials, which dealt with commercial matters and which had been conducted by legal professionals since the medieval period, on the whole attracted far less controversy, with two exceptions – firstly, contested cases of inheritance and imposture, and secondly, the travesties of justice which were to be found from time to time in the unreformed Court of Chancery (a court of conscience originally designed to mitigate the severity of the common law courts, but before 1800 fossilized by its very commitment to comprehensive justice). Inheritance cases involving the claims of impostors depended upon acts of recognition in which we see the convergence of the rhetorical tropes of proof common to both literary and legal interpretation (Eden 46–50): the most prominent example, which resonated through the literature of the second half of the nineteenth century, was the case of the Tichborne Claimant (1871–4). After leaving England to seek his fortune in 1854, Sir Roger Tichborne, the heir to a vast Hampshire estate, was believed to have drowned off the coast of South America. In 1866, a butcher from Wapping called Arthur Orton slipped quietly into England from the Australian colonies to lay claim to the identity of Sir Roger and his vast inheritance; the threat to the social order thus posed by the return to England of bushrangers and convicts in the colonies recalls the plot of Dickens's *Great Expectations* (1860–1). When his case reached the courts in 1871, the jury heard evidence for 102 days before deciding that the claimant was not Roger but Arthur: he was consequently prosecuted for perjury in 1874 and sentenced to 14 years' imprisonment with hard labor. Trollope's *Ralph the Heir* (1871) was published concurrently with the first of the two Tichborne trials, and he returned to probe questions of impostorship further in *Is He Popenjoy?* (1878). Marcus Clarke's *For the Term of His Natural Life* (1874) and Charles Reade's *The Wandering Heir* (1873) also offered thinly fictionalized accounts of the case – in Reade's analysis, the hearing was "the greatest conflict of direct and heterogeneous evidence ever known in this country before or since" (269). And if Clarke, Reade, and Trollope were attentive to the political implications of personal inheritance in their works – the Burkean sense that social relations and therefore political stability depend upon the performance of accurate acts of recognition – it was George Eliot who was to make these anxieties a dominant motif of her mature fiction (Semmel 1–15). Eliot spent a day in the public gallery of the Tichborne trials in mid-January 1872, when she had just completed Book IV of *Middlemarch* (1872). Eliot described the evidence that she heard as of "great interest" and she was clear in her own mind that the Claimant was an impostor (*Letters* V, 337). It is possible that her immersion in the case influenced both her representation of Bulstrode's moral imposture and the development in which the stranger Rigg unexpectedly inherits Stone Court. *Middlemarch*, like the Tichborne trial, is preoccupied with questions of representation – whether and under what conditions one person can stand or advocate for another (Mr Brooke for the people in Parliament, Farebrother for Fred in pursuit of Mary's hand, Dorothea for Lydgate following the death of Raffles).

Debates concerning the theory of representation were shaped by responses to the passage of the Reform Acts of 1832 and 1867 (Gallagher 222–30); they also underpinned the reform of the Court of Chancery. Under mounting criticism by mid-century, common law and equity procedures were increasingly aligned with one another before Chancery was abolished as a separate jurisdiction in the Judicature Acts of 1873–5. Rejecting Chancery's insistence that an interest in property is the defining test of any claim for participation in the governance of a democratizing nation, what Dickens promotes in his extraordinary attack on Chancery in *Bleak House* (1852–3) is the *national* interest – a collection of common interests based on merit and worth and not restricted to any one social class by virtue of birth or property ownership (Schramm 2012: 217–42). It is hard to assess whether *Bleak House* played any quantifiable part in the eventual demise of the Court of Chancery as a separate jurisdiction. James Fitzjames Stephen (1829–94), a lawyer, historian, and perceptive though hostile critic, felt that Dickens had seized upon an old scandal only to enhance the apparent prestige of fiction: as Chancery had attempted to reform itself throughout the 1830s and 40s, the novel, he felt, made sense only if it was set in the 1820s (Stephen 1857: 130). Modern historians have likewise concluded that nineteenth-century law reform "was largely managed by lawyers," who sought "piece-meal, pragmatic reform" (Lobban 117). But *Bleak House* offers us extensive evidence of Dickens's participation in a wider 1850s socio-cultural dialogue about the proper work of the "conscience." Like Alfred Lord Tennyson and F. D. Maurice, Dickens "responded to the mid-Victorian reorganization of his country's traditions and institutions by examining the national conscience": all were involved in a larger Victorian conversation about the origins of our moral sense and how it is best activated and trained (Petch 134). In its attention to the processes of deliberative decision-making and its interrogation of the evidence upon which ethical action should be founded, literature offered a privileged forum for the dissection of the individual conscience at work. Literary representations of subjectivity often depended upon quasi-forensic processes of accusation and (self-)defense: the integrity of character was best "proven" when put to the trial. As John Henry Newman observed in *Apologia pro Vita Sua* (1864), "religious men would rather be in error with the sanction of their conscience, than be right with the mere judgment of their reason" (Note G); his sanction draws its force from Austin's definition of a law as "the command of a sovereign enforced by a sanction" (Stephen 1900: III, 321). To the religious imagination, the conscience is an intuitive faculty, whereas to the utilitarians the conscience was conditioned by reason into a habit – an idea resoundingly endorsed by Darwin's theory in *The Descent of Man* (1871) of a conscience habituated by social instincts. But the sovereign self, the self with a conscience, is assumed by both intuitionists and utilitarians, and is at the heart of Victorian legal thought.

Implicit in this investigation of the origins of moral discernment was the question of gender. The rise of the professions in the Victorian period functioned as a reconfiguration of patriarchal power. The law valued masculine common-sense, and male processes of adjudication, as in tort law's reliance, when establishing responsibility for a civil wrong, on the imagined actions of "the reasonable man." Tulkinghorn's relentless pursuit of Lady Dedlock in the interests of Sir Leicester and the baronetcy in *Bleak House* was only the most explicit example of a ubiquitous phenomenon, and women would not be permitted to practice as a barrister or a solicitor in England until 1922. At a time when women were excluded from both the franchise and the representation of their own interests in courts of law, literature offered a forum for self-expression and the advocacy of women's struggle for narrative and political equality (Krueger 1–24). The novel conferred recognition on the important feminine qualities of charity, forgiveness, and mercy, and thus positioned women's stories as complementary to the male public sphere much as Equity supplemented the work of the more rigid Common Law.

Bleak House offers the most sophisticated example of this dynamic at work: in a novel committed to the representation of witness testimony which the courts would prefer to exclude, Esther, the illegitimate daughter of "Nemo" – No-One –

simultaneously creates the form of the tale with her compelling first-person account of events and embodies Dickens's charitable manifesto: "I thought it best to be as useful as I could, and to render what kind services I could, to those immediately about me; and to try to let that circle of duty gradually and naturally expand itself" (ch. 8). Unlike the moribund Court of Chancery, Esther discharges her trusts and responsibilities promptly, enabling Dickens to reclaim the principles of Equity as a property of literature and of the sentimentally-educated reader (Dolin 85–7; Polloczek 244; Watt 47). As Matthew Bagnet observes, "the noun-substantive, Goodness, is [of] the feminine gender" (ch. 49). Eliot also claimed an important role for her fictional women in the imagination of a more just society: drawing on the model of Portia, she allows both Esther Lyon in *Felix Holt* and Dorothea Brooke in *Middlemarch* to intervene actively in the quest for justice for the male protagonists. Esther's merciful intercession wins Felix's eventual pardon for manslaughter and effects some form of equitable reconciliation between Harold Transome and his suffering mother; a more formal legal model serves as the organizing principle of the closing chapters of *Middlemarch*. When Lydgate is wrongfully suspected of complicity in the (possible) murder of Raffles by Bulstrode, Dorothea undertakes to act as his counsel in conversation with their neighbors. But unlike a professional representative, she embraces advocacy from a conviction of his innocence: "You don't believe that Mr Lydgate is guilty of anything base? I will not believe it. Let us find out the truth and clear him!" As Farebrother notes, "a woman may venture on some efforts of sympathy which would hardly succeed if we men undertook them" (ch. 72). Clearly Eliot sees Dorothea's feelings here as generous and benevolent – like Dickens, she suggests that women preside over a particularly charitable jurisdiction of judgment – yet, at the same time, Eliot saw no need for women to play a more prominent role in public affairs: Dorothea's efficacy as an advocate is indeed predicated upon the restriction of her role to neighborly and matrimonial relations. A similar ambiguity characterizes the representation of working-class defendants in Victorian novels: the speech of Stephen Blackpool, Felix Holt, and Jem Wilson is often upheld as a model of integrity, even as their creators Dickens, Eliot, and Gaskell expressed reservations about the extension of the franchise. In Gallagher's analysis, "[l]iterary practice [is the] primary mechanism for social reform [and a]s such, it becomes an alternative, at least for the foreseeable future, to political representation" (224).

The legal system in Victorian England used, as it does today, the services of a divided profession: rights of audience in the higher Crown courts were restricted to barristers, who were instructed by solicitors, who in turn dealt directly with clients. Barristers were considered gentlemen, guided in their conduct by ideals of self-sacrificing public service; they enjoyed considerable autonomy and independence, although they were bound by a code of conduct that hardened as the century progressed. A man who hoped to practice at the Bar would typically attend Cambridge or Oxford to read for a degree other than law, then would undertake a five-year apprenticeship in one of the London Inns of Court (the Inner Temple, Middle Temple, Gray's Inn, and Lincoln's Inn), before being "called to the Bar" (as were Charles Reade in 1843, and Wilkie Collins in 1851). It was possible to earn a good income at the Bar: the young protagonist of Thackeray's *History of Pendennis* (1848–50), considering how best to make a living, eyed up "those prodigious prizes which are sometimes drawn in the great lottery of the Bar" (ch. 29) and which might reward the right combination of diligence and good luck. In fact, as *Pendennis* also acknowledges, early years at the Bar were often financially precarious – Fitzjames Stephen, for example, began work at the Bar in 1854, and four years later was making only £50 a year – but, once established, able orators often became both wealthy and well-known. Fitzroy Kelley was reported to have earned £25,000 in 1859, and estimates of the earnings of Charles Austin in 1857 vary from £40,000 to £100,000 (a median income for a barrister in the provinces in the 1850s was the £800–900 per year earned by Charles Rann Kennedy). In the 1880s, Charles Russell (who had successfully defended the Irish politician Charles Parnell before a special judicial commission in 1888–9) charged £500 to accept a brief and £100 per day thereafter. To put these figures in perspective: the prime minister's annual salary was £5,000 and annual judicial salaries in the higher courts ranged from £5,000 to £8,000.

On the other hand solicitors, and attorneys, before the latter term was abolished in 1875, were considered the lower branch of the profession: Victorian novels often represent them as "commercial men," or detective-like figures, prepared to dirty their hands in the service of their clients or in pursuit of profit, although family solicitors such as Tulkinghorn in *Bleak House* clearly attained a degree of financial comfort and respectability. Estimates for a reasonable solicitor's salary in the period range from £500 in private practice to twice that in a local government post, or up to £3,000 if employed as a proctor in the Court of Doctors' Commons (a court of matrimonial and admiralty disputes, abolished in 1867). Whilst solicitors had limited rights of audience in court, they enjoyed their own monopolies on the drafting of documents and conveyancing work. Dickens's novels in particular are peopled by practitioners of all types of legal work: from the proctors of Doctors' Commons, epitomized by Mr Spenlow in *David Copperfield* (1850), to the "pettifogging" Dodson and Fogg and the eloquent but seemingly amoral barrister Serjeant Buzfuz in *The Posthumous Papers of the Pickwick Club* (1836), and the bombastic Attorney-General in *A Tale of Two Cities* (1859). Even Esther's father "Nemo" is employed as a law-writer, one of the humble scriveners who eked out a living on the margins of the extended profession.

Education for aspiring legal professionals became more formalized in the course of the century: for the lower branch of the profession, the Law Society was established in 1825, proceedings against dishonest practitioners were first taken in 1834, and the Solicitors' Act of 1860 instituted an examination system; for barristers, the Inns of Court appointed Readers in 1847 and a Council of Legal Education in 1852, and organized compulsory Bar examinations from 1872. Reform and more effective professional training brought the two branches of the profession closer than ever before: the role of solicitor rose in status as the century progressed. At the same time, provincial bars were established at such major centers as Birmingham and Manchester, and while

London remained the hub of the legal system, the provincial administration of justice in Assizes and Quarter Sessions was supplemented, in 1846, by the establishment of County Courts. This devolution of legal authority represented an intensification of legal culture within provincial life. And the style of advocacy practiced at the criminal bar also changed over time: the florid oratory employed by the so-called "Irish school" of Old Bailey practitioners (notably Charles Phillips, whose controversial career Dickens followed very closely) was superseded by more measured and less emotional address. The presentation and interpretation of evidence became increasingly, as Bentham had hoped, a question of "science."

When Victoria ascended the throne in 1837, the court system had been a jumble of overlapping civil, ecclesiastical, and common law jurisdictions: one case involving church rates had woven its way through eight courts, from an ecclesiastical court of first instance to the House of Lords over a period of 16 years (1837–53), involving a total of 38 judge sittings (Waddams 259). And the empire took problems of jurisdiction beyond the British Isles. A struggle between Canada and the United States over the extradition of a fugitive slave, John Anderson, was complicated when the English Court of Queen's Bench presumed to exercise jurisdiction in Canada by issuing a writ of habeas corpus, and the substantive issues of extradition and natural justice were overshadowed by the related questions of imperial authority and colonial independence. Indeed, English legal culture was most rigorously tested in imperial jurisdictions. Fitzjames Stephen, the legal member of the Viceroy's Council in India from 1869 to 1872, saw himself as a legal missionary, spreading "the Gospel of the English," which was its law. This gospel was challenged on a number of fronts: by Rudyard Kipling, who suggested that the imposition of Empire was fraught with moral hazards for the empire-builders; and by Robert Louis Stevenson, in whose Pacific tales the English legal system is brought into contact with native systems of justice, and found wanting.

Although problems with uncoordinated jurisdictions were slow to resolve, substantive legal reform was more extensive in the Victorian period than at any time in English history since the revolutionary era following the Civil War. The effects were several. Firstly, the reach and power of positive law was increased and consolidated: "The whole of England is now policed and patrolled," it was said at the end of the century (Odgers 130). Secondly, a legislative network of basic public education (1870, 1876), health services (1848, 1875), and a carefully tiered system of local government (1888, 1894) characterized a general shift in social discourse from character-centered individualism to welfare collectivism (Wiener). Thirdly, the gradual movement towards democracy in the Reform Bills of 1832, 1867, and 1884 brought with it the legalization of trade unions (1871) and significant changes to employment law – reflected in a change of terminology from "master and servant" to "employer and workman" – culminating in the no-fault Workmen's Compensation Acts of 1897 and 1900. By century's end, legal practice, legal education, and the institutions of adjudication would have been unrecognizable to the practitioners of the previous century.

Theory

The theory and philosophy of law in Victorian England were shaped by seven Englishmen: Bentham and Stephen, noticed above; John Austin (1790–1859), Henry Sumner Maine (1822–88), Albert Venn Dicey (1835–1922), Frederick Pollock (1845–1937), and Frederic William Maitland (1850–1906). Although they all practiced to some degree, only Stephen enjoyed a full professional career in the law, and with the exception of Bentham they were all primarily involved in legal education. They discovered precedents and suggestions for their own theories and methods in Roman law and in the writings of German jurists, and their recurrent resource for contrast and comparison with English law was the Code Napoléon of France. Their methods were analytical, historical, and comparative, and it was their common aspiration to establish law as a science. The Official Law Reports, instituted in the 1860s and edited by Pollock, in which judicial precedents were systematically recorded, acquired an important place in the establishment of legal science. Pollock was also the founding editor of the first academic law journal in English, the *Law Quarterly Review*, the first issue of which appeared in 1885 (although by this time John Westlake had served as England's one founding member of the *Revue de droit international* in 1868). The next year Maitland helped found the Selden Society (named after the sixteenth-century jurist John Selden) to advance the knowledge of the history of English law, primarily through the publication of manuscript sources. In turning to textual sources, Maitland brought the scientific methods of late nineteenth-century historiography to bear upon the law. All these jurists explore English law as a set of cultural and linguistic practices that are the expression of the community they affect – "It is we who are guilty of our own law," as Maitland put it (*Westminster Review*, 1879) – and their writings focus, from varying legal perspectives, the tension between authority and individualism that pervades Victorian thought.

Bentham believed that the replacement of case-law by a code would necessarily establish a science of legislation. "Codification" is Bentham's neologism (*OED*, 1817), and it became a catch-phrase for law-reformers throughout the nineteenth century. It had no greater devotee than Stephen, who having spent three years codifying Indian law believed that codification would have brought to English law the certainty of Bradshaw's *Railway Guide* (Stephen 1895: 347). Suggesting predictability as well as certainty, the comparison reveals the extent to which a legal code might curb judicial discretion. This was crucial to Bentham's intention to thwart the power of the conservative combination of "Judge and Co.," who accordingly anathematized it in the name of individual judgment. Unlike Bentham, Austin did not oppose judge-made law, but he made it the basis of his call to codification as a rationalization of the existing system. Austin's theory that the principles on which cases are decided could themselves be codified and turned into statute-law was based on the inductive model of scientific method: "For what is that process of induction by which the principle is gathered before it is applied, but this very process of codifying such principles, performed on a particular occasion, and performed on a small scale?" (II, 666). The analytical method demonstrated by this argument reached its apotheosis in the work of Pollock. There natural science, civil law, case-law, even ethics, are conditioned by precedent, habituated by custom, and aligned in a system of analogical relationship whose principle of uniformity is reached through the inductive method.

A foundational principle of Bentham's attempt to establish a science of legislation had been his repudiation of "legal fictions," procedural pretenses the purpose of which is to give jurisdiction. As a dictionary definition from 1854 had it, "A 'Fiction in Law' is an assumption of a thing made for the purposes of justice, though the same thing could not be proved and may be literally untrue" (Stone 127). Bentham hated such pretenses: to him they were manifestations of language in its least controllable form. But Maine in 1861 accused Bentham of ignoring the role of legal fiction as a way of making law, one of the three "agencies by which Law is brought into harmony with society," the other two being Equity and Legislation (20). Maine extended the meaning of the term beyond its sense as false averment, "to signify any assumption which conceals, or affects to conceal, the fact that a rule of law has undergone alteration, its letter remaining unchanged, its operation being modified" (21–2). The semantic leverage afforded by this daring redefinition liberates the spirit from the letter of the law. To Maine, fictions are creative instruments of change, a species of virtual legislation which transforms a system of laws while concealing that transformation. Maine appeals to the double-language of case-law, in which each decision subtly alters established precedent while purporting to be its mere continuation. Fictions are a way of doing things both with and without words, for while the language of the law does not change, its meaning is on the move. Dicey's analysis of the reform of the law concerning the property of married women might be offered as an example of Maine's evolutionary pattern of law reform in Fiction, Equity, and Legislation (Dicey 369–96). This was a reform that had culminated in legislation, had begun in equity, and had turned on fiction. Under the Equitable jurisdiction of the Court of Chancery, it was possible for a married woman to "possess separate property over which her husband had no control whatever" (Dicey 377). But marriage settlements in Equity (as such arrangements were called) were for the rich; the poor were vulnerable to common-law rights of the husband. (Dicey adduces Thackeray's *Barry Lyndon* to exemplify the husband who abuses his common-law rights.) The Married Women's Property Act of 1870, thanks to a legal fiction, secured for all married women "the rights which the Court of Chancery had secured for those women who enjoyed the advantage of a marriage settlement." In Dicey's memorable words: "The rules of equity, framed for the daughters of the rich, have at last been extended to the daughters of the poor" (386, 395). Fiction and Equity had contended with the might of the Common Law to produce progressive Legislation.

To Stephen the procedures by which the law was applied constituted the strength of the English common law, as represented by a system of criminal justice driven by private litigation, rather than by the public inquiry of the French inquisitorial system (Stephen 1863: ch. 5). The adversarial practices of English law are continuous with the individualism of Victorian culture, and indeed the canonical texts of Victorian individualism are frequently cast as adversarial discourse, and are thus in some measure modeled on the law. Mill's *On Liberty* (1859) depends on images of conflict and adversarial process. Law supplied Mill with a language for his discussion of individual judgment, in which all opinions must be given a "hearing." In a brace of Mill's *Westminster Review* essays (1838–40) progressive and conservative modes of thought clash in the case of Bentham v Coleridge, and his *Autobiography* (1872) brings opposed philosophical schools into the relationship of Intuition v Experience. Newman's *Apologia* propounds, as its title suggests, the case for the defense in Kingsley v Newman, and also an advocate's case for the Roman Catholic Church and its clergy. Wilde's exercise in self-justification, *De Profundis* (1905), written in jail during 1896–7, recasts Wilde v Queensberry as Wilde v Lord Alfred Douglas. And in Hopkins's response, in "The Wreck of the *Deutschland*" (1876), to the Protestant culture of Germany as represented by the anti-Catholic laws from which five Franciscan nuns were escaping, his poetic voice is cast in impassioned advocacy on behalf of Christ against Luther.

Stephen's argument for the superiority of the English system is based on his belief in cross-examination as the best instrument for the sifting and testing of evidence. Whereas the inquisitorial procedure, in which someone may be examined on the same matter on several occasions, results in evidence "like handwriting scratched out and altered so often as to become, at last, one unintelligible mass of blotches and scratches" (Stephen 1863: 459), the adversarial procedure brings the crucial evidence into immediate focus. Cross-examination is the key technique of the adversarial method, and Stephen's lucid account of it (1863: ch. 5) can stand as a defense of the English system against the case made by Trollope in *Orley Farm*. Trollope criticizes cross-examination as the bullying of witnesses, and yet his novel is written by the practice against which it protests. The most striking feature of its narrative manner is the use of many narrated monologues in which the characters subject themselves to rigorous cross-examination as they interrogate their own motives. Cross-examination is part of the grammar of their interior lives, and their various and conflicting loyalties are tested, with the help of the narrative voice, by the language of the law. Such intrasubjectivity is integral to the performative analysis of legal discourse in Browning's *The Ring and the Book* (1868–9): the series of monologists incorporate other viewpoints than their own by "quoting" arguments and objections which they can then answer, and the extended composition of two opposing lawyers' arguments is nestled at the core of the poem (books 8 and 9).

"Evidence is the basis of justice," Bentham had claimed in his *Rationale of Judicial Evidence* (1827). The many substantial Victorian reforms of the law of evidence in the nineteenth century culminated in the Criminal Evidence Act of 1898, which gave the criminal accused the right to testify on oath at his own trial, and fascination with the epistemology of evidence developed across the century. Stephen's introductory remarks on "The Nature of Evidence" could have prefaced *Middlemarch*: "All the facts with which we are acquainted, visible or invisible, internal or external, are connected together in a vast series of sequences which we call cause and effect, and the constitution of things is such, that men are able to infer from one fact the existence, either past or future, of other facts" (1863: 235–6). Inference, like induction, is a process of reasoning from effects to causes which underlies many forms of inquiry, but the mind may be baffled by the ambiguous epistemological spaces in which evidence is constituted. In Stevenson's *Strange Case of Dr Jekyll and Mr Hyde* (1886) the narrative is focalized through the lawyer Utterson, whose legal imagination is challenged by the unraveling of events which he tries to construe as evidence. The confidence with which he casts himself as Mr Seek is confounded by the mysteries of Jekyll's laboratory, which are beyond the reach of legal science (Jekyll is a Doctor of Civil Law as well as a Doctor of Medicine). Collins's *The Moonstone* anticipates Stevenson in its supersession of conventionally legal evidence, as Franklin Blake investigates a mystery to which the key is his own unconscious behavior.

In contrast to these destabilizing anticipations of the modern fascination with the unconscious, Victorians generally stressed conscious responsibility, and throughout the period the language of legal identity informs the sense of moral accountability (Rodensky 3–91). Gladstone thought the qualities necessary to the exercise of the franchise were "self-command, self-control, respect for order, patience under suffering, confidence in the law, regard for superiors" (Wiener 144). His 1864 phraseology echoes the advice of Pallas to Tennyson's Oenone (1832): "Self-reverence, self-knowledge, self-control, / These three alone lead life to sovereign power" ("Oenone," ll. 142–3). As the subsequent lines of the poem reveal, "sovereign" here has legal force, as indeed it does for Mill in *On Liberty*: "Over himself, over his own body and mind, the individual is sovereign" (ch. 1). The criminal law was a discourse of responsibility, part of a broader Victorian "discourse of character" (Wiener 38) built upon the individual sense of right and wrong. For Stephen it was "absolutely necessary that legal definitions of crimes should be based upon moral distinctions" (1863: 82), and he uses the concept of "malice" because it is his criterion of legal responsibility for criminal intention. Victorian notions of criminal intention and responsibility were complicated, however, by the case (1843) of Daniel M'Naghten, who in attempting to assassinate the prime minister Sir Robert Peel killed his private secretary, and was tried for murder. Because medical evidence suggested that M'Naghten was suffering severe delusions of persecution, the judge directed the jury to find him not guilty on the grounds of insanity. The M'Naghten Rules (as they are still known) evolved from subsequent debate among the judges summoned before the House of Lords: to establish an insanity defense, the accused had to be under such a defect of reason "as not to know the nature and quality of the act he was doing, or, if he did know it, that he did not know he was doing what was wrong" (*R. v. M'Naghten* (1843) 8 ER 718). In his *General View* Stephen acknowledged that if the existence of "moral insanity" and "irresistible impulses" were proved, it "would disprove malice" (1863: 95); later he would argue that the law should acknowledge mental diseases – irresistible impulses, delusions, morbid excitements – which destroy the power of self-control. On these grounds, it could be argued that Porphyria's lover (Browning, 1842) would not have been held legally responsible for his actions.

Conceptions of sanity were implicated in the legal doctrine of the sanctity and liberty of contract. As George Jessel said (1875): "If there is one thing more than another that public policy requires it is that men of full age and competent understanding shall have the utmost liberty of contracting, and that their contracts when entered into freely and voluntarily shall be held sacred" (Cornish and Clark 269). For Maine the condition of individualism is the power to contract, which is in turn the condition of social development. Contract is the jurisprudential principle of discipline in Maine's individualist vision, and the obligation of contract represents "the complete reciprocity and indissoluble connection of rights and duties," which Maine figures as a chain of law between the contracting parties (290). Where Bentham, in his reaction against the conservative ideology of Blackstone and Burke, had disavowed any form of social contract other than the greatest happiness of the greatest number, Maine's stress on reciprocal obligation invoked a terminology of rights and duties, which implied a social contract subtending agreements between individuals. The terminology ran through the social thought of the period: in Carlyle's *Chartism* (1839) it was used to differentiate between the nexus of Cash Payment (individual contract) and the nexus according to the law of nature (comprehensive social contract); Mill tried to avoid it in *On Liberty*, but found himself compelled to consider the nature of social obligations; and in *Culture and Anarchy* (1869) Matthew Arnold, with both Carlyle and Mill in mind, tried to put the terms into relationship by subsuming them in the concept of "welfare."

Maine's language instantiates a web of social obligations, for chains are infinitely extendable, even into universal contracts: "For so the whole round earth is every way / Bound by gold chains about the feet of God" (Tennyson, "Morte d'Arthur" [1842], ll. 254–5). Once a chain has begun, as George Eliot might ask, where will it end? This was a real legal question, and it followed from the basic rhetorical model of contract law as formulated by William Anson, for whom contract is created by the acceptance of an offer: "Acceptance is to Offer what a lighted match is to a train of gunpowder" (*Principles of the English Law of Contract* [1879], 7th edn 1893). Anson's analogy exploded into the courts in the landmark case of Carlill v Carbolic Smoke Ball Co. (1892–3). The question here was whether the defendants' advertised offer of £100 to anyone who, after using their product in accordance with the printed directions, contracted influenza, constituted an intention to enter into legal relations. The defendants maintained that their offer was too vague to be taken seriously, and that a unilateral contract was not legally possible; but they had deposited £1,000 in a bank account "showing our sincerity in the matter," and when Mrs Carlill caught influenza and her husband brought an action, the judges took the advertisement at its word and found for the plaintiff. Novelists, once again, found otherwise. In *Our Mutual*

Friend (1865) the links in Maine's socially-binding chain of law do not hold: Wrayburn complains of "people's breaking promises and contracts and bargains of all sorts" (book 2, ch. 2), and the will of Robert Baldwin is a *mise en abyme*, an internal symbol of misdirected will (book 3, ch. 6). *Our Mutual Friend* depicts Maine's world turned upside down, and indeed throughout Victorian literature contracts, wills, and settlements are the occasion of conflict. The settlement is best understood as an intergenerational family contract whereby inherited lands belong to the family rather than to the individuals who comprise the family at a particular time. Because of this institution's infinite capacity for focusing tension within families, settlements in fiction are invariably the site of the conflicting demands of social contract and individualism. In the compounding uncertainties of *Daniel Deronda* (1876), heralded by the gambling with which the novel so strikingly opens, and configured by wills, settlements, and threatened disinheritance, these conflicting demands are unresolved. But a settlement could also be a catalyst for self-determination against family identity. Female independence in Victorian literature is frequently signified by a woman's rejection of what is legally hers to inherit: Dorothea Casaubon rejects the will of her husband in *Middlemarch*, and Esther Lyon turns from the Transome estate in *Felix Holt*. Aurora Leigh's refusal of Romney's offer of marriage is a powerful assertion of gendered independence: by rejecting his reduction of love to a "simple law-clause" she liberates herself from the patriarchal system of settled estates (Barrett Browning, *Aurora Leigh* [1856] II. 785).

In his claim that the movement of progressive societies "has hitherto been a movement *from Status to Contract*" (141), Maine's "hitherto" embodies a challenge which signifies a crisis: whither contract, and the individualism it expresses, in the increasingly regulated context of English society? In various ways, as the century developed, the law curbed and inhibited the Benthamite principle of laissez-faire. The growth of liability insurance, and of the limited liability company, meant that responsibility was focused less upon individuals, and was distributed more generally throughout social mechanisms (Wiener 203); and within criminal law a shift in emphasis from moral condemnation to social regulation enhanced the law's function as the instrument of public order (Wiener 260). In Dicey's extreme view, the Factory Acts of the mid-century decisively signaled the defeat of individualism by collectivism: this legislation "introduced socialistic enactments into the laws of England" by recognizing "the principle that the regulation of public labour is the concern of the State" (Dicey 237–8). Trollope responded to such irritants in the legal culture by turning to the imaginary spaces of the new world. In *The Way We Live Now* (1875) Winifred Hurtle's courageous individualism is validated by the summary justice of Oregon and Kansas, which the novel offers as a refreshing contrast to the moribund practices of English law; and her story challenges the reader's imagination with the possibilities of a new legal frontier.

See also 1870; CLERICAL, MEDICAL; FICTION, HISTORIOGRAPHY; SKIN

REFERENCES

Austin, J. (1885) *Lectures on Jurisprudence; or, The Philosophy of Positive Law*, 2 vols, 5th edn, rev. and ed. R. Campbell. London: John Murray.

Beattie, J. (1986) *Crime and the Courts in England, 1660–1800*. Oxford: Clarendon Press.

Cairns, D. (1998) *Advocacy and the Making of the Adversarial Criminal Trial 1800–1865*. Oxford: Oxford University Press.

Cornish, W. R., and G. Clark (1989) *Law and Society in England 1750–1950*. London: Sweet and Maxwell.

Dicey, A. V. (1905) *Lectures on the Relation between Law and Public Opinion in England during the Nineteenth Century*. London: Macmillan.

Dolin, K. (1998) *Fiction and the Law: Legal Discourse in Victorian and Modernist Literature*. Cambridge: Cambridge University Press.

Eden, K. (1986) *Poetic and Legal Fiction in the Aristotelian Tradition*. Princeton: Princeton University Press.

Gallagher, C. (1985) *The Industrial Reformation of English Fiction: Social Discourse and Narrative Form 1832–1867*. Chicago: Chicago University Press.

Gatrell, V. A. C. (1994) *The Hanging Tree: Execution and the English People, 1770–1868*. Oxford: Oxford University Press.

Krueger, C. (2010) *Reading for the Law: British Literary History and Gender Advocacy*. Charlottesville: University of Virginia Press.

Langbein, J. (2003) *The Origins of Adversary Criminal Trial*. Oxford: Oxford University Press.

Lobban, M. (2003) " 'Old Wine in New Bottles': The Concept and Practice of Law Reform, c. 1780–1830." In *Rethinking the Age of Reform: Britain 1780–1850*, ed. A. Burns and J. Innes. Cambridge: Cambridge University Press.

Maine, H. S. (1986) *Ancient Law: Its Connection with the Early History of Society and Its Relation to Modern Ideas*. New York: Dorset Press.

Mill, J. S. (1980) *Mill on Bentham and Coleridge*, ed. F. R. Leavis. Cambridge: Cambridge University Press.

——(1989) *On Liberty*. Cambridge: Cambridge University Press.

Odgers, W. B. (ed.) (1901) *A Century of Law Reform: Twelve Lectures on the Changes in the Law of England during the Nineteenth Century*. London: Macmillan.

Petch, S. (1997) "Law, Equity, and Conscience in Victorian England." *Victorian Literature and Culture* 25, 123–39.

Polloczek, D. P. (1999) *Literature and Legal Discourse: Equity and Ethics from Sterne to Conrad*. Cambridge: Cambridge University Press.

R. v. *M'Naghten* (1843) 8 ER 718.

Reade, C. (1903) *The Wandering Heir*. London: Chatto and Windus.

Rodensky, L. (2003) *The Crime in Mind: Criminal Responsibility and the Victorian Novel*. Oxford: Oxford University Press.

Schramm, J.-M. (2000) *Testimony and Advocacy in Victorian Law, Literature, and Theology*. Cambridge: Cambridge University Press.

——(2012) "Dickens and the National Interest: On the Representation of Parties in *Bleak House*." *Law and the Humanities* 6, 219–44.

Semmel, B. (1994) *George Eliot and the Politics of National Inheritance*. New York: Oxford University Press.

Stephen, J. F. (1857) "The License of Modern Novelists." *Edinburgh Review* 106, 124–56.

——(1863) *A General View of the Criminal Law of England*. London: Macmillan.

Stephen, L. (1895) *The Life of Sir James Fitzjames Stephen*. London: Smith, Elder.

——(1900) *The English Utilitarians*, 3 vols. London: Duckworth.

Stone, M. (1985) "Dickens, Bentham, and the Fictions of the Law: A Victorian Controversy and Its Consequences." *Victorian Studies* 29, 125–54.

Sutherland, J. (1991) "Wilkie Collins and the Origins of the Sensation Novel." *Dickens Studies Annual* 20, 243–58.

Waddams, S. M. (1992) *Law, Politics, and the Church of England: The Career of Stephen Lushington 1782–1873*. Cambridge: Cambridge University Press.

Watt, G. (2009) *Equity Stirring: The Story of Justice Beyond the Law*. Oxford: Hart Publishing.

Welsh, A. (1985) *George Eliot and Blackmail*. Cambridge MA: Harvard University Press.

——(1992) *Strong Representations: Narrative and Circumstantial Evidence in England.* Baltimore: Johns Hopkins University Press.

Wiener, M. J. (1990) *Reconstructing the Criminal: Culture, Law, and Policy in England, 1830–1914.* Cambridge: Cambridge University Press.

FURTHER READING

Frank, C. (2010) *Law, Literature, and the Transmission of Culture in England, 1837–1925.* Farnham: Ashgate.

Grossman, J. (2002) *The Art of Alibi: English Law Courts and the Novel.* Baltimore: Johns Hopkins University Press.

Lacey, N. (2008) *Women, Crime, and Character: From Moll Flanders to Tess of the d'Urbervilles.* Oxford: Oxford University Press.

Schor, H. (2013) *Curious Subjects: Women and the Trials of Realism.* Oxford and New York: Oxford University Press.

Schramm, J.-M. (2012) *Atonement and Self-Sacrifice in Nineteenth-Century Narrative.* Cambridge: Cambridge University Press.

12

Medical

Lawrence Rothfield

As the young Pip is being brought upstairs to visit Miss Havisham, in chapter 11 of Dickens's *Great Expectations* (1861), he meets "a gentleman groping his way down" who turns the boy to the light to examine his face, questions him briefly, advises him with a frown, "You behave yourself!", and then releases him and continues downstairs. It is not until years later that Pip comes to know this man with the "disagreeably sharp and suspicious eyes" as Jaggers, the lawyer. Jaggers's legalistic view of humanity as guilt-ridden – "I have a pretty large experience of boys, and you're a bad set of fellows" – dominates the novel, not just because Jaggers sits in the center of the web of non-relations linking Miss Havisham's upstairs world of great expectations to Magwitch's downstairs world of crime, but also because the kind of power Jaggers exercises over Pip is only the most potent version of the punitive impulse we see at work throughout: in Pumblechook's browbeating, Mrs Joe's "tickling," and Pip's own internalized "oppressed conscience."

Yet even as Dickens registers this disagreeable dominance, he hints at another perspective Jaggers might have represented in a different world:

> With these words he released me – which I was glad of, for his hand smelt of scented soap – and went his way downstairs. I wondered whether he could be a doctor; but no, I thought; he couldn't be a doctor, or he would have a quieter and more persuasive manner.

As Pip's momentary interpretative puzzlement shows, doctors and lawyers in the mid-Victorian period occupy roughly similar positions within the cultural imagina-

---

A New Companion to Victorian Literature and Culture, First Edition. Edited by Herbert F. Tucker.
© 2014 John Wiley & Sons, Ltd. Published 2014 by John Wiley & Sons, Ltd.

tion. Both attend to individuals in need, both make house calls, and both wash their hands after seeing their clients; both have aptitudes for diagnosis based on physical observation, "large experience," and questioning. But such similarities only heighten the differences between the two sorts of professional. Jaggers discharges his duties by executing the intentions of Miss Havisham rather than tending to her infirmities, and when he washes his hands it symbolizes his disavowal of responsibility rather than self-consciousness about the medical benefits of cleanliness. His "manner" is accusatory, repellent, and guilt-inducing, not the "quiet and more persuasive" manner of a physician, whose ideal type Dickens portrays in *Little Dorrit* (1857) as imbued with "an equality of compassion no more disturbed than the Divine Master's of all healing was" (ch. 25).

"Manner" here stands, as it does everywhere in Victorian culture, not just for politeness but for something deeper: a way of exercising power and manifesting authority. And for Dickens, at least, the physician's power seems remarkably exempt from the critique leveled against lawyers and the policing of the liberal individual subject they help enforce. Yet the obliqueness of Dickens's positive allusion to medical power here is perhaps as relevant as anything the passage above implies about Victorian attitudes toward medicine itself. It is as if medicine's exemption from criticism were purchased at the cost of near-invisibility. Not only in Dickens, but in Victorian literature more generally, one finds a conspicuous absence of medical themes – of stories centrally *about* doctors interacting with patients, struggling against diseases, illness, or injury – at least until the 1870s. While there are a few attempts to depict medical men, most notably in Thackeray's *Pendennis* (1850), Trollope's *Barchester Towers* (1857) and *Doctor Thorne* (1858), and Conan Doyle's insider's view in his short-story collection *Round the Red Lamp* (1894), such depictions tend to focus on the social and cultural standing of the apothecary or physician rather than showing doctors at work or in love. Even here, however, there is surprisingly little in Victorian literature, compared to the number of works that feature lawyers or churchmen.

One explanation for this may be that these latter professionals also qualified as "gentlemen" for those in higher society, with all the doors this opened not just literally but imaginatively for novelists, while most doctors could only aspire to such status, as one of Trollope's snobs in *The Vicar of Bullhampton* (1870) makes clear: "She would not absolutely say that a physician was not a gentleman, or even a surgeon; but she would not allow to physic the same absolute privilege which, in her eyes, belonged to the law and the church" (ch. 9). Lawyers or churchmen could be imagined as suitable romantic interlocutors in a way that medical men, for the most part, could not. Moreover, medical careers lacked the dramatic possibilities for cross-class mobility and conflict inherent in the lives of nonprofessionals – orphans, governesses, and industrial entrepreneurs, for instance – without offering writers the imaginative compensation of a well-established intra-professional code of manners that could enable a novelist like Trollope or Eliot to take clerical life as a synecdoche for the broader culture. There was, of course, a story to be told about the emergence of the modern medical profession from the ancient corporate hierarchy of physicians, surgeons, and apothecaries (each with its own privileges, coat of arms, ceremonies, dress, and rituals) into the structural form we are familiar with today: the division between general practitioners and consultants or specialists affiliated with hospitals. But while a few Victorians – Thomas Wakley, founder in 1823 of *The Lancet*, or Florence Nightingale – stood out as heroic figures battling for the medical good, the history of Victorian medicine lacked the kind of sharp break with corporate structures that would enable novelists to depict physicians as romantic world-historical individuals or even careerist wannabes.

Indeed, given the motley arrangement of colleges and societies, the *ad hoc*, apprentice-like nature of medical training, and the relatively low prestige, pay, and possibilities for advancement associated with work that involved manual labor, medicine hardly qualified as a career until well into the latter part of the century. Unlike lawyers or clerics, who could imagine themselves climbing a career ladder that in principle extended into the stratosphere of politics or the higher echelons of the Church, aspiring physicians, surgeons, and apothecaries of the early Victorian era faced a slowly crumbling but still discouraging array of intellectual, social, and jurisdictional restraints on ambition. The typical student either apprenticed directly, or spent four years or so desultorily reading, attending lectures in private medical schools, and ward-walking before being crammed for an examination in which, an irate writer to *The Lancet* (1848) complained, "scanty physiology and pathology, decked out in respectable Latin, will stand higher than mere professional excellence, marred by a false concord, or a fault of prosody." Those with family connections then made their way through nepotism into the London elite or settled for a quiet life in towns and villages outside the 15-mile limit that legally defined the privileged zone of London practitioners licensed by the Royal College of Physicians or the College of Surgeons. As London itself ballooned into a megalopolis, increasing numbers of underemployed medics began to develop a "general" practice within the city limits, taking second licenses enabling them to practice surgery as a physician or give medical advice as an apothecary; but despite the efforts of Wakley and others to tear down all the institutional walls, the general practitioner remained more or less an underling with dim prospects.

After the passage of the Medical Registration Act of 1858, which abolished regional licensing and formally installed the hospital as the seat of medical instruction, the lot of the average physician improved somewhat. At the very least, it was now possible to imagine a great career beginning in a provincial medical school and ending in a London hospital at the pinnacle of what was now a unified profession. Those in this new order who made it to the top as consulting physicians could imagine that there were no limits to medical power; hence the flowering, in the late Victorian period, of larger-than-life representations of physicians as both godlike and demonic. But even – indeed, especially – after the passage of the Medical Act, licensing was by no means rigorously enforced, leaving the average practitioner in an ongoing struggle for authority against folk healers, midwives, and other traditional providers of medical aid, as well as a slew of quacks and charlatans who now poured into the medical marketplace. Promising electric cures for nonexistent diseases, competing fiercely for medical trade by unabashedly advertising, or even luring unsuspecting patients into "museums" of anatomical curiosities connected directly to examining rooms, these medical entrepreneurs made life miserable for the rank-and-file practitioner. Unable to perform medical miracles that might clear a career path in this crowded field, the average doctor was doomed to a life of accommodation and ingratiation, bone-setting and pill-prescribing, with at best the hope of respectability, at worst the specter of penury. In short, medicine was not the stuff of which dreams or plots of great expectations are made.

If the average medical career did not lend itself easily to thematization, however, changes in medicine's social structure nonetheless did make themselves felt culturally in a variety of ways. Woodcourt in Dickens's *Bleak House* (1853) and Tom Thurnall in Kingsley's *Two Years Ago* (1857) embodied Wakley's reforming impulse (though not particularly memorably), and Nightingale provided the template for a number of vocationally hungering heroines of the 1860s and 1870s, including Dorothea Brooke in Eliot's *Middlemarch* (1872). *Middlemarch* also stands out, of course, as the only Victorian novel to provide a fully realized characterization of a physician caught up in the murky professional politics of the period. Yet even Eliot found it necessary to deviate from the average in order to make a medical life narratable. Her Tertius Lydgate is an odd bird in the English context, trained not in London but in Paris and Edinburgh, where medical visionaries made it possible to conceive of medicine as a heroic undertaking which could lead to an epic life or tragic failure; even so, Eliot ultimately feels compelled to apologize to her readers in the book's "Finale" for defining as a tragic figure one who ends as "what is called a successful man."

But the relative paucity of explicit literary representations of physicians does not mean that medicine is marginal to Victorian culture. On the contrary, as Pip's comment indicates, medicine's quietness of manner is an indicator of its persuasiveness. Indeed, Victorian medicine has been so persuasive that we tend to overlook the astonishing changes it imposed on British culture, transformations quite as profound as those associated with the Industrial Revolution, running so deep that we no longer can recognize their originally revolutionary character. In the course of Victoria's lifetime (1819–1901), smallpox vaccination was made compulsory; the postmortem autopsy became routine; anatomy and pathology were established as standard elements of a medical school education; inhalation anesthesia was introduced; physicians discovered that at least some diseases were transmitted not by atmosphere-corrupting poison seeping from decomposing organic matter but by germs; antiseptic surgery began to be practiced; preventive and occupational medicine as well as public health and sanitary medicine were founded. The general practitioner appeared, along with the professional nurse and a range of specialists in fields such as psychiatry, neurology, sexology, and obstetrics. New kinds of disease and patient identities came into being: possession was redefined as hysteria, sodomy as homosexuality, hypochondria as neurasthenia, pregnancy as a medical condition. The hypodermic needle was perfected, along with injectable drugs like cocaine, supplementing the use of opium, morphine, and other pain-killing medications and helping consolidate and complicate the concept of addiction and the figure of the addict. Artificial insemination was invented by the Victorians, as was vivisection, and circumcision was made routine. There also emerged a slew of medical ideas and practices which mercifully have not survived, or have survived as jokes: now-vanished disease entities such as spermatorrhea, masturbatory insanity, monomania, hysteria; bizarre or kooky practices such as clitoridectomy, wet dressing, the cold-water bath, electric medicine, mesmerism, and phrenology.

These various technological, conceptual, and professional innovations each had an impact on Victorian culture. Taken together, they amount to a vast extension of the powers and capabilities of medicine. Doctors by the end of the nineteenth century were simply able to do more to, with, and for their patients – not only because they had a much wider array of diagnostic and therapeutic techniques available to them, nor because some of these techniques actually eased suffering or even in rare cases cured or prevented disease, but because the domain of medicine expanded dramatically. In what can only be called a massive medicalization of Victorian life, aspects of existence and forms of behavior that formerly had been either not problematized at all or thought of in nonmedical terms came to be understood as matters in which health and disease were at stake.

Describing medicalization in this way makes it seem a rather sinister event, a sort of power grab. And indeed in some manifestations Victorian medicine did involve a seizing upon groups – women, the poor, those with distinctive sexual habits or emotional makeups or cognitive capacities – whose difference could be defined as pathology in need of monitoring, therapy, regulation: in need, in short, of discipline.

The most egregiously coercive of these disciplinary medical practices were those connected to social medicine and the public health movements, which took shape in the early Victorian period through what social historian Frank Mort has called a "medico-moral" political alliance between medics and moral reformers. Spurred by the cholera epidemic of 1831, doctors, clerics, and local officials who had earlier collaborated only when dealing with prisoners or lock-hospital patients began focusing on the urban poor, whose immoral lifestyle was thought to make them agents of contagion. This new focus is reflected in literature in the subgenre of industrial fiction that flourished during the 1840s, when Elizabeth Gaskell and other reform-minded novelists led readers into dank Manchester basements where sewage seeped up from the earth floors and drunkenness, licentiousness, and class resentment festered. Correlating working-class unrest with unsanitary conditions on one hand and lax morality on the other, such novels helped the Victorian bourgeoisie symbolically to transform a political crisis into a social problem by locating the roots of conflict in conditions at once pathological and vicious.

Concern about political unrest from below, and efforts to repress the unruly poor or send in clerics to help relieve their suffering and counsel submission, were of course nothing new. What *was* novel in the Victorian period was the involvement of medicine in such policing, and – particularly important for students of Victorian literature and culture – the concurrent effort to justify such policing by defining the body politic in specifically medical terms. Earlier eras had defined state power by appeals to a metaphysical notion of the body politic (a notion allegorized in the conception of the king's two bodies); more recently, Thomas Malthus had redefined the body politic in the nightmarishly materialist terms of political economy, as a mathematically predictable entity – population – defined by its natural tendency to reproduce until checked by the laws of nature, laws enforced by diseases (among other agencies). As Mary Poovey (1988) has pointed out, the Victorians built on Malthus's foundation of a body subject to disease while rejecting its law-bound determinism for a more therapeutically optimistic vision of the population, which they renamed "the social body."

Fusing (or rather confusing) medical and ethical norms, the metaphor of the social body was at once more flexible and more far-reaching than the older metaphors of the body politic or population had been. A body defined in medical terms necessarily would exhibit disorder not simply as outbreaks of political violence or the dismal inevitability of sexual reproduction, but in subtle processes occurring in the hidden depths whence diseases emerge. Thus, for example, James Kay, one of the leading figures in the early public health movement (and a man who began his medical career publishing papers on brain and circulatory diseases), could speak of "the moral leprosy of vice" as "capable of corrupting the whole body of society, like an insidious disease." Leprosy was an ancient trope for moral disfigurement, of course; what was new was the medical twist Kay gave to it by emphasizing its gradualness as a pathological process. In doing so, he was simply extending to the social body the logic of medical research that Eliot's Lydgate expressed more nobly as aimed at piercing "the obscurity of those minute processes which prepare human misery and joy, those invisible thoroughfares which are the first lurking-places of anguish, mania, and crime, that delicate poise and transition which determine the growth of happy or unhappy consciousness" (ch. 16).

Lydgate, however, represented a very different brand of physician from Kay, a clinician rather than a public health official, and the reference to "minute processes" for a clinician would have meant something very different from what it meant for a practitioner of social medicine. Even within social medicine itself, the social body went through several different incarnations over the course of the century. It is important, therefore, to look more closely at the rhetorics of pathology that came into play, because different theories of disease causation gave rise to quite distinct sorts of "therapeutic" interventions and literary practices.

Social medicine relied on the miasmatic theory of disease causation, which held that epidemic influences in the atmosphere become malignant when combined with the poisonous effluvia arising out of decomposing organic matter. Scientifically reasonable in its materialism, easily graspable and illustratable – think of the fever-bearing fog that seeps through Dickens's London – and yet also traceable to human agents, miasma theory allowed early sanitary reformers to argue that bad personal habits could engender disease as well as moral decay, and lent scientific legitimacy to the call to empower public health officers not just to isolate and quarantine those found to be already infected, but to enter into households and "improve" living conditions to prevent disease.

By the 1860s, however, the miasmatic theory had been largely discredited, after epidemiologists discovered that death rates from cholera correlated directly with the pumps and cisterns of specific London water companies, leading to the conclusion that the disease was transmitted by bad water rather than bad air. Social medicine then turned to a different rhetoric of pathology that helped shift the focus of medico-moral power and redistribute authority within the sanitary movement. Doctors specializing in venereal diseases, the most notorious of whom was William Acton, called for health officers to turn their attention away from diseases transmitted by miasma in order to focus instead on the danger to the social body posed by syphilis and gonorrhea, and on the need to monitor the agents of these contagious diseases. In principle, such an appeal was neutral with regard to who the agents might be; in calling for the state to take over the administration of public health, doctors set themselves up as objective scientific reformers opposed to the inept moralistic meddling of philanthropic amateurs. In practice, however, the public health measures enacted in the 1860s – most notably the Contagious Diseases Act of 1864 – proved to be, if anything, more biased than earlier policies. Only the target had changed, from class to gender. The new public health initiatives identified prostitutes rather than the working poor as agents of infection, giving wide latitude to local physicians and police in identifying suspected carriers. As a result, women found that their mere presence on the streets had been redefined as a medical danger; indeed, within the medically dubious physiology of sex purveyed by Acton and his followers, female sexuality was defined as both dangerous to others and pathological *per se*, as opposed to male sexuality, which Acton argued was uncontrollable by nature and therefore both unregulable by law and a feature of health in men.

While the Contagious Diseases Act was repealed within a few decades, it portended a much more long-lasting and frightening development within medico-moral policing: the medicalizing not only of sexuality but of other categories of deviance as well. Seen as an event within the history of Victorian medicine, sexual policing appears as part of a broader development of medical surveillance. Beginning in the 1860s, psychiatrists began to discriminate between a number of different sorts of "partial" or "latent" insanity, replacing the earlier catchall legal defense of monomania with a spectrum of neurasthenias; Victorian psychologists began to distinguish among cognitive disabilities (retardation, imbecility, cretinism, etc.); and sexologists created what Foucault has called "a mosaic of perversions" that medicalized behaviors such as fetishism, sodomy, and even masturbation. Such efforts came to a head in the late 1880s and early 1890s, when Richard von Krafft-Ebing, Professor of Psychiatry at Vienna, published *Psychopathia Sexualis*. Confusing as Krafft-Ebing's logic was (he waffled on whether the pathologies he was describing were congenital or the effects of degeneration), his book was incredibly influential in establishing in the public mind the conviction that figures such as the "lust-murderer" and the "invert" were not just criminals but pathological types. Max Nordau's equally popular *Degeneration* (first translated in 1895) simply extended Krafft-Ebing's medical argument from individuals to intellectual groups of "sick" artists.

Whether they supported medical policing or were themselves the target of it, Victorian writers were caught up in this movement. Inevitably its fantasies of sensationally lost self-control, pursuit by normalizing authorities, radically alterable sensibility, and degenerative morbidity found cultural expression. From Mary Elizabeth Braddon's Lady Audley — confined for life in an asylum because a physician is willing to declare that "there is latent insanity! . . . She has the cunning of madness, with the prudence of intelligence . . . She is dangerous!" (ch. 37) — to Browning's Guido Franceschini to Stevenson's Mr Hyde and Wilde's Dorian Gray, late Victorian literature is replete with hounded, haunted figures who represent the dangerously pathological.

Looking back on these fictions and the medical ideas underlying them today, it is difficult to understand how anyone could have taken them seriously. They seem to show that when the social body is taken as a real thing, the metaphor opens the door for mischief, enabling bad medicine and tendentious social policy to masquerade as real, disinterested science, and giving rise to grotesque fictions. In clinical medicine, on the other hand, where doctors focus on anatomies rather than behavior, individuals rather than groups, one might expect to find a more even-handed application of medical practices across classes and genders. Yet even here, notoriously, a double standard prevailed for the bodies of the poor and women. In the Anatomy Act of 1832, for example, as Ruth Richardson has brilliantly shown, the need for cadavers in medical research led to passage — in the face of widespread political opposition and even rioting — of a measure that singled out the destitute for dissection. (As late as 1864, in the figure of Betty Higden in *Our Mutual Friend*, Dickens could still movingly evoke the terror this Act generated in elderly poor facing the possibility of dying in the workhouse without money to pay for burial.) And the anatomical conceptualizing of the body as an economy of vital forces connected by a network of tissues did not prevent physicians from claiming that the female body was both more sensitive physiologically and distinctly organized with the uterus as the center of its anatomical web; the result was an array of horrendous medical interventions directed at women (ovariotomy, clitoridectomy, the rest cure).

Given that all these coercive horrors were legally sanctioned, it is difficult not to take the opposition we began with, between Jaggers's lawyerly bullying and the quietly persuasive manner of a doctor, as an ideological ruse masking a fundamental equivalence or at least strategic alliance between legal and medical power. This jaundiced view of Victorian medicine, developed in the earlier work of Foucault and his followers, stresses the essential continuity between the overtly punitive and repressive power of the police and the softer but perhaps more constraining power exercised by agencies like medicine. The police force us to behave; the doctor orders us, but we usually follow these orders consensually. As a result, as D. A. Miller puts it, the disciplinary force inherent in medicalization "never passes for such." In Miller's brilliant reading of the Victorian novel, novelists themselves participate in this disciplinary project – not by representing triumphant doctors and compliant patients, but by "putting in place a perceptual grid in which a division between the normal and the deviant inherently imposes itself" (18).

The Foucauldian approach to medicalization brings into high relief a crucial tendency within Victorian culture. But it does so at the cost of giving a slanted and partial account of what was in reality an extremely complex and uneven development. Medical power picked out women, the poor, and deviants for special scrutiny, it is true, but focusing exclusively on double standards misses the more fundamental point that Victorian medicine aimed at subjecting *all* bodies to its gaze. The Anatomy Act itself, for example, began as an effort to persuade all citizens that it was their duty to donate their bodies to science (as Jeremy Bentham did his), not as the punitive measure addressed only to paupers that it ultimately became. Similarly, women were thought to be more susceptible by nature to hysteria, given their higher general level of sensibility and anatomical organization, but since the fundamentals of physiology applied to both sexes, men could and did suffer from hysteria too.

Moreover, medicine's relation to juridical and moral practices was not always collaborative. In some cases one might even argue that doctors were downright progressive. For example, sexologists – including Krafft-Ebing himself – stood in the vanguard of those calling for decriminalizing same-sex sodomy, and they did so on the basis of biological and medical arguments. And as A. J. Youngson and Mary Poovey (1995) have shown in very different ways, the mid-century battle over the introduction of chloroform anesthesia into midwifery pitted doctors against clerics who maintained that the pangs of labor resulted from God's curse on the daughters of Eve. This is not to say that submitting to chloroform anesthesia was an unalloyed good, only that in assessing the effect of this sort of medicalizing it is important to take account of the context in which doctors were operating.

The negative view of medicalization obscures these struggles for power in Victorian culture, since it defines all forms of power as equally bad and equivalent in operation. It also fails to distinguish between different *kinds* of concern. If, for example, doctors worried about sexual matters, they did not all worry for the same reasons. Acton and the sexologists may have focused on sexual diseases, but they were considered oddballs by the vast majority of clinical practitioners, most of whom treated sexual matters as impinging on health only where they affected basic physiological functions such as digestion, respiration, secretion, sensation, or reproduction. Masturbation was a worry because it overstimulated the bodily economy, but so did overwork, overeating, and speculating; as an irritant, masturbation could be the cause of a nonsexual disease such as epilepsy, and could be prevented, according to an 1834 *Lancet* article, by "counter-irritation to the part affected" (ouch!) or by a diet of fish and grains. The interchangeability of masturbation with overeating and the weirdness of the prescription points up the fact that sexual matters were not for the most part pathologized in themselves.

Finally, viewing medicine through the lens of policing power reduces what medicine did to a single effect, that of subduing the untamed, unregulated social or sexual body to docility. Victorian medicine did foster a vision of the patient as compliant, as what one guide to aspiring practitioners calls "clinical material" to be fingered. This was, after all, the era that developed a set of distinctions – between voluntary and involuntary physiological functions, between controlled actions and reflex actions, between sensibility and sensation, between the signs reported by the patient and the symptoms revealed by physical examination, between individual reports and statistical evidence – which peeled the life of the body off from that of the self who inhabited it. The Victorians also were the first to realize this ideal by developing first mesmerism and then effective anesthetics like ether and chloroform as well as painkilling drugs such as morphine and cocaine.

But dissociating the self from the body – whether by defining what is happening to the body as a case, reducing patients to statistics, numbing the body or rendering the self insensible – does not mean that the self is destroyed or rendered simply docile. The aim of social medicine, after all, was not just preventive, but hygienic: as William Farr, inventor of what came to be known as "vital statistics," put it in an article on hygiene in *The Lancet*, social medicine sought "to increase the *sum of vitality* by extending individual life to its full term (averting death); by obviating sickness; and by increasing the energy of all the vital forces, whether nutritive, formative, locomotive, or sensitive and intellectual." More generally, as Bruce Haley has shown, Victorian culture envisioned such vitality not as an absence of disease, but in positive terms that made the quest for health a privileged form of self-development. A case, in other words, can be interesting, and not just for the doctor: as Henry James's Milly Theale puts it, her own illness can assume "the beauty of the idea of a great adventure, a big dim experiment or struggle in which she might more responsibly than ever before take a hand" (*The Wings of the Dove* [1902], ch. 13). Less romantically but more daringly, the participation of many late-Victorian intellectuals in what we call, after all, a drug *culture* shows that they were well aware that anesthetics could be used for exploring new kinds of aesthetic experience. Aestheticism itself derived much of its force from the daring claim to be turning the analysis of the experience of beauty into a kind of vivisection of oneself (as Oscar Wilde's Lord Henry puts it) that located the origins of strange maladies in "some pearly cell in the brain, or some white nerve in the body" or "some strange poisonous germ" (*The Picture of Dorian Gray* [1891], ch. 11). The darker side of this experimentation was brought out in science fiction depicting chemical and vivisectional exploration run amok, as in Robert Louis Stevenson's 1886 *Dr Jekyll and Mr Hyde* (Jekyll buys his house once belonging to a "celebrated surgeon" and, "his own tastes being rather chemical than anatomical" [ch. 5], turns the former dissecting rooms into a laboratory for self-experimentation) and H. G. Wells's *The Island of Dr Moreau* (1896).

It is important to note that such fictions, relying as they did on the assumption that physiology and pathology were essentially matters not just of the body but of cells, and taking an experimental attitude toward the body, could only emerge (in

England, at least) relatively late in the century. Here we must emphasize one last kind of uneven development in Victorian medicine: an unevenness of scientific knowledge within medical practice. Celebrants of progress like Macaulay may have included "the science of healing" among the many things the Victorians had "carried to a perfection which our ancestors would have thought magical" (118), but the reality was that English medicine lagged behind its counterparts on the Continent. The scientific knowledge was there: by the 1840s, chemists had shown that one could identify albumen in urine, making it possible to diagnose granular kidney disease at an earlier stage; tumors and nervous physiology were being investigated at the cellular level in the 1830s by German physiologists. In England itself, the 1832 Anatomy Act made it increasingly evident that doctors needed to "open up a few corpses," in the famous words of the father of pathological anatomy, Xavier Bichat, in order to be properly educated. Yet as continental medicine was moving into cellular pathology and microscopy, English medical education still did not include formal training in pathological anatomy. As a result, even the gains made in the early nineteenth century by French medicine – most fundamentally, the conceptual linking of physiology or normal vital functions (digestion, respiration, secretion, sensation) with pathology or abnormal functions, and the localizing of these functions in tissues rather than in organs or humors – were only gradually absorbed into English medical practice. Doctors trained in Bichatian medicine could distinguish pericarditis from myocarditis or endocarditis, where their English counterparts continued to speak of "inflammation of the heart" (Bynum 32), unless trained in Paris or Edinburgh. Eliot highlights precisely this unevenness by having the French-trained Lydgate diagnose what the other Middlemarch physicians call Casaubon's "fit" as "fatty degeneration of the heart" using Laennec's recently introduced stethoscope.

Pre-cellular but tissular physiology may have been avant-garde to many doctors, but it provided metaphors and analogies that had a powerful impact upon Victorian society, in large part because they differed from the dominant medical metaphors of the body. While proponents of social medicine relied on an essentially eighteenth-century medical epistemology of what Poovey (1995) calls "anatomical realism," radical critics of modernization used the more up-to-date language of pathological anatomy to redefine the problems suffered by the social body. Thomas Carlyle, for example, argued in "Characteristics" (1831) that the social body, like the individual body, consisted of a "vital articulation," and in *Sartor Resartus* (1833) he defined this articulation as a forming of "organic filaments" into "Pericardial Nervous Tissue (as we named it) of Religion." The force of the analogy lay in the diagnosis it enabled Carlyle to make, as well as in the therapeutics he could then reject or embrace: just as the vital forces inherent in living tissue were distinct from the forces inherent in inorganic nature ("what the Physiologists call *irritability*" being considered irreducible to either chemical processes or galvanic reflexes), so, Carlyle declared, vital social forces were distinct from the "spasmodic, galvanic sprawlings" of merely reflexive religious practices or the mechanistic relations of the cash nexus. A few decades later,

from the left, Marx would ridicule the political economists (whose fears had paradoxically helped spawn the social body metaphor in the first place) for not looking
deeply enough into society to recognize that the social body was an evolving
organism.

If the organic and tissular metaphors for the social body opened up the possibility
for radical critique of a new kind, they also opened up the more general possibility
for a kind of social thought. What we now call sociology was founded by the Victorians out of the sense that society needed to be analyzed not as a set of rules or laws
– as was the case for economics and political economy – but as a complex system of
organic functions that define norms and demand adjustments. Nowhere is this assumption more densely elaborated than in the work of the founder of the discipline, Herbert
Spencer. Spencer borrowed from the latest medical physiology the structure for his
theory that social organisms, like plants and animals, develop from homogeneity to
heterogeneity, and combined it with Darwinian elements to produce a kind of sociological fantasia of progressively differentiated interdependency and diffuse causality
of "insensible gradations." Ultimately Spencer's vision would inform not only sociology but also the novel, providing the metaphorical underpinning for George Eliot's
and Thomas Hardy's realism, with its reiterated reference to social relations as weblike,
variegated, complexly determined, and involved in gradual, almost imperceptible
change.

Eliot's fiction, as Henry James observed, marks a limit to the development of
the English novel; as I have argued elsewhere, the emergence of cell theory and
evolutionary biology called into question the physiological perspective that grounded
her analyses of social life. Within a few decades of her death Victorian medicine
would itself be reorganized almost beyond recognition both epistemologically and
institutionally, as the Pasteurian focus on germs gave rise to Lister's antiseptic
surgery, as scientifically centered medical education became the norm, and as the
National Health Service bureaucratized the medical profession while massifying the
social body.

Even as it was passing away, however, Victorian medicine spawned one last great
cultural work: Conan Doyle's detective fiction. Trained as a doctor at the very moment
when the new science was displacing the old, Conan Doyle was somehow able to
apotheosize nearly all the culturally significant features of Victorian medicine. These
include its affiliation with social policing (Holmes's "deductions" are modeled on the
diagnostic technique displayed by Conan Doyle's medical school professor, Dr Joseph
Bell, but he uses this technique to help identify socially dangerous individuals rather
than "those minute organisms that disseminate cholera and fever, tubercle and anthrax"
as Bell [1893] does); its unevenness as a science and as a procedure (inscribed in the
hierarchical difference between Holmes's scientifically specialized way of seeing and
the simpler yet more human viewpoint of the general practitioner Watson); its uneven
application across genders (as in "A Scandal in Bohemia," where the double standard
is both exhibited and exposed); and its capacity to define cases in a way that at once
reduces persons to diagnosed, detected individuals and makes them interesting as *cases*

(a term whose ambiguity returns us to the mutual relations of medicine and the law). If we can still feel the pleasures and anxieties of reading *The Adventures*, it is at least in part because, in spite of Freud on the one hand and the technologizing and bureaucratizing of medicine on the other, we can still identify with both doctor and patient as the Victorians created them. In that sense, we remain – in spirit at least – other Victorians.

See also GROWING OLD, PASSING ON, SEXUALITIES; SKIN, PARAPETS

REFERENCES

Bell, J. (1893) "Introduction" to A. C. Doyle, *A Study in Scarlet*. London: Ward, Lock & Bowden.

Bynum, W. F. (1994) *Science and the Practice of Medicine in the Nineteenth Century*. Cambridge: Cambridge University Press.

Farr, W. (1835–6) "Lecture on the History of Hygiene." *The Lancet* 1, 773–6.

Foucault, M. (1978) *The History of Sexuality, Volume I: An Introduction*, trans. R. Hurley. New York: Random House.

Haley, B. (1978) *The Healthy Body and Victorian Culture*. Cambridge MA and London: Harvard University Press.

Kay, J. P. (1832) *The Moral and Physical Condition of the Working Classes Employed in the Cotton Manufacture in Manchester*. London: James Ridgway.

Krafft-Ebing, R. von (1908) *Psychopathia Sexualis, with Especial Reference to Contrary Sexual Instinct*, trans. G. Chaddock. Philadelphia: F. A. Davis.

Macaulay, T. B. (1835) "Sir James Mackintosh." In *Critical, Historical, and Miscellaneous Essays and Poems*. London and New York: Chesterfield Society.

Miller, D. A. (1988) *The Novel and the Police*. Berkeley: University of California Press.

Mort, F. (1987) *Dangerous Sexualities: Medico-Moral Politics in England Since 1830*. London and New York: Routledge and Kegan Paul.

Nordau, M. (1895) *Degeneration*. New York: D. Appleton.

Poovey, M. (1988) *Uneven Developments: The Ideological Work of Gender in Mid-Victorian England*. Chicago: University of Chicago Press.

——(1995) *Making a Social Body: British Cultural Formation, 1830–1864*. Chicago and London: University of Chicago Press.

Richardson, R. (1988) *Death, Dissection, and the Destitute*. London: Penguin Books.

Spencer, H. (1868) *Essays Scientific, Political, and Speculative*. London: Williams and Norgate.

Youngson, A. J. (1979) *The Scientific Revolution in Victorian Medicine*. New York: Holmes and Meier.

FURTHER READING

Carpenter, M. W. (2009) *Health, Medicine, and Society in Victorian England*. Santa Barbara: Praeger.

Darby, R. (2005) *A Surgical Temptation: The Demonization of the Foreskin and the Rise of Circumcision in Britain*. Chicago: University of Chicago Press.

Foucault, M. (1975) *The Birth of the Clinic: An Archaeology of Medical Perception*, trans. A. M. Sheridan Smith. New York: Random House.

Gallagher, C. (1986) "The Body versus the Social Body in the Works of Thomas Malthus and Henry Mayhew." *Representations* 14, 191–209.

Gilman, S. L. (1985) *Difference and Pathology: Stereotypes of Sexuality, Race, and Madness*. Ithaca: Cornell University Press.

Jacobus, M., E. F. Keller, and S. Shuttleworth (eds) (1990) *Body/Politics: Women and the Discourses of Science*. New York: Routledge.

Jordanova, L. (1989) *Sexual Visions: Images of Gender in Science and Medicine Between the Eighteenth and Twentieth Centuries*. Madison: University of Wisconsin Press.

Oppenheim, J. (1991) *"Shattered Nerves": Doctors, Patients, and Depression in Victorian England*. New York: Oxford University Press.

Pamboukian, S. (2012) *Doctoring the Novel: Medicine and Quackery from Shelley to Doyle*. Athens: Ohio University Press.

Peterson, M. J. (1978) *The Medical Profession in Mid-Victorian London*. Berkeley: University of California Press.

Rothfield, L. (1992) *Vital Signs: Medical Realism in Nineteenth-Century Fiction*. Princeton: Princeton University Press.

Showalter, E. (1986) "Syphilis, Sexuality, and the Fiction of the Fin de Siècle." In *Sex, Politics, and Science in the Nineteenth-Century Novel: Selected Papers from the English Institute, 1983–1984*, ed. R. B. Yeazell. Baltimore: Johns Hopkins University Press.

Sparks, T. (2009) *The Doctor in the Victorian Novel: Family Practices*. Burlington: Ashgate.

Swenson, K. (2005) *Medical Women and Victorian Fiction*. Columbia: University of Missouri Press.

13
Military

John R. Reed

The first thing to understand about the armed services of nineteenth-century Britain is that they were entirely determined by class difference. The commissioned officers were understood to be gentlemen, the noncommissioned and warrant officers might possibly have gentlemen among them, but the common soldiers and sailors were, for most of the century, seen as a separate and grossly inferior breed. It is necessary, then, to regard members of the services in distinct categories, since conditions in the service were different for masters and men.

Commissioned Officers

The army and the navy provided thoroughly desirable professional opportunities for men in nineteenth-century Britain, but there were complicating features in both services that made them unpopular choices for a large part of the population. Some of these were peculiar to one service, but others were common to both. There was, to begin with, the question of class already mentioned. Officers were gentlemen and therefore professionals. Officers for both services were recruited from the aristocracy, the gentry, and the middle classes. An officer, as a professional man, found himself having to deal with men who could seldom be considered fit companions for him. In the navy this meant that officers consorted with one another and, on shipboard, formed an elite that constantly had to reinforce its elitist qualifications. In the army the officers, with greater freedom of movement, nonetheless kept mainly to themselves,

A New Companion to Victorian Literature and Culture, First Edition. Edited by Herbert F. Tucker.
© 2014 John Wiley & Sons, Ltd. Published 2014 by John Wiley & Sons, Ltd.

though obliged to supervise men generally less amenable to discipline than sailors. A military officer would thus constantly be obliged to prove himself worthy of his position and his authority and be prepared to risk his life in circumstances that included combat, inclement weather, and disease, all in the company of men he generally was taught to regard as inferiors. For many young men considering career options, these features of military life alone would make it unattractive. Dickens, however, was more sympathetic to the men in the ranks than to officers. He mocked blustering officers in *The Pickwick Papers* (1837) and pilloried Major Joey Bagstock in *Dombey and Son* (1848). By contrast, in *Bleak House* (1853) he rendered favorable portraits of ex-trooper George Rouncewell and ex-artilleryman Matthew Bagnet. Army officers in fiction and on the stage were often associated with sexuality, both as objects of desire and as seducers. Captain Hawdon is an example in *Bleak House*, but perhaps the most notable instance in Victorian fiction is the noncommissioned officer Sergeant Troy in Hardy's *Far from The Madding Crowd* (1874).

The general perception through much of the nineteenth century was that sons of the aristocracy and gentry were the best source for army officers because of their familiarity with horsemanship, the use of weapons for hunting, and their habit of directing the activities of inferiors. Although a large number of army officers were from such families, as the century continued more and more officers tended to come from the middle classes. Thackeray, an astute observer of army types, recognized this trend in his fiction. In *Vanity Fair* Rawdon Crawley is the son of a baronet, but George Osborne and his friend Dobbin are sons of men made well-to-do by trade. In *The Newcomes* Jack Belsize is from a titled family, but Colonel Newcome is from the established middle class.

The navy presented a slightly different situation. There tradition held that the humblest person could rise to the highest rank on merit alone, something utterly impossible in the army. Horatio Nelson was held up as an example of such progress. But although Nelson had been born into a modest family (his father was a minister of the Church of England), he was scarcely of humble origins. He began under good auspices and benefited much from the interest of his friends, including an uncle who was a captain in the navy and subsequently became its Comptroller. In any case, by the beginning of the nineteenth century the rough professional from humble life had effectively disappeared. Nonetheless, although the rags-to-riches pattern was highly unlikely in the navy, opportunities for cross-class movement existed there to some degree, as they did not in the army. The tendency to admit potential officers into ships at a very young age, often as young as 13, meant that much of their training occurred on the job, though after achieving midshipman status a young man would still have to pass appropriate examinations to gain his lieutenancy. Then through service, merit, and "interest" (the common term for patronage), he would rise to commander (with command of a relatively insignificant vessel), captain, and finally post captain, which meant that he was put in command of a substantial ship, such as a frigate. From this point onward, his promotion was by seniority. A naval officer who did not disgrace himself could not be removed from the active list. In effect, he held tenure, though this did not guarantee him service in a ship or on land; when not on active service he was entitled to half pay. As the nineteenth century progressed, the Lords of the Admiralty paid greater attention to the formal education of potential officers at their own schools and on training ships, and changes were gradually made in the half-pay system. In the 1870s new examinations affected the military as they did the civil service. Most significantly, the purchase system was abolished.

The purchase system allowed for the official sale of military commissions below the rank of general. Military service tended to run in families, with sons following their relatives into navy or army. The famous Lord Cochrane, later tenth Earl of Dundonald, began his military career along with his brother in His Majesty's 104th Regiment of the Horse Guards, but Thomas quickly changed to the navy in his uncle's frigate the *Hind* (Lloyd 7–8). Sometimes this tradition was followed out of family honor or patriotic feeling, but in many families the military was seen as a likely source of income, especially for a younger son. This was often the case in Ireland, where social rank was not always accompanied by a commensurate income. Whatever the reason for established families' sending their sons to be officers in the navy or army, there was always some room for newcomers. Lord Malmesbury asserted in 1855 that military patronage was not dominated by interests of the younger sons of the landed classes, and subsequent research supports this claim. Half the army officer corps at mid-century was middle class, and the nonaristocratic and nonlanded character of the Indian army was even more marked (Bourne 87).

If class was important, so were income and interest. Army commissions could be bought and sold until roughly the third quarter of the century. Although this practice was theoretically controlled, with established prices for the various officer ranks, in practice there was a good deal of "illegal" negotiation. These purchases were overwhelmingly at the junior ranks, where young men were beginning their careers. The highest ranks were not open to purchase. Certain regiments were more prestigious than others. The most desirable were the cavalry and infantry Guards regiments, which served the Royal Household. Their uniforms were appropriately elegant, and they had the advantage of largely ornamental service in the London area. In the period 1834–8, for example, 76 percent of promotions to lieutenant were purchased, as were 80 percent to captain, and 72 percent to major, with only 58 percent to lieutenant-colonel (Harries-Jenkins 73). This system of purchase did not obtain in the Royal Navy, where all patronage was in the gift of the Lords of the Admiralty; nonetheless, interest here (the lobbying of relatives, members of Parliament, and other influential people) played a significant part. In both services promotion was possible through merit during combat or accomplishments over time. In the navy promotion beyond the rank of captain went entirely by seniority. In the army seniority was important, but there were many exceptions. In the letters and memoirs written by military men during the nineteenth century, promotion is a frequent subject.

But even if promotion was possible for young men without powerful interest, not everyone could afford to become or remain an officer. Military pay was notoriously inadequate for the expenses incurred by officers, who had to pay for their own uniforms, weapons, and other paraphernalia and who had to live in a manner worthy of a gentleman. An officer's pay in the navy was equated not with his rank or seniority, but with the post that he occupied. *Rank* (first lieutenant, captain, admiral, etc.) qualified an officer for certain assignments, but the assignment (in a frigate or man-of-war, in a battle zone or on peacetime patrol) or *posting* determined reward. Most young officers required money supplements, either from their own resources or from their families. In 1867 a lieutenant might earn £118 12s 6d and have interest and expenses of £53 19s 5d, leaving an annual remainder of £64 13s 1d. For a major, with greater obligations, the amounts would be £292, £249 10s 4d, and £42 9s 8d (Harries-Jenkins 87). To contemplate a career as a military officer, then, was to anticipate a long period of economic dependence, and it is largely for this reason that families with comfortable incomes were the likeliest to place their sons as navy and army officers.

As we have seen, a principal attraction for becoming an officer in the navy or army was that it brought with it the recognition of gentlemanly status. But there was an added allure for the higher-ranking officers. Unlike some other professionals, especially early in the century, officers were admitted to good society and to elite clubs. The daughters of officers of higher rank were entitled to presentation at court. When John Ruskin listed what he called the five great intellectual professions, he placed the Soldier first. All of these professions required self-sacrifice, but the soldier's (and implicitly the sailor's) was the most obvious. Ruskin said the reason the world "honours the soldier is, because he holds his life at the service of the State" (*Unto this Last* [1860], Essay I). Many honors and rewards were available to officers. For outstanding service in action they might receive special honors, such as the Order of the Bath, or even be knighted. With continued excellent service they might rise in the ranks of the aristocracy. Wellington, for his great service, rose all the way to a dukedom. Such forms of recognition usually were accompanied by substantial financial rewards. Naval officers had special opportunities for additional sources of income. During wartime captured enemy ships could be adjudged prizes and the value of the prize distributed among those associated with the action, according to a regular scale by which those concerned – from the admiral of the fleet down to the common sailor – received their share. For the senior officers these rewards could be substantial, running into thousands of pounds. Another source of income was the transporting of treasure, known in the navy as freight. Here the rewards could be enormous. Captain Frederick Chamier, who went on to become a novelist, brings his autobiography to a close with his return from the West Indies in command of a ship with a freight worth upward of 700,000 dollars; for this assignment he anticipated a very comfortable reward.

Chamier was one of a group of novelists who wrote in a Victorian subgenre most often associated with Captain Frederick Marryat, the naval novel. These were rousing tales usually involving young men rising into the officer ranks. Marryat's *Peter Simple* (1834) and *Jacob Faithful* (1834) are perennial favorites, enjoyable as adult or juvenile fiction. The army had its subgenre too, most notably represented by the novels of Charles Lever, such as *The Confessions of Harry Lorrequer* (1839) and *Charles O'Malley* (1841). Lever has survived best among the military novelists, though others, like William Hamilton Maxwell and Captain Michael Rafter, had respectable reputations in their day.

Gentlemanly status, honor, and opportunities for social and financial reward all made the role of naval or military officer attractive, but the advancements, recognitions, and awards were not distributed with an impartial hand. We have already noted how those with wealth could afford to purchase choice commissions in the army and those with personal influence could see to it that early promotions and attractive assignments went to their friends and family. Officer positions continued to appeal to young gentlemen and their families because the navy's reputation was high after the Napoleonic Wars and remained extremely high throughout the nineteenth century. The army's reputation was less secure, but on the whole it fared well in public opinion, generally improving as the century continued. But the realities of naval and military life through most of Victoria's reign were not as glorious as they might appear.

In the navy there was a large surplus of officers, many of whom remained on half-pay almost their entire careers. Here again interest was important, for the person with influential friends would find himself with a ship to command while others cooled their heels at the Admiralty offices hoping for any assignment. Captain Frederick Marryat made a good income from his popular novels, but while he was ashore writing them, he was still hoping for active service. The peculiarity of the naval service was that, although promotion was by seniority after the attainment of a captaincy, there was no obligation on the Admiralty to appoint any officer to an active assignment by reason of seniority. Because for most of the century there was a redundancy of naval officers, a young man's prospects without financial and political resources were not especially good. Moreover, the opportunities for service were not the best. One might command a prison ship going to Australia. There was still the slave trade, which remained a viable possibility until the 1880s, and there were surveying and exploratory ventures. Closer to home there was coast guard duty, an important assignment in the earlier part of the century. If the end of war eliminated most possibilities for prize money, the slave trade still offered such opportunities both on the west and east coasts of Africa; but this service was offensive in many ways, not the least being the danger of disease and the risky method of using ships' boats for most of the cruising activity on the east coast of Africa. Substantial rewards were also possible for coast guard officers who managed to catch smugglers; such officers were selected for their rectitude and capacity to resist temptations to illicit activities themselves, although vigorous smuggling diminished as the century wore on.

Some officers left British naval service either entirely or for a time to serve other nations. Lord Cochran commanded the Peruvian and later the Greek navy, but the huge rewards he was promised did not materialize. Lieutenant Lloyd Mathews left the service to lead an Arab sultan's army at Zanzibar. Generally speaking, however, these adventurers were the rare exception. Captain Alexander Maconochie made a reputation in the convict colony at New South Wales as an innovative penologist, and brought his system home to England, where he became a much-appreciated reformer. A navy officer, by virtue of his position, surely had the respect and admiration of the general population. But unless he had the good fortune to be already well placed in the social hierarchy, he had to be largely content with that respect and admiration.

The half-pay officer of either service was so familiar a figure in Victorian society that he appeared regularly in the literature of the time, frequently as the genteel but impoverished father of a novel's heroine. One of the best-known half-pay officers in Victorian fiction is the retired army officer Captain Brown in Elizabeth Gaskell's *Cranford* (1853), who is described as follows: "He was a half-pay Captain, and had obtained some situation on a neighbouring railroad, which had been vehemently petitioned against by the little town; and if, in addition to his masculine gender, and his connection with the obnoxious railroad, he was so brazen as to talk of being poor – why, then, indeed, he must be sent to Coventry" (ch. 1). Instead, however, his kindliness and disciplined habits make him a favorite in the town.

The situation was different for the army. There was always sufficient occupation for the officers of this branch of the service because the empire made enormous demands on Britain's armed forces, especially the land forces. There was India to be subdued and policed. Here an officer could manage, one way and another, to acquire a considerable fortune. Many became senior administrators in India, especially after the East India Company ceded control to the government. There were two important outbreaks of war in the middle of the century – the Crimean War (1854–6) and the Indian Mutiny (1857). The former called forth from Tennyson "The Charge of the Light Brigade," "The Charge of the Heavy Brigade," and *Maud*. There was much popular poetry on this subject, but also some worthwhile, if more obscure, recognition of the fighting man, as with Sir Francis H. Doyle's "The Return of the Guards, 9th July 1856." The Crimean War turns up in contemporary fiction as well, for example in Charles Lever's *Davenport Dunn* (1859). Tennyson responded to the Indian Mutiny with "The Defence of Lucknow," and there was an outpouring of literary treatments of this event (see Brantlinger; Herbert). The army was involved in many lesser but nonetheless important struggles during the later part of the century, such as the Afghan Wars (1839–42, 1878, 1880), the wars against Ashantis and Zulus (1873–4 and 1879), conflicts with the Boers (1880 and 1899–1902), and the Egyptian campaigns (1882–4). Although high honors were rarer during most of the century than they had been during the Napoleonic Wars, knighthoods, baronies, and higher stations were still possible for outstanding military service. Sir Garnet Wolseley achieved a Viscountcy through distinguished service in Burma, the Crimea, India, China, Canada, and Africa, crowned by the relief of Khartoum. Most officers had to content themselves with lesser positions if they chose to leave the service and accept them. Those who did became minor administrators, prison wardens, railway officials, and the like. Well-known officers were occasionally asked to serve on important boards. Some military figures were elected to Parliament. The Scottish aristocrat Lord Cochran was a Radical MP for Westminster while still on active naval service, and General Sir Edward Bruce Hamley was elected Conservative member for Birkenhead when his military career was drawing to a close. The hero of George Meredith's *Beauchamp's Career* (1875) is a naval officer who is unsuccessful in his campaign for a seat in Parliament as a radical. Meredith had assisted his friend Frederick Augustus Maxse in a similar but successful campaign.

Uncommissioned Officers

Beneath the captain and lieutenants in the navy was a second elite group comprised of marine officers, the ship's master, surgeon, purser, and chaplain. These men were frequently gentlemen or of gentlemanly bearing. For the surgeon and chaplain, practice aboard ship was inferior to decent positions ashore. The master (responsible for navigation), surgeon, purser (in charge of the ship's stores), and chaplain were warrant officers, petty officers who received their warrants from the Navy Board rather than commissions from the Admiralty, as other officers did. There were, in a large ship, several other warrant officers, chief among them the gunner, boatswain, and carpenter. These three generally remained with the same ship and therefore had a degree of career stability unavailable to those above and below them in the ship's hierarchy, but they were not classed with the gentlemen.

In the army, there was nothing quite comparable to the navy structure beneath the commissioned officers' ranks, but there were the quartermaster, responsible for food, clothing, and equipment, and sergeants responsible for various duties, such as the paymaster sergeant, the hospital sergeant, and so forth. Then there were drummers, and corporals, the latter the lowest rank that could in any way be regarded as an officer's rank. Captains in the army were equivalent to lieutenants and warrant officers in the navy, lieutenants to mates, and ensigns to midshipmen. Men from the ranks could rise to sergeant and upon occasion quartermaster.

The Men

Conditions for ordinary sailors and soldiers improved markedly during the nineteenth century. At the beginning of the century sailors had to endure cramped and unhealthy quarters and long voyages, fed on miserable fare. Scurvy and dysentery were still significant health hazards along with accidents of various kinds, many associated with severe weather. Ordinary seamen in the navy had ratings or ranks, but these were not so distinct as the ranks of officers. Still, a sailor could move from seaman to able-bodied seaman on up to boatswain or even master, by gradual steps. The overwhelming majority remained ordinary seamen. They signed on to a ship – or, early in the century, were impressed for service against their will – for the term of a ship's commission, generally a three-year assignment. At the end of that time the ship might receive a new commission, be put up for repairs, or be retired. If the ship was going out of commission the ship's company was paid off and the hands sought new berths or retired from the service. During the Napoleonic Wars there was a chronic shortage of seamen, many dying from combat and disease, and others deserting in large numbers. After the wars a smaller navy and improving conditions for seamen made it generally easier to man the navy, and a sailor with a good reputation could always find some berth.

A sailor's pay was minimal and paid out at widely separated intervals; there were some arrangements for directing money to families, but often a sailor's dependents had to wait a considerable time for assistance. It was difficult for seamen to marry, partly because of the difficulty of financial arrangements and partly because the men were away for long periods of time. But many did get married, often to women with employment of their own on shore. Seamen did not, however, lack female companionship. When ships were in port, women flocked to them by the hundreds and sometimes were illegally concealed on the ship and sailed with the men, even assisting, at times, during sea battles. By mid-century this practice was extinct.

Discipline was severe and usually immediate. Captains had great authority and often exercised it sternly, considering obedience and attention to duty crucial to the welfare of the ship. The most common form of corporal punishment was flogging. During the first half of the century there were many debates about the value of flogging, which gradually gave way to other means of discouraging bad behavior and encouraging good. During the Napoleonic years sailors often remained on board ship for many months, even years at a time, not having shore leave because captains feared they would desert, as they often did when they had an opportunity. Many British deserters took service with American vessels. The conditions established during the Napoleonic years set the pattern for many years to follow and reforms in the navy and the army were allowed only grudgingly. Most practices died away, in fact, mainly with the gradual disappearance of the generation that had experienced the Napoleonic Wars. One of the chief improvements in the ordinary seaman's lot during the nineteenth century was, along with more comfortable and more sanitary conditions aboard ship, the institution of long-term service, which made the navy sailor's career more secure. For the first half of the century sailors bore the reputation of being good-naturedly rough when sober and disgustingly brutish and dissolute when drunk. This image improved with time until, near the end of the century, the "bluecoat" was viewed with pride and respect.

The soldiers of Wellington's army were regarded as the nation's trash. Although preferred recruits were men from the militia, many joined up to avoid obligations and penalties of various kinds – from criminal prosecution and sexual liability to financial debt or simple poverty. Army pay was bad and often intermittent, and, during wartime, conditions were dreadful. Medical assistance was crude and inadequate, an issue that received dramatic attention during the scandals associated with the Crimean War, made prominent by the new immediacy of war reporting in the press and by the improvements instituted by Florence Nightingale, which made her a popular heroine. Punishment for offenses was harsh, ranging from flogging to hanging. There were few established barracks for soldiers at the beginning of the century, so that they were often billeted upon the citizenry, a policy that did not improve public attitudes toward them. But regular garrisons were established as the century progressed. One positive feature in the soldier's life was his uniform: many memoirs of enlisted men indicate that the right to wear a uniform influenced their decision to enlist. A soldier's pride in his uniform might extend to national patriotic feelings, but it was characteristically limited chiefly to his regiment or unit. A notable example was the Rifle Brigade with its distinctive green uniforms. Through the Victorian period, however, with its increasing sense of imperial power, the association of uniform with national identity increased. During the Napoleonic War a soldier's daily food ration was supposed to be a pound of meat, one and a half pounds of bread or biscuit, and a third-pint of rum or a pint of wine, but even these amounts were often not forthcoming in the field. Improvements in the commissariat were slow but steady during the century, though the blunders of the Crimean War proved that they were still inadequate at mid-century.

At the beginning of the century enlistment was for 20 years, effectively the active period of a man's life at a time when men were considered old at 50. There were few provisions for retirement, except for some few wounded in battle. Soldiers could marry, but only six wives per company were allowed to travel on service. Earlier, camp-followers were commonplace with the army, but well before mid-century women were prohibited from accompanying either service. Most army service was abroad, in India, the West Indies, Canada, and elsewhere as needed. Regiments were not supposed to enjoy more than five years at home to every ten abroad.

Apart from the prestigious Household regiments, whose troops ordinarily remained in England, the cavalry was the premier service for enlisted men, though the artillery and engineer corps were also desirable. During the nineteenth century artillery gradually became more important, whereas the significance of the cavalry waned. Improvements in weaponry kept the ordinary infantryman essential. The military strategists were slow to change battle tactics, and as late as the Egyptian campaigns of the 1880s soldiers were still forming battle squares as they did in the Napoleonic days. But much of the fighting required of soldiers during the Victorian period involved skirmishing and irregular methods. Precise, long-distance repeating rifles and Gatling guns changed the dynamics of battle, but the infantry was still required for final assaults upon fortifications and for the routing of enemy troops in the field. From the 1830s onward, reforms improved housing, sanitary, and dietary conditions, reduced the severity of punishments, especially flogging, and instituted positive inducements such as good conduct medals. Short-term, renewable enlistment improved the quality of recruits, and better educational and training programs ensured a more professional rank and file.

Nineteenth-century Britain saw a steady but ultimately dramatic transformation of its armed services. Each became more technical and more humane; each changed from an aristocratic and loosely organized structure to a democratized and precise system. Navy and army officers remained prominent professionals, but whereas the navy retained its luster, the army senior officer corps was badly tainted by the disasters of the Crimean War. A series of reforms gradually established in both services better basic educational preparation, better professional training, and finally, with the reforms of 1870, open examinations for commissions and the abolition of patronage and purchase as modes of promotion. The armed services were now becoming not only a profession, but professional as well. The fervor for empire during the last quarter of the nineteenth century enhanced the honor of the military officer once more, elevating figures like Gordon and Kitchener to national heroic status. The shock of the Boer War failures aside, Great Britain approached World War I with a growing sense of modern naval and military competence. The greatest improvements were those affecting the enlisted men, who moved from barbarous conditions to relative comfort. By the end of the century the navy and the army, both officers and men, had the respect of the civilian population.

At the beginning of the nineteenth century popular culture offered stereotypes of the drunken but carefree sailor, and the riotous and low-bred soldier, along with the bluff but honest navy captain and the sexually seductive army officer, most likely from a regiment of dragoons. These stereotypes persisted in popular songs, theatrical performances, and conventional fictional narratives of the time. But growing up alongside these stereotypes were different, more individualized images of the men of the armed services. We have already noted Dickens's tendency to offer a more positive view of the enlisted man. In *North and South* (1854–5) Mrs Gaskell complicates Margaret Hale's problems by involving them with her brother's naval delinquencies. Charlotte Yonge makes the two principal male protagonists in *The Clever Woman of the Family* (1865) military officers. Both have been wounded in the service of their country during the period of the Indian Mutiny; both are morally upright and dependable, their military self-discipline and capacity for self-sacrifice being stressed as the basis of their trustworthiness. By the end of the century the aura of Empire had conferred on both army and navy a heroic character. This is evident not only in the balance of applause with scrutiny that Rudyard Kipling's works provide, but also in the uncritical championing of military power in the large body of writing for young boys represented in the writings of authors such as Mayne Reid and G. A. Henty. When Queen Victoria died in 1901, the army and navy, as complete institutions, were enjoying a level of prestige that they had scarcely experienced before.

See also 1870; HISTORIOGRAPHY; SKIN, SHORES

REFERENCES

Bourne, J. M. (1986) *Patronage and Society in Nineteenth-Century England*. London: Edward Arnold.

Brantlinger, P. (1988) *Rule of Darkness*. Ithaca: Cornell University Press.

Harries-Jenkins, G. (1977) *The Army in Victorian Society*. London: Routledge and Kegan Paul.

Herbert, C. (2008) *War of No Pity: The Indian Mutiny and Victorian Trauma*. Princeton: Princeton University Press.

Lloyd, C. (1947) *Lord Cochrane: Seaman–Radical–Liberator: A Life of Thomas, Lord Cochrane 10th Earl of Dundonald*. London: Longmans, Green.

FURTHER READING

Ballard, G. A. (1934) "The Navy." In *Early Victorian England 1830–65*, 2 vols, ed. G. M. Young. London: Oxford University Press.

Barnett, C. (1970) *Britain and Her Army 1509–1970: A Military, Political and Social Survey*. New York: William Morrow.

Baynham, H. (1969) *From the Lower Deck: The Royal Navy 1780–1840*. London: Hutchinson.

——(1971) *Before the Mast: Naval Ratings of the Nineteenth Century*. London: Hutchinson.

Black, J. (2009) *War in the Nineteenth Century: 1800–1914*. Cambridge: Polity Press.

Fortescue, J. (1934) "The Army." In *Early Victorian England 1830–65*, 2 vols, ed. G. M. Young. London: Oxford University Press.

Lewis, M. (1948) *England's Sea Officers: The Story of the Naval Profession*. London: G. Allen and Unwin.

—— (1965) *The Navy in Transition 1814–1864: A Social History*. London: Hodder and Stoughton.

Markovits, S. (2009) *The Crimean War in the British Imagination*. Cambridge: Cambridge University Press.

Myerly, S. H. (1996) *British Military Spectacle: From the Napoleon Wars Through the Crimea*. Cambridge MA: Harvard University Press.

Peck, J. (1998) *War, the Army, and Victorian Literature*. New York: St Martin's Press.

Skelley, A. R. (1977) *The Victorian Army at Home: The Recruitment and Terms and Conditions of the British Regular, 1859–1899*. London: Croom Helm.

Spiers, E. M. (1980) *The Army and Society, 1815–1914*. London: Longman.

Strachan, H. (1984) *Wellington's Legacy: The Reform of the British Army, 1830–54*. Manchester: Manchester University Press.

—— (1985) *From Waterloo to Balaclava: Tactics, Technology, and the British Army, 1815–54*. Cambridge: Cambridge University Press.

14

Educational

Thomas William Heyck

Education in nineteenth-century England and Wales produced a number of very different experiences and career patterns for teachers. (The educational systems of Scotland and Ireland were so different that this chapter will deal with England and Wales only.) These experiences and patterns were profoundly affected by a set of common social and cultural factors: the rapid expansion of demand for education for all levels of society and at all levels of learning; the formation of class divisions in the social structure; the secularization of both thought and institutions; and rigidity in assumptions about gender differences. Schooling at all stages of education, from universities down to elementary schools, expanded during the Victorian period, as England for the first time became a "schooled society." This expansion greatly increased the number of teachers and made them more important to society. Moreover, all levels of Victorian educational institutions became secularized – that is, they shifted from the orbit of the Christian churches to that of secular authorities. At the beginning of the century most teachers at the higher levels were clergymen and almost all were under the supervision of Christian churches or agencies; at the end of the century few were clergy and many worked outside the influence of any denomination. Together, the expansion and secularization of education encouraged teachers in England to take significant steps towards professional autonomy and status; yet the complications of class and gender made for very different aspirations, standards of living, and careers.

Class and gender constituted the main divisions in Victorian society. The sense that Britain in the course of industrialization and urbanization had become divided into

A New Companion to Victorian Literature and Culture, First Edition. Edited by Herbert F. Tucker.
© 2014 John Wiley & Sons, Ltd. Published 2014 by John Wiley & Sons, Ltd.

three broad layers – the landed, middle, and working classes – and that these classes competed over the distribution of wealth and power, significantly shaped politics, identity, and social relations. The vocabulary of class dominated assumptions about both a person's place in the social structure and the proper function of social institutions. Education did not escape class thinking; thus the Victorians generally assumed that there should be different kinds and levels of schools, with different educational objectives, for each social class. At the same time the conviction that men and women differed not only biologically but also in intellect, psychology, and emotions, supported a belief in the "separate spheres" – the public for men and the private for women. This strong sense of different gender roles contributed powerfully to both the evolution of Victorian educational institutions and the careers of women teachers. For all these reasons, whether in terms of the quantity or of the quality of life, it made all the difference whether a teacher in, say, the 1820s was a woman trying to scratch out a living as mistress of a "dame school," or a man serving as headmaster of an elite public school; or whether a teacher in the 1890s was a male fellow at reformed Oxford or Cambridge, or a female teacher in a state elementary school.

The University Teachers

As Jude Fawley, the idealistic but poor stonemason in Thomas Hardy's novel *Jude the Obscure* (1895), discovers to his own bitter disappointment, university education in early Victorian England was open strictly to upper-class males; consequently, university teachers themselves were men almost exclusively from landed and professional families. Until the 1830s there were only two universities in England and Wales – the ancient universities of Oxford and Cambridge – and despite the later foundation of additional universities, Oxford and Cambridge remained much the wealthiest and most prestigious. The two old English universities in the first decades of the century were extremely small, with no more than 1,500 students between them. Moreover, they remained what they had been since the Reformation of the sixteenth century, quasi-seminaries of the Church of England. They had essentially religious functions: the training of the clergy of the established Church and the education of the nation's social elite in Christian morality. Given these functions, "Oxbridge" emphasized not research but what was taken in the day to be a liberal education – classics at Oxford and mathematics at Cambridge – because these subjects were thought to give unique mental and moral discipline. Further, the two universities were organized on the collegiate model, which meant that they were federations of relatively autonomous colleges in which the teachers and students lived and worked. Though a small number of chaired professors delivered lectures, the great majority of instruction was done by the college tutors, who taught on the tutorial or "catechetical" method, which they regarded as the best method for moral training.

This situation meant that there were few careers in university teaching in early nineteenth-century England. The tutors were drawn from the ranks of the fellows of the colleges, of whom there were only about 540 at Oxford and 350 at Cambridge. All of the fellows had to be graduates of one of the two universities, but only about 20 percent of the fellows actually taught; the others enjoyed the income of their fellowships while they prepared for the bar or studied for ordination. As for the tutors, the only requirements for their posts other than a degree were that they had to take holy orders in the Church of England, usually within seven years of winning their fellowships, and that they had to remain unmarried. Underlying these requirements was the assumption that a celibate clerical teaching staff was best for the essentially moral and religious educational objectives of the universities. But these requirements dictated that for the great majority of tutors the main career pattern led *out* of the universities, into parish appointments, rather than *up* within the universities. If a college tutor did not want to become ordained or wished to marry, he would have to leave the university. In Anthony Trollope's novel *Barchester Towers* (1857), for example, the clergyman Mr Arabin becomes a tutor while he waits for a parish living to open up. Those who remained enjoyed lifetime appointments in the often luxurious surroundings of their colleges, where they lived isolated from the world yet with no prospects for promotion inside the university. Inevitably, the lack of careers in education elicited from many tutors uninspired teaching, and this tendency was reinforced by the centrality of the honours exams, which were crucial for all serious students. The tutors had to teach strictly for the exams, which turned them into crammers of routinized information and examination skills.

By mid-century, however, both the universities themselves and the careers of the professors and tutors had been transformed by a powerful reform movement. The campaign to reform the English universities derived from a number of different sources, all drawing on the Victorian belief in progress. One was natural science, which traditionally played only a minor role in Oxford and Cambridge. By mid-century, status-hungry natural scientists were claiming positions in the universities commensurate with science's growing research achievements, not least in evolutionary biology and geology. English natural scientists wanted to improve their own professional standing and cultural authority by dislodging the clergy from their monopoly over the universities' endowments, and to have the universities conform to the scientific ideals of research and specialization. Another force for reform was utilitarianism, which sought to make the ancient universities more useful to the activities and values of the middle class – to business and industry, but also to political and social progress generally. To the utilitarians it seemed inefficient that Anglican clergymen taught secular subjects, in which they were unlikely to be specialists. A third impulse towards university reform came from the English Nonconformists (i.e. non-Anglican Protestants). The Nonconformists felt that they comprised the central corps of England's rapidly growing commercial and industrial class, and they resented their exclusion from the faculty and student body of the universities by the religious tests. These three broad forces resulted in the foundation in 1828 of University College, London, which joined the Anglican King's College, London in 1836 to form the University of London; and from the 1850s they brought about the establishment of provincial universities in England's largest industrial cities.

Meanwhile, the reform movement found support among the dons (faculty members) within Oxford and Cambridge. Some of the internal reformers shared the values and goals of the scientists, utilitarians, and Nonconformists. Others were motivated by evangelicalism and romanticism to reinvigorate the old universities so as to produce a morally and spiritually elevated cultural elite, who in turn might restore the cohesiveness of English society. But the most important element among the internal reformers was the tutors who wanted to establish genuine careers in university teaching. They were responding in part to the increasing seriousness of their students and their parents, who were themselves much influenced by evangelicalism. Such people wanted the tutors to provide better teaching and a more intense work ethic. And many tutors were frustrated by the demand that they teach the same subjects and texts repeatedly, regardless of their own special interests and abilities, in order to cram students for the examinations. They wanted to become masters of their special subjects, to require that a much larger proportion of fellows share the teaching, to open the fellowships to competition, and to erect a career hierarchy *within* the universities for professional teachers. To establish a structure for professional careers, they wanted to abolish the requirements for holy orders and celibacy, and to designate the professorships as the top rungs on their academic career ladder.

As a result, Oxford and Cambridge became much more "professional" institutions in the 1850s and 1860s, and this change profoundly affected the lives of the dons. Royal Commissions on Oxford and Cambridge led to legislation for the two ancient universities in 1854 and 1856; and the tutors themselves adopted higher standards of teaching as well as certain practices that encouraged specialization. Both universities were opened to Nonconformist students by the abolition of the requirement of subscription to the Anglican Thirty-nine Articles; and in 1871 subscription by the fellows was also abolished. New courses of study in natural science, law, modern history, and moral science were adopted. The tutors at both universities began to divide up the broadened curriculum in order to specialize in teaching. Most fellowships were opened to competition by examination, and a much larger number of them was devoted to teaching. The requirement that fellows remain unmarried was gradually abolished by the 1880s, and as a result an increasing number of tutors no longer actually resided in their colleges. The professoriate was established as the top rung on a career ladder to which the tutors might aspire. Many earnest tutors, hopeful of instilling in their students an ethic of Christian morality and public service, sought to "reach" the students through athletics and close friendship. The character of John Hardy, an idealized tutor in Thomas Hughes's novel *Tom Brown at Oxford* (1858), epitomized the new professional don: Hardy not only makes reforms in his college in order to keep undergraduates out of trouble, he also encourages serious reading by students and takes a very active role in collegiate and university rowing. Hardy is a professional teacher, deeply learned in his special subject and a conscientious tutor. Oxford and Cambridge colleges were full of real-life Hardys from the 1850s on; and, as the character of Henry Grey in Mrs Humphrey Ward's *Robert Elsmere* (1888) shows, the ideal don was alive and well three decades after *Tom Brown at Oxford*.

In the last 30 years of the century, however, the academic profession in England began to change again. For one thing, provincial university colleges at Manchester, Birmingham, Leeds, and Liverpool reached autonomous university status, and they added an element to the university system that was devoted not only to research and to "modern" subjects but also to the German-style "professorial" lecturing, as opposed to the tutorial method of teaching. The teaching staff at these "red brick" universities, arranged in a hierarchy of lecturer, reader, and professor, clearly had professional career structures organized around research as well as teaching. Some of the professors, like the chemist Henry Enfield Roscoe of Manchester, established close connections with local industries.

Nevertheless, Oxford and Cambridge remained by far the wealthiest and most prestigious institutions of higher education in England, and their graduates tended to monopolize the highest posts at the red bricks. Within the ancient universities themselves, the tutors continued to define their work as educating the nation's political and social elite, but they found that scholarship and research had become much more important in their careers. One reason for that development was the increasing value assigned by English society in general to professional expertise: professionals were increasingly seen as the "new gentry" of Britain, and professionalism required specialized knowledge. But another reason was that the placing of the professors at the top of the academic career ladder had the unanticipated consequence of valuing "learning" (research) over teaching. In their reform campaign the tutors at Oxbridge had sought to retain control over teaching; hence they had identified the professoriate with learning rather than teaching. Research scholarship thereby gradually became a qualification for a professorship. By the end of the century research had been widely accepted alongside teaching as one of the essential functions of Oxford and Cambridge; thus not only were the professors supposedly distinguished by their contributions to scholarly knowledge, but also the tutors had become harder-working, specialized, and laicized professionals who sought to combine research with teaching.

It was also the case by the end of the century that not all university teachers were men. Women had been excluded from the universities by the Victorian assumptions that women were not suited by temperament or intellect either for the clergy or for public life, and that they were not capable of the sustained, rigorous work required by the university studies. Moreover, through the first half of the century, not even middle- and upper-class women could obtain a strong secondary education, still less the training in Latin and Greek that was the prerequisite for matriculation at either university. And many proper Victorians, men and women alike, felt that advanced education would spoil women's cherished innocence and nurturing instincts. During the course of the century increasing numbers of women, and a few male advocates like John Stuart Mill, argued that women were in fact as intelligent and as capable of higher education as men; but proposals that women be admitted to Oxbridge roused reactions of either shocked indignation or raucous laughter. One clerical opponent of admission of women to Oxford declared in a sermon in 1884: "Inferior to us [men] God made you [women], and inferior to the end of time you will remain" (Brittain 69). The persistent and touchy defensiveness of the Victorian establishment to the prospect of women's university education found early expression in Tennyson's *The Princess* (1847), a work whose ideological evasiveness earned it a second lease of life as light operetta in Gilbert and Sullivan's *Princess Ida* (1884).

Despite such opposition heavy and light, women reformers and their male allies worked persistently in the 1850s and 1860s for coeducation at Oxbridge. Their efforts formed one aspect of a broad-ranging feminist movement that sought to open public life and the professions to women, and to end what Mill in 1869 called "the subjection of women" to males. Emily Davies, for instance, having failed to get the University of London opened to women, sought to establish a college for women in Cambridge. Similar efforts were made at Oxford. By the end of the 1870s two women's colleges had been founded at Cambridge (Girton and Newnham) and two at Oxford (Somerville and Lady Margaret Hall). The universities would not allow the young women of these colleges to take their degrees until the twentieth century, but step by step in the late-Victorian decades women won the right to take the regular university examinations, to attend lectures offered by the tutors and professors of the men's colleges, and in general to enjoy official recognition of their presence. At the same time, the women's colleges, which from the outset had female heads, began to appoint women as their own teaching staff. By 1900 the four colleges employed more than 50 women tutors and lecturers, whose career aspirations copied those of their male counterparts in combining research scholarship and teaching. They worked in close, high-minded association with their students, for the women's colleges emphasized both ladylike decorum and a family atmosphere as well as high intellectual ideals. Meanwhile, the provincial universities and university colleges abandoned their barriers to women students, and by the 1890s most had small but growing numbers of women lecturers, mainly in French, music, and English literature. These pioneer women teachers produced increasing numbers of women graduates, many of whom would go on to staff secondary schools for women, and thus generate more women applicants to the universities.

The Public School Teachers

Until fairly late in the century secondary education for boys in Victorian England was available only in the old endowed grammar schools and the even more prestigious "public" schools. The public schools had been founded in the sixteenth century to train young men for the Church and public service, and by the nineteenth century were not "public" in any real sense at all, save that they were not owned by any one individual and not conducted mainly for private profit. Most public schools were actually private, boarding schools offering training in the classics to sons of the well-to-do, and all had close ties to the Church of England. At the beginning of the century there were only nine of these institutions in England (Eton, Harrow, Rugby, Winchester, Westminster, Shrewsbury, Merchant Taylors', St Paul's, and Charterhouse), but the number grew, especially after 1850, as the public school system expanded to meet the demand generated by the expanding middle class. The public schools supplied most of the students to Oxbridge; but the social prestige of the public schools was enormous in its own right. In a time when a university degree was not always the necessary qualification for ruling-class employment, the schools gave a boy the deportment, accent, habit of authority, and connections ("the old school tie") that opened to him a myriad of positions in Church and State. To send a son to a public school marked social and financial "arrival" for middle-class families. The Victorian public schools transmitted aristocratic attitudes and ideals to middle-class boys; thus, though they reflected anti-utilitarian and anti-industrial values, the public schools were among the most important of all English social institutions.

However, the public schools at the beginning of the nineteenth century had fallen into disorder, disrepute, and financial trouble. Although the headmasters and staff were Anglican clergymen, their treatment of the boys combined permissiveness and brutality. The teachers were poorly paid and of a lower social status than many of their students, who held their teachers in sovereign contempt. The teaching staff were remote from the students and allowed them outside of class to behave as they pleased. In class, on the other hand, the headmasters and assistant masters enforced discipline and diligent memorization of the lessons by constant flogging with birch and ash rods. Hostility between teachers and students was the typical result, and outright student rebellions, which sometimes had to be put down by armed force, were not uncommon. At the same time, uncontrolled bullying of the younger boys by the older was universal, as was the practice of "fagging," whereby senior boys demanded personal services from the juniors. Enrollments fell in all the schools; Charterhouse, for example, had 489 students in 1825 but only 137 in 1832.

Conditions in the public schools began to improve in the latter 1820s, when they entered a period of reform and expansion that was to last several decades. The leading reformer was Thomas Arnold, who became headmaster of Rugby in 1828 and transformed it into an immensely influential model school. He was celebrated in the most famous public-school novel, Thomas Hughes's *Tom Brown's Schooldays* (1857). But Arnold did not bring about the alteration of the public schools single-handedly, for there were other reforming schoolmasters; and all were responding to criticism from a growing number of politicians as well as to the impulses of evangelical religion and the demands of the middle class. Arnold was typical in that he saw the public schools as essentially religious. To him, life was a struggle between good and evil, and in school, outside of the control of their families, boys needed firm guidance to avoid evil. Arnold wrote: "It is *not* necessary that this school be a school of 300 or 100 or fifty boys; but it *is* necessary that it be a school of Christian gentlemen" (Gathorne-Hardy 72). Thus, he set out not only to improve the teaching at Rugby but also to shape the character of the boys. As he said many times, "What we must look for here is, 1st, religious and moral principles; 2ndly, gentlemanly conduct; 3rdly, intellectual ability" (Stanley 95). To these ends, Arnold raised the status and pay of his assistant masters, moved the boys from independent "dames' houses" in the town to houses in the school headed by carefully recruited housemasters, enlisted the senior boys (the sixth form) as prefects to enforce discipline, and took over teaching the sixth form himself, as well as the office of chaplain and chief preacher. Arnold retained corporal punishment and did little to change the Rugby curriculum, but his kind of reforms spread among the other public schools (18 Rugby boys went on to serve as headmasters of public schools). Victorian public schools became morally serious, intensely religious institutions that consciously engaged in "character-building," preparing an expanding ruling class for their duties as governors of the nation and empire.

The reformed public schools proved to be immensely attractive to the richer elements in the middle class who wished to have elite status. Enrollments in all the schools recovered by about mid-century, and from the 1850s new public schools were founded and old grammar schools were converted into full-fledged public schools. Although it is not easy to distinguish the public schools from all the other 500 or so private schools that sprang up to educate middle-class British boys in the nineteenth century, a good estimate is that in the 1890s there were between 64 and 104 public schools in Britain as a whole, with many more claiming that exalted status. The public schools served only a tiny proportion of the age group (they had only about 7,500 students in 1865 and 20,000 in 1890), but their graduates dominated admission to Oxbridge, ordination to the clergy, entry into the professions, officerships in the army, posts in politics, and appointments in the imperial and domestic civil services. As one Victorian expert on the public schools declared, "The great Endowed Schools are less to be considered as educational agencies, in the intellectual sense, than as social agencies" (Staunton xxix–xxxi).

In the late-Victorian period the public schools for boys changed somewhat from the Arnoldian pattern, becoming in the process more in-turned, regimented, and above all devoted to athletics. Headmasters of Arnold's generation did not emphasize sports and games; to them, as to Arnold, the cherished "manliness" of character meant Christian religiosity, independence, and a mature sense of personal responsibility. But in the second half of the century "manliness" came to connote loyalty, physical courage, endurance, and discipline, as well as Christian morality. The schools became institutions inculcating "muscular Christianity," the cult of athleticism, and patriotism, which together encouraged a distinct anti-intellectualism. Clearly, there was a strong resonance between the imperialism and militarism of the late nineteenth century and the cultivation of sports in public schools. It was in the late-Victorian period that the saying "Waterloo was won on the playing fields of Eton" was concocted and attributed to the Duke of Wellington. But compulsory sports, like the simultaneous regimentation of the students' lives, were also responses to problems that were internal to the public schools – namely, the perpetual problem of disciplining the students and the perceived need to distract them from the sexual impulses of adolescence. A boy who had been trained to severe self-discipline and tired out by daily sports was thought less likely to engage either in rebellious behavior or in the sexual activities inherent in an all-male environment.

The careers of the headmasters and their assistant masters reflected the centrality of the public schools to upper-class Victorian life. Headmasters from the time of Arnold through the end of the century enjoyed not only dictatorial power over their schools but also the prestige and pay of eminent professional men. Because of the religious function of the schools, the headmasters all were clergymen (the overwhelming majority of them Anglican priests, though a few Catholic and Nonconformist schools were established), the first lay headmaster of Rugby winning appointment only in 1903. Most were of relatively high status before becoming headmasters, being offspring of professional families and graduates of either Oxford or Cambridge. Their pay put them well up in the ranks of well-to-do professional men: in the 1860s the headmaster of Rugby made £3,000 a year, those of Eton and Harrow even more. Since their work was regarded as essentially religious, successful headmasters could expect to be promoted into important posts in the Church of England. A common career pattern would begin with a boy going to a public school, then to Oxford or Cambridge; after taking his BA he would have a college fellowship, followed by a period of teaching at a public school, a headmastership, and then a cathedral deanship or a bishopric. Six of the eight Archbishops of Canterbury appointed between 1860 and 1960 had been public school headmasters. But the headmasters carried heavy loads: they stood *in loco parentis* to the boys; they were expected to be both good teachers and inspirational preachers; and they had to worry about keeping the numbers of students at their schools up and, as Oxford and Cambridge increasingly valued merit by examination, about the success of their boys in university academic competition.

One of Thomas Arnold's most important reforms was to raise the status and quality of his assistant masters. So widespread were the effects of this reform that appointment as an assistant master in a public school became a very desirable position for a young graduate of one of the ancient universities. Indeed, fellows of Oxbridge colleges wishing to get married often went into schoolteaching. Moreover, since the assistant masters for the first two-thirds of the century were almost always ordained, they found that college fellowships, parish livings, and assistant masterships were largely interchangeable. There was much traffic of clergymen among the three types of post. The pay of assistant masters put them solidly among the middle class, though young teachers often had to delay marriage until they had been promoted. In the 1870s, for instance, when the standard salary for a college fellow was £200, the average salary of assistant masters at the bigger public schools was £250, clearly a middle-class income but not enough for a gentleman to support a home, family, and the requisite three or four domestic servants. A few – most of them classics teachers – made much more: the average pay and perquisites of Rugby's 13 classics assistant masters in 1861 was £966, which placed them among the Victorian upper middle class. In some cases, in order to retain excellent teachers, the headmasters appointed them as housemasters, because housemasters enjoyed the board-and-room payments of their students and thus could make as much as £1,500 a year (Honey ch. 5; Gathorne-Hardy 106–9).

During the course of the century public schoolmastering took the first halting steps towards becoming a profession in itself. After the reforms of the Arnoldian period, most assistant masters in the public schools for boys took their teaching seriously, and their promotion in terms of salary and posts depended largely upon merit. They did not, however, take much interest in teacher training, because both they and their headmasters believed that the main requirement of a public school teacher was simply to be a gentleman. In the late-Victorian period, headmasters increasingly valued athletic prowess and coaching ability among their assistant masters. Teaching in a public school became a profession in the senses that the schoolmasters eventually separated from holy orders and thought of their careers as confined to the schools themselves. The Victorian public school teachers gradually became laicized: as late as 1870, for instance, a majority of teachers at ten leading public schools were ordained, but in 1889 only 28.7 percent were, and in 1906 only 13.3 percent. Yet the lay schoolmasters, whose career hopes now focused on promotion to a headmastership and not to ecclesiastical preferment, faced a problem in the fact that, until the end of the century, the headmasterships all required ordination. The teachers' resentment was one of the early signs of the same kind of emerging professional consciousness seen in the universities; other indicators in the late-Victorian period included a desire among assistant masters to have pension funds for their retirement years and security of tenure against the traditional power of the headmasters. But the prevailing tradition of the "gentleman amateur" and the culture of passionate loyalty to one's own school prevented the assistant masters from going very far along the road to professionalization during the nineteenth century.

After mid-century, public schools for girls began to be built, and these institutions provided a growing number of secondary teaching posts for women. The public schools for girls were the result of dissatisfaction in middle-class families with the educational opportunities for their daughters. At the beginning of the century families of gentle status (aristocracy, gentry, and middle class) educated their daughters either by hiring governesses or by sending them to private schools operated by gentlewomen who were down on their luck and in need of income. To be a governess was among the least happy walks of life for a Victorian lady, and a woman of good family – say, the daughter of a poor clergyman – would resort to it only because she needed income and had few other choices for "respectable" work. The pay was very poor – in the first half of the century less than £50 a year plus board and room. Nevertheless, by the 1850s there were more than 21,000 governesses in Britain. Governesses often had little education themselves, though by mid-century a significant number were able to obtain training in teaching. For the most part, governesses taught the "accomplishments" – subjects regarded as useful to middle- and upper-class girls, such as music, French, drawing, and needlework – but often they had to teach subjects – geography, arithmetic, history – about which they knew little themselves. Moreover, families hired them because of their gentle status but then often treated them with contempt. Charlotte Brontë, who worked for a time as a governess, wrote in 1839: "I can now see more clearly than I have ever done before that a private governess has no existence, is not considered as a living and rational being, except as connected with the wearisome duties she has to fulfill" (Renton 74–5). She was to depict the position of governess in even more depressing terms in *Jane Eyre* (1847).

Mistresses of private schools for girls present a somewhat different story. While many banked on their middle-class status as ladies to attract students, usually no more than ten or twenty in number, to their little boarding schools, others became committed to obtaining expertise in teaching. By strenuous efforts in self-education, study abroad, and attendance at teacher-training colleges, these women teachers sought to make themselves pedagogical experts, not purveyors of the traditional liberal education. Many imported new theories of "child-centered education" from the Continent. Thus, unlike male public school masters, they hoped to win professional status as experts in pedagogy. Their campaign for professional status was difficult, partly because of the continuing assumption that women were not suited for the professions, and partly because their work as teachers was undervalued. Schoolmistresses rarely made more than £300 a year, from which the expenses of the school had to be paid. Moreover, they taught ladies' accomplishments as well as academic subjects to girls whose sole goal in life was marriage to a gentleman; nevertheless, by the 1860s, many schoolmistresses had developed a group consciousness as professional teachers.

By mid-century the desire among feminists and some middle-class families for more prestigious education for young women began to produce better secondary schools for girls, and this movement ironically would work against the model for schoolmistresses as experts in pedagogy. The prestige of the boys' public schools insured that the new schools for girls would be private boarding schools modeled on the traditional male public schools. The most influential public schools for girls were Cheltenham Ladies' College, founded in 1854 and led from 1858 by Dorothea Beale, and Roedean, founded in the 1880s by the Lawrence sisters, Dorothy, Penelope, and Millicent. By the 1890s there were more than 200 private schools for girls, of which more than 20 were regarded as full-fledged public schools. The majority of all these schools adopted the same emphasis on religion, moral training, and sports as the boys' schools.

The public schools for girls created professional teaching careers for women in their posts of headmistresses and assistant mistresses. In their quest for professional standing, these women had to distinguish themselves from both the private schoolmistresses and the working-class women who taught in the nation's elementary schools. To be sure, an element of the ideal of the teacher as pedagogical expert influenced the new girls' public schools. One headmistress wrote: "Parents will have to realise that the teacher is an expert professional and is entitled therefore to the deference shown to the skilled professional opinion of the doctor, lawyer, or architect" (Pedersen 46). But over time the prerequisite for women public schoolmistresses was a university degree, not pedagogical training. Some received advanced education at Queen's College and Bedford College (London), which had been established in the 1840s to give better training to governesses but which developed into university-level institutions. As London and the provincial universities gradually opened themselves to women, aspiring public schoolmistresses in the late-Victorian period could earn degrees from them. Increasingly, however, education in one of the women's colleges at Oxford and Cambridge became the prerequisite for a post at one of the public schools for girls. By the same token, the relatively high status of these positions and the idealism of the schools attracted more than half of all the women who had studied at Oxford and Cambridge. The subjects they taught were confined neither to the accomplishments of the lady schoolmistresses nor the classics of male public schoolteachers. English and foreign literatures predominated, but women teachers also offered mathematics and sciences. Since the career opportunities for public schoolmistresses were so limited, the schools had little turnover and both excellent and poor teachers could be frozen in place for decades. Nevertheless, by the last 20 years of the century public headmistresses were not only preparing their students for roles in the public sphere, but also themselves achieving distinction as experts in scholarship, local government, and civic affairs.

The Elementary School Teachers

The so-called "elementary" schools of Victorian England were for the working class. However, for the first three-quarters of the century many members of the working class had no access to schooling at all, for there was no state school system until 1870. The prevailing assumption held that the state ought to interfere as little as possible in the workings of the economy and society. Education was a matter for religion: as one Bishop of London put it, "The church is the authorised and recognised organ and instrument of national education" (Midwinter 37). Further, working-class boys and girls were supposed to go to work before they were ten years old and to work full time after they were 11. For those that had the time and money, early- and mid-Victorian England had only a patchwork quilt of different types of private or "voluntary" schools. For example, there were thousands of Sunday schools, first established by the various Christian denominations in the latter part of the eighteenth century. The Sunday schools became an important social institution in urban working-class communities, but they could not offer any education beyond the most basic. Their teaching staff were volunteers, devoted to teaching the rudiments of reading and religion. There were some small "charity" schools for the poor that had been set up in the eighteenth century by philanthropists for religious purposes. A few model schools like the utilitarian knowledge factory run by Mr M'Choakumchild in

Dickens's *Hard Times* (1854) were established by Victorian middle-class progressives to advance what they called "the march of mind." Other private schools, usually very cheap (charging as little as nine pence a week, or a little more than £1 a year), were set up by men or women, often unsuccessful tradesmen or shopkeepers, who were simply trying to make a living. Pip attends one of these in Dickens's *Great Expectations* (1861). These schoolmasters and schoolmistresses were often unqualified, and most of the schools were very small and disappeared when the founder–teacher failed, moved on, or died.

But the most important types of school before 1870 were established by two religious foundations – the (Anglican) National Society and the (Nonconformist) British and Foreign School Society. Even they fell far short of reaching the entire working-class population. The National Society and the British and Foreign School Society became semi-official in the 1830s, when they received recognition by the state in the form of an annual grant for the construction of additional schools. However, the continuing inadequacy of the school "system" as a whole is shown by the illiteracy rate: by a conservative estimate, one-third of all men and half of all women in England and Wales in the 1850s were illiterate by even minimum standards. Perhaps a quarter of all parishes in England and Wales had no school at all. Some middle- and upper-class Victorians regarded this situation as dangerous to religion and public order; but more conservative people felt that education of the working class would itself be politically dangerous and destructive of the deference properly demanded from working people.

Teaching as a walk of life in the elementary schools was profoundly shaped by these conditions. The managers of both the charity schools and those run by the two denominational societies took cheapness as their key consideration. An adult teacher (at first, most of them men) might make as much as £60 a year, which was only the equivalent of the wages of a semi-skilled worker but enough to discourage a philanthropic organization from hiring more than one per school. In order to serve more students both of the denominational societies adopted the "monitorial" system that had been invented in the last years of the eighteenth century, whereby a single adult teacher, training older children as monitors to teach the younger, might supervise the teaching of up to 500 students. Since the monitors, rarely more than 12 or 13 years old and barely educated themselves, received only a few weeks' training as teachers, the monitorial system provided instruction by rote memorization at best. Their skill level allowed them only to drill their students in the most basic three Rs according to rigidly planned lessons. Teachers in the monitorial system assumed that the students were passive recipients of information as well as stained by original sin and inclined to wicked behavior. Teaching therefore had to be a process of forcing students to memorize factual information while applying corporal punishment for discipline. The teachers themselves were regarded by the middle and landed classes as nothing more than tradesmen; indeed, the upper classes thought it important to recruit adult elementary teachers from the working and lower-middle classes so that the teachers would not rise socially "above" their pupils. The teachers were not treated as professionals and thus were of distinctly lower status than the public schoolmasters and schoolmistresses. Obviously, the monitorial system bore an analogy to the factory system in industry; and the monitorial system combined with the mechanical mode of teaching – memorably depicted in Dickens's *Hard Times* – to keep the role and status of the teacher comparable to that of a factory worker.

In an effort to improve elementary education, James Kay-Shuttleworth, secretary to the Education Committee of the Privy Council, inaugurated the "pupil–teacher" system in 1846. Kay-Shuttleworth meant to work major changes in the training and provision of teachers, but his pupil–teacher plan can be seen as an outgrowth of the monitorial system. By it, boys and girls between 13 and 18 years of age could be given apprenticeships in teaching. For a small salary these pupil–teachers both taught classes and received training in teaching each week. After completing an apprenticeship a pupil–teacher could apply for a scholarship to one of the teacher-training colleges (which were in fact secondary schools) that had been established in the 1830s and 1840s. Whether attending a teacher-training college or not, a pupil–teacher could obtain certification of teaching competence after government examination. Finally, Kay-Shuttleworth's scheme provided small augmentations to the teacher's salary for mentoring pupil–teachers. By 1861 there were 14,000 pupil–teachers and 35 teacher-training colleges – 17 for men, 14 for women, and four co-educational.

The pupil–teacher system of 1846 had a significant positive effect on the elementary school teachers' competence and status. It gave them higher incomes, a system for certification of skills, and a quasi-civil service standing. In 1861, the Census moved teachers to the occupational category of "professions." A Royal Commission in 1861 found that the average pay for certified schoolmasters was £94 3s 7d, which was the equivalent of the pay of a skilled artisan, and some schoolmasters were also given housing. Certified women teachers earned less for the same work: in 1861 certified women teachers made an average of £62 4s 10d, which was about the same as an *uncertified* male teacher (Newcastle Commission 63–7). Most teachers still worked alone in their schools, save for their pupil–teacher apprentices; but many had good relations with the local Anglican clergyman, who often was the chief figure in the local school council.

Kay-Shuttleworth had never intended to make professionals of the elementary teachers: "We hoped to inspire them with a large sympathy for their own class. To implant in their minds the thought that their chief honour would be to aid in rescuing that class from the misery of ignorance and its attendant vices" (Tropp 14). Nevertheless, many teachers, who by the 1850s felt that they stood in an anomalous position – above the workers by their own estimation but not regarded as equals by middle-class and professional people – believed that their social rank ought to be higher than merely working class. *The School and the Teacher*, a schoolteachers' journal, declared in 1855: "It is no strange thing that men who in education, tastes and habits, have all the qualifications of 'gentlemen,' should regard themselves as worthy of something very much higher than the treatment of a servant, and the wages of a mechanic . . . What in short the teacher desires is, that his 'calling' shall rank as a 'profession'" (Tropp 26). Of particular annoyance to the teachers was the government's policy of excluding them from serving as Her Majesty's Inspectors of the schools; these well-paid posts were reserved strictly for university graduates (the most famous being Matthew Arnold), none of whom had any training or experience as elementary school teachers.

The higher pay, improved training, and consequent status restlessness of the elementary teachers eventually generated a reaction among influential middle- and upper-class people who felt that elementary teachers were seeking to rise above their proper station. One school manager in Wales accused teachers of extravagance "in their houses, mahogany furniture, sofas, etc., when painted deal would do" (Tropp 20). Another critic of the teachers, an Anglican clergyman, said that the claims of the teachers were pretentious, and that until the teachers "are taken from the same rank of society and have undergone the intellectual training and the social discipline which is absolutely necessary to the doctor, the lawyer and the clergyman . . . I must confess myself to be one of those . . . who cannot accede to the national schoolmaster a rank on the level with the learned professions" (Tropp 37). The Newcastle Commission, which reported in 1861, heard much testimony along these lines and concluded that a large portion of students were not well taught, in part because the best-trained teachers found it hard to do the drudgery of teaching. Hence, the Commissioners recommended ending the pupil–teacher system of 1846 in favor of "payment by results" – paying teachers according to the results earned by their students in national examinations. Robert Lowe, the Palmerston administration's chief educational official, issued in 1862 a Revised Code establishing a new set of rules for elementary schooling based largely on the findings of the Newcastle Commission and his own commitment to the doctrines of Political Economy. Payment by results became the main educational principle of the day: teachers would be paid according to attendance records and the performance of the students on examinations administered by the Inspectors. Pay for pupil–teachers and their mentors was abolished.

The elementary school teachers found the Revised Code disastrous to education and a blow to their own professional aspirations. The number of pupil–teachers and applicants to the training colleges declined rapidly. At the same time as university tutors were developing careers as professional teachers and research scholars, elementary teachers had to teach strictly to the exams, and thus to drill their students incessantly to give memorized answers to the texts and problems that they would face. The exams themselves became artificial performances by students for the Inspectors, with anxious teachers standing by nervously. Matthew Arnold, perhaps the most thoughtful of all the Inspectors, regretted that the Revised Code made it impossible for the Inspectors to explore "the intellectual life of the school" as a whole, for the Inspectors had no time for anything except examining each student. Moreover, he stated in 1867, "The work of teaching in school is less interesting and more purely mechanical than it used to be." Under the 1846 system, he wrote, the teacher had felt he was "a fellow-worker with the national government"; but now "he is told that he has greatly overrated his importance and that of his function" (Arnold 112–14).

Not surprisingly, the teachers suffered a blow to their morale and to their fledgling attempts to form professional associations. These efforts had begun as early as the 1830s but had yielded national associations (one for Anglican and one for Nonconformist elementary teachers) only in the 1850s. In the latter 1860s the teachers' morale began to recover, and their associations began to apply political pressure on Parliament to raise teachers' status. Their renewed efforts were made more urgent by passage of the Reform Act of 1867, which extended the vote to most urban working-class males. As Robert Lowe himself told Parliament, "I believe it will be absolutely necessary that you should prevail upon our future masters to learn their letters" (*Hansard* 1549). Elementary education for the working class seemed more important than ever before, not least to the teachers. In 1870 teachers of all denominations, after many years of dispute over religious issues, reached agreement endorsing religious education (Bible study for all in national schools, plus a "conscience clause" that would excuse those whose families objected). They formed the National Union of Elementary Teachers (NUET), which set out to elevate the status of the teachers by securing appointment of teachers to the Inspectorate, tenure against clergy interference, adequate salaries, retirement pensions, exclusion of unqualified people from teaching, and control over the examinations admitting teachers to the profession. In the last 30 years of the century they made significant progress on all of these items, except for the professional monopoly implied by the last two.

Meanwhile, the Gladstone government passed the vitally important Education Act of 1870, which established the first state school system in Britain. The Act was extremely controversial because it incorporated all the voluntary denominational schools into the system and thus established new, nondenominational schools and school boards only in localities where the denominational schools were inadequate or nonexistent. As late as 1900 a majority of elementary schools in England and Wales remained denominational. Moreover, payment by results continued to prevail until 1895 and thus to dominate teaching. And schoolteachers, especially in the villages, often had to do extra duties as required by the local clergyman, such as playing the organ and training the church choir, even though the NUET won agreement to the principle of letters of appointment that specified the teacher's duties. But whatever the controversial aspects of the 1870 Act, it radically expanded the school system – and the number of teachers. In 1870 there were 12,467 certified teachers (about evenly divided between men and women); in 1895 there were 52,941 teachers (two-thirds women), relatively few of whom had been trained in teacher-training colleges. The number of pupil–teachers also grew, from more than 14,000 in 1870 to more than 29,000 in 1895 (almost 80 percent of whom were women). But the teachers had not won the right to exclude uncertified and poorly paid teachers, and by 1895 there had been a twenty-four-fold increase of uncertified teachers (Tropp 114).

By the end of the century the elementary school teaching force in England and Wales was composed of a relatively small core of trained and certified teachers working amidst a very large number of untrained and uncertified teachers and pupil–teachers. To be sure, teachers' pay had improved: in 1895 the average salary of certified male teachers stood at £123 a year and that of a female certified teacher £80. But these wages were still little better than those of a skilled artisan or barely educated clerk. Most teachers continued to be recruited from the working class. They still felt socially anomalous, isolated from the working class by their superior education but not accepted as equals by the clergy or other professionals. Moreover, their relative social mobility concerned many middle-class people, who resented the teachers' claims to middle-class or professional standing. The teachers' unsettled position in society was reflected in their thinking about their national association (renamed the National Union of Teachers (NUT) in 1883). Was it a trade union or a professional association? Like a union, the NUT did try to influence Parliament and the government; but otherwise it did not behave like a union. Instead, it devoted itself to improving the status of the teachers, on grounds that raising their social position would improve education and therefore English society generally. But if the teachers were as yet socially neither fish nor fowl, contemporary social observers like C. F. G. Masterman forecast a promising future for them in a society that increasingly demanded an educated population. Masterman wrote in his famous *The Condition of England* (1909) of "the new type of teacher":

> [The teachers] are not only doing their work efficiently, but are everywhere taking the lead in public and *quasi*-public activities. They appear as the mainstay of the political machine in suburban districts, serving upon the municipal bodies, in work, clear-headed and efficient; the leaders in the churches and chapels, and their various social organizations. They are taking up the position in the urban districts which for many generations was occupied by the country clergy. (67)

At the end of the nineteenth century, to conclude, teaching in England remained divided into three very different walks of life. The university dons and the public school teachers retained their traditional elite connections and relatively high social status as educators of the ruling class. To be sure, there were distinct differences in quality of life between the Oxbridge dons and the teachers at the provincial universities, for the professors and fellows at Oxford and Cambridge enjoyed an elegance in their surroundings, as well as contact with the top levels of society, that were unavailable to most red brick teachers. But all university faculty members were well along the way to careers as specialized and professional teacher–scholars, and the professors clearly held prestigious positions as "scientific" research scholars. Women in increasing numbers were winning their way into university teaching, though not even in the twentieth century did they achieve anything like equal numbers to men. Like the university teachers, public school teachers (except for the headmasters) had become laicized by 1900, and they thought of their careers as moving within the circle of public schools themselves. The rapid increase in the number of public schools gave them a much expanded range of opportunities. But instead of moving towards professional training as teachers or research scholarship, public school teachers had been caught up in the cult of the amateur who must reach his students through patriotism, school loyalty, and organized sports.

The number of elementary school teachers had increased rapidly after passage of the Education Act of 1870, and by 1900 these teachers showed clear signs of consciousness of themselves as professional teachers. Women constituted the fastest-growing group among the elementary school teachers, even though the social assumptions of the day allowed them to be paid less than men. Overall, the importance of the teachers to English society had risen as the English political public realized that education of the working class had become essential for the nation's political and economic strength. By 1900 the state had taken responsibility from the churches for elementary education, and there was a growing sense that secondary education for the masses would also have to be provided. The teachers in 1900, as in the 15 years after 1846, worked as quasi-civil servants. Yet the teachers' pay had not risen much faster than the overall cost of living. Moreover, they were still recruited largely from the working class and, despite their generally improved training, they still found that middle- and upper-class people did not accord them the status as professionals that they claimed. In the early twentieth century schoolteaching would provide a way out of traditional working-class occupations for young people like D. H. Lawrence, but teachers had a long way to go before acquiring professional, or even middle-class, standing.

See also 1870; GROWING UP, MOVING OUT; CLERICAL, MEDICAL, ADMINISTRATIVE; LITERARY CRITICISM; SKIN

REFERENCES

Arnold, M. (1889) *Reports on Elementary Schools, 1852–1882*. London: Macmillan and Sons.

Brittain, V. (1960) *The Women at Oxford*. London: George G. Harrap.

Gathorne-Hardy, J. (1977) *The Old School Tie: The Phenomenon of the English Public School*. New York: Viking Press.

Hansard's Parliamentary Debates (1867) Third series, vol. 188. London: Cornelius Buck.

Honey, J. R. de S. (1977) *Tom Brown's Universe: The Development of the Victorian Public School*. London: Millington.

Masterman, C. F. G. (1960) *The Condition of England*. London: Methuen.

Midwinter, E. (1970) *Nineteenth Century Education*. London: Longman.

Newcastle Commission (1861) Report of the Commissioners appointed to inquire into the state of Popular Education in England. *British Parliamentary Papers*, 21, Part I. London: HMSO.

Pedersen, J. S. (1991) "Schoolmistresses and Headmistresses: Elites and Education in Nineteenth-Century England." In *Women Who Taught*, ed. A. Prentice and M. R. Theobald. Toronto: University of Toronto Press.

Renton, A. (1991) *Tyrant or Victim? A History of the British Governess*. London: Weidenfeld and Nicolson.

Stanley, A. P. (1846) *The Life and Correspondence of Thomas Arnold*. London: B. Fellowes.

Staunton, H. (1865) *The Great Schools of England*. London: S. Low, Son, and Marston.

Tropp, A. (1957) *The School Teachers: The Growth of the Teaching Profession in England and Wales to the Present Day*. London: Heinemann.

FURTHER READING

Armytage, W. H. G. (1955) *Civic Universities: Aspects of a British Tradition*. London: Benn.

Bamford, T. W. (1960) *Thomas Arnold*. London: Cresset Press.

Bill, E. G. W. (1973) *University Reform in Nineteenth-Century Oxford: A Study of Henry Halford Vaughan*. Oxford: Clarendon Press.

Brock, M. G., and M. C. Curthoys (eds) (1997) *History of the University of Oxford. Volumes 6 and 7: Nineteenth-Century Oxford*. Oxford: Clarendon Press.

Brooke, C. N. L. (1993) *A History of the University of Cambridge. Volume 4: 1870–1990*. Cambridge: Cambridge University Press.

De Bellaigue, C. (2007) *Educating Women: Schooling and Identity in England and France, 1800–1867*. Oxford: Oxford University Press.

Engel, A. (1983) *From Clergyman to Don: The Rise of the Academic Profession in Nineteenth-Century Oxford*. New York: Oxford University Press.

Heyck, T. W. (1982) *The Transformation of Intellectual Life in Victorian England*. London: Croom Helm.

Mangan, J. A. (1981) *Athleticism in the Victorian and Edwardian Public School*. Cambridge: Cambridge University Press.

Rich, R. W. (1933) *The Training of Teachers in England and Wales during the Nineteenth Century*. Cambridge: Cambridge University Press.

Rothblatt, S. (1968) *The Revolution of the Dons: Cambridge and Society in Victorian England*. London: Faber.

Searby, P. (1997) *A History of the University of Cambridge. Volume 3: 1750–1870*. Cambridge: Cambridge University Press.

Smelser, N. J. (1991) *Social Paralysis and Social Change: British Working-Class Education in the Nineteenth Century*. Berkeley: University of California Press.

Sparrow, J. (1967) *Mark Pattison and the Idea of a University*. Cambridge: Cambridge University Press.

Wardle, D. (1976) *English Popular Education, 1780–1975*. Cambridge: Cambridge University Press.

15
Administrative

Michael Hunt

Administration has been an important element of government throughout history, being in essence the means by which the wishes of a ruler are carried out. It was practiced amongst others by the ancient Chinese and by the Romans. Historically in the United Kingdom its principal purposes for national government might be summarized as the collection of revenues for the king and the maintenance of law and order including the administration of justice. The extensive array of national government services that exist today, devoted not least to social welfare, simply did not exist when Victoria ascended the throne. At the level of local government the principal units for administrative activity were the unsystematized and inadequately resourced self-governing parishes, responsible (amongst other things) for the maintenance of roads and for the relief of the poor, and the counties, principally domains of the wealthy landed gentry who accepted responsibility for the delivery of justice. In addition some towns, known as Municipal Corporations, had responsibility for the delivery of a range of functions including poor relief and the administration of justice. Any review of administrative change in the Victorian period has to take account of both the expansion in government activities that took place during those years (and the reasons for those changes) and also the changed structures through which those activities were delivered.

These changes arose, of course, because of changes in both the economic and the political environment. The early part of the Victorian period may loosely be described as a period of laissez-faire, a period, as W. H. Greenleaf has suggested, of disinterested state activity. But the move from what Greenleaf has described as libertarianism to collectivism was well under way. Libertarianism, he suggests, essentially referred to the right of an individual to be free from arbitrary activity by the state and to have the right to own and dispose of his property (including his own labor). The role of the state was simply to ensure that those rights were preserved. Associated with this was the view that power should be diffused, partly to prevent the growth of an overbearing autocratic state (or an overbearing autocratic monarch) and partly also to ensure that the costs of the state did not become too large and thus, by imposing taxation, impact on the choices that a free man might take. This brief summary scarcely does justice to a range of interlocking ideas and traditions, some of them still to be found in the British political culture today, which are an essential prerequisite to understanding the incremental development of Victorian administration.

One obvious limitation of libertarianism was that it seemed to favor those in positions of power more than the peasantry. Collectivism, stimulated particularly by the Industrial Revolution of 1750–1830, recognized by contrast that the community interest might need to take precedence over individual interests – indeed that individualism alone might be inimical to the interests of the majority. Putting it slightly differently, collectivism implied that the weaker members of society might need the strength of the state to preserve and enhance their own interests in a positive way. But collectivism was far from the dominant ideology in the United Kingdom by the end of Victoria's reign even if some of its ideas were implicitly accepted by many members of the working classes and by their representatives in the growing Trade Union and Labour movements. Moreover, collectivism and libertarianism were not opposites but each comprised a variety of different forms which might appropriately be regarded as "adjacent steps in a progression" (Perkin 110). Needless to say, such progression, viewed from the perspective of administrative reform, was anything but smooth.

It may be worth noting (among other reasons, so as not to be completely insular) that the tensions referred to above – between the individual and the collective, or between classes – were peculiarly evident in English administration. While the history of administration on the Continent during this period parallels England's in many respects (for example, as to the smallness of the civil service in comparison with today's) there were also significant differences. Prussia and France were notably in advance of England when it came to the coherence and centralization of public administration. In large part this was because their respective state governments were much more highly centralized and authoritarian. France, of course, had experienced a revolution in the late eighteenth century which, whilst it disposed of rule by a monarch and a ruling class, nevertheless retained the centralized controlling administration that had been a feature of its previous form of rule. Subsequently Napoleon Bonaparte put in place many of the structures of a reformed administrative state that have lasted until the present day. Prussia's highly organized bureaucracy, within a monarchical system, was principally designed to support its military aspirations. The greater coherence of the civil services in Prussia and France embodied less of the ambivalence about class, and of the tension between the individual and the collective, that were so characteristic of Victorian administration.

Amongst a number of political theorists whose ideas influenced the development of British administration in the nineteenth century Jeremy Bentham (1748–1832) is especially significant. To the Victorians he was the legal and administrative reformer *par excellence*, a man who had first set his sights on English law and the English constitution, then gradually extended them to every imaginable institution: prisons, schools, factories, workhouses, and the workings of government more generally. Bentham embodied many of the age's characteristic conflicts. Obsessively rational, he actually disbelieved in rights of any kind, subordinating all such abstract principles, which he dismissed as "vague generalities," to the sole good of pleasure and the sole evil of pain. Ethics he summed up in the famous Greatest Happiness Principle, which asserts that it is the single obligation of individuals and legislators to "maximize" (a word of Bentham's coinage) the happiness of the greatest number of beings whose interest is in question. If it happens that the question is about a given nation, then it is all the inhabitants of the nation whose pleasures must be considered; if the scope of the question is "international" (another Bentham coinage), then the pleasures of everyone in the nations under consideration must be consulted. Always eager to follow a thought out to a logical conclusion, Bentham readily extended his ethical horizons to include the pleasures and pains of "all sentient beings." The Greatest Happiness Principle had already been expressed by others in almost the same terms, but Bentham was uniquely rigorous in maintaining it as the fundamental ethical principle and in following out its logical implications.

One characteristic Victorian tension is apparent already in the Greatest Happiness Principle, that between the individual and the collective. For on the one hand the principle locates the good solely in pleasure as actually experienced by individuals, while on the other it refuses to value any one individual's pleasure over another's. It is no wonder then that Bentham has been hailed both as the champion of radical individualism and the champion of the state. And, given his influence, it is no wonder either that Victorian thinking about administration – and government more generally – betrays this same split, laying down a tradition of laissez-faire with one hand while the other invents the welfare state and the bureaucracy of regulatory government. This is also reflected in the writings of John Stuart Mill, who like Bentham adhered to a utilitarian philosophy. In his 1859 treatise *On Liberty*, he refers to "the greatest dissemination of power consistent with efficiency; but also the greatest possible centralisation of information and the diffusion of it from the centre" (139). Time would show whether these two precepts were compatible with one another.

In practical political terms the catalysts for the changes that took place in Britain during the nineteenth century included factors such as the gradual loss of power by the monarchy and its concomitant accretion by Parliament. Coupled with this was the even more gradual increase in the representative nature of Parliament, facilitated by a succession of Reform Acts which gradually extended the right to vote. One effect of this franchise extension was the recognition by MPs that they had to pay attention to the needs of the middle and poorer classes, rather than simply other members of the upper classes, if they were to secure election. Economic factors included the Industrial Revolution, which facilitated the movement from a largely agrarian society to one where manufacturing and commerce were increasingly important. This led to a distribution of incomes that was rather more complex than before, which, in turn, facilitated industrial production because of an increased demand for goods and services. This increase was supported by an increase in the population which further increased domestic demand. Industrial production and thus economic wealth were also encouraged by an improvement in transport facilitated by the development of the canal system. None of these factors led directly to an increase in administration, nor did any changes in either the nature or the delivery of services occur quickly. Nevertheless, the Victorian era witnessed a growing realization, by both public and government, that some of the conditions experienced by many of the most vulnerable in society were no longer acceptable in a changing political and economic climate, and that state intervention was essential to inhibit the worst of these abuses.

The Industrial Revolution was significant for other reasons. The opportunities for work offered by the expansion of industry involved the movement of substantial numbers of the population from the countryside to the towns. For most, living conditions were appalling – overcrowding in poorly built houses without sanitation provided a breeding ground for diseases of many kinds. Work was often dangerous, wages were poor, and hours were long. In particular the social structure based around the parish system began to break down: its traditionally understood system of rights and responsibilities that had maintained a tolerable way of life in rural society, as well as a system of law and order, could not withstand the pressure of crowded urban living. As a result crime increased, and it is no accident that one of the earliest significant reforms of the nineteenth century involved the establishment of a police force in London, the largest of the cities. Poverty increased and was addressed by the Poor Law Amendment Act of 1834. Other examples of nineteenth-century legislation related to conditions in factories and the employment of children and women underground in the coal mining industry. But all of these responses to perceived social problems were essentially *ad hoc*. They represented a specific attack upon a specific problem usually preceded by publicity and public disquiet about a particular social evil. In addressing the problem the intention was to deliver what was minimally necessary to remove the evil, thus ensuring that state expenditure was as low as possible and also that the responsibility for self-improvement remained with those who were being lightly assisted. Harling notes that "the Victorian state's attempts to impose market discipline on the poor obliged it occasionally to intervene in the market itself in an effort to make the living and working conditions of the poor broadly tolerable. Thus the line between *laissez faire* and state intervention was constantly renegotiated because it was obvious to everyone that strict non-intervention would create unsustainable social tensions" (26). However, since intervention was assumed to be the exception rather than the rule, progress in resolving social problems was inevitably incremental and slow. MacDonagh suggests that because immediate solutions to problems rarely proved sufficient, it was almost invariably necessary to revisit the problem with further legislation which involved new administrative arrangements.

The format principally adopted for dealing with social problems was regulatory – that is to say, the government wished to prevent the problem occurring and was prepared to pass legislation for that purpose. This usually involved delegation to subnational or *ad hoc* bodies acting as inspectors although, as Moran notes, in many cases the inspectors lacked any real powers and opted for a conciliatory approach rather than attempting to prosecute offenders. The 1834 Poor Law, for example, established an administrative Central Board, which operated through local Boards of Guardians in areas formed by combining parishes. The function of the Boards of Guardians was to regulate the workhouses established to provide employment for the poor and destitute. This limited approach was adopted for a number of reasons including central government's lack of expertise in dealing with problems; difficulties of communication which meant that it would take some time for central administration to become aware of breaches of the law; and the feeling that the ultimate responsibility for solving the problem lay with the poor themselves. There was thus a moral tone to the solutions adopted. Alongside this was the moral attitude that the state should be as frugal as possible in its expenditure; the solutions adopted therefore made only minimal demands on the national exchequer. It need hardly be added that there was little attempt to see an interconnectedness among problems (such as housing and poverty and education). While such a systemic grasp of social networks engrossed Dickens's novels after 1850, his earlier works – notably the first part of *Oliver Twist* (1837) – provided a valuable and critical insight into the minimalist approach adopted by the early-Victorian state to dealing with social problems.

It was the need to resolve social problems in more than an *ad hoc* way that provided the motive and the structure for a system of local government in England. The 1848 Public Health Act established Local Health Boards to be responsible for the supply of water, drainage, sewerage, and street cleansing in sanitary districts based on the unions of parishes that existed for the poor law. Additionally it established a central body to oversee the work of the Boards. It thus confirmed a structure that formed a basis for a system of local government which was to remain in place for the next century as well as confirming the principle of central supervision over the work of these authorities.

Central Government

Britain's central government in the early to mid-nineteenth century was of limited size by comparison with its continental neighbors. One writer has estimated that it comprised only about 21,300 employees in 1833, many of these working in the revenue departments (Lubenow 18). Departments were not well funded. Indeed most were fairly small, certainly small enough for ministers to make most of the major decisions. The job of the civil service was simply to service ministers – to provide them with papers when the need arose and, if necessary, to help prepare legislation. There was little or no coordination between the departments; Chapman and Green-away confirm that their disaggregated nature reflected the fact that they developed at different times and in response to a variety of different requirements. They therefore operated as discrete bodies, each developing its own processes and procedures to respond to the tasks it was required to undertake. Moreover, they adopted their own recruitment and promotion procedures. In many cases recruitment was corrupt in the sense that there were no particular requirements for admission to a paid position, so that recruitment and advancement frequently depended on whom one knew rather than on any innate abilities. This did not necessarily mean that departments were staffed by incompetent or inefficient officials, but it did mean that there could be no certainty about the quality of the service delivered.

There is perhaps no better account of this variety than the opening chapters of Trollope's early novel *The Three Clerks* (1858) which is a closely autobiographical record of his own early days as a civil servant within the postal system. Trollope's particular brand of realism both makes for a highly detailed and accurate portrait of life in the civil service and challenges the kind of simplification that both reform-ers and supporters of the status quo were apt to fall into when the call for administrative reform became popular in the middle of the century. In short, an office of the Victorian civil service might be a very dreary place indeed, with little or no useful work being done by ill-schooled and ill-mannered clerks. Or it might be a model of intelligence and industry, staffed by the very brightest and most able men of the time.

Some of the complexity of this situation is also apparent if we compare Bentham's approach to administrative reform with probably the most famous literary accounts of maladministration from the period, Dickens's accounts of Chancery – the institu-tion for resolving legal disputes – in *Bleak House* (1853) and the Circumlocution Office in *Little Dorrit* (1857). Legal reform and administrative reform are of course two dif-ferent things, but they tended to coalesce in Bentham's mind (as in Dickens's) insofar as they raised questions about corruption and inefficiency and insofar as Bentham recognized that the one reinforces the other: a procedural maze conveniently masks corrupt aims, and corrupt aims of course divert institutional energies from their legitimate functions. But the greatest evil for both these authors always is waste of energy. While somebody's pockets are filled and there is the appearance at least of gainful employment, nothing needful is actually done.

Dickens was peculiarly enraged by any combination of inefficiency and corruption and found as fertile a ground for his anger in the civil service as he had in Chancery. His satire was widely noticed, and *Little Dorrit* brought the term "Circumlocution

Office" into currency (Trollope used it the very next year in *The Three Clerks*). Nevertheless, Dickens shows himself to be seriously divided by the contrasting demands of
individualism and collectivism in approaching social problems. He looks to individuals both as targets for blame and to provide the real basis for reform, and he
decries the excuses of individuals who seek protection under the umbrella of "the
system." (A rejected title for *Little Dorrit* was "Nobody's Fault," an ironic comment
on the tendency to let institutional responsibility hide that of individuals.) But as
much as he distrusted politics and government, he also recognized that good-hearted
individuals could not by themselves bring about the kind of fundamental change
that was needed, and so he joined and spoke on behalf of the privately organized
Administrative Reform Association upon its founding in 1855. In good Victorian
fashion his fierce interest and faith in the individual were balanced by an authoritarian strain that admired the police and other institutions that seemed able to act
powerfully and decisively (able to act themselves, that is, rather like individuals).
Much of his frustration with government officialdom was precisely that, as often as
not, it did *not* govern.

There are peculiar obstacles to understanding the Victorian perspective on administration, and Dickens himself may, oddly, be among these. We who have seen the
evolution of bureaucracy in the twentieth century easily think of Kafka when we read
Bleak House or *Little Dorrit*, and we may think of those novels as striking at something
peculiarly modern. Dickens certainly was prescient in imagining in Chancery a great,
pervasive, and monstrously evil institution populated mostly by rather ordinary
people; and the Circumlocution Office, with its perfection of the principle of HOW
NOT TO DO IT, also seems immediate and recognizable. But Dickens would have been
horrified to think he was pointing towards the future or that things could possibly
get worse; all his effort was bent towards abolishing dysfunctional historical relics.
Chancery is a medieval institution, literally and figuratively; it is appropriately central
in a world that seems, on every level of *Bleak House*, incapable of escaping its own
past. The Circumlocution Office is likewise meant to portray something musty and
antique, precisely the sort of labyrinth of outmoded and irrational practices that
"reform" of a Benthamite stamp was intended to sweep away, not through sheer
destruction, but by replacing it with something very possibly bigger and better,
something altogether efficient and modern.

The debates generated by Dickens's attacks are instructive. His contemporaries in
the law and the civil service sometimes complained that he took the objects of his
satire from the newspapers and targeted abuses that had already been identified and
largely remedied. They also complained that he did not know enough about the
institutions he satirized to make useful criticisms and that he overlooked the real
achievements especially of the civil service. There was some truth to these charges.
Chancery had been the subject of a series of leaders in *The Times* just before the writing
of *Bleak House*, and reform of government departments had already begun. But neither
Chancery nor the civil service would see fundamental reform completed within Dickens's lifetime.

Centralized Reform

What then prompted reform of the central administration? As Chapman and Greenaway explain, reform did not arrive suddenly (23). From the 1830s onwards there had been demands for substantial reductions in the size of the "civil establishment." By the late 1840s these demands were being countered by the suggestion that the primary requirement was for increased efficiency rather than simply economies. This led to a series of independent reviews of government departments, particularly in relation to their staffing. Foremost amongst those advocating reform was Sir Charles Trevelyan, the Assistant Secretary to the Treasury, who had long held the view that the efficiency of the civil service might be improved by dividing the work undertaken into intellectual and mundane tasks and then recruiting people on the basis of their abilities to perform one or the other of these distinct sets of tasks. Since the Treasury was represented on all of the departmental review committees, Trevelyan was in an excellent position to ensure that his views were heard and to influence the committees' reports. Subsequently it seemed to some of those involved in the individual departmental reviews that the time had come to consider, across departments rather than simply within them, the ways in which staff were recruited and promoted. This led to a more general review of the organization of the civil service undertaken by Trevelyan together with Sir Stafford Northcote, a former civil servant.

Ideas for reform of central government were complemented by the reforms taking place at the Universities of Oxford and Cambridge, which removed much of the corruption that had come to be associated with the award of degrees from these institutions. Inspiration was also drawn from the example of the East India Company. Initially a trading company dating from the seventeenth century, it expanded its activities during the eighteenth century to include responsibility for the maintenance of law and order in India, acting in that regard under the auspices of British imperial power but at the same time clearly pursuing its own commercial interest in political stability. Although oversight of its non-commercial activities was slowly regained by the British government during the late eighteenth century it was not until 1834 that the company became, in effect, a government agency. Its significance for reform of British central administration is that, by the beginning of the century, the East India Company had established a school which provided appropriate training for a pool of men from whom recruits to its service might be drawn. This had led to the development of an efficient service whose officials successfully managed the varied demands of governing a huge and varied country more or less independently of the UK government. Whilst its selection processes were hardly open, in many other ways its training and promotion procedures provided a model for other administrations to copy.

Northcote and Trevelyan's *Report on the Organisation of the Permanent Civil Service* was published in 1854. Its findings amply corroborated some of the lampooning of the service to be found in the literature of the time. For example, it noted that

Admission into the civil service is indeed eagerly sought after but it is for the unambi-
tious and indolent or incapable that it is chiefly desired. Those whose abilities do not
warrant an expectation that they will succeed in the open professions, where they must
encounter the competition of their contemporaries, and those whom indolence of temperament, or physical infirmities render unfit for active exemptions, are placed in the
civil service where they may obtain an honourable livelihood with little labour, and with
no risk; where their success depends upon them simply avoiding any flagrant misconduct
and attending with moderate regularity to routine duties. (4)

The report's recommendations followed from this analysis: that men would be
recruited on the basis of their ability; that, in proof of ability, there should be a
coherent system of examinations; and that these examinations would be conducted
by a central board. The latter recommendation resulted in the creation of the Civil
Service Commission in 1855, and this organization played a formative role in establishing the high standards subsequently expected of senior civil servants. In order to
attract the best recruits the examinations would be competitive and "on a level with
the highest description of education in the country" (i.e. the reformed Universities of
Oxford and Cambridge). There would be a proper distinction between "intellectual"
and "mechanical" work, in order that the ablest recruits should not find themselves
working on routine tasks; and there would also be opportunities to move around different sections of the office to which they were recruited. This provision for mobility
was intended to broaden officials' experience and make best use of their abilities, as
well as to counter the corruption caused by favoritism.

One effect of the link to the highest standards of education was to ensure that only
the upper classes would have the opportunity to reach the top posts in the service,
since only their families would be able to afford the costs associated with studying at
Oxford or Cambridge. Furthermore, members of the "lower" classes were unlikely to
receive the education necessary to meet those Universities' entry requirements. Some,
such as Gladstone, thought this barrier to be no bad thing, although Queen Victoria
apparently expressed concern that "competitive examinations might fill the public
offices with low people without breeding or feelings of gentlemen." Evidence suggests
that her fears were unfounded.

Although the report's analysis of administrative problems could hardly be dis-
puted, its findings attracted widespread criticism, and, initially, little progress was
made towards reform. Some impetus towards change arose from public disquiet
about administrative failings at the time of the Crimean War, when inadequate
preparations for winter warfare led to many thousands of deaths among British soldiers from disease and exposure. However, it took many years before Northcote and
Trevelyan's report was fully implemented, resulting in the creation of a civil service
that survived without substantial reform until well into the second half of the twentieth century.

Three features of that service are worthy of comment. The first, already mentioned,
is the continuing significance of class divisions. Government, whether undertaken by

politicians or by senior permanent officials, remained the preserve of the upper classes until well beyond the end of the Victorian era. Whilst the poorer classes, as they gained an education, and the emerging middle classes were recruited into the civil service, they were not by and large recruited into the most senior ranks because they did not have the requisite university education. Even in the unlikely event that they did acquire such an education they still faced the almost insurmountable barrier of coming from the wrong class – an indefinable but nevertheless critical barrier which almost certainly prevented their passing the selection panel. The division of the civil service into grades, with recruitment to a particular grade dependent on previously acquired educational qualifications, thus usually prevented even bright recruits without a degree from moving upwards through the service.

A second and associated issue related to the requirement to be a "gentleman." This was a Victorian criterion as impossible to deny as it was difficult to define. Was gentlemanliness a matter of "breeding" (itself a highly ambiguous word referring both to actual birth and to education) or of some innate merit not tied to family, such as an aptitude for sheer hard work that might lead to a significant rise in station? Trollope argues in *An Autobiography* (1883) that civil servants ought to be gentlemen, but recognizes the difficulty in defining the term and also plainly includes in its compass a much wider circle than that of men so secure in their rank as to be above self-interest. It was assumed that gentlemen would have a well-rounded education that acquainted them with the classics, literature, or other subjects associated with the arts. In consequence, they were likely to be largely unfamiliar with contemporary developments in science and technology. This was not thought to be a serious problem and less significant than the need to overcome the sterner problem of corruption under the old system of appointments. In their desire to recruit the best and most able men by a system of competitive examinations the authors of the Northcote–Trevelyan Report thought it desirable to make the scope of the examination as wide as possible. The report noted that "Men capable of distinguishing themselves in any of the subjects we have named and thereby affording a proof that their education has not been lost upon them, would probably make themselves useful wherever they might be placed" (14). This might not have mattered too much in a non-interventionist era when the scope of government was relatively limited. However, the preference for recruiting and promoting graduates with a generalist knowledge, rather than utilizing and developing particular specialisms, was also to remain a feature of the service until well into the latter part of the twentieth century.

Thirdly, although it might be difficult to specify the nature of being a gentleman, one clear characteristic was that he would know how to behave. In particular he would know how to retain confidences. Hitherto government had been largely regarded as an elite and therefore private activity carried on by gentlemen who understood, without needing to be told, that it was improper to discuss private matters outside a small circle of trusted acquaintances. Vincent has noted that honor in the civil service (including privacy) was preserved by its members' attachment to the culture and attitudes of an elite. The unwritten rules associated with this culture were tested by (among other factors) the increase in government business in the nineteenth century and the consequent need to employ staff who were not members of the elite.

> Thus the more honour had become identified with secrecy, the more secrecy had become vulnerable to the socially inferior. The personality which would observe and respect the conventions of discreet reserve could not be manufactured. Neither ambition nor application were any substitute for a good background and the right sort of education. (Vincent 81)

This dilemma motivated the passage of secrecy legislation designed principally to prevent those who could not be relied upon to observe the rules from causing embarrassment by leaking information, hitherto regarded as private, to those outside government and especially to the press. Again, the closed nature of administration, complemented by further prohibitive legislation in the early part of the twentieth century, was to remain a longstanding feature of British government.

We can illustrate all these developments from the experience of contemporary writers. Like Trollope, Matthew Arnold became a civil servant for reasons chiefly financial. He was socially far better connected than Trollope, however, and came to his appointment as one of Her Majesty's Inspectors of Schools with help from his mother (widow of the celebrated headmaster of Rugby) and Henry Petty-Fitzmaurice, third Marquess of Lansdowne, who was head of the cabinet's Education Council and had recently employed Arnold as his private secretary. Although he came to his post by way of classic patronage, he filled it with care. This is complication number one. For 35 years, during all the years of his rise to eminence as one of England's finest poets and its finest critic, an international celebrity who lectured at home and abroad, Arnold worked earnestly at his terribly demanding job. Much of his work involved long railway trips across England and Wales (and eventually France, Italy, Germany, and Switzerland) to report in the most minute detail on hundreds of schools, hundreds of teachers and pupil–teachers whom he was required to examine individually (according to his best biographer, Arnold once orally examined 307 pupil–teachers in a single day), and thousands of students, whose examination papers he likewise read individually (Honan).

The experience deeply impressed him. In a famous passage from his 1866 essay "My Countrymen" Arnold writes:

> Your middle class man thinks it the highest pitch of development and civilisation when his letters are carried twelve times a day from Islington to Camberwell, and from Camberwell to Islington, and if railway-trains run to and fro between them every quarter of an hour. He thinks it is nothing that the trains only carry him from an illiberal, dismal life at Islington to an illiberal, dismal life at Camberwell; and the letters only tell him that such is life there.

This is the first-hand experience of someone who had actually spent hours and hours in railway carriages and who had plumbed the mind of the middle class through spending even more hours observing its schools and teachers. But what is also evident here is another characteristically Victorian tension or ambivalence – complication number two – which characteristically appears whenever matters administrative are in question. On the one hand, Arnold is a dutiful laborer in the Benthamite mold (and a denizen of the small civil service world: Arnold's patron Lord Lansdowne was the son of Bentham's patron). To a very considerable degree, Arnold believes in the state and he believes in authority and conformity, reason and efficiency. He believes, necessarily and professionally, in "inspection." But he is, on the other hand, far from prepared to make a fetish of such merely mechanical goods as reason or efficiency. The complaint about the emptiness of a life that is in a merely mechanical sense comfortable and well-managed is scarcely original; it carries on a theme first sounded among the Victorians by Carlyle. But its significance here is that it comes from a person so centrally and officially placed. John Stuart Mill provides a very similar example. He was literally brought up at Bentham's knee, came to his post in the East India Company through family connection (his Benthamite father James), served it dutifully for many years, but likewise chafed against the administrative ideal of the merely efficient and rational, and in *On Liberty* championed the spontaneous and the individual in almost Arnoldian terms.

What shape had Victorian administration assumed by the end of the century? At the level of local government, the demands that had led to action on specific problems such as health, poverty, and education had resulted in structural reforms which had been codified into a system of elected local authorities. Naturally, social reform was not the only driver of change; the rise of a new middle class, the growing collectivization of the working classes reflected in the increasing power of trades unions, and the demand for reform of the suffrage were equally significant factors. The system of local government was codified in Acts of 1888 and 1894 which established elected local authorities to administer (principally) a range of social welfare functions. The Acts took account of demographic changes but made little attempt to consider whether the functions now devolved on local authorities were appropriate or, in resource terms, sustainable. They thus embedded tensions, not least with central government, which were to reappear continually during the twentieth century.

The central administration had expanded in the number of government departments and their responsibilities, as well as in the size of staff employed. The debate about the role of the state, whether it should be minimalist, regulatory, or the embodiment of collectivist principles, was not resolved. Unlike some other European countries, notably France with its tradition of state involvement and control, Britain has never resolved the issue of the role of the state in society. Perhaps the resulting flexibility and adaptability have allowed it to survive. However, whilst many of the seeds for an increasingly interventionist state were sown during Victoria's reign, administrators were, for the most part, slow to develop administrative systems that recognized the changing nature of the state. There were exceptions, among them the work of Edwin Chadwick on sanitation, which has not been discussed in this chapter. Further, it may be unreasonable to expect a dominant ruling class to have easily ceded power to those whom it had been long accustomed to rule. Nevertheless, despite its faults, much of the edifice of Victorian administration lasted well into the twentieth century. Northcote and Trevelyan's *Report*, for example, provided the basis for a civil service that bore comparison with any other during the century that followed.

Literature had been influential in bringing about change. The novels of Dickens, Trollope, and Arnold have already been referred to; later authors like Wilde, Gissing, and Shaw had little difficulty in satirizing the class distinctions that characterized much of British society and administration. They were joined by composers of light opera: Gilbert and Sullivan's *The Mikado* was set in Japan but instantly recognized by audiences as a commentary on the British system of government; *Iolanthe*, which satirized the pomposity of the ruling classes, was also successful. It is perhaps instructive that the British have been able to sit lightly to their rulers and, paradoxically, to combine deference with the ability to make fun of them. It is unlikely that this would have been possible had they not, for the most part, felt that their needs were being addressed through the administrative structures that had been established, or had they lacked confidence that the political and administrative changes taking place, however slow and piecemeal they might be, would in time allow those needs to be met.

Acknowledgment

The author acknowledges with gratitude permission to include extracts of text from the chapter contributed by Robert Newsom of this companion.

See also 1832, 1870; LEGAL; SAGE WRITING

REFERENCES

Chapman, R. A., and J. R. Greenaway (1980) *The Dynamics of Administrative Reform*. London: Croom Helm.

Greenleaf, W. H. (1983) *The British Political Tradition: Volume One, The Rise of Collectivism*. London: Routledge.

Harling, P. (2006) "The Powers of the Victorian State." In *Liberty and Authority in Victorian Britain*, ed. P. Mandler. Oxford: Oxford University Press.

Honan, P. (1983) *Matthew Arnold: A Life*. Cambridge MA: Harvard University Press.

Lubenow, R. (1971) *The Politics of Government Growth*. Newton Abbott: David and Charles.

MacDonagh, O. (1977) *Early Victorian Government 1830–1870*. London: Weidenfeld and Nicholson.

Mill, J. S. (1912) *Three Essays*. Oxford: Oxford University Press.

Moran, M. (2003) *The British Regulatory State*. Oxford: Oxford University Press.

Northcote-Trevelyan (1854) Report on the Organisation of the Permanent Civil Service. *British Parliamentary Papers*, 26, 1713. London: HMSO.

Perkin, H. (1977) "Individualism Versus Collectivism in Nineteenth Century Britain: A False Antithesis." *Journal of British Studies* 17:1, 96–112.

Vincent, D. (1989) *The Culture of Secrecy: Britain 1832–1998*. Oxford: Oxford University Press.

FURTHER READING

Annan, N. (1955) "The Intellectual Aristocracy." In *Studies in Social History: A Tribute to G. M. Trevelyan*, ed. J. H. Plumb. London: Longmans.

Blake, A. (1989) *Reading Victorian Fiction: The Cultural Context and Ideological Content of the Nineteenth-Century Novel*. Basingstoke: Macmillan.

Childers, J. (1995) *Novel Possibilities: Fiction and the Formation of Early Victorian Culture*. Philadelphia: University of Pennsylvania Press.

Collini, S. (1991) *Public Moralists: Political Thought and Intellectual Life in Great Britain 1850–1930*. Oxford: Clarendon Press.

Finer, S. E. (1952) *The Life and Times of Sir Edwin Chadwick*. London: Methuen.

——(1972) "The Transmission of Benthamite Ideas 1820–50." In *Studies in the Growth of Nineteenth-Century Government*, ed. G. Sutherland. Totowa: Rowman and Littlefield.

Gilmour, R. (1993) *The Victorian Period: The Intellectual and Cultural Context of English Literature, 1830–1890*. New York: Longman.

Harrison, R. (1983) *Bentham*. London: Routledge and Kegan Paul.

Houghton, W. E. (1985) *The Victorian Frame of Mind, 1830–1870*. New Haven: Yale University Press.

Hume, L. J. (1981) *Bentham and Bureaucracy*. Cambridge: Cambridge University Press.

Pellew, J. (1982) *The Home Office 1848–1914: From Clerks to Bureaucrats*. London: Heinemann.

Poovey, M. (1995) *Making a Social Body: British Cultural Formation, 1830–1864*. Chicago: University of Chicago Press.

Roberts, D. (1960) *Victorian Origins of the British Welfare State*. New Haven: Yale University Press.

Shuman, C. (2000) *Pedagogical Economies: The Examination and the Victorian Literary Man*. Stanford: Stanford University Press.

Snow, C. P. (1970) "Dickens and the Public Service." In *Dickens 1970*, ed. M. Slater. London: Chapman and Hall.

Stansky, P. (ed.) (1973) *Government and Society in Victoria's Britain*. New York: New Viewpoints.

16
Financial

Christina Crosby

Trollope advances in *An Autobiography* (1883) his "theory" that

> the love of money is so distinctive a characteristic of humanity that . . . sermons
> [preached against it] are mere platitudes called for by customary but unintelligent piety.
> All material progress has come from man's desire to do the best he can for himself and
> those about him, and civilization and Christianity itself have been made possible by
> such progress. Though we do not all of us argue this matter out within our breasts, we
> do all feel it; and we know that the more a man earns the more useful he is to his fellow
> men. (ch. 6)

For all its bluff assertion of common sense, there *is* a distinctly theoretical element
to this statement, and if Trollope here appears the crassest of materialists, one must
acknowledge a certain idealism in his praise of the love of money. For money, after
all, is the universally equivalent and acceptable form of value; and it is this fact
that gives money its charm. "The enjoyment of money ownership undoubtedly contains an idealist element," Georg Simmel writes in 1900, several decades after
Trollope:

> the pleasure of money ownership as such is one of the most abstract enjoyments and is
> most remote from sensual immediacy since it is exclusively experienced through a
> process of thought and fantasy. It resembles the joy of victory which is so strong in some
> people that they do not even ask what they gain by such a victory. (329)

A New Companion to Victorian Literature and Culture, First Edition. Edited by Herbert F. Tucker.
© 2014 John Wiley & Sons, Ltd. Published 2014 by John Wiley & Sons, Ltd.

Possessing £100, one can enjoy prospectively all of the commodities it might purchase, including the most abstract: an investment that will return even more, money making money.

The pleasures of literature, too, are abstract, experienced through thought and fantasy – however sensual – and this point of intersection may be the place to begin thinking about the relation of money and finance to literature, or, more specifically, to consider how value is represented in Victorian novels. To note that money looms large is to observe the obvious, but it is worth our while to consider the matter more closely. Certainly the love of money starts, sustains, and resolves plots, establishes character, and makes a whole rhetoric of value available to Victorian writers who represent money as the condition of possibility for all good things even as they excoriate money-getting as a sign of moral decline. Moreover, the relations of capital shaped literary production, influencing both the content and the form of nineteenth-century novels: the triple-decker, for instance, is specific to developments in the Victorian publishing industry. One could develop this argument further, following Jameson's reading of the relations of form to content: "form is . . . the final articulation of the deeper logic of the content itself," and in this sense money informs Victorian literature in the strongest sense – gives it the form its content requires (329).

To ask how the domains of money and literature articulate is to pose a foundational question about representation and value, and value is no simple thing. What counts as valuable, and how is value represented? These are questions about form that Mary Poovey addresses through the study of "historical epistemology," seeking to understand how value is made intelligible and to study the significance of value in the intertwining of ethics and economics. She takes as her starting point the sixteenth-century development of double-entry bookkeeping that required a merchant to balance his accounts, in token of his probity and credibility. The emergence of numbers as the most widely credited "modern fact" contributed to the development of classical political economy, where moral virtues and empirical data are mutually informing. From the feeling of satisfaction that Adam Smith took to be the universal human response to systematic description, he advanced his theory of a providential, abstract order that "produced effects that, at least in theory, could be measured or counted." This theorizing of quantitative data became in time the "paradigmatic use of numbers in the modern fact" (Poovey 216). Such numbers seemed descriptive, not persuasive (mathematical, not rhetorical), yet to be meaningful they required interpretation – the work of political economy as it developed into empirical science. Smith's political economy "aligned the observations one's eye could provide with the assumptions the philosopher held, and opposed both to language intended simply to persuade" (248). Wealth relieved want, stimulated culture, and elaborated a vast network of cooperation through competition. As Dugald Stewart, an influential follower of Smith, wrote in 1794, each individual is "led by an invisible hand" in pursuing what appears to be his own self-interest but the economist, working at a higher level of abstraction, recognizes as a harmonious, natural order. "It is this view of Political Economy that can alone render it interesting to the moralist, and can dignify calculations of profit and loss in the eye of the philosopher" (quoted in Poovey 275).

Explicitly moral claims of political economy like Stewart's receded over the course of the nineteenth century into the data-based discipline we know simply as economics. As this disciplinary knowledge became increasingly specialized, and the money form of value was increasingly abstracted into an array of financial instruments, commentators created a new genre of writing that popularized political economy and explained to an educated public how markets work. In contrast, persuasive rhetoric that makes explicitly moral claims took up residence, and became increasingly formalized, in literature and literary criticism. Novels strove to articulate value in literary language that increasingly required the reader's active interpretation. Where political economy gathered and interpreted quantitative data, literature sought to persuade readers of fictional worlds rich in qualitative values characterizing protagonists and antagonists, and enacted through plot. Knowledge about value bifurcates: on the one hand an empirically disciplined economics analyzes economic data and advises government, while on the other hand imaginative literature develops a highly nuanced language of moral value and an increasingly formal complexity, both of which appear detached from any calculation of "getting and spending." The "problematic of representation," however, "the gap that separates the sign from its referent or ground" deeply correlates all these forms of representing value (Poovey 5). This is the history we must recuperate if we are to understand what has been lost as economists and professors of literature elaborate their disciplinarily separated – and often rhetorically opposed – work in the contemporary university.

Catherine Gallagher, in *The Body Economic*, traces a different division within the writing of Victorian novelists, political economists, and social reformers: not between economics and literature, but rather between "bioeconomics" and "somaeconomics." Her conclusion contests Poovey's, as Gallagher discerns a continuity in concern for both moral and economic value across all the texts she reads. She begins with the Revd Thomas Malthus, who considered that a Providential God so created mankind that improvident reproduction inevitably creates a population that grows beyond "the power of the earth to produce subsistence," making sinful sexual relations their own punishment. From this "bioeconomic" premise followed one important strand of ideas about economic and ethical values: labor is a bodily sacrifice that creates value, which is then circulated and consumed by the body of the nation. "Somaeconomics" is Gallagher's term for the other major strand of theorizing value, which focused on the pleasures and pains of economic actors, from Jeremy Bentham's utilitarianism to the "marginalist" work of Stanley Jevons, who in the 1870s challenged the labor theory of value by considering the way a consumer's sensual feelings determine value with reference to the scarcity or abundance of a commodity. From this standpoint Gallagher, using the methods of New Historicism, discovers shared tropes that draw the texts of political economy and imaginative literature together. In Dickens's *Hard Times*, the circus that seems the antithesis of the hard work of factory labor is not in fact a playground. Rather, all of the circus performers work, and the work wears their bodies down – a novel rendering of bioeconomical truths, just as Dickens recounts in letters how the productive labor of writing and editing is exhausting his energies. George Eliot, in a complementary fashion, worries lest she may have written so much as to tire the public and devalue her labor in their eyes. *Daniel Deronda* is animated by similar concerns: Gwendolyn comes to realize the somaeconomical truth that in her fabulously wealthy husband's eyes she is just one more prize, worthless once he has broken her spirit; Daniel is haunted by the fear that he is of little use to anyone, until he learns he is Jewish, finds himself immeasurably valued by Mordecai, and takes up his Zionist vision. Thus Gallagher argues that the work of imaginative writers demonstrates the power and range of economic ideas, even as economists continue through the nineteenth century to theorize the values of the market in relation to moral goods. Literary and economic texts alike are animated by the question of how to value life itself.

The immense number of *things* represented in novels and Victorian archives becomes in Elaine Freedgood's work the starting point for theorizing how the imaginary spaces of novels register both economical and ethical values. *The Ideas in Things* revisits the two cardinal axes of representation, metaphor and metonymy, and makes out a fresh case for the importance of the latter. Metonyms, figures of contingency that can seem to disrupt the symbolic unity of a text, are shown in Freedgood's historically oriented work to turn the things in a novel towards the world beyond its covers. She identifies objects with metonymic functions that invite critical attention by virtue of appearing repeatedly in a novel: in Gaskell's *Mary Barton* a family's calico curtains signal their working-class respectability; in *Jane Eyre* the mahogany furniture the heroine encounters in houses of the well-to-do reinforces her own poverty; because the "Negro head" tobacco that Dickens chooses for Magwitch in *Great Expectations* is favored by convicts transported to the supposedly "empty" continent of Australia, the brand links him to that criminal world and to the British disregard for Aboriginal lives. Each of these commodities is a social hieroglyphic that conceals as much as it reveals, which is why for Freedgood the things of realism need to be read in the vast archive of print awaiting the researcher: "Social relations hide in things" (54). The hard-pressed workers of enterprising capitalists in the north of England turn out calico for export that immiserates handloom weavers in India; the value of imported mahogany washes away the soil of Madeira and Jamaica as the forests of those colonized islands disappear; Magwitch returns from his exile and his tobacco, with its whiff of the indigenous, comes with him. Figuratively weak but informatively strong, such metonymies can carry one out of the text of the novel, into the teeming Victorian world of things, the values materialized in them, and the histories they entrain. Investigating those histories, Freedgood reads the undeclared social relations of Victorian capitalism.

Money is every bit as much a hieroglyph as a commodity, perhaps even more, because it circulates quite anonymously and leaves no trace in its travels. Economic value can assume many forms, of course, including the form of commodities, but money is sovereign over all; money is the shape all commodities must take, ideally in their prices and actually in the process of exchange when money changes hands. Both the pleasures of money ownership and the pain of being without money are determined by the particular logic of this form of value, and its peculiarities are crucial to thinking further about what literature might have to do with economic life. I will argue that literature both accommodates and helps to render intelligible the abstractions and contradictions of money as money becomes a more and more imposing and insistent part of life in nineteenth-century Britain. At the same time, the money-form of value presents insoluble questions that can be tracked in many Victorian novels. How might reading novels help Victorians to comprehend the mysteries of value and the abstractions of money? How might literature make pleasurable the derealizations of the money-form and the distance from sensual immediacy it requires?

Banking: The Mobilization of Money Power

Students of nineteenth-century Britain know that the three great facts of that time and place are capitalization, industrialization, and urbanization, the transformation of local and agrarian economies and ways of life into the modern world of steam and iron, metropolitan centers, and worldwide interdependences. Britain under the queen sees the triumph of capital and the consequent unrelenting drive for innovation and expansion; as Hobsbawm notes of the nineteenth century, "revolutionary change became the norm" (46). By mid-century business cycles of prosperity and recession spread across national economies (32), and by the 1880s the world is united by international markets and the consolidation of colonial ventures into empire. This "take-off into sustained growth," as the economists call it, could not have happened without the concomitant development of systems of finance to fund new enterprises, from the manufacture of the most familiar consumer goods (cotton cloth, most notably, but also all sorts of household items) to the development of hundreds of miles of railroads and huge public works projects like docks or sewers. Only if capital were available when and where it was needed could this economic system flourish as it did. The creation of new commodities and incitement to economic growth depended upon the development of a national banking system and of increasingly complex markets in financial instruments like stocks and bonds.

Such developments began long before the nineteenth century, only to grow exponentially from 1800 on. The Bank of England, founded to finance the government of William of Orange in the late seventeenth century – and to provide a steady stream of interest income from the national debt for stockholders – retained its monopoly on joint-stock banking until 1818: before that date banks within 65 miles of London were prohibited from having more than six partners. The Bank of England became by necessity the bank of last resort and the first institution to try directly to control the economy through raising or lowering the interest (or "discount") rate charged for lending money. Its early monopoly and its incipient role as a central bank also encouraged the establishment of hundreds of private banks both in the country and in London: 940 country banks were operating by 1814 (King 9), often from a first-floor room in the substantial house otherwise occupied by the banker and his family. These banks often developed out of other commercial activities and were part of "a face-to-face society of friends, cousins, and business associates," and bankers flourished to the degree that they were seen as men of unimpeachable credit, able to display wealth and status (Mathias 135). Yet provincial banks were also part of the increasingly specialized business of supplying loanable capital to increasingly distant and even unknown debtors. Indeed, banking helped to create, then had to confront and manage, the ever more complex circuits of capital; bankers had to make up (in concert with industrialists, the government, and merchants) the various financial instruments which enabled business to be conducted over time and space. No longer face-to-face, money and commodity transactions depended on credit in the form of bills of exchange, accommodation bills, promissory notes, Treasury bills, Exchequer bills, bills of lading, bills of sale, drafts, cheques, stocks and bonds, and, of course, bank notes (see the Appendix to this chapter).

Crisis and Credit

These forms of transaction are different from, yet related to, the personal faith in the local bankers called for in this 1816 letter to the *Newcastle Courant*:

> That we may receive credit *from* [the bankers] let us give credit *to* them, and then mutual confidence will once more be reestablished . . . These remarks are for the public good and the result of a strong conviction that this *running* and *hunting* down the credit of our banks is a *chase* in which no wise man ought to join. It may be "sport" to some now, but if persevered in it will be death hereafter. (Phillips 79)

Not just the Bank of England but provincial banks issued their own notes: promises to pay on demand a certain quantity of specie (or Bank of England notes understood to be always convertible into gold). A banker, however, does not hold a reserve of liquid value equivalent to his liabilities, and the danger was always that there would be a run on the bank that would force the banker to stop payment if he could not quickly realize his investments. But in a crisis no one is a buyer and everyone (including the banker) is trying to sell to raise money to meet the bills (or bank notes) presented for payment. Commodities, whether goods in a warehouse or the assets a bank holds in the form of debts (bills, stocks, bonds, and so on), languish on the market. A monetary crisis thus flushes the contradictions of money into the open: because it is useful not in itself but as the universally equivalent form of value, its usefulness can be realized only in exchange. Furthermore, useful things, the whole various world of goods and services, are worthless unless exchanged for money. To "give credit" to the bankers was thus to believe in them and in their notes, to credit that those notes *were* money in order to avoid the economic death consequent on a failure of circulation.

That such credit was tenuous is evident in the ongoing nineteenth-century debate over how much money should be held in reserve proportionately to notes in circulation. A run on one bank would destabilize others as well, for, as Phillips puts it, "each holder of 'rag' [paper] money being anxious to have it changed into gold" (1), the bank notes would come flooding back to the issuing banks. Country bankers in such a crisis would turn to London and borrow money to meet the demand, as happened in 1825, the first major crash of the nineteenth century. When the firm of Pole, Thornton, and Co. threatened to break (which it eventually did, involving 44 other, smaller country banks in its collapse), the young Henry Thornton went with John Smith, an older and well-established banker from another firm in Clapham, to meet the Directors of the Bank of England. His sister reports on this meeting in a letter to a family friend:

> John Smith began by saying that the failure of this House would occasion so much ruin that he should really regard it as a national misfortune, and also that what he had seen of the conduct of one of the Partners at a crisis of extreme peril, had convinced him that, could it be saved for the moment, it might be well managed in future; he then turned to Henry and said, "I think you give your word the House is solvent?" Henry said he could. "Then," says John Smith to the Directors, "your money is safe." . . . "Well then," said the Governor and Deputy Governor of the Bank, "you shall have four hundred thousand pounds by eight tomorrow morning, which will I think float you." (Shannon 101)

As the economic crisis deepened, however, Pole, Thornton continued to be drawn upon by smaller country banks desperate for cash, and not even the £400,000 could save them. Yet the credit of Henry Thornton emerged from the crisis unimpeached, and within weeks he was a partner in the banking house of Williams and Co., as his sister reports:

> A happier person I have seldom seen than Henry, after fourteen hours of intense work, but so pleasant he says, people pouring in with all their congratulations and their accounts – so that in spite of the numbers, who having wanted to pay their Christmas bills drew out of the House small sums – the number of new friends who paid in left them with a much larger sum than they had in the morning when they opened. (Phillips 108)

The bankruptcy of Pole, Thornton was occasioned by unsuccessful speculations by one of the partners, which undermined the bank's assets, and by the fact that the fortune of another partner was much in land and thus impossible to realize quickly in cash. Despite the personal connections and good name of Henry Thornton, the firm was forced first to stop payment, then into bankruptcy. The failure of convertibility prompted outcries of "'Away with Old Rags. Gold for ever!'" (Phillips 2), but by the 1820s money was by no means gold alone, and the long process of the dematerialization of money (which in the twenty-first century is largely made up of electronic impulses) was well under way.

The monetary form of value thus steadily eroded the significance of face-to-face, interpersonal credibility; the pleasantness of Henry's receiving both congratulations and cash because people believed in him was clearly a local phenomenon, soon overtaken by impersonal exchanges over greater and greater distances. Yet the waning significance of individual credibility and the steadily increasing abstraction of credit should not obscure the fundamental fact that banks no less than individuals depended (and still depend) on the public's belief in their worth and stability, and public trust in the value of their bank notes. The monetary crises which repeatedly wracked the nineteenth century, ruining widows and orphans, throwing men and women out of work, bankrupting large firms and small, were understood to be crises of confidence – of belief, faith, and credit. The fact that economic crises are the consequence of interrelated forces, far too contradictory to be solved by monetary policy (though economists have long hoped differently), in no way obviates the need for public trust in money and confidence in the financial and governmental institutions understood to secure its value.

Certainly the crisis of 1825, "one of the most violent of the century," demonstrates both the increasingly complex and impersonal relations of the early nineteenth-century economy, and the very local and devastating effects of a general collapse of the economic system. This crisis, which was the first of the century but by no means the last to shatter fortunes and ruin firms, followed on a boom fueled by the floating of bonds for South American republics and South American mining projects; the Bank of England simultaneously was expanding credit to the government and to the East India Company; plentiful credit led to the buying of commodities and securities with borrowed money in order to sell again at a profit; an excess of imports led to a drain of gold abroad. When the South American mining projects collapsed, the bank restricted credit to build up its reserve of gold; confidence in convertibility was shaken, and owners of paper money wished to realize it in cash (this is the point at which Pole, Thornton, and Co. broke, taking with it those country banks whose assets they held). Finally, the panic spread beyond financial institutions, as merchants and manufacturers, unable to borrow and desperate for money to pay bills coming due, dumped their commodities on the slumping market. This crisis and the others which followed at about ten-year intervals (1837, 1847, 1857, 1866, 1878, and 1890) led repeatedly to cries of "gold for ever!" But an economy driven to expand cannot return either to gold or to barter. Indeed, despite controversies about the relation of paper money to gold which continued for the whole of the nineteenth century, various forms of "nominal money" (Goux 19) continued to be developed and refined, to the point where Walter Bagehot could declare in 1873 that the London money market is "by far the greatest combination of economical power and economical delicacy that the world has ever seen . . . Concentration of money in banks, though not the sole cause, is the principal cause which has made the Money Market of England so exceedingly rich, so much beyond that of other countries." Great industrial projects and worldwide trade both were predicated on the ready availability of that concentrated money. As Bagehot puts it, "English trade is become essentially a trade on borrowed capital, and . . . it is only by this refinement of our banking system that we are able to do the sort of trade we do, or to get through the quantity of it" (15, 17).

Debt (which is to say credit) is the condition of wealth and economic expansion, for borrowed capital is needed to finance industry and commerce on such a scale; and capital lent returns to the banks in the form of deposits which are lent out again. These successive transactions actually increase the supply of money. Banks thus create money in the form of multiple deposits and bank notes and, conversely, decrease money when they fail.

Money Making Money

As economic relations became more complex, distant, and anonymous, personal credit mattered less and other forms of credit mattered more. As early as 1802, in "An Inquiry into the Nature and Effects of the Paper Credit of Great Britain," Henry Thornton's father traced the circulation of a £10 bill of exchange: drawn first by a farmer on a corn factor (who agreed to pay at a certain specified date in the future for corn delivered to him by the farmer), the bill passed from the farmer to a grocer (at a "discount," whereby the farmer lost some of the value of the bill for the advantage of ready money), from the grocer to a sugar baker, from the sugar baker to a West India merchant, from the merchant to a country banker (who, redeeming the bill from the corn factor at full value on the due date, pocketed the difference between £10 and the discounted value he paid the merchant who needed ready money). "The bill, in this case, will have effected five payments," Thornton writes, "exactly as if it was a £10 note payable on demand to bearer. It will, however, have circulated chiefly in consequence of the confidence placed by each receiver of it in the last endorser, his own correspondent in trade" (King 33).

But this face-to-face confidence, which closely associates trade "correspondence" with personal "responsibilities," and the ethical–affective register of "credit" with the economic form of the bill of exchange, could not continue to sustain the economy. For as the demand for capital increased in the industrializing north, country bankers turned increasingly to the growing market in bills not only as an investment, a way to put their assets to work, but also as a way to borrow even more assets (King 27). By conflating a bill of exchange with a bank note, Thornton in 1802 ignores the signal fact of discount, the fact that money could make money. As W. T. C. King observes in his *History of the London Discount Market* (we would now call it the money market),

Financial dealings in bills arise when they are viewed, not merely as acknowledgments of indebtedness or for payments to trade creditors, but as a means of raising money by the sale of the bills (and the debts they represent) to third party financiers . . . although the tangible commodity in the Discount Market is the bill of exchange, the commodity in which the market *deals* is not bills but the loans made by the purchase of bills. (xvii)

A banker is a dealer in debts, and, indeed, the assets that a bank holds are, precisely, debts that when discharged will bring in more money than the bank paid to buy them. As the economy expanded with this exponential abstraction of exchange value, finance became increasingly specialized, and with the development of a market in bills came bill brokers who served as intermediaries between buyers and sellers. Finance also became increasingly anonymous and speculative.

In his 1834 book on banking, J. W. Gilbert notes unhappily the intimacy between banking and speculation:

It is the object of banking to give facilities to trade, and whatever gives facilities to trade gives facilities to speculation. Trade and speculation are in some cases so nearly allied that it is impossible to say at what precise point trade ends and speculation begins. . . . Wherever there are banks, capital is more readily obtained, and at a cheaper rate. The cheapness of capital gives facilities to speculation, just in the same way the cheapness of beef and beer gives facilities to gluttony and drunkenness. (quoted in Marx 1967: 406)

This impossibility of distinguishing with certainty between legitimate trade (confined to the making and exchange of useful goods) and the vice of speculation (devoted to nothing but money) haunted nineteenth-century writers, especially after the Joint Stock Companies Act of 1856. Before that date, any shareholder in a firm was liable, should the firm fail, "to the last shilling and acre" of his property no matter how small his investment: a condition of unlimited liability that effectively prevented the sale of stocks of small denomination and severely restricted opportunities for investment. After 1856, however, any seven or more persons could register a "memorandum of association" and create a corporation with limited liability (thus the familiar "Inc." and "Ltd." following the names of certain firms since mid-century). In consequence the value of quoted securities – the written proofs of ownership of stocks, thus negotiable instruments – traded on the Stock Exchange increased nearly twenty-fold over the course of the century, from £600 million in 1802 to over £11,000 million in 1913 (Morgan 139), an enormous quantitative increase that intensified worries of moral decline.

An anonymous 1876 article in *Fraser's Magazine* on "Stockbroking and the Stock Exchange" begins with the requisite wonder at how the national debt, not only of Britain but of governments around the world, has "swollen prodigiously," and proceeds to observe that for the purposes of the stockbroker it is much the same whether the "securities" he deals in are based in industrial undertakings or commerce, or are mere loans necessitated by a national bankruptcy or an ambitious war. His business is to buy and sell and get gain out of these bits of paper; and it is of the essence of that business that quantity should have weight with him, not quality, and of quantity it cannot be denied that the modern stockbroker has enough. (85)

As "bits of paper" the stocks are rhetorically depreciated, just as the security offered by "securities" is ironically undercut by the quotation marks. If the quantity of these stocks is assured (though one might wonder whether it is possible ever to have "enough" of pure quantity), evidently their quality is questionable, as is that of the men who deal in them:

> For [stock exchange members] the market value of a given stock is never gauged by its intrinsic worth so much as by the speculative furor of the moment . . . It is this that explains the marvelous effect of lies in the course of any one day's dealing. . . . It is business founded on opinion and on the chance of the moment. A thousand temporary influences are at work appealing to the passions of the hour with ten-fold the force of the permanent conditions or surroundings of the stock. (91)

Ruled by their passions, the stockbrokers work in "an elaborately organized gambling hell" and "the most upright men in it do things themselves, and are familiar with doings in others, such as anyone with sound moral vision would shrink from and shudder at" (93). The metaphors of vice and contagion here accord well with other nineteenth-century characterizations of financial dealings as a fever, or frenzy, or mania, or panic – all excessive, all overwhelming, all diseased.

Quantity versus Quality

This opposition between moral value and financial value is seemingly redressed at the close of the *Fraser's* article in an appeal to "open competition": "Mere rules and regulations will do nothing; publicity and the risks and moral safeguards of open competition are what is wanted to clear the air of this important centre of business from its moral miasma" (102). But this appeal is as illogical as it is bracing: the author remains as troubled by the contradictions of finance as was Gilbert four decades earlier, for neither can say at what precise point virtuous business ends and vicious speculation begins. That an "important centre of business" is a "gambling hell," and securities are but bits of paper is a dilemma produced by the logic of money and the necessity, in an economy organized by production for the market, of turning money into capital: making money and commodities make more money and commodities, or, in the case of finance capital, making money make money. As *Fraser's* says of the stockbroker, "His business is to buy and sell and get gain out of these bits of paper; and it is of the essence of that business that quantity should have weight with him, not quality."

Market value is measured in money, and money itself is purely quantitative, abstracted from any particular good or service. The qualitative, *intrinsic value* of the stock, the actual railroad or mine or national debt in which it confers a share, does not appear in its *quoted value* of so many pounds, shillings, and pence.

Just as the enjoyment of money is "remote from sensual immediacy," so is money itself. Yet money is absolutely necessary whether to realize a business venture or to experience a sensual enjoyment; one must have money to exchange for commodities. This is the contradiction of money: it is the most desirable of things yet has no use except when it passes from one's hands; it is purely quantitative yet, as Simmel observes, "has the very positive quality that is designated by the negative concept of lack of character" (215). *Pecunia non olet*; money has no odor, as the Roman emperor Vespasian observed to his son of the revenues he derived from taxing public toilets. In the money-form, value bears no trace of its origin or destiny. This deodorant property suggests one reason why "the biggest British fortunes were made in commerce and finance, not in industry, and by the late nineteenth century there were more millionaires among merchants, bankers, and ship owners than among landowners" (Cassis 2). Indeed, pure capitalists tend to profit from economic crises like those which recurred throughout the nineteenth century: "the big bankers usually make a steady profit out of these dangers . . . The services of money, as the neutral tool of economic processes, have to be paid for regardless of the direction or pace of these processes" (Simmel 215).

Finance capitalists who did not savor of the factory or mine actually found it easier to move into aristocratic circles than did industrialists, and were better able to maintain upper-class status while carrying on business; further, they had more access than industrialists to political power (Cassis 2). Nevertheless, the fact that the only positive quality of money is a negative troubles Victorian writers, who emphatically link this negativity to the absence of moral qualities. Much of Victorian fiction is sustained by the contrast between material wealth and moral worth, and bankers and financiers are more often villainous than virtuous in the pages of novels. In Eliot's *Middlemarch* (1872) the cowardly Bulstrode, who controls the fortunes of the town as the local banker, contrasts poorly with the philistine but generous manufacturer Vincy and even more with the idealized Caleb Garth, who reverences the "business" of surveying and building. Dickens's representation of the hypocritical banker Bounderby in *Hard Times* (1854) is as grotesque in its way as his characterization in *Little Dorrit* (1857) of the aptly named financier Merdle (whose name recalls the French *merde*). Even the quiet world of Mrs Gaskell's *Cranford* (1853) is deeply disturbed when the country bank in which meek and saintly Miss Matty's money is invested fails, leaving her destitute.

These specific representations of bankers and banking are motivated by the opposition of quantity and quality, but novels which have nothing to say about banking are also organized by the contrast between economic value and intangible but weighty moral worth: carriages, heavy plate, and large accounts at the bank often belong to morally bankrupt characters; and when the virtuous characters do well in the end, it is the good things of the world that are valorized by being in their possession, not the other way around. Even Trollope, who forthrightly declares his faith in "the love of money" as the basis of civilization and Christianity, is sure to punish those in his novels who love nothing else. Whatever sympathy he has for the great financier Melmotte, that character comes to a horrible end in *The Way We Live Now* (1875), and the value of landed property is confirmed even as credit, and fortunes made of credit-money (stocks, mortgages, notes), vanish into thin air. In these texts and many others, money is valued according to a moral calculus; the literary, whether Dickens's grotesque melodrama or Trollope's doggedly realistic representation, evidently endorses values which cannot be weighed and measured by the banker's scale or entered into his accounts.

Melodrama and the Money-Form of Value

Because money is the universally equivalent form of value, a commodity must assume the form of money to realize its value – it must be sold. It does not in fact disappear, of course; but it assumes what Marx calls in *Capital* a "phantom-like objectivity," present, but at a spectral remove mediated by its equivalence to money, which must stand in for commodities if they are ever to be, in fact, used (Marx 1977: 128). The tropes of *Our Mutual Friend*, from the most local metaphor to the most encompassing figuration, enact a representational process that melodrama actually shares with its ostensible opposite, money. That is, the melodramatic form of the novel stages the money-form of value in its narrative discourse even as Dickens insists that money is lethal, a corrupt and corrupting thing. The text is replete with figures of equivalence which obsessively transform objects into animated entities, and people into lifeless objects; further, it is dominated by a register of filth and decay which creates the novel's organizing metaphor: money is death. But even while making a spectacle of money that reveals it to be a baleful influence on human life, the text helps to accustom readers to the contradictions, dematerializations and rematerializations, displacements and ghostly embodiments of the money-form of value, and does so by the very form of its melodramatic revelations. For in melodrama, too, the material world has but a "phantom-like objectivity," and the things of this world are meaningful only relative to the immaterial realm of good and evil which is the real stuff of melodrama. The presence of this moral realm is what makes melodrama so moving: one sees virtue misrecognized and endangered by vice; one longs to save the threatened heroine or child who is alone in a fallen world and unloved; one gladly suffers this pathos in the hope of reunion with a lost unconditional love (often imagined as maternal and domestic); and one experiences the melodramatic world as everywhere invested with moral significance.

Our Mutual Friend opens with a classically melodramatic tableau that divides Gaffer Hexam from his lovely, motherless daughter Lizzie at his scavenging work on the

Thames. Gaffer trades on death, for the bodies he finds in the river yield an inquest fee when he turns them over to the coroner; more immediately, their pockets yield up money which he robs, coins filthy from the rotting body and polluted, but good money nonetheless. The further Gaffer reaches for money, the further he is from Lizzie and the closer to death; and his own end – when he overreaches, falls into the river, is caught by his rope and drowned – is forecast here. Moreover, the setting makes concrete the moral of the scene, for the oozy river and the disintegrating body establish material decay as inseparable from the getting of money. Lizzie shrinks from her father with a "look of dread or horror" when he stretches over the stern to rifle the pockets of the corpse.

From the first, then, the story is explicitly about money, which Dickens represents as something which fastens on living life, corrupts, and kills; he figures money as fatal to the quality of life and even to life itself. In *Our Mutual Friend* not only do rotting corpses in the polluted Thames yield money to the waterman Gaffer and his like, but we discover in a parallel plot that waste is a valuable commodity. The mounds of dust (everything from ashes and broken crockery to dead cats) are the goods which have funded the substantial fortune that weighs so heavily on the lives of the protagonists. The odor of rot and decay thus pervades the book as Dickens confounds the maxim that money never stinks. Yet in the novel everybody wants money because everything can be changed into money – indeed, the heaps of dust have almost all been sold, transformed into the fortune of £100,000 deposited in the Bank of England – and money can buy anything. Dickens insists on the alienating power of money by subjecting all the things in the novel (and the people are among the things) to a melodramatic logic which spectacularly displays money as corrupting and deadly. By the end of the novel the money which has been insistently figured as stinking and deadly is nonetheless redeemed, and the hero and heroine are rewarded with a huge fortune that has been made from garbage. From the very beginning, the text has determined that material things (whether corpses and garbage or the highly varnished furniture of the *arriviste* Veneerings) are but the bearers of immaterial moral concepts. That is, all the stuff which fills the richly detailed material world of *Our Mutual Friend* has value insofar as it is equivalent to something else: the immaterial realm of virtue and vice, moral damnation or salvation.

Melodrama thus enacts in language the derealization necessary to the money-form of value; further, it redeems the violence of this abstraction and makes it pleasurable, even comic. The popularity of theatrical as well as fictional melodrama in the nineteenth century suggests that the pleasures of the mode were much appreciated – a conclusion which seems reasonable given the relation between melodrama and the money-form of value. For money, too, is predicated on the dichotomy of the concept and the thing, the ideal and the real, and in Victorian Britain money changes everything. The revolutionary fact of production for the market ensures that money is the beginning and end of economic life, and economic life revolutionizes all other ways of life.

If Dickensian melodrama is a comforting representation of the abstractions attendant on exchange equivalence, Ruskin's later writings on political economy show a darker, indeed desperate, side of the violence of abstraction and the logic of money. The desperation comes from his acute sense of the presence of the embodied world and his attention to sensual life – his early writings were devoted to aesthetics, after all – yet for Ruskin as for Dickens the ruin of the phenomenal world betokens a graver death of the spirit. In a private letter he reports his state of mind subsequent to writing *Unto this Last*, a set of essays on political economy first published in 1861: "I am still very unwell, and tormented between the longing for rest and lovely life, and the sense of this terrific call of human crime for resistance and of human misery for help, though it seems to me as the voice of a river of blood which can but sweep me down in the midst of its black clots, helpless" (quoted in Ruskin viii). He figures his torment in the same terms that he uses to represent economic circulation in his essay "The Veins of Wealth":

> The circulation of wealth in a nation resembles that of the blood in the natural body. There is one quickness of the current which comes of cheerful emotion or wholesome exercise; and another which comes of shame or fever. There is a flush of the body which is full of warmth and life; and another which will pass into putrefaction.

> The analogy will hold, down even to minute particulars. For as diseased local determination of the blood involves depression of the general health of the system, all morbid local action of riches will be found ultimately to involve a weakening of the resources of the body politic. (137)

By the conclusion of the essay this is no longer an analogy, but a fully realized truth: "the true veins of wealth are purple – and not in Rock, but in Flesh" (143).

Flesh, however, is but the embodiment of spirit, for ultimately Ruskin wishes his readers to ponder "whether, among national manufacturers, that of Souls of a good quality may not at last turn out a quite leadingly lucrative one" (144). Ruskin, like Dickens, writes of bodies and things temporal to address things spiritual. One consequence of his faith in moral quality is his readiness to abandon the gold standard for what we might call the "good standard." Thus for Ruskin all money is, finally, fiduciary, a matter of belief alone, and not a value materialized in gold or any other commodity:

> The intricacy of the question has been much increased by the (hitherto necessary) use of marketable commodities, such as gold, silver, shells, &c., to give intrinsic value or security to currency; but the final and best definition of money is that it is a documentary promise ratified and guaranteed by the nation to give or find a certain quantity of labour on demand. (138)

Money, then, is textual and immaterial, though legally guaranteed in "civilized nations" to have material effects, and all fundamental economic problems resolve into questions of faith and belief. The material condition of England, with its deadened, desperate workers living in squalor and its rich, grasping merchants living in luxury, is the emanation of broken faith. As in Dickensian melodrama, the material world bears this immaterial, moral truth: neither blood nor gold is valuable in itself; both are only figures in a higher, spiritual calculus.

Realistic Representation and Credit

The double discourse of value which melodrama exploits is also at work in the *Autobiography* of Trollope, an author who sets himself resolutely against the pathos and popularity of melodrama. The "loudness and extravagance of [the] lamentations" of a writer like Ruskin are objectionable to him because unreal: writing that asserts itself so insistently is incredible because faithless to the world it purports to represent (ch. 20). "I am realistic," Trollope declares, which is to say "anti-sensational" (ch. 12). In this spirit he recounts a routine of work that enabled him to produce enough books, and to sell them for enough money, to rank as the most prolific, if not the greatest, author in the English language. The *Autobiography* produces a carefully elaborated theory of writing, despite Trollope's repeated insistence that he thinks of writing as a trade or craft as down-to-earth as shoe-making. According to that theory, realistic writing is the best writing, writing which disappears as such and leaves the reader with the impression of a world unmediated by language. Such literature is produced by writing in the best way, which is to say according to the demands of a rigorous schedule. To be precise (and Trollope always is), the best writing is done under the "hot pressure" of the requirement to produce 250 words every quarter hour. With his watch set before him on the desk as he wrote, counting the words as he went, day after day and year after year, Trollope gave himself over to a reality which he imagines as fully calculable and measurable: so many minutes, so many words = so much reality represented. The public rewarded him with a substantial income from his novels, travel books, and stories, money which is tallied to the last penny at the end of his account.

Trollope is above all credible. That the peculiar credibility of his writing should be an effect of his submitting to the illimitable demands of quantity suggests that reading his novels is an education in the senses – not in any lushly sensual way, but in developing a taste for more, in renewing one's interest. As E. S. Dallas writes of Trollope in 1859, "He writes faster than we can read, and the more the pensive public reads the more does it desire to read" (Smalley 103). As Dallas's irony suggests, there is no time to be pensive when reading a Trollope novel, no time to be lost in thought any more for the reader than for the writer. A Trollope novel gives immediate and absorbing pleasure, but when one is finished reading, the pleasure, which lies in the immediacy of the reading, and not in reflection, fades. To renew it, one must read another, and another, and another. This desire for more of the same suggests that Trollope's realistic representation serves to accommodate readers not only to the pleasures of equivalence and quantity, but to the need to renew that pleasure and the faith that, if only they can get their hands on the next book, more pleasure will follow. If melodrama naturalizes the money-form of value, Trollopian realist writing celebrates consuming on credit. Victorian literary modes as apparently antithetical as realism and melodrama thus both suggest the interrelation of the literary and the economic, and show how literary form makes the strangely dematerializing effects of money, credit, and capital familiar and even enjoyable, though the joy be so strong that one may not ask what is gained in such a pleasure, and what lost.

Appendix: Financial Instruments

Bank notes   Paper money issued by private banks, convertible to gold money (or Bank of England notes) on demand. Bank of England notes were declared legal tender in 1833, and the Bank Act of 1844 decreed that the Bank of England was to be the only bank of issue; all other notes were to be withdrawn from circulation.

Bill of exchange and accommodation bill   "Originally used only by merchants, [a bill of exchange] was not unlike a check. Merchant A out in the country instructed Merchant B in London to whom he had sent goods to pay C an amount equal to the value of the goods on such and such a date. B agreed by writing 'accepted' across this written instruction from Merchant A; the result was a bill of exchange. From being a technique used by merchants, however, the use of bills broadened into a way for private individuals short of cash to raise money. Either you wrote the bill out instructing yourself to pay or, if your credit was lousy, you wrote out instructions to a friend with *good* credit to play the part of Merchant B and pay C to whom you owed money or from whom you were borrowing. This second arrangement was called an 'accommodation bill'" (Pool 270).

Bill of lading   A document detailing the cargo in a shipment; it could be assigned as security for a loan.

Bill of sale   "A document giving rights in household furniture and other similar personal property. It worked like a mortgage; one gave a bill of sale on one's household goods to the person from whom one borrowed cash and if one didn't repay him in time he took the goods" (Pool 271).

Bonds   Issued by both governments and corporations, bonds are purchased by investors who periodically receive a set amount of interest and are promised repayment in full on a pre-determined date.

Drafts and cheques   Documents drawing on an account on deposit at a bank, made out to bearer.

Promissory note   "A form of personal debt . . . This transaction represented a loan of money upon the debtor's promise to pay the amount plus the interest, which was usually quite steep, by the end of a specified period. The loan might be extended or a new loan made at the end of the period, a process called 'renewing.' Promissory notes had to be drawn up in a prescribed form, bearing an official stamp; the stamp itself was sometimes used as a reference to such loans . . . To 'accept' a note for a friend is to countersign it, indicating that one accepts the responsibility of repaying the note should the original debtor, one's friend, fail to do so" (McMurty 49).

Stocks   "Ownership shares in a corporation. They are sold initially by the corporation and then traded among investors. Investors who buy them expect to earn dividends as their part of the profit" (Morris and Siegel 34).

Treasury bill and Exchequer bill   Bills issued by the government; they were redeemable with interest at the end of a set period, and could be bought and sold on the market. These are distinct from the "funds," government securities in the form of annuities which paid an invariant rate of interest, 5 percent. The "Consols" were nine different annuities that were consolidated into one; these annuities paid 3 percent a year, and could be bought and sold, but not redeemed (Pool 290).

See also COMMERCIAL; POETRY, FICTION

REFERENCES

Anon. (1876) "Stockbroking and the Stock Exchange." *Fraser's Magazine* n. s. 5, 84–103.

Bagehot, W. (1873) *Lombard Street: A Description of the Money Market*. New York: Scribner, Armstrong, and Co.

Cassis, Y. (ed.) (1992) *Finance and Financiers in European History 1888–1960*. Cambridge: Cambridge University Press.

Freedgood, E. (2006) *The Ideas in Things: Fugitive Meanings in the Victorian Novel*. Chicago: University of Chicago Press.

Gallagher, C. (2006) *The Body Economic: Life, Death, and Sensation in Political Economy and the Victorian Novel*. Princeton: Princeton University Press.

Goux, J.-J. (1988) "Banking on Signs." *Diacritics* 18: 2, 15–25.

Hobsbawm, E. J. (1964) *The Age of Revolution: 1789–1848*. New York: New American Library.

Jameson, F. (1971) *Marxism and Form: Twentieth-Century Dialectical Theories of Literature*. Princeton: Princeton University Press.

King, W. T. C. (1936) *History of the London Discount Market*. London: George Routledge and Sons.

McMurty, J. (1979) *Victorian Life and Victorian Fiction: A Companion for the American Reader*. Hamden: Archon Books.

Marx, K. (1977) *Capital*, vol. 1 (1867), trans. B. Fowkes. New York: Vintage Books.

——(1967) *Capital*, vol. 3 (1894), trans. F. Engels. New York: International Publishers.

Mathias, P. (1983) *The First Industrial Nation: An Economic History of Britain 1700–1914*, 2nd edn. London: Methuen.

Morgan, E. V. (1965) *A History of Money*. Baltimore: Penguin Books.

Morris, K. M., and A. M. Siegel (1997) *The Wall Street Journal Guide to Understanding Personal Finance*. New York: Lightbulb Press.

Phillips, M. (1894) *A History of Banks, Bankers, and Banking in Northumberland, Durham, and North Yorkshire, Illustrating the Commercial Development of the North of England from 1755 to 1894.* London: Effingham, Wilson and Co.

Pool, D. (1993) *What Jane Austen Ate and Charles Dickens Knew.* New York: Simon and Schuster.

——(2008) *Genres of the Credit Economy: Mediating Value in Eighteenth- and Nineteenth-Century Britain.* Chicago: University of Chicago Press.

Ruskin, J. (1909) *Unto This Last and Other Essays on Art and Political Economy,* ed. Sir O. Lodge. London: J. M. Dent and Sons.

Shannon, H. A. (1953) "The Coming of General Limited Liability." In *Essays in Economic History,* ed. E. M. Carus-Wilson. London: Edward Arnold.

Simmel, G. (1978) *The Philosophy of Money,* trans. T. Bottomore and D. Frisby. London: Routledge and Kegan Paul.

Smalley, D. (ed.) (1969) *Trollope: The Critical Heritage.* London: Routledge and Kegan Paul.

FURTHER READING

Baucom, I. (2005) *Specters of the Atlantic: Finance Capital, Slavery, and the Philosophy of History.* Durham: Duke University Press.

Goux, J.-J. (1990) *Symbolic Economies: After Marx and Freud,* trans. J. Curtis Gage. Ithaca: Cornell University Press.

Poovey, M. (1998) *A History of the Modern Fact: Problems of Knowledge in the Sciences of Wealth and Society.* Chicago: University of Chicago Press.

Poovey, M. (ed.) (2003) *The Financial System in Nineteenth-Century Britain.* Oxford: Oxford University Press.

Pressnell, L. S. (1956) *Country Banking in the Industrial Revolution.* London: Oxford University Press.

Rosenberg, J. (2011) *Critical Enthusiasm: Capital Accumulation and the Transformation of Religious Passion.* Oxford: Oxford University Press.

Valenze, D. (2006) *The Social Life of Money in the English Past.* Cambridge: Cambridge University Press.

Woodmansee, M., and M. Osteen (eds) (1999) *The New Economic Criticism: Studies in the Intersection of Literature and Economics.* London: Routledge.

17
Industrial

Herbert Sussman

Early Industrial England

Like Charles Dickens, Benjamin Disraeli, and even Friedrich Engels, Thomas Carlyle felt impelled to see for himself the most significant phenomenon of his time, "a system of life constructed on a new principle" (Briggs 12), a wholly unprecedented marvel, the new industrial cities of the English midlands. Of Birmingham in 1824 Carlyle wrote:

> Torrents of thick smoke, with ever and anon a burst of dingy flame, are issuing from a thousand funnels . . . You hear the clank of innumerable steam-engines, the rumbling of cars and vans, and the hum of men interrupted by the sharper rattle of some canal-boat loading or disloading. . . . I have looked into their iron works where 150,000 men are smelting the metal in a district a few miles to the north; . . . their tubs and vats, as large as country churches, full of copperas and aqua fortis and oil of vitriol; and the whole is not without its attractions, as well as repulsions. (Froude 1882: I, 232)

Carlyle's rhetoric of awe exemplifies the wonder of his age at the transformation in the 1820s, 1830s, and 1840s of Birmingham, of Bradford and Leeds, Manchester and Sheffield, from small villages to smoky cities. But what appeared as miraculously sudden to Carlyle and his age was, in hindsight, the coming together of changes dating from at least the later eighteenth century, a confluence of existing technologies and new inventions within a particular economic system. The mule and spinning

A New Companion to Victorian Literature and Culture, First Edition. Edited by Herbert F. Tucker.
© 2014 John Wiley & Sons, Ltd. Published 2014 by John Wiley & Sons, Ltd.

jenny invented in the eighteenth century for mechanizing the weaving process required increased power; mills shifted from the power of the waterwheel to the power of the steam engine, already in use in coal mines; the steam engines turning the shafts and belts of the mill needed coal; transport of coal from these mines brought the steam engine on wheels, the railway. And the seemingly unlimited production of woven cloth needed swift and economical transport by railway and steamships from the industrial city to consumers both domestic and global.

Driving this process was the desire to replace hand-labor by the machine. Weavers working in their own cottages in the Yorkshire countryside became obsolete; these destitute hand-loom operators lingered at the edge of industrialism and in its literature as real casualties and imaginative symbols of those whose craft and livelihood were destroyed by mechanization. For industrialism demanded centralization, the concentration of operatives in the new spaces of mills that housed the mechanized looms. A large population of skilled and often unemployed workers attracted new factories. Operatives must be within walking distance of the factory; a supporting population must be in place to feed and clothe these workers. And, in an economic system driven by entrepreneurial zeal and quick profit, and as yet unhampered by government regulation of such matters as air quality and sewage disposal, the industrial city expanded without constraint. Between 1821 and 1831 the population of Manchester increased by 45 percent.

For these industrial cities men and women left the drudgery of agricultural life in England, and sailed from impoverished Ireland, in search of a new way of life. To the mill-owners they were "operatives" or "hands"; Engels and Marx invented the name "urban proletariat." A preferable name now for this way of life that had never before existed is "industrial workers" or simply "workers," following Williams's brilliant account of the transformation in the meaning of "work" and "worker" during the early industrial period:

> The specialization of *work* to paid employment is the result of the development of capitalist productive relations. To be *in work* or *out of work* was to be in a definite relationship with some other who had control of the means of productive effort . . . Time other than that spent in paid employment is significantly described as "your own time," "free time," or as "holiday" . . . or as "leisure time." (335–6)

This division of time into only two categories, "work" and "leisure," is dramatized by the internal conflict of Tennyson's "Lotos-Eaters" and encapsulated in the singular paradox of Miss Havisham employing Pip to "play, play, play!" (*Great Expectations*, ch. 8).

In leaving the agricultural village the workers were themselves transformed. Left behind were the rhythms of the natural world; mechanization took command (Giedeon). They no longer rose to cock's crow or ceased work at sunset. Rather, with their fellow operatives they rose for their shift to the mechanical time of the clock, the standardization of time being at the heart of the industrial system. Gas-lighting allowed work after dark; the working mill illuminated in the night became an icon of the unnaturalness of the age.

As a space and an institution, the factory was at once continuous with earlier disciplinary institutions such as the school and the army, and yet totally unprecedented. Under the division of labor, the central principle of efficiency within industrialism, a worker repetitively re-produces a single part or engages in an unchanging function. In such labor the worker is removed or alienated from the making of the total product as well as from the surplus value that accrues to the product in excess of the cost of his own labor. The working body is assigned a position in space, must bend to the regular rhythm of the steam engine, of the belts, pulleys, and spinning machines, must work at a specified speed defined by mechanical operations. Under constant visual surveillance, set to a specific unchanging task, like the prisoner, the soldier, or the student, the factory worker exists as a body within a complex system of "bio-power" (Foucault). In contrast to the farm and field, a way of life within living memory, in the factory there was no time for talk or joking, only the adapting of emotional rhythms to the methodic rhythms of the machine.

In the early decades of industrialism the factories and textile mills were busy with men and women, and also with children. At the early industrial moment children were crucial to the enterprise, since their small bodies and tiny fingers were of particular value in tying threads amid the clashing machinery. Only in 1833 did Parliament pass regulations to exclude children under nine from textile mills and limit those aged between nine and thirteen to forty-eight hours a week or nine hours in one day.

It is estimated that half the workers in the mills were female. These included young unmarried women often fresh from the countryside, as well as women married and unmarried who had lived their entire lives within the industrial society. Removed from the social supervision of family and of a traditional society, working alongside men, subject to the sexual power of supervisors, and often independent of spirit, the mill girls acquired a reputation for sexual looseness or, depending on one's perspective, sexual freedom. But it was expected by factory girls and by working-class society that they would eventually marry and take responsibility for home and children, with the husband supporting the family with his wages.

These new gender roles – husband as breadwinner, wife as childcare giver, unmarried son or daughter as factory worker – are generated by one of the most significant shifts created by industrialism, the separation of the workplace from the home. In agricultural society, labor and family life, workplace and domestic space exist within the single space of the farm. Husbands and wives, sons and daughters all participate according to gender roles in planting, in feeding the animals, in the harvest, in performing the endless tasks of farm life. But with the centralization of factory labor the husband, and unmarried sons and daughters as well, had to leave the home each day to earn their daily wage, while the wife stayed behind to care for the young children. From these material circumstances there developed the powerful nineteenth-century ideology of two separate spheres, the masculine public sphere of work, the private female sphere of domesticity, the competitive realm of business, the moralized space of the home. Of course, the boundaries of male and female spheres were highly permeable, especially for the working class. Given the vagaries of employment in industrial capitalism, married women often had to work, leaving the children without adequate care. And the muscular labor in mill and coal mine belied the supposed physical weakness of females.

Nor did the home life of the workers necessarily fit middle-class ideals of domesticity. The houses were "one or two-storied cottages in long rows, perhaps with cellars used as dwellings . . . These houses of three and four rooms and a kitchen" were "badly ventilated, damp, and unwholesome . . . [and] at least one family sleeps in each room" (Engels 60, 106). Given the need that workers' homes lie within a short walk of the factory or mill, the working-class district of once red, soon sooty brick was packed tightly near the equally sooty mill or factory at the center of the industrial city. The result was a rigorous segregation of the industrial town by social class.

Within these working-class districts there existed a range of status and of economic well-being – from the skilled artisan and mechanic, to the unskilled laborer, to the Irish, who were seen as a distinct species. Furthermore, in spite of the middle-class tendency to see workers as an aggregate, they presented, as any large group will, a spectrum from the dissolute to the disciplined, from the enthusiastic Methodist to the distinctly irreligious. Still, for all these differences, there emerged a cohesive working-class consciousness (Thompson), about which it is possible to generalize. In contrast to the individualist competitiveness of the middle class, there flourished a general sense of cooperation, of mutuality, seen for example in the Friendly Societies for mutual benefit and care. Workers identified themselves as members of a group or a class defined by difference from the masters or owners, held together by a powerful and always at least potentially radical political culture grounded in opposition to those with economic power.

There was also a distinct working-class intellectual and artistic culture. Although no public schooling was available for workers before 1870, two out of three industrial workers in the 1840s and 1850s were literate, with near universal literacy achieved by the end of the century. Through widespread individual reading and the growth of educational initiatives for the workers such as the Mechanics' Institutes, the working-class intellectual became a common figure, exemplified by Saunders Mackaye in Charles Kingsley's *Alton Locke* (1850) and in real life by the education reformer William Lovett. Academic canonization of the middle-class poetry and fiction of the period has obscured the oral and the print culture of the Victorian workers, which is now being recuperated. There were working-class newspapers, literary periodicals for factory girls, politically radical fiction, theatre, poetry often in the form of broadsides and ballads (Vicinus), and, at the close of the century, a wealth of working-class autobiographies (Gagnier).

The workers comprised, to use a favorite Victorian figure, a single nation, a class defined against another equally unprecedented social class, the owners of the mills and factories. Here again, a new way of life demanded a new name. To the Victorians these men were "masters"; to Carlyle they were "Captains of Industry"; to Marx and Engels "capitalists." We might call them industrialists or, more simply, owners.

In their entrepreneurial zest and instinct for technological innovation, the first industrialists the world had ever seen – for England was the first industrial country – seemed to act out the script of the "self-made man" promulgated by Samuel Smiles in *Self-Help* (1859), and widely accepted as Victorian gospel. That their power derived from wealth rather than from aristocratic birth, from the building of factories rather than the inheritance of land, created an entirely unprecedented form of power that challenged the traditional, hierarchical society into which most of them had been born. Furthermore, this acquisition of power and wealth was deeply individualistic, for in the early industrial period, from the 1820s through the 1860s, before limited liability laws and corporate ownership, the owner himself was fully at risk, his personal fortune tied up with the fortune of the mill, his personal credit and reputation fused with the credit of the factory. For good or for ill, this engagement with the enterprise based on private ownership grounds the intense identification of self with mill in such industrialists as Thornton of Elizabeth Gaskell's *North and South* (1855) or Robert Moore of Charlotte Brontë's *Shirley* (1849).

Unlike the workers, the owner was not bound by the inflexible sound of the opening bell. He chose to live in the outlying area, the newly invented suburbs removed from his factory in the central city. The constructed space of the new industrial city quite effectively separated the classes, concealing the actual living conditions of the workers from the sensibilities of the bourgeoisie. In Manchester beyond the working-class quarters, Engels wrote in 1845,

> lives the upper and middle bourgeoisie, the middle bourgeoisie in regularly laid out streets in the vicinity of the working quarters . . . the upper bourgeoisie in remoter villas with gardens . . . or on the breezy heights of Cheetham Hill, Broughton, and Pendleton, in free, wholesome country air, in fine, comfortable homes, passed once every half or quarter hour by omnibuses going into the city. And the finest part of the arrangement is this, that the members of this money aristocracy can take the shortest road through the middle of all the labouring districts to their places of business, without ever seeing that they are in the midst of the grimy misery that lurks to the right and the left. (79)

Here, in the suburban homes of the middle class, appeared most vividly the effect of separating home from workplace – the creation of the male and female, public and private spheres. The breadwinner took the omnibus to the mill; his wife and daughters remained at home, supposedly engaged in domestic activity. But in the homes of the middle class unmarried and married women had no real activity, although the "management" of a large staff of female servants was often seen as the analogue of male management of industrial workers. The drudgery of female servants carrying coal upstairs, scrubbing floors, and cooking was never recognized as contradicting the mistress's internalized middle-class belief in the mental and physical frailty of woman.

From the need of the bourgeoisie to comprehend and mitigate industrialism, or – from a more critical perspective – to control the workers and justify their own power, there emerged from this early industrial moment a new literary form, the industrial novel. Industrial novels by middle-class authors for middle-class readers include Frances Trollope's *The Life and Adventures of Michael Armstrong, the Factory Boy* (1840); Benjamin Disraeli's *Coningsby* (1844) and *Sybil, or The Two Nations* (1846); Elizabeth Gaskell's *Mary Barton* (1848) and *North and South* (1855); Charlotte Brontë's *Shirley* (1849); Charles Kingsley's *Alton Locke* (1850); and Charles Dickens's *Hard Times* (1854).

Whether written by Gaskell, the wife of a Manchester clergyman, or Dickens, a casual visitor to the midlands from London, the shape of the industrial novel replicates the shape of the industrial city. For the middle-class writer, representing working-class life necessarily involved a journey, socially between classes, geographically between districts, imaginatively between cultures – a journey analogous to colonial exploration. Henry Mayhew records his own travels into the unknown country of the poor in *London Labour and the London Poor* (1851). Dickens's *Bleak House* (1853) is structured around such expeditions to the sites of poverty, as are the philanthropic activities in George Eliot's novel of provincial life, *Middlemarch* (1872). As middle-class scout, the novelist returns with word of this unknown territory, but in doing so maintains and even strengthens the bourgeois perception of the workers as Other, reinforces as inevitable the distance and the difference between the two classes, the two nations.

For the middle-class novelists, for the middle class, and of course for the workers, the great question of the day was the relation between the classes, between workers and owners. Since in these decades the relation between capital and labor was a problem without precedent, a variety of models emerged. A communal or socialist pattern is exemplified by Robert Owen, who at New Lanark provided as early as the opening decade of the century housing and childhood primary education, sharing control with his workers in a community that became in the 1820s and 1830s a model for utopian settlements in America as well as for labor unionism and the cooperative movement. Some industrialists shaped their way of life, as Carlyle urged them to do in *Past and Present* (1843), on the style of the preindustrial rural gentry, as a paternalism with reciprocal responsibilities. An aristocratic or even feudal structuring of industrialism had a strong appeal, as in Disraeli's novelistic vision of industry as controlled and ameliorated by the noblesse oblige of an aristocracy of birth.

But the dominant model for the relation between owners and workers became not community but competition. Industrial capitalism admits no ties of responsibility, but only the nexus of contract, "cash-payment" in Carlyle's term (*Past and Present*, book 3, ch. 10), and is grounded on the equation of the laws of the market with the laws of nature. The law of gravity cannot be repealed; the law of supply and demand cannot be abrogated. Industrialists opposed parliamentary regulations that would compel children to attend school no less than two hours per day and compel owners to fence machinery so that working children would not be mangled in the gears and pulleys. The reasons provided were that such external government interference would disrupt the "natural" functioning of the free market. In many ways, the contradiction between such assumed economic determinism and moral choice structures the industrial novel (Gallagher).

According to the ideology of laissez-faire the capitalist purchases labor from another individual, the worker, who sells his or her labor in competition with other workers. The natural law of supply and demand then regulates wages; the "iron law of wages" arranges that wages never drop below subsistence, since if they did so the operatives needed to run the mill would starve to death, posing a distinct problem for the owners. Within laissez-faire economics, then, each person becomes an isolated unit acting in the marketplace. Industrialism is not so much a walk of life as it is a continuous scrimmage. Atomistic competitiveness transforms all everyday behavior into self-interest:

> They crowd by one another as though they had nothing in common, nothing to do with one another, and their only agreement is the tacit one, that each keep to his own side of the pavement, so as not to delay the opposing streams of the crowd, while it occurs to no man to honour another with so much as a glance. The brutal indifference, the unfeeling isolation of each in his private interest becomes the more repellent and offensive, the more these individuals are crowded together, within a limited space. (Engels 58)

The workers, however, did not see the bond of cash payment as inviolable natural law. Instead, they considered their own rights as "free-born Englishmen" to be inalienable (Thompson) and, denied the vote, looked to collective moral protest to obtain these rights. The largest workers' political protest of the early industrial period was Chartism, named for the "People's Charter" of 1,200,000 signatures calling for such reforms as universal male suffrage, the removal of property qualifications for election to Parliament, and the secret ballot. The Charter was presented to Parliament on several occasions in London during the 1830s and 1840s; each time Parliament overwhelmingly refused to consider it.

From the bourgeois political standpoint, workers who rejected atomistic competitiveness to join in collective, albeit peaceful, political action, such as Chartism, became dangerous. In the industrial cities the sheer number of people confined to a small space and no longer regulated by the hierarchical structures of the village seemed a source of potential revolution. As an aggregate, workers were figured in a politically charged vocabulary as a mass (as in the phrase "mass society"), the crowd (with implications of the loss of control), or the mob (sub- or nonhuman force beyond reason). Carlyle's favored tropes for the preindustrial lower orders in *The French Revolution* (1837) were the volcanic eruption, the tempest, and the ocean deeps; and Gaskell epitomizes the metaphoric transfer to factory conditions when she has Margaret Hale see "the slow-surging wave of the dark crowd come, with its threatening crest, tumble over, and retreat" (*North and South*, ch. 21).

The contradiction between workers in groups as a threatening mob and individual workers as sympathetic British subjects structures the middle-class imagination. The industrial novel turns on members of the middle class forming affective relations with individual workers, such as the working-class autodidact, thus presenting workers as human beings with a subjective life (Poovey). For Gaskell, the individual workers are noble, but only inasmuch as they resist absorption into the crowd. Dickens represents the workers of Coketown as machine-like, undifferentiated, "people equally like one another, who all went in and out at the same hours, with the same sound upon the same pavements, to do the same work" (*Hard Times*, book 1, ch. 5); and yet the plot turns on the virtue of the individualized working man, such as Stephen Blackpool, a virtue measured by his tormented resistance to the temptation of joining a union.

This fear of the crowd or mob does much to explain the intense government repression in the early nineteenth century of what the age called "combination," the organization of working men into what we would call unions. In working-class political culture principles of association, community, and mutuality were, as Chartism demonstrates, valued as means of asserting political and economic power. This collective consciousness remained strong, as shown by the continuing growth of unions in nineteenth-century England. But to the owners and the government the association of working men into unions with strong leadership posed a clear and present danger to the dominant power structure. This fear of workers becoming organized is registered in the bourgeois industrial novels' representation of union organizers and all leaders of the working class as deceptive, bloodthirsty villains: witness *Hard Times*, *Shirley*, and *Sybil*.

With the failure of paternalism or mutuality and in spite of continuing episodes of violent class warfare – the Luddite frame-breaking in Yorkshire in the 1810s depicted in *Shirley*, Peterloo (1819), Bloody Sunday (1887) – the dominant form of struggle between capital and labor became economic. The industrial strike became the central agon of the early industrial age and the dramatic center of the industrial novel. Dickens journeyed from London to Preston to observe a strike that he made the focus of *Hard Times*. A walkout is the plot crux of *North and South*.

And yet, although class conflict occupies the center of the industrial novel, incidents of violence and industrial disputes are regularly subsumed within an overarching courtship plot. If industrialism had separated the middle-class woman from the activity of industrialism, the process also generated by reaction a desire among women somehow to influence the public sphere from which they had been excluded. The movement of Margaret Thornton (*North and South*) or Shirley Keeldar (*Shirley*) between the male and female sphere, between factory and home, can be read as a protofeminism suggesting that women be given agency within the public sphere of industrialism. But the closure in marriage between the hard industrialist and the soft female also clinches the ideological work of the industrial novel. This bourgeois literary form represents – and indeed seeks to effect imaginatively – a mediation whereby laissez-faire industrialism grounded on economic law may be moralized and feminized, so as to enable the system to endure, but remain under bourgeois control.

Time/Space/Consciousness/Culture

For the industrial worker walking on cobbled streets amid brick houses, fields and woods that lingered in memory had disappeared from daily view, as had sun and sky now obscured by what John Ruskin called the pestilential "Storm-Cloud of the Nineteenth Century" (1884). Even the vestiges of the natural in the urban landscape, particularly the rivers on which all industrial cities had been founded in the days of water power – the "slime pools" of Manchester's Irk "from the depths of which bubbles of miasmatic gas constantly arise" (Engels 83), Coketown's "river that ran purple with ill-smelling dye" (*Hard Times*, book 1, ch. 5) – signaled the fouling of the natural world by industrial and human waste.

But the transformation of William Blake's "green & pleasant Land" into an England of "dark Satanic Mills" (*Milton*) should not be overstated. Industrial development was confined to a range of cities in the midlands; the cherished countryside of village and field largely remained unchanged. Early Victorian England had become, in Gaskell's terms, an industrial north and an agricultural south. Even in the manufacturing districts, in the days before urban sprawl a clear boundary marked the edge of the industrial city and the preindustrial country; in coal districts sheep grazed in the next field from the pit heads. Workers could easily take expeditions to a rural world that started at the edge of town. As recorded in the literature of industrialism, the easy physical movement from central city to sheep fields and country inns, from industrial north to rural south not only registers the varied landscape of the period, but also enables a complex genre of industrial pastoral, a physical and also a psychological journey into the rural world that remained a vivid memory for the first industrial generation.

The city/country opposition that industrialism strengthened was also paradoxically reduced by industrialism, and particularly by the railway. Indeed, it was the introduction and rapid spread of railways in the 1830s that most radically altered the Victorian categories of space and time. Space may be described as the distance between two points on the map, but in experiential terms this physical distance is measured not only in miles, but also in the time taken to traverse this space; a place may be described as "two hours" away. For those living in the 1830s and 1840s who still recalled travel on stage coach over muddy roads, space seemed to collapse with the coming of "railroad speed." To the first railway generation the space-time between city and country, between the metropolis and the rural home, between industrial towns, had virtually been eliminated. And since the government had demanded that railways provide special low fares, a Victorian of any class using the Bradshaw railway guide could move with heretofore unimaginable swiftness. Magic and fantasy provided the only rhetoric, as shown in Carlyle's letter of 1839 describing his first experience of railway travel:

> Out of one vehicle into another, snorting, roaring we flew: the likest thing to a Faust's flight on the Devil's mantle; or as if some huge steam night-bird had flung you on its back, and was sweeping through unknown space with you. (Froude 1884: I, 144)

For travelers, railway speed provided an entirely new form of visual perception, the world seen from the window of a speeding train. Objects in the background remained relatively stable while the foreground virtually dematerialized as the eye/brain registered streaking impressions rather than the solid physicality of the material object (Schivelbusch). Some writers attempted to register this new mode of experience. Elizabeth Barrett Browning's "The Cry of the Children" (1844), Tennyson's "Locksley Hall" (1842) and *Maud* (1855), Dickens's vigorous prose in *Dombey and Son* (1848, ch. 20) are exemplary. In J. M. W. Turner's painting *Rain, Steam and Speed: The Great Western Railway* (1844) the hard outlines of the iron locomotive dissolve, fuse with the storm to offer pure energy, the speed of industrialism itself.

But most Victorian writers and artists joined in a counter-revolution, repudiating the industrialization of space, time, and perception by valorizing alternate forms of cognition and the art of the preindustrial times. The railway lurks as an absent presence, whose rejection shapes Victorian aesthetics and art. Ruskin, the most influential art writer of the age, is exemplary. His descriptions of Venetian architecture in *The Stones of Venice* (1851–3), for example, assume a virtually motionless viewer occupied intensely with the foregrounded detail of a sculpted capital as the implicit antithesis of the railway traveler glimpsing a distant cathedral from a moving train. Similarly, the Pre-Raphaelite artist's equally obsessive detailing of a foreground pond or wall necessitated spending days and even freezing nights in immobile observation (Schivelbusch).

The railway expanded mechanization of time beyond the space of factory and mill. In the preindustrial world the time rung by the church clock varied slightly from village to village. Such local times posed no particular problem for an agricultural society, but running trains on the different times of different localities would mean shattered metal on the track. Thus, what we now call "standard" time was set for the entire country by the railway and sustained by the telegraph. The entire population now moved in a mechanical synchrony. Time, no longer grounded in the revolution of the planet or the rising of the sun, became an artifice, a human construct to which all events referred. Quite appropriately, if quite foolishly, the anarchists in Conrad's *The Secret Agent* (1907) seek to blow up the Greenwich Observatory and thus Greenwich Mean Time.

Again, although literature in some few instances registers this mechanical time, notably in the opening of the aptly titled *Hard Times*, the imposition of a mechanical time on the entire population generated a literary and artistic counter-revolution, a valorization of an oppositional, pre- or anti-industrial time. George Eliot endows

Adam Bede with a sense that his carpentry work is regulated only by inward satisfaction: "I can't abide to see men throw away their tools in that way, the minute the clock begins to strike, as if they took no pleasure i' their work" (*Adam Bede*, book 1, ch. 1). By the end of the century writers became increasingly occupied with time as measured by feeling or mood, not by a clock outside the self. This occupation with irregular rhythms of the psyche, with duration, with the inner flow of natural feeling is exemplified in the impressionism of Walter Pater's "Conclusion" to *The Renaissance* (1873): "For art comes to you proposing frankly to give nothing but the highest quality to your moments as they pass, and simply for those moments' sake."

The way industrialization thus generated aesthetic counter-formations took material form in the shape of the industrial city. At the center of Manchester the Manchester Art Museum was built in Gothic style, its colored patterned brick and hand-carved ornament challenging the severe functional style of the surrounding factories. At the center of industrial Birmingham the city fathers built an art museum in classical style, its white stone, severe columns, and carved pediment presenting a similar contrast to the urban environment. Arriving at a Victorian railway station, the traveler passed from the street through a medieval, classical, or Egyptian façade, then entered the train shed, a vast hall of prefabricated iron columns supporting a roof of standardized glass panes, ingenious products of industrialism, in which the smoking locomotive waited.

Establishing a preserve of space sacred to art at the center of the city or covering the fact of the train with a façade from times gone by exemplifies the ambivalence of an industrialized society toward the new way of British life that was producing great wealth, and great poverty. In creating an astonishing material culture and technology, industrial capitalism generated its antithesis. As much as industrialism invented the railway and the textile mill, industrial capitalism also invented "culture," music, literature, painting, sculpture, and architecture valued as activities that "attack what was seen as the 'MECHANICAL' character of the new civilization then emerging: both for its abstract rationalism and for the 'inhumanity' of current industrial development" (Williams 89).

A like ambivalence was lived out by the industrialists themselves, who resided outside the manufacturing city, often married into the landed gentry, bought ancient country houses, and took pride in acquiring Italian Renaissance paintings as well as richly colored Pre-Raphaelite art, rather than representations of gritty industrial England. This opposition of culture and industry is inscribed and mediated within the industrial novel. In *North and South* an Oxbridge man teaches Greek to a captain of industry. In *Hard Times* the factory and the circus are opposed.

But Dickens wrote only one industrial novel, as did Charlotte Brontë. Working within the discourse of "culture," Victorian writers and artists chiefly turned away from their own industrial age, refused to attach any aesthetic or imaginative value to the technological wonders of their time. Emily Brontë wrote of a primal world isolated from the weavers of Yorkshire, George Eliot in *Middlemarch* and *Adam Bede* of society on the brink of industrialization. Tennyson wrote of a lady weaving not in a mill but in a tower on the road to Camelot, Robert Browning of Renaissance artists rather than textile designers, Arnold of an ancient Greek philosopher rather than a contemporary inventor. Industrial workers appear only indirectly, coded in legendary terms as Tennyson's overworked, leisure-besotted Lotos Eaters. The industrial landscape appears as a dream landscape in Browning's "Childe Roland to the Dark Tower Came." As an exception, like the female writers of industrial novels, Victorian women poets such as Elizabeth Barrett Browning, Caroline Norton, and Eliza Cook bring reformist sympathy into poems criticizing the factory system.

Because our twentieth-century perception of the early industrial age has been filtered through this Victorian tradition of culture that privileges art over industry, the justifiable pride of workers, technologists, engineers, and just plain citizens in their very great, very human accomplishments has been denigrated, or written out of memory. Victorians by the tens of thousands flocked to the Great Exhibition of "The Industry of All Nations" in 1851. Within this technological tradition, the industrial machine becomes a prosthesis, an enhancement of human capacity. An extant photo of Isambard Kingdom Brunel before huge metal links of anchor chain bespeaks his vast pride, and that of his society, in the creation of iron-hulled steamships to carry Victorians swiftly across the Atlantic.

From the factory, specifically from the textile mills, also emerged the dominant apparatus of the late twentieth century, the intelligent machine. In the Jacquard loom, patterns punched into paper cards ran the complex weaving operations. On the model of this loom, Charles Babbage conceived of his never completed "Analytical Engine," the first modern computer, a universal machine that could be programmed to perform different functions. This blurring of the boundary between the category of the human and the mechanical remains one of the most lasting legacies of the first industrial age.

The New Industrial Age

By the 1860s the structure of industrialism had changed. Workers continued to toil in factory and mill, but under new limited liability laws ownership of a factory and mill by a single master gave way to ownership by a corporation. The entrepreneurial vigor of the independent capitalist whose fortune was one with his firm disappeared; his place was taken by a new figure, corporate or managerial man, divorced from contact with the worker, separate from the activity of production. The white-collar worker, the clerk, and the accountant employed in a large office and preoccupied with job security, promotion, and pension, each a prop of the lower-middle-class status he was desperately concerned to maintain, became the central figure in the new landscape of corporate industry. So, too, the landscape of the industrial city shifted. The population at the center of industrial cities declined as the outer ring filled with respectable suburban terraces from which clerks commuted by tram and railway to their offices in the central city.

Working-class women, primarily unmarried women, of course continued to work. The entry of middle-class women into the work force in the later nineteenth century was an overdetermined development, but one enabling factor was the creation of respectable female employment in the managerial domain that stood at one remove from the factory floor. Starting in the 1880s the job of office assistant or secretary gradually shifted from a male to a female activity. The literature of the later decades of the century engaging the condition of women turns not on how females might moralize the male sphere of industry, but rather on how they might learn new technologies and participate in the managerial sphere. The association of the female with the newly invented typewriter is represented in works as diverse as *Dracula* (1897) and George Gissing's *The Odd Women* (1893).

During the later nineteenth century class conflict was not resolved, but it assumed a different shape. Against the fierce arguments of the early industrialists, by mid-century the principle of government regulation of working hours and factory safety had been established. The work day for the textile mills had been set at ten and a half hours, the work week at 60 hours, and the worst abuses of child labor had been eradicated. By the late 1860s large trade unions, organized along craft or occupational lines, had become legal. With some exceptions, such as Bloody Sunday of 1887 when police violently broke up a socialist meeting in Trafalgar Square, class conflict had been absorbed into the political process. By the end of the century the Labour Party had become a powerful force.

By the 1860s workers in England still toiled in factories and in mills, railways still ran, industrial cities still bellowed smoke into the air, but industrial novels had ceased to be written. We can only speculate as to the reasons for the strange death of this genre. Perhaps there was no longer the shock of the new, as the industrial world of the midlands was absorbed into common consciousness, unremarkable as a tree or a flock of sheep to a countryman. Perhaps, too, the salary man puttering in the small garden of his respectable semi-detached house did not offer the heroic possibilities of a captain of industry such as John Thornton or the broad comic possibilities of a Bounderby. Unlike their contemporaries Frank Norris in America and Émile Zola in France, bourgeois English writers turned from the ongoing oppression and struggle of the working class.

The turn of late-Victorian high literature and art from the practice of realism and the subject of industrialism marks the triumph of the domain of "culture" (Gallagher; Poovey). Asserting the autonomy and the identity of the aesthetic and the psychological continued the project of "culture" begun with the coming of industrialism, constructing an alternative realm to the industrial. Henry James's valorization of psychological complexity, Pater's locating the "real" in the flux of inward sensation, Whistler's transformation of London warehouses to bits of color in his Nocturnes all manifest the desire for a counter-world of pure immaterial feeling, eradicating from art the material forms, working people, and energy of the industrial.

At the end of the nineteenth century the saga of industrialism found a new hero, the imperialist. However multiform the reasons for the intense expansion of British and European colonialism in the 1880s, certainly one major impulse was that the limitless productivity built into industrial capitalism demanded global markets, particularly with saturation of the domestic market. Whatever role the imperialist actor took – explorer of lands unmapped by Europeans, officer or soldier in an imperial army conquering and controling indigenous peoples, colonial administrator, colonial merchant – his way of life maintained industrialism by guaranteeing consumers abroad for the patterned cloth and the metal knives that continued to pour from the mills and factories of Manchester and Birmingham.

See also 1851; MOVING OUT, SEXUALITIES; COMMERCIAL; FICTION; PARAPETS

REFERENCES

Briggs, A. (1993) *Victorian Cities*. Berkeley: University of California Press.

Engels, F. (1984) *The Condition of the Working Class in England, from Personal Observation and Authentic Sources*. Chicago: Academy.

Foucault, M. (1977) *Discipline and Punish: The Birth of the Prison*, trans. A. Sheridan. New York: Pantheon.

Froude, J. A. (1882–84) *Thomas Carlyle: A History of the First Forty Years of His Life, 1795–1835*, 2 vols. London: Longmans, Green.

Gagnier, R. (1991) *Subjectivities: A History of Self-Representation in Britain, 1832–1920*. Oxford: Oxford University Press.

Gallagher, C. (1985) *The Industrial Reformation of English Fiction: Social Discourse and Narrative Form, 1832–67*. Chicago: University of Chicago Press.

Giedion, S. (1948) *Mechanization Takes Command: A Contribution to Anonymous History*. New York: Norton.

Poovey, M. (1995) *Making a Social Body: British Cultural Formation, 1830–64*. Chicago: University of Chicago Press.

Schivelbusch, W. (1986) *The Railway Journey: The Industrialization of Time and Space in the 19th Century*. Berkeley: University of California Press.

Thompson, E. P. (1966) *The Making of the English Working Class*. New York: Vintage.

Vicinus, M. (1974) *The Industrial Muse: A Study of Nineteenth Century British Working-Class Literature*. New York: Barnes and Noble.

Williams, R. (1985) *Keywords: A Vocabulary of Culture and Society*. New York: Oxford University Press.

FURTHER READING

Babbage, C. (1989) *The Economy of Machinery and Manufactures*. New York: New York University Press.

Bizup, J. (2003) *Manufacturing Culture: Vindications of Early Victorian Industry*. Charlottesville: University of Virginia Press.

Freedgood, E. (2003) *Factory Production in Nineteenth-Century Britain*. New York: Oxford University Press.

Jennings, H. (1995) *Pandæmonium 1660–1886: The Coming of the Machine as Seen by Contemporary Observers*. London: Papermac.

Ketabgian, T. (2011) *The Lives of Machines: The Industrial Imaginary in Victorian Literature and Culture*. Ann Arbor: University of Michigan Press.

Rabinbach, A. (1992) *The Human Motor: Energy, Fatigue, and the Origins of Modernity*. Berkeley: University of California Press.

Sussman, H. L. (1968) *Victorians and the Machine: The Literary Response to Technology*. Cambridge MA: Harvard University Press.

Ure, A. (1835) *The Philosophy of Manufactures: An Exposition of the Scientific, Moral, and Commercial Economy of the Factory System of Great Britain*. London: Charles Knight.

Weiner, M. (1981) *English Culture and the Decline of the Industrial Spirit*. Cambridge: Cambridge University Press.

Woodward, L. (1962) *The Age of Reform, 1815–70*. Oxford: Oxford University Press.

18
Commercial

Jennifer Wicke

The Uncommercial Traveller (first edition, 1861), Charles Dickens's extraordinary collection of sketches of British life, begins with what its first-person narrator, a traveling writer not to be confused with Dickens himself, calls a "negative introduction": by presenting his "brief credentials" as the opposite of those held by a commercial traveler, in short, by listing what the uncommercial traveler is *not*, Dickens's disingenuous stand-in outlines the terrain of Victorian commerce:

> No landlord is my friend and brother, no chambermaid loves me, no waiter worships me, no boots admires and envies me. No round of beef or tongue or ham is expressly cooked for me, no pigeon-pie is expressly made for me, no hotel-advertisement is personally addressed to me, no hotel-room tapestried with greatcoats and railways wrappers is set apart for me, no house of public entertainment in the United Kingdom greatly cares for my opinion of its brandy or sherry. When I go upon my journeys, I am not usually rated at a low figure in the bill; when I come home from my journeys, I never get any commission. I know nothing about prices, and should have no idea, if I were put to it, how to wheedle a man into ordering something he doesn't want. As a town traveller, I am never to be seen driving a vehicle externally like a young and volatile pianoforte van, and internally like an oven in which a number of flat boxes are baking in layers. As a country traveller, I am rarely to be found in a gig, and am never to be encountered by a pleasure train, waiting on the platform of a branch station, quite a Druid in the midst of a light Stonehenge of samples.

If we reverse the negatives in this paragraph, a panoramic visual catalogue of the contours of commercial life at mid-century magically appears, the trick revealing

A New Companion to Victorian Literature and Culture, First Edition. Edited by Herbert F. Tucker.
© 2014 John Wiley & Sons, Ltd. Published 2014 by John Wiley & Sons, Ltd.

the rabbit of commerce hidden within the twists and turns of the passage. Dickens's narrator professes to travel not on business *per se*, but for "the great house of Human Interest Brothers," and to "have rather a large connection in the fancy goods way." The book as a whole is an ethnography of Victorian commerce, with the narrator a type of travel-writer *manqué*, who is also free to indulge in fictionalization. The metaphor of the writer as traveling salesman, who brokers human interest and who delivers the language of fiction as fancy goods, already establishes the pervasiveness of commerce in the period, the dissemination of its special vocabulary, and the mediating nature of literature as a fancy goods business in its own right.

To discuss "commerce" in Victorian literature and culture is a tricky negotiation, almost seeming to call for the same device of negative definition deployed by Dickens. The challenge for this chapter is to extricate commerce from its companion terms and practices. It is easier to say what commerce is not, than what it is: we can perhaps agree that commerce is business, although immediately the latter word requires more specificity, since commerce is not restricted to industry, despite industrialization's role as the driving engine of modern commerce. On the other side of the coin, literally, commerce cannot be confused, although it always threatens to be, with the circulation of money, or with money in the abstract, since commerce is not restricted to finance, albeit intimately connected with wealth in all its forms. Dickens's homegrown if negative descriptions of a traveler immersed in the warm bath of commerce can helpfully delineate the outlines of commercial culture for us: commerce might truthfully be said to be all that is not uncommercial – and that turns out to be a remarkably small set of activities, in Victorian Britain as elsewhere.

More than this, the word "commerce" is a cultural coinage, a discursive entity as much as a "real" state of affairs. The discourse of commerce reflects upon itself across the Victorian century, in the form of philosophical and political critiques, in literary works of poetry and prose, in the guise of economic history and flamboyant rhetoric alike. "Commerce" permits a huge volume of cultural work to be done, and unlike the realms of capitalist industry or capitalist high finance, whose discourses were largely reserved for experts, Victorian commerce has a discourse which cuts across boundaries of class and education, political persuasion and profession, ranging from the popular to the rarefied: everyone talks about commerce in Victorian Britain, everyone employs its vocabulary, and almost anyone can buff or tarnish its discursive surface. Commerce as a word or category has this nebulous, fantasmatic side to it: it is brought into being, or recognized, in and through a special and specific language, nominally a culture-wide possession, but often as not through the back-door of what it is *not*.

After all, following out the arc of Dickens's antinarrative, commerce is embedded in or exemplified by the menu at a restaurant, a glass of sherry, railway schedules, paved roads, tourist outings, magazine advertisements, shoe polishing and sales techniques. Commerce covers virtually all of the exchanges between and among human beings in daily life, from the most humble and limited personal errands, to shop-going, businesses of commissions and sales, international trade, and imperial commerce. Our category for commerce has to be broad enough to admit the pies sold by the village baker, the large commercial firm of the sort depicted in *Dombey and Son* (1848), the funeral home business and Covent Garden marketplace, the manufacture and distribution of books by publishers such as Chapman and Hall, who put out *The Uncommercial Traveller*, and the public lecture-tour manager: the agent, say, who brought such profit to Dickens through commercializing his readings that the great uncommercial traveler himself died from exhaustion. This handful of examples should be enough to indicate the wide parameters of commerce, and also to indicate its long past, which stretches back to prehistoric societies.

As the Victorian theorist of political economy Karl Marx was to demonstrate in *Capital* (1867), the fruit of years of research and writing from his carrel in the British Museum's Reading Room, capitalism was a relatively modern phenomenon in history, originating in Renaissance Europe and only culminating in the later eighteenth century as a decisive rival capable of superseding – and overthrowing – the agricultural *ancien régime*. By mid-century, as Marx began his seminal work and Queen Victoria had settled into her long reign, capitalism had become the most descriptive single word for the British economic system. Commerce now emerged under the general heading of capitalism, the latter word being indeed a synonym for organized commerce. It is a synonym which cannot be allowed to slip into tautology, however – even in Victorian Britain, as in Europe and the United States, capitalism did not encompass all of commerce. Marx's genius, in following his great Victorian mentor Charles Darwin (without the latter's knowledge, of course), was to discern the forest of capitalism out of the discrete trees of commerce, to deduce what he thought of as the natural laws governing that forest of human making, and to chart its historical evolution over time, even as Darwin's *The Origin of Species* (1859) formulated the evolutionary laws governing the natural world.

One way of locating Victorian commerce would be to trace the capitalization of its commerce, staying alert to those commercial practices or forms that persist as vestiges of ages-old commercial behavior outside, or in relation to, the capitalist concentration of the market. One small literary example of the persistence of older modes of commerce within capitalist commerce is the portrait of the hand laundry run by Old Betty in Dickens's *Bleak House* (1853). Her laundry, whose mangle is famously turned by the lost boy Jo, is a manifestation of noncapitalist commerce, a cottage industry as it were, except that Betty is only able to launder for enough money to buy those few manufactured staples she and everyone else rely upon for food, clothing, and shelter – her commerce takes place in a shadowy corner of the ever-expanding house of capitalist commercialization. Eventually, poverty forces the elderly Betty to try to elude the workhouse by traveling the roads until her death, an uncommercial traveler of another kind. Victorian literature is a privileged site for witnessing the collisions of earlier with later modes of commerce, not all of them so catastrophic as Betty's, some even more so. As a heuristic tool for interpretation or a lens with which to view Victorian culture, commerce enables a more internally differentiated, dare one say heteroglossic glimpse of socioeconomics than an analysis of capital tends to do; theories of capital perhaps necessarily elide the coexistence of commercial forms, and again perhaps necessarily occult the creativity, as well as the destructiveness, of commercial behavior. Betty's fate, like Jo's and any number of other Victorian literary characters', is a synecdoche for the immiseration of millions of actual people; at the same time, even Marx observed the powerful benefits of capitalist commerce, and acerbically noted their absence in "backward" Asian societies under "Oriental despotism" (ch. 12).

Coming at commerce from the other direction, that is, by way of money and finance instead of capitalist industrialization, leads to some of the same ironies and complexities. Commerce did not and does not always involve money, as there can be trades for goods or services which bypass the money form. Commerce in the sense of human commercial exchange is self-evidently ancient, and includes the practices of barter, the public market or bazaar, trade, and even slavery. Some of these types of commerce survive well into the Victorian era, coexisting with financial activities in many cases. The literary staging of this overlap between nonmonetary commerce and financial commerce – i.e. nonmarket and market commerce – occurs repeatedly in the work of Thomas Hardy. His pseudo-imaginary county of Wessex is largely rural and agricultural but contains several market towns, and many of his works feature the surviving rural tradition of the market fair as a pivot of their action. These traveling market fairs were held at regular intervals in the larger towns – thus their name – and drew people from far-flung villages to join in trading their wares or foodstuffs, at the same time as they enjoyed entertainments like music, dancing, games, and festivals. Hardy depicts startling customs still obtaining at the market fair, such as the public auction or sale of wives, along with less disturbing medieval remnants like puppet shows or contests of skill. *Tess of the d'Urbervilles* (1884) is only one of several books which represent the vigorous market fair tradition gradually being eroded or invaded by what Carlyle first called "the cash nexus," and we may call the modern market – invisible, anonymous, abstract. Tess Durbeyfield, oldest daughter of a poverty-stricken family of small farmers, sets out early in the tale for the market fair, loaded with the jars of honey her mother hopes to have her exchange there, for other food items and for a chance to hear the newest songs. By the novel's end, Tess has been imprisoned for murder, and is hung from the prison gallows on the hillside, while below in the town the market fair commences again. Before this fatal crux is met, Tess travels restlessly throughout her small pocket of Wessex, which increasingly becomes inhospitable to barter or exchange. Eventually, driven by poverty and eviction, she hires on as a farm laborer working for wages, side by side with a menacing threshing machine, harvesting grain to be sold at markets outside the county, and even outside the country, far from the music of any market fair. The selling of the grain novelistically threshed by the character Tess, and even the selling of "grain futures" in the financial markets, based on predicted rates of production, are both indubitably "commerce." So, however, is the business transacted in the pub secreted behind closed curtains in a village neighbor's living room, and the purchase of the ordinary jar of marmalade which Tess uses emptied as a marker for her dead child's grave. Commerce in Hardy's market fair persists in an intermediate state, where money is only part of the commercial equation.

"Commerce," then, is a ductile word, capable of many meanings, but perhaps best captured by the sense of trading hands, whether exchange passes literally from hand to hand or takes place on a more systemic plane – the "macrolevel" of commerce, where trade is king. The denigrating sense of the phrase "to be in trade" persists as a sneer and a smear to this very day in Britain. Even commerce that produces staggering wealth carries a whiff of the hand-to-hand materiality of "trade," and it is correspondingly disdained – only high finance or land-based wealth can purify commerce of its lower-class vestiges – and a title, as many a Victorian gentleman came to recognize, didn't hurt either. In *A History of Commerce* (1907), the major text of its period, the economist Dr Clive Day of Yale declares emphatically that in "the study of the development of commerce in different countries we shall take up first the country which at the beginning of the nineteenth century, and at its end as well, held the leading position, England" (344). Victorian Britain was the unequivocal leader of the entire world, because it was the world leader in trade. In addition to the careful historical and statistical researches which describe this preeminence, Day's analysis includes an account of the politics of trade that allowed for Britain's supremacy. In the modern world as in the ancient, trade is carried out between countries or nations. The importance of this for an understanding of Victorian commerce cannot be underestimated, since it was through exports and imports that Britain became a commercial powerhouse. Even in 1907 economic historians could see the significance of three major developments of the latter half of the nineteenth century:

> (1) The English people were the most advanced, in industrial and mercantile ability, of any people in the world. . . . (2) The geographical situation of England, and the physical resources of the country, especially its coal, made the English superior to most peoples and equal to any, in this age of transportation and manufacture by steam. (3) The commercial policy of the government allowed the people to make the most of their advantages. (Day 367)

What Day meant by the last of these three reasons, although hardly the least, was the huge political upheaval that brought about free trade in Victorian England.

The critical political maneuvers which changed commercial policy were effected by parliamentarian Sir Robert Peel's bills of 1842, which secured the reduction of crippling tax duties on 750 items, and of 1845, which abolished 430 out of 813 import duties. Until the reform movement began in the 1820s, Britain had languished under restrictive taxes which hindered trade at every turn, and which forbade "free" trade in every instance. Customs tariffs on imports were astronomical, and duties on exports equally prohibitive. So paralyzing were these taxes that smuggling was actually a regulated profession, with a tariff modeled on, but of course lower than, the regular tariff. Smuggled goods, such as silk handkerchiefs, were openly brandished – Day recounts that a member of the House of Commons whipped his out of his pocket and said, "Here is a foreign ware that is totally prohibited. Nearly every one of you has a similar illicit article in his pocket. So much for your prohibition" (355). Such a pocket handkerchief veto was augmented intellectually when London merchants with a vested interest in the free swish of silken scarves urged a return to the principles of free trade outlined by Adam Smith in his *Wealth of Nations* (1776). The restrictions imposed by the government even extended to a ban on the emigration of skilled workmen, who were seen as an "export" the government refused to allow. The reform movement eased emigration procedures, so that the free trade in goods was accompanied by a freer trade in human skills across national boundaries. The irony of this facet of reform in light of the international slave trade – an embedded feature of Victorian global commerce despite the national Abolition Act of 1833 – cannot be overlooked.

William Gladstone's bills of 1853 and 1860 capped a free-trade campaign whose most visible struggle had involved repeal of the corn laws. Importation of grain was prevented by the high custom duties which the landed classes, and their aristocratic representatives in Parliament, had demanded; while Britain in the nineteenth century was decisively becoming a manufacturing, not an agricultural, economy, the aristocracy still held sway in government. The Anti-Corn Law League movement began outside Parliament, with a mercantile group who insisted that the high price of basic foodstuffs brought on by the protection of British grain, when it was produced so much more cheaply elsewhere, was a life-or-death question for commerce and thus for the body politic. Laborers could not afford to buy bread on their wages; the crop failures of 1841, and the Great Hunger in Ireland of 1845 and after, indicated clearly that Britain could no longer afford to produce its own food, let alone export it. The repeal of the corn laws in 1846 was "a momentous act in English history. It marks the formal and final recognition that England had grown from an agricultural to an industrial and commercial state" (Day 387). Any number of Victorian literary works illuminate the ostensibly dry debates over commerce in corn, wheat, and barley, casting into sharp relief their human ramifications. An extremely poignant charting of these ramifications occurs across the oeuvre of Charles Lever, an Anglo-Irish novelist whose effervescent Irish sporting-life novels give way over time, and in the aftermath of the famine, to an engagement with political and economic forces which together have conspired to obliterate so many Irish lives, through death or forced emigration. Ireland was perforce an agricultural colony, not allowed to develop commercially outside of British control, and the devastation wreaked there by the failure of the potato crop was due in part to the refusal either to import foodstuffs or to set aside its own harvest, earmarked for exportation to England, for the feeding of the starving Irish populace. Writing in Britain, and as a member of the Anglo-Irish ascendancy, Lever nonetheless conveys the agony of these commercial machinations as they filter down to real people. His final work, *Lord Kilgobben* (1872), is set squarely on a desolate bog, whose boundaries are so inhospitable to commerce that they form a no-man's land.

England's emergence as a commercial colossus gave growing power to the middle classes in Parliament and in civil society, even as it shifted the tenor of world relations. Victorian Britain's imports exceeded even her massive exports by century's end. The table of commercial trade levels for 1880 is eye-opening; imports amounted to $1,720,000,000; exports to $1,700,000,000. The imbalance may strike a reader as belying the nation's commercial strength. Far from it – what this statistic reveals about Victorian commerce in Britain is the liminal quality of its importations. The ship-owning nature of British commerce meant that Britain was carrying goods and passengers all over the world – a form of profitable export hidden within the import column. England received huge commissions on facilitating trade between other countries, another export masquerading as an import. Finally, the British empire entailed capital investment around the globe; Britain's many imports from its own colonies were further exports disguised as investment dividends and stock options. While two-fifths of British trade was with all the combined countries of Europe, another one-fourth was with its colonies, especially British India, of which Victoria had been named Empress; in the third place at century's end was trade with a single country, the United States. The special trading relationship between Victorian England and the United States has implications of a postcolonial kind, which reverberate in such major events as the US Civil War. Dickens's *Martin Chuzzlewit* (1844) gives a jaundiced version of this active commercial alliance, wherein a morally bankrupt and corrupt United States tricks innocent Britishers into immigration by proffering a vision of paradise that turns out to be a fraudulent land deal.

Free trade is a misnomer in the most egalitarian of times; when imperialism reached its height by the 1880s, the phrase became more than a misnomer – it was a scandal. There is nothing "free" about trade in a colonial or imperial relationship, and as Britain commanded the largest world empire since ancient Rome, its commercial trade increasingly took place under the sign of empire. Possibly the greatest late Victorian political economist was J. A. Hobson, the man who explained British imperialism, and argued against it, or at least certain forms of it, at the historical zenith of British commerce. Hobson's *Imperialism* (1902) examined the transmutation of commerce into the differing forms of imperialism, which each had their own mode of commercial production, whether the extraction of raw materials was paramount, or the creation of new consumer markets in the case of settled colonies, or the extension of financial markets, as in the stock speculation on far-away imperial ventures in mining or railroad construction. He joined another unlikely Victorian, the Polish Joseph Conrad, in protesting the most virulently exploitative forms of imperialism, such as the genocidal imperialism of the Belgian Congo: King Leopold's atrocities there served as the basis for *Heart of Darkness* (1899), for Hobson's own critique, and for the concerted efforts of the anti-Leopold league they both belonged to. In another register, more analytic than ethical, Hobson pointed out the tension between the economic interests of empire and nation – he saw that imperial commerce would negatively affect everything from prices to employment levels back at "home." This commercial split between global, imperial markets and homegrown, national activity, which Hobson had the prescience to see, shows once again what we glimpsed above in Hardy's fiction: that Victorian commerce, for all its might, was less univocal and less monolithic than we might think. To be sure, the goals of commerce are not altruistic – the profit motive is forever at the fore. Still, there is commerce, and then there is commerce. In those kindly merchants the Cheeryble brothers (*Nicholas Nickleby*, 1839) Dickens depicts – not without special pleading and sentimentality, to be sure – the flip side of Mrs Jellyby in *Bleak House*: the brothers preside like Santa Claus twins over a firm run for the benefit of its British workers. The Quaker brothers in Mrs Gaskell's *Sylvia's Lovers* (1863) offer another portrait of commerce as the milk of human kindness. For these Victorian writers the civilizing mission of commerce begins, and belongs, at home.

One remarkable apologist for commerce as the quintessence of civilization, where fraud and exploitation are exceptions to a splendid rule, was the Victorian economic historian/ideologue H. Gordon Selfridge, who waxes poetic in his opening peroration to *The Romance of Commerce*, a 1902 book whose title surely says it all: "To write on the subject of Commerce or Trade and do the subject justice would require more volumes than any library could hold, and involve more detail than any mind could grasp. It would be a history *in extenso* of the world's people from the beginning of time" (1). Selfridge properly widens his canvas of commerce to include all of time and human history, but then zeroes in nonetheless on the glories of English merchants and traders. Rather endearingly, he proposes that the most salient human talents are commercial, so much so that any worthwhile human endeavor is mercantile. Selfridge anoints all people ("except the idlers") as merchants, his highest accolade, and credits their efforts as commercial in essence. "We give this title exclusively to the man who buys and sells merchandise, but the artist sells the work of his brush, and in this he is a merchant. The writer sells to any who will buy, let his ideas be what they will. The teacher sells his knowledge of books – often in too low a market – to those who would have this knowledge passed on to the young . . ." And so on *ad infinitum*, with the doctor, the lawyer, the statesman, the preacher, the actor, the farmer, the employee: "all have something to dispose of at a profit to themselves, and the dignity of the business is decided by the manner in which they conduct the sale" (2–3). Selfridge's bestowal of his mark of favor upon so many professions, endeavors, and ways of life, is actually an incisive move: it has taken nearly a century to acknowledge without a knee-jerk recoil that commercial practices enmesh literature, art, education, religion, science. Selfridge embraces this fact a little too ardently and uncritically, but his apotheosis of commerce is nonetheless a helpful corrective to the entirely minatory view of commerce as an interloper and a threat. For every merchant prince or capitalist owner, there is also an equivalent to Mr Venus, the eccentric shopkeeper of Dickens's *Our Mutual Friend* (1865), who plies his trade as the articulator of skeletons and bizarre taxidermist, selling moribund, fantastical marvels of a necrophiliac's dream. There is a market, it would seem, for anything.

The "wild romance and adventure," the "fantasies of commerce" Selfridge wishes to wring from his account of commerce, have affinities with art-making; he wants to invest the domain of commerce with the aura of art, and vice versa. In another uncanny and surely unwitting imitation of Marxist analysis the book argues for the totality of commerce in human life:

> Just as in a beautiful tapestry there must be the groundwork, the foundation upon which the design is woven, so has Commerce acted as the underlying warp and woof in the development of civilization . . . Or to change the simile, Commerce is the foundation upon which nations are built; but it is also the superstructure, and provides the bands of steel which support every part of the national edifice. (348)

Granted, this is over the top rhetorically, but the echoes of "base" and "superstructure," the emphasis on interwoven indistinguishability, pose a problem for those who would see the paragraph as pure ideology. If it is nothing but that, how then does it anticipate the very terms used to critique what has come to be called the ideology of capitalism? Selfridge's paean to commerce wonderfully typifies the positive Victorian outlook on commerce, yet its rhetorical fabric reveals once again the puzzling, elusive nature of commerce as a discourse: commerce is groundwork, but also foreground, base but also superstructure; it is the tensile strength of the threads that make up the cloth of society, while it is also the evanescent sheen of color and the shimmering design inscribed in that tapestry. There is an echo here of the indeterminacy found in Conrad's famous description of narrativity in chapter one of *Heart of Darkness*, where the narrator Marlow says that in contrast to the seaman's tale, which wraps a nutshell around a kernel of meaning inside, his story unfolds only "as a glow brings out a haze." The "spectral illumination of moonshine," suggesting a meaning so lambent and diffuse that it cannot really be located, exists in tandem in the book with Marlow's (and presumably Conrad's) Victorian paean to work – "work has a kind of truth to it" – and with the ambivalence each brings to the commercial work of empire. Selfridge, too, exalts work (commerce in its active form) with such effusions as "work may be full of excitement, of satisfaction, of joy and happiness" if accompanied by "the springs of imagination," in the "alchemy" that is Commerce (358). He is unexpectedly Conradian in seeing commerce as both stalwart and gossamer, a haze around a glow around a nut with kernel intact: in other words, an essentially imaginative affair.

There is a canker in the romantic rose of commerce, however, and that canker is advertising. Selfridge will not award advertisement any commercial laurels; for him, it is a parasitic worm on commerce's body. Advertising inevitably lies, according to him, and "we need a new philosophy here" (424). Selfridge turns out to be wrong; as historical hindsight lets us see, advertising *was* the new philosophy, and Victorian commerce is unthinkable without it. A thread of argument across this chapter involves the mediated nature of Victorian commerce: commerce does not go unaccompanied, as Selfridge might have it, into its multifarious transactions. Commerce in the Victorian period and afterwards required a mediating nimbus, usually conferred by advertising. Of course, advertising taken separately is also commerce, and the establishment of advertising agencies in 1845 in Britain, and in 1865 in the United States, marked the beginning of a unique commercial history, as advertising became a business, and its agencies "shops." Commercial exchanges of all sorts, from the local to the global, from the Victorian era forward needed the conduit of an advertising message to funnel goods, to announce their availability, to explain their superiority, to blazon their identities. The goods of commerce were invisible, as H. G. Wells may have surmised, without their advertising cloaks. Not all of Victorian culture is as resistant to advertisement as Selfridge appears to be, and Victorian literature especially is replete with references to, and adjudications of, this new commercial philosophy.

Anthony Trollope's novel *The Struggles of Brown, Jones, and Robinson* (1862) is a storehouse of commercial references; its first sentence invokes the commercial aspects of reading in the Victorian age, when its narrator, one George Robinson, modestly demurs at having his name on the title page of what he insists is a memoir. "It will be observed by the literary and commercial witnesses" (i.e. readers) to this "transaction" (i.e. the book), he says, that he had no wish to court a "lawsuit" from the firm of Brown, Jones, and Robinson by having his "name advertised as the author of this account." What follows is a satirical send-up of a legal disclaimer-cum-advertisement for the book the reader currently holds in hand, as Robinson traces his conversations with the other members of the firm on the issue of authorship. It quickly becomes apparent that the firm these three contentious partners belong to is an advertising firm. Robinson's narrative is a doubled one – as he scores points off his "vain" and "old-fashioned" partners he simultaneously gives us a rhapsodic business lesson: "Advertise, advertise, advertise. And I say it again – advertise, advertise, advertise! It should be the motto of British commerce." Robinson clues us in to the new demands of commerce:

> It won't suffice now-a-days to stick up on a blank wall a simple placard to say that you have forty thousand best hose just arrived. Any wooden-headed fellow can do as much as that. That might have served in the olden time that we hear of twenty years since; but the game to be successful in these days must be played in another sort of fashion. There must be some finish about your advertisements, something new in your style, something that will startle in your manner. If a man can make himself a real master of this art, we may say that he has learnt his trade, whatever that trade may be. Let him know how to advertise, and the rest will follow.

Robinson's clarion call sets the tone of a work that wittily professes to recount "the commercial, not the domestic histories" of the firm of Brown, Jones, and Robinson, as it sticks to the last of advertisement. Chapter two is ushered in on a reverent note of worship: "O Commerce, how wonderful are thy ways, how vast thy power, how invisible thy dominion!" Despite the palpable irony hovering over Trollope's deadpan treatment of this discourse, his book beautifully displays the invasion of advertisement into all styles of writing, including the literary, and exposes by default the invisible omnipotence of the commerce it accompanies.

Buried in the Victorian triple-decker *No Name* (1862) is a veritable dissertation on advertising philosophy. Wilkie Collins's novel is chock-full of commercial nuggets of the greatest interest, but to touch only on advertising is to hit a mother lode. Without sketching the action of this complex book, it suffices to know that Magdalen Vanstone, the No Name of the title, who has been stripped of her surname and inheritance by a latter-day revelation of illegitimacy, is living incognito as a traveling actress. She is attended in her exile by the Wragges, a dubious couple consisting of the acute and devious Captain Wragge, and his slow-witted but deeply good and probably battered wife. The trio are staying in the neighborhood of Vauxhall Gardens, the fabled public amusement park, now defunct: "where the beauty and fashion of London feasted and danced through the summer seasons of a century – spreads, at this day, an awful wilderness of mud and rubbish; the deserted dead body of Vauxhall Gardens mouldering in the open air." On the "site where thousands of lights [once] twinkled" now "Commerce is not turbulent, nor is the public consumer besieged by loud invitations to 'buy.'" The dead body of commerce is a forlorn, even a tragic spectacle; and the silencing of voices exhorting customers to buy, however hectoring to the ear, is evidently a loss, a kind of death. Collins situates a major section of the narrative at the crossroads of older commerce – the once-magical Vauxhall Gardens – with newer possibilities, provided by advertising, department stores, and theater, and largely imaginary in kind.

> Mrs. Wragge was seated at the table, absorbed in the arrangement of a series of smart circulars and tempting price-lists, issued by advertising trades-people, and flung in at the cab-windows as they left the London terminus. "I've often heard tell of light reading," said Mrs. Wragge, restlessly shifting the position of the circulars, ". . . here's light reading, printed out in pretty colors. Here's all the Things I'm going to buy when I'm out shopping tomorrow. Lend us a pencil, please – you won't be angry, will you? – I do so want to mark 'em off." She looked up at Magdalen, chuckled joyfully over her own altered circumstances, and beat her great hands on the table in irrepressible delight . . . Her hands began to drum on the table louder than ever, until Magdalen quieted them by presenting her with a pencil. Mrs. Wragge instantly recovered her dignity, squared her elbows on the table, and plunged into imaginary shopping for the rest of the evening.

Mrs Wragge's childlike delight in her imaginary shopping is more than slightly pathetic, but bathos aside, her pleasure in conjuring a shopping world out of light reading is portrayed as a redemptive respite from her travails at home. The ads on pretty paper are accepted as fiction, rather than reviled as lies, and Mrs Wragge's mental shopping exercises her imagination as few things can in the "wilderness" of her uncommercial, unhappy surroundings. She catalogues her potential purchases with the exacting precision of a crazed accountant:

"Give us the pencil," said Mrs. Wragge, shuffling the circulars in a violent hurry. "I can't go to bed yet – I haven't half done marking down the things I want. Let's see, where did I leave off? *Try Finch's feeding-bottle for infants*. No! There's a cross against that: the cross means I don't want it . . . *Elegant cashmere robes; strictly oriental, very grand; reduced to one pound, nineteen, and sixpence. Be in time. Only three left*. Only three! Oh, do lend us the money and let's go and get one!" (Third Scene, ch. 1)

Mrs Wragge does get her strictly oriental robe later in the book, as a commercial consummation devoutly to be wished by the reader; Magdalen Vanstone, through other means than shopping, i.e. via the chicanery of a sham marriage, gets her name back. The posters advertising her performances under an assumed name have made her a household word, a desirable commodity, and thus commerce has given her leverage in the marriage market. Both transactions are commercial, and nominative, and they are so in reciprocally determinative ways. Advertising, on the positive side of its ledger, does provide a name and thus a habitation for desire, and Collins's novel reveals the unsettling limbo of modern commerce, where nothing can have no name.

Inability to fix the parameters of commerce, and susceptibility to its glamour, in contradistinction to its grubby practicalities, affects most of the key Victorian critics of commerce. Although Selfridge begins his book with an epigraph from John Ruskin, wherein Ruskin declares there to be "five great intellectual professions existing in every civilized nation," with Merchants (ranked number two) figuring among Soldiers, Pastors, Physicians, and Lawyers in their unique duty "to provide for" the nation, Selfridge was in fact Ruskin's opponent in the Victorian debate about commerce. Ruskin, along with other Victorian social prophets like Thomas Carlyle and William Morris, was obsessed with commerce and its depradations, and in his massive works dealing with commerce single-handedly established a large corner of the market on discourse about commerce, as distinct from commercial discourse. In a centenary volume of 1912 celebrating Ruskin's birth, the late-Victorian economist Hobson meticulously delineates Ruskin's abiding importance. Hobson acidly refers to the contempt excited in the business mind by Ruskin's claim to be "a teacher of the science and the art of political economy." Seeing him as an interloper in the field, Ruskin's critics asked, "But what could an art critic, a literary dilettante, know about the business world? To the academic, as to the business man, it never seems to have occurred that wealth is primarily a quality, not a quantity, and that the understanding or appreciation of that quality demanded qualifications which Ruskin had, and they had not." This fascinating declaration of the qualitative dimension of commerce or business, of its inherent aesthetic and Ruskin's concomitant skills in teasing out those qualities, accompanies Hobson's critique of political economy after Adam Smith, and explains his preference for Ruskin over John Stuart Mill and other experts. Smith's liberal vision of the discipline was supplanted by a "degrading process," in Hobson's words, where political economy became the "bondslave of the rising manufacturing and trading classes, who needed it to work their intellectual mill." Ruskin's knowledge of both work and consumption, and his "subtle mastery of words," allowed him a wider purview than the hired guns of economic thought could command. "Everywhere the loose materialism of commerce has obscured the human significance of industrial terminology as of industrial processes themselves." The very words of commerce – value, profit, consumption – have an extraordinary significance, for which Ruskin may be the best guide. How one chooses to gloss these words changes what they mean, and what constitutes commerce (Hobson 1920: 83–4).

Hobson is as acutely aware of Ruskin's blindnesses as of his insights. Ruskin valorized the landed gentry, possibly thanks to his enjoyable carriage rides in the country as a small child, and he ultimately idealized the upper classes as "composed of the best bred, the most energetic and most thoughtful of the population." These blind spots aside, however, what Ruskin's treatment of commerce provided was a shift from a quantitative economy to a qualitative economy, based on "vital satisfaction" rather than pecuniary value. Hobson, who should know, goes so far as to call this teaching "genuinely revolutionary," for its insistence upon consumption and not production as the final goal of economic activity. Consumption, Ruskin saw, entailed the resolution of commercial into human values, for value could be measured only in the form of the "vital use" people can enjoy from what they consume – whether wholesome food or beautiful art. Ruskin states it thus: "A horse is no wealth to us if we cannot ride, nor a picture if we cannot see, nor any noble thing be wealth except to a noble person" ("The Political Economy of Art," 1857). By putting the end-value of consumption before the fore-value of production, Ruskin vigorously transformed the configuration of commerce at the intellectual level, as his admonitions about the conditions of work and the division of wealth did on the social. Ruskin founded the Guild of St George in 1871 on the principle that "the highest wisdom and the highest treasure need not be costly or exclusive." The seeming gulf between Ruskin's nuanced version of commerce and Selfridge's encomia to it is bridged by Hobson's choice of adjectives to describe the greater theorist of commerce: the "pure romance" trailing all of Ruskin's thought, which "belongs to the literature of power."

The svelte epilogue to Ruskin's massive oeuvre on commerce could be Oscar Wilde's chic essay, "The Soul of Man under Socialism" (1891). A savagely anti-Victorian Victorian, Wilde offered a take on commerce surprisingly akin to Ruskin's aristocratic socialism, in its emphasis on the human benefits of wealth and prosperity. Any number of important Victorian cultural movements, from the Pre-Raphaelite circle of artists and poets to the decadent movement of which Wilde was a leader, participate in an oppositional commercial discourse. Oppositional, yet often reliant on commercial prosperity or even commercial technique. For Wilde, wealth and commerce should not be shunned, because it is they that provide the means for the flowering of individual talents and tastes. That Wildean flowering would depart from Ruskin's moralized ideals, perhaps, but Wilde concentrates just as Ruskin does on the consumption end of commerce, the "vital use" to which goods can be put, in order to make a case for idyllic self-actualization. Where they part company is over the issue of modernity. Wilde embraces contemporary commerce, with its machines and tools for living, and excoriates the nostalgic yearning of Ruskin and Morris for feudal, preindustrial England. One can perhaps credit Wilde's Irishness with his ability to see the contradictions implied in William Morris's vaunted return to artisanal handwork. The handmade objects Morris favored and produced – whether fabrics or pottery or wallpapers or the gorgeous publications of his Kelmscott Press – were incredibly expensive, out of the reach of ordinary people; it was their machine-made knock-offs that made huge commercial profits for Morris and his Firm. A commercial spade should be called a spade; the plantation system of land usurpation in Ireland during Morris's and Wilde's lifetime sufficed to quench the glow from that picture of precapitalist England. Art, including the aesthetics of identity, depends on commerce for Wilde, and there can be no escape into the past from the mechanisms of modern commerce. Nor does there need to be: commerce will free people to be artists. The irritating grain of contradiction hidden in the Wildean artistic pearl is crystallized in the essay's harping on middle-class tastes (very bad) and middle-class culture (worse). For an artist who was veritably a creature of commercialization – in the multiplication of his image in advertising, popular music, lecture performances, gossip columns and public spectacles, and the international popularity of his work – Wilde protests a bit too much. He draws the line where commerce encroaches too far on art, and labels it Philistinism. That high culture high-water mark defies the deeper message of his own work, and his life, which makes clear how hard it is to separate the bathwater of commerce, publicity, and popularity from the baby of art, autonomy, and self-fashioning.

The apotheosis of commerce in Victorian times is encapsulated in its chief invention, the department store. Other than the book, to which we shortly turn, there is no Victorian site so apropos for the consideration of commerce. What the book and the department store have in common derives from their being repositories of commercial transaction, mediated by language in the case of the book, and by spectacle in the case of the store. To trot out that pesky but useful Victorian eyewitness Selfridge again: he closes his romantic book on commerce with a chapter on what he calls "The Great Distributing House," his name for the department store. An extraordinary – and no doubt extraordinarily expensive – foldout is included in the leaves of this chapter. When unfolded to its full and stunning length, it is a schematic rendering in red ink of the distributional calculus of the store, from its "flower mounting" and "baby linen" stock to its "aero firm alarm system," its "mess hall attendants," "glove repair" section, staff magazine, sewage maintenance operations, purchasing department, and foreign offices. The vast web of interrelated commercial activities centrifugally spun by the department store is the nexus of commerce inscribed in one place. Some of the visionary impetus of the department store as Commerce centralized and fantasized arose from Prince Albert and his plans for the Crystal Palace at the world-famous Exhibition. That expanse of soaring glass, giving architectural support to the anthology of British commerce housed within, translated within a few decades into the structure of the department store, which was at once an exhibition hall, a palace of dreams, and a bureaucratic hub.

Victorian literature is littered with department stores, or their avatars, the gleaming shop windows before which so many characters stand transfixed. While Michel Foucault's notion of nineteenth-century power as a panoptical regime of the eye has become a staple of theoretical approaches to Victorian culture, it might be wise to stop short of the surveillance paradigm and to give proper attention as well to the magical properties of the commercial palace. Edmund Gosse's exceptional memoir *Father and Son* (1907), a painful account of the inevitable estrangement of a nineteenth-century Calvinist father from his *fin de siècle* secular son, movingly describes the latter's childhood escape from the austerities of Christian fundamentalism by way of the enchantments of the store, the shop window, and advertisement. He was never allowed to buy anything on these forays, yet received a vicarious baptism in commerce, as it were, when the family's serving-maid went down the street to make a purchase for herself, and "if I did not hold the rose of merchandise, I was very near it" (ch. 5). Echoing both Romantic and spiritual language, Gosse's "rose of merchandise" may appear oxymoronic or appalling, but he touches on what many late Victorians recognized for themselves as consumers: the transfiguring romance that was commerce made of its venue the department store an everyday sacrament.

If commerce is a discourse as well as a set of economic practices within Victorian culture, as I have been arguing, then the metalevel of the discourse of commerce involves the book trade. Books are commercial commodities of exchange, and no arena of commerce saw a greater change during the Victorian period than the book market. In the Victorian period the decisive switch to modern forms of the production, distribution, and consumption of the book (and magazine and newspaper) took place. Terry Lovell's *Consuming Fictions* (1992) explores this Victorian territory: the best medium for circulating the discourse about commerce – the novel, newspaper editorials, magazine articles, political cartoons, pamphlets, and ads, etc. – was created by commercial means.

The ultimate cautionary tale for the commercialization of the book trade, and thus the commercialization of literature and domesticity, must be George Gissing's *New Grub Street* (1891). Written near the end of the century which had wrought such major changes in literary production, Gissing's book is a *cri de coeur* for the author dispossessed by the grubby new traffic in books. The novel is a veritable archeology of the *fin de siècle* book trade. Its characters include a thinly veiled autobiographical portrait of a serious novelist who is impaled on the cusp of the transition from the Victorian triple-decker, a man of letters whose literary reviews and essays come to depend on the sheer exploitation of his daughter's research for him at the British Museum Reading Room, a male author in search of an old-style patron, a female author who leaves him in the commercial dust by playing the market for all it is worth. *New Grub Street* ends tragically and hyperbolically, with suicide, blindness, starvation, and the immolation of a precious manuscript in a fire, a twilight of the gods of "pure" literature on the bonfire of trade.

There was another, and less morbid, side of the commercial story to tell. Just as Mrs Wragge got a reprieve from her violent homelife in the fantasies of shopping granted her by advertising's light reading, so the cadre of women writers in the Victorian period found a (partial) haven from gender discrimination in the very commercialism which was anathema to writers like Gissing. The brisk trade in books, centralized around publishers and increasingly independent of either elite patronage or university ties, made it possible for women to enter literature and its precincts in great numbers. The spectrum ranges from the greatest of Victorian literary writers, like Charlotte Brontë and George Eliot, who had masculine *noms de plume* but were widely celebrated, and others like Elizabeth Gaskell who wrote under their own names and were enormously popular. Writing was indeed one of the few professions women could hold in Victorian society, even pseudonymously, and women's writing of the period is as imbricated by and in commerce as male writing – and perhaps more so.

George Eliot's masterpiece *Middlemarch* (1872) enacts the paradoxes of commercialism for the Victorian world of literature and for the female gender within the world of Victorian culture alike. Predicated on the historical anonymity of its main protagonist, Dorothea Brooke Casaubon Ladislaw, who unlike her prototype St Theresa, who founded a reforming order of nuns, cannot become a famous reformer, but is destined for the "hidden life" of marriage and motherhood, *Middlemarch* is heady with the details of commerce – wealth, property, trade, debt, business, profession, credit. This is a novel which can date the action of a chapter by a commercial and political allusion – "It was just after the Lords had thrown out the Reform Bill" is the sentence which opens chapter 84's intense, if oblique, reflection on the trade reforms earlier mentioned in this chapter. The pure-spirited Dorothea brokers the commercial failures and successes of her many acquaintances, thanks to her inherited fortune; the novel dwells on commercial debt and professional exigencies with a fierce business acumen. As a Victorian woman, and not a heroic nun, Dorothea is prohibited from a public career herself – she can only mediate the careers of men like Dr Lydgate, whom she offers to rescue financially.

> "It would be quite worth my while," said Dorothea simply. "Only think. I am very uncomfortable with my money, because they tell me I have too little for any great scheme of the sort I like best, and yet I have too much. I don't know what to do. I have seven hundred a year of my own fortune, and nineteen hundred a year that Mr. Casaubon left me, and between those three and four thousand of ready money in the bank. I wished to raise money and pay it off gradually out of my income which I don't want, to buy land with and found a village which should be a school of industry. . . . So you see that what I should most rejoice at would be to do something good with my money." (ch. 76)

Dorothea is forced into philanthropy because she cannot exercise her own money commercially. Her "scheme" (as it is called throughout the novel) is dedicated toward the public good, of course, and not to commercial profit, but there is nothing commercially innocent about either Dorothea or George Eliot for that matter. While Dorothea ultimately gives up her fortune to marry a reforming member of the House of Commons, in defiance of her landed-class origins, one could construct a gendered commercial allegory out of Eliot's narrative to set beside the story of the triumph of the bourgeoisie that others have noted within it. Unlike Dorothea, George Eliot, albeit not as Mary Ann Evans, *is* able to enter public life, through the door of commerce represented by the book. *Pace* Gissing, she thereby recognizes that, tainted as commerce may be in contrast to the worlds of art and philosophy, all human exchanges however aesthetic or intellectual will include commerce, and will take place in some sort of market. The pure "marketplace of ideas" does not exist. Moreover, Eliot's work suggests that in any event such a marketplace would only be a utopia for a few – who, under Victorian conditions, would inevitably be wealthy men. Commerce is ineluctable, Eliot sees, and to shun it or demonize it entirely is to live blind to one's own conditions. For certain groups, and women of all classes would surely be included here, to say nothing of female intellectuals, commerce can paradoxically offer an arena less beset by exclusion, prohibition, or tradition.

Dorothea Brooke's story, set within the context of George Eliot's novel and then within the large context of Victorian culture, is an allegory of the mediating powers of commerce, to harm and blight as well as to enable, and of commerce's own abiding need for the mediation of creative artistry and agency. Dorothea's fictive tomb may well lie unvisited, but Eliot's Victorian masterpiece is not now and never went unread. The commercial traffic around her book, and every other Victorian book one could cite, is messy, often crude, sometimes vulgar, and always arbitrary. If it had not been marketed, circulated, advertised, and promoted, *Middlemarch* could never have reached anyone's attention, could never have entered into the melee of commercial exchanges which constitute the literary market, and might have gone as unremarked as Dorothea's gravesite. Commerce is fierce, unjust, and unequal, but it can resurrect books, ideas, and even people in the afterlife of its market. The skeins and the schemes of commerce, in their resemblance to literature's skeins of language and narrative schemes, can sometimes intertwine to result in surprisingly creative, transformational energies. Improbable though it may seem, in this George Eliot is commerce's prophet. What allows commerce to play this role in awakening the resurrecting powers of attention Eliot cites through her treatment of Dorothea, and thus to exemplify the market-driven rise of women writers in Victorian culture, is the endpoint of the arc of all commercial exchanges of whatever kind in acts of consumption that, in the case of the commerce in books, goes beyond their purchase, a preliminary stage for the consumer of books, to figure consumption as another name for reading. Victorian literature extends beyond the eighteenth-century practice of comparing books to victuals, including such toxic foodstuffs as drugs or poison, to a self-reflexive and parabolic fascination with reading as the ultimate act of commerce with a text. Among the key fables of Victorian commerce as a kind of consumption-cum-congress with words, and thus the site of transgressive or transformational possibilities for literary and cultural commerce, are Christina Rossetti's narrative poem "Goblin Market," and Bram Stoker's *Dracula*, each of which addresses the paradox of consuming oneself in an act of being consumed. As such, these polar parables of consumption bring the contradictions and complexities of Victorian commerce into the sharpest relief.

Published in 1862 in the volume *Goblin Market and Other Poems*, and illustrated by the author's brother, the poet and Pre-Raphaelite artist Dante Gabriel Rossetti, Christina Rossetti's long poem has rightly become a *locus classicus* for changing critical notions of gender, culture, and aesthetics of the Victorian period. Viewed through the lens of commerce, the poem has it all, from its location in part in the titular marketplace of the "goblin men," whose call "Come buy, come buy!" literalizes the market exchanges that undergird Victorian society, to its evocation of the commodity exchange of women's bodies for money in prostitution and in the economic stringencies of the Victorian marriage market. The poem is redolent of advertisement, with a persuasive lexicon of temptation that draws two sisters, Laura and Lizzie, who fetch water from a stream near the orchard market, into the seductive purchase and consumption of the goblin merchants' array of rare fruits. Laura initially succumbs to the alluring market display on a solo venture out for water, and having no money with her trades bodily objects – a lock of hair and a "tear" – to the goblin men for enough fruit to suck down in a trance-like frenzy of consumption: "She sucked until her lips were sore" (line 136). Lizzie remains impervious to the marketing cries, in part thanks to her memory of the cautionary tale of Jeanie, who has died after consuming these same fruits, but Laura suffers from no longer being able to hear the goblin calls and locate the fairy-like marketplace in order to satiate her fruit hunger again. Wasting away from lack of the magical fruit she can no longer consume, and unable to grow any more fruit on her own from the seed she has saved, Laura is near death when Lizzie undertakes a mission to the goblin market, armed with a silver penny, in order to transact some commerce in the rare fruits and save her sister's life. Lizzie's resolutely commercial approach to the exchange is rejected by the merchants, who have initially invited her to eat with them, but become violent and abusive when she refuses to eat the fruit herself and tries to buy it with coin. Assaulted by fruit, but penny intact, Lizzie races home in hopes the dying Laura can be saved by consuming the dregs and juices of fruit from her body in an act of consumption both homoerotic and Eucharistic, as Lizzie cries to Laura: "Eat me, drink me, love me," she cries, exhorting her to "suck my juices" (lines 468–71). While repulsed by the bodily pulp, the next day Laura is restored to life, and the sisters live on to old age and to the telling of the tale. With all the valences of gender, sexuality, market forces, and spiritual templates melded in this sweet and deadly fruit, "Goblin Market" marks a point of arrival for Victorian literature, a marketplace of no return, where the consumption of poetic words and of their ethical import dovetails with the consumer's new-found place in culture, impossible to extricate from the pulp of words and coin that constitutes the self.

Bram Stoker's *Dracula* of 1897 carries consumption as the crux of commerce, and its curse, into the genre of the novel and toward the end of the Victorian period, at a stage when opting out of consumption, as Lizzie manages to do until she, too, recognizes its inexorable involvement in the salvation of her sister, is understood as impossible, and the only question remaining is who will consume who first. Stitched into the global fabric of imperial commerce and its entirely unequal market exchanges, and alert to the consuming power of New Women (Stoker's mother was a famous feminist) and unorthodox, queer consumers of every kind (Stoker's lifelong bond was to the actor Sir Henry Irving he served as manager), *Dracula* recounts a collaborative stalking and staking of Count Dracula that summons to the fore the newest modes of commerce and consumption, from the mass media and modern cultural forms its vampire hunters embrace – shorthand, telegraph, proto-telephone, gramophone, typewriter, photography, cinema, advertisement, electric illumination, rapid transportation – to the routes and roots that empire has exposed in the commercial trails and traces it leaves. The attempt to extirpate vampirism from modern London entails fighting the fire of consumption with more of the same. If vampirism in Dracula is posited as a type of contagious consumption whose hallmark is a reproductive process that consumes lifeblood in order to create a legion of new, albeit undead, consumers, the fight against it requires every new type of consumption and artifact of modern commerce, including the typewriter needed by Mina, she who happily possesses what Van Helsing calls a "man-brain," as she transcribes the manuscript of their battle and in doing so both finds its target, the Count, in the very crosshairs of commerce, and creates the text that we as readers consume. Victorian commerce gives birth to the modern consumer in an act of literary reading.

See also 1851, 1870, 1897; FINANCIAL, INDUSTRIAL, PUBLISHING; FICTION, SAGE WRITING

REFERENCES

Day, C. (1907) *A History of Commerce.* New York: Longmans, Green.

Hobson, J. A. (1897) *On Imperialism.* London: Chapman & Hall.

——(1920) "Ruskin as Political Economist." In *Ruskin as Prophet: A Centenary Study*, ed. J. Howard Whitehouse. New York: E. P. Dutton.

Lever, C. (1872) *Lord Kilgobben.* London: Harmsworth Press.

Lovell, T. (1992) *Consuming Fictions.* London: Verso.

Selfridge, H. G. (1902) *The Romance of Commerce.* London: William Bredon & Sons.

FURTHER READING

Altick, R. D. (1957) *The English Common Reader: A Social History of the Mass Reading Public 1800–1900.* Chicago: University of Chicago Press.

Armstrong, I. (2008) *Victorian Glassworlds: Glass Culture and the Imagination.* Oxford: Oxford University Press.

Bigelow, G. (2003) *Fiction, Famine, and the Rise of Economics in Victorian Britain and Ireland.* Cambridge: Cambridge University Press.

Bowlby, R. (1985) *Just Looking: Consumer Culture in Dreiser, Gissing and Zola.* New York: Methuen.

Brewer, J., and R. Porter (eds) (1992) *Consumption and the World of Goods.* London: Routledge.

Campbell, C. (1987) *The Romantic Ethic and the Spirit of Modern Consumerism.* Oxford: Oxford University Press.

Freedman, J. (1990) *Professions of Taste: Henry James, British Aestheticism and Commodity Culture.* Stanford: Stanford University Press.

Frost, S. (2012) *The Business of the Novel: Economics, Aesthetics, and the Case of Middlemarch.* London: Pickering and Chatto.

Gagnier, R. (2000) *The Insatiability of Human Wants: Economic and Aesthetics in Market Society.* Chicago: Chicago University Press.

Gallagher, C. (2006) *The Body Economic: Life, Death, and Sensation in Political Economy and the Victorian Novel.* Princeton: Princeton University Press.

Hadley, E. (2010) *Living Liberalism: Practical Citizenship in Mid-Victorian Britain.* Chicago: University of Chicago Press.

Helsinger, E. K. (1991) "Consumer Power and the Utopia of Desire in Christina Rossetti's 'Goblin Market.'" *ELH* 8, 903–33.

Hendrickson, R. (1970) *The Grand Emporiums.* New York: Stein and Day.

Hobsbawm, E. J. (1987) *The Age of Empire.* Cambridge: Cambridge University Press.

Houston, G. (2005) *From Dickens to Dracula: Gothic, Economic, and Victorian Fiction.* Cambridge: Cambridge University Press.

Lynch, D. (1998) *The Economy of Character: Novels, Market Culture, and the Business of Inner Meaning.* Chicago: University of Chicago Press.

Nunokawa, J. (1994) *The Afterlife of Property: Domestic Security and the Victorian Novel.* Princeton: Princeton University Press.

Pocock, J. G. A. (1985) *Virtue, Commerce, and History.* Cambridge: Cambridge University Press.

Rappoport, J. (2011) *Giving Women: Alliance and Exchange in Victorian England.* Oxford: Oxford University Press.

Richards, T. (1990) *The Commodity Culture of Victorian England.* Stanford: Stanford University Press.

Said, E. (1993) *Culture and Imperialism.* New York: Alfred A. Knopf.

Tucker, H. F. (2003) "Rossetti's Goblin Marketing: Sweet to Tongue and Sound to Eye." *Representations* 82, 117–33.

Wicke, J. (1992) "Vampiric Typewriting: Dracula and Its Media." *ELH* 59, 467–93.

19
Artistic

Julie Codell

In William Thackeray's *The Newcomes* (1853–5), the artist Clive Newcome upholds the gentleman artist, epitomized in the former century by Sir Joshua Reynolds, while in the same pages Clive's father snobbishly refuses to dine with an artist from the lower classes. Fiction's portrayal of the artist as bohemian fed a popular stereotype, but it was one challenged repeatedly by artists themselves, by the organizations on which they relied, and by a resourceful art press that propagandized for respectability. A word introduced by Thackeray, according to the *OED*, "bohemian" referred to a gypsy-like literary or artistic person, whose "irregular life or habits" probably bespoke a comparable shiftiness in moral character. At times a sympathetic, harmless, comic figure, as in Henry Murger's *Scènes de la vie de Bohème* (1851) and George du Maurier's *Trilby* (1894), the bohemian appeared diabolically anti-social in Oscar Wilde's *Dorian Gray* (1890) and seductively immoral in Morley Roberts's *Immortal Youth* (1896). Artists in poems by Felicia Hemans, Alfred Tennyson, Robert Browning, and Dante Gabriel Rossetti were troubled figures caught between individual desires and serving the public good. Women artists were represented more benignly in fiction: the artistically talented protagonist of Charlotte Brontë's *Jane Eyre* (1847), for example, and the artist heroines in Anne Brontë's *The Tenant of Wildfell Hall* (1848) and Margaret Oliphant's *The Three Brothers* (1870).

The central problem around which artistic discourses circulated was the status of the artist. Artists' professional standing reflected changes in ideas about gender, class, education, and money. In the eighteenth century artists were generally divided, as in *The Newcomes*, between well-off Academicians, regularly exhibiting at the Royal Academy (RA) and rewarded by upper-class patronage, and less-educated artisans

A New Companion to Victorian Literature and Culture, First Edition. Edited by Herbert F. Tucker.
© 2014 John Wiley & Sons, Ltd. Published 2014 by John Wiley & Sons, Ltd.

who earned little from painting and often engaged in lucrative printmaking (e.g. William Blake). From mid-century on, artists' status, benefiting from the rising art market of the 1860s, changed radically: they became celebrities and were hailed for contributing cultural capital to a national identity and embodying such English traits as individuality, love of domesticity and landscape, narrative content, and talent for color.

Conflicts from the eighteenth century between idealism and commercialism, however, continued into the nineteenth. Victorians reinterpreted the commercial success of artists as a sign not of their greed but of their unity with the British public, their work ethic, and their domestication as responsible citizens and normal paterfamilias. Discussing his success and sales, Pre-Raphaelite artist William Holman Hunt satirized the fictional bohemian:

> it was amusing to read references to painters as generally leading a lazy, cigar smoking life. The only artists I ever knew who achieved work of note in any sense whatever, went first through a steady training of several years, and afterwards entered their studios with as unvarying a punctuality as business men attend their offices, worked longer hours than these, and had fewer holidays, partly because of their love for art, but also because of their deep sense of the utter uselessness of grappling with the difficulties . . . except at close and unflinching quarters. (I, 344)

Hunt's mention of the studio acknowledged its importance in literature as a charged site: the antithesis of ordered domestic life in a conventional novel like Anthony Trollope's *Last Chronicle of Barset* (1867), but in the art press lauded as a place of hard work. The home studio, a new Victorian architectural genre, mitigated charges of bohemianism. It synthesized economic success, social status, domestic order, and professionalism. *The Art Journal* and *The Magazine of Art* augmented series on artists' lives with photos of their grand studio homes, and books on artists called their studies "shrines" in token of their denizens' celebrity professionalism.

Studios were cleansed of bohemian moral ambiguities, such as unchaperoned models. But their size and wealth generated another debate over whether a studio should be luxurious for socializing or simple for working. Helen Zimmern represented Alma-Tadema's luxurious 66-room home as a site of moral virtue, underscoring Victorian anxiety lest studio homes seem to signify grasping commercialism and ostentatious social ambition that would deflect artists from their higher calling (29). Zimmern claimed that Alma-Tadema was not "led astray by success," but was "self-exacting, self-critical." (Inasmuch as her language – "splendid," "remarkable," "superb" – was promotional and hyperbolic, Zimmern of course participated in the very phenomenon she meant to disclaim.) Similarly, Frederic Leighton's fashionable Holland Park house reflected his character: "generous . . . unpretentious size . . . charming" (*The Magazine of Art* 1881, 1–32). John Everett Millais's home reflected English good sense and prosperity without "affectation . . . not obtrusive or self-assertive" (*The Magazine of Art* 1881, 290).

In the studio home, economic success became a sign of virtue. Unlike the grand eighteenth-century homes of Academicians like Joshua Reynolds that had aspired to aristocracy, the Victorian home studio became "an inspirational tool and material proof of the professional approach" that "removed the suspicion of amateurism," a social cleansing that secured a professional identity, at least for the most successful artists (Walkley xxiv). Despite these changes, however, artists' training remained unaltered since the 1768 founding of the RA as both an art school and a near-monopolistic exhibition site. Before attempting to enter the Academy, young boys could attend Sass's Academy (later renamed Cary's Academy) in London, opened in 1817 by Henry Sass (1788–1844) and caricatured by former student Thackeray in *The Newcomes*.

The RA, semi-private and only partially supported by the government, was created to promote the arts in Britain through education and exhibition and to counteract the long-standing dominance of royal commissions by foreign artists such as Hans Holbein and Anthony Van Dyck. Students at the Academy learned to draw by copying Old Master paintings and casts of classical and Renaissance sculpture. But early on, the RA was attacked by artists for weakness in drawing, where French training was strong. *The Builder* in May 1856 recommended in blatantly economic terms that artists outside the Academy "take the tide of patronage while at its flood" (10 [May 1856], 257). The most persistent complaints concerned limitations on membership (40), members' large number of exhibition submissions (eight per year), the privileged status of oil painting, and an annual exhibition decried as a shop. Academicians' works were hung "on the line," roughly in the middle of the walls, while thousands of non-members' works in rooms with three-story high ceiling were "skied" at the top of the high walls, unseen by the public, critics, and other artists.

In response to these criticisms, a few rival societies appeared early in the century: the Royal British Artists (established in 1819 to correct the RA's discrimination against landscape painters), the Society of British Artists (1824), two competing watercolor societies (1804 and 1832), a Society of Engravers (1802), and the British Institution (1805). In 1863 a Royal Commission investigated the RA's restricted educational and membership practices. The Academy thereafter tried new market-ing strategies and more openness, a special Press Day in 1871, mass circulation of RA reviews, season tickets in 1876, and publication of *Royal Academy Pictures* from 1888.

Informal groups emerged in ostensible resistance to the RA. Yet even the revolu-tionary, short-lived Pre-Raphaelite Brotherhood (1848) had rules on admitting members, meetings, adopting resolutions, voting, and restricting members' public behavior. The St John's Wood Clique (1860s and 70s) was composed mostly of Academy Associates, the category for RA members recently admitted. After mid-century, many British artists studied in France in the atelier system of individual master and pupils, bringing improved draftsmanship and styles like Realism, Impres-sionism, and Art Nouveau back to England.

Debates within these societies and the RA were couched in terms of "monopolies," "exclusivity," and "free market" competition. The RA reacted to outside criticism by arguing that only its members, being no less professional than doctors and lawyers, should police their institution. Economic language and government investigations conflicted with what was the cardinal development of the Victorian period in this regard: artists' claim to the status of *professionals*. Ultimately, the concept of professionalism itself papered over these conflicts by making success a virtue and a sign of national identity that joined artists and the public.

The professions are "very much a Victorian creation" (Reader 2), one on which the fortunes of the fine arts shed revealing light. During the century the Victorian art world expanded far beyond early societies, or elite Academicians, and the topic of professionalism affected art as it did other fields, including literature. Artists' new relationships to the wider public became increasingly speculative and dependent on the free market, threatening their claims of professional autonomy. Art unions – not to be confused with the later phenomenon of trade or labor unions – that helped redefine this relationship sprang up in Europe and the United States, reaching England in the late 1830s. The London Art Union, the largest, was formed in 1837 at the suggestion of the House of Commons Select Committee on the Arts and Manufactures, reflecting the government's newly active role in promoting art for the public. People subscribed to art unions for one guinea annually and received one engraving in return. Art unions' contests, awarding prints of popular paintings, contributed to the mass dissemination of Victorian art from the 1840s to the 1860s.

Professionalism synthesized three economic claims: market autonomy to control the cost of services; a "calling" motivated by public service, not economic need; and special expertise or knowledge that contained surplus value (public good) not measurable by supply and demand. H. Byerley Thomson wrote in 1857 that "professions and the professional classes . . . form the head of the great English middle class, maintain its tone of independence, keep up to the mark its standard of morality, and direct its intelligence" (5). The first attempt to count professionals was made in 1841; art's designation as a profession appeared in the 1861 census when artists totaled 4,643. The number of artists rose to 11,059 by World War I, as compared to only 3,434 authors, editors, and journalists.

As a calling, a profession was marked by autonomy in the marketplace – setting one's own price for one's expertise. For professionals, the overt exchange of money was considered vulgar and ungentlemanly (Reader 36). Paula Gillett argues that Victorians viewed the professional's high remuneration as "recognition *of* service rather than payment *for* service," leaving the artist's idealism unsullied (54). Sales were handled by servants, dealers, or professional societies' staff. Artists claimed that their proper rewards were honorific: awards, titles, and national museum acquisitions.

Ambiguities nevertheless marked artists' (and writers') professionalism throughout the century. They had no examination ladder or absolute certification, as other professions did, to distinguish professionals from amateurs. Amateurs competed in the market with professionals, and the public, regardless now as always of expertise, considered itself an adequate judge of aesthetic merit. In the open marketplace anyone was free to criticize and judge art and artists, creating a central conflict between professional autonomy in the market and inexpert consumption. Artists' professional identities undergirded their upward mobility but could not police borders between professionals and amateurs. Owning cultural, not material, capital, and not belonging exclusively to a single social class, artists and writers did not exist professionally in the same way as did doctors or lawyers. The intangibility of professional products meant that the professional's product was "inextricably bound to the person and the personality of the producer . . . *the producers themselves have to be produced* if their products or commodities are to be given a distinctive form" (Larson 14). For artists, this meant arguing that their products were not simply paintings or sculptures, but ideas, or didactic lessons or comments on daily life. Many Victorian artists accordingly participated in public self-promotion and marketing through networks of critics, patrons and the press, and their own writings and lectures that constructed them as gentlemanly, quintessentially English, and idealist.

Debates in the 1850s and 1860s about whether to make exhibitions open or restrict them by membership in the sponsoring organization entailed further questions about whether aesthetics or economics guaranteed quality, and whether exhibition practices were too shop-like (Newall 27). Many criticized exhibitions for treating art like merchandise, endorsing sentimental subjects to satisfy consumer demand, and inducing ungentlemanly competition. Others argued that these practices reflected the free-market mentality that characterized Englishness. In 1800 art writer Edward Edwardes argued for a free market, but Richard and Samuel Redgraves in 1866 promoted cooperation, brotherhood, and sociability as constituting professionalism. They recognized that any artist's price fluctuations affected Victorian artists as a group.

Artists' professional public identities rested on a nexus of the art press, critics, and dealers, all of whom had a stake in artists' celebrity status and appearance of respectability. The art press enjoyed a wide circulation. The *Art Journal*'s monthly circulation increased from 700 in 1839 (when it was called the *Art-Union*) to nearly 25,000 in 1851 (*The Art Journal* 1851, 301). This press endorsed artists' new celebrity, wealth, and sociability, reported on prizes, commissions, and prices, and deployed New Journalism methods – interviews, hyperbolic advertising language, gossip columns – to induce spectating and buying. Economics saturated professional art discourse in the press. Promoting "art commerce," Samuel Carter Hall wanted the newly commenced *Art-Union* to show "the commercial value of the Fine Arts," that "beauty is cheaper than deformity," that it is sound policy and patriotism "to resort to native artists . . . in every branch of Art-manufacture" and to pay them better (I, 210). Hall bragged, "*I had to create a public for Art* . . . to make the work respected as well as popular" (197) by blending "information and instruction with interesting and useful intelligence," to replace consumers' purchases of Old Masters with acquisitions of works by living British artists (199). An essay entitled "The Business Side of Art" (*Art Journal* 1888, 249) recognized an excess of supply over demand in art and recommended expanding the art market by dividing it into coteries, something new professional societies began to do after 1880 (Codell).

Such interventions bear out Pierre Bourdieu's thesis that art is produced not only by artists but also by art discourses in "reproductions, catalogues, art journals, museums," which become "a stage in the production of the work, of its meaning and value" (110). That *all* commentary – criticism, catalogues, biographies, cartoons, media, and exhibitions – competes in "a struggle for the monopoly of legitimate discourse about the work of art, and consequently in the production of the value of the work of art" (Bourdieu 36), was already evident to Hall and to Marion Harry Spielmann, editor (1887–1904) of *The Magazine of Art*. Spielmann believed in the mutual benefits of linking art and commerce, and he treated commercial success as a sign of both artistic quality and national unity of taste. On this view creativity and commercial success were not opposed for Victorian artists, as they were for the French avant-garde. The art press thus transformed art production into a business whose enterprising artists mirrored middle-class values: social decorum, the gospel of work, a concern with moral character, and an identification of high culture with the nation.

The art press promoted artists' production as rightfully commercial for the sake of the consumer: it assured readers of art's investment value. Successful artists endowed their purchasers with cultural and symbolic capital as artists' names became brand names. *The Art Journal* noted when its favorite artists' prices went up, as if their stock had risen. Despite claims of high-minded educational intentions, these publications were a form of trade journals addressed not only to practitioners, but also to the public, informing readers about sales, prices, artists' new speculative income sources (advertising, "artistic" postcards, home furnishings), talented young artists whose works would appreciate over time, auctions and exhibitions to encourage the public to buy British art. Treating beauty as a surplus value, an author in *The Art Journal* argued that "taste is a marketable commodity, which being of so much value is worth getting honestly, and by fair purchase" (*The Art Journal* 1871, 295).

Culture and consumption constructed each other, and Victorian artists knew it. Charles R. Leslie in his 1843 biography of John Constable (1776–1837) stressed Constable's economic knowledge and careful negotiations over money and commissions. Leighton's 1888 presidential address at the Liverpool Art Congress argued that artists must blend nationalism ("greatness," "pride") and economics ("national prosperity"). For Leighton, artists could make the public better consumers of art and thus contribute to national prosperity, as well as national culture. He insisted that art should not be divorced from "industrial production," because their marriage could shape consumer demand; he called the public "purchasers" and artists "suppliers," who contributed to Britain's economic well-being (Barrington II, 343, 350, 358–61).

Like literary authors, whose self-comparison to mechanical inventors underscored their position "as market agents" (Ruth 8), artists laid claim to economic knowledge as a badge of professionalism that distinguished them from amateurs (motivated by love) and from artisans (motivated by need). This position, however, still remained subject to criticism: the painter Edward Poynter, for example, in a lecture of 1871 complained that English art students wanted to sell before they were trained. But G. D. Leslie claimed that money inspired artists, and he condemned the RA for forbidding students from selling their schoolwork. He argued that Old Masters "by no means despised the remuneration" and that geniuses often sprang from humble circumstances and so appreciated "the advantages of wealth" (*The Art Journal* 1882, 71–2).

The positions we have been reviewing were not only contested but in certain respects internally contradictory. Jonathan Freedman argues that Aestheticism, a movement that included both Leighton and Poynter, synthesized aesthetics and commodification by positioning artists as professionals through a set of negotiations among art production, economics, and society whose effect was "to accomplish the commodification of 'culture' itself." The resulting "sphere of autonomous high culture" was accessible through taste or education or "the acquisition of goods whose possession would confirm the high cultural status of their consumers." Ironically, these goods often "turned out to be artifacts that critiqued commodity culture itself" (xii–xii). This wry critique of Aestheticism makes explicit the definitive structural contradiction that this chapter has been suggesting was constitutive of the artist's Victorian place: a "complete but complex entanglement with the development of a cultural apparatus at once thoroughly professionalized and wholly commodified." Bearing a "monopoly of knowledge," the artist appeared disinterested, while staging a successful career into the bargain (xix).

In literature, too, the relationship between the artist and the public was conflicted. In Tennyson's "The Palace of Art," the soul as artist lives apart from society until realizing that she should integrate with others and serve humanity. John Ruskin attacked artists for dining with patrons or owning expensive carriages. He promoted an ideal of innocent, childlike artists above and beyond concerns with status and money (Codell 79–96). Rossetti's Chiaro in "Hand and Soul" (1849) seeks fame but is miserable until an image of his soul tells him to paint a spiritual art for the good of others, not for personal fortune. In Robert Browning's painter poems "Pictor Ignotus" (1845) owes the anonymity of his eponym, which means "unknown painter," to a refusal to commercialize; "Andrea del Sarto" (1855) broods on the consequences of the speaker's having sold his genius out; and even "Fra Lippo Lippi" (1855), often taken as the poet's alter ego, is defined by the struggle between pleasing patrons and expressing himself in a fresh artistic style.

The idealist side of professionalism was boosted by the creation of the Slade Professorships at Cambridge, Oxford, and the University of London, all founded in 1869 by collector and philanthropist Felix Slade's bequest. Many Slade Professors were artists. Artists' rise in status was also reflected in their attaining positions as museum directors, art administrators, and titled knights. Millais was created a baronet in 1885, the first artist to have a hereditary title. Leighton was knighted (1878) and made a baronet (1886). Burne-Jones received an honorary degree from Oxford (1881) and became an Honorary Fellow (1882; he studied there but left before receiving a degree) and a baronet (1894), horrifying both his socialist wife Georgiana and his socialist friend William Morris. Poynter, the first Slade Professor at University College London (1871–5), directed the National Gallery (1894–1904), supervised the Tate Gallery's opening, received an honorary degree from Cambridge (1898), and was made a baronet (1902). From the 1880s on, artists' professional societies all became royal societies, entitling their presidents to be knighted – a practice formerly reserved for the RA, as the speaker of Browning's "Youth and Art" (1864) offhandedly records while regretting the sacrifice of bohemian love to established success: "I've married a rich old lord, / And you're dubbed knight and an R.A." (ll. 59–60).

This rise in status was further promoted by the press genre of the heroic artist biography, a culture industry that indulged in a form of branding by the repetition of epithets: manly Millais, cosmopolitan Leighton, idealist G. F. Watts, and so forth. Artists as circulating commodities became national heroes in serialized biographies that shaped Victorian concepts of art, artists, genius, and aesthetic worth. Biographies reiterated the trope of struggle rewarded by success ("no man ever became great without working assiduously," *The Art Journal* 1855, 45) across middlebrow periodicals like *The Nineteenth Century*, *The Fortnightly Review*, *The Athenaeum*, and in America *Scribner's*. *The Art Journal* series "British Artists: Their Style and Character" (1855) was illustrated by engravings of paintings that could be removed and placed on parlor walls, further bonding artists with the public. That in 1861 one biographer was already berating artists' overexposure in the press (*The Art Journal*, 133) is not surprising, given the ambivalent compromise the period repeatedly struck between art's ineffable aura and its mass-cultural marketing. For biographers' insistence that successful artists were motivated by selfless duty was a "misrecognition" (Bourdieu 39–41), meant to replace economic motives with higher ones. Archdeacon F. W. Farrar insisted that Hunt made less money than if he had "merely followed the practice of the ordinary run of painters" (Farrar and Meynell 16), a misrecognition and defense of Hunt's high prices. Another biographer insisted that popular and populist William Orchardson, who "never prostitutes his high abilities to pander to lasciviousness," painted "in the manner of a healthy-minded and sane man of affairs and man of the world" full of "excellent robust virility" (Little 15).

New Journalism interviews offered a sensational simulation of the artist's creative inner life. Richard Salmon argues that the interview simultaneously represented intimacy and undermined it, making subjects "products to be circulated and consumed" (159). The interviewer claimed to reveal an "authentic" self, whose celebrity was deemed worthy of the "cultural distinction which the interview confers upon its subject" (162). But as in any market exchange, there was a price to pay: the artist-celebrity became "public property":

the public whose favourable suffrage he has won by his works . . . desire – and the desire is legitimate and perfectly reasonable – to learn some of his life and history. . . . that would penetrate even the solitude of his studio and . . . even the sanctity of his domestic hearth – . . . This is the penalty . . . each pays for his position and popularity. (*The Art Journal* 1856, 41)

"Suffrage" implies that the public is enfranchised to pry into artists' lives, because these lives determine history and define the age (so ran Carlyle's vision of biography's grand purpose). The Victorian culture industry, replicating industrial capitalism's structures and values to secure readers' identifications with artists, twinned cultural legitimacy with economic achievement.

The art world became internationalized and complex, embracing critics, dealers, curators, framers, print shops, and proliferating display venues. Above all, artists befriended writers and journalists and were themselves authors of autobiographies, diaries, press articles, and lectures subsequently published, a professional strategy to address the buying public directly and shape artists' public image as professionals. Artists and critics engaged in exchanges that benefited both of them. Critics, who were often also biographers, provided advertisement, defined reputations as a form of capital, created markets for themselves and for artists, and influenced consumers' preferences by validating consumers' self-images through notions of proper taste. Critics gained authority through frequency of publication: William Michael Rossetti wrote almost 400 art essays for English and American periodicals from 1850 to 1878. An artist's biography might appear in multiple places: the life of James Clarke Hook that F. G. Stephens wrote for the *Portfolio* (1871) was expanded for *The Art Journal* (1888) and later published in an *Art Annual* that same year. Critics and artists were often close friends or even family: Butler's brother-in-law Wilfred Meynell wrote her biography, and W. M. Rossetti wrote about his Pre-Raphaelite brethren.

Artists' letters to Stephens, an original Pre-Raphaelite Brotherhood member and *Athenaeum* critic for 40 years, exemplify this knowledge exchange whereby artists deployed journalism's circulation for economic benefit. The insider information Stephens obtained about artists' pending projects and RA pictures, and secret Academy elections, gave support to his own public authority. When Leighton offered to help Stephens if "in need of a paragraph to fill a gap in this week's number" (Stephens' letters, Bodleian MS Don e 69, #25, January 18, 1864), this was a typical *quid pro quo* exchange, feeding the same New Journalism focus that was exemplified by Spielmann's gossipy "art causerie" column in *The Graphic*.

Artists' negotiations behind the scenes allowed them to address the public without losing their professional claim for art's higher purpose. Within these symbiotic exchanges, critics visited studios to see and understand works likely to be "skied" at the RA. Artists requested publicity for one-picture mini-exhibitions. Critics ventriloquized artists in the press and helped them meet patrons, find studios or publishers or venues, and in the process educated the public. Even here labor remained a measure of value: clocking hours spent in the studio, a common topos, assured the public of a painting's worth. Critics gave essential support to artists straddling two contradictory measures of economic worth – invested labor and professional knowledge. Artists exploited their networks, aware that when one artist's prices fell they all suffered, thus indicating a sophisticated understanding of how speculative markets work. Dealers too played a vital role promoting artists and internationalizing the London art market. Most prominent were Louis Flatow and Ernest Gambart, who held one-work exhibitions and paid large sums for artists' copyright, making their money by then selling prints of popular works. William Powell Frith's *Derby Day* (1858) earned him £1,500 and inspired Flatow to commission a second painting, *The Railway Station* (1862), for the enormous sum of £5,250, which Flatow more than recovered by exhibiting the painting to over 21,000 spectators who paid to see the work and bought reproductions. William Agnew paid £20,000 for Hunt's *The Shadow of Death* (1873). Dealers' one-artist shows also benefited women artists: Barbara Leigh Smith Bodichon exhibited at Gambart's French Gallery and sold out all her works in one solo show's opening in 1861. Gambart famously paid Hunt £5,000 for the rights to engrave *The Light of the World* (1853) and £5,500 (about £2 million today) for *The Finding of the Saviour in the Temple* (1860), which Gambart exhibited in 1861 with dramatic lighting as a one-work show. Gambart charged spectators at a rate like the RA's, one shilling for entry and sixpence for the catalogue; such circumspect ambition was rewarded when in 1898 he was made a Member of the Royal Victorian Order.

Refining and professionalizing their role, these dealers invented the modern commercial art gallery. Galleries partnered with professional societies to exhibit and sell members' works all year round, instead of only during the spring "season"; the Institute of Painters in Water Colours, for example, merged with the commercial Dudley Gallery. But there remained a fine line to tread: such commercial venues, along with advertising and press coverage, eroded artists' idealist professional claims. Amateurs exhibiting in these galleries also undermined artists' professional image: the Dudley Gallery's first exhibition call netted 1,700 works, of which the accepted 519 were mostly by amateurs. Foreign influences, too, challenged English artists' market share. *The Art Journal* and *The Magazine of Art* condemned English and French Impressionists' exploitation of novelty for commercial success, and Ruskin followed suit with his 1878 attack on Whistler for flinging paint "in the public's face" – a conflation of canvas with consumption. Frith told readers that such newfangled art was a poor investment (*The Magazine of Art* 1889, 7).

By the 1880s, following a recession that deflated the art market, the art world became decentralized: professional societies emerged for painter-etchers (1880), medallists (1891), portrait painters (1891), and pastellists (1899), catering to new middle-class consumers' diverse interests and limited resources. Specialized publications proliferated in the 1890s: the *Savoy*, the *Studio*, the *Yellow Book*, and the *Century Guild Hobby Horse*, and short-lived periodicals (*Pageant, Rose Leaf, Chameleon, Butterfly*) that served these niches. *The Magazine of Art* ended in 1904, *The Art Journal* in 1912, each replaced by specialist publications that disguised economics beneath a new veil of aesthetic mystifications.

The emergence of these professional societies shows how artists, like other late-Victorian professionals, banded together to control the market and optimize new relations with consumers, even as they sought to resolve conflicts between professionalism and mass marketing. In "Whence This Great Multitude of Painters?" (1892), Marcus Huish, editor of *The Art Journal*, lamented the excessive number of painters in a limited market, the blurred distinctions between professional and amateur, and government failure to encourage design schools for the working class. This last theme resurrected a mid-century debate over the assignment of the lower classes to design schools and of the middle and upper classes to the "fine" arts:

> now there is hardly a household of which one member does not belong either professionally or as an amateur, to the artistic community. Fifty years ago the two hundred artists who exhibited at the Royal Academy and Water Colour Societies comprised almost every member of the profession; now the list of exhibiting artists extends to nearly five thousand names and it increases by hundreds yearly. (Huish 720)

Societies and galleries together were listed in *The Year's Art* (edited by Huish), complete with an alphabetical list of British artists that by 1909 had doubled in length from the 100 pages of 1888.

Societies sought to distinguish themselves from the Royal Academy by eclectic non-partisanship and open memberships. In 1870 the British Institution applied a universal suffrage method. The Old Watercolour Society in 1881 allowed a varying number of associateships. Membership in the New English Art Club was relatively open, with election possible by majority vote even when the candidate had not submitted a work for consideration. The Society of Lady Artists expanded its membership in 1886, insisted that members be professionals, and charged non-professionals a fee to exhibit. Despite these innovations, however, societies often replicated the Academy's organizational structures and practices, using existing networks of critics, dealers, and the press. They sought Academicians, well-known collectors, and peers as honorary members to attest economic viability and social respectability. The art press promoted societies' liaisons with galleries through free advertising, a controversial practice traditionally provided for the RA; and press critics wrote catalogue introductions for societies' exhibitions.

Societies also provided art education and schools: the New English Art Club taught life drawing classes for men and, separately, women. Societies contributed to a growing international market by inviting foreign artists to show in England and by dominating English sections of exhibitions held abroad: society officers formed the selection committee for the 1908 Franco-British Exhibition in Brussels. Requiring members to produce new works annually, societies tried to stimulate the slack market by promoting scaled-down inexpensive media (watercolors, drawings, small bronzes). Organized to sell art, societies were, in a development telling for our purposes, registered with the Board of Trade. Artists often joined several societies to maximize their market shares. John Lavery joined the RA, Scottish societies, a society for oil painting, and societies in Munich, Paris, Vienna, Brussels, San Luca, Rome, Milan, and Madrid. Whistler, despite his ostensible disdain for societies, had almost as many memberships.

The unique Grosvenor Gallery (1877–90) promoted Aestheticism, yet exhibited prominent Academicians (e.g. Leighton and Poynter). Founded by the wealthy couple Coutts Lindsay and Blanche Rothschild Lindsay, the gallery highlighted works by Burne-Jones and Whistler. Its pictures were spaced far apart in deliberate contrast to the RA's cheek-by-jowl hanging, and a single artist's works were grouped together. The first gallery to be electrically lighted in 1883, the Grosvenor had a private salesroom for year-round display of works priced by the artists. The opening, attended by the Prince and Princess of Wales, was where Ruskin was first affronted by Whistler's Nocturnes. The Grosvenor's attempt to make money with a restaurant infuriated Burne-Jones and two staff who resigned to create a spin-off, the New Gallery (1888–1910). Both galleries were economically useful to a small number of artists, as were the Show Sundays in successful artists' studios attended by the rich.

At the first Grosvenor exhibition in 1877 there were ten women out of 64 invited artists. Over its 14 years, the Grosvenor showed over 1,000 artists, only a quarter of whom were women (a lower ratio than at the RA); and women's works were 17 percent of the total exhibited, most of them moreover "hung in the less prestigious rooms" (Marsh 1997: 47). The second half of the nineteenth century saw an increase in the number of one-woman exhibitions, from three in 1850 to about a hundred in 1914 (Yeldham 115). Some women did well at international exhibitions. Ruskin thought women should learn drawing skills, but, despite his excessive praise of Kate Greenaway, he believed women's art was inferior. Charles Lock Eastlake, RA President and Director of the National Gallery, whose wife Elizabeth Rigby Eastlake was a prominent art critic, promoted women's work and recommended five women to enter the Academy school in 1860; the Academy admitted 13, then stopped admitting them from 1863 to 1868, and then admitted them with restrictions (no life classes). In 1865 1,652 women and 5,249 men were painters or sculptors (Reader 173). The University of London's Slade School of Fine Art (1871) admitted women, who also gained equal overall university status in 1878.

The expansion of societies' membership generally benefited women who became members and later, often many years later, full participants. In 1890 the Royal Watercolour Society, experiencing a membership decline, allowed women to vote and attend meetings, but not to participate in business matters until 1923. Despite the fact that two RA founders were women highly renowned in their lifetimes – painter Angelica Kauffmann and miniaturist Mary Moser – women did not become full Academy members until Laura Knight joined in 1936, and women were barred from the RA schools because life classes were deemed inappropriate. Never more than 25 percent of the RA's student body, women often went abroad to study in Germany or in France's atelier system with master artists. Women submitting work for RA exhibitions often used their initials, not full names. Sisters of artists in the Pre-Raphaelite circle, like Joanna Boyce (sister of George) and Emma Sandys (sister of Frederick), gained entry into closed male circles; although they remained tangential, many women artists were influenced by the Pre-Raphaelites and some were trained by them.

Women's marginalization by the RA meant they were not invited into other societies, which were intent on claiming Academicians as members. The British Institute and the Society of British Artists allowed women to exhibit but reserved membership for men. Both watercolor societies forbade any but members to exhibit. Limited membership meant limited exhibition opportunities. Nevertheless, some women artists became highly successful: to Bodichon, Butler, and Greenaway may be added Louise Jopling, Evelyn De Morgan, Eleanor Fortescue-Brickdale, Henrietta Ward, Kate Bunce, Helen Allingham, Evelyn Pickering, and Henrietta Rae, among others.

Eliza Cook's Journal asserted, "Society has no conventional prejudice against it. A woman may be an artist and a 'lady'" (Cherry 82). George Eliot commented in 1857 to Sara Hennell, upon seeing a work by French animal painter Rosa Bonheur: "What power! This is the way women should assert their rights!" (quoted in Losano 1). But many Victorians felt that professionalism conflicted with acceptable femininity. Earning money clashed not only with professional ideals, but also with acceptable behavior for middle-class women whose work was properly non-remunerative and domestic or philanthropic. Women artists advocated equal right to work, though not always electoral enfranchisement, while their art adhered to conventional subjects: Ward's patriotic genre subjects, Butler's battle scenes, Rae's classical nudes, Bodichon's imperial paintings of Algeria.

Women governed their professional societies according to many of the same principles as men. The Society for Female Artists' founder Harriet Grote argued that art's progress meshed with commerce and promoted art for the mass market (Grote 196–200); after 1859, this society's catalogues included prices to improve sales. Press reviews justified women's professional status on the benefits of labor itself, their contributions to the circulation of goods, and the inherent value of the accumulation of capital: the same arguments, in short, that were made for male artists' contributions to the nation (*English Women's Journal* 1858, 205). The Census in 1841 listed 278 women as artists, while in 1851 the number of women artists rose to 548, in 1861 to 853, and in 1871 to 1,069. Nevertheless, the deck remained stacked against them throughout the century: when in 1898 the RA exhibited 1,474 works by 853 artists, only 126 works were included by only 77 women, fewer than 10 percent (Marsh and Nunn 1989: 27).

Women's educational, ideological, social, and economic difficulties were further complicated by the ways in which gender inflected, and exacerbated, the ambiguity, inconsistency, and suspicion that, as this chapter has shown, haunted Victorian notions about the "artist" and the "professional." The Society of Female Artists in 1857 became the Society of Lady Artists in 1872, and then the Society of Women Artists in 1899. From the biological, to the social, to a classless generic designation, these name changes reflected women's changing professional status and determination to shake associations with amateurism and biological destiny.

See also 1851, 1897; SPECTACLE, PUBLISHING; PARAPETS

REFERENCES

Barrington, E. (1906) *The Life, Letters and Works of Frederic Leighton*, 2 vols. London: George Allen.

Bourdieu, P. (1993) *The Field of Cultural Production*, ed. R. Johnson. Cambridge: Polity Press.

Cherry, D. (1993) *Painting Women: Victorian Women Artists*. London: Routledge.

Codell, J. (1995) "Artists' Professional Societies: Production. Consumption and Aesthetics." In *Towards a Modern Art World*, ed. B. Allen. New Haven: Yale University Press.

Farrar, F. W., and A. Meynell (1893) "William Holman Hunt." *Art Annuals* 1–32.

Freedman, J. (1990) *Professions of Taste: Henry James. British Aestheticism and Commodity Culture*. Stanford: Stanford University Press.

Gillet, P. (1989) *Worlds of Art: Painters in Victorian Society*. New Brunswick: Rutgers University Press.

Grote, H. (1862) *Collected Papers*. London: John Murray.

Hall, S. C. (1883) *Retrospect of a Long Life from 1815 to 1883*, 2 vols. London: Bentley.

Hunt, W. H. (1905) *Pre-Raphaelitism and the Pre-Raphaelite Brotherhood*, 2 vols. London: Macmillan.

Huish, M. (1892) "Whence This Great Multitude of Painters?" *The Nineteenth Century* 32, 720–32.

Larson, M. S. (1977) *The Rise of Professionalism: A Sociological Analysis*. Berkeley: University of California Press.

Little, J. S. (1897) "The Life and Work of William Q. Orchardson, R.A." *Art Annuals* 1–32.

Losano, A. (2008) *The Woman Painter in Victorian Literature*. Columbus: Ohio State University Press.

Marsh, J., and P. G. Nunn (1989) *Women Artists and the Pre-Raphaelite Movement*. London: Virago.

——(1997) *Pre-Raphaelite Women Artists*. Manchester: Manchester City Art Galleries.

Newall, C. (1987) *Victorian Watercolours*. Oxford: Phaidon.

Reader, W. J. (1966) *Professional Men: The Rise of the Professional Classes in Nineteenth-Century England*. New York: Basic Books.

Ruth, J. (2006) *Novel Professions*. Columbus: Ohio State University Press.

Salmon, R. (1997) "Signs of Intimacy: The Literary Celebrity in the 'Age of Interviewing.'" *Victorian Literature and Culture* 25, 159–77.

Thomson, H. B. (1857) *The Choice of a Profession*. London: Chapman and Hall.

Walkley, G. (1994) *Artists' Houses in London. 1764–1914*. Aldershot: Scolar Press.

Yeldham, C. (1984) *Women Artists in Nineteenth-Century France and England*, 2 vols. New York: Garland.

Zimmern, H. (1886) "L. Alma Tadema. Royal Academician. His Life and Work." *The Art Annual* 1–32.

FURTHER READING

Allen, B. (ed.) (1995) *Towards a Modern Art World*. New Haven and London: Yale University Press.

Barker, E., N. Webb, and K. Woods (eds) (1999) *The Changing Status of the Artist*. New Haven and London: Yale University Press and the Open University.

Codell, J. (2012) *The Victorian Artist: Artists' Life Writings in Britain, 1870–1900*. Cambridge: Cambridge University Press.

Corbett, D. P., and L. Perry (eds) (2000) *English Art 1860–1914: Modern Artists and Identity*. Manchester: Manchester University Press.

Dakers, C. (1999) *The Holland Park Circle: Artists and Victorian Society*. New Haven and London: Yale University Press.

Fletcher, P., and A. Helmreich (eds) (2013) *The Rise of the Modern Art Market in London, 1850–1939*. Manchester: Manchester University Press.

Kriz, K. D. (1997) *The Idea of the English Landscape Painter: Genius as Alibi in the Early Nineteenth Century*. New Haven and London: Yale University Press.

Macleod, D. S. (1996) *Art and the Victorian Middle Class: Money and the Making of Cultural Identity*. Cambridge: Cambridge University Press.

Orr, C. C. (ed.) (1995) *Women in the Victorian Art World*. Manchester: Manchester University Press.

Smith, G. (1998) *The Business of Watercolour*. Aldershot: Scolar Press.

20

Spectacle

Joss Marsh

Victoria's reign was the era not only, as educational catchphrase had it, of "learning by looking," but also of *living* through looking. The nineteenth century saw an explosion in visual technologies: the kaleidoscope (1815), the daguerreotype and the photograph (1826/1835), the stereoscope (1849), the cinema (1895), besides the optical toys and physiological experiments that preceded it (like the thaumatrope, zoetrope, and "wheel of life"), the resurgent magic lantern, and the techniques of photomechanical reproduction that saturated the world in images from the 1880s. And that explosion was underpinned by what Jonathan Crary has called the philosophical "reorganization" of human vision between about 1810 and 1840. The nineteenth-century break with classical models – Renaissance perspective, "objective" geometrical optics – signaled the birth of a new type of "subjective observer," enmeshed in a visual environment that became more and more abstract as the century lengthened. As such, he was "both a product of and at the same time constitutive of modernity in the nineteenth century" (Crary 9).

The "reorganization" Crary charts found persistent expression in the new language and imagery of literature, a trait especially remarkable in the works of Dickens, but noticeable even in run-of-the-mill publications like an 1871 shilling guide to *The Educational Places of Amusement in London*. Here, we read, Covent Garden market must be viewed "very early on Saturday morning" to be seen "as a *spectacle*" (xii); the British Library is a "phantasmagoria of the human mind" (22); the South Kensington Museum is "a beautiful kaleidoscope" (26); the Crystal Palace at Sydenham offers not only (courtesy of casts and reproductions) the greatest collections of Art, Nature, and Science but "fairy scene[s]" in the shrubberies (93) and an unrivaled "panorama" from

A New Companion to Victorian Literature and Culture, First Edition. Edited by Herbert F. Tucker.
© 2014 John Wiley & Sons, Ltd. Published 2014 by John Wiley & Sons, Ltd.

the upper terrace (89); while London demands at all times of all visitors that they keep open their "greedy eyes" (44). Light, vision, movement, and virtuality were as much keynotes of Victorian spectacle and exhibition as were the profit motive of capitalistic enterprise and the educative impulse of expanding democracy. Their history is also a history of the present.

Victorian "show business" centered firmly in London, feeding the expanding appetite of an urban population that swelled from one to three million between 1801 and 1861. "Exhibitions then," Richard Altick records in his indispensable *Shows of London*, "were as much of an institution as the theater" (221); in any "moderate" year, metropolitan sightseers alone spent £4 million annually (420). Even the Duke of Wellington was an inveterate showgoer, who enjoyed reenactments of the Battle of Waterloo in 1827 and 1849, and left orders with Madame Tussaud's in 1835 to update him on new additions to her famed waxwork Chamber of Horrors. The eight railway lines opened between 1836 and 1848 made it possible for foreigners and country visitors, too, to "see the lions" – not just the ancient menagerie at the Tower of London, as originally meant, but all the sights of the town. (The animals moved to Regent's Park Zoo in 1834.) *En route*, from the train windows, the new visitors enjoyed nineteenth-century observers' first experience of moving pictures.

In the year Victoria came to the throne, until some time after the Great Exhibition of 1851, the bulk of London's attractions were the same that had charmed pennies from pockets for centuries. Freaks, fat boys, bearded and fireproof ladies, dwarves (live and embalmed), "learned" pigs, and exotic creatures: early Victorians suffered like their fairgoing ancestors from what *Punch* caricatured as "Deformito-mania" (September 4, 1847: 90). They wondered at the same clockwork inventions, though by the 1840s these included a speaking automaton – imaginatively recalled by Charlotte Brontë in *Jane Eyre* (1847, chs 19 and 23) and George Eliot in *Middlemarch* (1872, ch. 32) – and the "Eureka" machine, which could turn out 60 Latin hexameters an hour. Doing the rounds of sights with his old nurse Pegotty in Dickens's novel of 1849–50 (ch. 33), David Copperfield visits some long-gone "perspiring Wax-work, in Fleet Street"; "Miss Linwood's Exhibition" at Leicester Square, a "Mausoleum" of needlework copies of Old Master paintings "favorable to repentance," which drew disconsolate crowds for nearly 40 years to 1846; the Norman Tower, which housed the royal armory (hence Wellington's fiat that no more than a hundred visitors be allowed in at any one time); and St Paul's Cathedral, reduced to a "two-penny show" by the notorious functionaries who controlled admission and – as at Westminster Abbey – charged extra fees for tombs, side-chapels, Nelson's remains, and all other exploitable features (the total could easily reach to five shillings).

Dickens's earliest work, *Sketches by "Boz"* (1836), added to the list of attractions such pleasure-grounds as venerable Vauxhall Gardens, London's premier *al fresco* entertainment, though distinctly flyblown in daylight. It was here that balloons were spectacularly launched in the 1830s, and that Wellington relived his Waterloo triumph. Surrey Gardens, which had a lake, specialized in the reconstruction of naval battles and "Pictorial Typoramas" – enormous modeled canvas "views" – of Vesuvius

(1837–8), the Great Fire of London (1844), etc., accompanied by fireworks at 9:30 p.m. sharp. In the later 1840s, concerts by Jullien's "monster" orchestra brought Surrey its greatest fame. Cremorne Gardens, to the north, were a favorite spot for dancing and assignations. Thomas Carlyle was one of the near Chelsea neighbors who complained about the noise. They were satisfied when Cremorne finally closed in 1878, 20 years after Vauxhall was sold for building lots. The age of the pleasure-ground was over: respectable public parks, like the Embankment Gardens (laid out in the 1850s), were the new order of the day.

For sheer staying power, the most successful of London's show-places throughout the century was Egyptian Hall, Piccadilly, an exotic architectural fantasy adorned with fake hieroglyphics. Here, from 1812, were miscellaneously shown the Natural History collection of its founder, William Bullock (1812), the first in England displayed in realistic postures and "habitat groups"; the ground-breaking Egyptian exhibition (1821) of the indomitable ex-fairground strongman Giovanni Battista Belzoni, discoverer of Abu Simbel, centered on a full-scale recreation of Seti's Tomb, dimly lamp-lit and low-ceilinged (to evoke the discoverer's first sensations), and expertly "dressed" (like a film set) with ancient artifacts; an artfully enlarged mastodon skeleton billed as the "Missouri Leviathan" (1839); George Catlin's paintings of Native American life, which cashed in on a vogue for travel writing in 1840, and were re-exhibited with a troupe of "Ojibbeway" Indians hijacked from Manchester in 1843, the year the Ethnological Society was founded; various electro-biological displays; and a group of South African Bushmen, who performed "the very kind of routine that monkeys sometimes were taught" in 1845 (Altick 280), with other "Kaffir," "Aztec," and aboriginal manifestations of the anxious interest in the human family that ushered in Darwin's evolutionary revelations.

Higher-class premises, like the Cosmorama Rooms in Regent Street, typified early Victorian practice by alternating between sacred and profane subject matter, and between the exhibition of single rare objects and discrete collections: Charlemagne's so-called manuscript Bible, shown in 1836, for example, or a display of disguises, manacles, and other criminal bric-a-brac timed to publicize the 1845 publication of memoirs by the real-life model for the all-seeing hero of nineteenth-century detective fiction, the former chief of the French Sureté, Eugène-François Vidocq. Complex models of foreign cities were popular through the century: Jude Fawley leans deep in study over a miniature Jerusalem in Hardy's last novel, *Jude the Obscure* (1895), exactly as pious showgoers examined Brunetti's 100-square-foot model of the Holy City in 1847. Near the bottom end of the social scale were shabby wonder-houses like Pollard's Museum in lower-class Lambeth. Beneath were the pavement exhibitors who showed Punch and Judy, peepshows, trained animals, telescopes, and mechanical figures, of whom Henry Mayhew's *London Labour and the London Poor* (1849–62) preserves intimate record.

Spectacle both moved off the streets and took to the road under Victoria. In London, as the law-and-order lobby gained ground, "rude and demoralizing amusements" and the "brutal exhibitions of cock-fights and bull-baiting" were forced to give ground

(*Educational Places* 32). Bartholomew Fair, where Wombwell's Menagerie and Richardson's Theatre once ruled the roost over giants, jugglers, fire-eaters, games of chance, infant prodigies, beer shops, and penny shows, was put down in 1840; Dickens's wonder-packed *Old Curiosity Shop* (1841) implicitly laments its passing. There was compensation, of course: London's resplendent shop and (later) department store windows – plate-glassed from the 1870s – were a world-famous show, though they could only be considered "free" – like city markets, sandwich men, billboards, or omnibus advertisements – if one discounted the hidden costs of capitalist spectacle. "Puffery" was standard practice: the seven-foot-high, perambulating Hat by which the London Hatter of Carlyle's *Past and Present* (1843) hopes commercially to be "saved" was its "topmost point as yet" (book 3, ch. 1); while the exhibits at mid-Victorian shows were often either ticketed for sale or displayed with an eye to attracting support for business or missionary ventures.

Astley's pioneer circus company stayed put in its London "Amphitheatre of the Equestrian Arts" through the century. But elsewhere the first great mass entertainment to which it gave birth in the 1770s packed its Big Top and spangled "properties" into wagons to tour the provinces. Eight well-known troupes were on the road in the 1830s; the 30 years from 1870 to the end of the century were the traveling circus's golden era. It was "wonder" that made circus "wander," suggests a linguistic slippage in Dickens's 1854 *Hard Times* (ch. 8), a novel that pits its spontaneous and "fanciful" joy against the mechanized grind of industrial "Coketown"; the self-styled "King" of the tenting circus, "Lord" George Sanger, called his Ring a "magic circle." But the "open road" was often "strewn with thorns" (Sanger 1). When his infant son dropped dead of convulsions, in the winter before Dickens wrote, Sanger had to parade through Stamford, Lincolnshire, smiling, with the corpse in the back of a van, to drum up the money to bury him. Such private hardships, like the crippling dangers of high wire, trapeze, and (in late century, when circus was mechanized) man-hurling cannon were no less a fact of its life than the invisible labor that enabled the circus illusion of effortless play to which hard-working Victorians responded rapturously.

The circus was unusual among Victorian spectacles in *really* delivering wonder. Others advertised their modernity in presenting a simulacrum. In 1794 a strange new building had risen above Leicester Square. Entering from the street after paying a shilling, spectators moved through a darkened passage to the center of the huge circular edifice, 90 feet in diameter. Inside, they emerged on a platform 30 feet wide, surrounded on all sides by a breathtaking view: London seen from the superb vantage point of Albion's Mills, on the south side of the river. The experience was no trick of mesmerism or magic carpet, but the effect of the first "panorama," a giant painted representation painstakingly constructed, in superb detail, that lived up to its ancient Greek name of an "all-embracing," 360-degree view. The brainchild of an Edinburgh portraitist called Robert Barker, the panorama was a logical fulfillment of *trompe l'oeil* traditions extending back to Roman times. What convinced the eye that what it gazed on was real was Barker's realization that, to offset the effects of circularity, what appears straight in nature must be curved in panoramic reproduction, and the spectator kept at a strict optimum distance from the image. Precluded by barriers and enclosures from seeing above, behind, or around the canvas, unaware (by design) even of the light-source that illuminated it, the spectator did not merely look at but stood within the illusion.

Handed down from Barker to his son and their partner Robert Burford, London's first panorama flourished until mid-century, giving character to the sometimes seedy Square as London's show business center. Pendennis takes in the view, in Thackeray's novel of 1848–50, without seeing his way any clearer to romance; David Copperfield is shown its splendor by Steerforth in Dickens's competing text of 1849–50, without seeing through his false friend, as if to extend the visual pun. The panorama was *the* early Victorian London show, a quintessentially urban art. Before cheap trams, the Underground, and workmen's railway fares brought green space and the grand amenities of suburban pleasure-sites within reach of city crowds in the second half of the century, the panorama offered virtual escape into a lost world of space, long vistas, and clear air. Uplifted by its bird's-eye view, like Dickens suspended above the city in the basket of a balloon in George Cruikshank's frontispiece to *Sketches by "Boz"*, spectators gained temporary visual power over the enveloping brick-and-mortar labyrinth in which they spent their lives.

That sense of vicarious experience was exaggerated by the Leicester Square panorama's greatest rival, the Colosseum near Regent's Park, erected in 1824. In the huge rotunda, 112 feet high, was installed the fruit of several years' recording of the burgeoning metropolis from atop St Paul's dome, 2,000 meticulous sketches by a Yorkshire land surveyor called Thomas Hornor. Transferred to canvas by a painter with an equal head for heights, Hornor's project offered a facsimile experience of the view without climbing hundreds of stairs or finding it obliterated by smog. To complete the illusion, visitors even stood on a replica of the cathedral's real viewing platform, reached by the first passenger elevator in London, and looked out at the spectacle through a three-dimensional mock-up of the scaffolding in place while Hornor had sketched. Instinctively, they drew back from the edge; some claimed they saw figures move across the canvas, or heard ghostly sounds of life ascending from the painted streets.

The Colosseum management invested (necessarily, given the cost) in very few standing shows, and ultimately were bankrupted. But as the great building's fortunes declined, a new attraction sprang up beside it in 1848: the Cyclorama, where four times a day customers could experience the sensational sights *and* sounds of the Lisbon earthquake of 1755 : "Never," said one Victorian man-about-town, "was better value in fright given for the money" (Edmund Yates, in Altick 158). Meanwhile, since the anxious days of the Napoleonic Wars, which made bodily touristic travel impossible, the original panorama and its other rivals had varied the scenes to which they transported spectators in illusive "reality": Dublin, Paris, Berlin, Rome, and (three times at Leicester Square) Constantinople, each city more glamorized by distance than the last. Before the railway brought Mont Blanc and other sublimities within reach, the panorama offered ordinary people a virtual "grand tour." "Moving panoramas," first introduced on the pantomime stage in the 1810s, took the illusion still further. In the 1830s vertical ones even made vicarious balloon flight possible. In 1848 the most popular show in town was New Yorker John Banvard's "monster" three-mile narrated excursion up the Mississippi, during which bluffs, prairies, cabins, wigwams, plantations, levees, and steamboats scrolled past the astonished spectator. Opening at Easter 1850, "The Overland Route to India" was seen by a quarter of a million people.

Serious Victorians took the panorama seriously, buying sixpenny guides to individual shows, and flocking in the 1840s to representations of the Holy Land: here was a spectacle that Evangelical scruple allowed one to view. The images' size played to what scholars call nineteenth-century art's "cult of immensity"; their superabundant detail may have helped create later taste for the photographic meticulousness and bold coloration of Pre-Raphaelite painting. Moreover, like the historical paintings of the period – Sir George Hayter's 170-square-foot picture of the House of Commons, for example (exhibited 1843) – the panoramas were intended to picture history as it was made. Rebellious Delhi and Lucknow, for example, were spectacularized for patriotic view in 1857–8 with nearly a newsreel's dispatch. However, just as their topographical function declined with developments in transportation, so the panoramas' topical role was eroded in mid-century by the technology that made possible pictorial papers like the *Illustrated London News* (founded 1842), though their sheer size still spoke to the nation's sense of imperial grandeur, and stylish comic commentary made a hit of Albert Smith's *The Ascent of Mont Blanc*, shown 2,000 times between 1852 and 1858.

Since panoramas depended for illumination on sunlight from concealed skylights, their hours of operation were limited to daytime, and strictly curtailed in foggy winters. Light was the greatest problem and desideratum of nineteenth-century representation as showmen conceived it. From the 1850s panoramic spectacle lost its status as the apogee of realism to the photograph or "sun picture," in which – as if by autogenesis – the world traced its own physical image by that very medium of light alone. Exploiting first the single-plate process patented by the Frenchman Daguerre, then the negative–positive technique discovered by England's Fox Talbot in 1835, photographic studios proliferated across London. The same promise of the real was the key to the final "domestication" of panoramic impulse by the portable home stereoscope of the 1860s (Altick 233). Simultaneously viewed, its left- and right-eye photographic images produced a compelling illusion of three-dimensionality.

Earlier Victorians paid to stare at a different spectacle that Daguerre sent to London in 1823: the diorama, a screen-like picture on canvas or lawn, painted in a combination of opaque and translucent paints, roughly 70 by 45 feet, granted dynamic brilliance and the dramatic illusion of depth by the influx of sunlight controlled through a series of skylights and windows in a specially designed and darkened auditorium. The interior of a cathedral was thus seen alternately bathed in light and shadowed by clouds; a storm brewed above the Swiss Alps. In the 1830s novel "trans-formation" effects – achieved by painting both sides of the screen, as in late eighteenth-century pantomime design – allowed views before and after an avalanche, or before and after the 1823 fire at Rome's St Paul basilica. As Altick remarks, it is hard to judge how far the diorama's play of light may have impacted the practice of painting, as did Turner's revolutionary handling of light (195). For writers it seemed to promise the redemption of history. Browning's historical epic *Sordello* (1840) gets underway by staging itself as a diorama project. "The memory," Eliot notes in *Middle-march*, "shifts its scenery like a diorama" (ch. 53): elsewhere, photography, prisms, the panorama, and lantern "images" all further her investigation of consciousness, psychol-ogy, and desire.

The diorama's appeal faded in mid-century, but its persistent rival, the magic lantern, survived and triumphed. Invented circa 1660, that new optical wonder had dwindled since to a street-show or seasonal entertainment, the province of itinerant showmen like the Savoyard Jos Leverge, who performed at the house of the popular antiquarian William Hone, on Twelfth Night 1818. His show had not changed for years, Leverge told Hone, since he had only "this one set of glasses" – two Bible scenes, and a much-circulated slide called "Pull Devil, Pull Baker," which delivered a short-changing baker into the jaws of hell (Robinson et al. 169). From the 1790s to the 1820s, a lantern-show of more notorious popularity held spectral sway in Britain: the "phantasmagoria" of Étienne-Gaspard Robertson and his rivals, devised (appropriately enough) in the Revolutionary 1790s. Projected invisibly, from behind a translucent screen, in disorienting darkness, with morbid patter and sound effects, it was the disreputable ancestor of the horror movie and monster show, and provided inspiration to Mary Shelley, Thomas Carlyle, Lewis Carroll, Robert Louis Stevenson, and many others. But under Victoria, newly powered by oxyhydrogen "limelight" (first used in lighthouses), and possessed from circa 1825 of a new optical phenomenon – "dissolv-ing views," which, courtesy of multiple or bi-lens lanterns and perfectly-registered images, allowed travel through space and time – the lantern became the spectacle of the century. By its means Temperance crusaders fought back the "demon drink," mis-sionaries convinced "natives" of the "reality" of Christ, scientists illuminated the secrets of nature, showmen devised grand "optical pantomimes" and multi-media "extravaganzas," ordinary men and women took virtual tours of the world, and parents convinced children of the wonders of fairyland. During its heyday in Britain, there was at least one lantern in every public institution, and a smaller-scale, sometimes "toy" lantern in almost every middle-class household, a forerunner of the modern spectacularization of domestic space. Some 1,000 professional lanternists lectured and performed daily in theatres, schools, scientific and working-men's institutions, museums, church halls, and elsewhere. The direct ancestor of cinema, the lantern competed with it until well into the silent era – even anticipating the advent of "moving" pictures, the ultimate light show and illusion of life, through ingenious mechanical slides (devised, for example, to mimic the movement of the heavens) and "Life Model" slide series, ancestors of narrative film, in which models were posed against real-life or painted backgrounds, to body out tales of salvation or stories from Dickens and his late-Victorian multi-media-manipulating descendant, the celebrity journalist, playwright, and balladeer George R. Sims.

Light, perspective, and optical pleasure were keynotes of the greatest exhibition of the nineteenth century, symbolically dividing the age of show and spectacles from the age of exhibition and public museums. The Great Exhibition of the Works of Industry of All Nations was held in London's central Hyde Park from May to October 1851. It had had a long genesis. Exhibitions of "arts and manufactures" had been held in Leeds, Sheffield, and Liverpool in the late 1830s and early 1840s, inspired by Mechanics' Institutes and artisans' schools of design. Abroad, the earliest industrial exhibition was held in a revolutionary "Temple of Industry" at the Paris Louvre in 1798. At home, Prince Albert and Henry Cole laid the last groundwork for a *popular* as well as *international* exhibition with an Exhibition of Ancient and Medieval Art in 1850. The Great Exhibition these two brought to fruition took in machinery and scientific instruments; raw and processed minerals and materials; architectural and engineering models; sculpture, mosaic, and musical instruments; "Indian curiosities" and other imperial products. Thirty-four nations participated, grouped together in the East Wing, while Britain alone dominated the West.

The Exhibition show-cased the machine as wonder: a "stupendous Locomotive Engine," for example, "capable of driving a train of 120 tons gross at an average speed of 60 miles an hour" (Timbs 125). It presented the product as power fantasy: "Not only has the surface of the earth been made to minister to the wants . . . of man," especially Englishman, rhapsodized the *Illustrated Exhibitor*, "but the solid contents of the globe itself have been formed into one vast laboratory, wherein the Great Master Mind has prepared ready to the hands of his pupils, the materials of dominion" (*A Tribute*). It was "the most lavish of shows, the apotheosis of the lofty ideal of 'rational entertainment'" (Altick 456). It whetted public appetite for systematic collection and display. It had numerous offspring, in the great expositions and World's Fairs that punctuated its century and the next across Europe, America, and the colonies. (Later London exhibitions were marred by commercialism and took up overtly national themes, like "Greater Britain" in 1899.)

Despite contrary claims (by Dickens, for example), the Exhibition did not simply sate public desire for mechanical spectacle and leave the imagination untouched. Its great success depended on the extraordinary design of the great greenhouse-like iron-and-glass building in which it was housed, erected in only four months by an army of London workmen, and inspired by study of the ribbed leaf formations of the giant African *Victoria regia* lily. Cruciform like a church in design, but three times as long as St Paul's Cathedral, covering fully 19 acres of ground, gardener Joseph Paxton's "Crystal Palace" brought all classes together in an elevating environment of space and light. The Exhibition it housed became a "Diorama of the Peaceful Arts," declared Charles Babbage, inventor of the calculating machine.

"The glass," however, as Wellington warned, "[was] very thin" (Altick 457). London's chief commissioner got a thousand extra men to police the crystal walls, while public figures like Dickens, Thackeray, Mill, and Forster, editor of the liberal *Examiner*, joined a Central Working Classes Committee to consider how to control attendance. Others feared catastrophic accidents, disease, and famine brought on by crowds; a few thought the Palace a second Tower of Babel (Allwood 18). But all precautions were proved unnecessary. In the six months it stood open, over six million people crowded into the Exhibition, over two-thirds of them from the provinces, and a huge number on cheap shilling days, without a single serious incident. The bogey of the insurgent crowd that had haunted the Victorian imagination was finally laid to rest; the "Workers" to whom the Exhibition was formally dedicated had shown themselves fit inhabitants of "the World's Hive." Spectacle had come into its own as a means of social control.

The Exhibition of 1851 triggered a Victorian museum explosion that had been a long time coming. Sir Hans Sloane had bequeathed his extensive collections, the core of the British Museum, to the nation in 1752. But access to this treasure-house was thwarted by dilapidated premises, incrementally rebuilt 1823–52 and (until 1997) part-devoted to library purposes. There were no scientists on the board of trustees, although the museum housed the nation's greatest natural history collections as well as antiquities (until mid-century, almost exclusively Greek and Roman remains). In the library there was no up-to-date catalogue, and overcrowded reading rooms brought on "museum headache" and "museum fever."

From the public's point of view, however, the worst problem was the museum's peremptory elitist policies. It took commoner William Hone 18 months to obtain access to the manuscripts on which in 1823 he founded the pioneer study of medieval mystery plays, *Ancient Mysteries Described* (where he incidentally recorded the conversation with the itinerant lanternist Jos Leverge, mentioned above). "Do you not think that one object of the Museum is to improve the vulgar class?" director Sir Henry Ellis was asked during a public inquiry in 1835. "I think the mere gazing at our curiosities is not one of the greatest objects of the Museum," he replied, in a snobbish riposte to the very topic of this chapter. Besides: "People of a higher grade would hardly wish to come to the Museum at the same time with sailors from the dock-yards and girls whom they might bring with them" (Altick 444–5).

Yet – again – when the British Museum was first opened during a public holiday, on Easter Monday 1837, and packed with 23,000 persons, not one breach of its peace occurred. Attendance leapt from 81,228 in 1827–8 to 897,985 twenty years later. Enlightened leadership and better funding expanded book collections from 150,000 volumes in 1827 to 520,000 in 1856 and over a million by 1871; the number of readers leaped to 188,266 by 1857; electric lights saved their eyes after 1878. Belatedly, the state had entered into competition with commercial show-business for the "leisure-time custom of the multitude" (Altick 454), recognizing the truism expounded by *Blackwood's Magazine* that museums "make the libraries of those who have no money to expend on books, and are the travels of those that have no time to bestow on travel," instilling knowledge "drop by drop, through the eye into the mind" (April

1842, 419). Gazing at its curiosities might, *pace* Ellis, minister to a very great object indeed.

Early Victorian museums were hybrid operations: spectacular, commercial, and educational. They recalled the extraordinary "jumble" Tennyson describes in the opening lines of *The Princess* (1847): costly curios, fossil ammonites, and Gothic fragments in the hall, model steamers and telegraphs in the yard, while above the "strange" spectacle a "maiden Aunt" takes it for "text," to "preach . . . / An universal culture for the crowd" (ll. 17, 107–9). At the Royal Institution, from 1801 through the 1880s, the inventor–educators Humphry Davy, Michael Faraday, and John Tyndall demonstrated their skills as popular showmen as well as advocates for science to society's upper 10,000. Other profit-minded or altruistic public men made the benefits of science visibly tangible for the masses. As much as *Chambers's Edinburgh Journal* or the utilitarian *Penny Magazine* (one of numerous periodical publications to take title and terms of reference from commercial spectacular culture: "repository," "bazaar," "magazine"), the Royal Polytechnic Institution on Regent's Street, founded in 1838, typified the popular "March of Mind." Here lectures explained the "atmospheric" or vacuum-driven railway, gun-cotton (cellulose nitrate) used for blasting, thunderstorms, and the potato blight that reduced Ireland to famine in 1845. A pneumatic telegraph, models of the ear and eye, brick- and pin-making machines, a "hydrostatic" bed, steam-engine designs, and two astronomical clocks were exhibited and demonstrated. From 1841, on the roof, as at the rival Adelaide Gallery (founded 1832), was a photographic studio. But the most famous attraction was a three-ton cast-iron diving bell in a deep-water tank, in which visitors who paid an extra shilling could be submerged. This topped even the Adelaide's steam-powered machine gun, discharged every hour, and its oxyhydrogen microscope-lantern displays of the thousands of microbes infesting a single drop of Thames water – the still-unsuspected cause of London's repeated typhoid and cholera outbreaks.

The Crystal Palace, moved to the suburb of Sydenham, enlarged, and re-erected in 1854, partook of the general hybridity. Ten of its "courts" offered the history of architectural styles, from Egypt to the Middle Ages, while others housed machinery in motion, a picture gallery, and scientific collections. In the grounds a fake Ichthyosaur disported with a fake Megalosaurus, next to "the largest geological model in the world." Hybridity could decline all too easily into mere novelty: the Palace became a stage to the tightrope-walker Blondin in the sensation-seeking 1860s, dwindling eventually into a giant hall of variety entertainment; the short-lived Royal Panopticon became the sinful Alhambra Music Hall in 1858. The Polytechnic, however, resolutely confirmed the marriage of Science and Art, even when mounting the lantern-driven "spectral optical illusions" of the popular lecturer "Professor" Pepper, "Chromatrope" displays (kaleidoscopic magic lantern light shows), and "grand optical pantomimes" powered by giant lanterns.

The greatest legacy of the Great Exhibition thus eventually proved not the physical building, but its clear profit of £186,000. This was the seed from which grew the great cluster of public museums that is modern-day South Kensington: the Museum of Practical Geology, opened two evenings a week from its commencement in 1851, and free on Saturdays; the later Natural History Museum, to which the British Museum's ill-kept and jumbled collections moved in 1881; and the South Kensington Museum, specializing in the ornamental and fine arts, first opened in 1852 as the "Museum of Manufactures," and later rebuilt as the Victoria and Albert Museum (begun 1899, opened 1908). Radical, utilitarian, and populist, the original institutions were children of the same political imperative that passed Forster's universal Education Act of 1870. Food exhibits gave workers practical lessons in health and housekeeping; new exhibition designs moved them through the halls in a linear fashion, as if to reinforce the institutions' belief in historical and evolutionary progress (Bennett 181), while the perusal of new rows of transparent cases also encouraged them to examine each other's behavior as well as the objects displayed (53–5); the museum became self-teaching, open to all. Between 1857 and 1883 the proto-V&A accommodated over 15 million visitors. The South Kensington institutions concluded, however – like the Great Exhibition itself – in putting Britain's power and riches on display; with the passing of the years their first projectors, like Henry Cole, resented their gathering emphasis on fine art and expensive purchase. Inexorably, though slowly, other collections scattered across the capital were consolidated: the Royal United Service Institution's, for example, was eventually absorbed into the Imperial War Museum. The laying out of the Kensington complex spurred expansion, too, of museums for the provinces, where legislation of 1845, 1850, and 1855 already set aside a small tax for the purpose. In 1860 there were 50 significant provincial museums; in 1900 there were 200. In the matter of art exhibition, however, Manchester had set an example, mounting the nation's first wide-ranging loan exhibition in 1857.

Public taste for art was both untutored and unsatisfied in the earlier years of Victoria's reign: London was the last great European capital, trailing Paris by 30 years, to build a national collection, funded by government and directed to public use. In the home, Britons slaked their thirst on engraved reproductions of inaccessible masterworks; in town, they patronized grotesqueries like an exhibition of "flowers" made entirely from fishbones. The painter Benjamin Haydon, having spent 42 years – as he announced in an extraordinary *Times* advertisement of 1846 – attempting to "elevate" the public taste in works like *The Raising of Lazarus* and *The Burning of Rome*, shot himself when the famous American midget Tom Thumb outsold him at Egyptian Hall by £600 to £5 13s 6d (Altick 414).

Like museums, early Victorian galleries were exclusive institutions. A very few noblemen's private collections were thrown open on select days, though never at times when working people could get to see them. Sabbatarianism kept both museums and galleries holy until 1896; Sunday opening was rejected by 376 votes to 48 in the House of Commons in 1856. In between, Sunday opening hours for public houses were extended to 1–3 p.m. and 5–11 p.m., giving fuel to the fears of institutions like the Royal Academy that cultural enfranchisement would irrevocably breach that "propriety" ensured by its one-shilling entrance fee. The National Gallery (opened 1824) did away with the fee, but repeatedly outgrew its premises until it was relocated at Trafalgar Square in 1839, and secured full control of its purpose-built buildings some time later. Attendance quadrupled from 127,000 in the 1820s to half a million in 1840, though some of the attendees may well have used the gallery as an indoor picnic spot and refuge from rain. By mid-century, public access to aesthetic experience finally answered to the democratization of subject matter exemplified by the crowded and spectacular genre paintings of W. P. Frith, like *Derby Day* (1858) and *The Railway Station* (1862), and presaged in the street scenes of eighteenth-century artists like Hogarth, whose bequest of paintings formed a core part of the Academy's collection.

Thus even art – like antiquities, like scientific wonder – could serve to quiet a working population that resented its lack of access to power from the Great Reform Act of 1832 through the Third Reform Act of 1884: this was the "modern museum idea" (George Brown Goode, quoted in Bennett 20). Paintings, concluded the author of *The Educational Places of Amusement in London* in 1871, were "silent monitors" of those who beheld them (37). *Silent monitors*: the phrase is a summary of the relationship Crary argues between the "panoptical" Benthamite surveillance that redesigned the nineteenth-century workshop, asylum, and prison as places where one was controlled by one's own visibility, and the spectacle of streets, shops, railways, parks and gardens, museums and show-places. "Looking" was not to be divorced from "being looked at," and both contributed to the "disciplining" of the Victorian subject (Crary 18, citing Foucault). But while, in the long view of political history, uplifting the people might also have meant keeping them down, on the day-to-day level of lived experience it also brought millions aesthetic pleasure, empowering knowledge, temporary release from toil, and the vision of worlds unseen.

See also 1851; ARTISTIC, COMMERCIAL; DRAMA; PARAPETS, SHORE

REFERENCES

Allwood, J. (1977) *The Great Exhibitions*. London: Studio Vista.

Altick, R. (1978) *The Shows of London*. Cambridge MA: Harvard University Press.

Bennett, T. (1995) *The Birth of the Museum: History, Theory, Politics*. London and New York: Routledge.

Crary, J. (1990) *Techniques of the Observer: On Vision and Modernity in the Nineteenth Century*. Cambridge MA: MIT Press.

The Educational Places of Amusement in London (1871) London: James Hogg.

Robinson, D., S. Herbert, and R. Crangle (eds) (2001) *The Encyclopaedia of the Magic Lantern*. London: Magic Lantern Society.

Sanger, G. (1926) *Seventy Years a Showman*. New York: Dutton.

Timbs, J. (1851) *The Year-Book of Facts in the Great Exhibition of 1851*. London: David Bogue.

A Tribute to the World's Industrial Jubilee (1851). Special issue of *The Illustrated Exhibitor*.

FURTHER READING

Assael, B. (2005) *The Circus and Victorian Society*. Charlottesville: University of Virginia Press.

Bailey, P. (1978) *Leisure and Class in Victorian England: Rational Recreation and the Contest for Control, 1830–1885*. London: Routledge and Kegan Paul.

Beard, M., et al. (1852) *Tallis's History and Description of the Crystal Palace, and the Exhibition of the World's Industry in 1851*. London: Tallis.

Buzard, J., J. W. Childers, and E. Gillooly (eds) (2007) *Victorian Prism: Refractions of the Crystal Palace*. Charlottesville: University of Virginia Press.

Cocks, A. S. (1980) *The Victoria and Albert Museum: The Making of the Collection*. London: Windward.

Durbach, N. (2010) *Spectacle of Deformity*. Berkeley: University of California Press.

Flint, K. (2000) *The Victorians and the Visual Imagination*. Cambridge: Cambridge University Press.

Gernsheim, H., and A. Gernsheim (1968) *L. J. M. Daguerre: The History of the Diorama and the Daguerreotype*. New York: Dover.

Greenhalgh, P. (1988) *Ephemeral Vistas: The Expositions Universelles, Great Exhibitions and World's Fairs, 1851–1939*. Manchester: Manchester University Press.

Horton, S. (1995) "Were They Having Fun Yet? Victorian Optical Gadgetry, Modernist Selves." In *Victorian Literature and the Victorian Visual Imagination*, ed. C. T. Christ and J. Jordan. Berkeley: University of California Press.

Malley, S. (2012) *From Archaeology to Spectacle in Victorian Britain: The Case of Assyria, 1845–1854*. Farnharm: Ashgate.

Miller, E. (1973) *That Noble Cabinet: A History of the British Museum*. London: Deutsch.

Otter, C. (2008) *The Victorian Eye: A Political History of Light and Vision in Britain, 1800–1910*. Chicago: University of Chicago Press.

Qureshi, S. (2011) *Peoples on Parade: Exhibitions, Empire, and Anthropology in Nineteenth Century Britain*. Chicago: University of Chicago Press.

Ritchie, J. E. (1858) *The Night Side of London*, 2nd edn. London: William Tweedie.

Sala, G.A. (1971) [1858] *Twice Round the Clock, Or, the Hours of the Day and Night in London*. Leicester: University of Leicester Press.

Toulmin, V., and S. Popple (eds) (2000) *Visual Delights*. Trowbridge: Flicks Books.

——(2005) *Visual Delights Two: Exhibition and Reception*. Bloomington: Indiana University Press.

21
Publishing

Richard D. Altick and James Mussell

Victorian publishers were the means by which two of the period's most powerful forces, entrepreneurial capitalism and technological advance, left their imprint on the form and content of literature. They were, as their predecessors the bookseller–printers had been, the indispensable middlemen between authors and readers. But in Victorian years the familiar three-party relationship, scarcely changed since Elizabethan times, grew more complicated; and the cash–payment nexus, as Carlyle called it, was more crucial in determining the quantity and quality of what the printer, another essential partner in the transaction, converted from manuscript into print. Publishers had to size up their authors' wares and anticipate what might be made from them once they were shaped and crafted into a different form for a complex and competitive marketplace. As the market for print increased over the century, it was complicated by the intersection of emerging mass readership with a proliferation of niche audiences. Publishers occupied a precarious balance point, as both purchasers of texts in their raw form and canny readers of the shifting marketplace itself.

The printed word was, more than ever, a commodity. Near the end of the century, in George Gissing's novel *New Grub Street* (1891), the leading male characters – three men seeking, with various degrees of desperation, to make a living by their pens – repeatedly speak of markets and trade: "Literature nowadays is a trade. Putting aside men of genius, who may succeed by mere cosmic force, your successful man of letters is your skilful tradesman" who turns out "marketable stuff" (8). Romantic notions of authorship seemed at odds with a publishing industry that had to allocate texts to types and market them accordingly. Yet Victorian publishing was creative

A New Companion to Victorian Literature and Culture, First Edition. Edited by Herbert F. Tucker.
© 2014 John Wiley & Sons, Ltd. Published 2014 by John Wiley & Sons, Ltd.

in its own right, developing new forms and genres to suit changing reading habits and readers. The situation of publishers specializing in new books discouraged risk-taking: monopoly meant high prices and low runs reliably aimed at a wealthy and well-demarcated readership. The price of new books remained inflated until relatively late in the century, but publishing was never just about new books. Literature was published in a wide range of forms across the period. There were expensive three-volume novels ("triple deckers") intended primarily for the libraries, but these were followed by a series of cheaper reprints, appearing at various points after a text's first publication, that extended its life for other sets of readers. Before appearing in book form a work of fiction might be sold in parts, spreading the cost of a text over multiple installments. New literature was also a staple of the periodical press, and editors became adept at selecting and promoting the texts that they thought their readers wanted. The periodical trade and book trade were closely related, with many publishers owning their own periodical titles in order to promote their wares. Literature even found its way into the newspaper: poetry, for instance, was a regular feature of the Chartist *Northern Star*; and from 1873 Tillotson's Newspaper Literature Syndicate distributed fiction to papers throughout Britain and, eventually, abroad.

The enormous enlargement of readership by the end of the century was partly the result of the spread of literacy in a population that had itself grown at an unprecedented rate. The ability to read, though not necessarily with ease and comprehension, was more widely shared than ever before, and the expanding middle class and to some degree the working class enjoyed an increased amount of disposable income that they could spend for nonessential purposes like books and periodicals. Reading aloud was common throughout the period, especially for those with limited access to print or too busy to read for themselves. Although silent reading did not fully replace communal reading, falling costs and increased leisure created more opportunities for the latter. At home, improved lighting – the transition from candles to oil lamps to gas to electricity – meant that reading, despite the small type in which newspapers and some magazines were printed, became more pervasive as a leisure-time activity; beyond the home, there was an expansion of possible sites for reading as new institutions such as subscription reading rooms, mechanics' institutes, and public libraries developed alongside (and often in opposition to) the continued proliferation of coffee houses and pubs (Vincent and Colclough 301–8). As railways added mobility to everyday life, they likewise added hours of tedium which books and papers were admirably suited to relieve (no record seems to exist of anyone reading with any comfort inside a jolting over-the-road coach). Whereas previously people would have been read to, they were now increasingly able to read for themselves; more importantly, many of those whose reading matter had been acquired at second hand – extracted and pasted into commonplace books, informally bought and sold, or simply passed from reader to reader – were able to buy material of their own, whether cheap reissues, penny fiction, broadsides, or numbers of periodicals and newspapers.

As the urban population grew it offered a more concentrated market for these commodities, one which became more easily reached as the old skeletal distribution system, consisting of booksellers in a few towns and hawkers in the country lanes, was replaced by a network of bookshops and newsagents in every sizable population center. These were supplied by the railways, which brought a daily flow of stock from the publishing warehouses and works, initially based in London and Edinburgh but eventually separated from the publishers' offices entirely. The book post, set up with special mailing rates in 1848, also provided a way to distribute literature (Colclough 241–2). New marketing techniques supplemented the staid announcements, no bigger than our classified ads, that were a staple of book-trade print advertising throughout the era. No firm, to be sure, went to the excesses practiced in the 1820s by Henry Colburn, the brash maverick who hyped his line of "silver fork" fiction, first by planting in newspapers scandal-tinged stories purporting to identify the blue-blooded originals of characters in a forthcoming novel, and then by inserting enthusiastic reviews in the periodical he owned. But when Dickens launched his weekly *All the Year Round* in 1859, a saturation publicity campaign called not only for posters on London buses but for a quarter-million handbills to be passed out in the streets. A few years later, Matthew Arnold's wife found herself walking down Regent Street behind a sandwich man advertising her husband's essay on Marcus Aurelius in the latest number of *Victoria Magazine*. On September 30, 1885, Cassell's arranged for posters to appear overnight declaring H. Rider Haggard's *King Solomon's Mines* "The Most Amazing Book Ever Written." By the end of the century, even the most sedate firms helped make celebrities out of their most popular authors by placing innocuous news items about them in the daily papers and arranging for home interviews, a new journalistic device that was fiercely resisted by some as unbefitting the dignity of the literary profession, in middlebrow magazines.

Alexis Weedon has argued that there was a "book hunger" between the 1830s and 1870s (157). In feeding this hunger, publishing, heretofore a cottage industry on the fringe of the nation's economy, developed into a major enterprise with an annual turnover of several million pounds that witnessed a fourfold increase in production from 1846 to 1916 (Weedon 57). As social and cultural interests multiplied in this increasingly complex society, new firms sprang up to cater to emergent sub-audiences, and old mainstream houses adopted specialties alongside their general lists. John Murray's already venerable firm was known for its guidebooks and travel narratives, the even older house of Longman for its textbooks, Cassell's for education-at-home titles in response to the Victorian self-help movement, Routledge for cheap reprints, Moxon for poetry, Bentley, Tinsley, and Macmillan for fiction.

Innovating publishers brought old print genres to new stages of development and invented new ones. Chapman and Hall's success with Dickens's *Pickwick Papers* in 1836, for instance, prompted a resurgence in part publication for new fiction aimed at middle-class readers. The period also saw a proliferation of differing book formats. The mid- and late-Victorian years shape up in retrospect as the golden age of children's books and magazines, engagingly designed and produced, not least with an eye toward nurturing future generations of adult book buyers. Other money-makers, devised specifically for the Christmas trade, were short fictions packaged as gift books – Dickens's *A Christmas Carol* (1843) and *The Chimes* (1844), and Thackeray's *The Kickleburys on the Rhine* (1850) and *The Rose and the Ring* (1855) – and lavishly illustrated holiday numbers of family periodicals, often featuring specially commissioned stories, music, and poetry. These in particular reflected publishers' growing awareness of the power of physical appeal to sell printed objects, which in turn encouraged the invention of state-of-the-art mechanical modes of illustration, printing, and binding. Books formerly were sold in sheets and bound to the order of individual purchasers; now cheap binding cloth and machinery to apply it to the folded sheets, and equipment to stamp lettering and designs on it, made "publishers' bindings" standard throughout the trade. These came in several qualities and degrees of decoration, so that some houses advertised whole hierarchies of editions of a standard author like Tennyson, in formats ranging from the luxurious and costly to the cheaply ornate.

This was the more energetic aspect of an industry otherwise noted at the time for its financial conservatism. All Victorian firms were organized as family concerns or partnerships; and, unlike printers, who had expensive plant costs and so needed additional finance, most publishers remained that way into the twentieth century. Having no easy means of raising additional capital at times when the ledgers were being written up in red ink, publishers remained dependent on cash flow, which required quick returns on investments, which in turn required that the product for sale find an immediate market. Production costs rose and fell with changes in the cost of raw materials, labor, and the introduction of new technologies. Because different print formats, pitched at particular price points in the market, entailed different production costs, publishers carefully calculated runs to maximize profitable return and minimize accumulation of unsold stock (Weedon 59–109). Vogues in books, especially fiction, came and went. The silver fork novel and the Newgate (criminal) novel of the pre-Victorian decades were succeeded by the Irish novel in the forties, the sensation novel in the sixties, and the "New Woman" novel in the nineties. Other special-interest genres, such as religious and sporting novels, had substantially longer lives. In a competitive trade affected, more than most merchandisers, by the popular appetite for novelty and by the quickening pace of everyday life, solvency was contingent on an astute sense of what the public wanted at the moment. "I hope it's not historical, Mr Trollope?" an employee of Hurst and Blackett famously asked that novelist when he brought in the manuscript of *The Three Clerks*. "Whatever you do, don't be historical; your historical novel is not worth a damn" (Trollope I, 147–8).

The word "bestseller" was not invented until the 1890s, but the idea it represented was current much earlier. It always was a relative concept, whether for the short term (a year or two) or the long (a decade, a generation). Early in the century, when an ordinary "serious" title such as a biography or a history was printed in an edition of

750 copies and the customary print run for a novel was at most 1,250 copies, Scott's successive volumes of poetry were clear record-breakers: *The Lay of the Last Minstrel* (1805) sold 15,000 copies in five years, and *The Lady of the Lake* (1810) 30,000 or more in the first year (Altick 262–3, 386). So Scott's Midas touch was already operative when he turned from verse to prose romances. The first printings of *Rob Roy* (1818) and *Ivanhoe* (1820) ran to 10,000 each; of *The Fortunes of Nigel* (1822) 7,000 copies were sold in London alone on the morning of publication (Altick 383).

Such sales, previously unimaginable, were harbingers of far greater successes in the Victorian years. Short-term bestseller figures are hard to come by, but these reported sales are representative: the first monthly numbers of *Nicholas Nickleby* (1838–9) and *The Mystery of Edwin Drood* (1870), 50,000 each; John Richard Green's *Short History of the English People* (1874), 35,000 in the first year; *King Solomon's Mines* (1885), 31,000 in the first 15 months; Robert Louis Stevenson's *Strange Case of Dr Jekyll and Mr Hyde* (1886), 40,000 in six months. These short-term sales may be compared with the steady sales of other titles over a period of years, usually in cheap reprints: Richard Harris Barham's three series of *Ingoldsby Legends* (1840/47–63), 52,000; Coventry Patmore's *The Angel in the House* (1854/62–96), between 200,000 and 250,000; *Alice in Wonderland* (1865–98), 180,000 (Altick 384–6).

These impressive numbers were dwarfed by the burgeoning periodical and newspaper press. The publications that dominated literary opinion early in the period – the quarterlies, the six-shilling *Edinburgh* (1802–1929) and *Quarterly Review* (1809–1967), and the monthlies like *Fraser's Magazine* (1830–82) – might not have sold much more than 10,000 copies, but publications such as the well-established sixpence *Evangelical Magazine* (1793–1904), which sometimes discussed literature as part of their wider offering, reached twice this figure. Periodical publishers were aware of the potential for large and sustained readership: the twopenny weekly *Mirror of Literature* (1822–47) achieved sales of around 80,000 and the (explicitly non-literary) *Penny Magazine* (1832–45) around 200,000 a week in its first year. Dickens's *Household Words* (1850–9) sold nearly 40,000 copies a week, and its successor *All the Year Round* (1859–95) managed to maintain sales of around 100,000. Slightly downmarket, but specializing in serial fiction and far outselling Dickens, were the penny weeklies: the *London Journal* (1845–1928, 500,000 at its peak), *Family Herald* (1842–1940, 300,000), and *Reynolds's Miscellany* (1846–69, also reaching 300,000). The shilling monthlies such as *Macmillan's Magazine* (1859–1975), *Cornhill Magazine* (1860–1975), and *Temple Bar* (1860–1906), which appeared in the 1860s and published the leading literary figures of the day, were in a different market but managed a respectable 30–50,000 copies a month. With the innovations of the "new journalism" in the 1880s and 1890s, records were broken again. George Newnes's *Strand Magazine* (1891–1950) was half the price, at sixpence, of the shilling monthlies, but its combination of short fiction, celebrity interviews, and lavish illustration allowed it to sell almost 400,000 copies a month by the mid-nineties.

Such quantities were made possible by several technological breakthroughs that revolutionized the printing industry. By the 1830s, the paper shortages that had dogged the industry were a thing of the past. The arrival of the Fourdrinier paper-making machine not only increased the amount available and reduced costs, but also allowed publishers more flexibility in terms of size (Weedon 64–70). Hand-operated presses, which had remained essentially unaltered for half a millennium, were replaced by steam-driven "printing machines," first used by newspapers but widely adopted for book work by the 1840s, when they doubled or tripled the rate of production (Dooley 78). A generation later cylinder machines, developed by Wharfedale in Britain and Hoe in America, increased the rate of production yet again (Dooley 80–3; Weedon 71). The production of images also underwent significant changes. Copper-plate and steel engravings were still used for up-market books, but the revival and increasing sophistication of wood engraving led to a proliferation of images across all sectors of the book and periodical press. Engraving became an industrial process, with engravers increasingly organized in a factory system. From the 1860s, photography was used to transfer the image, removing the need for it to be drawn on the block; photomechanical reproduction, introduced in the 1870s, removed the hand of the engraver entirely. This new way of printing broadened the repertoire of printed images while also making it easier to set them alongside letterpress (Beegan 72–97). Type-setting, however, continued to be done by hand until the very last Victorian years, when the Monotype and Linotype machines were introduced from the United States. But the lack of mechanization in the composing room was no bar to swift production: as standing type represented tied-up capital, authors could expect to receive proofs within weeks of turning in their manuscripts. Only six weeks elapsed between the publisher George Smith's acceptance of the manuscript of *Jane Eyre* (1847) and the appearance of the finished book in shops (Sutherland 47–8).

Equally important, by the 1840s the stereotyping process came into its own. This meant that, instead of tying up quantities of expensive, hand-set type for reprints that might never be called for, a printer could make a metal (later papier-mâché) impression of the pages for later use, thus freeing the type for other jobs and at the same time preserving the pages for future printings as needed. It was this money-saving capability that made it possible for publishers to build up a profitable backlist, render-ing them less vulnerable to shifts in taste. Stereotyping enabled publishers to undertake collected reissues of the works of living and still productive authors such as Dickens and Bulwer-Lytton without having to set a new edition. Sometimes these progressively cheaper editions came from the original publisher or by arrangements with him, but as copyrights expired, other houses brought out their own editions. A market for stereotypes was created, and provided an easy way for new firms to enter the market. By the end of the century cheese-paring paperback reprints might cost as little as sixpence. One effect of this practice was to prolong an author's reputation beyond its natural life: because they were cheap and stayed in print, the books continued to be bought even when their author was no longer popular (St Clair 415–17).

Stereotyping put downward pressure on the price of new works as publishers rec-ognized that costs could be recouped over subsequent editions; the publication of new literary works remained a monopoly, however, so publishers kept those prices high.

While the average price of most nonfiction eventually declined, in part because the quarto format gave way to the cheaper (because smaller) octavo, the inflated price of original fiction in book form was artificially maintained for most of the century. Although some one- or two-volume novels continued to appear, from Scott's *Kenilworth* (1821) onward the standard format of fiction was three volumes (hence the term "three-decker") costing 31s 6d, or a guinea and a half, or 10s 6d per volume. This was a price beyond the means of all but the wealthiest purchasers, but the publishers had a ready market in the circulating libraries, most famously Mudie's Select Library (established 1842), to whom they sold at discounts of up to 60 percent of the bookshop price. Mudie also advertised extensively, complementing the publishers' own campaigns, and his advertisements, stating how many copies of a particular title he stocked, were the best publicity a book could have. It was a cozy arrangement for all concerned, except the reader who wanted to own the books he or she read. The publishers were saved the expense of marketing the product at retail, and the libraries put Benthamite economics to profitable use by multiplying the number of readers a single copy would serve. Readers who subscribed a guinea a year to Mudie's were entitled to take out a volume at a time; another guinea allowed them to borrow up to four (Griest 17–18, 38–9).

This was a form of snobbery easily purchased ("Select"): as mentions in many novels attest, the conspicuous presence of "books from Mudie's" in a home was a token of genteel social standing, if not necessarily of discriminating taste. To be sure, one disadvantage of the system was that it empowered Mudie to wield what amounted to a veto power over the production of fiction. Publishers obtained their sense of public taste and tolerance second-hand, not through retail sales but through Mudie's conviction that he knew what his subscribers wanted to read, or rather what he, a fervent evangelical moralist, wanted them to read – or be protected from. The publishers' (and authors') primary market, so to speak, was not people but a faceless commercial institution. It is no surprise that when Mudie's became a private company in 1864, 50 per cent of the shares were bought by John Murray, Richard Bentley, and other publishers (Shattock 8).

This near-monopoly on the distribution of original fiction – it might today be called a conspiracy in restraint of trade – was sustained by publishers and circulating libraries at a time when common sense, as well as the ascendancy of free trade as economic orthodoxy, held that a cheapening of the manufacturing process should be reflected in cost to the consumer. Year in and year out, for eight decades, the guinea-and-a-half price was sacrosanct, despite repeated protests from free-trade politicians and from authors who wanted a wider, uncontrolled market. Only in 1894 did the rickety vessel finally founder, when an ultimatum by the circulating libraries effectively ended the arrangement (Griest 171–5). This landmark book-trade event was celebrated by Kipling in a ballad titled "The Three-Decker," first published in the well-established weekly *Saturday Review* (1855–1938). Ostensibly a lament over maritime obsolescence, like Turner's painting of *The Fighting Temeraire Tugged to her Last*

Berth to be Broken Up (1839), its true subject was made clear by its epigraph: "The three-decker novel is extinct."

This matter, however, should be kept in perspective. Since Mudie's is always written about in connection with its pernicious effect on the fiction of its time, it must be remembered that novels were not the only kind of books it stocked in large quantities. Of the five million volumes it circulated between 1842 and 1888 only a third were fiction, and of the 960,000 it bought between 1853 and 1862 only about half were novels, as against 215,000 volumes of history and biography and 125,000 of travel and adventure. Mudie, it is true, bought 2,000 copies of *The Mill on the Floss* in 1860, but five years earlier he had bought 2,400 of the third and fourth volumes of Macaulay's *History of England* and had to set aside a special room to check them out to importunate borrowers.

The hunger of readers with more modest incomes was somewhat appeased by the introduction of five- or six-shilling one-volume reprints appearing after initial demand for the expensive library edition was exhausted. The short-lived firm of Colburn and Bentley (caricatured as Bungay and Bacon in Thackeray's *Pendennis*, 1848–50) started their "Standard Novels" series in 1831, and it was here that six of Jane Austen's novels were first reprinted (1833). The next step in this cheapening process occurred at mid-century when publishers began marketing single-volume reprints in eye-catching pictorial board covers ("yellowbacks") designed to catch the eye of the customer on the move. Routledge's "Railway Library" appeared the same year W. H. Smith took over the stalls on the London and North Western Railway (1847); Bentley responded with his own shilling "Railway Library" in 1852–3; and W. H. Smith used Chapman and Hall's imprint to launch their own half-crown (2s 6d) series in 1862 (Shattock 8; Colclough 248). Different houses had different policies when it came to reprints, but 6s was standard, falling to 3s 6d in the 1870s. By the 1880s, 60 percent of books were being sold at this price directly to purchasers. For publishers, each of these reprints had its own break-even point, but in combination they could be used to recoup costs over a number of different editions (Eliot; Weedon 97–107). The timed release of these cheaper reprints meant that the same text found different readerships at different moments.

Literature, and fiction in particular, had such appeal that it could not be met by book publication alone. Most readers obtained new literature in various serial formats that included part issues of a single work and numbers of periodicals and newspapers. These serial publications spread the cost of new works over several parts but, perhaps more importantly, provided access to them prior to publication in book form and long before they would be reissued in an affordable format. For publishers, serial publication was a useful way to mitigate some of the risks inherent in publishing. It allowed them to gauge the market, minimizing the chance of unsold stock, while recovering costs over the run. And, of course, serial publication provided a useful advertising opportunity. Each number kept the publisher's name before readers and furnished space, usually in a wrapper, to promote other titles for sale.

Part publication burst into view when it was employed for *Pickwick Papers* in 1836–7. Priced at an affordable shilling and sold over the counter like conventional periodicals, these monthly (less often, weekly) 32-page illustrated paperbound "parts" reached a large public that seldom if ever ventured inside a bookshop. It was in this form that Dickens was catapulted to early fame, with the fifteenth number of *Pickwick* selling the then unearthly total of 40,000 copies. In the next two decades several other novelists, including Thackeray with *Vanity Fair* (1847–8), *Pendennis*, and *The Newcomes* (1853–5), published their new novels in parts. In the fifties and sixties the part issue was gradually superseded by the new shilling monthlies, but several of Trollope's novels appeared in numbers, and Dickens clung to the practice to the end of his life. George Eliot's *Middlemarch* (1871–2) was published by Blackwood, in a gamble calculated to boost sales and circumvent the libraries, in eight 5s parts and on an unusual bimonthly rhythm. Each part cost the same as two monthly numbers of *Blackwood's Magazine* (2s 6d) but each was almost book-length and so also competed in the market for books. The gamble paid off: *Middlemarch* sold just over 5,000 copies of these parts, realizing over £6,000 profit. The first expensive (42s) book edition was made up from the few leftover copies of the serial and so sold modestly; however, the subsequent four-volume guinea edition sold 3,000 in March 1873, and the 7s 6d single-volume edition managed 13,000 in May 1874 (Sutherland 108–205).

The clear demand for literature made it a valuable component of periodicals and newspapers. The groundbreaking monthlies *Blackwood's*, *Fraser's*, and the *New Monthly Magazine* (1814–84) complemented the serious literary criticism of their ponderous quarterly predecessors with a livelier tone and original literature of their own. Joined by *Tait's Edinburgh Magazine* (1832–61) and *Bentley's Miscellany* (1837–68), the names of these publications explicitly promoted their publishers. Expensive literary annuals issued for Christmas, such as the *Forget Me Not* (1823–47, 8s), specialized in fine engravings and verse and were at the top end of a vibrant seasonal market. Literature was also a staple of cheaper publications. The *Mirror of Literature* lived up to its name by reprinting, often without attribution, content from a wide range of other publications, offering it up weekly to its readers for twopence.

It was in the 1850s that publishers of periodicals really embraced the appeal of literature. Dickens's *Household Words* was a deliberate attempt to reach deeper into the lower middle and upper working class and poach readers from more sensational (and often radical) weeklies such as the threepenny *Lloyd's Weekly Newspaper* (1843–1931) and penny *Reynolds's Miscellany*. None was illustrated like the penny weekly *London Journal*, which often devoted the engraving on its front page to its serial fiction. The combination of illustration and literature was also typical of the mid-century monthlies, which, paying some of the highest fees in the business, supplied publishers with a regular showcase for their house authors as well as for promising young talent who might, in the future, provide them with book-length manuscripts. At a shilling, the monthlies were priced the same as a single part of a serial work, but often included two or three serials at once, so that readers got more for their money. For almost 30 years the shilling monthly provided the main source of new literature for middle-class readers, until in 1891 the sixpenny *Strand Magazine*, which offered literature as part of its range of explicitly "light" reading, used new production methods to increase dramatically the amount and range of its visual material. What is striking about the periodicals of the period is how commonly literature – or its discussion – was featured in the various genres. The *Illustrated London News* (1842–1989) carried fiction from 1843; its rival, the *Graphic* (1869–1932), did likewise from its first number. As Graham Law has shown, weekly newspapers, both provincial and, eventually, metropolitan, became an important market that in the 1870s allowed publishers to syndicate content in a number of titles. Even someone like W. T. Stead, who took a nonconformist dislike to fiction, recognized its importance and attempted to incorporate it into both his (failed) attempts to launch a daily newspaper (Brake 13).

These different print genres all left their mark on the way literature was written. Gissing described his author-character Edwin Reardon as being both restive and cynical under the "astonishing system" imposed on workaday novelists by the tyranny of the triple-decker (220). This fossilized and procrustean format, including large type, wide spacing, and as many blank pages as possible – the printers' way of coping with the problem of making more out of less – obviously called for an intolerable amount of literary padding to swell into the obligatory three volumes. Reardon, as he said, "kept as much as possible to dialogue; space is filled so much more quickly, and at a pinch one can make people talk about the paltriest incidents of life" as makeweight. At the same time, novelists had to stretch their plots and complicate matters with subplots and to indulge in "lengthy description of locality" and "deliberate analysis of character and motive," which, in terms of sheer craftsmanship, may or may not have been bad (227).

Serialization entailed its own demands upon authors. The celebrated formula attributed to Wilkie Collins, "Make 'em cry, make 'em laugh, make 'em wait," summarized the most obvious requirements imposed by serialization. Besides one or more dramatic episodes relevant to the ongoing narrative, each installment should contain a judicious balance of sentiment and humor, and, above all, it should end with a suspenseful situation that would ensure a healthy sale of the next number. Novelists had to fashion a product that was both complete (i.e. contained a good shilling's worth of mixed obligatory ingredients) and left readers impatient to get on with the story – next month. As Dickens's surviving working papers richly testify, writers confronted problems of structure, arrangement, pace, and emphasis that had to be solved as they proceeded, within the strictly ordained physical limits of each installment, under the inexorable pressure of deadlines, and without a chance to review and revise what they had written before the printer's errand boy, often enough waiting at the door, took it away. Some adjustments could be made in proof, but only hurriedly and still within the unbreakable confines of the number. Both structures could be in play at the same time. Dickens's *Great Expectations*, for instance, was written for *All the Year Round* and published in 36 installments from December 1, 1860 until August 3, 1861. At the end of the issue for February 16, 1861, the note "This is the end of the first stage of Pip's expectations" in effect wrote the three-volume structure into the serial. Certainly, the combined exigencies of three-decker publication and serialization were largely responsible for what some modern readers, unschooled in both print genres, consider the verbosity, inordinate length, qualitative unevenness, and sometimes sheer formlessness of much Victorian fiction.

Serialization brought novelists closer to their audiences and made them more responsive to their expectations than ever before. Dickens and Thackeray cultivated a familiar style suitable to regular appearances at their readers' firesides, reducing the barriers that print ordinarily imposed between writer and reader. Month-by-month sales figures, moreover, supplied an instantaneous measure of buyers' satisfaction; reacting to this early warning system, novelists could change course while there was still time. When in 1843 the monthly sales of *Martin Chuzzlewit* fell alarmingly below the level set by Dickens's previous novels, he took the drastic step of moving his characters to America, a land of immediately topical – satirical – interest. Serialization also enabled writers to receive feedback directly from readers and, if they liked, to act upon it. Dickens, learning that his depiction of Miss Mowcher in *David Copperfield* (1850) offended some Jewish readers, made rather awkward amends in a later number. Thackeray, hearing a fellow diner make a casual remark about closing a puppet box, promptly adopted it as the closing metaphor in *Vanity Fair*. Trollope, overhearing a clergyman at his club complaining to another that he was bored by Mrs Proudie, then appearing weekly in *The Last Chronicle of Barset* (1866–7), went home and killed her off. Serialization meant that authors lived alongside their readers while their works were being published and so produced a literature that was peculiarly attuned to the passing moment.

By the early nineteenth century the profession of letters, in the sense of a full-time occupation, was still sparsely populated and socially stigmatized. But the new economics of publishing as influenced by the technological revolution, the growing visibility and acceptance of the products of the press in the ordinary byways of life, and a better appreciation of the potential market, went some way toward gentrifying Grub Street, even though, as Gissing's title implies, it was far from being razed. Full-time authorship, especially novel-writing, appeared to be a viable (and, to the inexperienced, easy) way to make a good living. There was a great deal more money in the literary pot, with increasing numbers of authors competing to share it. As early as 1843, in a now totally forgotten novel, *Joseph Jenkins: Or, Leaves from the Life of a Literary Man*, the hack journalist James Grant said, on unspecified authority, that "in London alone, the number of persons who have adopted authorship as a profession, and who have no other means of subsistence, is from 3,000 to 4,000. To these are to be added the thousands who have commenced a literary career with a view to following it as a profession." Grant went on to say that the total number of those who either were surviving by some form of writing, or had quit within the past 20 years, was "about 10,000." It followed that only a minuscule portion of would-be professional authors succeeded in making a "permanent and ample living" at their desks (III, 169–70). In his *Fifty Years Ago*, published in 1888, Walter Besant, founder of a professional guild called the Society of Authors, estimated that there were then in London alone "fourteen thousand men and women who live by writing," of whom all but a thousand were "in some way connected with journalism" (195).

The methods of payment underwent a revision that occupied most of the century. The old subscription system, by which friends and patrons of an author underwrote the cost of publication by promising to buy one or more copies, had virtually disappeared in favor of two widely employed practices. One was the outright sale of a work's copyright. In exchange for a lump sum from the publisher, the author totally surrendered the property to the publisher, and if the publisher subsequently made a handsome profit from it, so much the worse for the author. In a variation of this arrangement, the publisher leased the copyright for a stated period, after which it reverted to the author, who was then free to offer it elsewhere. The much-used alternative was publication on a profit-sharing basis, in which author and publisher split the proceeds after the publisher had recovered his costs. As a regrettable number of unwary writers learned the hard way, this was a common means of defrauding writers. More than a few sharks lurked in the depths of Victorian publishing, as was demonstrated by the experience of both Emily Brontë and Trollope, whose debuts were grievously mismanaged by one T. C. Newby. Such occurrences were not uncommon in those years, and they ultimately contributed to the adoption, by the end of the century, of the more straightforward and easily policed royalty system.

One effect of this conception of literature as a dependable generator of income was to demystify the art as romanticized by Shelley and Carlyle: the formerly hieratic was coarsened into the crassly materialistic. Aspirants to the profession of letters came to measure their hoped-for success as much in pounds sterling as in popular acclaim. A few writers did find Golconda. Smith, Elder lured George Eliot away from Blackwood by offering £10,000 for *Romola* (1863); she settled for what she regarded as an even better deal, £7,000 for the copyright, with the proviso that it would revert to her after six years. Longman credited Macaulay with £20,000 on the third and fourth volumes of his *History of England* (1855), and had enough left over to pay Benjamin Disraeli £10,000 for his last novel, *Endymion* (1880). At the height of Trollope's popularity in the sixties his income from writing averaged a very comfortable £4,500 a year, two or three thousand per novel. The success of Conan Doyle's Sherlock Holmes stories ensured he could demand some of the highest rates in the business. The *Strand* already paid contributors well (and on acceptance rather than publication): Doyle was paid £4 per thousand words for the first six stories, earning £200; for the next six he demanded £50 a story, earning £300; and for the next 12 he asked for, and got, £1,000 (MacDonald 141–2).

There were increasing sales to be made abroad, too. The manufacture of books for export was a major part of publishers' business throughout the period, and stereotypes made it easy for publishers to sell texts to foreign publishers (Weedon 187–92;

St Clair 417). For authors, the international market meant a further set of negotiations with publishers. The American rights to *Middlemarch* earned from Osgood, Ticknor and Co. £1,200 for the author, who also obtained £327 from Asher and Co. in Berlin and £200 for the serial rights in Australia (Haight 437–8). Prior to the implementation of international copyright, such negotiations were based on privileged access: authors would provide publishers with the text of a work as quickly as possible so that the publishers could beat their rivals. The Berne Convention (1886) and the International Copyright Act (1891) in the United States secured the rights of authors abroad; for publishers, these international agreements increased the value of their copyrights at the expense of the long-established culture of reprinting foreign works.

Such success was not possible without publicity, and success tended to generate more publicity in turn. To get published, authors had to consent to be packaged and presented, appear in publishers' lists, and, in many cases, indulge in a form of self-promotion that teetered on the vulgar. Although access to the profession was relatively open – it required no equipment beyond an inkwell, pens, a quire of paper, and postage; no capital other than an education and the appropriate contacts – the attendant publicity could expose the author to an uncomfortable level of scrutiny. This was particularly problematic for successful women writers, who found their fame at odds with the expectations of femininity. Literature provided women with an important opportunity for remunerative work, and the period saw many women enter the market and thrive. Margaret Oliphant, to take one of the most prolific, wrote nearly 100 novels and over 300 articles over a long career supporting her extended family. Writers could get only so far publishing anonymously or pseudonymously; to achieve public renown as an author meant revealing the authoring mind. As women writers often found, this meant advancing a gendered body, with its own history, that was then invoked to hold their writing to account.

Since money was at the root of the transactions between publishers and authors, their relations were radically adversarial. Authors suspected that publishers were out to cheat them and complained, like Swinburne and any number of authors today, that they did not spend enough on advertising. Publishers, for their part, were convinced that authors did not understand how business operated or the extent to which profits were hostage to the caprices of popular taste. Trollope, himself a shrewd bargainer, dealt with 16 different publishers during his busy career but made close friends with none of them. The advent of the literary agent in the 1880s, whose role was to negotiate the best possible deal for the author, further exacerbated relations. Sometimes, to be sure, the business connection ripened into personal cordiality, even apart from publishers' recognition that self-interest required them to cultivate and retain the money-spinning writers on their lists. Some successful publishers and their star authors belonged to the same London clubs. Tennyson and Edward Moxon had a friendship that ended only with Moxon's death. Later, Tennyson was on equally warm terms with Alexander Macmillan, who was also Matthew Arnold's friend. Charles Kingsley was godfather to Macmillan's children. George

Smith, one of the most sympathetic and open-handed of publishers, was a close friend of Thackeray, the Brontë sisters, Browning, and Ruskin. From the literary standpoint, perhaps the most fruitful of these half-professional, half-personal friendships was that between George Eliot and John Blackwood. Their voluminous correspondence is replete with discussions of production and sales, of authorial problems on her side and suggestions about such matters as style and characterization on his.

In this latter regard, Blackwood performed the function served in other firms by the "literary adviser" or in-house reader, a type of professional employee who seems to have come into being during the 1830s. This person, usually university-trained and an established author in his own right, became indispensable when heads of firms had to devote themselves to management, with less time to spare for the editorial side of the business than in more spacious days. He (or she, in the case of Geraldine Jewsbury, who worked 15 years for Richard Bentley) was paid to deal, in the first instance, with the slush pile of unsolicited manuscripts as well as new work by writers already published by the firm, and then to give the head of the house advice on the ones that survived the first cut. Advisers also might be charged with recruiting new authors to the firm, in the capacity of a modern acquisitions editor. Although paid by the publisher, these readers were the forerunners of the literary agent; in fact, the lawyer and editor John Forster worked both sides of the street, as Chapman and Hall's longtime literary adviser and the friend and sometimes the agent of Dickens, Leigh Hunt, Carlyle, Bulwer-Lytton, and Walter Savage Landor. His successor at the firm, George Meredith, is enduringly remembered as the seer with the clouded crystal ball who rejected such eventual hits as Mrs Henry Wood's sensational *East Lynne* (1861). He also turned thumbs down on Samuel Butler's *Erewhon* (1872) and early productions of George Bernard Shaw; but on the other hand he was an early champion of Gissing, among others (Gettmann 188). The history of Thomas Hardy's attempt to become a novelist is largely that of his struggles with publishers and their advisers, including a sympathetic Meredith, to conquer their nervousness over his use of realistic detail.

The predominance of fiction in the marketplace meant that this was where the money was to be made. With poetry the "churn" that defined the market for literature – the demand for new works – did not apply in quite the same way (Weedon 92). While it is true that the first nineteenth-century bestsellers were not novels but expensive editions of poetry (Scott, Byron, Moore), original editions subsequently were priced to sell to what publishers evidently considered to be a small market of poetry lovers. Tennyson's and Browning's successive volumes cost six or seven shillings each, significantly less than the per-volume cost of a three-decker, and they were published in smaller runs resulting in a lower return. Occasionally publishers sought to apply to volumes of poems the same formats they used so successfully with novels, but to no avail. Moxon had unsuccessfully experimented with part-issue, then the latest thing in aggressive publishing, by bringing out Browning's *Bells and Pomegranates* (1841–6) at irregular intervals, in eight booklets priced from 6d to 2s 6d. Smith,

Elder's serialization of *The Ring and the Book* a quarter-century later fared little better, taking 12 years to sell the first edition of 3,000 copies. Moxon's Illustrated Edition of Tennyson for the carriage trade (1858), a lavish production in the format and at the price of a guinea-and-a-half novel, but containing in its single volume only the contents of the poet's 1842 collection, sold just half of its 10,000 copies. Rather than look to book publication, poets had to rely on publishing in periodicals and newspapers, where there was a steady demand for new work. As Kathryn Ledbetter has shown, publishing in the periodical press (while professing to be aloof from it) allowed Tennyson to capitalize on his fame and so promote his books. After *Idylls of the King* sold the first 10,000 copies of its run of 40,000 in a week, Tennyson received £250 for a single poem, "Sea Idylls," to adorn the launch of the new *Macmillan's Magazine*. In the first few weeks after publication in 1864 *Enoch Arden and Other Poems* sold 40,000, including 2,500 bought by Mudie; and 20,000 copies of *Demeter and Other Poems* (1889) were snapped up in the first week. When Tennyson moved from Moxon to Alexander Strahan in 1869 he was paid £5,000 a year for five years for his copyrights (Eliot and Nash 435).

If, at the end of the century, publishers had become better at reaching more readers, this success was built on a number of previous, unsuccessful attempts at expansion beyond the markets that they knew. Scott's publisher went bankrupt before realizing his 1820s dream of saturating the mass market with cheap books selling "not by thousands or tens of thousands, but by hundreds of thousands – ay, by millions!" (Lockhart VI, 31). Around the same time the newly formed Society for the Diffusion of Useful Knowledge (SDUK) was launching two series of "useful" (scientific and utilitarian) and "entertaining" (somewhat less heavy) volumes, sold in sixpenny fortnightly parts. These had the implicit purpose of weaning their intended working-class readers from the cheap radical publications whose easy availability and inflammatory messages seemed to threaten the nation's stability. But their popularity was short-lived if not wholly illusory, and the 200,000 weekly circulation of the SDUK's *Penny Magazine* proved unsustainable. These and other costly experiments in the first half of the Victorian period taught publishers valuable lessons. Idealism about an immense, largely untapped market "out there" had led them to misjudge popular taste. Apart from a strong interest in religious publications, which in any case was more typical of the lower middle class than of the working class, what the poorest, least educated public turned out to want was not so much uplifting books and periodicals on "useful" subjects as the red meat of their demonstrably favorite reading fare, the weekly papers that served up ample portions of sensation, salacity, sex (in high places), crime, and radical politics – in all but the last respect, the direct forebears of today's London tabloids.

Collins's article "The Unknown Public," published on the front page of Dickens's *Household Words* for August 21, 1858, attests to the ignorance of middle-class publishers as they tried to find a market for what they thought lower-class readers ought to read. However, the success of Dickens's weeklies suggests that middle-class values increasingly constituted a sort of common-ground and that fiction played a role in consolidating it. Certain pieces of legislation helped. The abolition of the newspaper tax in 1855 opened the way for cheapened daily papers: the *Daily Telegraph* went down to a penny in 1856 and other London papers followed suit, and dailies sprang up for the first time in provincial cities. Newspaper reading for the first time became as much a habit of day laborers as of gentlemen in clubs, and the profit and power that accrued from catering to it bred a new kind of plutocrat, the so-called press baron. Forster's Education Act (1870) was widely heralded as producing a generation of literates. And, to meet the expanded need these rising readers represented, printing presses with ever-greater capacity and the adoption of chemically treated wood pulp as the main ingredient in machine-made paper cheapened the product. It was no accident that the very word "pulp" came to designate magazines containing, as the *OED* puts it, "sensational or poor-quality writing." One momentous but still little-studied effect of mass-market publishing was to encourage a simplified prose style, suited to the limited comprehension of many readers, which, inverting a law of cultural gravity, had a trickle-up impact on the style of the higher journalism and literary writing in general.

In this outpouring of books and magazines, justifiably advertised as "miracles of cheapness!," there was plenty to satisfy every taste. "Shilling shockers" issued in weekly parts and "penny dreadfuls" complete in 32 pages continued the robust tradition of thrillers stemming from the Gothic romances that were published throughout the century. For those preferring canonical authors there were, for example, a shilling edition of Shakespeare's complete works, purchasable in penny numbers; Waverley novels by Scott at 3d; a 473-page illustrated Byron at 7d; and a sixpenny *Sartor Resartus*, which sold 70,000 copies in 1882, a year after Carlyle's death. In 1896, former business partners Stead and Newnes both launched penny series: Stead's "Penny Poets" was the first of three series that together constituted what he called his "Masterpiece Library"; Newnes's "Penny Library of Famous Books" concentrated on unabridged, recent popular classics (Altick 315; Eliot and Nash 440–2). All these triumphs of price-cutting were paperbacks, and they were textually as well as physically shoddy, with strenuously small type often printed in double columns. Yet this sacrifice in quality was itself a mark of innovation, as the success of these cheap publications testified.

Amid all the vicissitudes, bad guesses, and lucky accidents that arose when two disparate and vigorous social entities, commerce and culture, were brought into uneasy partnership, Victorian publishing was, in the long run, genuinely "creative." It made readers of millions of people who would not otherwise have exercised their semi-literacy beyond labels on merchandise and posters on walls and buses; for better or worse, it revolutionized literary culture by making Britain into what no country had ever been before, a nation of avid novel readers; under its patronage, the clerisy – the intellectual elite – prospered, and had a decisive influence on the acts and opinions of the age. The form and content of Victorian literature, and by reflection the characteristic tone of society at large, would have been very different if produced under another set of circumstances.

See also 1897; ARTISTIC, COMMERCIAL; POETRY, FICTION, SAGE WRITING, LITERARY CRITICISM

REFERENCES

Altick, R. D. (1957) *The English Common Reader: A Social History of the Mass Reading Public, 1800–1900*. Chicago: University of Chicago Press.

Beegan, G. (2008) *The Mass Image: A Social History of Photomechanical Reproduction in Victorian London*. Basingstoke: Palgrave.

Besant, W. (1888) *Fifty Years Ago*. London: Chatto and Windus.

Brake, L. (2011) "The Advantage of Fiction: The Novel and the 'Success' of the Victorian Periodical." In *A Return to the Common Reader: Print Culture and the Novel, 1850–1900*, ed. B. Palmer and A. Buckland. Farnham: Ashgate.

Colclough, S. (2009) "Distribution." In *Cambridge History of the Book in Britain, Volume VI: 1830–1914*, ed. D. McKitterick. Cambridge: Cambridge University Press.

Dooley, A. C. (1992) *Author and Printer in Victorian England*. Charlottesville: University Press of Virginia.

Eliot, S. (1985) "The Three-Decker Novel and Its First Cheap Reprint, 1862–94." *The Library* 6, 38–53.

——, and A. Nash (2009) "Mass Markets: Literature." In *Cambridge History of the Book in Britain, Volume VI: 1830–1914*, ed. D. McKitterick. Cambridge: Cambridge University Press.

Gettmann, R. A. (1960) *A Victorian Publisher: A Study of the Bentley Papers*. Cambridge: Cambridge University Press.

Gissing, G. (1891) *New Grub Street*. London: Smith, Elder.

Grant, J. (1843) *Joseph Jenkins: Or, Leaves from the Life of a Literary Man*, 3 vols. London: Saunders and Otley.

Griest, G. L. (1970) *Mudie's Circulating Library and the Victorian Novel*. Bloomington: Indiana University Press.

Haight, G. S. (1968) *George Eliot: A Biography*. Oxford and New York: Oxford University Press.

Law, G. (2000) *Serialising Fiction in the Victorian Press*. Basingstoke: Palgrave.

Ledbetter, K. (2007) *Tennyson and Victorian Periodicals*. Aldershot: Ashgate.

Lockhart, J. G. (1837) *Memoirs of the Life of Sir Walter Scott, Bart.*, 7 vols. Edinburgh: Robert Cadell.

MacDonald, P. (1997) *British Literary Culture and Publishing Practice, 1880–1914*. Cambridge: Cambridge University Press.

Shattock, J. (2012) "The Publishing Industry." In *The Oxford History of the Novel in English*, vol. 3, ed. J. B. Taylor and J. Kucich. Oxford: Oxford University Press.

St Clair, W. (2004) *The Reading Nation in the Romantic Period*. Cambridge: Cambridge University Press.

Sutherland, J. A. (1976) *Victorian Novelists and Publishers*. Chicago: University of Chicago Press.

Trollope, A. (1883) *An Autobiography*, 2 vols. London: Blackwood.

Vincent, D., and S. Colclough (2009) "Reading." In *Cambridge History of the Book in Britain, Volume VI: 1830–1914*, ed. D. McKitterick. Cambridge: Cambridge University Press.

Weedon, A. (2003) *Victorian Publishing: The Economics of Book Production for a Mass Market, 1836–1916*. Aldershot: Ashgate.

FURTHER READING

Erickson, L. (1996) *The Economy of Literary Form: English Literature and the Industrialization of Publishing, 1800–1850*. Baltimore: Johns Hopkins University Press.

Feltes, N. N. (1986) *Modes of Production of Victorian Novels*. Chicago: University of Chicago Press.

Flint, K. (1993) *The Woman Reader, 1837–1914*. Oxford: Clarendon Press.

Gillies, M. A. (2007) *The Professional Literary Agent in Britain, 1880–1920*. Toronto: University of Toronto Press.

Hughes, L. K., and M. Lund (1991) *The Victorian Serial*. Charlottesville: University Press of Virginia.

Jordan, J. O., and R. L. Patten (eds) (1995) *Literature in the Market Place: Nineteenth-Century British Publishing and Reading Practices*. Cambridge: Cambridge University Press.

Peterson, L. (2009) *Becoming a Woman of Letters*. Princeton: Princeton University Press.

Rose, J. (2001) *The Intellectual Life of the British Working Classes*. New Haven: Yale University Press.

Webb, R. K. (1955) *The British Working Class Reader, 1790–1848: Literacy and Social Tension*. London: Allen and Unwin.

Weedon, A., and S. Colclough (eds) (2010) *History of the Book in the West 4: 1800–1914*. Aldershot: Ashgate.

Part Four
Kinds of Writing

22
Poetry

E. Warwick Slinn

I

In 1853 Matthew Arnold enacted a defining event in Victorian poetry: he withdrew from publication *Empedocles on Etna*, the title poem of his previous volume (1852). Poetry should "inspirit and rejoice," he wrote in his famous 1853 Preface, but *Empedocles on Etna*, he said, did neither. In portraying the sustained agonizing of a philosopher–poet, whose suffering found no release in action other than a leap to his death in the crater of Mount Etna, this poem failed to "charm" or "delight."

Because Arnold's aesthetic values were inherited from antiquity – from Sophocles who "saw life steadily and saw it whole" – and from Romanticism – which emphasized the virtues of homogeneity (in consciousness) and cohesion (in form) – he was determined to argue, in spite of his own poem's potential subversiveness, that poetry's "eternal objects" are those "elementary feelings which subsist permanently in the race, and which are independent of time." Thus, he hoisted his aesthetic flag to the masthead of humanist essentialism, influencing whole generations of subsequent readers to the extent even of minimizing features of his own poetry. While that poetry is still admired for its plangent and elegiac lyricism, Arnold's continuing struggle to relieve fellow sufferers from the "strange disease of modern life" ("The Scholar-Gipsy," 1853, 1. 203) tends to be accompanied by a sense of division and irresolution rather than deliverance. His claim in the essay on Maurice de Guérin (1862), for instance, that poetry may reconcile self and world is hardly enacted in poems where speakers are fenced in cloistral rounds, separated from buried lives, or

A New Companion to Victorian Literature and Culture, First Edition. Edited by Herbert F. Tucker.
© 2014 John Wiley & Sons, Ltd. Published 2014 by John Wiley & Sons, Ltd.

trapped on darkling plains. So it makes sense to read Arnold's poetry in terms of Romantic irony rather than Romantic metaphysics (Ryals), and to attend to the repressed poem, *Empedocles*, with its problematic explorations of what can be known, felt, and understood, as more indicative of the radical features of Victorian verse than even Arnold cared to admit.

Arnold's seminal declaration that *Empedocles* embodied a growing cultural emphasis on "the dialogue of the mind with itself" (Preface 1853) points to its concern with self-consciousness and the conditions of subjectivity. Indeed, "mind" suggests that separation of self from world so famously promulgated by Cartesian idealism, the dualistic consequences of the formulaic *cogito ergo sum* ("I think, therefore I am"), where the thinking mind turns in upon itself. Internal dialogue, no matter how divided, would sustain that dualism and its accompanying illusion of a separate, essential self. But the poem is about more than internalized division. It is also about the representations of mind: about not just the conditions of subjectivity, but the means of representing it, about its relationship with language therefore, and about whether indeed subjectivity may be separated from the constructive processes of those very representations. Hence the protagonist himself fears that consciousness may be lost or obliterated in language, "overlaid . . . with words" (II. i. 29–30), or that he may be imprisoned forever in the very forms, modes, and "stifling veils" of mind and thought (II. i. 354).

In these fears Empedocles demonstrates the humanist and idealist desire for a transcendent ego, for that power of origination which was so seductive a feature of Romantic idealism, where the speaker may author herself without falling prey to the modes of otherness. Yet Empedocles is a poet and physician who doubts the value of representation, rejecting the functions of art and action. He presents the dilemma of a person who is no longer able to make meaningful contact with the world through language: the fragments and parables which represent beliefs about the world are regarded by Empedocles as but fragments and parables, linguistic fabrications. In him there is a loss of faith, therefore, not only in providence, but in the creative and communicative possibilities of art.

Although once a youthful idealist and poet like Callicles, whose songs attempt to woo him away from his climb up the crater, he no longer trusts the forms of his earlier trade. To that extent the possibilities for redemption and cohesion through language remain but the trappings of Callicles's hopeful lyricism. In its place Empedocles manifests a fundamental melancholy that may indeed, as Arnold feared, characterize the poetry of an age (Riede). By the end of the poem, Empedocles's only alternative is to submit to the materiality of death, to enact meaning by refusing the difference between sign and referent, refusing representation in order to embrace, indeed become, the thing itself. His suicide is hardly a grand action embodying the transcendent joy of a teleologically defined universe, but it is nevertheless conceived by Empedocles in triumphant terms. What is crucial to his perception of this final act, therefore, is its testimony to his own role as agent, its function as the enactment of a freely choosing and independent mind. Consciousness, representation, language, and agency: these are the issues which dominate Arnold's repressed poem and which persist elsewhere in Victorian poetry. The action of *Empedocles on Etna*, combined with Arnold's act of suppression, focuses a defining historical moment because it combines the poetic portrayal of the rupture of humanist idealism with the simultaneous and self-conscious attempt to hide that rupture, to sustain in its place the creative and restorative possibilities of poetic language.

II

While it has been common enough to observe the way Victorian poetry evinces contemporary qualities of introspection, questioning, and perplexity, the example of *Empedocles on Etna* teaches that it is not sufficient to observe these themes without also recognizing that their representation in poetry renders them different from the univocal, polemical writings of the period. Victorian poetry is quite simply more sophisticated, more politically, intellectually, and emotionally complex, than has often been credited. It is increasingly being analyzed as a poetry of multiple linguistic actions which generate themes of public crisis and social politics, from gendered bodies to nation-building, as well as the mixed anxieties of private crises. Such discursive processes, figuratively and formally constituted as both affirmation and critique, relate in more subtly various ways to the cultural debates and structures of their time than are suggested by the passive metaphor of "reflection." Victorian poets continued the Romantic disruption of neo-classical decorum (with its hierarchical list of genres from trivial lyric to serious epic); but through innovative dramatic modes and an experimental variety of longer forms, they also developed a sense of dynamic heterogeneity which questioned the assumptions of Romantic lyricism, their main inheritance.

Scholars increasingly emphasize the disruptive counter-side of Romantic writing itself, its disjunctions and mixed genres, the struggles of the speaking subject to establish authenticity. Yet the phenomenological inheritance of the Romantic odal hymn ("Ode: Intimations of Immortality," 1807; "Ode to the West Wind," 1820) bequeathed to Victorian poets a lyric voice which presented itself as autonomous, self-conscious, atemporal, and male, and an aesthetic which promoted the possibilities of attaining through metaphor a transcendent universality not bound by time, class, or gender. Several of the Victorian male poets appear to have realized all too quickly the contingency of this practice, and the women poets were faced with a choice about gender conformity – a choice of being written and thereby appropriated by a patriarchal poetics, or opposing that structure and being banished to its margins. Whether gendered through or against the hegemony, however, from the 1830s and 1840s the cultural value of the lyrical voice was in trouble. Its assumed singularity and transparency proved multivalent and mediated. Its expressiveness, its metaphorically flaunted ideality, its atemporal formalism, were increasingly to be recognized as contingent, discourse-based, and ideologically colonized.

Some poets continued writing conventional lyricism, affirming the values of personal feeling, whether as women's celebration of community (identifying consciousness with unmediated inwardness) or as men's celebration of women (identifying consciousness with externalized desire). But others were more questioning. They conducted various experiments in poetic dramatization, whether Elizabeth Barrett Browning's attempt to represent an assertive independence for female speakers, Christina Rossetti's daring exploration of erotic sublimation, or the ironies of consciousness proposed by Robert Browning, Tennyson, Clough, and Meredith. The attempts to structure feeling in terms of aesthetic stability and universality fell afoul of language which slipped from control. Consequently, readings of Victorian poetry now emphasize its fractured and ambivalent status, whether in terms of the deconstruction of lyrical homogeneity, the ironies of subjective production, or the feminism of patriarchal subversion. What was once represented as a poetry of sentiment and thoughtlessness, or "rumination," which related uneasily to the Romantic requirements of organic unity or mellifluous splendor, becomes now read as problematic structuring, process, and contestation.

Our current understanding of poetry is characterized by recognition of what ought to be obvious in poetic forms, the way poetic language draws attention to itself as language, to its status as sign. So students of Victorian poetry have become attuned to the implications of idealist language (Armstrong 1982), printed voices (Griffiths), and performativity (Slinn). Current criticism also develops what Herbert Tucker (1993) has called "cultural neoformalism," which aligns poetic affectiveness with historical specificity, and which can mean attending to social and ideological contexts (Sinfield; Armstrong 1993; Blair), to national identity (Reynolds), poetic agency (Slinn), or gender construction (Leighton; Billone). The poetic word, then, as self-consciously displayed and deployed in Victorian verse, is being read less as the focus for private expressiveness and more as the point where self and world are constructed – the focus for relationships, structured through the intersections of radical otherness and internalized desire; and the locus where subject production, gender difference, and secular power coalesce in moments of conflicting, excessive, frequently confounded utterance.

III

Working within the combined hegemony of utilitarianism and political economy, Victorian poets, with their interest in more symbolic means of signifying, sought to enforce values other than those provided by the capitalist market. Utilitarianism of course also provided them with considerable political and ethical impetus. While they opposed its materialist principles, that opposition nevertheless provided cultural definition, and the writings of William Johnson Fox and Jeremy Bentham offered to early Victorian poets a democratic politics and a theory of fictions (Armstrong 1993). Unfortunately, utilitarianism in its more homogenized and economic form left poets few choices: relegation (poetry is culturally trivial), incorporation (poetry celebrates the delights of commodification), or marginalization (poetry portrays an area of special experience, but remains politically unimportant). The more mythic–symbolic poets who followed Coleridgean idealism – Tennyson, Barrett Browning, Arnold, Christina Rossetti, Swinburne, Michael Field – generally affirmed areas of special, usually spiritual or metaphorically personal, experience. But whereas Shelley's political poetry, Friedrich Engels reported, was read and understood by the working class, these idealist poets tended towards an ultimately middle-class aestheticism and liberalism. Although the claim of special experience sustained a place in which to assert their ethical and aesthetic values, it inevitably facilitated their incorporation into hegemonic aims. In accepting marginalization they sustained and were structured by the very system they sought to challenge (Sinfield 17–21).

Yet to the extent that poetic language, more intensively figured than other forms of writing, draws attention to its condition as text, the poetry itself may display a covert radicalism, through representing the means of representing, the means by which hegemonic belief structures were sustained. As suggested by Arnold's *Empedocles*, Victorian poetry frequently enacts a form of expressiveness which in the very act of producing itself as commodity, as material sign, simultaneously provokes a deep sense of resistance to that commodification, whether as an aspect of psychology (Robert Browning's "Pictor Ignotus," 1845), form (*Aurora Leigh*, 1857), temporal presence (Tennyson's "Tithonus," 1860), or theme (Christina Rossetti's "Goblin Market," 1862). In this, it is radically (in the root sense of that term) and inquisitively political, even if, as some cultural theorists would argue, that resistance emerges from the economic institutions of capitalism itself.

Within Victorian poetry, then, commodification functions covertly as the economic and material other to aesthetic and moral value. This dialectical relationship means that the marginalized area of poetic experience, the figuration of feeling and the figuration of figuration, leads back to the materialist center, the figure as itself material. Hence, the poem indicates its own modes of production, both as a physical object and as an instrument in the making of cultural value. Moments of deep poetic crisis therefore tend to incorporate moments of semiotic self-awareness, as, for example, in the climactic episode of Tennyson's *In Memoriam*.

Published at mid-point in the century (1850) and quickly requiring several editions, *In Memoriam* emerged privately from Tennyson's grief at the death of Arthur Hallam, his close friend at Cambridge, and publicly from the widespread religious doubt which accompanied the early nineteenth-century increase in new scientific knowledges and questioning of established biblical and political authorities. It focuses therefore an array of cultural issues. The poem fully acknowledges the potential incoherence of a universe without a controlling deity; yet it also forges a brilliant poetic fusion of apocalyptic and scientific discourses. Affirming finally a teleological goal, Tennyson offers, at least momentarily, a reassuring fiction of closure. "Next to the Bible," Queen Victoria is reported to have told him, "*In Memoriam* is my comfort" (Sinfield 1). But this is not just a poem portraying historical agonizing over faith and doubt. Tennyson also pushes the language of representation to its extremes, relocating the boundaries of conventional thought as he registers, for instance, two crucial shifts in cultural perception. Through a revisionary image of nature ("red in tooth and claw," sec. 56), he replaces the benevolent, feminized nature of pastoral Romanticism, signaling a move from Romantic valorization of the natural object to Victorian poetic use of nature as an imagistic resource field; and through metaphors of material dissolution ("The hills are shadows, and they flow," sec. 123) he marks the expanded historical consciousness emerging from the new geological time scales. Further, and remarkably, he tests the boundaries of poetic construction. When relating the mystical experience of renewed contact with the dead Hallam (sec. 95) he cleverly deploys the language of paradox ("silent-speaking words" and "love's dumb cry") to diffuse the boundaries between literal and figurative, and thus to initiate the climactic moment when the dead man's "touch" is indeterminately literal and/or figurative in an ecstatic release from the binary structures of spirit and matter: "all at once it seem'd at last / The living soul was flash'd on mine." The sentence threatens to lose coherence: "The steps of Time – the shocks of Chance – / The blows of Death." At which point the poet struggles with the stylistic necessity of structuring the perception in conventional speech: what "matter-moulded forms" are appropriate, or even possible? Herein lies the focus of radical doubt – that uncertainty which observes not only the vicissitudes of faith or the consequences of new knowledge, but also, with Arnold's *Empedocles*, the problematic of representing the ineffable, of thinking and perceiving outside the requirements of language.

This moment of intensely private experience also acknowledges the role of public and symbolic value in the construction of poetic language. Insofar as doubt focuses on spiritual values, it focuses also on the symbolic constitution of (cultural) wealth, so that while *In Memoriam* overtly deals with the abstractions of faith, those abstractions are rooted in the materiality of loss, the loss, for instance, of Hallam's "touch." The climax of the poem therefore is a moment when touch, both literally and figuratively, is restored. Such moments are to do with formalizing, finding "form," which for Victorian poets means physical manifestation, "meaning" incarnate, poetic creativity linked homologously to spiritual incarnation. The biblical Word made flesh parallels symbolic meaning in the poetic and material word, which in turn necessitates the commodified word, Tennyson's "truths" which are made "current coin" (sec. 36). Much of the Victorian poetry of spiritual crisis similarly explores these boundaries and homologies, probing lines of division, suggesting an interpenetration of flesh and spirit, or conversely positing belief as the mere reflexiveness of metaphoric thinking: Arnold through his devastating image of cultural and spiritual displacement, "Wandering between two worlds, one dead, / The other powerless to be born" ("Stanzas from the Grande Chartreuse," 1855, ll. 85–6); Robert Browning through the dialectical coils of skeptical bishops and sensual monks (1855), or the ironic reflexivity of Caliban's natural theology (1864); Barrett Browning through the possibilities of a New Jerusalem in *Aurora Leigh*; Clough through his doubly dividing and divisible "Dipsychus" (1850–69); Christina Rossetti through the liminality of convent thresholds (1858); and Hopkins unceasingly, whether through a divinely inspired and poetically realized "shipwrack" ("The Wreck of the *Deutschland*," 1875, 1. 248) or the sacral interconnectedness of "Brute beauty" ("The Windhover," 1877, 1. 9).

During the century the intensively physical aspect of the intermingling of symbol and material becomes increasingly apparent. In Augusta Webster's "A Castaway" (1870), for example, Tennyson's "coin" of spiritual truth becomes the explicitly economic "coin" of a courtesan's life (l. 555). Again the image is both literal (the woman's body as an object of exchange) and figurative (her life is defined, culturally and morally, by how it is "spent"), thus constituting the meeting point of political economy and female worth, and dramatizing in the process the means by which women are ideologically commodified. In such a moment the poet's interest in symbolic value coincides with the economy's focus on market value, both sets of value being focused through the single material image. Again, poetic focus on symbolic meaning enacts a relationship between idealist value and commercial product. That relationship was consummated by Dante Gabriel Rossetti and William Morris when they engaged directly in the physical production of their writing. As Morris well knew, the making of art always confronts the resistances of the material: language incarnate means not just themes and images but papers, bindings, and markets.

IV

The possibility for figurative language to enact its own self-referentiality is one key to what is radical in Victorian poetry. Furthermore, as suggested for *In Memoriam*, it is a reflexiveness which incorporates historical and political contexts. In *Maud* (1855), for instance, the condition of England and the condition of the deranged hero are represented "as utterly congruent and as reciprocally determined" (Tucker 1988: 407). Crucially, however, linguistic self-reference or self-enactment, simultaneously formal and thematic, is a feature of what has become recognized as the main Victorian contribution to poetic form, the dramatic monologue. Conventionally associated with Robert Browning (though his own term was "dramatic lyric" or "dramatic romance"), it was nevertheless invented contemporaneously by Tennyson, and dramatic poems (employing speakers other than the poet) by Felicia Hemans and Letitia Landon predate the early monologues of both Tennyson and Browning.

In many respects the dramatic monologue was an unprecedented poetic phenomenon. From its inception in the 1830s and 1840s, its use spread rapidly, flooding the literary market and requiring puzzled reviewers to learn to describe its idiosyncrasies and implications. It appeared in numerous variants and was employed by an incredible array of poets, both men from Tennyson to Swinburne, and women from Hemans to Webster. As a literary form it was utterly immersed in the cultural conditions of its time – philosophical, aesthetic, political, and especially psychological.

In the first half of the century the concept of psychology was shifting from an earlier focus on the human soul or mind, as distinct from the body, to embrace both mind and body through mental pathology – aberrations and diseases. Central to this movement was a changing definition of insanity, and it is that which most relates to the advent of dramatic-psychological poetry. The understanding of madness broadened from loss or impairment of reason, through deluded imagination, to what the French called "rational lunacy" (*folie raisonnante*) or the British "moral insanity." After J. C. Prichard's *Treatise on Insanity* (1835), insanity became widely known in England as a quasi-moral condition: a "morbid perversion of the feelings, affections, and active powers," often coexisting with "an apparently unimpaired state of the intellectual faculties" (Prichard, cited in Faas 45). The boundaries between the mad and the sane were thus being blurred, and this possibility of a rational yet morbidly, even comically, excessive mind clearly fascinated Tennyson ("St Simeon Stylites," 1842; *Maud*) and Robert Browning ("Porphyria's Lover," 1836; "Too Late," 1864). At the same time, moral insanity also rendered intense passion somewhat precarious. Any hint of excess could suggest mental imbalance: merely "moral delinquency," for instance, or when a "modest female" acts in a "bold" and "indecent manner" (Faas 45). Poets exploited all of these aspects. By choosing aberrant or excessive speakers, they kept poetry as a genre for passion, though no longer in the discredited terms of Romantic lyricism; they also encouraged the reader to become an active participant and to contemplate the political as well as the psychological significance of the passion indulged: "I am not mad: I am black," asserts Barrett Browning's infanticidal slave mother ("The Runaway Slave at Pilgrim's Point," 1848, l. 218).

Accompanying the professional psychological development was an even broader tradition of introspection, which emerged from the growing desire to define the nature of selfhood in the late eighteenth and early nineteenth century. Self-analysis had been established by figures such as Locke, Hume, Hartley, Reid, and Priestley as a primary prerequisite to study of the mind, and this, combined with an equally strong Romantic aesthetic emphasis on expressiveness fueled by philosophical idealism, meant that by the early Victorian age there was a widespread obsession with self-scrutiny (Shaw 47–74). It was also claimed by some psychologists that the only way to understand the insane was to identify with their plight, to imagine what it must be like to see with their eyes. These are also the techniques of the Romantic poet, the powers of sympathetic identification, what Arthur Hallam praised as the young Tennyson's "power of embodying himself in ideal characters" (Armstrong 1993: 340), or what Fox equally admired in Tennyson as "the secret of the transmigration of the soul" (Faas 61).

Philosophically, the dramatic monologue can be read as a response to Romantic idealism and the crisis of dualism (body and soul, material and ideal, public and private, culture and nature) inherited from Western metaphysics and the Cartesian *cogito*. The form challenges dualism through representing the self not as a separate unit, but as tied to linear history and an open cultural system. It also represents the contradictions and differences of the self in language, continually enacting the doubled subject as both homogeneous "true person" and heterogeneous, disappearing moment of speech or signification (Martin 28–31). Foregrounding textual difference and its constitutive processes, the monologue form thus shifts aesthetic ideologies from homogeneity and wholeness to continuity and incompletion. Combining lyric with narrative and dramatic elements, it disrupts atemporal universality, introduces mimetic particularity, and emphasizes the dialogical nature of language, challenging as it does so idealist notions of the essential and single self.

The political implications of the form emerge from Robert Browning's responses during the 1830s to the contemporary theories of John Stuart Mill, which led him to realize how it might be possible to stage a cultural critique through the structuring processes of a poetic monologue. Mill's famous account of poetry as the expression of "overheard" feeling was parodied in Browning's early monologues, "Porphyria's Lover" and "Johannes Agricola" (1836; later called "Madhouse Cells," 1842), showing how the solipsism of isolated personal feeling leads to delusion and visions of omnipotence. Mill's distinction between poetry and rhetoric effectively produced what Isobel Armstrong calls a "poetics of exclusion" (1993: 137), denying to poetry externality, agency, or the validity of public knowledge. Browning circumvented Mill's lyrical cul-de-sac, Armstrong argues, through ideas derived from the liberal milieu both he and Mill shared. W. J. Fox's theories, for example, drawing on features of drama (dialogue, relationship, objectification), allowed for cultural criticism, showing how psychological conditions are grounded in history. These theories did not, however, allow for the function of constitutive fictions (crucial to an art-form based on dramatic illusion), and for that Browning turned to the godfather of utilitarianism, Jeremy Bentham. For Bentham, fictional constructs are potentially iniquitous, yet culturally indispensable; essential to language and conceptualizing, they intervene substantively in the world, effecting choices and actions. By combining these dramatic and fictive theories Browning thus constructed a poetic which is both culturally interventionist and an escape from solipsism (Armstrong 1993: 148–51).

One consequence of the claim for intervention is a recurring play with the possibilities for agency: the dramatic monologue offers a tacit paradigm for the exigencies of subjective and subjected action. It displays, for instance, an array of acts which play upon the meaning of assertiveness. Such acts exhibit an enormous emotional and psychological diversity, ranging (to take the political just in terms of the female other) from the tyranny of negation ("Porphyria's Lover") and ideological construction (D. G. Rossetti's "Jenny," 1870), to the rebellion of the woman *as* other (Barrett Browning's "Runaway Slave") and the self-appraisal of political economy by one of its products (Webster's "A Castaway").

As the form is developed it becomes fundamentally dynamic. The substantial monologues of Robert Browning's maturity, for example, display an endlessly dynamic process of spoken subjectivity. Numerous borders are approached or transgressed as speakers proffer various versions of "the dangerous edge of things" ("Bishop Blougram's Apology," l. 395), that liminality where our fascination follows not simply ambivalence (Blougram's "tender murderer" etc.), which is too static a nomination for Browning, but interplay, a discursive restlessness which has barely been identified or understood. Speakers become linguistically bacchanalian, energetically excessive, representing in order to re-present, as if living in a textualized culture means, as in the world of commodities, an unceasing proliferation of signs. Such proliferation induces psychological uneasiness and a consequent search for a security of persuasiveness or affirmation that is rarely attained, because words are discursive, achieving signification only through movement and mobility. Some monologues dramatize the dilemma of speakers sympathetically, in the tradition of soliloquies, while others suggest ironic discrepancies that severely limit or even undercut speakers' claims to certitude: their ludic excess ("St Simeon Stylites"), solipsistic omnipotence ("My Last Duchess," 1842), subtlety of revenge (Barrett Browning's "Bertha in the Lane," 1844), enabling blindness ("Andrea del Sarto," 1855), or eroticized spirituality (Christina Rossetti's "The Convent Threshold," 1858). But whatever complexities of sympathy and irony may be induced, dynamic restlessness remains endemic, and its accompaniment of multiplying structural differences tends to confound attempts to define the form as a fixed genre. At the same time, the widespread writing of poems that exhibit varieties of contestation, where expressiveness is placed in a context that objectifies its process (Arnold's "Stanzas from the Grande Chartreuse"), or where a speaker objectifies herself for self-scrutiny (Webster's "By the Looking-Glass," 1866, or "Faded," 1870), marks a cultural phenomenon of monologues that are recognizably "dramatic." The formal features of this hybrid mode almost certainly rest upon a rhetorical ambiguity that "pulls together the intimacy of reading and the detachment of spectacle" (Reynolds 160). By this means the politics of textual and cultural construction are held up for scrutiny, and the ideological assumptions of the classic "overheard" lyric are analyzed and rewritten.

V

Ideological formations in Victorian England as in all societies engendered certain patterns and conformities for gender and class relationships. Within the predominant bourgeois, patriarchal, capitalist formations, gendered positions in particular were assumed to be essential (fundamentally true) and were inhibiting as well as empowering for all classes and sexes. Yet various poetic representations of the way men read and write women, or how women might read and write themselves, began to question this essentialism. There was both the "Woman Question" and what could be called a "Condition of Manliness Question" (Sussman); and both questions for poets related inevitably to creativity as well as sexuality. Lyric poetry, for instance, as a genre associated with feeling, was culturally feminized and subject thereby to both formalist and psychological control. The idealist-based, expressive poetics which generally prevailed during the century enjoined all poets to develop a "healthy" release of emotions: that meant insanity, for both men and women, was the threatened price for either repressed or excessive passion. This injunction included working-class poets who were exhorted to write inspirationally, that they might model for others a balanced expression of feelings which could otherwise turn morbid (or sociopathic).

Women in this context faced the difficult – because naturalized – barrier of gender prejudice. If women poets transgressed the feminine requirements of the demure and sympathetically sentimental, they were deemed "coarse," unnatural; if they conformed to the ideological feminine, they were deemed merely women and thereby muted. In *Aurora Leigh*, for example, Romney tells Aurora what to expect from male readers: they will judge not what is "mere work" but "mere woman's work," producing certainly "the comparative respect," but that means "the absolute scorn" (II. 232–6). Even for women to have their poems read within established circles entailed overcoming male attitudes which regarded women themselves as the poem, not their writing. Again Romney, famously, states the case: women "give us doting mothers, and perfect wives, / Sublime Madonnas, and enduring saints," but they provide "no Christ," and therefore no "poet" (II. 220–5). While self-sacrificing purity was expected of women, the ideological and scriptural authority of masculine redemption and creation was not. Christina Rossetti challenges this expectation through Lizzie's role in "Goblin Market," and *Aurora Leigh* tells the story of Aurora's persistence with poetry and her eventual integration of both love and work, both sexual and poetic identities.

In the poetry of high culture the inscription of woman as textual object, as in herself a poem to be read, is also sustained by the literary conventions of courtly love, where the woman is passive, inaccessible, idealized, and silent. The complaining poet, frustrated by the unavailability of remote and enduring charms, is by definition male. The point of writing the poem is not to seek sexual consummation, but to sustain the structural relationship between desiring male subject and desirable female object, a structure which constitutes the poet as active agent. For as long as the poet speaks, he maintains his sexual identity as acting, expressive male.

When, conveniently, the desired object is silent, it may be more easily interpreted, rendered mysterious, or endowed with cosmic significance. Hence, in D. G. Rossetti's sonnet sequence *The House of Life* (the paradigm of Victorian courtly idealism; 1870/1881), a woman is that strange code, the "meaning of all things that are" ("Heart's Compass," l. 2), and Rossetti's liberal male speaker in "Jenny" enacts the classic bourgeois reduction of woman to sign, textualizing the female body within male discourse: "The woman almost fades from view," and what is left is "A cipher . . . A riddle" (ll. 277–80). Clearly, lurking in the courtly tradition is a politics of appropriation, which Robert Browning exposes ironically in poems where men declare eternal love for women who never knew they existed: "Cristina" (1842), "Evelyn Hope" (1855), "Too Late." These men introspectively and passively reenact courtly fantasies, but psychic appropriation may also be dangerous if the figurative power of the poet is enacted literally. In D. G. Rossetti's "True Woman: Her Love" (1881) the celebration of reciprocal love rests upon the unquestioned assumption that the woman's passion is "a glass" (l. 3) which mirrors the man's desire. But that same assumption allows Porphyria's lover to strangle her in accordance with what he believes to be her "darling one wish" (l. 57).

Women poets, then, if they would write of love, confronted a tradition which required their silence (Billone), idealizing the feminine only to disempower it. So they sought strategies for intervention. Barrett Browning employs parody in "Lady Geraldine's Courtship" (1844), while in *Sonnets from the Portuguese* (1850) her method is more elaborate, writing as both poet–lover and beloved in a reflexive relationship with a beloved who is also poet–lover. A complex of roles and reversals empowers the speaker to write and speak for herself, and the sequence ends in an acclaimed interdependence. Christina Rossetti took an opposite strategy in *Monna Innominata* (1881), a sonnet sequence conceived as something of a reply to *Sonnets from the Portuguese*, where she writes as one of the unnamed, silent women. Whereas Barrett Browning sought a place for the woman poet within and through received discourses, Christina Rossetti attempts to act outside them, speaking for the women whom they marginalize and repudiating their worldly assumptions by having her speaker surrender instead to divine love. While Rossetti may shift the terms of the amatory relationship, the radical structural element remains: when her persona speaks of spiritual love, she speaks as a desiring poet of a remote beloved, God. A logocentrically grounded structure of desire which engages unequal agents remains, then, difficult to elude, although in the brief lyric "Day-Dreams" (1857) Rossetti employs another, more subtle strategy. Here she explores the structural ambiguities of courtly relationships through a speaker of undefined gender, who observes and interprets the beloved who "doth not answer" (l. 26). Read in terms of the full possibilities provided by this gender uncertainty, the poem suggests the complex female identity, simultaneously passive and active, which is denied by an appropriating, distinctively male (poet's) gaze; here courtly structures themselves are used to expose and diffuse their assumptions.

Another dominant gender influence on poetry was the doctrine of separate spheres, the bourgeois domestic ideology which immured women in the home while men could wander free. In Robert Browning's "Meeting at Night" and "Parting at Morning" (1845), the contrasting moments of an unnamed speaker who enters the world of private sexual fulfillment at night, only to return to the public world of commercial "gold" the next day, would be gendered male (Sussman 104–6). An accompanying moral double standard which required women to emulate the impossible ideal of the virgin mother while men were encouraged to sow their seed variously, and to the homosocial approval of their peers, produced many poems about mothers and the requirements of self-effacement (treated ironically in "Bertha in the Lane"), and about prostitution. Women poets from Barrett Browning to Adelaide Procter and Webster resist the denigration of prostitutes, and several poems by men portray the self-justifying casuistry of male complicity ("Jenny," Robert Browning's *Fifine at the Fair*, 1872). In "Lord Walter's Wife" (1862) Barrett Browning brilliantly attacks men's evasions of their own ambivalence and the hypocrisy which transfers moral responsibility to women.

The increasing complexity of nineteenth-century sexuality and the proliferation of its coded performances makes it another area where poetry is generically suited to explore the problematics of discursive representation. Certainly poems display an array of gender-related issues, dramatizing uncertainties, blurring boundaries, exposing the textual artifice of differences: male femininity in *The Princess* (1847) and *In Memoriam*, or the speaker's cry for a new masculinity in *Maud*; redefined roles for women in *Aurora Leigh*; Robert Browning's representations of homosocial rivalry and the undercurrents to heterosexual success; sisterhood in "Goblin Market"; Clough's and Patmore's explorations of the factitiousness in sexual and religious thinking; Swinburne's combination of dissidence and innocence; the lesbian poems of Michael Field. Many women wrote to affirm the feminine, though few eluded being structured through reference to bourgeois categories (Armstrong 1993: 323). They commonly wrote, for example, about "home, the market, mothers and muses" (Leighton x), and attempts such as that by Michael Field to construct a separate aesthetic realm through a muse which fuses Sappho, Virgin, and Tiresias (see Chris White, in Leighton 148–61) rest upon categories of established metaphysics. But that is not to militate against their role and influence within contemporary culture. A poem such as *Aurora Leigh*, while it now provokes reservations in some readers about its feminism, quickly became cited within debates about the Woman Question.

If women wrote in relationship to bourgeois culture, so too did working-class poets. The forms and sentiments of their expression, for instance, are frequently the forms and sentiments of middle-class culture. The Parnassians among them, so labeled by Brian Maidment (1987) as those who sought recognition for their cultural achievement, frequently combined neo-classical forms with Romantic natural imagery. Employing Spenserian stanzas (Charles Swain's *The Mind*, 1832; Thomas Cooper's *The Purgatory of Suicides*, 1845), sonnet stanzas (John Rogerson's "Manchester," 1844), couplets (John Prince's "The Death of the Factory Child," 1841; Thomas Cleaver's "Night," 1848), and a form of truncated rhyme royal (Ebenezer Elliott's well-known "Steam at Sheffield," 1840), they wrote repeatedly with moral indignation, pathos, and pastoral idealism, traditional sentiments to which their traditional stanzaic forms represented a social–historical hearkening back. Prince's "Factory Child," for example, conducts an outraged lament for the death of a boy factory worker exhausted by his labors. The child dies heroically after a sequence in which his mother's memories of his naturalized childhood, when like a young Wordsworth he "knew each sylvan and sequester'd nook" (l. 79), contrast savagely with the industrially wasted body. Tone and imagery are melodramatic, although the outrage maintains the dignity of clearly focused anger.

The mixed elements of this poem indicate the larger dilemma of the working-class poet. There are confused aims and methods, for instance, as Prince mixes elegiac pathos with the hyperbole of political protest, and the "kind philanthropists" who are called on "to emancipate the British slave" (ll. 129–32) remain idealistically classless and so effectively powerless. Prince's use of conservative sentiment rather than political analysis is basically an appeal to moral justice and common humanity, which may be easily read as the dissemination of middle-class British liberalism; yet what better way of appealing to the sympathies of those with political influence? Unfortunately, the middle-class readers who did read this poetry tended to focus precisely on its literary weaknesses as a way of deferring its political challenge. The more aggressive language of the Chartist poets, for instance (Elliott, Gerald Massey, or W. J. Linton, whose doggerel epic *Bob Thin – or, The Poorhouse Fugitive*, 1845, tied weaver Bob's life to the history of British capitalism), was described as an "unpoetic" linguistic violence which threatened poetry itself (Maidment 288). The conservative, even at times anachronistic, literary ideology of these self-taught poets is no doubt a mimicry which performs their colonized condition, but their energetic and moralizing presence nevertheless became an acknowledged part of the Victorian literary scene. As their work became noticed by middle-class readers like Carlyle and Kingsley, aspects of artisan history and conditions "were made relevant to early Victorian industrial culture" (Maidment 100).

VI

Finally, a brief polemic: in an age which produced huge works, the poem which stands as the colossus astride Victorian verse is *The Ring and the Book* (1868–9). There are strong competitors in *Aurora Leigh* (1857) and Tennyson's *Idylls of the King* (1859–85), both of which present complex narratives of social and political significance, and both of which incorporate a variety of genres – autobiography, satire, treatise, lyrical prophecy in *Aurora Leigh*; lyric, tragedy, romance, epic in *Idylls of the King*. The *Idylls* stood for a long time as the monumental achievement of Victorian indirection, constructing from the medieval materials of Arthurian legend an epic vision of Britain's imperial splendor and internal decline. As Arthur's impossible morality fails to sustain the Round Table, the poem transforms Tennyson's repeated theme of loss into a symbolic mythos of changing order. Here, as in Arnold's *Empedocles*, is recognition that the inherited values of humanism and patriarchal instruction will no longer suffice.

Aurora Leigh offers a now canonical Victorian statement of women's claims to social and artistic equality. Through its challenge to the conventional feminine, it makes a radical break with its age, although it also enjoyed immense popularity. It flaunts "the woman's figures," exposes debilitating discrepancies between the idealized "natural" and the actual, describes slum dwellings and the working-class poor, represents male brutality and the humiliation of rape victims, displays the competitiveness between women provoked by patriarchal commodification, approaches the potential for same-sex relations between women, and above all dramatizes the experience of a female poet in a bourgeois society. In short, it combines the classic feminist themes of the age: education, love, marriage, creativity, sexual politics.

The Ring and the Book, however, produces a level of formal experimentation and ironizing self-reference that adds an epistemological cutting-edge not found in the other two works. The thematic exploration of truth, through a maze of public opinion, legal fictions, and church structures, combined with a methodological awareness which examines creativity and cultural construction, places the poem at the heart of

Western history and metaphysics, and thus at the heart of what was most innovative in Victorian poetry and poetics. It is at once the apotheosis and the critique of the influential Western traditions of idealism and humanist essentialism.

Its demands on readers are legendary. Twice the length of *Paradise Lost*, its sheer size and sustained textual intensity make reading a daunting task. The poem recounts a Roman murder story three times in book I and then through ten discrepant variations from the three protagonists (young wife, aged husband, idealistic priest), members of the populace, lawyers, the Pope, and through further reports in the final book, where there would be an end "had anything an end" (XII. 1). But plot is hardly the point. The poem is intent upon problematizing representation. Its concerns lie with evidence, eyewitness accounts, hearsay, history, narrative, imagination, institutional patterning. What happens, the poem asks, to morality, belief, and identity in a culture where signs and discourses multiply and defer, yet where we cannot know otherwise than through "worth of word" (I. 837)? The poem disperses all centers, confusing readers from Henry James onwards who have sought to restore some locus for belief and meaning, a center of consciousness. In all this *The Ring and the Book* culminates those repetitive obsessions of Victorian poetry nominated by Arnold's *Empedocles* – consciousness, representation, language, and agency. It also enacts an evanescent historical margin between Romantic phenomenology and a postmodernist culture of endless differentiation, proliferating simulacra, textualizing representations without closure.

See also 1897; SEXUALITIES; MEDICAL, FINANCIAL, INDUSTRIAL, PUBLISHING; LITERARY CRITICISM

REFERENCES

Armstrong, I. (1982) *Language as Living Form in Nineteenth-Century Poetry*. Brighton: Harvester.

—— (1993) *Victorian Poetry: Poetry, Poetics and Politics*. London: Routledge.

Billone, A. C. (2007) *Little Songs: Women, Silence, and the Nineteenth-Century Sonnet*. Columbus: Ohio State University Press.

Blair, K. (2006) *Victorian Poetry and the Culture of the Heart*. Oxford: Clarendon Press.

Faas, E. (1988) *Retreat into the Mind: Victorian Poetry and the Rise of Psychiatry*. Princeton: Princeton University Press.

Griffiths, E. (1989) *The Printed Voice of Victorian Poetry*. Oxford: Clarendon Press.

Leighton, A. (ed.) (1996) *Victorian Women Poets: A Critical Reader*. Oxford: Blackwell.

Maidment, B. (ed.) (1987) *The Poorhouse Fugitives: Self-Taught Poets and Poetry in Victorian Britain*. Manchester: Carcanet.

Martin, L. D. (1985) *Browning's Dramatic Monologues and the Post-Romantic Subject*. Baltimore: Johns Hopkins University Press.

Reynolds, M. (2001) *The Realms of Verse 1830–1870: English Poetry in a Time of Nation-Building*. Oxford: Oxford University Press.

Riede, D. G. (2005) *Allegories of One's Own Mind: Melancholy in Victorian Poetry*. Columbus: Ohio State University Press.

Ryals, C. De L. (1990) *A World of Possibilities: Romantic Irony in Victorian Literature*. Columbus: Ohio State University Press.

Shaw, W. D. (1987) *The Lucid Veil: Poetic Truth in the Victorian Age*. London: Athlone.

Sinfield, A. (1986) *Alfred Tennyson*. Oxford: Blackwell Publishers.

Slinn, E. W. (2003) *Victorian Poetry as Cultural Critique: The Politics of Performative Language*. Charlottesville: University of Virginia Press.

Sussman, H. (1995) *Victorian Masculinities: Manhood and Masculine Poetics in Early Victorian Literature and Art*. Cambridge: Cambridge University Press.

Tucker, H. F. (1988) *Tennyson and the Doom of Romanticism*. Cambridge MA: Harvard University Press.

——(ed.) (1993) *Critical Essays on Alfred Lord Tennyson*. New York: G. K. Hall.

FURTHER READING

Armstrong, I., and V. Blain (eds) (1999) *Women's Poetry, Late Romantic to Late Victorian: Gender and Genre, 1830–1900*. Basingstoke: Macmillan.

Bristow, J. (ed.) (2000) *The Cambridge Companion to Victorian Poetry*. Cambridge: Cambridge University Press.

Cronin, R., A. Chapman, and A. H. Harrison (eds) (2002) *A Companion to Victorian Poetry*. Oxford: Blackwell.

Hughes, L. K. (2010) *The Cambridge Introduction to Victorian Poetry*. Cambridge: Cambridge University Press.

LaPorte, C. (2011) *Victorian Poets and the Changing Bible*. Charlottesville: University of Virginia Press.

Maynard, J. (1993) *Victorian Discourses on Sexuality and Religion*. Cambridge: Cambridge University Press.

Prins, Y. (1999) *Victorian Sappho*. Princeton: Princeton University Press.

Tucker, H. F. (2008) *Epic: Britain's Heroic Muse 1790–1910*. Oxford: Oxford University Press.

23
Fiction

Hilary M. Schor

There would seem to be two reasons not to read another critical essay about the Victorian novel. The first is, quite simply, that everyone already knows enough about it. Even the most rapid survey course in English literature will pause at *Hard Times* or *Jude the Obscure*; film and television versions of the Brontës and George Eliot continue to win audiences; the annual parade of *Christmas Carol*s and the spectacle of over-stuffed Penguin paperbacks in airports would argue that the Victorian novel has won its place at the heart of our culture.

That very cordial relation between those eminent Victorians and us might suggest the *other* reason we do not want to think further about Victorian fiction: some of the best criticism of the novel has suggested that it is not only overly familiar, but down-right bad for us. Novels, it has variously been argued, are an integral part of a system of individual discipline and social formation that took its current, powerful form in the mid-nineteenth century, and has been shaping (and mis-shaping) individual readers and the culture in which they read ever since. In their forward-moving and morally progressive plots, their emphasis on individual solutions, their mirroring of a diverse but finally all-inclusive social sphere, the novels inscribe their readers more comfortably, and therefore more insidiously, within a master-plot of cultural control. As D. A. Miller (1987) argues, the way novelists contrast our unbounded subjectivity to the various boxes, cells, and coffins their novels contain seems to argue ourselves "open" or uncontained – the most dangerous and containing fiction of all. And as Lennard Davis (1987) asks, in a simpler and equally compelling critique of our eagerness to abandon ourselves to "novel" beings: is there not something very odd about

A New Companion to Victorian Literature and Culture, First Edition. Edited by Herbert F. Tucker.
© 2014 John Wiley & Sons, Ltd. Published 2014 by John Wiley & Sons, Ltd.

the spectacle of an airport full of readers poring over novels, and not even moving their lips?

This essay will not begin by disrupting either of these notions. Certainly, something we recognize as the Victorian novel did win a distinct cultural authority and has continued not only to be a popular form, but to represent "high culture" for many readers, both amateur and professional. The Victorian novel is, for many of us, still the most accessible and most beloved form of "masterpiece," with or without television costume dramas. And certainly with that cultural power come other forms of power – though I would hope to complicate a little the chicken-and-egg question of how literature comes to matter to people, and what difference literature makes in the "real world." This essay can perhaps best begin by excavating the unspoken ideas on which both the easier assumptions rest: the first, that there is some "natural" relationship between the real world and its fictional representation; and the second, that the Victorian novel played an altogether complicit role in representing that world. But let me first raise some questions about what we mean by the "Victorian novel," and whether we are all sure we know what we are reading when we carry these novelistic packages around.

When an undergraduate begins her Victorian novel survey, she is likely to confront a row of orange- or black-backed paperbacks, each with the reassuring apparatus of an introduction, footnotes, and a dim black-and-white apparition of an author on the inside cover. The book is invariably fronted either by a crowd scene at a fairground, railway station, or bazaar of commodity culture, or else by a solemn-faced, Whistler-esque heroine, staring earnestly back at her reader, promising the moral revolutions of the inner life. Victorian novels come to us, that is, poised between questions of outer and inner, public and private life; they tend to contrast and finally to oppose the individual to social forces; they promise that we will find a similar equilibrium in our own lives.

Before the class has even begun, that is, our undergraduate student already has missed some of the initial strangeness of the Victorian novel. For many first-time readers of Victorian fiction, it may be enough to point out that *all* nineteenth-century novels did not appear in the first instance with orange and black backs. While many contemporary editions attempt to recreate some conditions of Victorian reading – including serial publication, three-volume publication, illustrations, and bindings – it is difficult to disrupt the homogeneity of twenty-first-century publishing practices. It is even more difficult to disrupt the homogeneity of literary inheritance and pedigree with which we approach the Victorian novel, one of the central factors convincing us that we understand what we are holding in our hands.

For if we return to our platonic "lit survey," in most courses (including my own) the Victorian novel comes "after the Romantics," which usually means the Romantic poets. It is a rare student (at the undergraduate or graduate level) who comes to the novel from the essays of Thomas De Quincey or Charles Lamb, or even from the *Sketches* of Boz. The Victorian novel, once approached in survey form, may be even further sealed off from extra-novelistic contamination: even in a course focusing on

Victorian literature, the novel is most often opposed to "poetry," usually the intensely psychological monologues of Tennyson and Browning, and to "nonfiction prose," usually the social rantings of Carlyle, Ruskin, and Arnold. The novel in this way occupies an uneasy ground between the individual and the collective, but its very form, the central plot moving an individual from childhood to moral revelation, seems to resolve the question, promising that we will all, like David Copperfield, become the heroes of our own lives, and hence see ourselves smoothly mirrored in the self-reflexive surface of a Victorian novel. It is that smooth surface which I want to shatter here. A different account of the rise of the Victorian novel would offer a more nuanced response to my initial claims, that we know all too well what the Victorian novel is, and that it is not terribly good for us. That other version might suggest that the Victorian novel has a more complicated history than novel-lovers and critics imagine, and that it poses more difficult problems of form and meaning, disclosing a less simplistic (and less socially complicit) account of individualism, society, and representation.

Let us return, then, to the novel's origins. The Victorian novel seems to most critics to have emerged with the spontaneity of its most famous early incarnation: much as the theory of gravity arose when a single apple fell from Newton's sky, so too the novel began with a single inspiration, the young Boz sitting down to write and "thinking of Mr Pickwick." As *The Pickwick Papers* (1837) emerged from Pierce Egan's flash tales of the London adventurers Tom and Jerry and the sketchy pages of Robert Surtees's *Jorrocks' Jaunts* (1838) and other such tales of sporting life, it became a novel that "placed before the reader a constant succession of characters and incidents," "painted in vivid colours" and "rendered . . . life-like and amusing." I am quoting from Charles Dickens's later preface to the novel, but the coincidence of Dickens's avowedly "realist" definition of his enterprise, its astonishing and culture-wide success, and its publication in the years surrounding Victoria's ascension, make *Pickwick* and its publication-mate *Oliver Twist* (1838) easy markers for the Victorian novel.

But this straightforward birth-narrative needs some roughing-up, or at least some hint of digression. *Pickwick* owes much more to the sketch tradition from which it emerges, and indeed the novels Dickens wrote in those early years bear much less resemblance to the more coherent later cultural productions of the late 1840s, the 1850s, and 1860s. To make clear the promised complication of the Victorian novel, we need to explore the other elements at work in *Pickwick*'s invention. Against what was Dickens writing, and what earlier strains of nineteenth-century fiction, in particular the novels of the 1830s, was he echoing, amplifying, and perhaps repressing?

The literary forms of the 1830s, like the other cultural artifacts of that decade, are incredibly diverse, and are largely lost to literary history. In contrast to the novels of the earlier Romantic period (Walter Scott and Jane Austen, in particular) the novel moved in the 1830s back into London – and into particular neighborhoods. The novels of the period are highly marked by social indicators: the novel of high society, or "silver fork" novel; the novel of lower-class and criminal life, or "Newgate" novel; the budding social-realist novel, focusing on factory and industrial–urban life; the novel of middle-class or "domestic" realism. Like the details rendered in these novels, their readers are imagined in highly particular ways: as male or female; as residing in particular neighborhoods or following specific social practices; as having certain relationships to reading, whether sentimental or cynical, tremulous or aggressive. These novels have no readership today, in part because they are not very well written by modern standards, by which I mean that they fail to present smooth, seamless prose offering a coherent narrative point of view from which to observe a variety of characters possessing coherent (and sense-making) selves. That is to say, they lack what the Victorians made inevitable: omniscience in the external and internal world, and a cohesion of social and individual perception. (When these do not cohere in Victorian and post-Victorian fictions, we know we are in the presence of madmen and postmodernists.) The earlier novels are also difficult to read because of their clunky, ill-fitting, and digressive novelist apparatus: glossaries, footnotes, chunks of text in foreign languages, and technical argot. (This is again to say, they are mad and more than a little postmodernist.) This same apparatus is linked, however, to my point about their different relationship to individual and social narratives. The 1830s novel does not assume that all readers move easily in all worlds: Edward Bulwer-Lytton's ancient Rome, in *The Last Days of Pompeii* (1834), is a milieu hardly more foreign than the England depicted in two other novels of his: either the dandiacal high society of his silver-fork novel *Pelham* (1828), which earned Thomas Carlyle's rage in *Sartor Resartus* (1834), or the thieves' dens of his Newgate novel *Paul Clifford* (1830). In both novels, Bulwer's habit of introducing untranslated passages of Latin, of painstakingly elaborating details of dress, manners, local custom, and map-making, and of "dropping" into poetry, make England as alien as Pompeii – and as "novelistic." The play of genres we instantly identify in the 1830s is indicative of a deeper play of social identity and anxiety over social representation.

We can clarify these issues by focusing on two representative figures: Carlyle and Dickens. Carlyle was the most influential reader of novels of the early Victorian period, and no one is more striking in his response to that prickly Victorian sage than his unwished-for disciple Dickens. Again, the tyranny of survey syllabi has exiled Carlyle to the "social critics" roster, but it is useful to remember that he attempted to write an historical novel before he turned to the essay (Oscar Wilde called Carlyle's 1837 *French Revolution* the greatest novel of the nineteenth century) and, more important, that his insanely didactic *Sartor Resartus* contains within its fragments of social vision and prophecy a *Bildungsroman*, the story of young Diogenes Teufelsdröckh, who moves from loss to gain, from doubt to certainty, from a love story to a prophetic vision, in true novelistic fashion. Critics who take Teufelsdröckh's admonition to "close thy Byron, open thy Goethe" (return to the world of natural wonder, not artificial, "literary" sensation) as a directive to turn from fiction to fact often fail to note the highly fictional nature of Diogenes's wanderings or his metaphoric perorations. Similarly, readers who take seriously Carlyle's inveighing against the novel in essays like

"Biography" (1832) should weigh equally his concession that even "the stupidest" novel written can contain something of value, some insight into the mystery and wonder around us, and in each human soul.

For the young Dickens, turning from the sketch to the writing of serious fiction (which for him, as for his contemporaries, meant the novels of Scott), the Carlylean imperative to turn to the wider social world, to place individual consciousness within the progress of history, was a weighty one indeed. But along with the charge to a wider vision came a different attention to individual consciousness, which was now imagined (like the readerly consciousness) as more uniform, and more homogeneous. This move is made clear by the physical appearance of *Oliver Twist*, the "parish boy's progress" which owes as much energy and melodramatic passion to the Newgate novel as it spends in denying this inheritance. This novel, unlike other contemporary novels of thieves, prostitutes, and street-Jews, has no glossary or footnotes explaining its slang; it buries its geography, so that readers are only occasionally aware of famous London landmarks or the changes in neighborhood (Nancy remarks in passing to Bill Sikes that they are near a prison near a slaughterhouse – almost literally burying the reference to Newgate prison); its workhouse-born hero and gutter-raised heroine both speak perfect English; and (despite its frequent shifts from broad comedy to horrifying pathos) it contains a denunciation of the "streaky bacon" of novels that blend theatrical melodrama and hardened realism. The author's preface contains a lengthy attack on the Newgate novels of Bulwer, Harrison Ainsworth, and Thackeray, and turns back to Hogarth for its defense of its vicious criminals and modest maidens. The novel all but wears a sandwich-board proclaiming its high literary calling, and one would hardly know from its pages that its young author was simultaneously completing the romps of Pickwick – unless one remembered, of course, that Pickwick himself spends several late numbers of the *Papers* in prison for debt, and listens to one gothic tale of criminal nightmare and masochistic love after another, in the interpolated tales that impede that portly pilgrim's progress.

Critics have written persuasively of the investment Dickens made in creating himself as a serious novelist in the 1840s, and have argued (perhaps unintentionally) that the novel grew up alongside him. But a specter haunts that progress as well – the edgy and less complacently "fictional" novels of the 1830s, with their different claims to realism. The glossary and footnote, awkward as they seem, point to a realization that readers do not all speak a uniform English, or populate an easily navigable urban landscape, or recognize the same forms of social interaction or party-going manners. All this anxiety over social representation continues strong in the early Victorian novel and its social whirl, as in the beginning of Elizabeth Gaskell's *Mary Barton: A Tale of Manchester Life* (1848) where "a Manchester tea-party" must be explained in careful terms. Readers know, by the end of the first chapter, not only how social relations develop between the characters, but how many tea-cups a family would have, and where they would be kept, and from whom others would be borrowed, all to make up the awkward and heart-warming opening scene. Similarly, when the narrator of Gaskell's *Cranford* (1853) asks her readers, "Do you ever see cows dressed in grey flannel in London?," she is harking back to some of these earlier anxieties about how socially placed readers read – yet now with little doubt that readers are ensconced within an urban, cosmopolitan world and expect different experiences to be served up to them with a minimum of fuss. By mid-century the coherence of the Victorian novel as well as its social success – indeed, its status as a *guarantor* of social cohesion – was well underway.

But this fictional coherence was made, not born, and a brief return to *Oliver Twist* makes the transformation clearer. I have said that *Oliver* dispenses with the technical aids of earlier novels: glossaries, footnotes, maps. How can it do this, and still "translate" a strange world to readers who might otherwise be lost in the alleys of St Giles? Most simply, by introducing Oliver himself, the "parish boy," a character who is, in the novel's terms, "green." By having a central character who is foreign to the novel's world, and setting him to learn the lingo, master the urban landscape and find his place, the novel can help us translate as well. Oliver is, in a sense, the novel's interpretive device, the space of the dictionary or wall-map – and since he rarely understands what is said to him or knows where he is, he performs this plot-function (and narratorial function) admirably. This is not to say that the narrator of *Oliver Twist* is smooth or invisible – like the clunkiest of Newgate or silver-fork narrators, he is jokey and intrusive and mock-ironic and mock-heroic by turns; and yet he need not do much of the work of interpretation which readers can now convince themselves they are doing on their own. The *process* of social movement has been made invisible; tiny novelistic touches that used to signal "the new" have been effectively superseded.

Why does the disappearance of these signposts matter to the history of the novel – or to the emergence of later, far more complicated experiments in realism such as *Middlemarch* (1872) or *Daniel Deronda* (1876)? Is it *Oliver Twist* that makes *Masterpiece Theatre* possible? In part, yes. After the move from *Pickwick* to *Oliver Twist* and on to *Nicholas Nickleby* (1839), *Barnaby Rudge* (1841), and *Martin Chuzzlewit* (1844), Dickens was committed to novels of increasingly complicated form, thematic development, and social vision – the commitment most critics see fulfilled in *Dombey and Son* (1848), the first of the "planned" novels and the first to proceed from a thematic, formal, and narratorial scheme: the depiction of Dombey's "pride," and his reformation at the hands of his loving daughter. As the character of the loving daughter develops, in fact, it becomes the site of greatest fictional experimentation for Dickens, in Esther Summerson's shared narration of the divided novel *Bleak House* (1853), as well as in Amy Dorrit's letters, fairy tales, and quiet observations that provide an internal commentary on the problem of "nobody's fault" in *Little Dorrit* (1857). One can argue that, both in the problems of documentary social realism Dickens engages during the 1850s and in his experiments with point-of-view and narrative uncertainty, the narrator of these novels is often, as *Dombey* would have it, "a daughter after all" (chs 16, 59).

As the focal role of the curious woman deepened, so too did the attempt to reconcile the individual subject to the broader social order; Carlyle's jeremiad in *Sartor* called out for a cleansing of the world, the transformation of the "actual" into the ideal, but it began with the world of the actual – and so, in turn, did the novels of the 1840s. If the power of 1830s fiction lay in taking seriously Romantic claims that the child was father of the man, and *society* the most important father of that child (a lesson most novelists seem to have learned as much from William Godwin as from William Wordsworth), then the fiction of the 1840s moves from the particular social novels of the earlier decade (Frances Trollope's *Michael Armstrong, Factory Boy*, 1840) to that wider blend of individual and world-historical narrative found in *Mary Barton* and in Disraeli's *Sybil, or the Two Nations* (1846). Suddenly, all of England is present in the novel – and all of England is expected to *read* the novels, precisely to learn what Carlyle called in his "Biography" essay the grand secret: "the significance of Man's Life."

The story of how the novel became the most significant genre of the age is more intricate than Carlyle's paean suggests. From our perspective, this importance goes without saying: as James Fitzjames Stephen noted in 1855, "Novels, in the proper sense of the word, are used for a greater number of purposes than any other species of literature" (97). The novel attracted as much opposition as praise: as one 1859 review fumed, "That fiction, except in the form of apologue or allegory, should have ever become an instrument to illustrate or enforce moral order or religious truths, or even practical lessons in the life it professes to delineate, is incomprehensible" (Anon., "Cheap Literature"). But by 1859 opponents were fighting a rear-guard action: fiction had become just such an instrument, and David Masson, always an astute reader of novels, suggests the reasons why:

> There are no symptoms yet that the Novel is about to lose its popularity as a form of literature. On the contrary, there is every symptom, that in one shape or another it will continue to be popular for a long time, and that more and more of talent will flow into it . . . The Novel, we have found, has been becoming more real and determinate, in so far as it can convey matter of fact, more earnest, in so far as it can be made a vehicle for matter of speculation, and more conscious, at the same time, of its ability in all matter of phantasy. (152)

This concoction of "fact," "speculation," and "phantasy" was a terrifically potent one, and it suggested that Carlylean mixture of physical reality and spiritual allegory which was (as Dickens himself suggested, in the language of "vivid colours" and "life-like and amusing" incidents) at once *of* this world and *heightening* it.

But the central note that Masson's description adds to our analysis is that of the novel's "earnestness," a note that we associate with the fiction of George Eliot, whose first novel, *Adam Bede*, appeared in the same year as Masson's review. Again, this is a sentence we would read through today almost without noticing, yet turning the riotous abundance of the 1830s into the morally serious fiction of George Eliot and her rivals was not so easy as all that. Doing so depended on a movement towards the general that the novels of the 1840s carried out with some strain. In contrast to those earlier novels, it is harder to consider *Dombey and Son* or even *Hard Times* (1854) "industrial fiction," despite their attention to changing conditions of "masters and men"; the task of locating the specifics of social discourse and historical change becomes even more difficult with a novel like *Felix Holt, the Radical* (1866), which almost explicitly disavows the social realm in favor of more "speculative" questions. If the Newgate fictions of *Paul Clifford* and *Eugene Aram* (1832) were already in part silenced by *Oliver Twist*, how much more deracinated is the discussion of prison life in *David Copperfield* (1850), where the embezzling swindler Uriah Heep is imprisoned as much for his upwardly-mobile class ambitions as for his crimes, or in *Little Dorrit*, where the murderer Blandois is among the characters who spends the *least* amount of time in prison, and is finally incarcerated not by the turnkeys but by the novelist, who buries him under a falling house. The only prison in *Little Dorrit* is the Marshalsea, the debtors' prison, already long since destroyed when the novel was published in the 1850s.

This is not to say that the social, political, trivial, fashionable, *local* interests of the novel of the 1830s are banished by the late 1840s, but only to say that many of the concerns explicitly addressed in these novels — and often explicitly addressed *to the reader*, in the form of narratorial direct address and readerly apparatus — had to be submerged into more general and generalizing narrative strategies that we now take for granted. For the seamlessness of omniscience and the perfect wisdom of narrators have become the stuff of fiction to us, completely naturalized as "the fictional." Narrators who single out male and female readers; parodies and pastiches of other literary genres; chunks of undigested poetry; old ballads and newspapers; addresses to readers in their homes, their clubs, their ballrooms, or their beds — where are these 1830s hallmarks in *Jane Eyre, David Copperfield, Dombey and Son*, or *Mary Barton*?

One place such things went was into a novel that is my best counter-example, one that seems today even more of an aberration in literary history than it did in 1848: *Vanity Fair*. The original subtitle of Thackeray's novel, "Pen and Pencil Sketches of English Society," accentuates one part of its relationship to its literary forebears; "A Novel without a Hero," its original title and the subtitle under which it was published, suggests how programmatically it violates the rules of its contemporaries. Indeed, that subversive, decentralizing energy is part of what still engages even the most novice readers: from the moment when Becky Sharp hurls Johnson's *Dictionary* at Miss Pinkerton, crying out "Vive Bonaparte," the novel seems to offer a consistent critique of both heroes and hero-worship. Precisely that refusal to concede to anyone a higher ground, no matter how much it might cheer readers who sense the moral certitude of George Eliot looming around the historical corner, turns *Vanity Fair* into an increasingly unstable ground for readers as well as heroes — or heroines. This novel, however in touch it might be with "phantasy," is committed to a world of sobering fact, and deeply anxious about the grounds of "speculation."

In fact, "speculation" (of moral, economic, and philosophical varieties) is at the heart of *Vanity Fair's* enterprise, in ways that look both forward and backward in the novel's history. On one hand, its "sketchiness" recalls the clumsier qualities of the novels of the 1830s, even if its play with genres is both more deliberate and more critical. One of the most brilliant moments in *Vanity Fair* is the scene at the beginning of chapter 6, when Amelia Sedley comes downstairs to welcome George Osborne, and the narrator imagines her descent in the voice of a Newgate narrator, a silver-fork narrator, and *The Mysteries of Paris* (Eugène Sue's bestseller, tr. 1845). As Thackeray revised the novel between its first and second editions, the parodies got shorter and shorter, until only a ghost of the past narrators remains; but his parodic and pastiching instincts, the instincts of a cultural *bricoleur* as much as a *raconteur*, still pervade the novel.

On the other hand, Thackeray's fascination with the style as well as the substance, the "stuff," of fiction, gives him a new interest in the problem of telling stories, an awareness of who is telling what to whom, that novelists of the earlier period could not match, and that made the later narratorial experiments of George Eliot and Henry James possible. What Thackeray seemed to sense in the various genres of the 1830s was the possibility of different relationships not just between characters and narrators, but between narrators and readers. The sense of geographical plotting, of the need for highly specific versions of narratorial intrusion, is among the most notable things in *Vanity Fair*, as the narrator addresses "Jones at his club" or the women readers who will scorn the meek Amelia Sedley. But the narrator will also thank his local informant, Tom Eaves, and (most startling of all) will remark on his own witnessing of other characters' behavior at the German resort of Pumpernickel, and remark on the parts of the story he has heard from William Dobbin himself. It is almost impossible to reconcile with any account of realism the versions of story and storytelling this novel puts forward – a difficulty that poses problems not only of literary form but of *social* reality. How are individuals, whether narrators or not, to judge, or even to tell, stories? Can the novel actually, as Dickens promised, occupy the space of the "life-like" and the "colourful" at the same time – and what life (or is it "whose"?) should it represent?

On the wrapper of the original monthly numbers of *Vanity Fair* appears a moralist preaching to his congregation while wearing donkey-ears – ears also worn by his congregants. The illustration echoes a famous passage in Carlyle's essay "Biography," in which the "distressed Novelwright" asks the critics how he knows "that this my Long-ear of a Fictitious Biography shall not find one and the other, into whose still longer ears it may be the means, under Providence, of instilling somewhat?" The essayist answers that "None knows," and therefore he should "write on, worthy Brother, even as thou canst, even as it has been given thee." This passage is quoted at the beginning of *Mary Barton*, published at roughly the same time, and it raises again questions about the status of fiction, about biography ("the significance of Man's life"), and about the relationship of the novel to the larger society, even as it suggests some of the difficulties the novel experienced in claiming Carlyle's larger social and moral project, "under Providence, of instilling somewhat." Thackeray could be as scathing as any about the cultural program of fiction-making: in his brilliant series of parodies *Novels by Eminent Hands* (1847) he imagines "A Plan for a Prize Novel," which is to write an advertisement novel trading in what we would now call product-placement.

> Look over the *Times* or the "Directory," walk down Regent Street or Fleet Street any day – see what houses advertise most, and put yourself into communication with their proprietors . . . Walk into the shops, I say, ask for the principal, and introduce yourself, saying, "I am the great Snooks; I am the author of 'the Mysteries of Mayfair'; my weekly sale is 281,000; I am about to produce a new work called 'The Palaces of Pimlico, or the Curse of the Court,' describing and lashing fearlessly the vices of the aristocracy: this book will have a sale of at least 530,000; it will be on every table – in the boudoir of the pampered duke, as in the chamber of the honest artisan . . . So, Mr Taylor, or Mr Haberdasher, or Mr Jeweller, how much will you stand if I recommend you in my forthcoming novel?" You may make a noble income in this way, Snooks.
>
> For instance suppose it is an upholsterer. What more easy, what more delightful, than the description of upholstery? As thus: –
>
> "Lady Emily was reclining on one of Down and Eider's voluptuous ottomans, the only couch on which Belgravian beauty now reposes, when Lord Bathershins entered, stepping noiselessly over one of Tomkin's elastic Axminster carpets. 'Good heavens, my Lord!' she said – and the lovely creature fainted." (536)

This parody is only a step away from the society novels of the 1830s and earlier 1840s, and a rare parody by Dickens in *Nicholas Nickleby* offers some of the same critique of the fiction of commodities; but Thackeray's more thorough-going critique suggests some of the doubt he carried over from the earlier genres – doubt, precisely, whether the novel could have any existence apart from commodity culture, any place "outside" the world from which to criticize it. When Becky Sharp thinks, later in *Vanity Fair*, "It isn't difficult to be a country gentleman's wife . . . I think I could be a good woman if I had five thousand a year" (ch. 49), she is both commenting on the price the world places on virtue (only those who have money can afford to rise above it) and revealing more than she thinks about her own complicity with the world she in some ways sees so clearly. The novel is performing some of the same double-cross: it is both commenting on the socially determined nature of personality (and morality), and laughing at its own place in social (moral) negotiations. This novel may not have a hero, but it offers a version of hero-worship to the goddess of seeing-through-everything, at the same time that it offers itself as a version of the ultimate commodity or status-object, the perfect piece of self-conscious self-representation.

Even the more conventional novels of the 1840s share some of this ambivalence about their status as both "fictions" and "social representations." The scandal Charlotte Brontë unwittingly provoked by dedicating a second edition of *Jane Eyre* to Thackeray, who had his own insane wife in custodial care, suggests some of the dangers of novels that were too "realistic," at the same time that the more extreme responses to Brontë's novel and its heroine's violent imagination suggested that its power of "phantasy" was an even more dangerous social instrument. Similarly, where *Mary Barton*'s effort to represent the "dangerous classes" to middle-class readers won the praise of Carlyle himself for its message of fear and hope, the very detail that seemed to promise true connection between workers and masters also won it the vilification of factory owners who felt misrepresented by its sympathetic realism. While the extravagant parody and self-critique that make up *Vanity Fair*'s speculations may seem beyond anything in the period, these speculations have much in common with the other novels of the 1840s, and raise some of the same anxieties of fiction-making that will haunt the fictions of George Eliot and others in the next decades.

Eliot's novels, from *Adam Bede* on through *Daniel Deronda*, are hardly "novels without a hero," though it is interesting to reflect on the ways in which they may be even more novels with heroines. Or rather, one can see them as posing in considerably less ironic form the problems Becky Sharp herself raised: what we might call the Napoleon question, or how one is to reconcile individual stories to world-historic events; and what we might call the cash-nexus-of-morality question, of how historic events or social structures make *possible*, as well as militate against, individual moral action. When Eliot asks in *Daniel Deronda* what is the relationship of Gwendolen Harleth's puny moral life to large historical change – or even why this small consciousness matters at all in light of large social events – she is raising a question that, as we have seen, is central to the history of the novel, and raises serious questions about the status of fiction itself. But the answer she gives is that it is, in some sense, women who will wage the real battle of consciousness, the struggle of individuals anywhere to achieve a consciousness of and beyond themselves.

In some ways it might seem that we have returned to the insights not so much of the Victorian survey course as of the book jackets it has produced: that wistful Whistler heroine, trapped by her own plot but craving a larger consciousness, as if, indeed, she wanted to be reading the book with all the people on the cover. When George Eliot asks, "why always Dorothea?," perhaps she is anticipating just such a dilemma – although her novel's full title (*Middlemarch: A Study in Provincial Life*) encourages us to draw the individual and social plots together, and reminds us that the originally projected novel "Miss Brooke" is only one part of the very complicated whole that is *Middlemarch*. But for Eliot, Dorothea's struggle to consciousness is not only part of the broad social struggle for reform in the 1830s, but the sign of one specific social failure: the failure to educate women for lives of moral usefulness and "speculative" genius. Dorothea's struggle, like that of many who struggle under "prosaic conditions" and "rest in unvisited tombs," will have largely been in vain – which is also to say, it will have been "fictional."

But the novel's setting in the time of the first Reform Bill might lead us somewhere other than into the social debates over the second Reform Bill in the 1860s, when the novel was written alongside Matthew Arnold's *Culture and Anarchy* (1869) and Carlyle's *Shooting Niagara* (1867). While the 1830s setting of *Middlemarch* will not lead us back into the generic complexity and formal incoherence of the novels of that epoch, it might lead us back to their insight that characters, readers, and narrators are all placed in various ways in their societies, and in their reading practices – which for George Eliot means their practices of sympathy, and their habits of moral imagination. It is that rushing of sympathy, that effort of imagination, which marks Dorothea as a sympathetic reader of her fellow Middlemarchians – which deters her into sympathy with Tertius Lydgate and his wife Rosamond, and prompts Rosamond's sudden and unexpectedly generous renunciation of the love of Will Ladislaw, and her assurance to Dorothea that it is she whom Will loves – "you are thinking," she says, "what is not true." It is a similar effort – to think only things that are true – that Eliot hopes we will make, when we turn to the unattractive Edward Casaubon or the hypocritical Nicholas Bulstrode, but even more so when we recognize that Dorothea's failure to achieve success is a socially determined failure. Even if *Middlemarch* does not expect that we will all read as women read, it expects us to recognize that women still read differently from men, and that, to be successful readers of novels *and* of our culture, we too might learn to read for the stories of those who "rest in unvisited tombs." In this sense the Victorian novel did indeed, as Miller suggests, "package" subjectivity in culturally appealing ways. But notice also that it continued to question its forms of containment: the wistful heroine continues to yearn for the vast canvas of the Victorian marketplace.

Our survey of the novel ends on a similarly wistful note. By the time of *Middlemarch*, or even *Felix Holt*, readerly practices had shifted again: the serial publication of *Our Mutual Friend* (1864–5) was an anachronism; the three-volume novel had gained a certain ascendancy, and publication in more magisterial journals like *The Cornhill Magazine* offered more variety of length and seriousness. The obsessive quarreling with three-volume form that marks George Gissing's brilliant social novels of the 1890s, like the equally obsessive quarreling between Thomas Hardy and the editors of literary journals in the same decade, suggests that some of the cultural authority the novel held in the period of "high" Victorian fiction was a more precarious thing than it looked. The splintering of the social novel back into more specifically targeted novels suggests a breakdown of social consensus as well. The experimental feminism of Dickens's great period (*Bleak House* and *Little Dorrit*) gave way to the "New Woman" novel, pitched for a new, urban, female readership; the sensation novel, which in its origins had coexisted with Dickens – *Bleak House* and *Great Expectations* appearing alongside *The Woman in White* (1859) and *Lady Audley's Secret* (1862) – now travelled further abroad in search of thrills; and the detective plots of these same earlier novels, with their social question, "What connexion can there be?" became monolingual investigators, asking which snake came down which bellpull to kill which man, and *cui bono*?

Who profits, indeed? We might question if *fin-de-siècle* novels were still "used for a greater number of purposes" than other forms of literature. The authority of the individual consciousness seems to give way in similar fashion: by the 1890s, the literary impressionism of James, Joseph Conrad, and Virginia Woolf can be seen as continuing the experiments in realism Dickens undertook when bringing the "colouring" of imagination to the life-like events of his characters, but in ways perhaps less "vivid." Bram Stoker's *Dracula* (1897) offers us a variety of media from phonography to telegraphy to telepathy; Gissing's *The Nether World* (1889) inscribes a chorus of London voices from Greek odes to slum argot to a lonely Dickensian heroine; Hardy's *Jude the Obscure* (1895) takes the wanderings of Oliver Twist all the way into the graveyard ("Done because we are too menny"); but all these experiments in form seem similarly to break off, as desolate as Little Father Time. Rudyard Kipling emerges as a rare purveyor of anything like Victorian realism at the end of the century, and even his expansive accounts of the "great road" and the small consciousness that was the boy Kim do not seem to sustain the remarkable reach and variety the Victorian novel offered at its height.

But something interesting happens to Victorian fiction if we take a giant leap forward. While a series of great modernist novels invoke the Victorians – James Joyce's *Ulysses* (1922) as sentimental source; Woolf's *The Years* (1937) as historical archive; Doris Lessing's *The Golden Notebook* (1962) as moral exemplum – I am more interested in the postmodernist versions of Victorian fiction that suddenly seem to be everywhere. Not only the costume-dramas of large and small screens, but Victorian pastiches seem to be "at home and receiving." A. S. Byatt's *Angels and Insects* (1995) and *Possession* (1990) and Andrea Barrett's *Ship Fever* (1996) have joined John Fowles's *The French Lieutenant's Woman* (1969); Kazuo Ishiguro's brilliant *Remains of the Day* (1989) enters the dark houses of Dickens's *Great Expectations*, Margot Livesey's *The Flight of Gemma Hardy* (2012) takes a modern Jane Eyre to Scotland and Iceland, and Salman Rushdie's *Midnight's Children* (1981) goes absolutely everywhere else. In recent years, the Victorian novel has invaded outer space as well: Ishiguro's *Never Let Me Go* (2005) is a newly speculative novel of origins that examines the inner life of clones; P. D. James's *Children of Men* (1992) begins with a course on the heroine's text; Neal Stephenson's *The Diamond Age* (1995) imagines a Victorian after-life of thousands of little Nells. It is unlikely that people will ever stop adapting Dickens (whose irascible brand-defensiveness made him nowhere near so adaptable in his lifetime as he has proven ever since), but I am considerably more intrigued by the return of the Victorian debates over the nature of fiction itself, and the multi-volume form these debates have taken. Like *Angels and Insects*, which is obsessed with the problem of material reality and the status of "material" fictions, Margaret Drabble's trilogy *The Radiant Way* (1987), *A Natural Curiosity* (1989), and *The Gates of Ivory* (1992) interrogates the nature of human and natural relationships in the greater sweep of history. In the final volume Drabble not only reinvents characters from her previous fictions but moves her central heroine to the war-torn fields of Cambodia, in search of a lost friend. It is truly as if the Victorian novel had encountered the killing fields – and as if those fields were not so unfamiliar after all.

I am calling Victorian the multi-plot and the multi-volume novel; but I am also identifying as Victorian the effort to enlist larger sympathies, expand the sweep of human history, and put the individual consciousness back into the arena of world-historical events, even where this effort entails inventing new (cyber)worlds. Earlier in this chapter I somewhat jokingly identified the confusions of the early Victorian novel as postmodernist, and it is perhaps not so startling that those displacements, as well as the greater effort at connection the later Victorian novels evinced, continue to shadow the progress of the novel. But this suggests a slightly different response to my initial question: Why return to Victorian fiction at all? It is less easy to identify the Victorian novel as a handy tool for cultural discipline when one sees the genre as itself more ragged than it initially appears; it is profoundly significant that novelists of our day, attempting to document the barbarism as well as the triumphs of the individual *and the social* consciousness, are returning to the Victorian experiments in consciousness and "phantasy."

Perhaps what this chapter has most attempted to prove is that we do not know everything we think we know about the Victorian novel – and much of what we hold most certain (the coherencies of our ideas about the coherencies of Victorian fiction) is least certain after all. The fact that the forms of the Victorian novel can still be used to *displace* what passes for knowledge about the world is what I continue to value about it – and the attempt made here to defamiliarize the novel is my own tribute to its ability to make us less complacent. The novel is, to use a favorite Victorian word, a very "curious" genre, one that both contains its own mysteries and refuses to conform to anyone's ideas about it – certainly not mine. Our world, ourselves as readers, and our most profound ideas about the novel itself are little more, still, than other forms of "Victorian fiction."

See also 1832, 1851; Growing Up, Passing on; Financial, Industrial, Commercial, Publishing; Sage Writing, Literary Criticism; Neo-Victorianism

References

Anon. (1859) "Cheap Literature." Reprinted from *The British Quarterly Review* in *Victorian Fiction: A Collection of Essays from the Period*, ed. I. B. Nadel (1986). New York and London: Garland Publishing.

Davis, L. (1987) *Resisting Novels: Ideology and Fiction*. New York and London: Methuen.

Masson, D. (1859) "British Novelists Since Scott." In *Victorian Criticism of the Novel*, ed. E. M.

Eigner and G. J. Worth (1985). Cambridge: Cambridge University Press.

Miller, D. A. (1987) *The Novel and the Police*. Berkeley: University of California Press.

Stephen, J. F. (1855) "The Relation of Novels to Life." In *Victorian Criticism of the Novel*, ed. E. M. Eigner and G. J. Worth (1985). Cambridge: Cambridge University Press.

Further Reading

Barthes, R. (1974) *S/Z: An Essay*. New York: Hill and Wang.

Bersani, L. (1984) *A Future for Astyanax: Character and Desire in Literature*. New York: Columbia University Press.

Brooks, P. (1976) *The Melodramatic Imagination: Balzac, Henry James, Melodrama and the Mode of Excess*. New York: Columbia University Press.

—— (1984) *Reading for the Plot: Design and Intention in Narrative*. New York: Knopf.

Copeland, E. (2012) *The Silver Fork Novel: Fashionable Fiction in the Age of Reform*. Cambridge: Cambridge University Press.

Duncan, I. (1992) *Modern Romance and Transformations of the Novel: The Gothic, Scott, Dickens*. Cambridge: Cambridge University Press.

Eigner, E. M. (1978) *The Metaphysical Novel in England and America: Dickens, Bulwer, Melville and Hawthorne*. Berkeley: University of California Press.

Gallagher, C. (1985) *The Industrial Reformation of English Fiction, 1832–1867*. Chicago: University of Chicago Press.

Grossman, J. (2002) *The Art of Alibi: English Law Courts and the Novel*. Baltimore: Johns Hopkins University Press.

Jaffe, A. (1991) *Vanishing Points: Dickens, Narrative, and the Subject of Omniscience*. Berkeley: University of California Press.

Levine, C. (2003) *The Serious Pleasures of Suspense: Victorian Realism and Narrative Doubt*. Charlottesville: University of Virginia Press.

Levine, G. (1968) *The Boundaries of Fiction: Carlyle, Macaulay, Newman*. Princeton: Princeton University Press.

—— (1981) *The Realistic Imagination: English Fiction from Frankenstein to Lady Chatterley*. Chicago: University of Chicago Press.

Marcus, S. (1965) *Dickens from Pickwick to Dombey*. New York: Basic Books.

Miller, A. H. (2010) *The Burdens of Perfection: On Ethics and Reading in Nineteenth-Century British Literature*. Ithaca: Cornell University Press.

Miller, D. A. (1981) *Narrative and Its Discontents: Problems of Closure in the Traditional Novel*. Princeton: Princeton University Press.

Newsom, R. (1988) *A Likely Story: Probability and Play in Fiction*. New Brunswick and London: Rutgers University Press.

Sutherland, J. A. (1976) *Victorian Novelists and Publishers*. Chicago: University of Chicago Press.

Tillotson, K. (1956) *Novels of the Eighteen-Forties*. Oxford: Oxford University Press.

Welsh, A. (1981) *The City of Dickens*. Oxford: Clarendon Press.

24
Drama

Alan Fischler

Contexts

"The most striking thing to a foreigner in English theatres is the unheard-of coarseness and brutality of the audiences," wrote Prince Hermann Pückler-Muskau after his 1826 visit to London. Shouted vulgarities regularly drowned out the performers, he said, and fragments of orange peel and other foodstuffs were showered by the denizens of the gallery upon the more expensive seats below. "The consequence of this is that the higher and more civilized classes go only to the Italian Opera, and very rarely visit their national theatre" (51).

As the qualifier "rarely" suggests, it is an oversimplification to say that the early Victorian bourgeoisie boycotted the theaters – exceptions might be made when Covent Garden and Drury Lane produced either original plays with literary pretensions or Shakespeare under such high-toned managers as William Charles Macready – but it is also substantially true. And the effects of their absence were ruinous for the West End playhouses presumed to be the preservers of English drama. To be sure, entertainment flourished elsewhere in England: in the provinces, where resident "stock" companies played their repertory in the Theatres Royal found in most major towns, and in the capital itself, where saloon theaters and music halls packed in the working classes of the East End, and where the King's Theatre (later Her Majesty's) served up opera to aristocrats. But in mainstream theaters, where only the cheap seats were consistently filled, where even the prices on these had periodically to be lowered from 1815 to 1860, and where the sole sources of financial

A New Companion to Victorian Literature and Culture, First Edition. Edited by Herbert F. Tucker.
© 2014 John Wiley & Sons, Ltd. Published 2014 by John Wiley & Sons, Ltd.

relief – aristocratic patronage and state subsidies – belonged respectively to the past and the future, the cultivation of the drama was not a profitable venture. Little wonder that, in 1847, Covent Garden abandoned plays and reconstituted itself the Royal Italian Opera House.

By the early years of Victoria's reign there was marginal improvement upon the Regency situation: at least the prostitutes whom Pückler-Muskau had seen soliciting in the foyers were expelled by Macready from Drury Lane in 1842. But worse remained. Through the first half of the century, a typical evening of theater began at 6:30 and ended in early morning, with half-price admission available between 8:00 and 9:00. This bargain was a boon to poorer patrons, who might miss the short comedy that opened the evening, but could still catch most of the featured melodrama, as well as the farce or pantomime that followed. But those who took advantage of this arrangement had often spent the preceding hours at the pub, and were drunk and dangerous by the time they arrived. Nor was the behavior described by Pückler-Muskau their worst. In 1809, when John Philip Kemble had attempted to raise prices at Covent Garden and add more seating for the gentry, the result was the "O. P." (Old Price) Riots, which lasted for 67 nights until Kemble caved in and apologized; as late as 1880, when Squire and Marie Bancroft reopened the Haymarket after upgrading some of the cheap seats, they were met with a similar outburst on the first night.

As the bourgeoisie were thus being warned against trespassing upon territory that the working class regarded as its own, they were also being admonished that attendance at plays constituted a trespass of another sort. In 1832 Charles Kemble complained to a parliamentary committee that "religious prejudice is very much increased," so as to "take away a great number of persons from the theatre who formerly used to frequent it" (Booth 1991: 22), and, indeed, the chorus of voices preaching against the theater ran up the scale from Low Church evangelicals to Cardinal Manning. Many in the middle class developed an almost superstitious fear of entering any establishment with "Theatre" in its name; thus, when Priscilla and Thomas German Reed opened for business in 1856, they were careful to call their hall a "Gallery," which presented "illustrations" instead of "plays." But the problem lay deeper than nomenclature. The values espoused by the Victorian middle class (in public, at least) revolved around devotion to duty, which meant submission of the individual will to the direction of some higher authority, be it father, husband, God, law, or the unwritten code of morality that trumped all else. But the values of the dominant genres of drama, as practiced in the early nineteenth century, were quite otherwise: melodrama moralized on the unjust restraints of law upon the poor, farce was preoccupied with avoiding or disentangling the bonds of matrimony, the climax of pantomime featured a magical transformation to a state of anarchy in which the protagonists could now wage nonstop comic warfare against the authority figures who had formerly balked them, and comedy continued to work variations on the basic plot handed down from the Romans, in which obedience to parents is set at naught if it conflicts with the fulfillment of erotic desires. And the essence of drama is that, unlike most other forms of literature, it is consumed in public. Under the eyes of the very neighbors whom the newly arrived bourgeoisie were so anxious to impress with their respectability, entering a playhouse, especially when it purveyed such politically incorrect fare, was simply out of the question.

So it was for the very best authors. When Victoria became queen, the number of buyers to whom they might sell plays without music totaled two. Such had been the case since 1660, when Drury Lane and Covent Garden were granted a monopoly (shared in summer by the Haymarket) on the presentation of spoken drama. These were the "major" theaters which, because of their special legal rights, were said to produce "legitimate" drama; all other playhouses were therefore "minors" and their plays, perforce, "illegitimate." The majors were also major in size – with the population of London almost tripling in the first half of the century, Covent Garden and Drury Lane expanded accordingly, to capacities of 3,000 and 3,600 respectively – but certain minor houses, such as the Britannia and Astley's, held even more. In such huge theaters, conducted mainly for uneducated audiences who, like the groundlings scorned by Hamlet, were "for the most part . . . capable of nothing but inexplicable dumb shows and noise," spectacle reigned supreme. In 1823 William Moncrieff's *The Cataract of the Ganges* was produced at Drury Lane with an actual cataract on stage, while the mandatory "sensation scenes" of later melodramas featured simulated shipwrecks, avalanches, boat races, and volcanic eruptions; in 1835, Edward Fitzball's *Paul Clifford* put on the Covent Garden stage a coach and six horses – hardly competition for Astley's, where plays were produced in a circus ring custom-built for equestrian drama. Moreover, the vast distance to the gallery required nothing short of bellowing on the stage, so that actors became strangers to subtlety who would not only "tear a passion to tatters" but do the same to the meaning of the text. Authors had small literary incentive to contribute to theaters in which their carefully wrought words would be bleated, unheard, or upstaged by an elephant.

Nor did they have much financial incentive. Managers purchased pieces outright from dramatists, and there was no additional remuneration if a play turned out to be a hit: thus, Douglas Jerrold received £60 for *Black-Ey'd Susan* (1829), even though it made £5,000 for the manager of the Surrey and eventually yielded £60,000 to T. P. Cooke, who played the sailor-hero William throughout his career. As late as the 1850s, authors typically earned a maximum of £50 per act. To make a living at such meager wages required prodigious productivity: Dion Boucicault, for instance, claimed to have written 250 plays (though "only" 141 of these can be verified), J. R. Planché produced 176, and "Fitzball's efforts seem almost incalculable" (Nicoll 1930: I, 76). Under these circumstances, originality, let alone quality, became an unaffordable luxury, and dramatists regularly resorted to adaptations of popular novels, or to outright translations. Managers had occasional pangs of conscience about promoting such practices: in 1843 the Haymarket offered a £500 prize for the best original comedy on British manners, but *Quid Pro Quo*, by Catherine Gore, did not exactly furnish the foundation of a new national school, as it disappeared after five weeks. In 1859 Fitzball had to acknowledge that contemporary English drama was still "almost all composed of translations" (I, 76).

Nonetheless, the dominant presence on the early Victorian stage was a native author: Shakespeare. In 1843, when the Theatre Regulation Act finally did away with the monopoly, the way was cleared for his works to be played in formerly "illegitimate" houses. Thus began the distinguished series of productions, covering 31 of Shakespeare's plays, which Samuel Phelps mounted at Sadler's Wells from 1844 to 1862; thus, too, was enabled Charles Kean's traversal of much the same territory at the Princess's from 1850 to 1859. Like other managers, Kean exploited the opportunities for spectacle in Shakespeare, yet his was spectacle with a difference: following the archeological fashion that Planché had begun in 1823, Kean not only consulted scholarly sources on the trappings appropriate to the period of each play but flaunted them on his playbills, with essays attesting to the historicity of his costumes and sets. With his Eton education and antiquarian authorities, Kean made his Shakespearean productions respectable – and he did the same for melodrama, acting both the title twins in Boucicault's *The Corsican Brothers* (1852) in a restrained and gentlemanly style that deliberately departed from the rant and bluster characteristic of this genre. The difference was not lost on Queen Victoria, who came five times to see this piece; though she was criticized for doing so, her attendance was the thin end of the wedge, and the emboldened middle class soon followed her through the ever-widening opening.

Meanwhile, eight years after providing Kean with the perfect vehicle, Boucicault effected another change of more lasting importance to the history of drama. Having proven the popularity of *The Colleen Bawn* in New York, Boucicault proposed to Ben Webster a novel financial arrangement for its run at the Adelphi, whereby, once house expenses were cleared, he and the manager would share the nightly profits. In 1841 Boucicault had sold *London Assurance*, his first hit, for £300; now, in the first year of its London run, *The Colleen Bawn* brought him £10,000. Later in the sixties, the Bancrofts began to pay Tom Robertson a set fee for each performance of his plays; though these "royalties" amounted to less than Boucicault got from profit-sharing, they too signaled the demise of the impoverishing system of outright purchase. With relief from the pressure of constant productivity, originality became an option, attracting more and better dramatists to the profession. It has been estimated that about 700 authors wrote for the English stage between 1800 and 1850; in the next 50 years, their numbers soared to beyond 3,000.

As playwrights rushed in where their predecessors had feared to tread, there were also more playhouses to employ them. With the theater gaining both respectability and accessibility (the latter thanks to new railways from the middle-class suburbs), and with the population of London doubling to six million in the second half of the century, conditions were prime for a building boom. In 1851 there were 19 theaters devoted to English plays in London; in 1899 there were 61. The boom also extended to music halls, which began to draw the working class from the playhouses into a more comfortable environment where they could enjoy a varied evening of entertainment while smoking and drinking; this class migration further promoted the gentrification of the theaters. The new theaters were mostly smaller, permitting playwrights now to make their points not through spectacle but dialogue, which inevitably became more literate as it became more audible; meanwhile, managers liberated from the need to fill thousands of seats each night by means of heterogeneous and ever-changing programs now gravitated toward more specialized repertory. One result was the paring of the playbill: Kean had dispensed with the afterpiece during his tenure at the Princess's, but the Bancrofts went even farther at the Prince of Wales's, eliminating the curtain raiser and limiting the evening to a single play. Moreover, the single play that remained was now allowed to run night after night. Kean led the way, staging 102 consecutive performances of *The Winter's Tale* in 1856; seven years later, Tom Taylor's *The Ticket-of-Leave Man* began a streak of 407 performances.

Not surprisingly, the chief beneficiaries of these changes were dramatists willing to suit the tastes of the newly available, temptingly lucrative, middle-class audiences. Preeminent among them was Tom Robertson. In the fifties he had been prompter for Madame Vestris, a premature pioneer who, as early as 1831, was providing other producers with a model of refinement and meticulous attention to detail; in the sixties he applied her lessons to recreating on the stage of the Prince of Wales's a cozy and carefully correct middle-class milieu that made the Bancrofts' bourgeois audiences feel at home. Even the hut in the last act of *Ours* (1866), supposedly situated in a military camp in the Crimea, was equipped with all the domestic props necessary to turn the final scene into a roly-poly-pudding-making party. In 1898 Arthur Wing Pinero affectionately memorialized the creator of these "cup and saucer comedies" in *Trelawny of the "Wells"*, where the playwright Tom Wrench (a thinly disguised Robertson) declares "I won't have doors stuck here, there, and everywhere; no, nor windows in all sorts of impossible places" but rather "Just where they should be, architecturally. And locks on the doors, *real* locks, to work" (Act 2). Indeed, Robertson's production methods, complemented by the refreshingly uninflated rhetoric of his dialogue, associate his mid-century plays with the movement toward realism then sweeping the arts in Europe.

Conversely, the major works of Robertson's protégé, W. S. Gilbert, constituted a retreat from realism: the libretti he wrote for Arthur Sullivan, like most of his other plays, are generally set in remote eras or locales – sometimes as far as Fairyland. But in such settings, Gilbert undertook the very practical task of catering to the post-Darwinian prejudices of his middle-class patrons. He developed a new approach to comedy, where duty and human law replace Providence as the source of the happy ending, and the authority of parents and magistrates is neither denied nor deflated. The most solid sign of his success was the Savoy Theatre, which Richard D'Oyly Carte built in 1881 expressly to house the Gilbert and Sullivan operas, and the loyal patronage of this house by prosperous burghers enabled such pieces as *The Mikado* (1885) and *The Gondoliers* (1889) to achieve runs of 672 and 554 performances respectively. By 1883 Henry Arthur Jones was complaining that "Victorian drama reeks of the spirit of successful tradesmen" (Booth 1969: II, 10), but managers smelled money in this trend and continued to adapt their operations accordingly. To accommodate the dinner hour of polite society, curtain times were pushed back as late as 8:30; to tap into the growing market of those at leisure during the day, matinees were introduced by the Bancrofts – experimentally during the run of Robertson's *School* (1869), then regularly in 1878 – and soon became established throughout the West End.

To a great extent, matinees were both for and about women, who made up a major part of the audience; and questions about the code governing their social – and, especially, sexual – conduct became increasingly prominent in the plays they saw presented. Daytime became the domain of avant-garde drama, as rising native playwrights might hire theaters in daytime as their only means of getting such pieces performed. By far the most famous (or notorious) matinees were those devoted to the works of Henrik Ibsen, which furnished the theatrical battleground of the nineties. At the head of Ibsen's supporters was the critic William Archer, who published translations of Ibsen's plays in 1889–90; first among his lieutenants was the then unknown George Bernard Shaw, whose screed entitled *The Quintessence of Ibsenism* was as much an attack on prevailing bourgeois attitudes toward home, family, and women as it was a defense of the Norwegian master. Shaw's work appeared in 1891, the same year in which J. T. Grein initiated the Independent Theatre with *Ghosts*, a play that touches on both incest and syphilis. Though not the first production of Ibsen's work in London (*Pillars of Society* had appeared as long ago as 1880) it was the one with the greatest impact. *Punch* responded with a regular feature devoted to "Ibsenity," while Clement Scott, long-time drama critic for the *Daily Telegraph* and senior spokesman for the conservative bourgeois perspective, declared *Ghosts* "an open drain," "a loathsome sore unbandaged," "a dirty act done publicly" (Rowell 129).

The hysteria of Scott's response suggests a desperate man who fears his side is losing – and so it was. The rebellion against the demand for moralism in the arts, which began with Pater and the aesthetic movement of the seventies and eighties, now escalated into outright rejection of the righteous code of respectability supposed to govern society. The essential agenda of Ibsen's plays was exposure of the rot beneath such hypocritical righteousness; in English drama of the nineties the particular focus became the sexual double standard and its persecution of "the fallen woman." Some playwrights, like Jones and Oscar Wilde, merely raised questions about the status quo, while others, like Pinero and Shaw, mounted full-scale attacks on it. But the very fact that such themes were being addressed meant that the English stage had again become a forum for serious consideration of ideas, for the first time since the early seventeenth century: witness Jones's 1895 book entitled *The Renascence of English Drama*. Yet the irony was that this rebirth only brought drama back to what it had been at the start of Victoria's reign: a critique of mainstream middle-class values.

Drama and Melodrama

Melodrama, quite simply, means drama plus melody; its initial attraction was that it let minor theaters dodge the monopoly that restricted productions of plays unaccompanied by music. One enterprising manager got away with presenting *Othello* by having a musician at the pianoforte strike a chord every five minutes during the performance, thus making it a melodrama. Underscoring of dialogue remained a prominent feature of the genre throughout the century, but it soon evolved other distinctive characteristics: liberal doses of pathos, clear-cut characterization in which the hard-working poor imbued with virtue (always rewarded) are sharply distinguished from the rich and powerful infected with vice, sensation scenes with spectacular – sometimes supernatural – special effects, and happy endings (often involving last-minute rescues) wrought by the hand of Providence. The preoccupations of melodrama varied – the prevailing fashion was first Gothic, then nautical, and finally domestic – as did its theatrical venues.

This "illegitimate" dramatic form was distinctly antilegal in its prejudices, which held the possessors of power to be the enemy. The popularity of brigand-heroes is exemplified by the appeal of Walter Scott's *Rob Roy*, which appeared in at least ten stage versions between 1818 and 1828. Peasants were also prime protagonists: the title character of J. B. Buckstone's *Luke the Labourer* (1826) is actually portrayed as a villain, but he has watched his wife starve to death in the wake of an employer's callousness and now does his vindictive deeds as henchman for an evil squire. Melodrama is more often unambiguous in its affirmation of the underclass: Jerrold's *The Mutiny at the Nore* (1830) shows the justice of the sailors' grievances, while John Walker's powerful *The Factory Lad* (1832) endorses the righteous rage of industrial workers displaced by machines. *Black-Ey'd Susan* paints law and authority figures in the blackest of colors: the title character's persecutors include a landlord, a bailiff, and her husband's captain, who attempts to rape her. William is condemned to hang for striking the drunken captain, but is saved at the curtain from the sentence of "His Beelzebub's ship, the Law" (Act II, scene i).

Though all these pieces played at minor houses, melodrama ironically became a staple event at the only two theaters with no need to circumvent the monopoly. Isaac Pocock's two most popular takes on romantic brigands, *The Miller and His Men* (1813) and *The Robber's Bride* (1829), were both produced at Covent Garden, which so coveted *Black-Ey'd Susan* that Cooke, in costume, migrated nightly over the Thames to play William again in an afterpiece. Jerrold's *The Factory Girl* (1832), with its protests against child labor and industrial working conditions, proved too strong for the nonproletarian elements in the Drury Lane audience, but *The Rent Day* was a hit for him in the same theater and year: its attack on the abuses allowed by an absentee landlord was perhaps made palatable by a dash of spectacle, as the first two acts began with tableaux vivants duplicating well-known paintings by Sir David Wilkie. The verse in which Edward Bulwer-Lytton decked much of *The Lady of Lyons*

(1838) may have elicited from Covent Garden audiences the respect due to "literature," but the radical politics of the piece were essentially those of melodrama: Claude Melnotte, as the prime repository of virtue in the play, is necessarily a peasant, which earns him the scorn of the aristocratic Pauline but in no way hinders his meteoric rise through the ranks of the revolutionary Napoleonic army, where plain merit is evidently rewarded.

The popularity of melodrama at the major houses may be accounted for by the simple fact that, with their high proportion of working-class patrons, it sold. So did Shakespeare, but the spectacle expected at productions of his work could easily empty pocketbooks: "Shakespeare spells ruin" became a maxim among managers. Far less popular, but often as expensive, were those contemporary dramas of "literary merit" that the legitimate theaters valiantly tried to cultivate and abysmally failed to harvest. The problem with both the poets and poetasters who wrote for the stage was their fascination with rhetoric, psychology, and philosophical abstraction – which did not offer much to early Victorian actors and audiences, for whom the essence of theater was sensational action. Joanna Baillie, for instance, published three series of *Plays on the Passions*, with each drama dedicated to exploring a different emotion; mercifully, only five of her 26 efforts actually reached the stage. *Virginius* (1820) by Sheridan Knowles reeked with historical grandeur, but its most appealing feature proved to be the melodramatic pathos of the father–daughter relationship: as Richard Hengist Horne complained, "We have Roman tunics, but a modern English heart; the scene is the Forum, but the sentiments those of the Bedford Arms" (Booth 1969: I, 76–7). The cold neo-classicism of Thomas Noon Talfourd would have better belonged in an eighteenth-century playhouse; both his *Ion* (1839) and Knowles's *Virginius* were hits mostly because each provided a meaty part for Macready. More worthy in its ambitions was Westland Marston's *The Patrician's Daughter* (1842), an attempt to breathe life into poetic drama by treating a contemporary political theme; though critics considered the archaisms and blank verse inappropriate, Marston repeated the experiment in *Anne Blake* (1852). The poetry of Horne's work was admired by such as Poe, Carlyle, and Elizabeth Barrett Browning, but theatrical managers smelled disaster in his heavy historical dramas, and not one was produced. The cultivated classicism with which Arnold imbued *Empedocles on Etna* (1852) and Swinburne *Atalanta in Calydon* (1865) would surely have made them caviar to the general; happily, neither had any apparent aspirations toward staging these static works. Robert Browning's plays may as well have remained unproduced: *Strafford* (1837), a treatment of the prelude to the Civil War which Charles I himself could not have followed without footnotes, lasted four nights at Covent Garden, and *A Blot in the 'Scutcheon* (1843) ran for three at Drury Lane. Browning's crabbed, elliptical syntax was simply inimical to the instantaneous communication which has to happen in a theater. The verse of Tennyson would seem more suitable, but even at the crest of bourgeois patronage it was not much more successful: *Queen Mary* (1876) disappeared after 23 performances, while the premiere of *The Promise of May* (1882) was hooted from start to finish. In 1879 Henry Irving refused the honor of producing

Becket at the Lyceum because, as he frankly told Tennyson's son, he did not think it would make any money; when he finally did bring it out in 1893, the year after the poet's death, he had the good sense to adapt it first.

Meanwhile, at mid-century, respectable Victorians in search of serious theater were left to choose between melodramas they could not attend and poetic dramas they could not stand – until Boucicault, then writing for Kean, stepped forth with a third alternative: "gentlemanly" melodrama. Meaning to market his product to polite audiences, Boucicault did not draw the hero of *The Corsican Brothers*, Fabian Dei Franchi, from the lower classes or imply that virtue was theirs only. More strikingly original was his portrayal of Château-Renaud, not as the standard snarling villain but as a well-mannered, credible aristocrat. In the sixties, when he began to write melodramas on his native Ireland and to produce them on both sides of the Atlantic, he took an apparently more dangerous tack, yet even this was calculated to permit maximum popularity. It is true that the hero of *The Colleen Bawn* (1860) is an all-purpose outlaw, while those of *Arrah-na-Pogue* (1864) and *The Shaughraun* (1874) are active in the Fenian cause, but it is also true that the villains are not the consistently benign English authorities but rather Irishmen who skulk for protection under English coattails. Boucicault was also closely associated with the trend toward urban realism, which began in the forties with such plays as Moncrieff's *The Scamps of London* (1843), billed as "A National, Local, Characteristic, Metropolitan, Melodramatic Drama of the Day." In Boucicault's hands, such local color became a cottage industry in a mobile home: *The Poor of New York*, produced there in 1857, was transformed for each city it toured, becoming successively *The Poor of Leeds, Manchester*, and *Liverpool*, and *The Streets of Islington, London, Dublin*, and *Philadelphia*.

More important plays on the underside of urban life were Taylor's *The Ticket-of-Leave Man* (1863) and *The Silver King* (1882) by Jones and Henry Herman. As in earlier melodrama, men who have lived outside the law are the heroes of these pieces; however, for the benefit of the upstanding middle classes who had now returned to the theaters, there is a crucial revision of values. Law is no longer the enemy of the virtuous; rather, the former criminal associates of Bob Brierly and Wilfred Denver dog the attempts of the former to lead a respectable life and persecute the family of the latter, while police detectives become instrumental to their salvation. Nor does law prosecute the burgomaster Mathias in Leopold Lewis's *The Bells* (1871); it was more gratifying for bourgeois audiences to see one of their own punished for his crime by his own properly guilty conscience.

Meanwhile, the black-and-white morality of melodrama remained much as it had been: a title like *The Lancashire Lass; or, Tempted, Tried and True* (1867) by H. J. Byron, speaks for itself. But the specific vices now on view were those that preoccupied the new middle-class audiences, so that the crimes condemned by melodrama became mostly marital and domestic, such as the bigamy of the title character in *Lady Audley's Secret* (1863), and the conduct of Lady Isabel, who not only elopes with a lover but abandons her children in *East Lynne* (of which the most enduring version appeared in 1874). Providence still intervened to punish the wicked:

Boucicault's *The Octoroon* (1861) is resolved by a *deus ex* (a literal) *machina*: an unattended camera decisively records the guilt of the murderer, who is told, "The eye of the Eternal was on you – the blessed sun in heaven that, looking down, struck upon this plate the image of the deed" (Act 4). But this was two years after *The Origin of Species*, and the subsequent progress of Darwinism made such stuff ever harder to swallow; thus, in the last decades of the nineteenth century and even into the twentieth, traditional melodrama retained its popularity primarily among less intellectually sophisticated working-class and provincial audiences. Meanwhile, the beleaguered clergy began to realize that the lessons of faith and morality so widely preached from the stage actually served to second their own sermons, and a new attitude toward theater emerged. The year 1879 saw the founding of the Church and Stage Guild; by the nineties, the Lyceum – especially respectable under the management of Irving – was said to be a favorite haunt of clergymen. And devout dramas on explicitly religious subjects, such as Wilson Barrett's *The Sign of the Cross* (1896) and Hall Caine's *The Christian* (1899), gained acceptance for the first time in the century.

In the midst of – indeed, because of – this flood of righteous piety, the "problem play" began its perilous voyage, with sexual morality its chief concern. Far too early an essay was Gilbert's *Charity* (1874), with its uncomfortably positive picture of Mrs Van Brugh, who has given her life to good works but is nonetheless ostracized when her bourgeois neighbors learn of her "past"; damned for sympathizing with "the fallen woman," the play closed after 80 performances. Likewise premature was Pinero's *Mayfair* (1885), condemned for its depiction of a woman who is tempted to pay back her husband's infidelity in kind. But the tide had evidently turned by 1892 when Wilde, working also at the St James's, scored a hit with *Lady Windermere's Fan*, which is plotted along strikingly parallel lines. *Lady Windermere*, like *A Woman of No Importance* (1893) and *An Ideal Husband* (1895), is melodramatic at its core: beneath the glossy veneer of the famous epigrammatic wit, the plots of all three are driven by a shameful secret from someone's past. Yet Wilde was no rebel, arranging instead to avoid the implications of his themes: Lady Windermere stops on the brink of adultery, and Sir Robert Chiltern never actually has to take the consequences of defying his blackmailer, so that the essential moral questions – about the price of sin in the one case and of rectitude in the other – remain unanswered. And the answers proffered in the problem plays of Jones were ultimately reactionary. Declaring himself "still in favour of what is called bourgeois morality" (Nicoll 1946: I, 169), he made mouthpieces of older, wiser males who, in both *The Case of Rebellious Susan* (1894) and *The Liars* (1897), dissuade young wives from answering their husbands' brutal insensitivity with infidelity; in *Mrs. Dane's Defence* (1900), the equivalent character heroically prevents a woman who was not wise in time from reentering respectable society.

But other dramatists dissented. In *The Second Mrs. Tanqueray* (1893), Pinero set his sights on the sacred double standard: when Aubrey sees his "poor wretched wife" tortured by the pressure of her past, he cries out against her former lover:

Yes, I do curse him – him and his class! . . . He has only led "a man's life" – just as I, how many of us, have done! The misery he has brought on me and mine it's likely enough we, in our time, have helped to bring on others by this leading "a man's life"! (Act 4)

Paula's suicide follows moments later, making the point still sharper. Archer justly called the play "epoch-making" (Nicoll 1946: I, 181) and it was also profitable: that Pinero made £30,000 on *Mrs. Tanqueray* did much to establish the theatrical viability of such pieces. There followed *The Notorious Mrs. Ebbsmith* (1895), his semi-sympathetic treatment of a feminist; a more interesting play about a woman with a will of her own was Harley Granville-Barker's *The Marrying of Ann Leete* (1899), in which Ann seems a sort of early Lady Chatterley when she rejects the effete aristocrat intended for her and chooses instead the apparently more virile gardener. More frankly sexual was *Alan's Wife* (1893), an Independent Theatre piece by Florence Bell and Elizabeth Robins, in which the title character declares her reason for having refused the local minister: "We can't all marry scholars, Mother dear – some of us prefer marrying men instead" (scene 1).

Shaw's comedies of the nineties dealt also with sexual politics, but his more "serious" plays of the period – *Widowers' Houses* (1892) and *Mrs. Warren's Profession* (1898) – put a socialist twist on the Ibsenite attack against bourgeois respectability by exposing the sources of the wealth that funds it: slum tenements in the one case, and prostitution in the other. Still, Shaw was not beyond taking a respectful backward glance at the plays that he and his fellow "new" dramatists had displaced: *The Devil's Disciple* (1897) was billed as "A Melodrama," and the interrogation scene at its core is clearly modeled upon the trial of Shaun the Post in *Arrah-na-Pogue*.

Comedy

In its attitude toward law and authority, early nineteenth-century pantomime was the comedic mirror to melodrama. Its parts were a short "opening," in which (most often) the heroine's father refused the hero her hand, and a much longer "harlequinade," which followed a magical "transformation scene" where the characters assumed identities derived from Renaissance *commedia dell'arte*: the hero became Harlequin, the heroine Columbine, her father Pantaloon, and his servant Clown. The harlequinade was a virtually nonstop chase, featuring abundant action but little or no dialogue; with its mischief, murder, and mayhem – much of it directed by Harlequin and Clown against Pantaloon and policemen – it was a holiday from normal restraints on behavior. Appropriately, pantomime was generally given at holiday time, especially Christmas and Easter, but even at such seasons its insurrectionary values were hardly in harmony with those of law-abiding burghers.

This problem was clear to Planché who, in his attempt to second Vestris's too early efforts to attract the patronage of polite society, created a new genre, for which he adopted the name "extravaganza." Structurally, extravaganza was panto-mime minus the offensive harlequinade; the transformation scene now became the grand finale, and the insatiable Victorian appetite for spectacle caused it to become continually more elaborate. Scenic designers such as William Beverley greatly enhanced the appeal of extravaganza, but it was the gentleness and gentility of Planché's writing that decisively distinguished it from pantomime: for all the puns and topical references, the dialogue has grace, and the airy magic of the fairy tales he adapted is allowed to emerge. Moreover, these tales have morals: Emeralda in *Riquet with the Tuft* (1836) and Laidronetta in *The Island of Jewels* (1849) are hero-ines whose selflessness is rewarded when their beloveds are transformed into handsome princes.

As the middle classes returned to the theaters, pantomime attempted to woo them by moving closer to extravaganza. After the retirement of Joseph Grimaldi, who reigned supreme as Clown from 1806 to 1823, the harlequinade had started to become shorter. By mid-century it was roughly equal in length to the opening and eventually became a vestigial tail irrelevant to the preceding plot. The script for *The Sleeping Beauty and the Beast* (1900), by J. Hickory Wood and Arthur Collins, calls for only a two-scene harlequinade and does not bother to specify the action of either; by contrast, that of *Harlequin Harper* (1813), by Thomas Dibdin, has 12 such scenes and gives blow-by-blow stage directions for the action of each. *Sleeping Beauty* was produced at Drury Lane, as were most of the works of E. L. Blanchard, who dominated the genre between 1852 and 1888; indeed, pantomime enjoyed a renaissance there under the management of Augustus Harris (1879–96), who lavished care on every aspect of his productions, spending as much as £20,000 on each.

Alongside pantomime and extravaganza there flourished burlesque, which was often confused with the latter. But there was a difference, as Planché asserted when *The Sleeping Beauty in the Wood* (1840) was "announced as an extravaganza, distinguish-ing the whimsical treatment of a poetic subject from the broad caricature of a tragedy or a serious opera, which was correctly termed a 'Burlesque'" (Rowell 70). An essen-tially parasitic form, Victorian burlesque also drew sustenance from Shakespeare, history, and contemporary melodrama, Planché himself resorted frequently to the subject matter of classical mythology as the basis of his own burlesques; indeed, Vestris began her managerial career with *Olympic Revels; or, Prometheus and Pandora* (1831), which he and Charles Dance named for her theater. A century later, Granville-Barker still found this piece praiseworthy for its "simplicity, delicacy," "taste and tact"; Planché, he said, "knows when to stop" (Granville-Barker 109). But the same could not be said for his successors. Burlesque soon degenerated into a riot of execrable puns, with little other point. The titles of such pieces as *Faust and Loose* (1886) by F. C. Burnand, and *The Corsican "Bothers"; or, The Troublesome Twins* (1869) by H. J. Byron, adequately indicate the content and character of the work of the two leading writers in this genre. Sharing pride of place with puns was transvestism, which allowed women in male roles to display their legs in tights. When John Hollingshead took it upon himself to see that "the sacred lamp" of the genre "was kept burning" in the seventies and eighties (Rowell 143), and made his Gaiety Girls an increasingly prominent part of his productions, the seeds were sown for the twentieth-century transformation of burlesque into striptease.

Farce, too, had its different phases. Throughout the era its stock-in-trade was a quick-paced series of complications and misunderstandings, the accumulating pressure of which was typically brought to bear upon a single frenzied protagonist. Until the seventies, characters and settings were generally as proletarian as the audience: *The Area Belle* (1864), by William Brough and Andrew Halliday, shows the housemaid Penelope receiving her suitors, including a policeman and a milkman, in the kitchen, while the title characters of *Box and Cox* (1847), by John Maddison Morton, are respectively a printer and a hatter who work different shifts and are unknowingly sharing the same room in a lodging house. And since both working-class prudery and official censorship proscribed sexual content, the energy thus repressed burst forth in the form of scurrying, screaming, and violence: Jerrold's *Mr. Paul Pry* (1826) has a red-hot poker thrust against him and a box of fireworks in which he is hiding ignited, while the title of Morton's *Slasher and Crasher* (1848) pretty well describes the behavior of its characters. As in melodrama, the enemy is law, particularly the legal bonds of matrimony. Escape from present chains is the object in Joseph Stirling Coyne's *Did You Ever Send Your Wife to Camberwell?* (1846); avoidance of prospective fetters preoccupies the heroes of Coyne's *How to Settle Accounts with Your Laundress* (1847) and *The Mudborough Election* (1865), by Brough and Halliday, in which Widgetts and Veskit, having each promised marriage to a woman as a way of wiggling out of a debt, now attempt to wiggle out of the marriage. Similar is *Box and Cox*, in which Box has pretended to be deceased for the last three years in order to escape his engagement, and where he and Cox – who is, of course, now betrothed to the same woman – toss coins and throw dice in hopes of losing Penelope Ann to the other.

As farce adapted to bourgeois audiences in the seventies, the characters became more socially elevated but their concerns remained the same. Gilbert's *The Realm of Joy* (1873), Boucicault's *Forbidden Fruit* (1876), and James Albery's *Pink Dominos* (1877) all deal with attempts at infidelity; though the authors substantially sanitized the French originals they adapted, and the adulterous intentions of the characters remain unconsummated, such mildly naughty fare was still too highly spiced for the upright bourgeoisie. Pinero, however, found the right recipe with a variation on holiday comedy, which involves a temporary departure from social norms but no full-fledged defiance of them. Thus, the title characters of both *The Magistrate* (1885) and *The Schoolmistress* (1886), and the clergyman Dr Jedd in *Dandy Dick* (1887), are all ultimately – and quite willingly – returned to respectability after their various lurches into lunacy. Nor is law malign: indeed, the plot of *The Magistrate* is disentangled only when a brother magistrate takes the situation in hand. By the end of the era the farcical ruse perpetrated by Jack and Charley in Brandon Thomas's *Charley's Aunt* (1892) is aimed not at avoiding but at achieving marriage with Kitty and Amy; that the play registered the longest run of the century (1,466 performances) signifies its success in appealing to all classes of society.

Meanwhile, in the first half of the century, the attempts of the major houses to produce "pure" comedy – unmixed with magic, mayhem, or men in skirts – yielded only occasionally better results than their efforts to mount poetic drama as an alternative to melodrama. Shakespeare, again, set the standard, but also lured authors into slavish imitation: Knowles's three comedies were bogged down in Elizabethan settings and self-consciously archaic language. Boucicault was more successful, but only a bit more contemporary, with *London Assurance* (1841), which affects not only the aristocratic manner but also the amorality of Restoration comedy in depicting a son's triumph over his father in a fully mercenary love competition. Bulwer-Lytton's *Money* (1840) is even less sympathetic to the sensibilities of the bourgeoisie: the title indicates its concern with the very basis of their social status, but it shows the pursuit of money to be the root of fraud and feigning. If middle-class patronage contributed to the popularity of either of these pieces, it was probably because of the intelligent productions and star performances that Vestris bestowed on the former and Macready on the latter.

In the fifties, however, just when Boucicault and Kean were remaking melodrama in an image acceptable to bourgeois audiences, Taylor began to do the same for comedy. In both *Still Waters Run Deep* (1855) and *Victims* (1857) a susceptible wife falls under the spell of a man after her money, but ultimately comes to appreciate the quietly heroic virtues of her husband, a retired businessman in the former piece and a stockbroker in the latter. *Our American Cousin* (1858) is today remembered for its unfortunate association with the assassination of Abraham Lincoln; in Taylor's time it was famous for E. A. Sothern's performance as the foppish Lord Dundreary, whose aristocratic idiocy provided a pleasing butt for bourgeois laughter. And in *New Men and Old Acres* (1869), written with Augustus Dubourg, Taylor arrives at the apotheosis of the British businessman: Brown is described as "one of England's merchant princes – one of the class which has made of this tiny island an empire on which the sun never sets" (Act 1), and his chivalrous behavior becomes the salvation of an otherwise helpless noble family. Thus, when Byron brought forth *Our Boys* in 1874, the way into the hearts of the middle class had been prepared for him. According to the critics, its sentimental portrait of the retired butterman Middlewick, who tries to play the heavy father but melts into kindness when he later finds his boy in straitened circumstances, was the prime cause of its phenomenal success: a run of 1,362 performances spanning three and a half years.

Byron, in turn, had already prepared the way for a better playwright by introducing his friend Robertson to Marie Wilton, who opened the renovated Prince of Wales's with *Society* (1865). Robertson's plays came to be identified with this theater, though a variety of venues housed the premieres of such works as *Progress* (1869), *Birth* (1870), and *War* (1871). These aggressive, one-word titles might make him seem a social critic, but he was not. To be sure, the anti-aristocratic prejudices of the melodramas from which Robertson learned his craft persist in his plays – the priggish pride of Lady Ptarmigant in *Society* and the Marquise de St Maur in *Caste* (1867) represents the chief problem for the young lovers of each play – but he stopped short of egalitarianism, which would not have pleased his nouveaux-bourgeois patrons who were still relishing their rise in society. "Caste's all right," declares George in the play of that name:

> Caste is a good thing if it's not carried too far. It shuts the door on the pretentious and vulgar; but it should open the door very wide for exceptional merit. Let brains break through its barriers, and what brains can break through, love may leap over. (Act 3)

In other words, love levels all ranks, but it does not therefore follow that ranks ought altogether to be leveled.

The most immediate heir to Robertson's gentle comedic style was Albery, whose *Two Roses* (1870) was a hybrid: new in its portrait of a lawyer of incorruptible integrity, and old in the manner of its resolution which – with its revelation of an old, dark secret and its explicit acknowledgment that Providence has wrought all – hearkens back to melodrama. But such, claimed Boucicault, was the kind of play the public preferred: "The public pretend they want pure comedy; that is not so. What they want is domestic drama, treated with broad comedy character" (Sawyer 74). Likewise, the most important comedies of the era's most successful playwright, W. S. Gilbert, were mixed up with both burlesque and music: the former is in the mockery of melo-drama so integral to *H. M. S. Pinafore* (1878) and *Ruddigore* (1887), while the latter derived from Arthur Sullivan's original scores – an element unknown in burlesque, where lyrics were written to fit existing music.

Equally original was Gilbert's crafting of comedy to fit the prejudices of the bourgeoisie – but this was a skill that he had to learn the hard way. In 1877 he brought out *Engaged*, possibly the best comedy of the nineteenth century but hardly the best received. Every character in the play speaks in the rhetoric of idealized love, and acts quite otherwise: Belinda, for instance, professes to love Belvawney "with an imperishable ardour which mocks the power of words" but will not marry him without "a little definite information about the settlements" (Act 1), while the Scots peasant Angus weeps sentimental tears in wooing Maggie, then sells her to Cheviot for two pounds. The critics raged: "From beginning to end of this nauseous play," fumed the *Figaro*, "not one of the characters ever . . . does a single action that is not inseparable from the lowest moral degradation" (Booth 1969: III, 391). Gilbert did not make the same mistake in his subsequent libretti for Sullivan. His characters there are brazenly benevolent – most notably the parents, who are almost never obstacles to the romantic aims of their offspring, and the magistrates, many of whom cheerfully patter about their own incompetence in the autobiographical songs Gilbert made famous, thus making themselves immune to exposure and humiliation. Middle-class audiences must have been relieved by this affirmative approach to char-acterization, so different from that of traditional comedy, and gratified to see law become a savior: while some rigid rule or code of conduct may create the initial problem in *Patience* (1881), *Iolanthe* (1882), *The Mikado*, and *Ruddigore*, it also pro-duces their happy endings.

Other authors carried Gilbert's practices into the next decade. In *A Pair of Spectacles* (1890) Sydney Grundy gilds Goldfinch, who is both landlord and parent, with the utmost goodness. Basil Hood, who also worked with Sullivan, brought many of the features of the Gilbertian light opera libretto into the next century, collaborating with Edward German on the popular *Merrie England* (1902). But Gilbert's own penultimate piece for Sullivan, *Utopia (Limited)* (1893), was not a brilliant success, and *The Grand Duke* (1896) was an outright failure. As the fashionable arts distanced themselves from bourgeois values, Gilbert's work went out of favor – but the new style proved ironically similar to that which he had been forced to abandon in the seventies. Just as sympathetic plays about fallen women now flourished, too late for *Charity*, so Wilde now picked up the pieces of *Engaged* to fabricate the greatest comedy of the nineties: *The Importance of Being Earnest* (1895). *Earnest* was indebted to *Engaged* not only for a number of situations but also for its overall approach to middle-class sentimentality: its high-sounding speeches are transparent coverings for actions that evince the vanity of Gwendolen and Cecily, the self-regarding snobbery of Lady Bracknell, the callous lust of Algernon, and the two-faced hypocrisy of Jack. If Wilde's play was not better than Gilbert's, yet the time was ripe for it, and it was enthusiastically received. Wilde's works were, however, distinctly superior to those of Pearl Craigie, such as *The Ambassador* (1898) and *The Wisdom of the Wise* (1900); though she thought herself his equal in wit, few readers would endorse her valuation.

The cynicism that marks much of Wilde's work for the stage was an unsuitable stance for the essentially idealistic Shaw, but he was nonetheless an iconoclast even when dealing with iconoclasm: in *Candida* (1895), for instance, he reverses the polarities of Ibsen's *A Doll's House* as a means of asserting that the dynamics of marriage are more likely to depend upon a strong woman who allows her husband to remain a child. *Arms and the Man* (1894) and *Caesar and Cleopatra* (1899) deromanticize war and history respectively – perhaps in reaction against the pomp and pageantry then puffing up the period pieces that Irving was producing at the Lyceum and Herbert Beerbohm Tree at Her Majesty's. Shaw even deromanticizes romance, mixing it with Darwinism in *You Never Can Tell* (1898), which reads like an early draft of *Man and Superman* (1903): both plays feature a male who fancies himself the pursuer but is actually the prey of a woman who embodies the Life Force that advances the species. And it was Shaw, of course, who embodied the advance of English drama as it crossed the threshold marking the end of the Victorian era and the start of a new century.

See also LEGAL, SPECTACLE; FICTION; PARAPETS

REFERENCES

Booth, M. R. (ed.) (1969) *English Plays of the Nineteenth Century*, 5 vols. Oxford: Clarendon Press.

—— (1991) *Theatre in the Victorian Age.* Cambridge: Cambridge University Press.

Granville-Barker, H. (1932) "Exit Planché – Enter Gilbert." In *The Eighteen-Sixties: Essays by Fellows of the Royal Society of Literature*, ed. J. Drinkwater. Cambridge: Cambridge University Press.

Nicoll, A. (1930) *A History of Early Nineteenth Century Drama, 1800–1850*, 2 vols. Cambridge: Cambridge University Press.

—— (1946) *A History of Late Nineteenth Century Drama, 1850–1900*, 2 vols. Cambridge: Cambridge University Press.

Pückler-Muskau, H. (1833) *Tour in England, Ireland, and France, in the Years 1826, 1827, 1828, and 1829*. Philadelphia: Carey, Lea, and Blanchard.

Rowell, G. (1978) *The Victorian Theatre, 1792–1914*, 2nd edn. Cambridge: Cambridge University Press.

Sawyer, N. W. (1931) *The Comedy of Manners from Sheridan to Maugham*. Philadelphia: University of Pennsylvania Press.

Further Reading

Archer, W. (1882) *English Dramatists of To-Day*. London: Sampson, Low, Marston and Company.

Booth, M. R. (1991) *Theatre in the Victorian Age*. Cambridge: Cambridge University Press.

Davis, J. (ed.) (2010) *Victorian Pantomime*. Basingstoke: Palgrave Macmillan.

——, and V. Emeljanow (2001) *Reflecting the Audience: London Theatregoing, 1840–1880*. Iowa City: University of Iowa Press.

Disher, M. W. (1949) *Blood and Thunder: Mid-Victorian Melodrama and Its Origins*. London: Frederick Muller.

Emeljanow, V. (1987) *Victorian Popular Dramatists*. Boston: Twayne.

Fawkes, R. (1979) *Dion Boucicault: A Biography*. London: Quarter Books.

Fischler, A. (1991) *Modified Rapture: Comedy in W. S. Gilbert's Savoy Operas*. Charlottesville: University Press of Virginia.

Huberman, J. H. (1986) *Late Victorian Farce*. Ann Arbor: UMI Research Press.

Jenkins, A. (1991) *The Making of Victorian Drama*. Cambridge: Cambridge University Press.

Meisel, M. (1963) *Shaw and the Nineteenth-Century Theater*. Princeton: Princeton University Press.

Planché, J. R. (1872) *The Recollections and Reflections of J. R. Planché: A Professional Autobiography*, 2 vols. London: Tinsley Brothers.

Powell, K. (1990) *Oscar Wilde and the Theatre of the 1890s*. Cambridge: Cambridge University Press.

—— (2007) *Women and Victorian Theatre*. Cambridge: Cambridge University Press.

Savin, M. (1950) *Thomas William Robertson: His Plays and Stagecraft*. Providence: Brown University Press.

Schoch, R. W. (2003) *Victorian Theatrical Burlesques*. Aldershot: Ashgate Publishing.

Scott, C. (1899) *The Drama of Yesterday and To-Day*, 2 vols. London: Macmillan.

Scullion, A. (ed.) (1996) *Female Playwrights of the Nineteenth Century*. London: J. M. Dent.

Shaw, G. B. (1932) *Our Theatres in the Nineties*, 3 vols. London: Constable.

Stephens, J. R. (1992) *The Profession of the Playwright: British Theatre, 1800–1900*. Cambridge: Cambridge University Press.

Tolles, W. (1940) *Tom Taylor and the Victorian Drama*. New York: Columbia University Press.

Watson, E. B. (1926) *Sheridan to Robertson: A Study of the Nineteenth-Century London Stage*. Cambridge MA: Harvard University Press.

25
Life Writing

Timothy Peltason

It is difficult to define, but impossible to ignore, the category of "Life Writing" in Victorian literature, a category that includes not only the many thousands of autobiographies and memoirs that were produced in the period, but the hundreds of biographies as well, and the many novels and poems that borrow the form or share the motives of biography or autobiography. "From my youth upwards," wrote Harriet Martineau in 1855, "I have felt that it was one of the duties of my life to write my autobiography." She was not alone, and unprecedented numbers of Victorians, impelled variously by duty or by inclination, by the desire to offer instruction, to bear witness, to give pleasure to themselves or others, left behind some written record of their lives. Many of these records were brief and artless, the only written work of persons little known in their time and forgotten in ours. Others were written by persons of considerable contemporary reputation like Martineau, a distinguished novelist, journalist, historian, and political economist. These works continue to be valued for reasons as various as their authors – because they offer irreplaceable information about important social struggles; because they satisfy our curiosity about the lives of remarkable people; because some of them are among the great books of the century.

It tells us much about the age that these autobiographies and memoirs were written at all. First, and most obviously, the Victorian taste for the writing and reading of autobiography connects with the allied, though distinct, taste for the writing and reading of biography. We look to the eighteenth century for the greatest biography in English, Boswell's *Life of Samuel Johnson*, but to the Victorians for a culturally significant increase in the production of biography. One of the monuments

A New Companion to Victorian Literature and Culture, First Edition. Edited by Herbert F. Tucker.
© 2014 John Wiley & Sons, Ltd. Published 2014 by John Wiley & Sons, Ltd.

of late Victorian scholarship is the *Dictionary of National Biography*, commissioned by the publisher and entrepreneur George Smith in 1882, largely executed by its first editor, Leslie Stephen, and published over 15 years (1885–1900) in 63 volumes, containing 29,120 lives. An equally impressive and quite different scholarly accomplishment is Henry Mayhew's four-volume work *London Labour and the London Poor* (1849–62), an investigation of the types and conditions of lower-class London street life, for which Mayhew interviewed hundreds of individuals who told him their stories. For Mayhew, as for so many of his contemporaries, the natural unit of investigation and exposition was the character sketch or brief life. Although many biographies of the period study the great figures of British and world history, the distinctive Victorian Lives were lives not just by, but of Victorians. The writing of biography was one of the chief means by which the Victorians presented their accomplishments and their ideals – the complex image both of what they were and what they aspired to be – to themselves.

To the extent that biographical subjects were taken as ideals, the taste for biography is connected also to the taste – indeed, the hunger – for heroes, a hunger that is connected in its turn to the central spiritual crises of the age. Thomas Carlyle, an enormously influential figure in his own time, if far less so in ours, wrote *On Heroes, Hero-Worship, and the Heroic in History* (1841), a book that proclaims as its theme that "The History of the World is but the Biography of Great Men." John Stuart Mill was a great reformer, writer, and activist, a leading figure in the administration of British affairs in India as well as in the history of philosophy and of political theory. Although he and Carlyle were radically, almost comically, different in temperament, they were early associates, and they had in common this reverence for heroic lives and for their place in the formation of character. "Long before I had enlarged in any considerable degree, the basis of my intellectual creed," Mill wrote in his *Autobiography* (1853–4, published 1873), "I had obtained in the natural course of my mental progress, poetic culture of the most valuable kind, by means of reverential admiration for the lives and characters of heroic persons" (ch. 4).

Inspired by Carlyle, but defining heroism downward, Samuel Smiles wrote *Self-Help* (1859), one of the bestselling books of the nineteenth century, a compendium not of heroic but of instructively successful lives, mostly in commerce, and all tending to illustrate the doughty virtue advertised in the title. It is easy to see the limitations of Smiles's method and message, to dismiss him as pious and conventional, politically quietist, an apostle of middle-class earnestness and uplift. But he was also an ardent champion of the rights of working people, including the right to better themselves through education and industry; and he was extraordinarily influential. The comfort and counsel Smiles gave to hundreds of thousands of readers began with the Leeds working men who first heard the lectures that later became *Self-Help*, but reached far beyond them to include numerous sequels comprising exemplary lives and translation of his most popular work into dozens of European and Asian languages.

If only the least guarded of autobiographers would put him- or herself forward as heroic, there were many who presented themselves as exemplary persons from whose experiences much could be learned. These autobiographers recognized that the best way to teach their lessons was not by the making of an argument, but by the telling of a life story. A widespread belief in the special powers of narrative, of story, is another of the large cultural facts with which the vogue for biography and autobiography is connected. Mill is particularly illustrative of this point, because he not only offers himself as an example, but conducts a book-long argument about the indispensability, indeed the inevitability, of teaching by example. In his case, the powerful teacher and example was his father, James Mill: "Though direct moral teaching does much, indirect does more; and the effect my father produced on my character, did not depend solely on what he said or did with that direct object, but also, and still more, on what manner of man he was" (ch. 2). Under his father's stern and systematic tuition, John Mill attained to an astonishing and costly precocity. He read Greek at three, taught Latin to his siblings at eight, and produced at fourteen an abstract of his father's lectures on political economy, which his father then used as notes in the writing of a major book on the subject. But he suffered, too, from his father's failure to recognize the emotional and practical needs that might have been met by a less extraordinary boyhood.

Starting in his later teens, Mill fell into recurrent depressions and breakdowns, the most serious of which forms the subject of the often-anthologized chapter, "A Crisis in my Mental History." Having trained all his childhood for a career as a reformer, the young adult Mill, suffering from lowness of spirits, asked himself whether even the fulfillment of his dreams of reform would make him happy and was crushed when "an irrepressible self-consciousness distinctly answered, 'No!'" Becalmed, depressed, Mill gradually felt his way forward into a better state, with the help of Wordsworth's poems – "They seemed to be the very culture of the feelings, which I was in quest of" – and with the new conviction of the importance of "the internal culture of the individual" (ch. 5). James Mill had neglected to teach his son that the social world he needed to live in, and that he was being trained to reform, was composed not of the abstraction "humanity," but of individual persons; it was a part of the healing and redirection of energies that brought Mill forward from his moment of crisis to recognize the animating effect of other people, and especially James Mill himself, on his own life. The relationship between intellectual positions is realized in Mill's *Autobiography* as a relationship between persons, and the son tells us what he has learned from his father – and how his learning has gone beyond that of his father – not just by describing the course of formal instruction but by evoking the human circumstances of the teacher and the learner both.

Harriet Martineau also knew the importance of teaching by examples, of embodying the abstract in the concrete. By an odd coincidence both she and Mill wrote their autobiographies in the 1850s under the mistaken impression that they were suffering from fatal diseases and must hurry to record their stories, but both then lived on for 20 more years. She narrates in *Harriet Martineau's Autobiography* (written 1855) the turning point of her life as a writer, when she hit upon the scheme for the *Illustrations of Political Economy* (1832–4). Unlikely as it may now seem, these stories, each written to illustrate a particular principle of the dismal science, were a great popular success, stretching eventually to nine volumes and earning Martineau her reputation and her modest fortune. "It struck me at once," she writes of her moment of inspiration, "that the principles of the whole science [of Political Economy] might be advantageously conveyed . . . by being exhibited in their natural workings in selected passages of social life" (I, 138). The idea just comes to her – as such ideas do so often in these Victorian narratives, leaving no way to explain the event save to tell the story. Discouraged by everyone to whom she attempted to explain her idea – including James Mill, who told her publisher that her "method of exemplification" would never work (169) – Martineau persisted dauntlessly, as she relates in some of her most affecting pages. Equally affecting is the opening portion of her narrative, which describes the emotional pains and frustrations of her childhood. Although her family was reasonable, loving, and comfortably situated, she spent her early years feeling frightened and cut-off, unable to alleviate her fears and self-reproaches by confiding in anyone, a victim of the poor fit between her own temperament and the stern, but hardly brutal, childrearing practices of her family; a victim, too, of a mysterious ailment that left her almost completely deaf by the age of 16. Her book is crowded with sharp but fair-minded observations and with the evidences of a character at once typical and extraordinary, vulnerable and indomitable.

Carlyle merits a special place in this chapter as both the author and subject of Victorian biography, and as a memoirist whose *Reminiscences* (1881) tells much about his own life in the course of offering biographical sketches of those closest to him, including his father and his wife. The most influential of his life writings is the hard-to-categorize *Sartor Resartus*, subtitled in the 1838 British edition "The Life and Opinions of Herr Teufelsdröckh." The book offers itself as an account by an anonymous "Editor" of "a quite new branch of Philosophy," the "Philosophy of Clothes," and "what seemed scarcely less interesting, a quite new human Individuality, an almost unexampled personal Character, that, namely of Professor Teufelsdröckh the Discloser." Both the professor's subject and his name, which means "Devil's shit," mark him as an object of satire. But the Teufelsdröckh Clothes-Philosophy, for all its absurdity, becomes the agent of Carlyle's earnest and inspired criticism of his contemporaries, as well as of a full-dress Romantic metaphysic. And Teufelsdröckh himself lives out crucial episodes of Carlyle's own life, so much so that the book is conventionally – if somewhat dubiously – listed as a Victorian autobiography.

If not quite that, it is clearly what J. A. Froude's 1882 biography calls it, "a revelation of Carlyle's individuality" (vol. 2, ch. 6). The one episode that, according to Carlyle, "occurred quite literally to myself" (vol. 1, ch. 7) is the spiritual crisis described in book II, chapter 7, "The Everlasting No." In language wholly unlike Mill's, Carlyle describes a crisis of purpose kindred to Mill's, a conviction that all of his life-projects were meaningless and the universe a lifeless mechanism: and then a process of conversion, spiritual without being Christian, in which the worst is fronted and a sense of purpose is restored. For Carlyle, as for Mill and Martineau, the path of healing is not a sequence of reasons, but a sequence of events to be narrated. "For it seems as if the demonstration lay much in the Author's individuality," as Carlyle says earlier of Teufelsdröckh, "as if it were not Argument that had taught him, but Experience" (book 1, ch. 8); nothing but a record of experience then suffices.

John Henry, later Cardinal, Newman was another of the great figures of the age who discovered at a crisis that the way to make his point most effectively was to tell his story, as he did in the *Apologia pro Vita Sua* (1864), literally "an explanation, or justification, of my life." After completing his studies at Oxford, Newman remained there as a fellow of Oriel College, a priest of the Church of England, and, in his thirties and early forties, one of the central and charismatic members of the Oxford Movement. For many of its members this movement led gradually, but inexorably, to Rome; Newman was converted to Roman Catholicism in 1845. Two decades later he wrote the *Apologia* in response to remarks by Charles Kingsley, a liberal clergyman who accused him of a sinuous and un-English dishonesty.

Newman wrote, then, with the particular focus and intention announced by his subtitle, "Being A History of his Religious Opinions." But what he wrote, though not the life-story that a biographer would have written for him, is nevertheless a narrative, a work of life writing rather than a religious treatise. In an earlier series of essays, collected as *The Tamworth Reading Room* (1841), Newman had written about the special power of human examples: "The heart is commonly reached, not through the reason, but through the imagination, by means of direct impressions, by the testimony of facts and events, by history, by description. Persons influence us, voices melt us, looks subdue us, deeds inflame us" (letter 6). These sentences help to explain why Newman turned to autobiographical narrative to make his case; in addition they display the rhetorical power that helped him to make that case so effectively. Writing of the relationship between the established Roman Church and what he famously called "the wild living intellect of man" (*Apologia*, ch. 5), Newman both described and embodied the impressive human result of that shaping conflict and thus refuted, in his own person, Kingsley's claims that the Roman Church suppressed and distorted human nature. "The energy of the human intellect 'does from opposition grow;' it thrives and is joyous, with a tough elastic strength, under the terrible blows of the divinely-fashioned weapon, and is never so much itself as when it has lately been overthrown" (ch. 5).

One of the great sentence-writers of a great century of sentence-writers, Newman was judged the winner of his debate with Kingsley not because his judges – the English reading public – were converted to Roman Catholicism, but because they found Newman's presentation of himself compelling and plausible. Newman persuades – if he does – by the vigor and particularity of his language, and what he persuades us of is not the truth of the Roman revelation, but the richness and plausibility of his experience of it. The argument from experience modulates into that distinct, but intimately related thing, the argument from personality, and Newman ends by producing what is more truly and completely a piece of life writing than he likely intended.

In section 5 of Alfred Lord Tennyson's *In Memoriam* (1850), a patterned sequence of lyrics that constitutes one of the central Victorian narratives of crisis and recovery, the poet expresses an ambivalence about self-disclosure: "I sometimes hold it half a sin / To put in words the grief I feel; / For words, like Nature, half reveal / And half conceal the Soul within." Later in this lyric Tennyson's figures are more clearly borrowed from *Sartor Resartus* – "In words like weeds I'll wrap me o'er / Like coarsest clothes against the cold" – but the earlier image of a dialectical relationship between revelation and concealment is also indebted to Carlyle, whose strategies of indirection in life writing were an imaginative and formal resource for Victorian poets and novelists.

Unlike William Wordsworth, whose autobiographical poem *The Prelude* (1850) is one of the great documents of nineteenth-century life writing, the major Victorian poets and novelists tended to make art of their experiences by reporting them obliquely. Both Tennyson and Robert Browning wrestle in their early poems with what Mill, in a note on Browning's first volume, referred to as "intense and morbid self-consciousness," and both needed to discover modes of writing in which they revealed themselves obliquely rather than directly. For Browning, this led to the dramatic monologue, a genre of which he became the master; his monologues, especially those of *Men and Women* (1855), offer some of the most remarkable character sketches in Victorian literature – chances for characters to step forward and tell their stories, to represent themselves in words. Tennyson's most successful early poems either avoided the first-person singular or attributed it to a fictional speaker. Even when the first-person makes its great appearance in *In Memoriam*, it is carefully placed by Tennyson: " 'I' is not always the author speaking of himself, but the voice of the human race speaking through him" (Tennyson I, 305). Not *always* the author speaking of himself, but often enough to be the form in which Tennyson could best represent his own grief and recovery after the death of his beloved friend, Arthur Hallam; speaking for the race as well, the poet of *In Memoriam* takes on the familiar autobiographer's duty to be at once a distinctive individual and an example.

Other poets wrote their lives in their lyrics, constructing larger narrative structures out of a sequence of lyric moments: George Meredith's *Modern Love* (1862), a loosely autobiographical account of marital crisis, is a notable example, as is Dante Gabriel Rossetti's sonnet sequence *The House of Life* (1870/1881). The most ambitious and full-dress instance of Victorian life writing in verse is Elizabeth Barrett Browning's *Aurora Leigh* (1857). This remarkable work is at once a novel in verse, a meditation on the condition of England and on the responsibility of artists and activists to remedy that condition, a diaristic faux-autobiography of its eponymous heroine, and an oblique and selective life history and self-portrait of its famous author. Reflecting on the need to embody the abstractions of social analysis in the concrete particulars of individual lives, and thus, by extension, on the need for poems like *Aurora Leigh* to be written, Aurora's cousin Romney says to her: "There's too much abstract willing, purposing, / In this poor world. We talk by aggregates, / And think by systems" (VIII. 800–2). Speaking clearly for her author, Aurora has proposed a remedy in lines that haunt Romney so effectively that he repeats them back to her many years and many lines later: "You will not compass your poor ends / Of barley-feeding and material ease, / Without a poet's individualism / To work your universal" (II. 475–8; VIII. 427–30).

Unlike these other Victorian poets, G. M. Hopkins did his life writing in prose and in the unshaped form of letters, journals, and diary entries, a collection that constitutes almost in spite of itself a revealing self-portrait. Like the letters of Keats, which they rival in interest, Hopkins's letters offer a vivid and distinctive sense of his character in addition to their illuminating remarks both on his own poetry and on the conduct of the imaginative life. The diary entries alternate between ecstatically focused observation of the natural world, philological speculation, overheard folktales and anecdotes, notes on reading, and odd bits of workaday information. The poet's voice is intermittently audible, his inquiring and anxiously self-questioning spirit everywhere discernible.

Opening the field of Victorian life writing to diaries, we widen it almost unmanageably and raise a sequence of new theoretical questions. Working without evident principles of organization or plans for publication, yet always performing for at least the virtual audience of the projected, judging self, Victorian diarists offer to contemporary readers not the interests of narrative or point-making argument, but still, at their best, the vivid and vicarious experience of another self, another life, another and now distant world of daily activity. When the diarist is distinguished for other accomplishments, as in the case of Hopkins, we bring one kind of curiosity to the diary, eagerly scanning it for explanation or supplement to what we already know and value. In other cases the diarist is known chiefly for the diary, and our interest begins and ends with the document itself and with all that it discloses of the world and character of its author.

Standing in for hundreds of extant Victorian diaries, we can select one celebrated instance for brief commentary. The diaries of Francis Kilvert, a clergyman, record his daily life as a curate in several rural parishes of Wales and southern England between 1870 and his early death in 1879. Originally more than a million words in nine volumes, the diaries were censored by Kilvert's widow, discovered among his family's papers in 1937 and excerpted in three published volumes, now out of print, before a great niece burned the original manuscript. Several one-volume abridgements are now available, highlighting different aspects of Kilvert's writerly personality, but all give ample space to his lyrical accounts of natural scenery, accounts which have always the virtue of seeming to place the reader in the scene, re-experiencing with Kilvert the intense pleasure of being alive to the created world in that place and moment. Just as prominent are Kilvert's many descriptions of fetching young girls, sometimes of his own class – he was poor, but a gentleman – more often not. Farm girls, shop girls, gypsy children: he notices dozens, perhaps hundreds, of them in rapturous and appreciative detail, often telling of his friendly and sometimes flirtatious exchanges with them, relishing their bodies and their beauties, but without Pepysian coarseness or any disquieting sense that he took advantage of his privileges of class or gender.

Kilvert records hundreds of other encounters as well with the great and small of his parishes, feelingly sympathetic to the sufferings of the poor and the sick, grateful for the patronage he received from some of his superiors, wry about the entitlement and demandingness of others, but never seeming to question the social and sexual proprieties of whose limiting, sometimes damaging consequences he shows us such ample evidence. He is excellent company, consistently illustrative of the hard-to-manage double truth that there are two great mistakes that we can make when studying the men and women of a distant time and place: the first is to believe that they are just like ourselves; and the second to believe that they are not.

The great Victorian novelists also found ways of engaging in life writing by blending elements of autobiography and biography into their fictions, notably into those novels that critics have called by the name *Bildungsroman*. This German word – literally "the novel of formation" – names a loose and unofficial category which includes such classics of Victorian fiction as *David Copperfield* (1850) and *Great Expectations* (1861), *The Mill on the Floss* (1860), *Jane Eyre* (1847) and *Villette* (1853), and such less-read but still central achievements as Meredith's *The Ordeal of Richard Feverel* (1859), Thackeray's *The History of Pendennis* (1850), Kingsley's *Alton Locke* (1850), William Hale White's *The Autobiography of Mark Rutherford* (1881), and Samuel Butler's *The Way of All Flesh* (1903). In their varying ways these novels derive their structures from the unfolding shape of an individual life, offering their central figures as examples, if not of conduct, then of development. The two greatest novels of the period, *Bleak House* (1853) and *Middlemarch* (1872), also contain within their more panoramic plots a central story of growth and development: in *Bleak House*, the first-person narrative of Esther Summerson; in *Middlemarch*, the "home epic" of Dorothea Brooke. Most of these central characters share defining traits or life events with their authors; a few are virtual self-portraits.

Only Anthony Trollope, of the major Victorian novelists, wrote an undisguised autobiography. Titled simply *An Autobiography* (1883), it is a curious and attractive book best known for the disarming frankness with which Trollope discusses his workmanlike approach to authorship and the money he earned from it. Trollope furnishes few details about his personal life or about his long and happy marriage, but he does offer in the early chapters an unsparing account of childhood awkwardness and misery, a misery for which he consoled himself by the construction of long, imaginary narratives. In the next chapters of his life, the more moving for being so plainly told, Trollope tells a story not of crisis and conversion, but of steady and gratifying self-development: he works hard and steadily at his career in the Post Office and then in his spare time at establishing himself as a novelist, gradually emerging into a successful adulthood. In the course of this plain-spoken account, and of his protestations that he had no special gift but persistence, Trollope's special gifts are clearly on display.

Dickens did write, though he never published, an autobiographical fragment that is quoted extensively in the biography (1872–74) written by his friend John Forster.

To compare the fragment with its fictional transmutation in *David Copperfield* is to discover yet again the uses of indirection in life writing. The single, searing episode that dominates Dickens's brief narrative and Forster's discussion is one in which the ten-year-old Dickens was sent to work by his parents in Warren's blacking factory, preparing and relabeling the bottles in which boot-polish would be sold. Although Dickens's life story is significantly different from that of David Copperfield, he shares with his hero defining attributes, ambitions, and childhood memories, chief among them this interlude of child labor. David is an orphan, sent to work by a cruel stepfather on the wine bottles in a warehouse. But his feelings of desolation and abandonment are exactly those of the young Dickens. "No words can express the secret agony of my soul as I sunk into this companionship . . . That I suffered in secret, and that I suffered exquisitely, no one ever knew but I. How much I suffered, it is, as I have said already, utterly beyond my power to tell": these sentences appear in both accounts. In the fragment, Dickens goes on to say that "No man's imagination can overstep the reality" of his sufferings, but this curiously flat and unconvincing sentence merely suggests that Dickens's own imagination could do justice to this episode only by doing just that, displacing it into the experience of an alter ego and into a fictional context in which comic and dramatic invention lightens and animates the intensities of sympathy. The great strength of *David Copperfield*, the immediacy of feeling with which it renders David's childhood experience, is a weakness of the autobiographical fragment in which there is nothing to complicate or disguise the picture of a person whose urgent and unmastered sympathies are with himself.

The biographer, too, must balance sympathy and judgment, and in the best Victorian biographies, of which Forster's is one, the challenge is met by means that may be compared to those of the poet and novelist, or the autobiographer. J. A. Froude's biography of Carlyle was really two two-volume works – *Thomas Carlyle: A History of the First Forty Years of His Life 1795–1835* (1882) and *Thomas Carlyle: A History of His Life in London 1834–1881* (1884), surrounded and interrupted by six more volumes, edited by Froude, of letters and reminiscences by Carlyle and his wife Jane Welsh Carlyle. In the judgment of some late Victorian reviewers, Froude failed in sympathy for Carlyle, and judged too harshly Carlyle's failure of others, notably of his wife. Late-twentieth-century readers are likelier to feel that Froude judged too leniently the intemperate and spiteful political judgments of some of Carlyle's later works. But they are also likely to recognize that Froude's discussion of marriage is deeply sympathetic to Carlyle, never more so than when registering the harshness with which Carlyle judged himself. The great subject of these fascinating volumes is the remorse that Carlyle experienced upon discovering as a widower the many unhappinesses his wife had suffered at his hands:

> There broke upon him in his late years, like a flash of lightning from heaven, the terrible revelation that he had sacrificed his wife's health and happiness in his absorption in his work; that he had been oblivious of his most obvious obligations, and had been

negligent, inconsiderate, and selfish. The fault was grave and the remorse agonizing. For many years after she had left him, when we passed the spot in our walks where she was last seen alive, he would bare his gray head in the wind and rain – his features wrung with unavailing sorrow. (1882, ch. 18)

"Unavailing" makes a powerful and quiet comment. Reading back and forth between the Carlyles' own letters and memories and Froude's incorporation of those documents into a text he makes his own, the reader can gain a full sense not only of Froude's subjects, but of his method, the method by which the biographer is true both to his documents and to himself as their interpreter. Autobiographers are free to apportion their attentions unevenly; they owe a duty to memory that is real, but still quite distinct from the duty owed by biographers to the written record and to their subjects. Unsurprisingly, then, autobiographers are likely to write much more of childhood – where memories are plentiful and documents scarce – or to turn their autobiographies to a specific purpose, the vindication of a particular position, the explanation of a particular change of heart: or else to produce records that are frankly miscellaneous and impressionistic. However truncated or rearranged, the life account of the skilled autobiographer will inevitably offer a sense of his or her character. In order to achieve the same goal – to do some justice to the biographical subject – the biographer must attend carefully to documents. Hence arises that special Victorian creation, of which Froude offers one distinguished example, the "Life and Letters," which includes wherever possible the words of its subject, and thus provides an occasion for reflection on the relationship between the words of the biographical subject, which are commentary already, and the biographer's commentary on them.

Another great example of the Victorian Life and Letters is Elizabeth Gaskell's *The Life of Charlotte Brontë* (1857), the account of one distinguished novelist by another. Referring at one juncture to "the conviction, which I have all along entertained, that where Charlotte Brontë's own words could be used, no others ought to take their place" (ch. 14), Gaskell quotes frequently and at length from Brontë's letters, but places herself in the narrative, too, as is justified both by her friendship with Brontë and by the resultant vividness and inwardness of the narrative. Her opening description of Keighley, near the Brontës' Yorkshire home, aims at capturing "the smack and flavour of the place" (ch. 3); the pages that follow capture the special flavor of Charlotte Brontë herself: diffident, eager, loving, sternly sure in judgment. Bringing to bear her own love and judgment, Gaskell makes clear, among other things, that the difficulties that Brontë may have presented were partly explained, and wholly dwarfed, by the difficulties that she had faced within what emerges as a tragic story of loss and early death – the deaths, first, of Brontë's mother and three siblings, and then her own.

What pained the child Dickens most – and the adult Dickens, too, looking back on the child – was the sense of sinking, of being "cast away" (Forster I, 21) into hopelessness and irremediable ignorance, in short, into the working class. It will not do simply to scold Dickens for snobbery or to make light of the horror he felt at the prospect of his fall. His loss would truly have been grievous – and so would ours – had his education been stopped and a life of hard labor started when he was first sent to the blacking factory. In fact, he was rescued by a small reversal of family fortune and restored to a life, not of gentlemanly leisure, certainly, but of invention and aspiration and upward mobility. In this he resembled the other writers we have discussed, most of whom worked hard to support themselves, but none of whom was among the great majority of Victorian men and women who lived lives of constant hardship and meager expectations like the one into which Dickens fell briefly and so traumatically.

It is striking how many men and women of the working classes did manage to educate themselves in spite of such obstacles and, with or without benefit of formal instruction, to tell their stories. The amplest Victorian collection of working-class stories is offered by Mayhew's *London Labour and the London Poor*. But many working-class men and women wrote their own stories, too. Many of these working-class texts are brief and fragmentary; predictably, they are dominated by different concerns and motivated by different needs from the autobiographies of Mill, Carlyle, Martineau, and Newman. But just as predictably, they share many of those authors' interests and concerns. Any of these texts gratifies our hunger for information and helps us begin to do justice to the variety, and often the terrible difficulty, of Victorian lives. Many of them offer other gratifications as well: the engagement of human stories compellingly and convincingly told; the surprise of unexpected affinities of feeling; a freshened and focused sense of the human realities that made – and that still make – political struggle so urgent and consequential.

Two of the more substantial and successful of these working-class autobiographies were the *Life and Struggles of William Lovett in His Pursuit of Bread, Knowledge and Freedom* (1876) and James Dawson Burn's *The Autobiography of a Beggar Boy* (1855). Lovett's is the more familiar and more satisfyingly shaped of the two, because he writes from a secure sense of himself and describes the growth of strong and clear, if also frustrated and conflicted, political commitments. Born in Penzance, at the extreme southwest corner of England, he tells a childhood story of daily struggles and pleasures, filled with anecdotes that convey a sense both of his own personality and of the difficulties of his social position. Barred from a sailor's or fisherman's life by seasickness, Lovett apprenticed himself to a ropemaker, and then, finding no work in subsequent years, retrained himself as a cabinet-maker, working against both the hardships of the economy and the workingmen's rules that would bind him to a single trade. Finally established in London, he describes the worldly frustrations and the new learning that together led to his political commitments. "Awakened to a new mental existence" by his reading on religious and political questions, and "forcibly struck" by the injustices of existing social and political arrangements, Lovett employs the familiar language of autobiographical self-discovery. But the milieu and the nature of the discoveries are distinctive. When he is kept from an important political meeting because he must finish and deliver a set of dining tables for a gentleman, the reader is reminded of the daily demands of a working life. When that meeting is brutally attacked by the police, and when one reasonable and modest demand after another is denied by the holders of power, the reader is likely to be forcibly struck, too, by the injustice of a hierarchical society and by the dignity and moral power of Lovett's character and position.

The Autobiography of a Beggar Boy is a fascinating, but far less heartening book. Burn tells the story of an unsettled and brutalized boyhood, a story that *ought* to be heartening if only because of the resiliency and persistence that enabled its author to survive and write it. But Burn never quite emerges from his difficulties, either into material comfort or into a settled sense of his identity and the meaning of his own experiences. He closes his book with effortful optimism and with an improving, Smilesian moral – "The battle of my life is well calculated to prove to young men what energy and determination of character are able to accomplish when rightly directed" – but the reader learns rather different things from Burn's book, which makes vivid both the particular circumstances and hardships of a poor and wandering life and the human and psychic damage that such a life causes.

One of Lovett's lighter and more engaging episodes describes how his future wife, an English girl serving as a lady's maid in France, broke off their engagement when she could not satisfy herself that he had a right view of the Christian sacrament of holy communion. Too principled to dissemble, Lovett accepted the separation, though it felt to him "like the parting of the mental and bodily powers." After a year's separation and study, he and his beloved opened with one another "a kind of controversial correspondence on [religion] . . . the result of which was that our religious opinions became perfectly satisfactory to one another, and terminated by her coming over to England and accepting me as her husband." The story is a charming and revealing one – for what it tells us of Lovett's principled uprightness, and his wife's, and of the creaturely eagerness with which they accommodated their principles to their love for each other. But it reveals also how omnipresent the subject of religion was – not just to clergymen like Newman, and not just as the background and metaphor-provider for spiritual struggles like Mill's or Carlyle's, but as an instructive and obstructive fact of social and family life.

Two more of the notable life writings of the period focus in their quite different ways on religious differences in Victorian family life. In *The Way of All Flesh* Samuel Butler tells the story of Ernest Pontifex, the son of a mean-spirited and narrow-mindedly pious father like Butler's own. Writing in the 1870s and 1880s (though the novel was not published until 1903, after Butler's death), Butler is bracingly astringent and un-Victorian, as so many Victorians were. "'I have been thinking,' [Ernest] said, 'that I may perhaps never recover from this illness, and in case I do not I should like you to know that there is only one thing which weighs upon me. I refer,' he continued after a slight pause, 'to my conduct towards my father and mother. I have been much too good to them'" (ch. 80). The relationship between the novel's narrator and its central character, both of whom seem to be Butler, is confusing – resulting not in an achieved strategy of indirection but just a wobbly point of view – and the novel loses its way at several points. But the story is an immensely appealing one even so, moving beyond its satiric inversions to endorse a humane and loose forgivingness of manner; an unsystematized following of impulse; a life writer's subordination of doctrines to persons: "Our most assured likings have for the most part been arrived at neither by introspection nor by any process of conscious reasoning, but by the bounding forth of the heart to welcome the gospel proclaimed to it by another" (ch. 64). "No man's opinions . . . can be worth holding unless he knows how to deny them easily and gracefully upon occasion in the cause of charity" (ch. 86). This is a limited point of view – you cannot make a religious movement or a political revolution with it – but also an extremely attractive one.

Edmund Gosse's *Father and Son* (1907) tells another representative and distinctive Victorian story of family struggle and the loss of faith. Unlike Butler, Gosse loves and respects the father from whom he must nevertheless separate himself. His story makes plausible and vivid both the religious urgencies of Philip Gosse – a scholar, a naturalist, and a deeply committed member of the Calvinist sect called the Plymouth Brethren – and Edmund Gosse's gathering sense that he was called away from his father by the world of humanistic understanding. It was the reading of fiction, for Edmund, that "did more than anything else . . . to give fortitude to my individuality." And when he tells the story of his public baptism at age ten, "the central event of my whole childhood," he does so with a novelist's eye for the complex human motivations and responses of all the actors involved – his father's pride and his own in such precocious piety; the doubtfulness of his spiritual examiners, vanquished by his fluency and by the impressive new furnishings of his family's drawing room. To see the event in such purely human terms, however, is next door to unbelief, and Gosse leaves his father's world behind, impelled by the very tastes and attributes that make his book so successful.

We encounter related but distinct challenges to orthodoxy in the autobiographies of three scientists, to use a word that only entered the language in 1834. Darwin's *Autobiography*, written in spare afternoon hours during the summer of 1876, is a frankly miscellaneous account of the childhood and career of the scientist who wrote the most consequential book of the century, *The Origin of Species* (1859), which did more than any other work to unsettle the faith of literate Victorians. Darwin writes to amuse himself, he announces, and because his narrative "might possibly interest my children or their children" (ch. 1). He is rightly aware that his life story possesses wider importance and interest, not because of the dramatic power with which he invests it in the telling, but because of the momentousness of what he has done. He tells the stories accordingly of how he came to take the exploratory voyage of the *Beagle*, from which so much else followed; and he "can remember the very spot in the road, whilst in my carriage, when to my joy the solution occurred to me" (ch. 7) of a central problem in the theory of evolution. Our knowledge of the eventual significance of his discoveries does make these stories of interest; it adds force, too, to the appealingly deflationary sequence in which Darwin reports first his "glow of pride" when Sir James Mackintosh said of him, "There is something in that young man that interests me." And then comments: "This must have been chiefly due to his perceiving that I listened with much interest to everything which he said, for I was as ignorant as a pig about his subjects of history, politicks, and moral philosophy" (ch. 1). A nice piece of self-irony, made nicer by the fact that it is Charles Darwin who offers it. Professing to write "as if I were a dead man in another world looking back at my own life," Darwin offers a sequence of convincingly spontaneous recollections out of which emerge fascinating brief portraits of his father and others, and, with increasing definition throughout the book, a nuanced and believable portrait of himself.

Thomas Huxley was a surgeon and an anatomist, a natural scientist and a paleontologist, a distinguished professor and public advocate for liberal education, and a polemical religious skeptic who earned the nickname "Darwin's bulldog" for his zealous advocacy of the elder scientist's theory of natural selection. In his brief *Autobiography*, Huxley writes with Trollopian matter-of-factness about the need to earn his bread and with a whiff of pretentiously un-pretentious self-admiration about the virtues of plain-speaking: "I have been obliged through life with saying what I mean in the plainest of plain language, than which, I suppose, there is no habit more ruinous to a man's prospects of advancement." But he earns the reader's admiration, too, with his straightforward account of a life of extraordinary achievement made possible by extraordinary effort. And the resistance that he faced makes understandable his conviction "that there is no alleviation for the sufferings of mankind except veracity of thought and of action and the resolute facing of the world as it is when the garment of make-believe by which pious hands have hidden its uglier features is stripped off."

Like Huxley and Darwin, the astronomer and mathematician Mary Somerville encountered resistance of many kinds, from the same religious establishment that was scandalized by their work, but also from her father and mother and the many others in her set who thought that education of any kind and particularly education in science was unsuitable to the female mind. A generation older than Darwin, Somerville writes affectingly of her girlhood in Scotland, of the persistence with which she sought out books and training of all kinds, but especially in mathematics, finding an uncle here, a sympathetic tutor there, encouraging correspondents in increasing number to recognize her exceptional talents and to help her on her way. As her story opens outward she flourishes gratifyingly, given a modest financial independence by a respectfully described first marriage and then, with the help of a beloved second husband who celebrated and encouraged his wife's exceptional talents, finding her way to productive relationships with the leading scientific minds of her age and to distinguished work both as an independent inquirer and as the English translator and expositor of the best Continental work in mathematics and astronomy. Living into her nineties, in full possession of her faculties and good health, Somerville is an enormously appealing figure, unapologetically conventional in her affirmations of religious faith, of received social hierarchies, and of the distinctively female pleasures of motherhood, housewifery, balls and fancy dresses, but also forthright in her advocacy of abolition, of women's education and suffrage, of the humane treatment of animals, and of the necessity to both personal and cultural health of unprejudiced inquiry into the nature of things. Like those of Francis Kilvert, Somerville's Victorian conventionalities can tempt the modern reader to condescension; but only an incautious reader will succumb to the temptation.

Three more books, dramatically unlike one another in their construction of the auto-biographer's task and unlike any others we have discussed, will complete our survey of Victorian life writing with a thesis-humbling reminder of how various the subject is. Oscar Wilde's *De Profundis* was written from prison in 1897, posthumously published in an abridged and altered version in 1905, the full text appearing only in 1962. Like so many life writings, *De Profundis* is generically hard to place, a long letter addressed to Wilde's estranged lover, Lord Alfred Douglas, detailing the troubled history of their relationship and of Wilde's own career, but also the story of Wilde's trial and imprisonment "for committing acts of gross indecency with another male person," a story that then modulates into a lengthy meditation on love, sorrow, society, and the figure of Christ. The result is a strange, manipulative blending of reproach and forgiveness, careful documentation and revisionist history, inimitable elegance of address and all-too-imitable self-dramatization. The dizzying changes that Wilde records and the instability of his tone as he records them seem a failure of will and control, rather than the controlled triumph of will over mere event that his most accomplished works celebrate. To say, as a more wholehearted admirer of *De Profundis* might wish to, that Wilde mastered circumstance would be to deny the full horror and brutality of the punishment he received and to underestimate the power of a brute stupidity to have its way in the world. But to say simply that he was defeated would be to ignore the gallant seriocomic performance of his own nature that sustained him, in prison and afterwards, and that is at once a legacy to his readers and a gift from his art to his life.

John Ruskin's *Praeterita* (1885–9) is an ampler work, as one might expect from the author who wrote 39 volumes of visionary commentary on art, architecture, literature, and society, in sentences rivaled in the nineteenth century only by those of Newman and Dickens for rhetorical power. Ruskin wrote *Praeterita*, he tells us, to give pleasure to himself and others and to pay homage to his parents, who were strict and indulgent in equal measures, and who loom large throughout the book, but especially in the opening chapters, which may be compared instructively with John Stuart Mill's account of his over-managed childhood. Writing for pleasure, Ruskin makes no mention of many painful episodes – his annulled marriage, the bouts of madness that interrupted his career and finally reduced him to silence. Although this last work is touched by both sorrow and anger, it has none of the inspired, but hectoring, fury of many of Ruskin's earlier writings. It does offer a wonderful account of Ruskin's childhood, and appreciative and varied reports on the places and objects of beauty that formed his character and that were the subjects of such great earlier works as *Modern Painters* (1843–60) and *The Stones of Venice* (1851–3). Like so many autobiographers of the period, Ruskin tells of crisis and recovery, of the discovery of vocation, of the transmutation, rather than simply the loss or the restoration, of religious faith. But uniquely, and somewhat confusingly, Ruskin tells not one but many such stories; it is a distinguishing feature of both his writing and his character that though he speaks often of the beauties of simplicity and order, he does so lushly and digressively. The way to simple clarity is effortful and complex; *Praeterita* is melancholy as well as mellow, a record of sublime sightings, but also of losses. At its best, the book brings Ruskin and his reader together to such extraordinary moments as the closing evocation of the night-skies of Siena – "the fireflies everywhere in sky and cloud rising and falling, mixed with the lightning, and more intense than the stars" – in the last and perhaps the finest paragraphs that Ruskin ever wrote.

To move next, and last, to the *Autobiography* (1899) of Margaret Oliphant (1828–97) will seem an anti-climax. This brief and broken narrative, strangely modest and even more strangely moving, was written in fits and starts by a prolific and successful writer of novels only recently made available again since her lifetime. These novels repay attention, but the *Autobiography*, authoritatively edited by Elisabeth Jay, is a good place for new readers to start and for this account to end. More than any other of the life writings here discussed, with the possible exception of *Sartor Resartus*, this is a book whose *tone* it is both difficult and crucial to determine. Oliphant is disingenuous at times, afflicted with a poor-me-ism, and an off-putting fondness for locutions like "my poor little unappreciated self." These are such evidently false modesties, however, and they are so quickly and unblinkingly noted as such by Oliphant herself, that they take their part in a complex and affecting self-portrait. Asserting her claims at one moment, denying or qualifying them at the next, Oliphant puts forth a steady, middle-voiced stream of shrewd, sharp, affectionate, ironic descriptions of both herself and others, especially of the succession of weak and erring men – husband, brother, sons – she had to support and direct. She tells a story of industry and self-sacrifice, of "a heart [that] contrived to rise whenever it had a chance," but that was cast down repeatedly by a series of crushing losses – a story interrupted by crisply phrased judgments that may strike the reader's ear as either bitter or brave, slyly aggressive or admirably undeluded. Finally, however, the book turns the tables and challenges that listening reader to imagine just what tone would be the right one in which to recount the deaths of Oliphant's mother, her two newborn sons, an infant daughter, her husband, her ten-year-old daughter, both her brothers – after years of total dependence upon her – and then, in their early thirties, her two, last, struggling sons. Looking back from the vantage point of all but the last of these deaths, she saw her life's happiness as embodied supremely in a moment "so curiously common and homely, with nothing in it . . . the moment after dinner when I used to run up-stairs to see that all was well in the nursery, and then to turn into my room on my way down again to wash my hands, as I had a way of doing before I took up my evening work . . . I can see it now, the glimmer of the outside lights, the room dark, the faint reflection in the glasses, and my heart full of joy and peace – for what? – for nothing – that there was no harm anywhere, the children well above stairs and their father below" (Oliphant 1990: 63–4). After the last death, and just a year before Oliphant's own, she ended her *Autobiography* differently, and starkly, with two one-sentence paragraphs:

> And now here I am all alone.
> I cannot write any more.

Trying to decide what to think of these last sentences in Oliphant's book, whether to find in them the sought-after intensities of melodrama or the found poetry of authentic feeling, we do not cease being readers of literature, but we remember also that we are reading a true story. Nearly all of the valuable critical writing about autobiography in recent decades has made the point, one way or another, that memoirs and autobiographies are the products of art and imagination and not just the documentary transcription of reality. But this important half-truth needs correcting and completing. It is true that biographies and autobiographies, like fictions, must be constructed; it is equally true, and necessary to remind ourselves, that they must be constructed *unlike* fictions, too, according to other laws and contracts. The category of Victorian life writing includes by courtesy those novels and poems that pose as truthful documents or that are known to have borrowed much of their matter from the life stories of their authors. But it is defined and anchored by the avowedly biographical and autobiographical narratives that make distinctly different truth claims – for all the powers of imagination that were required in their construction – and that thus offer to the contemporary reader distinct pleasures in reading and distinct forms of access to that familiar and deeply entangled Victorian couple, Letters and Lives.

See also GROWING UP, MOVING OUT; PUBLISHING FICTION, SAGE WRITING

REFERENCES

Forster, J. (1966) *The Life of Charles Dickens*, 2 vols. London: J. M. Dent.

Huxley, T. H. (1909) *Autobiography and Selected Essays*. Boston: Houghton Mifflin.

Martineau, H. (1877) *Harriet Martineau's Autobiography*, 3 vols. London: Smith, Elder.

Oliphant, M. (1990) *The Autobiography of Margaret Oliphant: The Complete Text*, ed. E. Jay. Oxford: Oxford University Press.

Smiles, S. (1958) *Self Help*, ed. A. Briggs. London: John Murray.

Tennyson, H. (1897) *Alfred Lord Tennyson: A Memoir by His Son*, 2 vols. London: Macmillan.

FURTHER READING

Amigoni, D. (1993) *Victorian Biography: Intellectuals and the Ordering of Discourse.* New York and London: Harvester Wheatsheaf.

——(ed.) (2006) *Life Writing and Victorian Culture.* London: Ashgate.

Arrowsmith, W. (1982) "Ruskin's Fireflies." In *The Ruskin Polygon: Essays on the Imagination of John Ruskin*, ed. J. D. Hunt and F. Holland. Manchester: Manchester University Press.

Atkinson, J. (2010) *Victorian Biography Reconsidered: A Study of Nineteenth-Century "Hidden" Lives.* Oxford: Oxford University Press.

Burnett, J. (ed.) (1974) *Annals of Labour: Autobiographies of British Working-Class People 1820–1920.* Bloomington: Indiana University Press.

——(ed.) (1982) *Destiny Obscure: Autobiographies of Childhood, Education and Family from the 1820s to the 1920s.* London: Allen Lane.

——, D. Vincent, and D. Mayall (eds) (1984–9) *The Autobiography of the Working Class: An Annotated Critical Bibliography*, 3 vols. New York: New York University Press.

Cockshut, A. O. J. (1974) *Truth to Life: The Art of Biography in the Nineteenth Century.* New York: Harcourt, Brace.

Corbett, M. J. (1992) *Representing Femininity: Middle-Class Subjectivity in Victorian and Edwardian Women's Autobiographies.* New York: Oxford University Press.

Danahay, M. (1993) *A Community of One: Masculine Autobiography and Autonomy in Nineteenth-Century Britain.* Albany: State University of New York Press.

Davis, P. (1983) *Memory and Writing from Wordsworth to Lawrence.* Liverpool: Liverpool University Press.

Gagnier, R. (1991) *Subjectivities: A History of Self-Representation in Britain, 1832–1910.* New York: Oxford University Press.

Henderson, H. (1989) *The Victorian Self: Autobiography and Biblical Narrative.* Ithaca: Cornell University Press.

Landow, G. (ed.) (1979) *Approaches to Victorian Autobiography.* Athens: Ohio University Press.

Machann, C. (1994) *The Genre of Autobiography in Victorian Literature.* Ann Arbor: University of Michigan Press.

Peltason, T. (1988) "Imagination and Learning in George Eliot, Mill, and Dickens." *Essays in Criticism* 38, 35–54.

——(1990) "Ruskin's Finale: Vision and Imagination in Praeterita." *ELH* 57, 665–84.

Peterson, L. (1986) *Victorian Autobiography.* New Haven: Yale University Press.

——(1999) *Traditions of Victorian Women's Autobiography: The Poetics and Politics of Life Writing.* Charlottesville: University of Virginia Press.

Pritchett, V. S. (1942) *In My Good Books.* Port Washington: Kennikat Press.

Reimer, G. T. (1988) "Revisions of Labor in Margaret Oliphant's Autobiography." In *Life/Lines: Theorizing Women's Autobiography*, ed. B. Brodzki and C. Schenck. Ithaca: Cornell University Press.

Ricks, C. (1996) "Victorian Lives." In *Essays in Appreciation.* Oxford: Oxford University Press.

Sanders, V. (1989) *The Private Lives of Victorian Women: Autobiography in Nineteenth-Century England.* New York: St Martin's Press.

Vincent, D. (1981) *Bread, Knowledge and Freedom: A Study of Nineteenth-Century Working Class Autobiography.* New York and London: Methuen.

26
Sage Writing

Linda H. Peterson

On the Origins of Sage Writing in Early Victorian England

Sage writing emerged in the early Victorian period as a distinctive form of nonfictional prose – one that confronted the new and difficult problems posed by modern industrial, urban life and that proposed solutions, whether specific modes of action or more general philosophical principles. John Holloway, the literary historian who gave the name "sage writing" to this body of Victorian literature, included both essayists and novelists in his analysis; for Holloway, the defining attribute of sage writing was an "interest of a general or speculative kind in what the world is like, where man stands in it, and how he should live" (Holloway 1), not the literary genre *per se*. Given this broad definition, we might conclude that virtually every historical epoch has had some version of sage writing, some prose form that has addressed social problems both speculatively and practically. Indeed, in our own era we recognize certain writers as "public intellectuals" and call a rhetorical form they use, often similar to "sage writing," by the terms "cultural criticism" and "cultural critique." Yet the Victorians are noteworthy for their commitment to identifying and analyzing social, political, economic, religious, and philosophical problems; and Victorian sage writers are noteworthy, too, for their development of a prose form that provided not only a site of analysis but also the rhetorical tools for conducting such analysis.

Victorians faced a number of problems familiar to us but new to them as early participants in a modern society: the development of industry with its sometimes

A New Companion to Victorian Literature and Culture, First Edition. Edited by Herbert F. Tucker.
© 2014 John Wiley & Sons, Ltd. Published 2014 by John Wiley & Sons, Ltd.

detrimental environmental and economic effects; the growth of cities and the problems related to rapid urbanization; new discoveries in science and the attendant challenge to religious authority; the expansion of democracy in a series of reform bills that gave the franchise to middle-class, then working-class citizens; campaigns for women's rights, including changes in marriage laws, educational opportunities, and career possibilities. All of these changes – and others – became the subject matter of Victorian prose and provoked much thought and debate. But sage writing would not have emerged so distinctively as a form had it not been for other significant influences.

Scholars focused on philosophical traditions cite the influence of German Idealism on the thinking and experimental style of writers such as Thomas Carlyle and George Eliot (Ashton), as well as of the Scottish Common Sense school for its principle that "the validity of the truth claims made by the sage cannot be separated from the rhetorical performativity of his language" (Budge). Scholars of print culture point to the dramatic increase in nineteenth-century periodicals and newspapers that gave sage writers a place to promulgate their ideas and reach increasingly diverse groups of readers. Between 1815 and 1835 periodicals like the *Edinburgh Review*, the *Quarterly Review*, the *New Monthly Magazine*, *Fraser's Magazine*, *Blackwood's Magazine*, and the *Athenaeum* – to name only some of the most prominent – expanded rapidly, increasing their sales as well as their payments to authors. By 1818 the *Edinburgh* and the *Quarterly* each approximated a circulation of 14,000; during the 1830s the circulation of the weekly *Athenaeum* rose from 3,000 readers to 18,000 (see Erickson 78–80). As circulations rose freelance writers, as they came to be called, discovered that they could earn 20, 30, and more guineas per sheet for their literary contributions, thus making it possible to pursue authorship as something more than a sideline or avocation.

Related to the growth of periodicals, then, was the rise of the man (or woman) of letters, the professional writer who made a living by the pen. Carlyle, the preeminent sage writer of the early Victorian period, argued that it was "the wondrous art of *Writing*, or of Ready-writing which we call *Printing*" that made possible the new "Hero as Man of Letters" (*Heroes and Hero-Worship*, 1841). The critic G. H. Lewes noted at mid-century that "in the present state of things a man who has health, courage, and ability can earn by literature the income of a gentleman," i.e. approximately £300 a year. Of course, not all writers who placed their work in periodicals were "sages." Many were hacks, grinding out pages for quick (and sometimes not so quick) payment. But, as Lee Erickson has argued, the sheer number of outlets for writing "soon made professional journalism a respectable profession and also made it necessary for the weekly and monthly magazines to hire full-time editors, subeditors, and staff writers who were salaried and who wrote when no one else would" (88). Carlyle started by writing for the *Edinburgh Review* and published his ground-breaking work *Sartor Resartus* (1833–4) in *Fraser's Magazine*. Eliot began as a subeditor on the *Westminster Review* and soon began writing major reviews for its columns. Harriet Martineau started by contributing to a small but influential Unitarian journal, *The Monthly*

Repository. Even John Henry Newman, not particularly known for his periodical writing, was influenced by the literary reviews of the early nineteenth century; as a boy of 14 he imitated the rivalry of the *Edinburgh* and *Quarterly* by writing "two periodicals – that is, papers called the 'Spy' and 'Anti-Spy.' They were written against each other" (Erickson 88–9).

If the rise of periodicals made possible the rise of the man and woman of letters, recent scholarship on professional authorship has suggested yet another factor spurring the development of sage writing: the *anxieties* created by authorship as a profession. To avoid the charge of writing hackwork or piecework, authors needed to justify their "brain work" and offer something more than the daily pap of newspaper reportage. James Eli Adams points out that Victorian writers were "explicitly concerned to legitimate vocations devoted to intellectual labor" because of the previously amateurish status of writing and because of "the perplexities that followed from the Victorian 'feminizing' of such labor." Carlyle assumed the role of the sage or prophet in part to justify his intellectual labor, in part to avoid the charge of dilettantism or dandyism, in part to set himself apart from ordinary journalists. When as a young man he considered moving to London to pursue writing as a profession, he wrote (somewhat jocularly) to a Scottish friend: "If I break forth some day in Cockney-land, like some John the Baptist, girt about with a leathern girdle, proclaiming anew with fierce Annandale intonation: 'Repent ye, ye cursed scoundrels,' for &c &c you will not think it miraculous" (Adams 12, 22–3). However ironic, the allusion to John the Baptist suggests that Carlyle intended to lift his writing to a higher, prophetic mode.

Of course, not all sage writers suffered the anxieties of Carlyle about their brain work or their cultural status. John Ruskin, the son of a wealthy importer of sherry and fine wines, had no need to earn money from his writing; Matthew Arnold, the son of an eminent Victorian educator, held a position as Inspector of Schools for most of his adult life, thus obviating the need to justify authorship as his profession; Walter Pater was, first and foremost, an Oxford don. Women writers like Harriet Martineau, George Eliot, and Frances Power Cobbe suffered anxieties about their professional writing – but of a different sort. For them, as for many women, the decision to enter a profession (and thus leave the domestic sphere) was the primary anxiety. Their need to demonstrate a capacity to do brain work, an activity many thought unsuited for women, sometimes led them to produce sage writing self-consciously in the mode of their male counterparts, sometimes to experiment with forms of writing different from men's. Nonetheless, as Alexis Easley has argued, the practice of anonymity and pseudonymity in periodical writing opened up new opportunities for women to perform as sages in the public sphere, given that their gender was unknown or disguised.

The Carlylean desire to make the writer a professional – more than that, to make the man of letters a modern hero – helped to formulate the concept of the "sage writer." In his essays and books Carlyle drew on the features of Old Testament prophecy (hence the sometimes interchangeable terminology of "sage" or "prophet"), as well as on traditions of eighteenth-century satire and nineteenth-century homiletics. And in Carlyle's turn to biblical and sermonic modes we can trace a final influence on the development of sage writing: the substitution of the secular sage for the religious minister or priest. As Carlyle himself argued in his seminal essay "Characteristics" (1831), "Literature is but a branch of Religion, and always participates in its character." By the beginning of the Victorian age, however, the clergy had lost some of its prestige and power, and as the century progressed, Victorian religion was repeatedly challenged by evolutionary science and other emerging fields of specialized knowledge. Thus, in Carlyle's prophetic words, "the ancient 'ground-plan of All' belies itself when brought into contact with reality; Mother Church has, to the most, become a superannuated Stepmother, whose lessons go disregarded; or are spurned at, and scornfully gainsaid" ("Characteristics").

Sage writers offered an alternative to the Church as a source of wisdom – about the problems of life on earth, for the most part, but sometimes even in regard to the hereafter. In *Heroes and Hero-Worship* Carlyle argued that this development was logical, even necessary. After his discussion of "The Hero as Divinity" and "The Hero as Prophet," Carlyle turned – in what he viewed as a historical progression – to "The Hero as Poet" and then "The Hero as Man of Letters." "The hero as divinity, the hero as prophet, are productions of old ages; not to be repeated in the new," he asserted. The modern hero, embodied for Carlyle in men of letters like Samuel Johnson, Jean-Jacques Rousseau, and Robert Burns, carries on the work of these older heroes by "discharging a function for us which is ever honourable, ever the highest": "He is uttering-forth, in such a way as he has, the inspired soul of him." This uttering-forth – this speaking and writing of genuine, original, divinely given truth – became the defining mark of the sage.

The Rhetoric of Sage Writing: Some Characteristic Strategies

Carlyle's early *Edinburgh Review* essays, "Signs of the Times" (1829) and "Characteristics," mark the emergence of sage writing as a form and introduce its classic rhetorical strategies. With the title of the first, Carlyle alludes to Christ's words in Matthew 16:3, "O ye hypocrites, ye can discern the face of the sky; but can ye not discern the signs of the times?" – a biblical allusion that signals his intention to assume the prophetic mode, and read the signs of his own times, analyze their meaning, and offer his pronouncement on the spiritual inadequacies of his age. With the second title, "Characteristics," Carlyle adapts the German term *Charakteristik*, meaning a sketch or characterization, thus again signaling an intention to analyze the dominant features of his age – which for him was a "Mechanical" one – and to pronounce judgment on its mistakes and misunderstandings. In both essays Carlyle assumes the role of sage and prophet, demonstrating intellectual discernment in analyzing society and spiritual integrity in calling for its reform.

Several features of Carlyle's essays became common in sage writing as other prose writers imitated or developed features of his style: in addition to biblical allusion, a penchant for aphorism, the use of metaphor, and a distinctive prophetic "voice." For example, Carlyle begins "Characteristics" with an aphorism or wise saying: "The healthy know not of their health, but only the sick: this is the Physician's Aphorism; and applicable in a far wider sense than he gives it." This aphorism may be Carlyle's original invention, perhaps an adaptation of Goethe's distinction between classicism as *gesund* and romanticism as *krank*, or perhaps a modern version of the well-known Bible verse, "They that be well need not a physician" (Matthew 9:12). Whether original or borrowed, the aphorism introduces in compact language the argument Carlyle intends to make throughout the essay: that a healthy society, like a healthy body, functions unself-consciously; that a sick society, like a sick body, is "too con- scious of many things . . . oftenest the fierce jar of disruptions and convulsions." Carlyle applies the aphorism first to the individual body and soul, then to the social body and body politic, and finally to what he calls "the Condition of our own Era." By beginning with an aphorism, Carlyle suggests through his rhetorical form that his words convey important truth.

Victorian sage writing is replete with aphorisms, as other examples from Carlyle's works suggest: "Wonder is the basis of Worship" (*Sartor Resartus*); "The true Uni- versity of these days is a Collection of Books" (*Heroes and Hero-Worship*); and "Blessed is he who has found his work; let him ask no other blessedness" (*Past and Present*, 1843) – all of which have sufficiently entered our cultural vocabulary that they are included in modern editions of *Bartlett's Familiar Quotations*. Other sage writers were equally famous for their aphoristic style: Ruskin, as in "Remember that the most beautiful things in the world are the most useless: peacocks and lilies for instance" (*The Stones of Venice*, 1851–3) or "All books are divisible into two classes: the books of the hour, and the books of all time" (*Sesame and Lilies*, 1865); Arnold, as in "Conduct is three-fourths of our life and its largest concern" (*Literature and Dogma*, 1873); and especially Eliot, as in "We are all of us born in moral stupidity, taking the world as an udder to feed our supreme selves." The source of this phrase, Eliot's novel *Middlemarch* (1872), is a virtual treasure-trove of original aphorisms, which may explain why she, known primarily as a novelist, is also known as a sage writer (see Price).

Such aphorisms evoked the prestige of wisdom writing, as seminally found in the Book of Proverbs or Ecclesiastes; they gave sage writers a vehicle for clarifying and condensing thought and simultaneously challenged readers to ponder the profound ramifications of the sage's words. When, late in the century, aesthetes like Oscar Wilde wanted to parody the Victorian sage – and steal his thunder – they too used this characteristic aphoristic style. Wilde's preface to *The Picture of Dorian Gray* (1890), for instance, is simply a list of aphorisms about art beginning with "The artist is the creator of beautiful things" and ending with the now-famous line "All art is quite useless."

Another feature of sage writing, the use of metaphors, especially a dominant structural metaphor, complements the aphoristic style. Just as the aphorism condenses the sage writer's argument into a crystalline sentence, so the metaphor crystallizes into an object or word the ideas or arguments the writer amplifies throughout the essay. In "Signs of the Times," for instance, Carlyle calls his era "the Mechanical Age"; and, in example after example, he follows out the implications of this metaphor in British life – from the machinery that has transformed British industry or the steam railways and steamships that now transport British trade, to the mechanical approach that dominates British philosophy, to utilitarianism and the concept of the "Machine of Society" that motivates British politics. Carlyle's criticism focuses on what this "mechanical" view of things omits: the dynamic and organic forces that are truly important to our life and development. Despite the negativity of his critique, Carlyle's metaphor leads him to prophesy "that Mechanism is not always to be our hard taskmaster, but one day to be our pliant, all-ministering servant; that a new and brighter era is slowly evolving itself for all men." Even his prophecy involves a metaphor, that of a taskmaster becoming a servant.

Much of what we today retain from Victorian sage writing involves metaphor: Arnold's "sweetness and light" to characterize the Greek heritage in Western culture (*Culture and Anarchy*, 1869) or his "touchstones" to determine what ranks as great literature ("The Study of Poetry," 1880); Carlyle's "steamroller" of a universe, smashing the hopes and aspirations of every human being who comes in its way (*Sartor Resartus*); or Ruskin's "queens' gardens" to locate the feminine influence in English culture (*Sesame and Lilies*) or his "storm-cloud" to describe the environmental and moral degradation of his age and its apocalyptic effects ("The Storm-Cloud of the Nineteenth Century," 1884). Such metaphors help to crystallize and envision thought. They are also, for some (but not all) sage writers, an alternative to traditional, logical forms of argumentation. For Carlyle in particular, the healthy understanding "is not the Logical, argumentative, but the Intuitive" ("Characteristics"). Thus, Carlyle tended to employ metaphor as a means of grasping what the logic of his contemporaries missed: "To figure Society as endowed with life," he argued in "Characteristics," "is scarcely a metaphor; but rather a statement of fact by such imperfect methods as language affords."

These features – the use of aphorisms, metaphors, and biblical allusions, the assumption of the role of social critic or latter-day prophet – produced in most sage writers a distinctive "voice." One early reviewer of Carlyle's work, John Sterling, noted that it "exhibits all the vehemence and self-reliance of a prophet" (Seigel 101) – and, indeed, *prophetic* is a term frequently used to describe the voices of Carlyle, Ruskin, and Arnold. (Arnold was called, by a disparaging reviewer, an "elegant Jeremiah," a phrase evoking the Old Testament prophet of doom and gloom but also acknowledging in a grudging way the cultured sophistication of Arnold's analyses.) According to George Landow, the prophetic voice of the Victorian sage derives from his peculiar stance:

> Whereas the pronouncements of traditional wisdom literature always take as their
> point of departure the assumption that they embody the accepted, received wisdom of
> an entire society, the pronouncements of the biblical prophet and Victorian sage begin
> with the assumption that, however traditional their messages may once have been, they
> are now forgotten or actively opposed by society . . . The style, tone, and general pre-
> sentation of the sage derive from the fact that his voice resides at the periphery; it is,
> to use a Ruskinian etymological reminder, an eccentric voice, one off center. (Landow
> 1986: 23)

By his eccentricity or marginality, the sage achieved a unique perspective on his
society and set himself off from the mistaken masses.

In addition to "eccentric" we might offer the words "elevated" or "disinterested"
to describe the sage's voice. The latter was the preferred term of Matthew Arnold,
suggestive less of an idiosyncratic stance than of a desire to remove the sage from the
immediate political fray and analyze matters with what Amanda Anderson has called
a "value-laden value-neutrality: impartiality, tact, moderation, measure, balance, flexibility, detachment, objectivity, composure" (115). In "The Function of Criticism at
the Present Time" (1864) and again in *Culture and Anarchy* Arnold argued that what
England most needed was not writers representing their own political points of view,
but rather "critics" who were "disinterested" – that is, above party politics, inhabiting
"the world of ideas, not the world of catchwords and party habits." Arnold's "critic"
(his term for our "sage") less frequently occupies the eccentric position of a Ruskin,
or the knowable political position of a Mill or Martineau, than he ideally strives to
articulate "the best that has been thought and known in the world" ("Sweetness and
Light"). The Arnoldian ideal of disinterestedness exerted a strong influence over later
sages, most obviously Pater, who removed sage writing nearly altogether from the
realm of politics into that of aesthetics, and whose definition of the critic's task
begins, citing Arnold, "To see the object as in itself it really is" (Preface to *The Renaissance*, 1873).

Whatever their rhetorical techniques or political commitments, sages were, above
all else, cultural interpreters. Whether they chose to adopt the prophetic voice (as did
Carlyle and Ruskin) or whether they instead modulated their voices within the bounds
of traditional rhetoric (as did Martineau and Cobbe), sage writers interpreted the signs
of their times. Thus, the premier technique of sage writing became the identification
and interpretation of ordinary, even trivial phenomena as keys to cultural meaning.
This technique was used with effect by virtually every Victorian sage and has been
passed down to twentieth-century cultural critics such as Joan Didion, Tom Wolfe,
and Hunter Thompson. Matthew Arnold used, for example, the murder of an illegitimate child by a woman named Wragg to critique the current state of British culture
in "The Function of Criticism" (1864). In the *Latter-Day Pamphlets* (1850) Carlyle
chose a statue erected in honor of George Hudson, the railway king, to reveal the low
level to which English heroism and hero-worship had fallen. In "What Shall We Do
with Our Old Maids?" (1862) Cobbe began with a report from the Convocation of
Canterbury to raise issues about women's education and employment. And Ruskin,

in a brilliant example of this technique in the essay "Traffic" (1862), focused on the architectural styles of the churches, schools, and houses of the industrial town of Bradford to interpret the current state of religion and commerce.

According to Ruskin, "All good architecture is the expression of national life and character; and it is produced by a prevalent and eager national taste" – an argument he had developed in *The Stones of Venice* and repeats at the beginning of "Traffic." Ruskin notes that the buildings in Bradford belong to two different architectural styles: churches and schools use the Gothic style, whereas mansions and mills "are never Gothic." What, Ruskin asks, does this peculiar phenomenon mean – given that, during the Middle Ages, all buildings were constructed in the same Gothic style, houses and churches alike? Ruskin interprets the modern division of architectural styles to mean that "at the root of the matter, it signifies neither more nor less than that you have separated your religion from your life." "Traffic" goes on to argue that the true religion of Bradford is commerce (*traffic*, in its nineteenth-century usage) rather than Christianity. The phenomena of everyday life become the occasion for – and evidence of – the sage's cultural analysis. Whatever the phenomena, the goal is critique and, ultimately, reform.

Women Writers as Cultural Sages

Holloway's *The Victorian Sage* (1953) included only one woman author: George Eliot. Eliot's high seriousness, her sense of "the high responsibilities of literature that undertakes to represent life" (111), and especially her brilliant use of metaphor, aphorism, and allusion, made her an undeniable candidate for sage status. Other women writers were omitted, however, and only in recent years has there been intense discussion about women writers who belong in this category – thanks to the ground-breaking work of Thaïs Morgan's *Victorian Sages and Cultural Discourse: Renegotiating Gender and Power* (1990) and anthologies such as Andrea Broomfield and Sally Mitchell's *Prose by Victorian Women* (1996) and Carolyn Christensen Nelson's *A New Woman Reader* (2001).

As contributors to Morgan's collection point out, Victorian women writers faced cultural prejudices that turned them away from sage writing as a genre. Proper ladies were not supposed to speak out; they were not supposed to meddle in politics or other public issues; they were, at best, supposed to compose domestic treatises, devotional tracts, or sentimental poetry – literary genres beneath the designation "sage." Even professional women writers who resisted these prejudices tended to be associated not with sage writing but with the novel. Women's success in fiction was so noticeable that Lewes (George Eliot's partner) commented:

> Of all departments of literature, Fiction is the one to which, by nature and by circumstance, women are best adapted. Exceptional women will of course be found competent to the highest success in other departments; but speaking generally, novels

are their forte. The domestic experiences which form the bulk of women's knowledge find an appropriate form in novels; while the very nature of fiction calls for that predominance of Sentiment which we have already attributed to the feminine mind. (Christ 21–2)

Lewes's view coincides with modern scholarly statistics: of the 11 Victorian women listed in the *Wellesley Index to Victorian Periodicals* with more than 50 entries to their name, half are better known as novelists than as nonfiction writers.

Even so, a significant number of Victorian women writers donned the prophetic mantle and wrote in the mode of the sage. Their work – what they wrote about, what rhetorical techniques they adopted, how they resembled or differed from their male counterparts – broadens our sense of sage writing in the Victorian period. Indeed, it makes us rethink the contributions of other prose writers, men and women alike, who have not usually been called sages but who added their voices to debates about the pressing social and political issues of their day.

Most prominent as a female sage writer in the biblical mode was Christina Rossetti, who in prose commentaries such as *Seek and Find* (1879), *Called to Be Saints* (1881), and *Time Flies* (1885) used the liturgical calendar and traditional Anglo-Catholic devotional practices to rearticulate spiritual wisdom and practical piety for modern readers. Most prominent in the classical prophetic mode was Florence Nightingale who, in *Cassandra* (written 1852), spoke out against the social pressure to marry and the trivialization of the lives of women who did not. "Why have women passion, intellect, moral activity," Nightingale asked, yet "a place in society where no one of the three can be exercised?" The title of Nightingale's prose piece – which names the visionary Trojan princess who prophesied truthfully but whose words were never believed – signals her own prophetic intentions. So, too, do Nightingale's adaptations of Old Testament prophetic strategies and her (mis)quotations of John the Baptist, who, in the New Testament, is figured as the "voice of one crying in the wilderness" (Landow 1990: 42–4). For Nightingale, the modern prophetess cries "in the crowd, 'Prepare ye the way of the Lord,'" and what she prepares for is a female Christ and female followers who will truly live by Christ's sayings. The self-designation as Cassandra may, however, suggest that Nightingale feared her message would not be heard or even that she was ambivalent about assuming the prophetic role (a conclusion supported by her decision not to publish *Cassandra* but to circulate it privately among friends).

Other women writers were less ambivalent. Martineau, Cobbe, and Eliza Lynn Linton also wrote as sages, though typically not in the prophetic vein of Carlyle or the classical, feminine mode of Nightingale. Martineau was proud of the fact that, as a child, she had attended a boy's grammar school and mastered the traditionally masculine subjects of rhetoric and composition; Martineau, Cobbe, and Linton all pursued careers as journalists, Linton becoming the first salaried woman reporter (for the *Morning Chronicle*) and Cobbe noting with pride that she daily went to the office to do her work "like a man." When these women wrote about contemporary social problems, they wrote in what Lewes would have deemed a masculine style, utilizing the rhetorical tools of *logos* and eschewing *pathos*. Martineau's style emphasizes balance, and her prose often depends on the hypothetical syllogism (If x is true, then y is true; if y is not true, then x is not true) – as in her argument in *Household Education* (1849) about women's intellectual capacities: "If it is said that the female brain is incapable of studies of an abstract nature, – that is not true: for there are many instances of women who have been good mathematicians, and good classical scholars." Cobbe similarly emphasizes a logical approach, as in "The Rights of Man and the Claims of Brutes" (1863), where she begins, "Let us endeavour to arrive at a clear analysis," or in "Wife-Torture in England" (1878), where she explicitly states that she will "avoid making this paper more painful than can be helped" – tactics that stress her reliance on masculine logic and her avoidance of feminine emotion or sensationalism.

The rhetorical approaches of Martineau, Cobbe, and Linton remind us that not all sage writers distrusted logic as Carlyle did, or explicitly invoked the biblical model of the prophet. Martineau, for example, employed a modern version of scientific prophecy that "predicts" the future by systematically studying the causes and influences of the past; according to Martineau's understanding of Auguste Comte and his positivist philosophy, every present event can be understood as the result of antecedent causes, and by projecting antecedent causes forward we can anticipate the future. Or, to cite the case of a male sage, Arnold may have been disparaged as an "elegant Jeremiah," but in his reliance on the tactics of classical rhetoric, his style is closer to Martineau's than to Carlyle's. Similarly, Mill was committed to the uses of logic in essays like *On Liberty* (1859) and *On the Subjection of Women* (1869), even if he explored its limits in his *magnum opus, A System of Logic* (1843).

Among women writers, Linton was most like the prophetic Carlyle in her approach and style, sometimes echoing his key words or metaphors. In her now-infamous (because antifeminist) "Nearing the Rapids" (1894), Linton picks up on Carlyle's antidemocratic essay "Shooting Niagara: and After?" (1867), which protested the passing of the Second Reform Bill and the extension of the franchise to men whom he considered uneducated and ill-prepared to be voters. In "Nearing the Rapids" Linton similarly comments with disdain on the extension of the franchise to independent women who were heads of house. To her, this extension would include far too many women of dubious morality, poor education, or provincial interests – none of whom could possibly contribute to "the perfection of good government," which she holds out as the ideal goal of granting the vote. Her opening phrase – "Those rash pilots, the Women's Rights men and women, bent on shooting Niagara and wrecking the old-time womanly ideal" – reinvents Carlyle's metaphor of pursuing a dangerous course. In other essays, however, Linton invented her own key phrases – as in her famous essay, "The Girl of the Period" (1868), a critique of the fashion-conscious, money- and status-mad modern woman. "The Girl of the Period" became so standard a phrase that it gave to the Victorians their own meaning of the acronym "GOP" – a sign, in itself, of their modern fondness for the quick tag or sound bite.

Other Sage Writing: A Complementary Tradition

If the prose of women writers expands our sense of the traditions and techniques of sage writing, it reminds us too that many Victorians who wrote about contemporary problems did not adopt the prophetic mode (even though they laid claim to wisdom) or deliberately assume an "eccentric" or "disinterested" perspective. We tend to distinguish between practical wisdom and special wisdom, the latter being the province of the sage. But many Victorian essayists preferred to write from the stance of the practical man or woman, emphasizing the commonsensical or even the mundane as their source of knowledge. Their writings, enormously popular and widely read in their day, are complements to the prose of a Carlyle, Ruskin, or Arnold and, in a different way, are "sage" as well.

In writing about the "State of the Country" in *Rural Rides* (1830), for instance, William Cobbett literally became the man on horseback, riding through the English countryside via fields and back lanes, observing the state of agriculture and the lives of rural laborers, and assuming the professional writer's privilege of commenting on what he observed. But Cobbett's perspective is that of a practical man who understands agriculture, who has written books on *Cottage Economy* (1822) and *The Woodlands* (1825), and who can thus speak as a man who has seen the "signs of the times" close up. His perspective is not that of the Arnoldian "disinterested" critic but that of a politically committed radical.

In *Rural Rides* Cobbett criticizes a political system that has allowed the lives of rural workers to become wretched, a system that relies on statistics rather than direct observation to prove things are fine and that foolishly believes protective tariffs on English grain will solve whatever agricultural problems there may be. Cobbett's writing is "sage" in that it is knowledgeable, but he does not particularly rely on metaphor or aphorism or biblical allusion. If his is a distinctive voice, it is because it has the earthy, even racy quality of an outdoorsman or because it reproduces the strident, forthright harangue of a political orator. "Radical," Cobbett liked to explain, "means, *belonging to the root; going to the root*":

> Our system of husbandry is happily illustrative of our system of politics. Our lines of movement are fair and straightforward. We destroy all weeds, which, like taxeaters, do nothing but devour the sustenance that ought to feed the valuable plants. Our plants are all *well fed*; and our nations of Swedes and of cabbages present a happy uniformity of enjoyments and of bulk. (I, 32)

His agricultural allegory typifies his political beliefs, but in its literariness it is relatively atypical of his commentary.

What Cobbett does employ, in common with other Victorian sages, is the telling anecdote, the revelatory phenomenon, the small detail that reveals the true state of things. As he rides through the fields around Cirencester, he observes that it is a "fine, clean, beautiful place" with laborers "pretty well as to dress and healthiness." How does he know? Because "the girls at work in the fields (always my standard) are not in rags, with bits of shoes tied on their feet and rags tied round their ankles, as they had in Wiltshire" (I, 24). If shoes tell a tale about rural fieldworkers, a donkey-cart tells a related tale about the gentry. In nearby Bollitree, Cobbett sees a "pleasant-looking lady" and "two beautiful children" riding "in a little sort of chaise-cart, drawn by an *ass*." This contrivance proves to Cobbett that the lady is an intelligent woman ("a real *practical radical*") and her husband a blessed man. Why? Because the donkey-cart avoids the expense of a carriage and pair of horses; it avoids "feeding those cormorants who gorge on the taxes" (I, 29–30) – and presumably it means that the man and his wife are reinvesting their wealth in the land. Such details are not disinterested in the Arnoldian sense, however; they reveal people's politics, whether the individuals know it or not.

Cobbett's practical and political writings about agricultural scenes represent a larger body of writing about rural England, the counterpart to Carlyle or Ruskin's commentary on urbanization and industrialization. If Carlyle drew his emblematic anecdotes from life in the city, Cobbett and his cohort – William Howitt, his wife Mary Howitt, and Mary Russell Mitford, to name a few of these rural sages – found them in the country. If Carlyle in *Past and Present* or Ruskin in *The Stones of Venice* looked back to the Middle Ages for their ideal social order, these writers recalled a traditional agricultural society in which both laborers and landowners lived well in peace, plenty, and social harmony. If Carlyle brought to his readers' attention the "Condition of England," Cobbett showed them the "State of the Country."

Some of this rural sage writing is overtly nostalgic. When Mitford wrote a series called "Our Village" in the 1820s and 1830s, the same period in which Carlyle published "Signs of the Times" and "Characteristics," the circulation of the magazine that carried her essays increased eightfold. London readers, as well as their country counterparts, devoured her sketches of life in a classic English village – the sort of village that industrialization and urbanization were destroying. Or, when William Howitt published his enormously popular *The Boy's Country-Book* (1839), a collection of tales based on his childhood in rural Derbyshire, London readers participated vicariously in rural pastimes and pursuits that were fast becoming extinct. On the face of it, Mitford's and Howitt's sketches of rural English life seem antithetical to Carlyle's analyses of modern urban existence: Mitford chronicles life in a small village, focusing on cottages and houses and the folks who live in them, taking her readers on a series of "walks in the country" to show them flowers, trees, and other country pleasures; whereas Carlyle discusses model prisons, new poorhouses, modern railways, and distressing features of urban life.

Yet these strains of writing, however different their authors' politics, are two pieces of the same Victorian prose puzzle – the one looking analytically at the modern scene, the other looking descriptively (and often nostalgically) at a lost Eden. The urban sage inveighs prophetically, critically, even angrily; the rural sage speaks practically, sensibly, sometimes lovingly and sadly. Victorian readers had both points of view available to them: they could think analytically about urban problems or they could mentally escape to a peaceful country village; they could consider English culture "disinterestedly" or they could lament the state of English agriculture and take a partisan political side.

Both strains of sage writing come together in the prose of George Eliot; indeed, Eliot makes a strong case for the importance of both perspectives in the work of the Victorian sage. When Eliot was still primarily a book reviewer and translator, she wrote an influential article, "The Natural History of German Life" (1856), that reviewed two German books by the author Wilhelm Heinrich von Riehl. This review flowered into an essay discussing the crucial role of community-building in the work of the modern sage, and soon became an argument for the necessity of a combined knowledge of rural and urban life as the basis for such work.

Riehl had compiled a book about the "general characteristics of the German peasantry" and their variations from geographical region to region. Eliot believed that similar sociological studies needed to be conducted of English peasants and workers. Otherwise, true sage writing, true insight into and advice about modern existence, could not be had. According to Eliot, many Victorian writers on contemporary issues failed to offer sound advice, let alone genuine wisdom, because they lacked this basic sociological information:

> The tendency created by the splendid conquests of modern generalization, to believe that all social questions are merged in economical science, and that the relations of men to their neighbours may be settled by algebraic equations, – the dream that the uncultured classes are prepared for a condition which appeals principally to their moral sensibilities, – the aristocratic dilettanteism which attempts to restore the "good old times" by a sort of idyllic masquerading, and to grow feudal fidelity and veneration as we grow prize turnips, by an artificial system of culture, – none of these diverging mistakes can coexist with a real knowledge of the People, with a thorough study of their habits, their ideas, their motives.

If Eliot here attacks certain strains of sage writing, the utilitarian as well as the nostalgic, she also argues for the importance of that complementary tradition of prose writing about rural life which is often omitted from our modern discussions of the Victorian sage. We cannot understand Victorian nonfictional prose without both. We need to expand our definitions of the sage and his (and her) rhetorical stances and techniques. The rural rides of a Cobbett or the village rambles of a Mitford inform the political, social, and literary contexts in which – and about which – Carlyle, Ruskin, and Arnold wrote. Indeed, they are part of the context and part of the literary tradition, whether or not we choose to call them "sage."

Whatever the designation, this complementary tradition gives us a broader perspective on Victorian nonfictional prose and its interconnections. Cobbett's detailed observation of the "State of the Country" influenced subsequent strains of both urban and rural writing – the urban in the rich, investigative sociologies of Edwin Chadwick (*Report on the Sanitary Condition of the Labouring Population of Great Britain*, 1842), Henry Mayhew (*London Labour and the London Poor*, 1861–2), or William Booth (*In Darkest England*, 1890); the rural in the radical utopian fictions of William Morris (*News from Nowhere*, 1890) or Samuel Butler (*Erewhon*, 1872). The influence may be more stylistic than ideological in some cases, more ideological than stylistic in others, but it is illuminating to read Mayhew's descriptions of mudlarks and scavengers while recalling Cobbett's accounts of rural fieldworkers. In future scholarship we might continue to explore such connections.

See also 1832; CLERICAL, ADMINISTRATIVE, PUBLISHING; LIFE WRITING, LITERARY CRITICISM

REFERENCES

Adams, J. E. (1995) *Dandies and Desert Saints: Styles of Victorian Masculinity*. Ithaca and London: Cornell University Press.

Anderson, A. (2001) *The Powers of Distance: Cosmopolitanism and the Cultivation of Detachment*. Princeton: Princeton University Press.

Ashton, R. (1980) *The German Idea: Four English Writers and the Reception of German Thought, 1800–1860*. Cambridge: Cambridge University Press.

Broomfield, A., and S. Mitchell (eds) (1996) *Prose by Victorian Women: An Anthology*. New York and London: Garland.

Budge, G. (2005) "Rethinking the Victorian Sage: Nineteenth-Century Prose and Scottish Common Sense Philosophy." *Literature Compass* 2: 1, online.

Christ, C. T. (1990) " 'The Hero as Man of Letters': Masculinity and Victorian Nonfiction Prose." In *Victorian Sages and Cultural Discourse*, ed. T. E. Morgan. New Brunswick and London: Rutgers University Press.

Cobbett, W. (1885) *Rural Rides . . . during the Years 1821 to 1832: With Economical and Political Observations*, ed. P. Cobbett, 2 vols. London: Reeves and Turner.

Easley, A. (2004) *First-Person Anonymous: Women Writers and Victorian Print Media, 1830–1870*. Aldershot: Ashgate Press.

Erickson, L. (1996) *The Economy of Literary Form: English Literature and the Industrialization of Publishing, 1800–1850*. Baltimore: Johns Hopkins University Press.

Holloway, J. (1953) *The Victorian Sage: Studies in Argument*. London: Macmillan.

Landow, G. P. (1986) *Elegant Jeremiahs: The Sage from Carlyle to Mailer*. Ithaca and London: Cornell University Press.

——(1990) "Aggressive (Re)interpretations of the Female Sage: Florence Nightingale's *Cassandra*." In *Victorian Sages and Cultural Discourse*, ed. T. E. Morgan. New Brunswick and London: Rutgers University Press.

Lewes, G. H. (1847) "The Condition of Authors in England, Germany, and France." *Fraser's Magazine* 35, 285–95.

Morgan, T. E. (ed.) (1990) *Victorian Sages and Cultural Discourse: Renegotiating Gender and Power*. New Brunswick and London: Rutgers University Press.

Nelson, C. C. (ed.) (2001) *A New Woman Reader*. Peterborough ON: Broadview Press.

Price, L. (2000) *The Anthology and the Rise of the Novel from Richardson to George Eliot*. Cambridge: Cambridge University Press.

Seigel, J. P. (ed.) (1971) *Thomas Carlyle: The Critical Heritage*. London: Routledge and Kegan Paul.

FURTHER READING

Amigoni, D. (2011) *Victorian Literature*. Edinburgh: Edinburgh University Press.

Anger, S. (ed.) (2001) *Knowing the Past: Victorian Literature and Culture*. Ithaca: Cornell University Press.

Brake, L., L. Higgins, and C. Williams (eds) (2002) *Walter Pater: Transparencies of Desire*. Greensboro: University of North Carolina Press.

Collini, S. (1991) *Public Moralists: Political Thought and Intellectual Life in Britain, 1850–1930*. Oxford: Clarendon Press.

Gross, J. (1969) *The Rise and Fall of the Man of Letters*. New York and London: Macmillan.

Harrison, A. H. (1990) "Christina Rossetti and the Sage Discourse of Feminist High Anglicanism." In *Victorian Sages and Cultural Discourse*, ed. T. E. Morgan. New Brunswick and London: Rutgers University Press.

Helsinger, E. K. (1997) *Rural Scenes and National Representation: Britain, 1815–1850*. Princeton: Princeton University Press.

Herbert, C. (2001) *Victorian Relativity: Radical Thought and Scientific Discovery*. Chicago: University of Chicago Press.

Landow, G. P. (1981) "Ruskin as Victorian Sage: The Example of 'Traffic.'" In *New Approaches to Ruskin: Thirteen Essays*, ed. R. Hewison. London: Routledge.

Leary, P., and A. Nash (2009) "Authorship." In *The Cambridge History of the Book in Britain. Volume VI, 1830–1914*, ed. D. McKitterick. Cambridge: Cambridge University Press.

Levine, G. (1968) *The Boundaries of Fiction: Carlyle, Macaulay, Newman*. Princeton: Princeton University Press.

——(2002) *Dying to Know: Scientific Epistemology and Narrative in Victorian England*. Chicago: University of Chicago Press.

Peterson, L. H. (2009) *Becoming a Woman of Letters: Myths of Authorship and Facts of the Victorian Market*. Princeton: Princeton University Press.

Ulrich, J. M. (2002) *Signs of their Times: History, Labor, and the Body in Cobbett, Carlyle, and Disraeli*. Athens: Ohio University Press.

27

Historiography

Edward Adams

Edward Gibbon's *Memoirs of My Life and Writings* (1796) is one of England's earliest examples of an autobiography, a model whereby numerous nineteenth-century historians envisioned their careers, and a testament to history's traditional status as narrative literature. Gibbon concedes that England has lagged behind other nations, particularly France, in producing great historians, but, with suitably false modesty, declares its redress by the brilliant scholarship and literary successes of David Hume, William Robertson, and himself: "The candor of Dr Robertson embraced his disciple. A letter from Mr. Hume overpaid the labor of ten years; but I have never presumed to accept a place in the triumvirate of British historians" (169).

Thirty-four years later, amidst the stirrings of the First Reform Bill, the Dickensian-named historian Nicholas Harris Nicolas recorded a very different state of affairs. The preceding decades had not fulfilled Gibbon's triumphalism. England again trailed its traditional rival France and a rising Germany. The corruption and laxity widely infesting English public life, which Reform would soon confront, were also regnant at the various depositories of records. Nicolas exposed this embarrassment as a crime against national glory and a nearly impassable barrier to researchers forced to pay exorbitant fees and kowtow to supercilious bureaucrats for access to public materials from which worthy histories of their nation might arise:

> In asserting that the History of England is not merely imperfect and erroneous, but that it is discreditable to a country which boasts of intellectual pre-eminence over surrounding nations, a statement is made of which every one who has devoted the smallest portion of time to the inquiry is fully persuaded . . . [W]henever a contemporary document is

A New Companion to Victorian Literature and Culture, First Edition. Edited by Herbert F. Tucker.
© 2014 John Wiley & Sons, Ltd. Published 2014 by John Wiley & Sons, Ltd.

discovered, and its contents are compared with our best historians, their narratives either receive elucidation which gives a new colouring to the transaction, or, as frequently happens, their representations are proved to be false. (1)

Observations on the State of Historical Literature (1830) was dedicated to Viscount Melbourne, the elegant representative of Regency-era vices that, Nicolas proceeded to demonstrate in detail, had resulted in this mess. Nonetheless Melbourne, as Lytton Strachey's modernist triumph of historical satire *Queen Victoria* (1921) dramatized, would find a role beside the young queen and within the great Reform project. Nicolas acknowledges only two figures between Gibbon's boast and his lament – "the only living authors entitled to the appellation of historians of England are Dr. Lingard and Mr. Sharon Turner" (3) – and their dull glow alongside their shining predecessors confirms his complaint's truth.

Nicolas's *Observations* might almost have inspired Trollope's Barsetshire novels, filled as it is with detailed unmaskings of sinecures, inside dealings, unfair rewards, and expensively-produced official volumes not unlike Septimus Harding's lavish history devoted to "Purcell, Crotch, and Nares" (*The Warden* [1855], ch. 1). Nicolas documents the "sums which have been paid by the Record Commission," and names the insiders who have rewarded themselves generously for leisurely labors over similarly lavish and, so he charges, utterly useless editions along with the aristocrats and dignitaries who rule this corrupt system without proper constitutional oversight. The result is a financial and historiographical disaster: "notwithstanding the expenditure of about 10,000 pounds per annum, Government virtually represses Historical knowledge" (v).

Whether or not Nicolas's brilliantly muckraking account of English historiography's sorry condition deserves credit for turning things around, it signals the dawning of several decades marked by a series of magnificent histories and historians whose literary achievement – as judged by prose style, narrative art, historiographical innovation, or even sales – only the Victorian novel rivaled. Moreover, this era witnessed a determined and successful effort to advance, if that is the right word, history from the status of a literary art (for that is how Nicolas still saw it) practiced by accomplished amateurs to that of an academic discipline guarded by professional norms and aspiring, by the end of the century, to the still more heavily-policed status of an objective science.

In this chapter, I will survey both the intellectual variety and the sheer number of major Victorian historians, which rendered the era a silver if not fully golden age of literary and scholarly achievement. It is useful to organize the mass of Victorian historical production in terms of two great shadows from which the Victorians, for all their achievements, struggled to emerge. Victorian historiography had, first, to confront the contemporary accomplishments of the Germans and, second, to escape the allure of traditional heroic history ("drum and trumpet" history), and embrace a modern conception of economic processes and social realities. In pursuing these aims, historiographers uneasily remembered Hume, Robertson, and, especially,

Gibbon, who had set a standard of intellectual sophistication, narrative sweep, and literary éclat that inspired the best Victorian efforts and often humbled them by comparison.

Nicolas's lament over the Regency period underscores this abiding anxiety of pre-emption. So does the reality that in 1897 J. B. Bury, author of numerous ancient histories and one of the historiographical stars of the day (especially for *History of the Later Roman Empire*, 1923), produced the definitive twentieth-century edition of Gibbon's *Decline and Fall*. This version replaced the formerly definitive 1838 edition by Henry Hart Milman, leading Victorian church historian and author of lengthy, Gibbon-inflected works from *The History of the Jews* (1829) and *The History of Christianity* (1840) to *The History of Latin Christianity* (1855). By the mid-twentieth century these editions of Gibbon, not their own histories, were Milman's and Bury's best known books. No comparable effort has ever been expended on any Victorian historian. Many histories deserve to be read for pleasure and edification, but not even Carlyle's *French Revolution* or Macaulay's *History of England* has inspired such care from succeeding scholars.

One further conditioning circumstance for this chapter demands preliminary mention. The career of Sir Walter Scott represents the most profound historiographical consequence, in any language, of the revolution in historical understanding brought about by 1789's events (Lukács). Scott first flourished as an original poet with *The Lay of the Last Minstrel* (1805) and *Marmion* (1808), then turned to the novel with *Waverley* (1815) and peaked with *Ivanhoe* (1819), though he regularly published new novels until his death in 1832. *The Life of Napoleon* (1827), his major historical work, was lauded by Goethe — the "richest, the easiest, the most celebrated narrator of the century undertakes to write the history of his own time" (quoted in Lockhart II, 575) — in terms insinuating that its success was less intrinsic than it was a function of Scott's reputation and subject matter. Even as a lightly-researched, fast-paced narrative of his lifetime's stirring events through the colorful lens of an epic biography, it was soon replaced by Archibald Alison's more popular and enduring (though as strict history equally dubious) *History of Europe from the Commencement of the French Revolution in 1789, to the Restoration of the Bourbons in 1815* (1833–43). This delightfully reactionary narrative (Americans roundly condemned its harsh judgments of their young democracy) sometimes exhibits a forward-looking dimension absent from Scott's, as in its innovative forty-first chapter: "It would be to little purpose that the mighty drama of the French Revolutionary wars was recorded in history, if the mainspring of all the European efforts, the BRITISH FINANCES, were not fully explained." Still, although Scott's *Napoleon* reflects in general the qualitative decline of his last works, his early poetry, rooted as it was in serious primary research on regional balladry, resulted from authentic and time-consuming historiography. His novels, which largely deserve their status as the first masterworks of historical fiction, similarly contain some serious research.

Two points about Scott's fiction arise here. First, the vitality of this new subgenre directly inspired a wave not just of similar fictions, but of scholarly histories. In the short term, Nicolas's patriotic alarm at the state of English historiography rang true; for Scott's most influential work *Ivanhoe*, in which he adapted to medieval England the formula he had previously reserved for relatively recent Scottish history, bore its first serious historiographical fruit in France, with Jacques Thierry's richly colored *History of the Conquest of England by the Normans* (1825). Very soon, however, the national, racial, and class issues unleashed by the French Revolution and novelized by Scott began to be researched, debated, and tested by a series of major English historians, climaxing in the grand narratives of Carlyle, Macaulay, Edward Freeman, J. R. Green, and William Stubbs – to whom I will return below.

The second point about Scott for our purposes is that his personal favorite among his novels was set only 20 years in the past. *The Antiquary* (1816) is just barely an historical novel, though it directly acknowledges the French Revolution. It accurately captures, as *Ivanhoe*'s facetious self-mockery does not, Scott's sense of his credentials as an historian – and fairly reflects the fussy, unphilosophical, and antiquarian practices which then held sway (as Nicolas concedes with reference to "the Society of Antiquaries of London," 23). The deeper irony here is that it was largely due to Scott that English historians began to conceive of their business not as the dry-as-dust accumulation of long-forgotten and eminently forgettable facts, but as the sustained research into and inspiring narration of matters that had helped shape the modern world. Thus during the years of Scott's decline preceding the First Reform Bill, Carlyle and Macaulay were studying Scott, coming to despise mere antiquarianism as well as his fictionalizings, but planning careers that would rival his in popularity and influence, while centering around innovative historiography and profound German philosophy.

In the Shadow of the Germans

Antiquarianism, largely a perquisite of narrowly educated and well-funded establishment clergymen thickly broadcast throughout the English countryside and often uninspired by their vocation, died a slow death. The increasing production of meticulous county histories was an important phenomenon that sometimes earned the praise of distinguished historians: "The expansion and extension of genealogical study is a very remarkable feature of our own time . . . Local history and minute archaeology have been of use in the same way" (Stubbs 1886: 50–1). Still, the sense that such amateur avocations were really a matter of idle hands lent to the devil's work appears as late as 1891, when Hardy's tragic *Tess of the d'Urbervilles* begins with "Parson Tringham, the antiquary, of Stagfoot lane" who "hunt[s] up pedigrees for the new county history" and cannot refrain from letting "plain John Durbeyfield, the haggler" in on his worse than useless discovery. A more profound example of the waste associated with such toils lies at the heart of Eliot's *Middlemarch* (1871), where the wealthy Reverend Edward Casaubon employs a curate to cover his church duties and devotes himself to an epic *Key to All Mythologies* – a Frankenstein's-monster assemblage of dead knowledge that belies my satirical description by never showing a hint of life, although it ensnares Dorothea Brooke into a passionless marriage. Fortunately, young Will Ladislaw, armed with a German education, arrives to slay these dragons. He reveals to Dorothea that "it is a pity that [Mr. Casaubon's scholarship] should be thrown away, as so much English scholarship is, for want of knowing what is done in the rest of the world. If Mr Casaubon read German he would save himself a great deal of trouble" (ch. 21). Later, when Dorothea confronts Will with her hope that Casaubon's meticulous antiquarianism might yet effect some advance in learning, Will drives a stake through the heart of his undead scholarship: "The subject Mr Casaubon has chosen is as changing as chemistry . . . Who wants a system on the basis of the four elements, or a book to refute Paracelsus? Do you not see that it is no use now crawling a little way after men of the last century – men like Bryant – and correcting their mistakes?" (ch. 22). Nietzsche, benefitting from a century of innovative German philosophical historiography, frames in *On the Advantages and Disadvantages of History for Life* (1874) the sharpest rebuke to antiquarianism – that it subjects the living present to the dead past – a fine description of Tess's fate and Dorothea's predicament. Eliot, however, who began her career by translating one of the greatest efforts of German scholarship, Strauss's *Life of Jesus Critically Examined* (1835), hardly required Nietzsche to explode dilettantish fact-collecting organized around obsolete theories.

Historicism was the fundamental achievement of nineteenth-century German thought and the centerpiece of the German Romantic university, whose strong influence on English university reform culminated in the appointment at century's end of the Munich-educated and half-German John Dalberg-Acton to Cambridge's chair of history. Acton embodied German thinking's productive reconsideration of all aspects of experience in historical terms. His far-reaching plan for the multi-volume and multi-authored *Cambridge Modern History* (1907–12) set a new standard of objective, impersonal professionalism that justly divides Victorian from twentieth-century historiography. Although the Victorian combination of serious historiography with personal style persisted well past Acton's posthumous achievement (witness the twentieth-century renown of Macaulay's great-nephew George Macaulay Trevelyan and his popular historical narratives), the rising German-inspired historiography had meanwhile stressed the recuperation of cultural artifacts rejected as primitive and fantastical by Gibbon's Enlightenment thinking.

Here emerge important parallels between German historicism and Romanticism broadly considered (see Berlin). The ballad-revival in Germany and England prefigured Romantic nationalism and marked the decline of French-dominated, pan-European Neoclassicism (see Trumpener). Scott, whose antiquarian interest in local vernacular ballads led to his historical novels, stood apart from his cosmopolitan eighteenth-century forerunners, who dismissed the historical value of ballads, of ancient national legends and myths. The opening of Robertson's *History of Scotland* (1759), particularly because it harbors patriotic intentions that presumably would welcome old legends, best reveals this prejudice of the Age of Reason:

The first ages of Scottish History are dark and fabulous. Nations, as well as men, arrive at maturity by degrees, and the events which happened during their infancy or early youth, cannot be recollected, and deserve not to be remembered. The gross ignorance which anciently covered all the north of Europe . . . (7)

Such hauteur paved the way for the intellectual revolution of Victorian historiography when in 1828 Julius Hare and Connop Thirlwall began translating the *History of Rome* by Barthold Niebuhr, the most influential of the German philosopher-historians. By dismissing the wholesale dismissal of primitive legends, the Germans made the historical origin and youth of cultures and nations pre-eminent, rather than their maturity and decline. Eventually, the obscure eighteenth-century philosopher of history Giambattista Vico would be seen as having anticipated the German breakthroughs, as Jules Michelet, the brilliant French Romantic historian, zealous lest the Germans get too much credit, made plain by making Vico available to European scholars. The opening pages of his *History of the Roman Republic* (1831) trumpeted Vico's precedence in a manner that nonetheless acknowledged the practical fact of German pre-eminence:

All that Niebuhr was to discover by his vast researches, [Vico] divined; he made patrician Rome stand out in strong relief, and revived its curiae and its gentes. Certainly, if Pythagoras remembered that he had, in a former existence, fought under the walls of Troy, these illustrious Germans ought perhaps to have remembered that they had already formerly lived in Vico. All the giants of criticism, already and at their ease, find a place in this little pandaemonium of the *Scienza Nuova* (1725).

Hare and Thirlwall's introduction of Niebuhr to England did not go unopposed by the reigning reactionary Toryism. Hare's 1829 *Vindication of Niebuhr's History of Rome* neatly parallels Nicolas's 1830 *Observations* on the verge of the coming era. It also recalls Gibbon's brilliant *Vindication* (1779) of the former cosmopolitan era – and refutes with rhetorical patience and documentary care the groundless accusations that Niebuhr's scholarship continued the skeptical tradition of Voltaire and thus encouraged innovation leading to revolution.

It was Thirlwall, however, who took the decisive next step and applied Niebuhr's techniques to his eight-volume *History of Greece* (1835–44). This path-breaking work was rapidly overshadowed by George Grote's *History of Greece* (1846–56), which both followed and challenged the Germans. Grote publicly declared that he would never have undertaken his work if he had known his old college fellow was laboring before him. Indeed their histories closely resemble one another – in length and scope, in ideology and historiography – but Grote, while never extreme or unreliable, surpasses and intensifies his predecessor. Both intended to answer William Mitford's Gibbon-inspired *History of Greece* (1784–1810), to correct its "erroneous statements as to matter of fact" and substitute "a juster and more comprehensive point of view" (Grote I, iii). Civilized repudiation of the view that heroic warfare was history's essence formed Thirlwall's theme, not only about ancient Greece but also within his own narrative, which consistently concluded its treatment of such matters on a tragic note. Thus about the Athenians' eventual condemnation of the hero of Marathon, a topic that had evoked Mitford's scorn for democracy, Thirlwall wrote, "if they conceived that nothing he had done for them ought to raise him above the laws . . . they were not ungrateful or unjust; and if Miltiades thought otherwise, he had not learnt to live in a free state" (II, 247). Themistocles, the hero of Salamis, is similarly judged. Grote goes farther by consistently thematizing Greek history (and, implicitly, his own narrative) as exemplifying the supersession of military heroism by intellectual progress: "intellectual superiority came to acquire a higher place in the public esteem as compared with military prowess" (I, 288). This theme forms the essence of his history: it explains his abandonment of the narrative where Alexander looms, and it guides this self-revealing appreciation of Thucydides: "the qualities necessary to the historiographer, in their application to recent events, have been developed with a degree of perfection never since surpassed. Men's minds have assumed a gentler as well as a juster cast; and acts come to be criticised with reference to their bearing on the internal happiness of a well-regulated community, as well as upon the standing harmony of fraternal states" (II, 355). Grote optimistically discerns the fundamentals of the modern, liberal ideal of international law to which we still aspire.

But it is the relation to German scholarship, the touchstone of historiographical progress in the nineteenth century, that best dramatizes Grote's winning self-confidence. Thirlwall sprinkles his text dutifully with "as Niebuhr has shown" and brief footnotes, but Grote densely footnotes to demonstrate his familiarity with numerous German historians along with a readiness to correct Niebuhr, which Thirlwall and the Germans seldom risked doing. Having learned from Michelet to appreciate Vico's precedence over the Germans, Grote rejects both the Italian's "divination" and Niebuhr's "vast researches," as dubious efforts to discern historical events behind the veil of legend. Instead his innovation is to admit the obvious, namely that "we now read as poetry and legend" what "was once accredited history" (I, viii), but then to apply this insight to a sustained analysis of how such thinking shaped the Greeks' later historical thinking and action. His argument culminates in a fully modern understanding of rational and mythic thinking in Herodotus. In effect Grote's *History of Greece* supplements Western historiography's pioneering effort by incorporating myth as interpretable fact, thereby not just narrating his own core values of intellectual freedom and progress but also embodying them. Thirlwall proffers a learned, up-to-date, and judicious mind, but Grote an exciting scholarly imagination striving ever forward.

Thomas Arnold, fourth and last of the major English Niebuhrians, suffered the double misfortune of selection by Lytton Strachey for satirical portraiture in *Eminent Victorians* (1918) and of tasking himself to rework Niebuhr's uncompleted series of essays on Roman history into one continuous *History of Rome* (1835–44) – and then himself dying before its completion. Although he sometimes quibbles with Niebuhr's claims, Arnold never challenges his guide's fundamental assumptions. Thus, instead of achieving Grote's impressive resolution of the fundamental tension between legend and history, Arnold's narrative bifurcates into scholarly chapters and imaginative retellings in a deliberately archaic style (these episodes inspired Macaulay's *Lays of Ancient Rome*, 1842). This compromise allowed Arnold to include the famous legends such as the rape of Sabine women by marking them as unhistorical, but prevented him from incorporating them into an integrated understanding.

This self-division reappears in the tension between Arnold's analytical learnedness and his sentimental contention that Roman history was guided by providence. He adduces the larger historical significance of Rome's defeat of Carthage in terms of Rome's destiny "to bind together barbarians of every race and language into an organized empire, and prepare them for becoming, when that empire was dissolved, the free members of the commonwealth of Christian Europe" (471). Such judgments, peppering Arnold's narrative, explain both his subterranean effort to rebuke Gibbon's skeptical, even anti-Christian history and the mockery with which Strachey later greeted that effort – for Strachey adored Gibbon. Nonetheless *The History of Rome* embodies a worthy homage to German historiography as well as an earnest challenge to the Gibbonian sneer. In contrast, the leading Roman history of the next Victorian generation possesses neither of these virtues. Charles Merivale's bland *History of the Romans* (1850–62) shares Arnold's religious alarm, yet avoids confronting Gibbon:

> I have now reached the point at which my great predecessor Gibbon commences, and much as I regret that the crisis should be unfolded to the English reader by one who, unhappy in his school and his masters, in his moral views and spiritual training approached it, with all his mighty powers, under a cloud of ignoble prejudices, I forbear myself from entering the lists in which he has long stalked alone and unchallenged. (VII, 496)

This retreat on Merivale's part underscores the philological and archaeological excellence displayed by Theodore Mommsen's contemporaneous *History of Rome* (1854–56). Mommsen was quickly translated into English, outsold Merivale even in England, and gained a Nobel Prize for Literature in 1902. The shadow of the Germans and Gibbon lay over Arnold and Merivale alike, but where one of them achieved qualified success, the other displayed ideological and scholarly timidity almost worthy of Casaubon.

The Shadow of Epic

Thomas Carlyle assumed, for the Victorians, the task of transferring and popularizing German thought that Coleridge had carried out for the Romantics. He so identified with his masters as to transpose his own life and thought, in *Sartor Resartus* (1833), onto an imaginary German philosopher. Moreover, though usually seen as sage or prose prophet, Carlyle was primarily a practicing historian, and German ideology and historiography of orality and legend shaped his monumental works from *The French Revolution* (1837) and *Oliver Cromwell's Letters and Speeches* (1845) to his vast (its hero is born around page 500 in my eight-volume edition) *History of Friedrich II of Prussia* (1858). While this last and most remunerative work most fully embodied Carlyle's ideas of "hero-worship" and "great man history," its march back toward military history and away from the forward-looking emphases of *The French Revolution* betrayed his credo that the future would belong to an industrial "tools and the man," not a Vergilian "arms and the man," theme (*Past and Present*, 1843).

This reversal characterizes the retrograde tendencies of many spectacular historiographical and publishing successes of the mid-Victorian period. Edward Creasy's *Fifteen Decisive Battles of World History* (1851), which pioneered a subgenre of the still-popular mode of military history, inspired Macaulay's reconceptualization of his originally "people's history"-inflected *History of England*, which outsold Dickens. Macaulay turned away, from what had begun in volumes 1–2 (1848) as a vigorous narrative of the English nation's largely bloodless revolution against James II's tyranny, to celebrate instead William III's epic contest with Louis XIV, across Europe and into independent-minded Ireland, in the even more popular volumes 3–4 (1855) and posthumous volume 5 (1859). A similar though subtler wavering between innovative social history and heroic militarism invests J. R. Green's bestselling *Short History of the English People* (1874). Among the period's leading historians, only William Stubbs resisted such calls to arms, though even he could not finally resist coloring his *English Constitutional History* with patriotic touches borrowed from *Ivanhoe*.

Enough is said elsewhere in this *Companion* about Carlyle and J. A. Froude to permit a comparatively brief treatment of their historical achievements. Both are better historians when they lack the heroes they earnestly theorized. In Carlyle's masterpiece *The French Revolution* – the Victorian era's polyphonic equivalent of Joyce's *Ulysses* (1922) – tragedy descends with the death of Mirabeau, the revolution's one great man, but the result releases literary brilliance of the highest order and vivid insight into the maelstrom of history. While Froude's multivolume *History of England* (1856–70) represents another stylistic and narrative triumph, and a cutting-edge example of archival research, its hollow paean to the Reformation through adulation of Henry VIII's visionary kingship seems more problematic than Macaulay's celebration of the Glorious Revolution in terms of William's genius. But Froude's *Life of Carlyle* (1882–4) entirely succeeds as a biography-based history of contemporary England, and it does so largely because of the doubts regarding its hero that caused Froude much public discomfort.

Froude was also attacked vigorously by Edward Freeman. Though the assaults arose less from Froude's occasional errors of transcription than from his Carlylean authoritarianism, Freeman's own histories embody a Germanic racialist ideology that now seems equally objectionable. Freeman not only pioneered the use of topographical, geological, and archaeological evidence, but also synthesized the piecemeal work of the previous generation of historians of Saxon England. His narrative masterpiece, the mammoth *History of the Norman Conquest* (1867–76), relates to earlier compendia of short treatises by Francis Palgrave and John Mitchell Kemble much as Thirlwall's and Arnold's synthetic narratives did to Niebuhr's collections. This branch of English historiography acknowledged the Germans' influence by studying the folk roots of English nationhood. To move from Palgrave on the Anglo-Saxons in the 1820s, still relying on older French scholarship and its Roman-centered theory of England's institutions, to Kemble in the 1840s, repeatedly confessing indebtedness to current German scholarship and a Teuton-centered theory of England's institutions, is to tell the principal story of Victorian historiography in miniature.

It is worth pausing over Kemble because he dramatizes the combination of lurking genocidal thought and openly progressive, well-nigh utopian longing that can make reading Freeman, Green, and even Macaulay such a bracing experience. For Kemble's dry studies become richly poetical when they turn to his theory of the "Mark," or folk-community, as a kind of imperial antidote-cum-apology. This theory influenced Tennyson's complexly English patriotism, but it inspired William Morris's more simply Germanic epic poems and romances of the 1870s–90s (along with his socialist politics) and thence J. R. R. Tolkien's narratives in the twentieth century. Kemble's notion of the Mark, though now discredited, appealingly masked the unpalatable story of genocidal conquest with a kindly vision of a Shire-like, pre-Norman, little Englandism:

> All over England there soon existed a network of communities, the principle of whose being was separation, as regarded each other: the most intimate union, as respected the individual members of each. Agricultural, not commercial, dispersed, not centralized, content within their own limits and little given to wandering, they relinquished in a great degree the habits and feelings which had united them as military adventurers; and the spirit which had achieved the conquest of an empire, was now satisfied with the care of maintaining inviolate a little peaceful plot, sufficient for the cultivation of a few simple households. (70–1)

One can almost hear Bilbo Baggins's "No more adventures!" Such bucolic incantation, however, barely masks the price paid by the original Britons for this Rome-slaying idyll.

Kemble's thinking shaped Freeman's conviction that the tragedy of 1066 and his hero Harold's death, not the earlier obliteration of Roman Briton, comprised the chief disaster of English history, one it would take centuries to correct:

> Harold now stood alone. By a fate of special bitterness, he had seen with his own eyes the fall of those nearest and dearest to him. The deed of Metaurus had been, as it were, wrought beneath the eyes of Hannibal; Achilleus had looked on and seen the doom of

his Patroklos and his Antilochos. The fate of England now rested on the single heart and single arm of her King. (Freeman III, 486)

This passage suggests how Freeman's sweeping narrative transcends the antiquarian essays bequeathed by Palgrave and Kemble. Freeman subjected their recondite studies and his own archaeological researches to multiple orgasms of battle, single combat, and tragic defeat – all climaxing at what he insisted on renaming Senlac, and we have returned to calling Hastings. Here the excesses of both the Niebuhr-inspired uncovering of truths behind oral legends and ballads, and the traditional allure of "arms and the man" that seduced Carlyle and Macaulay, blossom in a narrative that, while it possesses undeniable pleasures, descends to the vulgar, even ridiculous: "The great campaign of Hastings was thus in truth a trial of strength between the greatest living captains" (III, 440); "the English hero fell crushed beneath the stroke of the Duke's mace" (III, 485). What is more, Freeman loads his narrative with references to the *Iliad* and *Odyssey*, even footnoting it with Homer (in Greek), as though ancient epics in the original language could guide advanced scholarship about 1066.

J. R. Green exemplifies the epic mode of Victorian historiography in a more subtle form. He does conform to the pattern of Victorians inspired by Gibbon to an historian's career (I, xiii). He also followed Gibbon and Nicolas in desiring to make historiography the crown of England's literature and elevate it to the premier position among rival literatures (I, xx). Such goals required history to be epic; accordingly, Green's narrative is filled with strategic, self-referential notices of epic poems and histories. Nonetheless, and here he pushes beyond Gibbon and Freeman, Green's gestures are intended to suggest that his is not merely a better, more civilized epic, but something radically different. Here, as in his democratic populism, Green echoes France's Michelet or even America's Whitman. Like Whitman's self-serving commentary on Homer and Shakespeare's violently aristocratic ideologies – "the grandest of those poems . . . preserve and typify results offensive to the modern spirit . . . in Homer lives the ruthless military prowess of Greece . . . in Shakespeare the dragon-rancors and stormy feudal splendor of medieval caste" (1174–5) – Green's analogous comments thematize his text's democratic departures from the aristocratic violence and political backwardness of traditional epic: "I have striven throughout that it should never sink into a 'drum and trumpet history'" (I, xxiv); "Lesser bards strung together his victories in rough jingle of rime and hounded him on to the slaughter" (I, 315). Green efficiently combines a range of progressive topoi: contempt for war, for its heroic agents, and for war poetry's outmoded and provocative stylings. His smoothly accessible, bestselling *Short History* realizes a democratic and anti-heroic goal of making the English people itself the protagonist, not any of its traditional warriors or kings, and in making that theme congruent with its imagined audience. Green echoes Whitman when he dares to critique Shakespeare: "Puritanism may fairly claim to be the first political system which recognized the grandeur of the people as a whole – Shakespeare knew nothing [of this]" (II, 877). Both Whitman and Green were progressively responding to Carlyle's authoritarian admirations, whether for Shakespeares or Fredericks, and simultaneously deploying Carlyle's theories as foils for their very different constructions of a new kind of epic and audience: as his title simply announced, a people's history.

On the other hand, at 1,903 pages, my lavishly illustrated four-volume American edition suggests that any anti-epic resonances in the title's "short" is qualified by its heroical and daunting length. This reversal leads to a more disturbing point. Green's desire to write a history of a whole people necessitates an expansiveness that belies his rhetorical and lowly self-representation. His bid to popularize the national theme commits him to valorizing the ultimate illiberal and undemocratic act. For Green's anti-epic innovations rely upon the most thoroughly Iliadic or Joshuan theme of all: the English people's formation as a unified nation capable of acting as the protagonist of his massive narrative rests upon the invasion, conquest, and barbaric extermination of the native Celts of Roman Britain.

> What strikes us at once in the new England is, that it was the one purely German nation that rose upon the wreck of Rome . . . But if England seemed for a moment a waste from which all civilization of the world had fled away, it contained within itself the germs of a nobler life than that which had been destroyed. The base of the new English society was the freeman whom we have seen tilling, judging, or sacrificing for himself in his far-off fatherland of the North Sea. However roughly he dealt while the struggle went on with the material civilization of Britain, it was impossible that such a man could be a mere destroyer. War was no sooner over than the warrior settled down into a farmer . . . (I, 24–5)

The last sentence, savoring of Kemble's naivety over the Mark, sums up the attitude toward heroic war in the remaining 1,900 pages. But the original horror of the Homeric-biblical epic conquest of Britain by Saxondom always lurks ominously beneath.

No career better reveals the ultimate trajectory of Victorian historiography beyond such poetical aspirations (and limitations) and toward the dominant twentieth-century condition of academic professionalism than that of William Stubbs. Although both Freeman and Froude eventually found themselves occupying chairs at Oxford, neither seemed at home there; it was Stubbs's professionalism that prepared for the coming Creightons, Maitlands, and Actons. His masterwork, *The Constitutional History of England* (1874–8), demonstrates the Victorians' debt to German scholarship, but wears its Germanic learning with a grace seldom found in its peers. Stubbs is also at ease when upholding the value of medieval history and accordingly demoting the traditional prestige of ancient Greece and Rome. Finally, although there remain traces in Stubbs of the awkward struggle against epic ambitions – and the desire for public notoriety and wide sales often accompanying such ambitions – he does not, even surreptitiously, glorify war. Furthermore, his more accessible lectures, subtitled with disarming frankness – "Delivered at Oxford, Under Statutory Obligation in the Years 1867–84" – explicitly recapitulate the evolution of Victorian historiography with their combination of clerical antiquarianism (Stubbs became Bishop of Chester), German learning and friendships, narrative sweep and interest, and, finally, learned professionalism. Stubbs's lectures consider carefully the practical reforms in history teaching at Oxbridge and beyond, even as he curiously surveys the achievements of his predecessors and peers.

Stubbs felt, all the same, that a heroic era of personal historiography was coming to an end. The preface to his *Constitutional History* seems compelled to ward off, albeit with undeniable grandeur, the challenge of epic:

> For the roots of the present lie deep in the past, and nothing in the past is dead to the man who would learn how the present comes to be what it is. It is true, Constitutional History has a point of view, an insight and a language of its own; it reads the exploits and characters of men by a different light from that shed by the false glare of arms, and interprets positions and facts in words that are voiceless to those who have only listened to the trumpet of fame. The world's heroes are not heroes to it.

Although Stubbs resists portraying pre-Norman England as the pure kingdom of Anglo-Saxon freedom sometimes imagined, still he cannot shake off the ideology and stirring visions of Green, Freeman, and Kemble (now infused by the more advanced philological historiography of Mommsen). He thus finds arguments to suggest that England was more heroically free and German (for within this tradition to be free and to be German were bound together) than any state in Germany itself: "If its history is not the perfectly pure development of German principles, it is the nearest existing approach to such a development" (I, 6). This logic appears later, shorn of its cautious phrasing, when Stubbs's exuberant climax on the Magna Carta echoes the racialist thinking that had found such lurid expression in the openly epic histories: "The Great Charter is then the act of the united nation, the church, the barons, and the commons, for the first time thoroughly at one . . . The nation becomes one and realizes its oneness" (I, 543–5).

Jerome K. Jerome's *Three Men in a Boat* (1889), best known for its hilarious mis-adventures on a Thames vacation, is also filled with brilliant parodies of such solemn evocations, in clanging schoolboy rhetoric, of English history. His elaborate send-up of the morning of Magna Carta could well have had Stubbs in mind: "we wait in breathless silence till a great shout cleaves the air, and the great cornerstone in England's temple of liberty has, now we know, been firmly laid" (ch. 11). Even Scott's *Ivanhoe*, which owed much to the French Revolution's vision of Gaul finally throwing off its ancient German-Aristocratic conquerors, and which tempered its concluding vision of a unified England freed of the Norman yoke by conceding that a French strain would persist within the national fabric, eschews such self-fulfilling circularities as "one . . . oneness." For better or for worse, the Victorian amateur pretension to literary nationalism, prefigured by Gibbon's boast and spurred on by Nicolas's anger, had not yet passed into Acton's ideal of impersonal objectivity.

Coda: The Threat and Promise of Scientific History

One blot on Acton's gentlemanly reputation is his sneering attack upon Victorian England's most idiosyncratic yet most forward-looking historian. Henry Thomas Buckle's *History of Civilization in England* (1857–61), as the product of a self-educated amateur, inevitably attracted the contempt of Acton's pedigreed professionalism. Buckle even recalls Casaubon (Acton's 1860s reviews could well have influenced Eliot's 1870s portrait) in his antiquarian-like isolation from the latest German philology, reliance on obsolete French scholarship (Voltaire remains the ideal), and comical prejudices (England is the acme of civilization and freedom). His thinking, rooted in eighteenth-century mechanical and meliorist dogma, was anathema to Acton's German-Romantic historicism, but it grew to incorporate meliorism's up-to-date political-economic heirs. Buckle thus escaped Casaubon's antiquarian singleness of retrospect and further anticipated the major, still hotly debated, ambition to leapfrog Acton's narrow ideal of history as an academic discipline. He boldly recast it as an exact science by redefining historical causation away from heroic or individual agency and in terms of more strictly measurable factors.

In the twentieth century, Isaiah Berlin and Hugh Trevor-Roper aped Acton in scorning this effort as a dead end, though one wonders why these self-proclaimed liberals cling to individual agency and decry not just Buckle's speculations, but even such a well-established principle as Smith's invisible hand. Certainly, Buckle's rank amateurishness rendered him an easy target: as just one example, his theory of how the "carboniferous" content of a culture's basic foodstuffs predicts its level of civilized freedom verges on self-parody. Still, in other Victorian hands his project for a scientific historiography flourished. W. E. H. Lecky's influential histories, particularly his *Rise and Influence of Rationalism in Europe* (1865), as well as Herbert Spencer's sociological-historical lifework, represent Comtean variations on Buckle's scientific theme that were strongly admired in their day. Their works, however, now seem less intriguing than his historiographical ideas, particularly because Buckle's awkward attempts attained unrivalled intellectual distinction in the more skillful hands of Henry Adams and H. G. Wells.

These pioneers move beyond Victorian historiography, but warrant attention here if only to recapitulate key themes. In its rich engagement with the inheritance of Gibbon, the eminence of Germany, and the allure of epic, Adams's career and especially his *History of the United States* (1889–91) recall and surpass any nineteenth-century English history or historian – in scholarship and artistry both. The success of this work owes something to Adams's representing it as, in every aspect, a failure: as the grandest of the many failures recorded in that autobiography of the nineteenth century, *The Education of Henry Adams* (1918). Adams's work on the *History* led to his long campaign – inaugurated by an 1894 address as president of the American Historical Association on "The Tendency of History" – to encourage historians to transcend stale nineteenth-century concerns, which his epic history had both fulfilled and exploded, and reconceive historiography scientifically. His subsequent writings applied such current theories as the second law of thermodynamics or the rule of phase to the movements of the human past.

Although Wells never enjoyed Adams's familial or intellectual prestige, his enormous popularity makes him a worthy pairing and bookend. First, in a series of science fiction classics, particularly *The Time Machine* (1895) and *The War of the Worlds* (1898), Wells adapted not physical or chemical, but Darwinian theories to the rise and fall of civilizations, species, and even planets that put Gibbon, German historicism, and epic heroism under a microscope and found their obsessions vanishingly small. Nonetheless in *Tono-Bungay* (1909), his most autobiographical novel, Wells confessed that the attractions of traditional war history and Gibbonian pomp had profoundly shaped his authorial self-fashioning – and, as for so many Victorian historians, represented seemingly inescapable burdens. The disaster of World War I, again as for so many others, ironically gave Wells the immediate energy to dispel such enchantments. *The Outline of History* (1920), a nearly two-thousand-page history of the world from interstellar origins through the emergence of life and its evolution toward fully self-conscious humanity, is perhaps the most unlikely bestseller (over two million copies) of the Modernist era. It explicitly praised Gibbonian epic, then roundly condemned it along with nineteenth-century historiography's nationalist and heroic emphases – whether French Revolutionary, German Romantic, or British Imperial – which, it maintained, had inevitably led to the debacle. As a cure, Wells recast history and historiography as a halting but sure march toward truly universal, democratic, and peaceful human self-understanding – a goal that would finally be achieved through exactly the kind of educational enterprise his work embodied. He simultaneously belittled the Victorian era's historiographical parochialisms surveyed here and subtly thematized a higher ideal present within it all along. For Wells's masterpiece did not spring *ex nihilo*, but grew from the deeply humane efforts of Voltaire, Buckle, Darwin, and Adams that had led the way.

See also 1832; MILITARY; SAGE WRITING; NEO-VICTORIANISM

REFERENCES

Arnold, T. (1953) *History of Rome*. New York: Appleton.

Berlin, I. (2001) *The Roots of Romanticism*. Princeton: Princeton University Press.

Freeman, E. (1876) *History of the Norman Conquest*, 4 vols. Oxford: Oxford University Press.

Gibbon, E. (1990) *Memoirs*. Harmondsworth: Penguin.

Green, J.R. (1892) *A Short History of the English People*. New York: Bigelow, Brown.

Grote, G. (1884) *History of Greece*, 12 vols. London: John Murray.

Jerome, J. K. (2008) *Three Men in a Boat*. New York: Oxford University Press.

Kemble, J. M. (1849) *The Saxons in England*. London: Longman.

Lockhart, J. G. (1838) *Life of Sir Walter Scott*, 2 vols. Philadelphia: Blanchard.

Lukács, G. (1983) *The Historical Novel*, trans. H. Mitchell. Lincoln: University of Nebraska Press.

Merivale, C. (1865) *History of the Romans*, 7 vols. New York: Appleton.

Nicolas, N. H. (1830) *Observations on the State of Historical Literature*. London: Pickering.

Nietzsche, F. (1980) *On the Advantages and Disadvantages of History for Life*, trans. P. Preuss. Indianapolis: Hackett.

Stubbs, W. (1878) *Constitutional History of England*. Oxford: Oxford University Press.

——(1886) *Seventeen Lectures*. Oxford: Oxford University Press.

Thirlwall C. (1844) *History of Greece*, 8 vols. London: Longman.

Trumpener, K. (1997) *Bardic Nationalism: The Romantic Novel and the British Empire*. Princeton: Princeton University Press.

Whitman, W. (1996) *Poetry and Prose*. New York: Library of America.

FURTHER READING

Adams, E. (2011) *Liberal Epic: The Victorian Practice of History from Gibbon to Churchill*. Charlottesville: University of Virginia Press.

Berlin, I. (1998) *The Proper Study of Mankind Is Man*. New York: Farrar, Strauss and Giroux.

Burrow, J. W. (2008) *A History of Histories*. New York: Knopf.

——(1981) *A Liberal Descent*. Cambridge: Cambridge University Press.

Collingwood, R. G. (1956) *The Idea of History*. Oxford: Oxford University Press.

Duncan, I. (2007) *Scott's Shadow: The Novel in Romantic Edinburgh*. Princeton: Princeton University Press.

Gooch, G. P. (1959) *History and Historians in the Nineteenth Century*. Boston: Beacon Press.

Grafton, A. (1997) *The Footnote: A Curious History*. Cambridge MA: Harvard University Press.

Levine, P. (1986) *The Amateur and the Professional: Antiquarians, Historians, and Archaeologists in Victorian England, 1838–1886*. Cambridge: Cambridge University Press.

Rubinoff, L. (1968) "Introduction" to F. H. Bradley, *The Presuppositions of Critical History*. Chicago: Quadrangle Books.

White, H. (1975) *Metahistory: The Historical Imagination in Nineteenth-Century Europe*. Baltimore: Johns Hopkins University Press.

28
Literary Criticism

David E. Latané, Jr

In the twilight of Georgian England, Dr William Maginn sat down, still in the con-
vivial company of brother scribblers for *Fraser's Magazine*, and wrote an unsigned
review of Mr Grantley Berkeley's novel *Berkeley Castle*, which exposed the aristocratic
pretensions of the author (an MP and son of an earl), and concluded, "*Berkeley Castle*
in conception is the most impertinent, as in execution it is about the stupidest, it has
ever been our misfortune to read. It is also quite decisive of the character of the author
as a 'gentleman.'" Maginn's review, while accurate to a "T," was also clearly fueled by
a stronger brew, as well as by the animosity he felt, being an inordinately learned but
somewhat unfortunate Irishman afloat in London, at snubs inflicted by semi-literate
English snobs. A duel ensued, in which both politician and critic missed their marks
several times. It was in the next year, 1837, that Victoria came to the throne. By the
time of her death, two long generations later, politics remained much the same; yet
literary criticism had become more polite, as well as more scholarly, professional, and
(metaphorically) on target. A. C. Bradley's *Shakespearean Criticism* (1904), hailed as a
masterpiece of psychological analysis and occasionally cited without caveat by critics
today, may be taken as an end point. Midway between these dates, Matthew Arnold
in "The Function of Criticism at the Present Time" (1864) famously defined criticism
as "*a disinterested endeavour to learn and propagate the best that is known and thought in the
world.*" For him, one word summed up the rule that should govern the critic:
disinterestedness.

For the student of criticism in the Victorian age, it might be safest to disrespect
the *dis-*, for Arnold's dictum was born as a counterweight to the prevalence of

A New Companion to Victorian Literature and Culture, First Edition. Edited by Herbert F. Tucker.
© 2014 John Wiley & Sons, Ltd. Published 2014 by John Wiley & Sons, Ltd.

criticism of the most crudely biased sort, in which gain for one's political party, religious sect, or bank account was transparently the motive. In 1802 the founding of the *Edinburgh Review* had opened a new era in periodical criticism, and the *Edinburgh*, its quarterly imitators, and new magazines such as *Blackwood's* established a "damnatory style" of anonymous reviewing which continued well into the Victorian era (Coleridge, *Biographia Literaria*, ch. 21; see also Woolford). Alongside outrageous condemnation went the art of "puffing," or broadsiding the reading public with favorable short notices (planted, for instance, in the columns of the *Literary Gazette* or the *Athenaeum*) as well as through longer articles. The pioneering publisher Henry Colburn was notorious for buying periodicals which then gave the novels he published very fine reviews indeed, and on occasion writers even abused anonymity by reviewing their own books. Carlyle showed at least one thinking writer's contempt for the state of criticism at the beginning of the reign when he republished his bad notices as a badge of honor in the 1838 edition of *Sartor Resartus*. By 1886, however, a leading critic like Arthur Symons could proclaim, "I have ever held that the rod with which popular fancy invests criticism is properly the rod of divination: a hazel-switch for the discovery of buried treasure, not a birch-twig for the castigation of offenders" (Preface to *An Introduction to the Study of Browning*).

Our standard accounts of Victorian criticism have tended to take the high road, emphasizing the work done by poet–scholars and men (rarely women) of letters such as Arnold, Cardinal Newman, G. H. Lewes, Walter Bagehot, Leslie Stephen, Symons, and "Vernon Lee" (Violet Paget). Though we may occasionally be more amused by the style of "Walt Whitman is as unacquainted with art as a hog is with mathematics" (1856; quoted in Woolford 111), it is the more thoughtful work, where "the critic . . . before abandoning himself to the oratorical impulse [classifies] the phenomena with which he is dealing as calmly as if he were ticketing a fossil in a museum" (Leslie Stephen, *Cornhill* 36 [1877], 723–37), which leads Harold Orel to remark that "We may legitimately wonder whether the techniques for analysing and evaluating literary texts used in our century are all that superior to those used by Victorian critics" (3). Canvassing the widest range of cultural activity, we now map the byways, as well as the bylines, of the lesser known or anonymous critics, to explore the "cultural work" or ideology of critics both mundane and outrageous (if not profound). Examining, for instance, the ways in which the shapings of literary criticism coincide with alterations in national identity or attitudes towards empire, we are quick to ask what it means when Carlyle's "Editor" in *Sartor Resartus* (book II, ch. 1) says, "Tombuctoo [sic] itself is not safe from British Literature." We are also exploring our master tropes of gender, class, and race, and finally, though self-interestedly, we are uncovering the Victorian story of how literary criticism established itself in university literature departments.

Arnold is of course an exceptional figure, born onto the intellectual center-stage. His father Thomas was an historian, theologian, famous headmaster of Rugby School, and then Regius Professor of Modern History at Oxford; his godfather was the

Tractarian divine and poet John Keble; Wordsworth was a family friend. Educated at Winchester, Rugby, and Oxford, Arnold won prizes and scholarships, obtained in 1845 a Fellowship at Oriel College, and was appointed to the largely ceremonial position of Oxford Professor of Poetry at age 34, although the income that allowed him to marry and start a family came from the more mundane job of government Inspector of Schools. From the point of view of the sociology of authorship, foregrounding a man like Arnold distorts one's view of the practicing literary critic in the Victorian era. More typical is the unknown William Henry Smith (1808–72), who wrote books of poems, plays, and philosophical dialogues that are not without merit (though utterly without success). A failure at the law, he made his meager living penning over 130 articles, chiefly on literary subjects, for periodicals such as *Blackwood's* at ten guineas a sheet. Sometimes his perceptions were keen; he is always thoughtful rather than contemptuous or puffing.

Still, Arnold remains the place to start in considerations of Victorian literary criticism. This is because he is more a superb propagandist for criticism (social, of course, as well as literary) than a practicing literary critic. Wilde, whose witty inversions of Arnoldian precepts are well known, owes an ironic debt to Arnold for making it possible to view "The Critic as Artist" (an essay of 1891), one perhaps superior to his or her putative subject. Arnold's critical ideal, in the words of René Wellek, compassed "curiosity, flexibility, urbanity, a free articulation of ideas" (IV, 156). Why then has Arnold attracted such widespread disapproval, even dislike, in our time?

Arnold's legacy has come under scrutiny as scholars have become increasingly suspicious of poses of objectivity that mask positions which advantage *sub rosa* particular groups or causes. For half a century, currents in contemporary Anglo-American criticism and theory have been energized by a repudiation of the Arnoldian stance; the cultural historian Raymond Williams, one of the first modern theorists to criticize Arnold severely, refused to reconsider: "I would have to be savage today, nothing less would do" (124). Terry Eagleton speaks for many when he remarks, "We are generally right to suspect that appeals to see the object as it really is can be decoded as invitations to see it as our rulers do" (166). Arnold is seen as a "worn out man of letters," "with a frippery of phrases about sweetness and light, seeing things as they really are, knowing the best that has been thought and said in the world, which never had very much solid meaning." But this last-quoted judgment is no modern assailant's but Arnold's own – a piece of self-mockery from "A Liverpool Address" of 1882 – and it should therefore give us pause. The more one actually reads Arnold, the more difficult it becomes to turn him into a straw man.

Arnold's earliest criticism appears in his letters of the 1840s, especially those to his friend, the poet and fellow Rugby student Arthur Hugh Clough. (Throughout the century some of the most acute practical criticism occurs in letters from one poet to another, the Brownings', for instance, or Hopkins's letters to Robert Bridges.) It was when he took the extraordinary step in his preface of censuring and excising some of his own poems from his collected volume of 1853 that Arnold's critical impulse first came to the public eye, as a champion of the classical mode against a prevailing, and by then seedy, Romanticism. His position was contested by G. H. Lewes in prose, and Elizabeth Barrett Browning in an epic poem, *Aurora Leigh* (1857), which advocates for narrative verse the appropriation of the contemporary subject matter of the novel. Arnold's greatest impact comes, however, in *Essays in Criticism* of 1865, a miscellaneous collection of his writing from the previous few years. Arnold lays out the case for disinterestedness, flexibility, objectivity, and a wide range of sympathy as he examines a range of authors, chiefly French. His abhorrence of criticism as a tool in the service of some extra-literary agenda, combined with Newman's anti-utilitarian ideal of a liberal education as an end in itself (*The Idea of a University*, 1873), might be seen as the bedrock of the Anglo-American approach to academic literary criticism for the next hundred years. Arnold's later writing, much taken up with social and religious matters, adds little that is new to his critical position as such.

In some ways the critical activities for which many know Arnold best – his rankings of authors, naming of "touchstones," and general fastidiousness – are least important. Arnold airs his blind spots (Chaucer was "not one of the great classics") where many others remain silent, or mouth pieties. As a practicing critic his range – compared for instance to Lewes's or others' who earned their living with the pen – is small, taking practically no notice of the novel, or American literature, or living poets. He wrote essays on minor French writers who interested him, and left us without his criticism on Dickens, or George Eliot. What he left us instead was the notion of criticism itself.

Criticism of the Literature of the Past

Arnold's first book-length critical study was *On Translating Homer* (1861), and, indeed, in the absence of an academic literary criticism, a characteristic feature of the times was a strong interest in literary history. *The Temple Bar*, for instance, was one of the early shilling magazines of the 1860s – a "London Magazine for Town and Country Readers." In its first year it published articles on Bacon, the *Kalewala* (Finnish epic), Herrick, "Ancient Classical Novelists," Rabelais, Herbert, Donne, Gray, and Shelley. While this historical criticism did not escape the vices that plagued the contemporary reviews, it did offer greater latitude for reflection, and it was distributed to a wider audience than discussions of the same topics generally are now.

Today, criticism primarily concerns the literature of the past; books such as this one introduce readers to topics and recommend further readings in professional journals and university press monographs. In the consideration of their literary heritage, as in everything, the Victorians were industrious; but nothing like our professional critical "industry" existed, and Ian Small is correct to caution that in our use of the phrase "literary criticism" to describe, for example, writings of both Ruskin and Roland Barthes, we "presuppose . . . that they are doing the same 'thing'" (18). Universities were few in number, and the study of modern languages and literatures was not part of the traditional curriculum. Scholars of ancient languages rarely wrote what we would recognize as literary criticism; their increasingly specialized work took the form of philological research and textual editing. The establishment of the first chair in English literature at the new University of London in 1828 portends the rise of professional (and professorial) criticism at century's end, which instigates "a growing tension between academic specialists and general reviewers which, arguably, has persisted to this day" (Habib 2). Nineteenth-century publishers meeting the needs of an enlarging reading public, as well as of colleges and schools with an English curriculum, began producing numerous editions requiring critical introductions in the modern style, as well as series such as *The English Men of Letters* (begun 1877). Series editor John Morley elicited many distinguished contributions: Trollope on Thackeray, J. A. Symonds on Shelley, Stephen on Swift, Chesterton on Robert Browning, Huxley on Hume. Canonical poets and novelists thus enhanced by critical appreciation had also to have their lives and works traced, and late Victorians rose to the call. The past lay all before them, and if by our lights their steps were wandering, they were seldom slow. Most modern critical histories begin with the Victorians. The ascent of the Shakespearean Bradley (1851–1935) is paradigmatic: from Professor of Modern Literature at Liverpool (1882–90), to Professor of English at Glasgow (1890–1900), and finally to Professor of Poetry at Oxford. The astonishing production of George Saintsbury (1845–1933), a journalist and then an Edinburgh professor, became possible in this climate. Unlike earlier Victorian critics, Bradley and Saintsbury did not write across a range of nonliterary subjects; they confined their efforts instead to what Leslie Stephen dubbed in 1876 "aesthetic criticism" (see his "Thoughts on Criticism, by a Critic"; also Brake).

The ancient text that had the most thorough-going, professional cadre of critic-interpreters was the Bible, and from the perilous field of German biblical hermeneutics came many Victorian innovations in secular criticism, filtered through intermediaries such as Coleridge, Carlyle, and Julius Hare. Despite protracted resistance fed by English parochial suspicion – "the Critic leaves no air to poison; / Pumps out with ruthless ingenuity / Atom by atom, and leaves you – vacuity" (Browning, "Christmas-Eve," 1850, ll. 911–13) – criticism of the Bible and the Graeco-Roman classics often took the form of sophisticated textual and interpretive commentary that accompanied new editions, for instance Connop Thirlwall's of Schleiermacher's *St. Luke* (1825), or Sir Alexander Grant's Hegelian commentary on Aristotle's *Ethics* (1857–8). From examples such as these, more complex philosophical approaches spread into literary criticism proper, as for instance in the writings of Walter Pater. Mundane practices, too – the compiling of a "canon" and the listing of commentary resulting in what Saintsbury called an "atlas of the actual facts" (quoted in Wellek IV, 422) – descend ultimately from treatments of the Bible.

Victorian responses to earlier British literature may be categorized by period. Romantic critics such as Coleridge, Lamb, and Hazlitt had opened up the Elizabethan era, not only in Shakespeare studies, but also in the recovery of many other dramatists and poets from previous centuries' neglect. Victorian scholars followed through with such monuments as the 11-volume Moxon edition of Beaumont and Fletcher (1843–6). Special note should be taken of the Victorian Bardology; it comprises numerous elements, many of them subcritical – Dr Bowdler's *Family Shakespeare* for instance, or Anon's 1862 *Shakespeare: Was He a Christian?* (others proved him atheist, puritan, and Catholic). The Victorian Shakespeare is above all a *national* poet, essential to Englishness. Carlyle's lecture in *Heroes and Hero-Worship* (1841) poses a hypothetical either/or: *Empire* or *Shakespeare?* "Indian Empire will go, at any rate, some day; but this Shakespeare does not go, he lasts forever with us; we cannot give up our Shakespeare!" Bagehot's essay "Shakespeare – The Individual" (1853) mines the plays to prove the Bard a "no nonsense" optimistic fellow who became "a person of capital . . . a gentleman to be respected" – in short, an honorary Victorian. The heroines are of particular interest; early in the era Maginn argues that Shakespeare's range compels him "to bring females prominently forward in every variety of circumstance," and that, with the slight exception of Lady Macbeth, these heroines are "pure, honourable, spotless, – ever ready to perform a kind action, – never shrinking from a heroic one" (*Bentley's Miscellany* II [1837], 558; see also Anna Jameson's 1832 *Characteristics of Women*, and Lootens 77–115). These greatly imagined women then stepped out of the confines of the script, like 60 paragons in search of an author, and into such bestsellers as Mary Cowden Clarke's *The Girlhood of Shakespeare's Heroines* (1850). Shakespeare and his characters exhausted, William Black late in the century invents a sister in his bestselling novel of 1884, *Judith Shakespeare: A Romance*. (It was left to Virginia Woolf to demolish the subtitle.)

Much of the more respectable effort is antiquarian and biographical. The first Shakespeare Society was founded in 1840 with the scholar–editors Revd William Dyce, Charles Knight, John Payne Collier, and James Halliwell at its core. This generation made many remarkable discoveries among Renaissance manuscripts – too many, in fact, for Collier was also a dedicated forger, and the Society was dissolved in 1851, its legitimate work under a cloud. Halliwell did, however, produce the century's most substantial biography of the Bard. When the New Shakspere Society called its first meeting in 1874, it was at University College, with the cranky F. J. Furnivall, master of Victorian literary societies, in the chair. Much of the sound and fury that ensued concerned textual matters, as members labored over minute theories of style or prosody to prove that this or that play preceded or followed another. Otherwise, respectability was maintained. But what sort of Shakespeare criticism did the Victorians leave us that built upon the landmarks left by Johnson, Coleridge, and Hazlitt? While individual essays such as Pater's on *Measure for Measure* stand out, the stronger critical minds did not produce their best on Shakespeare.

The literature of the eighteenth century was sometimes treated by Victorian critics in a "yes, but" fashion. Critics dismayed at Byronism preferred Pope. In fiction, masters such as Fielding were used as a yardstick; the rich humor and variety of human life in *Tom Jones* were used to measure each successive wave of novels-of-the-day. As public literary life began to reflect a more narrow, middle-class sense of decency, however, squeamishness arose about writers like Swift, Sterne, and Smollett who treated frankly the indecency of the body and the realities of social relations. We are somewhat bemused, I think, by Thackeray on Sterne: "The foul Satyr's eyes leer out of the leaves constantly: the last words the famous author wrote were bad and wicked" ("Sterne and Goldsmith," in *English Humorists of the Eighteenth Century*, 1853). Sterne is contrasted with the "sweet and unsullied page" of Dickens. Criticism of this sort by poets and novelists is hardly disinterested; reproving a licentious eighteenth century was perhaps one way of keeping Mrs Grundy from complaining about contemporaries. The eighteenth century went on to become the focus of a wider debate. In an interesting "Dialogue on Poetic Morality" published in the *Contemporary Review* (1881), Vernon Lee writes:

> Our modern familiarity with the intellectual work of all times and races has made people perceive that in past days indecency was always a part and parcel of literature, and that to try and weed it out is to completely alter the character of at least a good half of the literature of the past. Hence, some of us moderns, shaken as we are in all our conventional ideas, have argued that this so-called indecency is a legitimate portion of all literature, and that the sooner it is re-introduced into that of the present the better, if our literature is to be really vital and honest. (698; reprinted in Stasny)

The endlessly debated question – should literature depict things as they ought to be (Romanticism) or as they have been and are now (Realism)? – is latent in all such discussions. What has become a *locus classicus*, that the novelist should "aspire to give no more than a faithful account of men and things as they have mirrored themselves" in the novelist's mind, is satisfyingly part of an historical novel set in the late eighteenth century, Eliot's *Adam Bede* (1859, ch. 17).

Among the learned and thoughtful critics of the previous century's literature, one stands out above the others. The work of Leslie Stephen (1832–1904) survives as one of the most original treatments in English of the relationship among literature and culture and society. Stephen, who is famous for all sorts of things – being an open agnostic, editing the *Cornhill Magazine* (1871–82), selecting the novels for Macmillan, founding and then writing 378 articles for the *Dictionary of National Biography*, fathering Virginia Woolf – devoted enormous energies to studying eighteenth-century England. His method, in one sense, is amateur, in that he confesses, "I at any rate love a book pretty much in proportion as it makes me love the author" ("The Study of English Literature"), but his scholarship and intellectual honesty take him beyond "appreciations" and "impressions." His own critics have found him cool, anti-aesthetic, overly intellectual, moralistic, and utilitarian. These very characteristics, however, might make his stock rise at present, when a view of literature as "a particular function of the whole social organism" (*English Literature and Society in the Eighteenth Century*, 1904) has its appeal. Stephen's work "was not only a pioneering clearing-away of the rubble, enabling Victorians to see the full dimensions of what the preceding century had accomplished; it remains today the most readable and informative introduction" to the age (Orel 122).

Theories of Poetry and Fiction

Victorian criticism of and response to Romantic-era writers is rich, copious, and almost impossible to categorize. The Romantics, despite their famously early deaths, were very much a real presence, whether in the flesh (Wordsworth, Landor, and Hunt) or in memory and memorabilia. One thing is certain: by 1893, with the publication of the Yeats/Ellis edition of Blake, Victorian taste-makers had delivered to the twentieth century the restricted, all-male canon of Blake, Wordsworth, Coleridge, Byron, Shelley, and Keats. One could assert that it was in the course of thinking through that quintessential Romantic question, "What is Poetry?" that this restriction came about. Bentham, when not comparing poetry to children's games, had given the pragmatic definition: poetry is writing that does not extend to the right margin of the page. Responses like those of Leigh Hunt in *Imagination and Fancy* (1844) – "poetry is imaginative passion" (Stasny 4) – go so far in the other direction as to be meaningless. John Stuart Mill's refinements in essays from the 1830s are more precise but take the same tack. Mill rejects the rhetorical, didactic, and intellectual aspects; poetry effects a sharing of emotions, and the best poetry appears to us as overheard song, rather than purposeful speech. The wide discussion of what is, after all, a purely theoretical question (readers recognized poetry when they saw it) gave the Victorians a consensus opinion that "poetry" was immediate, passionate, imaginative, lyric. Ultimately this meant, despite famous attempts to thin the flock (e.g. Arnold's dubbing Shelley an "ineffectual angel, beating in the void his luminous wings in vain"), that the answer to the question "What is Poetry?" could be given as that roll call of six Romantic names.

Early Victorian criticism – from Arthur Hallam's precocious analysis of Tennyson, to Mill's brief but influential excursion, to Keble's Oxford lectures – attempts to consolidate the innovations of the Romantics. (Shelley's "Defence," it might be mentioned, was also first published in 1840.) Faced with the phenomena of the time, theories of poetry and accounts of poetic practice veered towards taxonomy. Thus, we have Hallam's poets of "sensation" and "reflection," Browning's "objective" and "subjective" poets ("Essay on Shelley," 1852), Bagehot's "pure," "ornate," and "grotesque" (1864), Buxton Forman's "idyllic," "psychological," "preraphaelite," and "renaissance" groupings (*Our Living Poets*, 1871), and the very complex systems of E. S. Dallas in

Poetics: An Essay on Poetry (1852). Dallas was educated at Edinburgh, and had a strong grasp of the German and Scottish philosophical traditions. He represents the closest thing to a Victorian "theorist," and in *The Gay Science* (1866) he breaks with the association psychology generally used to explain literary effects. For better examples of theoretically informed and imaginative criticism, one must go to the Continent, to Taine, Sainte-Beuve, or Nietzsche, whose *Gay Science* (1882) is with good reason better known.

The Romantic novel cast no such shadow over the Victorians; though Walter Scott was omnipresent, he was not oppressive. Victorian critics developed a theory of realism in part by demolishing the steady stream of unrealistic or silly novels that issued from the press. Comparisons were often made to painting (Hogarth and Wilkie, or the "Dutch School" that Eliot admires in *Adam Bede*) as well as to the new art of photography. In an omnibus look at novels by women, Lewes declares in 1852 "that only *that* literature is effective, and to be prized accordingly, which has *reality for its basis*" (Olmsted II, 40). This criterion, which valorizes both Austen and Brontë, appeared again a few years later when Eliot attacked "mind-and-millinery" novels in which "a child of four and a half years old" talks in "Ossianic fashion" ("Silly Novels by Lady Novelists," Olmsted II, 281). Countervailing the dominant theory of realism, however, was a principle of amusement, which licensed other modes, giving rise to the controversy over sensation fiction that began in the 1860s, and subsequently to a critical divide between the "art" of fiction and more popular narrative modes. Olmsted remarks that the "period roughly 1880 to 1900 saw more writing directly concerned with the art of fiction than had appeared in the previous half-century" (III, xiv). Henry James in "The Art of Fiction" (*Longman's Magazine*, 1884) observes that the English novel "had no air of having a theory . . . a consciousness of itself behind it – of being the expression of an artistic faith, the result of choice and comparison" (Olmsted III, 287). The belated Victorian theoretical effort gave rise to the art novel (Meredith through Joyce), and brought this subgenre closer to the status of poetry, in sophistication and prestige, as well as in profitability.

Gender, and the Woman Critic

Literary criticism and commentary were diffuse and unspecialized throughout the era, and current cultural-studies approaches allow us to see more of this wide field. In addition to probing the 48 mainstream monthlies and quarterlies indexed in the *Wellesley Index to Victorian Periodicals, 1824–1900* (a key reference work which identifies authors for most anonymous articles), we are also recovering criticism from such unlikely places as Margaret and Beatrice De Courcy's *Ladies' Cabinet of Fashion, Music, and Romance* (1836–7), which includes, alongside colored fashion plates of morning visiting dresses, articles such as "Modern Swedish Literature," "Coleridge's Poems," and "Influence of Female Intellect upon Literature"; or from the Chartist

Northern Star, where we find an interesting dialogue, "Critic and Poet," and an essay on "The Beauties of Byron" that emphasizes the poet's politics. These investigations, carried out in large part by members of the Research Society for Victorian Periodicals, are changing the shape of critical history, giving us nonmale or nonbourgeois perspectives on established writers such as Dickens or Browning, and sometimes pointing towards interesting writers submerged or marginalized in received literary history.

It has been estimated that about a fifth of publishing writers were female, chiefly novelists or authors of children's literature, and that women wrote a relatively small percentage of literary criticism. More recent studies have revised the figure upwards and emphasized how public intellectuals such as Harriet Martineau "made gender itself a critical concept" (Kimberly Adams, in Habib 93). Gender issues in the criticism may be examined from several perspectives, not just the sex of the critic. Reception historians have scrutinized in increasingly subtle ways the fate of women writers at the hands of the reviewers, and we are also studying how gendered figures of speech used early in the century produced more concrete, though still radically unstable, critical categories, such as "manly" or "feminine." New scholarship based in queer theory reads subtexts more than contexts, exploring for example how criticism uses these terms to "participate in an aesthetic minoritizing discourse whose project is to construct an alternative masculinity" (Morgan 320). While we must be alert here to the orbit of the "hermeneutic circle" (Matthew 7:7) there is ample evidence in Victorian criticism supporting such a rich subtextuality; in commenting on Tennyson's *The Princess* (1847), Aubrey de Vere explores how Ida's "Amazonian philosophy" might "extirpate from the soul of man those feminine qualities which the masculine nature, if complete, must include . . . We dare not, however, undertake the exposition of all Mr Tennyson's hidden meanings" (*Edinburgh Review*, 1849; in Stasny 210). Alongside these more theoretical approaches to gender, scholars continue to identify in the periodical archive significant female practitioners of the art of criticism.

There is no doubt that women authors were treated differently from men, both in the initial reviews and in more retrospective estimations and attempts to define movements or the *Zeitgeist*. While attitudes change (for better and for worse) over the course of the century, one might begin with the notion of a double standard, based in part on the stereotypical shortcomings of the female intellect, coupled with the equally stereotypical superiorities of the female heart. This meant that critics were quite happy to judge favorably within a "separate sphere," but reluctant to rate women's writing equitably when it was perceived to step outside that magic bubble. Thus, the women poets who came into prominence from 1820 to 1850 (Hemans, L. E. L., Barrett Browning) had to fulfill the generic saintliness of "woman," and at the same time match the ideal of the *sui generis* poet-genius. The ensuing dissonance meant that in poetry "nineteenth-century feminine literary canonization became a virtual recipe for critical disappearance" (Lootens 10). But because reviewers were anonymous, and many novelists were as well, some attempts at stereotyping went spectacularly awry.

An *Athenaeum* reviewer, for instance, states definitively of one of Rhoda Broughton's novels, "the author is not a young woman, but a man, who, in the present story, shows himself destitute of refinement of thought or feeling, and ignorant of all that women either are or ought to be" (Casey 155); another reviewer believed that Tennyson's anonymous *In Memoriam* (1850) came from "the full heart of the widow of a military man."

We are just beginning to sort out the complexities of reviewing and reception in the nineteenth century. While egregious cases of gender bias are easy to locate, reviewers were powerless to banish women from literature, unlike the law and other professions. Gaye Tuchman and Nina Fortin mount a complex argument in *Edging Women Out* (1989) to show that women's authorship declined over the course of the century, as men seized prose fiction, formerly marginalized and despised, and enforced their new preeminence through the control of reviews. Ellen Casey (1996), however, in her examination of over 11,000 anonymous reviews of fiction in the weekly *Athenaeum* finds scant evidence for an "edging out," and instead uncovers a record of amelioration towards the end of the century in the damage wrought by the double standard. Other feminist critics, focusing on the reception of the "new woman" novelists of the 1890s or on the diminution of the reputation of George Eliot after her death, support the view that embattled male critics mounted more focused gender-biased attacks, thus enabling the late-Victorian canonization of male novelists like Hardy and Conrad.

It was hostile reviews of *Tess* (1891) and *Jude* (1895) that helped edge Hardy into poetry, which is the genre most paradoxically gendered. While some feminist critics view official poetic theory and practice as almost entirely phallocratic, poets were stigmatized as weak and effeminate throughout the period, from Dickens's sketch of the "Poetical Young Gentleman" (1838), to such caricatures of the aesthetes as Gilbert and Sullivan's "Bunthorne" (*Patience*, 1881) or the Irish poet "Joyday Flowers" in Sarah Grand's *The Winged Victory* (1916). Even more than in prose fiction, however, gender was related to style, and male and female poets were expected to keep to their respective sides of the road. The brawny and bearded Tennyson, paradoxically, was attacked most frequently with gender terms. Alfred Austin, in a sally so notorious it might have come from an alley rather than a respectable publisher, finds the laureate typical of the "feminine, narrow, domesticated, timorous Poetry of the Period," and goes on to fault a descriptive passage because "There is no dust, and clang, and hot blood in it . . . still life is not a masculine, but a feminine propensity" (Bristow 124–6). Tennyson's natural propensities, apparently, are insufficiently red in tooth and claw. From a different angle Swinburne sees Tennyson's pernicious influence in the "idyl" form: "It is naturally on a lower level than that of tragic or lyric verse. Its gentle and maidenly lips are somewhat narrow for the stream . . . It is very fit for the sole diet of girls; not very fit for the sole sustenance of men." Swinburne's utopia of an art that is "noble and chaste in the wider masculine sense" was perhaps wider than others would allow (Bristow 9–10).

Gender is also factored into reviews according to the presumed or implied audience. The prototypical novel reader was a young girl, with a "passive, languorous body displaying itself on a sofa and neglecting domestic duties as it 'devoured' the texts" (Ferris 18). One major function of Victorian criticism was to censure such fare, and praise literature that would be safe for the "young person." In poetry, however, chaste verse suitable for girls was generally chastised. Bagehot, for instance, makes some brilliant comments about the austerity and tactility of Wordsworth, noting that his poetry had become "the Scriptures of the intellectual life"; he then adds, "And therefore he has had a whole host of sacred imitators. Mr Keble, for example, has translated him for women" ("Hartley Coleridge" [1852] in *Literary Studies*). This in fact may be true; a case could be made that the extraordinarily popular *Christian Year* found its audience among religious, primarily female readers, who responded to the way it bent the tones of Wordsworth's secular poems to the round of the ecclesiastical calendar. The intent of remarks like Bagehot's, however, is not to analyze but to sneer. Thus G. K. Chesterton in 1914: "There is a moment when Carlyle turns suddenly from a high creative mystic to a commonplace Calvinist. There are moments when George Eliot turns from a prophetess into a governess. There are also moments when Ruskin turns into a governess, without even the excuse of sex" (*The Victorian Age in Literature*, 157).

Of the many women who wrote literary criticism, chiefly for periodicals, the best-known names earned their fame as poets or novelists. Elizabeth Barrett contributed critical essays to R. H. Horne's *A New Spirit of the Age*, an important volume of 1844; Mary Ann Evans (George Eliot) wrote extensively for the *Westminster Review*, Margaret Oliphant was a loyal *Blackwood's* writer, and Mary (Mrs Humphry) Ward reviewed for *The Times*. Oliphant, following in the footsteps of versatile earlier writers like Anna Jameson, is a particular force on the literary scene in the last 40 years of the century, generally (in line with *Blackwood's*) taking a conservative stance. Others we are just now disentangling from the archive, in effect creating them as "authors." One such is Edith Jemima Simcox, who appeared in the first issue of the important new critical organ *The Academy* (1869) and wrote as well for *The Contemporary Review* and *The Nineteenth Century* in the 1860s to 1880s (Fulmer 105). By 1900 some women had earned separate reputations as critics, notably Vernon Lee, whose work extends into the modern era. Because women critics, like their male counterparts, frequently wrote under the cover of anonymity, the extent to which gendered features can be discerned and elaborated into a separate aesthetic continues to be a source of debate (Wilkes 7). Oliphant's and Eliot's commentaries demonstrate that aesthetic solidarity along gender lines can be slight.

Aesthetic

René Wellek observes that 1850, the Victorian noon, could also be considered the midnight of English literary criticism; promising critics such as Mill and Carlyle had taken to "history and social pamphleteering," and poetic theory was "a remote derivative of popularized romanticism" (IV, 141). He goes on, however, to outline four strands that would provide a new platform for twentieth-century criticism: a new historicism, a new classicism, a new realism, and a new aestheticism. The changes become most evident in the last decades, and are "related to changes in the nature of *intellectual* authority in all disciplines of knowledge, changes which coincided with the wholesale professionalization and institutionalization of knowledge" (Small vii). "Isms" and "izations" have been with us ever since. Of all of Wellek's strands, "aestheticism" most clearly illustrates the growing interdependence of criticism and literature, for it takes its departure from critical precepts rather than from the manifold interdependence, which had been paramount previously, between individual writer and reading (buying) public. The godfathers of Victorian aestheticism are found in a newly canonized Keats, whose letters were first published in 1848; in Pre-Raphaelitism and the exhortations of Ruskin and Morris; and in the discussion of mid-century French imports such as Gautier and Baudelaire. Swinburne's *William Blake: A Critical Essay* (1868) is an important marker: a young poet furthers his career with a book-length critical study of the unknown Blake, using the occasion to ridicule a "British brigade" of "Philistia" obsessed with "moral custom" (a nod to Arnold's recent attack on philistinism); to praise "a living critic of incomparably delicate insight" (Baudelaire); and above all to proclaim "Art for art's sake first of all." The dual thrust of Swinburne's *Poems and Ballads* (1866) and his critical essays might for once justify that overused term "an intervention." He provoked some of the last masterpieces of the condemnatory style, notably from John Morley and Robert Buchanan, whose "The Fleshly School of Poetry" (*Contemporary Review*, 1871), was a decisive attack on Swinburne's friend D. G. Rossetti as well. From the 1860s on, with varying levels of intensity, combat was waged over "art for art's sake."

Aesthetic criticism placed great emphasis on the subjective nature of our apprehension of the art object, and twentieth-century criticism that traces the phenomenology of the act of reading descends from Pater & Co. Like Leslie Stephen, but from the other side of the blanket, Pater has a filial relation to Arnold, but with a significant twist. Ellis Hanson has recently shown how Pater's more narcissistic version of disinterestedness raises hackles that coalesce around the term "languid." Though disparaged by modernists such as Eliot, Pater is the most clearly modern critic of his time; he develops in fairly systematic and interesting ways his corollary to Arnold's dictum about seeing "the object as in itself it really is" — that one must first "know one's impression as it really is, to discriminate it, to realize it distinctly" (Preface to *The Renaissance*, 1873). Small argues that this emphasis on the subjective impression represents "an attempt to reinstate the value of literature in order to protect its autonomy: to preserve it, as it were, from competing explanations of its value provided by the newly professionalized literary historians, philologists, and textual scholars" (8). In Pater's case, however, criticism is a form of autobiography, and the "autonomy" of literature or art takes second place to the inevitable, quasi-tragic isolation of the perceiving mind. His quest is to bridge the chasm between subject and object through the appreciations of art, and in this he is the late-century heir to Romanticism, continental and insular. Ruskin's 1857 drawing manual notes how we must recapture "what may be called the *innocence of the eye*," so that we may deconstruct the world into "flat stains of colour" (*Elements of Drawing*, letter 1). Pater would like to train the mind to use the many-colored stain of the art object to reconstruct the world (as he would quickly add, "for me"). Pater's criticism is also notable for understanding what we would now call the "intertext": "Product of myriad various minds and contending tongues, compact of obscure and minute association, a language has its own abundant and often recondite laws" ("Style," *Appreciations*, 1889). Literary artists are thus by necessity "scholars" alive to the ways in which a living language leaves traces powerful enough to efface the intention of the "author." From the artist as scholar it is a short step to the "Critic as Artist," and thus to Pater's somewhat unwelcome disciple, Oscar Wilde.

Throughout the century, creative work had embodied criticism, sometimes with telling effect as in Aytoun's parodic *Firmilian: A Spasmodic Tragedy* (1854), which coined the name for a poetic "school" that it then laughed out of existence. Wilde's position is more radical, and his status as a critic is open to debate; he can be cast in the train of "dandies, scoffers and professional immoralists" (Warner and Hough II, 2) who took their cue from the conclusion to Pater's *Renaissance*. And the myth of his life can obliterate any sense of what he wrote, which can then be passed off as a witty but unoriginal recycling of Ruskin, Pater, and Whistler. But beneath the integument of the aesthete, who glories in the notion that "All art is quite useless" (Preface to *Dorian Gray*, 1890), Wilde's critical stance bears close attention, as a conscious reaction against the authority of the academic or scholarly communities – as opposed to individual "sages" – that had usurped cultural authority by the 1880s. Wilde's cultivation of celebrity status, as well as his demimonde friendships, can thus be read as "a *strategic* reaction against this new equation which identified intellectual value with scholarly seriousness and with the restricted practices of academic institutions" (Small 113). Wilde's criticism is thus a kind of anticriticism, his "Mr W. H." a travesty of the Shakespeare industry, his "The Critic as Artist" an apotheosis of flippancy, even when his perceptions are on target. Implicit in his inversion of Arnold ("the primary aim of the critic is to see the object as in itself it really is not") is the recognition that artists themselves work through such misprision. Wilde thus takes the final step from Pater's "for me" and into the abyss of the free play of signifiers explored by poststructuralist critics.

Conclusion

We read Victorian literary criticism for two reasons: to find out what was said about literary texts that we wish to understand and enjoy; and also to discover what the criticism reveals about the processes of reception and canonization, and thus about the ideological structures of Victorian literary culture in general. Scholars of Shakespeare or Austen, horrified at adding to the bulk of criticism with which they must wrestle, too easily consign Victorian criticism to the dustbin of "historical interest only." Much of contemporary criticism and theory – including the so-called postmodern – has its origins in the nineteenth century, particularly in the interrelations of practical criticism with philosophical theory in England and Germany during the first decades, and in the reactions to the mid-Victorian emphasis on utility and morality in art. And the academic scholarship that filled journals such as *Notes and Queries* (founded 1849), *PMLA* (founded 1889), and the "proceedings" of various author societies has a direct, enumerated connection to our own practice. At the same time much has changed, and many critics now begin their activity without the *a priori* that literature has an aura, and can thus be differentiated in a meaningful way from other forms of writing. In Hegel's highly pertinent terms, fine art "can heal the breach" between the "merely external" world and the "spirit": "Art's peculiar feature, however, consists in its ability to represent in *sensuous form* even the highest ideas, bringing them nearer to the character of natural phenomena, to the senses, to feeling" (Preface to *The Philosophy of Art*). Browning's "Fra Lippo Lippi" (1855) somewhat inverts Hegel's emphasis, when he says that, because the artist allows us to see the sensuous phenomena in new light, "they are better, painted – better to us, / Which is the same thing" (ll. 303–4; Pater, take note). In such company Louis Althusser, an influential theorist writing in 1984, can seem positively Victorian:

> Art (I mean authentic art, not works of average or mediocre level) does not give us knowledge in the strict sense . . . What art makes us see, and therefore gives to us in the form of "seeing," "perceiving" and "feeling" (which is not the form of knowing) is the ideology from which it is born, in which it bathes, from which it detaches itself as art, and to which it alludes. (*Essays on Ideology*, 174)

The ideological critic here finds an ally, rather than a target, in the "authentic" work of art. Althusser has substituted "ideology" for the "ideal" that Victorians, following their Romantic predecessors, felt art might allow them to glimpse, but within his argument art actually occupies an extra-ideological perspective. So from Hegel to Althusser runs an aesthetic that, applied within literary criticism, axiomatically grants rights and privileges to those poems and novels that are finally "Art." The last thing to say about the Victorians' literary criticism – but probably the first thing to remember – is that for them, while the tide was out for faith, the sea of art was still at the full.

See also 1897; EDUCATIONAL, ARTISTIC, PUBLISHING; POETRY, FICTION

REFERENCES

Althusser, L. (1984) *Essays on Ideology*. London: Verso.

Brake, L. (1986) "Literary Criticism and the Victorian Periodicals." *Yearbook of English Studies* 16, 92–116.

Bristow, J. (ed.) (1987) *The Victorian Poet: Poetics and Persona*. London, New York and Sydney: Croom Helm.

Casey E. M. (1996) "Edging Women Out?: Reviews of Women Novelists in the *Athenaeum*, 1860–1900." *Victorian Studies* 39, 151–71.

Chesterton, G. K. (1914) *The Victorian Age in Literature*. New York: Holt.

Eagleton, T. (1991) *Ideology: An Introduction*. London and New York: Verso.

Ferris, I. (1992) "From Trope to Code: The Novel and the Rhetoric of Gender in Nineteenth-Century Critical Discourse." In *Rewriting the Victorians: Theory, History, and the Politics of Gender*, ed. L. M. Shires. New York and London: Routledge.

Fulmer, C. M. (1998) "Edith Simcox: Feminist Critic and Reformer." *Victorian Periodicals Review* 31, 105–21.

Habib, M. A. R. (ed.) (2013) *The Cambridge History of Literary Criticism, Vol. 6*. Cambridge: Cambridge University Press.

Hanson, E. (2012) "The Languorous Critic." *New Literary History* 43, 547–64.

Lootens, T. (1996) *Lost Saints: Silence, Gender, and Victorian Literary Canonization*. Charlottesville: University Press of Virginia.

Morgan, T. E. (1993) "Reimagining Masculinity in Victorian Criticism: Swinburne and Pater." *Victorian Studies* 36, 315–31.

Olmsted, J. C. (ed.) (1979) *A Victorian Art of Fiction: Essays on the Novel in British Periodicals*, 3 vols. New York and London: Garland Publishing.

Orel, H. (1984) *Victorian Literary Critics: George Henry Lewes, Walter Bagehot, Richard Holt Hutton, Leslie Stephen, Andrew Lang, George Saintsbury and Edmund Gosse*. London: Macmillan.

Small, I. (1991) *Conditions for Criticism: Authority, Knowledge, and Literature in the Late Nineteenth Century*. Oxford: Clarendon Press.

Stasny, J. (ed.) (1986) *Victorian Poetry: A Collection of Essays from the Period*. New York and London: Garland Publishing.

Tuchman, G., and N. E. Fortin (1989) *Edging Women Out: Victorian Novelists, Publishers, and Social Change*. New Haven: Yale University Press.

Warner, E., and G. Hough (eds) (1983) *Strangeness and Beauty: An Anthology of Aesthetic Criticism, 1840–1910*, 2 vols. Cambridge: Cambridge University Press.

Wellek, R. (1965) *A History of Modern Criticism, 1750–1950*, vols 3–4. New Haven: Yale University Press.

Wilkes, J. (2010) *Women Reviewing Women in Nineteenth-Century Britain: The Critical Reception of Jane Austen, Charlotte Brontë and George Eliot*. Aldershot and Burlington: Ashgate.

Williams, R. (1979) *Politics and Letters: Interviews with New Left Review*. London: New Left Books.

Woolford, J. (1982) "Periodicals and the Practice of Literary Criticism, 1855–64." In *The Victorian Periodical Press: Samplings and Soundings*, ed. J. Shattuck and M. Woolf. Toronto: University of Toronto Press.

FURTHER READING

Armstrong, I. (ed.) (1972) *Victorian Scrutinies: Reviews of Poetry, 1830–1870*. London: Athlone Press.

Dale, P. A. (1977) *The Victorian Critic and the Idea of History: Carlyle, Arnold, Pater*. Cambridge MA: Harvard University Press.

Dames, N. (2010) "On Not Close Reading: The Prolonged Excerpt as Victorian Critical Protocol." In *The Feeling of Reading: Affective Experience and Victorian Literature*, ed. R. Ablow. Ann Arbor: University of Michigan Press.

Robinson, S. C. (1996) " 'Amazed at our Success':
The Langham Place Editors and the Emergence
of a Feminist Critical Tradition." *Victorian Periodicals Review* 29, 159–72.

Small, I. (ed.) (1979) *The Aesthetes: A Sourcebook.*
London: Routledge and Kegan Paul.

Swaab, P. (2012) *The Regions of Sara Coleridge's
Thought: Selected Literary Criticism.* New York:
Palgrave Macmillan.

Thompson, N. D. (1995) *Reviewing Sex: Gender and
the Reception of Victorian Novels.* Basingstoke:
Macmillan.

Tucker, H. F. (2001) "Arnold and the Authoriza-
tion of Criticism." In *Knowing the Past: Victorian
Literature and Culture,* ed. S. Anger. Ithaca:
Cornell University Press.

Warren, A. H. (1950) *English Poetic Theory, 1825–
1865.* Princeton: Princeton University Press.

Part Five

Borders

29

Permeable Protections: The Working Life of Victorian Skin

Helena Michie

Arnold J. Cooley's *The Toilet and Cosmetic Arts in Ancient and Modern Times* (1866) offers a characteristic mid-Victorian testimonial to the wonders of skin:

> [Skin] not merely acts as an organ of sense, and a protection to the surface of the body, but it clothes it, as it were, in a garment of the most delicate texture, and of the most surpassing loveliness. In perfect health it is gifted with exquisite sensibility, and while it possesses the softness of velvet and exhibits the delicate hues of the lily, the carnation, and the rose, it is nevertheless gifted with extraordinary strength and power of resisting injury, and is not only capable of repairing, but of actually renewing itself. (197)

Cooley's paean to skin is typical of Victorian popular-science books in its rhapsodic tone. It is also characteristic of that genre that his admiration of skin is expressed in two different registers: the aesthetic and the scientific. Skin, with its "delicate hues" and "velvet" texture, is a sensuous as well as a sensual object. Even more wondrous, however, in an age newly preoccupied with science and particularly with microscopic discovery, is its anatomical function. Skin's beauty and softness belie its strength, and its scientific properties are themselves beautiful.

Cooley becomes even more rhapsodic when he turns more explicitly to what he sees as the functions of the skin:

> It is absolute perfection. It combines within itself the powers of an organ of sense, of excretion, secretion, respiration, and nutrition. The integrity of its function is not only

A New Companion to Victorian Literature and Culture, First Edition. Edited by Herbert F. Tucker.
© 2014 John Wiley & Sons, Ltd. Published 2014 by John Wiley & Sons, Ltd.

highly conducive to health, but is absolutely essential to its perfect enjoyment, to both corporeal and mental vigour, and to beauty. (201)

In this summary of skin's "powers" Cooley stresses the lexicon of science: words like "excretion," "secretion," "respiration," and "nutrition" point to mid-Victorian scientific models of the body as an intersection of various discrete "systems." Cooley moves from what would be read as scientific language to broader but still medicalized notions of health and, finally, in the last word of the passage, to – or, rather, back to – "beauty." Skin, then, exists on and marks the border of two worlds; it demonstrates the beauty of science and embodies what Victorians called the science of beauty.

If, in the idiom of this section of our book, skin lives on the border between beauty and science, it is also of course a border in another sense. Skin belongs to and defines the individual body, but it is also, as the Cooley passage suggests, not quite *of* the body. Cooley cannot resist the metaphor of clothing as he searches for the appropriate figurative language in which to – well, clothe – skin. Skin "clothes it [the body], as it were, in a garment of the most delicate texture, and of the most surpassing loveliness." The collapse of skin into clothing is a common one; in part this might be a result of a puritanical reflex that draws the eye from the naked body by defining it as clothed. Dressing the skin in figurative language adds yet another layer of protection: the word "garment" over which Cooley hesitates allows him to rhapsodize about skin without seeming to celebrate nakedness.

Perhaps there is something else at work here and in similar formulations of the skin as garment. Skin also participates in another paradox that we see in Cooley and elsewhere. Skin is a protection from outside forces; in Cooley's account it actively "resists" injury and protects the body inside it. But it is, of course, also remarkably permeable, allowing for the passage of air and moisture (our enduring euphemism "perspiration" covers both) into and out of the body. Definitional of the "outside," skin also protects what is inside. While that "inside" is not anatomized in Cooley's popular science – we see no organs, no blood, no muscles, for example – it is nonetheless an ontologically powerful entity that William Cohen argues Victorians tended to think of as equivalent to the self:

> Both tactile membrane and enclosure, the skin is a permeable boundary that permits congress between inside and outside, whether that interior is conceived in material or metaphysical terms. The skin thus forms the border not only between bodily interior and exterior but also between psychical and physical conceptions of the self. (65)

If skin defines the difference between self and other we can begin to think in terms of a final paradox: the universality of skin (we all have it) and its role in defining the particularity of a specific body or groups of bodies. Victorian understandings of race and gender invite us, as it were, to linger on the surface of the skin and to read its meanings. Cohen summarizes: "As a social signifier . . . the color, texture, and appearance of the skin have often been presumed to testify to what resides within or beneath it" (65) . If we return to the skin of the opening passage from Cooley, we will see that it is marked by Cohen's "social signifiers." This is not the generalized, human skin one might expect from Cooley's invocation of science. It is, instead, skin of a particular color, and texture, a skin with "hues of the lily, the carnation and the rose," a skin unblemished by wrinkles or age spots, a skin that seems to belong and arguably to define a young, white woman. The irony of these social markings is that they are legible to us precisely because the skin is "unmarked" in the literal sense: it is very lack of marks that allows us to see the skin in the Cooley passage as belonging to a particular social body.

Victorian representations of and attitudes towards skin, then, are informed by a series of paradoxes of inclusion and exclusion: skin defines and protects the self, but is never quite sufficient to the task. Skin is celebrated but only on the condition that we avert our eyes from its surface, from its connection with nakedness. Skin defines the self, but that self is both messy and mysterious. Finally, skin is a universal attribute of humanness, but it is inevitably marked by and used to produce and maintain social difference. The remarks that follow attempt to examine the first three paradoxes in terms of the last by examining some specific instances of the social signification of skin. I begin by looking at what a focus on skin can add to a history of the permeable body and then in two parallel sections, "Second Skin" and "Sunshine," try to show how skin's (always insufficient) protective functions were deployed in discussions of sanitation and colonization.

Permeable Membranes

Mikhail Bakhtin proposes that Western culture relies on a long-standing distinction between what he calls the "classical" or "aristocratic body" and the "grotesque body" of the populace or, later, the working class. The classical body, associated with high culture, is often literally represented as being on a pedestal: something to be gazed up at. More importantly for our purposes, the classical body has been historically represented as impermeable, a body perfect and whole in itself, without orifices or openings. The grotesque body, on the other hand, is porous, its boundaries blurry: depictions of the grotesque body focus on its lower portions – on its buttocks and genitals – as well as on other orifices, typically, as cultural historians Peter Stallybrass and Allon White put it, on the "gaping mouth" that dominates the lower portion of the face.

The "bourgeois body," the body of the middle-class subject or individual, is based on classical standards:

> The grotesque body stands in opposition to the bourgeois individualist conception of the body, which finds *its* image and legitimation in the classical. The grotesque body is emphasized as a mobile, split, multiple self . . . and it is never closed off from either its

social or ecosystemic context. The classical body on the other hand keeps its distance.
In a sense it is disembodied. (Stallybrass and White 22)

The Victorians inherited and, some would argue, perfected this notion of the bourgeois body with its roots in classical aesthetics. I contend that although there are
many Victorian depictions of the poor as "gaping mouths" – think, for example, of
Oliver Twist asking for more, and of the numerous depictions of real and fictional
starvation in texts from the "hungry forties" – the skin became a privileged site for
representing anxieties about permeability. Cohen's reading of Anthony Trollope's
1861 short story "The Banks of the Jordan" (also known as "A Ride Across Palestine") does a remarkable job of connecting that tale's almost casual racism with the
narrator's deep anxieties about the integrity of his own skin and the susceptibility of
white skin to bruising, flaying, and gender misrecognition (72). According to Cohen,
skin fails the narrator as a marker of difference when he is improbably taken in by a
crossed-dressed young woman who accompanies him across Palestine. These failures
challenge the skin-based economy of difference on which the narratives of tourism
and English superiority depended. Indeed, tourism and settler colonialism, along
with emerging scientific understanding of the skin, make dermatological readings of
Victorian texts extremely compelling. Although Cohen relies in part on Didier
Anzieu's *The Skin Ego* (1989) for a trans-temporally psychoanalytic account of the
functions of skin in protecting the psyche while also allowing for exchange, I would
argue for a historically specific version of the connection between skin and self in the
Victorian period.

Second Skins

Victorian instantiations of Stallybrass and White's bourgeois body, closed off and
protected from the outside world, owed much to Victorian individualism, which
expressed itself in a variety of contexts, from the increasingly privatized structure of
middle-class housing to the almost hysterical privileging of female virginity, to
medical discourses about the need for each person, each body, to be surrounded by a
certain number of cubits of fresh air at all times. All these elements that kept bodies
apart from one another can be seen as a sort of superstructure of protection that suggested at the same time a natural separation of classes, races, and genders and
revealed the necessity of building barriers beyond the skin. That superstructure
included clothing and homes, forms of etiquette and city planning, all of which were
in some way extensions of the body's own protective mechanism – the individual
skin, impossibly vast and yet so intimately folded about the self. It is of course possible to see these larger boundaries as compensatory for the risks that attended
permeability: the carriage with its hard shell and small windows protected the
woman of leisure from the streetwalker, who might, deprived of the second skin of
wood and canvas, brush up against her. The contamination that was imagined to

ensue might be physical or moral or both, but it would certainly testify to the insufficiency of the skin as a barrier.

The middle-class home became a second skin, protecting its inhabitants not only from other people, but from what was thought of before the later-Victorian triumph of germ theory as "effluvia" (contaminants in liquid form) or "miasma" (contaminated air). In the opening few chapters of Elizabeth Gaskell's *Mary Barton* (1848) we are introduced to a series of working-class homes, descending literally and figuratively further and further away from middle-class standards. First, we see the home of John and Mary Barton; in the relatively prosperous times in which the book begins, the home is filled with objects signifying a certain standard of luxury: a Japan ware tea tray, a cheaper version of a Pembroke (folding) table frequently found in middle-class houses, all kinds of plates and glasses, and even triangular pieces of glass "to save carving knives and forks from dirtying table-cloths" (ch. 2). All of these domestic accoutrements have in common the construction of barriers between body and food; although we do not see one, the casual mention of "table-cloths" (in the plural no less) suggests both a form of clothing and a skinlike swathing of hard surfaces. Perhaps more important than these objects, however, are those that define the perimeter of the home, keeping the outside world at bay. The blue and white checked muslin curtains, of which Elaine Freedgood has written eloquently, serve as a barrier defining inside from outside; the narrator tells us that when they are drawn they "shut in the friends met to enjoy themselves." Echoing the softness of the table-cloths, the curtains oppose the comforts of home to the harshness of the world. The Bartons enjoy a further level of protection: "[t]wo geraniums, unpruned and leafy, which stood on the sill, formed a further defense from outside pryers." Curtains and flowers merge (or cover) function with aesthetics, softening the edges of what Giorgio Agamben would call "bare life." Although Gaskell makes it clear in her long description of the Barton home that it is not one with which middle-class readers would be familiar, its ethos of cleanliness, coziness, and integrity would have been instantly recognizable.

The second home the narrator describes is that of Alice Wilson, John Barton's sister and aunt to the novel's titular heroine. Her home in the cellar of a nearby building is also spotlessly clean, but it is lower in class and in topography than the Bartons'. As with the Bartons' home, the window of Alice's cellar is a particularly fraught place: "As the cellar window looked into an area in the street, down which boys might throw stones, it was protected by an outside shutter, and was oddly festooned with all manner of hedge-row, ditch, and field plants" (ch. 2). The narrator quickly informs us that these are the plants Alice uses in her role of nurse and midwife; they are useful but give off "no very fragrant odor." The threat from the outside is specified here; the menace is not from unnamed "pryers" but from stones that have an origin and are attached to particular agents. The herbs, while valued in a certain context, are "odd" to middle-class tastes; they replace through class devolution the scented geraniums of the Barton house. While this home is as clean as the Bartons', Gaskell makes visible Alice's struggle to keep it that way: "The floor was bricked, and scrupulously clean, although so damp that it seemed the last washing would never dry up." Dampness oozes through the floor despite Alice's best efforts at washing away the outside world.

Alice's cellar, and Alice herself, still cling to middle-class values and middle-class binaries. The third working-class home in *Mary Barton*, however, breaks down all separation between inside and outside. This is the cellar that John Barton visits after hearing that his friend William Davenport's family is sick and starving after Davenport has lost his job at the mill. That this visit – and this home – represent a further drop in class and condition is made clear in the narrator's representation of the scene as a crisis in hygienic border control:

> As they passed, women from their doors tossed household slops of every description into the gutter; they ran into the next pool, which overflowed and stagnated . . . our friends were not dainty, but even they picked their way, till they got to some steps leading down into a small area, where a person standing would have his head about one foot below the level of the street, and might at the same time, without the least motion of his body touch the window of the cellar and the damp muddy wall right opposite. (ch. 6)

Here a pervasive Victorian concern over poverty and sanitation reform is emphatically expressed through the absolute permeability of the Davenport home with its broken windows, muddy walls, and puddles of excremental slop. The outside has taken over, so that the reader is asked to picture "three or four little children rolling on the damp, nay wet, brick floor through which the stagnant, filthy mixture of the street oozed up." The house is so dark, so wet, so filthy, that even the Gaskell narrator cannot tell us how many children are present, or where the street ends and the floor begins.

Gaskell was writing out of a tradition that saw domestic buildings as protection from all kinds of ill, and the streets as dangerous places. Mary Barton's aunt Esther flees into the street with a lover and becomes a prostitute, haunting the novels' homes, but never returning to inhabit them. Esther's exposure to the world makes her ill; by the end of the novel, she dies of various undiagnosed or at least unnamed causes: a fetid combination, perhaps, of consumption, syphilis, alcoholism, and madness, whose individual etiologies need only be traced to the contrast between inside and outside, the street and the home, in order to be satisfactorily understood.

Discourses of health and illness often depended on this idea of home as second skin. Florence Nightingale, one of the last holdouts against germ theory, was particularly, but by no means uniquely, adamant about the connection between homes and health. In her 1860 manual for homemakers entitled *Notes on Nursing*, Nightingale included a section on the "Health of Houses," which proposed five "points" that would ensure domestic health: "pure air," "pure water," "efficient drainage," "cleanliness," and "light." All of these points involve the regulation through windows, doors, and drains of light, dirt, air, and water. Many of Nightingale's suggestions for the prevention and treatment of disease involve opening the right window, closing doors, and regulating the apertures of the house according to the time of day. Her confidence that a regimen of fresh air could cure smallpox might seem surprising, but it is very much part of a larger understanding of houses and of bodies, a noteworthy act of faith in the power of literal and metaphoric skins.

If houses are a second skin, what of the body's first layer of protection? Nightingale's account of the importance of skin to health sounds very much like her account of the health of houses. Nightingale begins her section of *Notes* entitled "Skin" by stating: "[i]n almost all diseases, the function of the skin is, more or less, disordered; and in many important diseases nature relieves herself almost entirely through the skin." In this paradigm, skin, even and especially during illness, performs a key function of getting rid of something for which Nightingale has a variety of names, but no precise definition. The function of the nurse/homemaker is to help the skin in its regulatory role:

> [T]he excretion, which comes from the skin, is left there, unless removed by washing or by the clothes. Every nurse should keep this fact constantly in mind, – for if she allow her sick to remain unwashed, or their clothing to remain on them after being saturated with perspiration or other excretion, she is interfering injuriously with the natural processes of health just as effectually as if she were to give the patient a dose of slow poison by mouth . . . The amount of relief and comfort experienced by the sick after the skin has been carefully washed and dried, is one of the commonest observations made at a sick bed. (93)

Nature "relieves" herself by passing toxins (to use a suitably imprecise but modern word) from the interior of the body to the outside through the skin. The patient feels "relief" when that layer of effluvia is removed. Relief, like the excreted toxins, passes through the boundary of the skin, but in the reverse direction.

Sunshine

In nineteenth-century Britain the sanitary concern with proper ventilation had its obverse: one of the primary threats to the skin was imagined to be the "open air." Cold and heat were equally damaging; Lola Montez (1858) insisted that the head be "dressed" before encounters with the outside (31). Of particular interest, because it brings together so many layers of Anzieu's "skin ego" and connects the racial with the individual at both the psychological and physical level, is Victorian discourse about the dermatological effects of sunlight. Although the Victorians did not yet have what we would recognize as a fully scientific discourse of sun damage, the idea of the susceptibility of skin to sun was part of both domestic and colonial discourses.

Many people, when they call Victorian women to mind, equip them with parasols protecting the fairness of their skin. Like many clichés about "the Victorians" this one has some truth to it. Along with bonnets and veils, parasols were part of a fashionable arsenal against the rays of the sun; if we look at the many paintings of women with parasols, we can see them as prosthetic skins. Like that other conical feminine accessory, the crinoline, parasols can be seen as defining a space around the individual female body, allowing middle-class women to walk untouched through and to define themselves against real or imagined crowds. Although they enhanced ideas of impermeable selfhood, parasols were also represented in aggregate. In William Powell Frith's panoramic paintings of Victorian daily life, for example, gender difference in crowds can be seen at a distance by the division between black hats (for men) and white or colored parasols (for women). In his *Derby Day* (1858) the mixed-gender crowd of spectators at the right of the painting is particularly full of open parasols. The crowd is represented spatially as a pyramid whose apex is a parasol protecting not only the woman immediately beneath its shade but, figuratively, the crowd itself. Mediating between the sunny sky and the colored mound of well-dressed spectators, the parasol suggests a flag or a banner triumphantly definitive of the crowd's nation, class, and place. The parasol celebrates the orderliness of the British crowd even at so public an event as the Derby, creating interstitial spaces among the massed bodies that individually make it up. Of course, this is possible, in the scheme of the painting, only on the right side of the painting in the space allotted to "ladies." There are places in the Derby, and in the painting, where no parasol could venture.

The fairness of complexion that was assumed to be endangered by the sun was also whiteness in the racial sense. In the case of managing whiteness, as in the case of protecting against disease, skin was seen as both crucial and insufficient. The phenomenon of "tropicalization," or changes in character and physique through sustained experience with the tropics, tells us something about the powers and limitations of skin as a way of defining and maintaining race. While in nineteenth-century US discourse the problem of racial difference seemed to be located in a representational history of reproduction and miscegenation, British discourse, as befitted a colonial power, tended rather to focus on a particular form of "going native" that registered in complicated ways on skin, clothing, and the relation between the two.

Tropicalization, of course, assumes a process of change, but also a process of adjustment. Skin, particularly the relatively pale skin we call "white," can of course change color and texture when exposed to the sun; this simple fact that accompanied the journeys of colonizers from "temperate" Britain to Africa or Latin America, India or Australia, became a way to express many anxieties embodied in the colonial and imperial projects. One such anxiety was that the merchants, sailors, and soldiers who undertook the direct work of empire would come back home to unsettle social arrangements on the home front. This is Sir Walter's appropriately superficial complaint in Jane Austen's *Persuasion* (1817) against sailors coming ashore after earning money and fame in the Napoleonic wars. Sir Walter has two objections to the navy: first, that it is "the means of bringing persons of obscure birth into undue distinction," and second, that it makes men unattractive by coloring and aging their skin. Sir Walter recalls a prime and to him monitory example: that of the forty-year-old Admiral Baldwin, whose "face the colour of mahogany, rough and rugged to the last degree," makes him look at least sixty (ch. 3). Class and complexion are intimately related here. The transformation of the skin – its bronzing and roughening – suggests a deeper transformation at the level of society. Sir Walter's comments on naval officers remind us that the sun produces not only darkening but aging in the skin-presumed-to-be-white. An advertising campaign devised in the late 1880s for the aggressively marketed commodity Pears soap brings out much the same connection between race and aging: a series of dark-skinned peoples were represented as being whitened by the application of Pears soap (Heath 171–2).

Advertising and colonizing campaigns naturally converged by the later nineteenth century, as multiple forms of encounter with tropical lands, especially those associated with settler colonialism, expanded the range of English bodies exposed to the sun. Women, too, were transformed by its rays. Thomas Atwood bemoans as early as 1791 the fact that "English white women in the West Indies . . . are not so remarkable for the pleasing florid complexion, which is peculiar to the sex in England" (quoted in Thomas 14). "Florid," I take it here, means not so much "red" as "pink," or even "like a flower," although the reddening of skin was often associated – in what was itself a striking ideological parallel to the colonial marking we are considering – with working-class occupations for women. Other writers note a change in (white) complexion analogous to the effects of disease. It is interesting that in these examples the primary effect is seen less as a literal darkening of skin pigment than as a metaphoric change linking exposure of the skin to the sun with discourses of health and sickness (Thomas 5). It would be easy to assume that the fear motivating all of these examples is that of becoming the racial other. While this anxiety was no doubt present, there is also a sense in which the epidermal transformations associated with tropicalization produced subjects neither native nor colonial in a strict sense; the changes registered on the surface of the skin were not easily reducible to a single identity.

Ryan Johnson, stressing the complexities of tropicalization, argues that British attempts to defend against the sun were not purely a matter of establishing difference between skin colors and races. In his history of British attitudes towards the tropics and health, he notes that Britons were advised to wear clothing that mimicked or at least functioned analogously to the skin of native peoples. Starting in mid century, the British were advised – counterintuitively, at least at the time – not to wear white clothing when the sun was at its height. The darker clothing that experts recommended was mostly worn during the day, to be replaced by more traditionally British fabrics and colors for evening wear when the sun went down and, presumably, rituals of cultural maintenance could take on their full force. These complicated sartorial practices, increasingly bolstered by the emerging science of color, constituted a form of mixing:

When adorned in clothing that was designed both to mimic "black" skin and blend the sartorial effects of metropolitan citizen and colonial explorer, the wearer was at once separated and connected with Britain and its tropical empire . . . Cloth believed to provide benefits naturally bestowed on local inhabitants reminded white Britons of the drastically different environment they were in, or would find themselves in; and rather than simply reinforcing and upholding a Britishness associated with metropolitan values, everyday tropical clothing reflects the . . . shifting, open, and ambivalent identity of the European civilizer. (536)

Victorian literature is full of characters associated with the tropics. The most famous of these is the racially ambiguous Bertha Mason Rochester from Charlotte Brontë's *Jane Eyre* (1847), the "mad" Creole wife whom the novel's hero confines in the attic of his ancestral home, Thornfield Hall. Bertha is famous in part because of the association of *Jane Eyre* with the early contributions of postcolonial criticism, which saw the novel (and its feminist critics) as privileging the triumphant white female subject – Jane herself – over her racialized (although possibly white) rival. Much of this work has also been invested in the identification of Bertha's probable race, and in the investigation of the meaning of "Creole" as a racial identification at the time the novel was written. (For a fine summary and extension of this work, see Thomas 1–2.) If Bertha's skin has been the subject of sustained inquiry, Rochester's might also be of interest in thinking through the phenomenon of tropicalization. Certainly by the time Rochester tells Jane the story of his first marriage in order to justify his attempt to deceive her into a bigamous union, Rochester is almost a parody of British racism and xenophobia. He associates the inhabitants of the West Indies, including and especially Bertha, with all forms of the climactically charged idiom of "intemperance" – from sensuality and drunkenness, to madness and violence. Rochester seems most concerned, however, with the idea that his wife's excesses might somehow infect him. He depicts his relationship with Bertha as as a form of contamination made possible by the structure of marriage itself:

Bertha Mason . . . dragged me through all the hideous and degrading agonies which must attend a man bound to a wife at once intemperate and unchaste . . . I was rich enough now – yet poor to hideous indigence: a nature the most gross, impure, depraved I ever saw, was associated with mine and called by the law and society part of me. (III, ch. 1)

We hear, under Rochester's complaint, the drumbeat of Victorian marriage law, which assumed, as the legal scholar William Blackstone had put it, that "man and woman are one flesh and that that flesh is the man's." The age-old metonymy of husband and wife, this "association" that allows for unspecified contamination, is based on a profound investment in the meaning of flesh.

Rochester struggles to assure Jane – and perhaps himself – that his morality, his essential self, acts as a barrier across which her sins (again the agent of infection is not quite named) cannot, ultimately, pass:

Jane – I approached the verge of despair: a remnant of self-respect was all that intervened between me and the gulf. In the eyes of the world I was doubtless covered with grimy dishonor; but I resolved to be clean in my own sight – and to the last I repudiated the contamination of her crimes, and wrenched myself from connexion with her mental defects. (III, ch. 1)

In this self-justifying narrative, Rochester tries to make it clear that the "grimy dishonor" that is a result of his marriage goes only skin deep. Underneath the grime he is "clean" and, ultimately, uncontaminated.

However complex the global politics of *Jane Eyre* may prove to be, Rochester's own attitudes towards the tropics and their effect on English bodies and subjects are quite straightforward. Other novels offer more nuanced tropicalized figures. Esther Summerson's fiancé Allan Woodcourt returns to England from a tropical shipwreck with a tan that marks him as a hero; his facial transformation contrasts with Esther's as she first tries to hide and then proudly displays the smallpox scars which signify her social vulnerability – and which seem to disappear when she marries Allan. In Gaskell's *Cranford* (1851), the colonially repatriated Peter Jenkins masquerades, before a maidenly middle-aged community including his own unsuspecting sister, as the aptly named showman Signor Brunoni, and in Kipling's *Kim* (1901) an Irish-Indian boy uses his equivocal complexion to enact a variety of roles in the great game of imperial espionage.

One of the most complex renderings of tropicalization and its imperial entanglements is William Makepeace Thackeray's *Vanity Fair* (1848), whose insistently pink and white complexioned heroine, Amelia Sedley, is both idealized and satirized by the narrator. Amelia's brother Jos, a mid-level civil servant in colonial India, enters the text and his mother's home bringing with him a range of presents from India, from the shawls he gives to the women in his family to the chilis that he famously foists upon the novel's anti-heroine, Becky Sharp. Despite his proclivity for curries, Jos when in England performs the role of the Regency buck, even to the extent of wearing buckskins:

A very stout, puffy man, in buckskins and hessian boots, with several immense neckcloths that rose almost to his nose, with a red striped waistcoat and an apple green coat with steel buttons almost as large as crown pieces (it was the morning costume of a dandy or a blood of those days) was reading the paper by the fire when the two girls entered, and bounced off the arm-chair, and blushed excessively, and hid his entire face almost in his neckcloths . . . (ch. 3)

Throughout the novel, Jos will take on a series of fantasized identities, including that of a soldier at Waterloo, for which he grows an impressively military mustache. His role playing is not simply a matter of insincerity or even of individual desire, however. Moving between countries, he enacts Englishness in different ways in each of them. His famous (and famously large) buckskins are at once a hyperbolic sign of the London man about town – the skin of a hypermasculine buck – and a darkened second skin that takes us back in time and place to his long sojourns in India. Jos's blush in this paragraph – the first of many when he encounters a potentially sexualized situation – may, of course, be read as a sign of both effeminacy and Englishness, a sign that survives the yellowing of his skin: "Jos still continued a huge clattering at the poker and tongs, puffing and blowing the while, and turning as red as his yellow face would allow him" (ch. 3). Jos can blush – but only up to a point. His face is a battleground, his blush an Englishness trying to get out, even as he is an Anglo-Indian trying to get back in. The blush itself is, of course, a sign of whiteness. For Charles Darwin in *The Expression of Emotion in Man and Animals* (1873) the blush, a reliable sign of the difference between humans and animals, occupies an anxiously ambiguous position in the differentiation among races. As Mary Ann O'Farrell notes (83), Darwin is preoccupied by the visibility of the blush as an emotional token, the outward confession of an inward state; while he announces his project as exploring "all the races of mankind," he nonetheless uses the visibility of the blush against white skin as a "norm" for his discussion of shame, a culturally ubiquitous phenomenon.

In extending the blush from Jos to Amelia, and finally to Dobbin, Thackeray complicates what might easily have been read characterologically as a sign of effeminacy in Jos. In fact, throughout *Vanity Fair* no mark upon the skin belongs to a single individual. Major Dobbin not only blushes, but shares with Jos a "yellow face," which by no means precludes his being an English "gentleman":

> We all know a hundred [men] whose coats are very well made, and a score who have excellent manners . . . but of gentlemen how many? Let us take a scrap of paper and each make out his list.

> My friend the Major I write, without any doubt, in mine. He had very long legs, a yellow face, and a slight lisp, which at first was rather ridiculous. But his thoughts were just, his brains were fairly good, his life was honest and pure, and his heart was warm and humble. (ch. 62)

A sign of the ubiquitous yellow fever that in this novel sickened and killed visitors to tropical lands from Jamaica to India, the yellow face suggests both susceptibility and survivorship, the two legs of tropicalization. Amelia must learn to prefer Dobbins's yellow face to the unmarked complexion of her unworthy late husband, George, whose picture she keeps over her bed as a reminder to be faithful to his memory. In *Vanity Fair* tropical exposure and illness darken the skin of the evil, the comic, and the virtuous alike; skin ultimately resists legibility as an individual characteristic and becomes the canvas on which larger historical movements (the Napoleonic war, colonialism) are written.

The literary examples I have used to talk about hygiene and sun resist any easy alignment with a moral or ideological position. Skin – marked or unmarked, tattooed or wrinkled, yellow or red or white – becomes the occasion for thinking through complex systems of difference – and also the failure of these systems. While the blush is gendered, and signs of sun on skin are part of a racialized discourse, these marks upon the skin cannot be read as indicating a single subject position. As skin tells us, the self is permeable, always vulnerable to threats from within and without.

See also MOVING OUT, GROWING OLD, SEXUALITIES; MEDICAL; PARAPETS SHORES

REFERENCES

Agamben, G. (1998) *Homo Sacer: Sovereign Power and Bare Life*, trans. D. Heller-Roazen. Stanford: Stanford University Press.

Anzieu, D. (1989) *The Skin Ego*, trans. C. Turner. New Haven: Yale University Press.

Bakhtin, M. (1984) *Rabelais and His World*, trans. H. Iswolsky. Bloomington: Indiana University Press.

Cohen, W. A. (2009) *Embodied: Victorian Literature and the Senses*. Minneapolis: University of Minnesota Press.

Cooley, A. J. (1866) *The Toilet and Cosmetic Arts in Ancient and Modern Times*. London: n. p.

Darwin, C. (1989) *The Expression of Emotion in Man and Animals. The Works of Charles Darwin*, vol. 23, ed. F. Darwin. New York: New York University Press.

Freedgood, E. (2006) *The Ideas in Things: Fugitive Meaning in the Victorian Novel*. Chicago: University of Chicago Press.

Heath, K. (2009) *Aging by the Book: The Emergence of Midlife in Victorian Britain*. Albany: State University of New York Press.

Johnson, R. (2008) "European Cloth and Tropical Skin: Clothing Material and British Ideas of Health and Hygiene in Tropical Climates." *Bulletin of the History of Medicine* 83, 530–60.

Montez, L. (1969) *The Arts and Secrets of Beauty with Hints to Gentlemen on the Art of Fascinating*. New York: Chelsea House.

Nightingale, F. (1969) *Notes on Nursing: What it is and What it is Not*. New York: Dover.

O'Farrell, M. A. (1997) *Telling Complexions: The Nineteenth-Century British Novel and the Blush*. Durham: Duke University Press.

Stallybrass, P., and A. White (1986) *The Politics and Poetics of Transgression*. Ithaca: Cornell University Press.

Thomas, S. (1999) "The Tropical Extravagance of Bertha Mason." *Victorian Literature and Culture* 27, 1–17.

Trollope, A. (1861; 1981) "The Banks of the Jordan." In *Complete Short Stories*, ed. B. J. S. Breyer. Fort Worth: Texas Christian University Press.

FURTHER READING

Aravamudan, S. (1999) *Tropicopolitans: Colonialism and Agency 1688–1804*. Durham: Duke University Press.

Benthien, C. (2002) *Skin: On the Cultural Border Between Self and World*, trans. T. Dunlap. New York: Columbia University Press.

Delgado, R., and J. Stefanic (eds) (1997) *Critical White Studies: Looking Behind the Mirror*. Philadelphia: Temple University Press.

Fanon, F. (1952; 2008) *Black Skin, White Masks*, trans. R. Philcox. New York: Grove Press.

Montagu, A. (1978) *Touching: The Human Significance of Skin*. New York: Harper and Row.

Penner, L. (2010) *Victorian Medicine and Social Reform: Florence Nightingale Among the Novelists*. New York: Palgrave Macmillan.

Poovey, M. (1995) *Making a Social Body: British Cultural Formation 1830–1864*. Chicago: University of Chicago Press.

Rylance, R. (2004) "Convex and Concave: Conceptual Boundaries in Psychology, Now and Then (But Mainly Then)." *Victorian Literature and Culture* 32, 449–62.

Spivak, G. C. (1985) "Three Women's Texts and a Critique of Imperialism." *Critical Inquiry* 12, 243–61.

30

On the Parapets of Privacy

Karen Chase and Michael Levenson

I

In the final movements of *Our Mutual Friend* (1865), Dickens at last bestows his reward upon John and Bella Harmon. Accepting the rich inheritance of his cruel father, John carries his astonished wife out of their modest cottage in Blackheath and leads her north and west through London, until they enter the stately precincts of urban privilege, where they arrive at a large townhouse that the reader has known as the "eminently aristocratic family mansion." The building has most recently belonged to the Boffins, the old Harmon servants, who are deferentially prepared to surrender both it and its accompanying fortune, but it has entered the novel as the special claim of the corrupt street-vendor Silas Wegg. As Wegg sits at his stall on the public thoroughfare, he gazes possessively on the walls of the building he has never entered, "our house": "It was a great dingy house with a quantity of dim side window and blank back premises." Of its inhabitants we know nothing, confined as we are to Wegg's fantasies projected on the concealed domain and yielding a hypothetical family with "names of his own invention": Miss Elizabeth, Master George, Aunt Jane, Uncle Parker (book 1, ch. 5). In the punishing critique of Wegg the domestic fantasist, close cousin to Wegg the blackmailer, Dickens enforces the power of the wall to act as the shroud of privacy. Here is a barrier resistant to the intrusions of a cunning predator, a wall strong enough, blank enough, to condemn the enemy to harmless dreams of an unseen interior – and what kind of wall is that?

A New Companion to Victorian Literature and Culture, First Edition. Edited by Herbert F. Tucker.
© 2014 John Wiley & Sons, Ltd. Published 2014 by John Wiley & Sons, Ltd.

Identified as "a corner house not far from Cavendish Square," the house falls within London's great northwestern expanse of Georgian architecture, the stout, persistent legacy of a century whose values could be abandoned more quickly than its buildings. The square-edged townhouse, with its unrepentant uniformity, its brick in neutral tones of grey or brown, and its façade adorned by nothing more than the repetitive pattern of rectangular windows, was for Dickens, as for many of his contemporaries, an architectural vacancy signifying the death of sensibility. The dully staring house was the close counterpart of a dully staring bourgeois respectability. The Georgian brick front was the stolid face of a cold privilege.

When Bella Harmon (née Wilfer) finally crosses the threshold of the aristocratic mansion, the novel penetrates the dull wall to find a living core. What the street-seller could only desperately imagine is now rendered as a vivid domestic phantasmagoria, replete with ormolu clock, ivory casket, a nursery, and even an aviary with tropical birds flying above "gold and silver fish, and mosses, and water-lilies, and a fountain, and all manner of wonders" (book 4, ch. 12). This figure of the pleasure garden behind impassive walls stands as one luminous icon of mid-century domestic desire. By the time John Harmon is finished with refurbishment, the old dingy mansion has become a "dainty house," as if to enforce the essential topographical truth: that even the unprepossessing Georgian façade can be redeemed by a household visionary (book 4, ch. 14). The fish, the birds, and the fountain create the comic extravagance of a domestic carnival, but Dickens knows himself to be pursuing an excess resident within the emergent norm. That even grim walls can contain a dainty interior – this is the first principle of Victorian domestic ambition in a gray climate.

We begin, then, by fully acknowledging the social force of the wall that divides street and house, that conceals and inspires the invention of a household universe, and that stirs the fantasies of those locked outside in physical and social separation. The story of Victorian domestic discourse is to a considerable degree a tale of moving walls, but at its start there emanates the allure of the immovable barrier that separates privilege from dispossession, and privacy from public life. The Census of 1851 enunci-ates the norm (and ideal) of the bounded household, which achieves "the exclusive command of the entrance-hall and stairs – and the possession of the free space between the ground and sky" (xxxvii). The wall is what converts free space into a series of domestic parcels, and while it stands within a complex array of social meanings – legal, economic, symbolic – it also stands as a conspicuous physical object, which signifies only through its heavy materiality.

The brick simplicity of the Georgian façade encourages an image of a flat plane marking the barrier between two realms, a plane appearing both solid and eerily sheer. One instant you are in the social domain, theater of visibility; in the next, you turn a key, or the butler opens a latch, and you discover the blanket of intimacy. Indeed, it may well have been the sense of flush proximity between the Georgian house wall and the neighboring street that incited a more aggressive flourishing of the household edge. When John Nash undertook his triumphalist urban renovation

for the Prince Regent, he lavished stucco on the palatial park terraces built for gran-
dees. After the dull brick of the previous century, the creamy paste not only
brightened the colors of the city, but it also invited a lordly elaboration of the
forward wall of home. Given the infamous malleability of stucco, which could be
smoothly molded atop a coarse underpinning, proud aristocrats, prosperous merchants, and successful professionals were able to adorn their homes with columns,
pediments, and window treatments, converting the front of the townhouse into a
commanding declaration of privilege.

   The mid-Victorians would come to revile the "fakery" of the material, which concealed the "truth" of structure beneath the pretense of classical dignity. And yet there
could be no turning back to the plainness of the Georgian surface. When the Queen
Anne style emerged so successfully in the second half of the century, it replaced the
creamy building paste with its own eager vision of a prosperous façade: red brick,
sash windows, prominent gables, and high chimneys. For all their stylistic differences, what Queen Anne shared with Nash's stucco was an ambitious construal of
household physiognomy, a refusal of gray brick blandness in favor of the assertions
of an articulate wall. The color and the ornament were one indication of house pride,
but the most conspicuous sign was the brazenly protruding doorway, extended
through muscular columns or, as the century wore on, through elaborate glass
awnings, stretching toward public space as if they were the advance guard of a militant domesticity. This elaboration of the house front, not only as a single proprietorial
wall but as one in a commanding line along the street, represents the material precipitate of a social victory: the extension of privilege from aristocracy and gentry to
the middle classes. In a district such as Cubitt's Belgravia, old and new types of
family distinction met and mingled, and in the high-shouldered presentation of their
robust façades they announced, even as they securely hid, the existence of pleasures
out of sight.

II

Kept outside though he is, Dickens's Wegg manages to pitch his stall "over against"
the wall of the town mansion, resembling "a leech on the house that had 'taken'
wonderfully" (book 1, ch. 5). When the Harmons assume residence and when
Wegg's schemes are fully exposed, he is told never to come outside the windows
again – as if possession of the house brought control wherever the wall cast its
shadow – and then in a last indignity he is flung into a scavenger's cart that happens
to be standing on the corner. The novel conducts this entire sequence in vengeful
tones representing the standpoint of the wealthy middle-class householder, and yet
through all its harsh presentation of the rights of domestic privacy, it continually
acknowledges the tumult just beyond the brick curtain. There are Wegg at his stall
and the scavenger at his cart, two figures standing for the ceaseless parade through
the public thoroughfare. "Uproar" is Dickens's chosen epithet, and as the work of

Henry Mayhew had shown those who had been too blind to see, the streets outside the home were swarming with the poor, the plaintive, the insistent, the cagy. To cross the threshold and to enter the street was typically to meet not only the street-seller in a stall, but also the crossing-sweeper eager to clear the way of mud and horse droppings, the groom tending the carriage, and the inevitable mob of boys. "Leech" is the cruel name that nevertheless evokes the social life on the threshold between home and street, where privilege draws the veil, while dispossession wails and waits.

Even behind the stucco and the brick, the cozy home could not run on sensibility alone. Keeping the poorer classes outside the door was one consuming task in the ceaseless negotiation between private and public life, but another was the hiring of workers to enter the house and to maintain its composure and distinction. The realms of Home and Street must be seen as two great systems, linked topographically as well as socially, whose complexity lies not only in their opposition but in their mutual dependency – the anxiety of the well-to-do to repel the indigent but also to choose carefully among them, in order to assemble the corps of servants within, who will become allies against the petitioners seen through the window.

The question of walled protection changes its aspect when the question is no longer how to construct an imposing barrier against the roaring streets, but how to arrange a pattern of rooms, corridors, and staircases in order to manage those household workers, who confuse the boundary between inner and outer. To keep servants was the surest mark of ascendancy into the respectable orders, families being ranked according to the number they kept, but in the very act by which the newly genteel classes ratified their triumph in the social arena, they were obliged to puzzle deeply over how to maintain distance from those brought so close. The great discourse of domestic management was at its heart a discourse of suspicion. The hapless maid, the incompetent groom, and the feeble governess were all irresistible subjects in popular journals and household manuals, but the center of fascination and fear was the actively malignant servant, the one who exploited the chances of propinquity, waiting for the right moment to steal the plate or to betray the family secret. Even when no foul deed is committed, there remains a foulness in knowledge alone. "Remember this, husbands, and wives, fathers and sons, mothers and daughters, brothers and sisters," warns Mary Elizabeth Braddon,

> Nothing that is done in the parlour is lost upon these quiet, well-behaved watchers from the kitchen. They laugh at you; nay, worse, they pity you. They discuss your affairs, and make out your income, and settle what you can afford to do and what you can't afford to do; they prearrange the disposal of your wife's fortune, and look prophetically forward to the day when you will avail yourself of the advantages of the Bankruptcy Act. (I, 149)

In the bewildering choreography of inside and outside, the servants represent the intrusion of the street into the deep recesses of home privacy, and the family that has drawn sharp lines between the household interior and the turbulent world must now turn to defend itself from outsiders in its midst.

The spatial response to the social disturbance was to build a universe of interior walls, a matrix of divisions that would not only protect against the invasions of servants but would allow domestic life to become a strenuous exercise in the articulation of human experience. As the "respectable" household assimilated the contrivances of industrial modernity, it became a scale model of the Victorian economy, dividing between the producers and consumers of domestic pleasure. At the rear and down below, the servants operated the machinery of "convenience," while the family enjoyed the passive virtues of "comfort." The spirit of manufacture, from which the gentleman's house was to be a refuge, entered the house in a disciplined squad of modern domestics whose role was to protect home life from the very disruptions which they exemplified.

The success of this complex operation required a rigorous architectural logic. According to Robert Kerr's influential formulation of 1864: whatever the size of the house, "Let the family have free passageway without encountering the servants unexpectedly; and let the servants have access to all their duties without coming unexpectedly upon the family and visitors" (1871: 68). The family must never catch sight of the scullery and the kitchen; the outer walks must be kept free from the servants' view. The starkness of this arrangement accords with the "foremost of all maxims," namely "that what passes on either side of the boundary shall be both invisible and inaudible on the other" (67). In the hands of a zealous architect and a wealthy client, walls could become the instruments of a radical differentiation within which forms of household pleasure and responsibility were framed in separate zones. Within grand Victorian architecture, "each territory was subdivided according to the activities that went on in it; this analysis of activities became more and more exact, and more and more activities were given a separate room" (Girouard 28). This describes the disposition of the country house, and nothing is plainer than that the general aspiration for the fully articulated house could only be fulfilled in the opulent houses of the wealthiest Britons. In the mid-sixties Kerr began designing Bear Wood for the owner of *The Times*, John Walter III. With its many scores of rooms (100 for the family, 97 for the servants) – including a gun-room, two beer-cellars, a schoolroom, an odd-room – it easily achieves that elaborate articulation of classes, sexes, generations, functions, and pleasures which is so widely accepted as a fundamental value, at once moral and architectural. A house such as Bear Wood is its own walled city, its own civil society.

At the end of his highly successful book *The English Gentleman's House*, which won him Walter's commission, Kerr includes a "table of accommodation," showing how walls and wealth moved in near-perfect synchrony. Forty thousand pounds will buy the discriminating topography of Bear Wood, but at ten thousand pounds one surrenders the gun-room; at five thousand pounds the billiard room vanishes; at twenty-five hundred, the morning room is relinquished; and at one thousand two hundred fifty pounds, the "very modest" bottom of Kerr's scale, both family and servants must make do with thirteen rooms each. At each lower rung in the ladder of gentility, the risk grows that children will be heard, servants will be seen, and privacy will be rudely assailed. The question, of course, is what will happen if one goes still further down Kerr's scale, if one carries through the logic of graphs and charts and diagrams, passing beneath the arbitrary limit of a thousand pounds to confront the hard-pressed circumstances in which most people lived? The book's silent and complacent assumption is that the downward movement of income will ultimately obliterate the articulation of household space, leaving a poor family to inhabit a home where walls disappear and distinctions perish.

Astonishingly, Kerr would soon go on to draw this brazen conclusion in public. During a series of meetings of the Royal Institute of British Architects (1866–7), he proposed what he called the "one-room solution." Given the dangerous housing crisis in the great cities, the only "unsentimental" and "professional" conclusion, he tells his colleagues, is to give the poor what they are willing to pay for and what speculative builders are willing to construct. He asserts that there are "degrees of delicacy" (Kerr 1866–7: 42), that the poor are not like the privileged, and the very poor are not like the poor. "Simple folk" require "simple dwellings," and to the charge that he advocates "pigging together in one room" (61–2), Kerr shruggingly replies that as professional men wanting to look reality in the face, they must accept "the expediency of keeping to the very lowest standard" (80).

A familiar distinction runs all through the conversation of these professional men at mid-century, the separation of the surging mass of the desperately poor from the "respectable" working classes, who keep their front doors closed, who keep their children off the street, and who live in whole floors rather than in single rooms. In fact, the more successful artisans now occupied individual terrace houses, modest versions of the middle-class norm, built along modest streets. The working-class ascent from room to floor to house seemed a validating arc of progress, the reassuring sign of assimilation to governing conventions of family privacy. But the success of an artisan elite only made the spectacle of mass failure more vivid.

III

Among those who held social power and the power of discourse, it was an article of complacent faith that the millions of poor who streamed through the cities had failed to comprehend the resources of the Wall. They were radically external creatures, whose exposure to open space, especially open urban space, deprived them of the indispensable pedagogy of home. In his exhaustive study of urban poverty, Henry Mayhew at once discovered a counter-world and confirmed a prejudice. The costermongers who hawked their wares in the street were "the Nomades of England, neither knowing nor caring for the enjoyments of home. The hearth, which is so sacred a symbol to all civilized races as being the spot where the virtues of each succeeding generation are taught and encouraged, has no charms to them" (43). The young girl who lives in the streets will resist the attempts to reclaim her; she suffers from a "muscular irritability" that "makes her unable to rest for any time in one place" (44). The poor appear as a great fluid or current, seeping past foundations and enclosures, enduring and then enjoying an escape from the boundedness so central to the prevailing definitions of home. As George Godwin tersely put it in *London Shadows*, "the health and morals of the people are regulated by their dwellings" (10). The loss of the physical delimitations of the house incited a release of mobile appetite and rootless passion. Poverty was in its essence an anti-domesticity.

Nevertheless, there remains an undercurrent within the new ethnographic journalism that suggests another way of construing the unwalled poor. In Mayhew himself, for all the reiterated emphasis on the savage repudiation of home, one finds a fascinated attention to the persistence of family life. Under the most appalling conditions of deprivation, parents and children cling together as micro-economies, contrived to eke out subsistence. He notes that children "are sent out by their parents in the evening to sell nuts, oranges, &c" (24); he praises those loyal girls without whose help the family would be sent to the workhouse; and in a summative mood he notes, "When, as is the case with many of the costermongers, and with the Irish fruit-sellers, the parents and children follow the same calling, they form one household, and work, as it were, 'into one another's hands'" (479). Mayhew is silent on the apparent contradiction between the refusal of home and the persistence of these intimate ties, but his own evidence suggests the need for a sharp conceptual distinction between "domesticity" and "family." The poor may live on the streets without the protections and solicitations of the cozy middle-class fireside; they may prefer the beer-shop or the penny gaff, warmed by the presence of many other bodies, to the damp of a bare room. But it is clear that forms of familial webbing remain decisive for many of Mayhew's poor, who must be understood as anti-domestic families, families without walls.

If so many Victorian opinion-makers refused to see family life on the uproarious streets, this must surely be due to the unchallenged assumption that the definition of a family was architectural as well as biological. Thus, the Registrar General of the Census intones that "It is so much in the order of nature that a family should live in a separate house, that 'house' is often used for family in many languages; and this isolation of families, in separate houses, it has been asserted, is carried to a greater extent in England than it is elsewhere" (*Census* xxxv). The very idea of a houseless family comes to appear a methodological anomaly and a national disgrace. If the poor move in hordes through the streets, it must be because the precious vessel has broken, spilling privacy into the public ways, where it can only wither and rot. The failure of the poor to enact the "isolation of families" is what brands them as savages.

But the challenge to walled isolation came not merely from the long day's swarming through the streets in search of a small sale, an odd job, or a wily cadging. The poor slept somewhere. At the point of exhaustion they too sought walls and a roof. Commonly, however, the architecture of poverty was not the self-contained house, but the corner of a room within a house in a court. Growing at such an extraordinary rate through the nineteenth century, the cities of Britain were ill-prepared to absorb their vast numbers. Old family houses were broken up into separate lodgings; new buildings crouched behind old buildings. The effect of the filling of rooms and the infilling of space was to create diverse systems of infamous courts, with hundreds of families squeezed together, facing one another across a narrow lane. "As by a fatal attraction," observes Thomas Beames, "opposite houses grow together at the top, seem to nod against one another, conspiring to shut out the little air which would pierce through for the relief of those beneath" (2–3). In Scotland and the north of England a familiar pattern was the arrangement of working-class housing into the notorious back-to-backs: two contiguous, parallel ranks sharing rear walls. Except at the end of rows each house would thus have common partitions with three others, leaving only the front exposed to any light and air; the walls were sometimes just a half-brick (4½ inches) thick; and to increase the density, the double rows would be matched with others, so that the one open side would face onto a narrow court (Burnett 67). In 1847 the *Quarterly Review* recounted the paradigmatic narrative of a young person arriving in London, who is directed to Duck Lane, St Giles's, Saffron Hill, Spitalfields, or Whitechapel, and then obliged to pass "through tight avenues of glittering fish and rotten vegetables, with doorways or alleys gaping on either side – which, if they be not choked with squalid garments or sickly children, lead the eye through an almost interminable vista of filth and distress" (144). The rookeries of the major cities were the moral and social counterparts to the great country mansions; in their most sprawling and intricate arrangements, they became a monstrous inversion of the fortified castle.

Inside this new system of walls, then, is a second, more deeply disturbing, provocation of the poor. If on the one hand they affront the norms of enclosed domesticity by coursing so visibly through the streets or attaching themselves like leeches to the façades of respectable homes, they are all the more offensive when they recede from view behind walls of their own. Godwin remarks that "If there were no courts and blind alleys, there would be less immorality and physical suffering. The means of escaping from public view which they afford, generate evil habits" (10). The relevant enclosure is not the individual household, providing that "exclusive command" of family space; it is rather the widely encompassing public barrier that surrounds the inhuman density of bodies and stirs images of a den, a nest, or a lair.

Within the pervasive decay of these wandering mazes there were special nodes of degradation, the lodging houses of the great cities, temporary dwellings for masses of the poor, who would fall together in the ill-tended rooms, crowded, filthy, verminous. Mayhew made the lodging houses a focus for his outrage and sorrow, and in parliamentary debates of 1851 Lord Ashley, soon to be the Earl of Shaftesbury, compelled the other honorable gentlemen in the room to listen to tales of horror. Ashley's premise was that "nothing produced so evil an effect upon the sanitary conditions of the population as overcrowding within limited spaces; and if people were in a low sanitary condition, it was absolutely impossible to raise them to a just moral elevation" (*Hansard*, cols 1259–60). From this high-minded principle he moved to chilling exposé, quoting the town clerk of Morpeth, who had described lodging houses that have no beds,

> but their occupiers are packed upon the floor, in rows, the head of one being close to the feet of another. Each body is placed so close to its neighbour as not to leave sufficient space upon which to set a foot. The occupants are entirely naked, except for rugs drawn up as far as the waist; and when to this is added that the doors and windows are carefully closed, and that there is not the least distinction of sex, but men, women, and children lie indiscriminately side by side, some faint idea may be formed of the state of these places, and their effect upon health, morals, and decency. (*Hansard*, col. 1263)

Such tales became almost routine at mid-century, leading to the passage of two Acts sponsored by Ashley in 1851 – the Common Lodging Houses Act and the Labouring Classes Lodging Houses Act – the first direct legislation on the problem of working-class housing.

According to the first of the two Acts, the Commissioner of Police must register lodging houses and must ensure the "well ordering" of the building and "the separation of the sexes therein." This requirement involved the ongoing inspection of the houses, an institutional resolve not fully appreciated by the targets of benevolence. For if, from the standpoint of privileged respectability, the courts and their lodging-houses were little more than "fever factories," from the perspective of inhabitants they were living communities vulnerable not only to fever but to the assaults of the authorities. Philanthropists who built model houses – cleaner, better equipped, fully supervised, and with higher rents – failed to grasp why their bounty was often refused, not recognizing that the greater cost was aggravated by the psychic burden of moral surveillance. Despite being a harsh critic of the moral degradation of court life, Mayhew discloses much evidence of the social formations created by these forcing-houses of collectivity. He records the case of a boy who had kicked at a policeman during a scuffle, noting that "The whole of the court where the lad resided, sympathized with the boy" (16). A young coster tells him that "all as lives in a court is neighbours" (40), and frequently one hears of the daily social ceremonies in the shared space between the clustered rooms: the gathering of men and women at the mouth of the alley, where they meet for a chat and a smoke. The physical arrangement of the court – the simple undifferentiated rooms so close beside one another, the narrow alley, and the common use of privies and water supply – brought about a "sharing of facilities in the private domain, a cellular quality of space in the public domain, and a threshold between public and private which was ambiguous and permeable" (Daunton 202). Within such a social topography the most decisive walls were the outer boundaries of the court, penetrated by a narrow entrance which opened into a world where meager accommodation (including the flimsy party walls) created a common life almost unimaginable to those of any substantial means.

IV

Indeed, insofar as respectable imagination gave itself to pictures of life behind the court walls, these were almost always pictures of foul blight, urgently demanding inspection if not eradication. In one of the most significant urban reconstructions of the first half of the century, the cutting of New Oxford Street broke up some of the most notorious rookeries of St Giles's. Hailed as a triumphant gesture of public hygiene, such engineering was also a defeat for social solidarity in hard-pressed conditions, for the effect of the sustained clearance was to redraw the relationship of private and public spheres, repudiating the rich ambiguity in favor of a stern differentiation between the determinate dwelling and the mere "connective tissue" of the street. The political result "was to 'open up' the city in order to make it visible for inspection" (Daunton 204). In fact, all through the century the cutting of new streets was as much an exercise in social engineering as a development in the lines of transport. When John Nash undertook the massive renovation of London, he saw the course of the triumphal Regent's Street as an opportunity to divide luxury from need: "my purpose was, that the new street should cross the Eastern Entrance to all the streets occupied by the higher classes, and to leave out to the East all those bad streets" (Crook 90). As with other such projects through the century, the street was at once a thoroughfare and a wall, a means of facilitating movement along its length, but also obstructing once easy movement across its width.

Still, no matter how wide the boulevard, how imposing the stucco or brick façade, how well-managed the servants, there persisted conspicuous signs of anxiety that the fortress of home remained vulnerable. In the early 1860s a great furor erupted on the subject of street music. The Italian organ-grinder became a figure of violent loathing for a large section of the professional middle-class, which defined its seriousness and its status in opposition to the tumult outside the window. Spurred by the anger of such luminaries as Dickens, Tennyson, and Charles Babbage, the parliamentarian Michael Bass took up the cause. He edited a volume of documents called *Street Music in the Metropolis*, at the center of which were the splenetic outcries of a cultural elite that saw the constant distractions in the thoroughfare as dangerously corrosive, putting physical health and intellectual vocation at serious risk. Here is one sign of the pathos of the household wall: no matter how impenetrable to the petitioning "leeches," it would always be vulnerable to sound (Picker 41–81). Ironically, the repeal of the window tax in 1851 had created a boom in the production of glass and had led to a brightening of the street wall with larger-paned windows, but this architectural improvement only exposed the home-dwellers more directly to the uproar on the street. The passage of Bass's Act made it easier to seek legal remedies from such noisemakers, but as long as the cities of Britain continued their steep growth in population and throbbed with the clamor of industry, no parliamentary act could ensure velvet domestic serenity.

Most frightening were the outbreaks of cholera in the middle decades of the century, especially the wave of illness in 1854, which in its attack on the parish of St James destroyed the comforting mythology of the immunities of wealth (Gilbert 36). The growing public health movement, ratified by the example of Florence Nightingale, was able to compel recognition of environmental threats to the integrity of home. Attention to domestic hygiene cannot stop at the threshold, because toxic vapors and foul air respect no laws of property; the hazards of inadequate drainage, open sewers, and exposed dung heaps can creep beneath the thickest walls; and there can be no healthy house in a diseased neighborhood.

Was there to be no peace anywhere for the triumphant middle classes? The aristocrats, the great gentry, and the barons of industry could enjoy the sanctuary of their country houses, perfectly intact at the end of long rural roads. Tennyson's *The Princess* (1847), in its rendering of the obedient multitudes permitted to spend a rare afternoon on the aristocratic green of Vivian-place, displays the easy governance of space enjoyed in the great country mansions. Their walls were as close to inviolable as the castles they imitated. But for the middle classes, who were growing in wealth and numbers – where might they hear the birds sing without the din of urbanism? The answer, of course, was in the suburbs. Beginning after the Napoleonic Wars and consolidating in the middle decades of the century, suburbanization offered a radical solution to the struggle between private and public domains. On the one hand, it allowed for the construction of a still more self-enclosed household space, either in the form of semi-detached or fully detached villas, which broke out of the linear patterns of urban terraced housing and offered the promise of walls surrounded on at least three sides by the pleasures of a garden. On the other hand, it secured a physical distance, becoming ever greater as railways confirmed the suburban boom, between the garden villa and urban pandemonium. In significant respects, the household wall was now stretched as wide as the train journey into the city.

V

Merely to watch the transformation of walls through the nineteenth century – the turn from Georgian gray and brown to creamy stucco and then Queen Anne's red brick, the internal partition into rooms and compartments, the infilling of urban space and the development of the maze of courts, the cutting of streets through that same offending maze, the march of walls into the green fields on the edge of town – is to follow a mobile topographical narrative, in which space is continually carved and molded, closed and opened. Then to restore people to the architectural scene is to recover a social drama of movement and barriers. In broad terms, the century of walls was a long disentangling of social mixtures. Architects devised ways to partition the house into male and female domains and to keep the family from its servants; city planners drove streets through the inner mysteries of poverty; building speculators developed suburban estates. As prosperous commercial magnates joined the world of the country house, many middle-class professionals rode the trains to the suburbs. The most fortunate of working-class families reached the dignity of terrace houses, but rising rents meant that the poorest were obliged to give up two or three rooms in order to test the awful efficacy of Robert Kerr's one-room solution.

From one perspective, then, the disposition of walls achieves the sharp clarity of articulated social space: the wealthy in the country, the middle classes in the suburbs, the artisans in their terraces, and the poor squeezed into their single rooms. But apart from those who enjoyed the astonishing privileges of the country house, the ordering of the social strata was an impure process, forever caught in forms of spatial snarl. The large urban centers continued to grow, and though many members of the middle class left on the suburban trains, others rose to take their place within the cities and found the same challenges to the life of household privacy. The movement of the laboring poor from courts and cellars into terraces was made unsteady by precarious economic conditions, so that any proudly rented house could break apart into the divisions of subletting: first a floor, then a room, then a corner of a room. Even for those seeking to make the suburbs their wall, history had ironies in store. What appeared in one decade as the safe distance from the vortex of the street was likely in the next to have been absorbed by the ooze of urbanism. Then, too, over-ambitious building speculators often had to lower the price on untenanted houses, giving the middle-class arrivals the surprise of working-class neighbors (Thompson 179).

The dream of impenetrable walls was the dream of an orderly society, tidily distributed according to function and fortune. No doubt for some – especially those wealthy few immured in rural settings – it must have seemed that the street was permanently distant and that the infolding of private virtue had been triumphantly achieved. And yet an abiding feature of the middle-class desire for enclosure, so widely embraced by other classes, is that after the scream of the railway, the spread of infectious disease, or the news of a violent crime, the act of self-containment must begin again. A house remains an object in social space, inevitably exposed to the winds of public life, and walls designed to keep inside and outside apart only sealed them in intimate antagonism.

See also 1851; Growing Up, Moving Out, Sexualities; Medical, Industrial; Skin

References

Anon. (1847) "Lodging-Houses." *Quarterly Review* 82, December.

Bass, M. (1864) *Street Music in the Metropolis*. London: John Murray.

Beames, T. (1852) *Rookeries of London: Past, Present, and Prospective*. London: T. Bosworth.

Braddon, M. E. (1863) *Aurora Floyd*, 3 vols. London: Timbley Bros.

Burnett, J. (1986) *A Social History of Housing, 1815–1985*, 2nd edn. London: Methuen.

Census of Great Britain, 1851 (1854) London: Longman, Brown, Green & Longmans.

Crook, J. M. (1992) "Metropolitan Improvements: John Nash and the Picturesque." In *London: World City, 1800–1840*, ed. C. Fox. New Haven: Yale University Press.

Daunton, M. J. (1990) "Housing." In *The Cambridge Social History of Britain, 1750–1950*, ed. F. M. L. Thompson, vol. 2. Cambridge: Cambridge University Press.

Gilbert, P. (2008) *Cholera and Nation*. New York: State University of New York Press.

Girouard, M. (1979) *The Victorian Country House*. New Haven: Yale University Press.

Godwin, G. (1854) *London Shadows: A Glance at the "Homes" of the Thousands*. London: G. Routledge.

Hansard's Parliamentary Debates.

Kerr, R. (1866–7) "On the Problem of Providing Dwellings for the Poor." *RIBA Proceedings* 17, 37–80.

——(1871) *The English Gentleman's House*, 3rd edn. London: John Murray.

Mayhew, H. (1861) *London Labour and the London Poor*, vol. 1. London: Griffin, Bohn.

Picker, J. (2003) *Victorian Soundscapes*. New York: Oxford University Press.

Thompson, F. M. L. (1993) "The Rise of Suburbia." In *The Victorian City: A Reader in British Urban History, 1820–1914*, ed. R. J. Morris and R. Rodger. London: Longman.

FURTHER READING

Ackroyd, P. (2000) *London: The Biography*. London: Chatto and Windus.

Arnold, D. (2005) *Rural Urbanism: London Landscapes in the Early Nineteenth Century*. Manchester: Manchester University Press.

Cierrad, I. (1999) *At Home: An Anthropology of Domestic Space*. Syracuse: Syracuse University Press.

Daunton, M. J. (1983) *House and Home in the Victorian City: Working-Class Housing 1850–1914*. London: Edward Arnold.

Dyos, H. J., and M. Wolff (eds) (1973) *The Victorian City: Images and Realities*, 2 vols. London: Routledge and Kegan Paul.

Koven, S. (2004) *Slumming: Sexual and Social Politics in Victorian London*. Princeton: Princeton University Press.

Jones, G. S. (1971) *Outcast London: A Study in the Relationship between Classes in Victorian Society*. Oxford: Clarendon Press.

McLaughlin, J. (2000) *Writing the Urban Jungle: Reading Empire in London from Doyle to Eliot*. Charlottesville and London: University of Virginia Press.

Mooney, G. (2009) "Diagnostic Spaces: Workhouse, Hospital and Home in Mid-Victorian London." *Social Science History* 33, 357–90.

Nead, L. (2000) *Victorian Babylon: People, Streets and Images in Nineteenth-Century London*. New Haven: Yale University Press.

Nord, D. (1995) *Walking the Victorian Streets: Women, Representation, and the City*. Ithaca: Cornell University Press.

Olsen, D. J. (1976) *The Growth of Victorian London*. London: B. T. Batsford.

Picard, L. (2005) *Victorian London: The Tale of a City, 1840–1870*. New York: St Martin's Press.

Tarn, J. (1973) *Five Per Cent Philanthropy: An Account of Housing in Urban Areas Between 1840 and 1914*. London: Cambridge University Press.

Walkowitz, J. R. (1992) *The City of Dreadful Delight: Narratives of Sexual Danger in Late-Victorian London*. London: Virago.

Winter, J. (1993) *London's Teeming Streets: 1830–1914*. New York: Routledge.

31

"Then on the Shore of this Wide World": The Victorian Nation and its Others

James Buzard

As if Victorian Britain did indeed enjoy the divine favor often claimed for it, clouds gave way to sunshine on the morning of May 1, 1851, just in time for Prince Albert, husband of the Queen, to open the Great Exhibition of the Works of Industry of All Nations at the so-called Crystal Palace in Hyde Park. Historians have tended to regard this event, as did mainstream organs of opinion at the time, not merely as the Prince's greatest achievement, but also as a summation or crystallization of the forces defining the Victorian age. All the peoples of the world – theoretically – were summoned to contribute their finest industrial and artistic products, their raw materials and crafted curiosities, to one grand display hosted by the indisputable leader in technological progress and commercial expansion, Great Britain. A spirit of peaceful competition was to prevail, marking the end of the turbulent 1840s, that decade during which economic crises and radical politics had rocked traditional regimes across Europe and, less dramatically but still disconcertingly, had called into question some certitudes of modern British society. One important aspect of the Exhibition was its determined appeal to the British working classes to come to London to see for themselves the scope and grandeur of the industries in which they played their part. The vista was to instill in them a greater sense of identification with the firms employing them, as well as with the nation those firms "represented" at the Exhibition. Proclaiming the "Hungry Forties" to be over, the Exhibition also encouraged much grander imaginings, seeming to herald the end to all international bellicosity and bloodshed: a prospering British subject of 1851 might be excused for taking the attitude which

A New Companion to Victorian Literature and Culture, First Edition. Edited by Herbert F. Tucker.
© 2014 John Wiley & Sons, Ltd. Published 2014 by John Wiley & Sons, Ltd.

one historian has labeled "Utopia Around the Corner" (Dodds 443–81). The transparency of the Crystal Palace itself – Joseph Paxton's glorified greenhouse – might have seemed a metaphor for the obstructionless free trade that would guarantee this new era of peace.

The sociocultural ramifications of the Great Exhibition are rich and diverse indeed. Of greatest concern here is the way the mid-Victorian extravaganza served as the vehicle for all sorts of questions, anxieties, and compensating ideas about the status and fate of the British nation. To judge by the promotional rhetoric, of course, there was little to question or be anxious about, and no need to compensate. The *Morning Chronicle* greeted the first of May by declaiming, "Now, punctual to the month and the day, the vast work is complete in all its noble symmetry. It is probable that no other people in the world could have achieved such a marvel of constructive skill within so brief a period. It is to our wonderful industrial discipline – our consummately arranged organisation of toil, and our habit of division of labour – that we owe all the triumph" (ffrench 186). In its enthusiasm, the newspaper had forgotten what the Archbishop of Canterbury tried to introduce into his benediction on the event: that Britain reigned supreme "not because of works of righteousness which we have done" but because God had mercifully chosen it to lead the world toward the light of reason and the free market. Still, however much it recommended Christian humility, the Archbishop's was plainly "the prayer of a successful people" (ffrench 190) whose empire, the largest in history, was shortly to grow even bigger.

What was there for such a people to be anxious about? Living up to its image, perhaps. In allotting display space to its guest-nations – and in reserving half of the space for itself – Britain tacitly claimed the right of the supreme industrial power to define each nation's place, in relation to its own, in the hierarchy of civilization. By "rhetorically positioning [itself] amidst the opposed examples furnished by rival countries," Britain aimed to produce an impression of a collective mental orderliness and rationality not to be matched by other peoples (Miller 72). Yet this national self-representation was in fact rather a makeshift affair, requiring to be propped up and spared excessive scrutiny. The history of the exhibition's planning stages is one, not of confident mastery or "noble symmetry," but rather of energetic, often frantic improvisation and compromise. Confident British supremacy was at least challenged by the fact that the "philosophical" system for classifying entries needed seemingly endless tinkering, and never satisfied everybody. The very success of the exhibition planners in securing many kinds of materials from many, if not all, of the world's countries put a severe strain upon the image Britain projected to the world and to itself: if the "system" for arranging all these things looked less like a confident deductive embrace of variety than like a patched-together set of expedients for not drowning in multiplicity, what would become of the image of Britain as the world's preeminent seat of rationality and organization?

What is more, the influx of goods was to be followed by a tidal wave of visitors to London, from elsewhere in Britain and abroad (about six million by the time the

Crystal Palace closed on October 11): what was to be done with them all? Editorial-izing in print and image, some Britons worried that this triumphant testimony to the nation's ingenuity and prowess would have the effect of swamping the capital city with foreigners. George Augustus Sala wrote of "The Foreign Invasion" in Charles Dickens's magazine *Household Words*. George Cruikshank's cartoon "All the World Going to See the Great Exhibition of 1851" shows the Crystal Palace perched atop a miniature globe which is covered by streams of people hurrying towards it, by ship, train, and caravan, from every point of the compass. In the image, Paxton's palace seems a vulnerable house of glass, and the confluence of visitors an advancing alliance of foes.

One convenient, and not too misleading, way of thinking of the British nine-teenth century is as a period bracketed by powerful fears of invasion. After the defeat of Napoleon at Waterloo in 1815, the prospect of a foreign army's actually penetrat-ing British territory did not resurface in any serious form until the rather more fantastic fears of a German invasion started to circulate toward the end of the century, informing such popular literary sensations as Erskine Childers's *The Riddle of the Sands* (1903). Later still, of course, there were the justified anxieties about the pos-sibility of a Nazi occupation during World War II. But if the long nineteenth century was an era free from actual threats from outside, it was also one for which the metaphor of invasion was remarkably and lastingly potent in mobilizing the desire for a national oneness. In certain novels written in the first decade of the twentieth century and presenting themselves as valedictories to the Victorian age – such as H. G. Wells's *Tono-Bungay* (1909) and E. M. Forster's *Howards End* (1910) – Britain appears menaced by alien forces, but these are not marauding armies; they are the less conveniently embodied, more insidious effects of trade (especially financial spec-ulation) and empire. With particular reference to the Forster novel, Fredric Jameson has argued that it is when an imperial nation has come to feel its dependence upon that which lies outside it as the central fact of its social existence that such a nation fosters in art the compensating image of itself as "a self-subsisting totality . . . a utopian glimpse of an achieved community" (58). I believe Jameson is wrong to locate such a dynamic as late as he does, and to associate it with modernism rather than nineteenth-century cultural developments: in their fictional recaps of the nine-teenth century, Forster and Wells were reprising a romance gesture that their precursors had long been performing, even in the so-called "realist" novel and in professedly international efforts like the Great Exhibition. The desideratum of an integrated totality "played a central role in narratives in the novel and imperial exhi-bitions alike" (Koenigsberger 6). In a variety of forms, Victorian culture seems to have confronted the offshore basis of its national way of life as something of an embarrassment and as a stimulus for the production of recuperative fictions of the nation's unity and self-reliance.

If global capitalism was not exactly born on May 1, 1851, it was consecrated on that day. Commodities were sacralized in the Crystal Palace, arrayed for admiration as if in the greatest imaginable emporium, yet lacking the sublunary element of price tags and so permitted to disclose their supposedly intrinsic value. The building itself was like the cathedral of a catholic capitalist order: made out of mass-produced, interchangeable pieces of iron and glass, it was laid out on the cruciform plan of Medieval cathedrals (even containing, alongside its myriad novelties, the seemingly anomalous "Medieval Court"). And if Prince Albert had had his way, the whole affair would have epitomized global capitalism in an even more striking fashion, for he had wanted all the articles to be shown "without reference to their country of production" (ffrench 211). A member of that small international elite placed above the commoner's relationship to nationality, the philosophical German Consort to the English Queen had benignly intuited what more recent observers have made a staple of comment on the spreading global market: that a truly free and international system of trade would render nations obsolete, sweeping them aside as capital sought markets wherever it could locate them, regardless of states and territories, of ethnic or religious ties. The fact that Paxton's structure was the least "site-specific" of buildings — made out of materials not bearing the signature of any particular terrain, capable of being taken down and re-erected in other locations — perhaps unintentionally contributed to the de-localizing aura of a capitalism straining to be set free of conditions and barriers. On some level, the energies behind the Exhibition pointed toward a vision of the possible future that not even the staunchest British opponents of trade barriers were prepared to contemplate for long. There were logistical reasons for the commissioners to reject Albert's design, but some anxiety over the glimpse it afforded of a future without boundaries may also have played a part in ensuring that the floor-plan would ultimately be laid out on national lines. When the Exhibition opened, items were arranged "on a geographical basis," and nations competed for the number of medals they could amass for being the "homes" of praiseworthy goods (ffrench 211).

We are accustomed to thinking of nations as the positive expressions of particular peoples' desires for self-determination; we are drawn to historical narratives about a people's emergence out of bondage into self-conscious nationhood. But as Eric Hobsbawm has pithily remarked, "Nations do not make states and nationalisms but the other way around" (quoted in Reynolds 40). If so, then under what circumstances do states, or certain of their members, find it necessary or expedient to invoke the national identities that supposedly pertain to them? The era that saw the rise of the nation-state as the predominant Western form of sociopolitical organization also provides ample evidence that, in the case of the West's dominant country, the category of the nation could function as a bulwark against implications of the very processes that had made it rich and powerful. Set entirely free, trade could dissolve the nation that promoted it; extended everywhere around the globe, empire could drain away or dilute the vital powers of the imperial center. Rather than something discovered by collective introspection, the identity of Britain throughout the nineteenth century was an ideal salvaged out of some prospect of danger or chaos which Britain itself had provoked. Rather than a goal attained once and for all, self-conscious British nationhood was the product of "a protracted and uneven process," and "its maintenance [was] always precarious and imperfect" (Poovey 55). I have argued elsewhere that the British novel played a critical role in the "autoethnographic" labor of imagining and shoring up an identity for England and Britain that might prove separable from and indissoluble by the forces of trade and empire (see Buzard 2005).

The establishment of territorial and conceptual borders was quite messy and protracted in the case of many Continental European nations, but "British boundaries after 1707 seemed settled once and for all, marked out by the sea, clear, incontrovertible, apparently pre-ordained" (Colley 17). This was the year of the Act of Union joining Scotland to England (and Wales, which had been united to England in 1536). For one British island there was now one British people, led by one (English) Parliament and, as had been the case since 1603, by one monarch. (The dominance of England within this new British union is the reason why, to the irritation of the Scots and Welsh, "England" and "Britain" continue to be equated with each other in loose common usage.) The sea that had long been an important natural defense for the inhabitants of the island now became, in the metaphor used by one proponent of the 1707 Act, a wall that fenced in the Britons, uniting them against outsiders (see Colley 17). However culturally diverse the Scots, Welsh, and English remained – to say nothing of narrower regional identities – their common interests seemed to be reinforced by events throughout the eighteenth and early nineteenth centuries. The British experience provides persuasive evidence for the claim that "the process by which individuals or groups embrace the concept of the nation as the most meaningful context for self-definition necessarily involves temporarily marginalizing other categories" (Poovey 55): this intermittent but recurrent marginalizing of their more local categories of identification was what Britain's various peoples learned to do, with varying degrees of strain.

The works of several early nineteenth-century authors aided in this task. Publishing in the wake of the 1801 parliamentary act which had formalized British control of Ireland and created the new United Kingdom of Great Britain and Ireland, authors such as Maria Edgeworth and Sydney Owenson (Lady Morgan) wrote novels and tales that argued the common destiny of Britain and its much-maligned neighbor and dependent. Such works were buttressed by "a liberal English discourse dedicated to producing ideological fictions through which Irish disaffection from English rule could be rhetorically minimized, managed, or resolved" (Corbett 4). Of course such efforts were only partly and temporarily successful, and rule of Ireland remained one of Britain's major recurrent challenges throughout the century, with the Irish repeatedly called upon to play the role of foils or "Others" for tendentious portraits of British or English national character (see A. Martin). A racialist discourse increasingly popular during the middle decades of the century contrasted "Saxon" (Teutonic) characteristics of rationality, self-discipline, and deferred gratification against Irish (and Welsh, and Highland Scottish) "Celtic" traits of spontaneity, imaginative free play, but also fecklessness, lending to English overlordship a specious air of the inevitable.

Appropriating and adapting the Edgeworth and Owenson model to the Scottish context, Walter Scott began in 1814 producing the series known as the Waverley novels, perhaps the century's most acclaimed works of fiction. It was Scott, above all others, who wrote the new British consciousness into existence. From his first novel, he signaled his desire to balance the claims of allegiance to the power centralized in London (he was a close friend of the Hanoverian King) with a determination to preserve all those cultural features that "distinguish us as Scotsmen" – and in so doing appeared to bear out Patrick Parrinder's assertion that in the longer tradition of the "English" novel, the "cultural nation," the body of a distinct people, and not the "political nation," or nation-state, has tended to be the focal point (17–20). Scott's *Waverley; or, 'Tis Sixty Years Since* is set in the time of the last Jacobite rebellion of 1745, and it manages to make repudiation of Bonny Prince Charlie's doomed campaign seem compatible with romanticization of it: the modern commercial Britain of English, Welsh, and Lowland Scots transcends yet retains, as commemorative artifact, the feudal Highland culture embodied in the rebel Fergus MacIvor. Scott was one of the most famous scions of a vibrant intellectual culture based in Edinburgh which, since the second half of the eighteenth century, had exercised a near-monopoly on the creation and institutionalization of British, and even English, identity. In *Ivanhoe* (1819), Scott gave memorable narrative shape to the originary myth of a hardy Saxon Britain straining to preserve itself under the "Norman yoke." The modern study of English and British history and literature, modern understandings of British imperialism, the "English" science of political economy, even the great *Encyclopaedia Britannica* and the *Oxford English Dictionary*, were all begun by Scotsmen (see Morse, ch. 2; Crawford, chs. 1, 2).

Chief among Britons' incentives to develop a working concept of British national identity was lasting conflict with Catholic France, which had sponsored that failed 1745 attempt to reinstate the Stuart line in Britain and which, more than any other country, served as Britain's defining opposite well into the nineteenth century. To a great extent, Britons' image of their nation as the preeminent defender of Protestantism – and its vaunted freedom of conscience and individual rights – had come to depend upon their conception of France as a priest-ridden, backward, and autocratic country all too eager to encroach upon British prosperity and territory. (Catholic Ireland after 1801 obviously had a different relation to the matter; only among the Protestant Orangemen of Ulster can there be said to have developed a United Kingdom identity comparable in rhetorical force to the British national identity attained by English, Scots, and Welsh.) Distrust of Catholicism, which Britons might regard as a kind of rival empire to their own, afforded a dependable resource for mobilizing British nationalism. Guy Fawkes Day (November 5) was an annual reminder of the time, in 1605, when Popish plotters "did contrive / To blow Old England up alive." The mob violence of the 1780s' anti-Catholic Gordon riots was not repeated in the next century, although reaction to the so-called "Papal Aggression" of 1850 suggests that violent feelings on the religious question could resurface at any time. What brought them up in 1850 was the Pope's decision to reinstate the Catholic diocesan hierarchy in England for the first time since the Reformation. Patriotic Protestants might well have felt the establishment of Cardinal Wiseman and his cohorts a fitting insult to crown that dismal experiment, the Oxford, or Tractarian, Movement, which had aimed at revitalizing the Anglican church but had wound up by making a Papist of its most prominent advocate, John Henry Newman. The 1864 dispute between Newman and Charles Kingsley over the truthfulness of Catholic clergymen provided another opportunity for chauvinists to insist upon the equation of Britishness and Protestantism. All the while, British Protestant missionary activity had manifested exponential growth around the world: the 1911 *Encyclopaedia Britannica* despaired of recounting the full history of "the hundred or more organized [missionary] societies of some size that have . . . come into being since the end of the eighteenth century, still less that of the three or four hundred smaller agencies" (XVIII, 587). Missionaries served not only as the exporters of British ideas, but as the dispatchers of alien ideas back to Britain, where they could assist in the rhetorical labor of defining Britishness by opposition.

Britain's longstanding animosity toward France was re-polarized when, during twenty years of warfare stretching from the 1790s to 1815, the rhetorically serviceable otherness of the French came to consist, not in Catholic backwardness, but in radical republicanism nurtured on Enlightenment ideas. Britons watched in horrified amazement as the democratic experiment of the French Revolution imploded in the Reign of Terror of 1793–4, then contorted itself into the aggressive Empire of Napoleon Bonaparte. Until the victory over Napoleon at Waterloo in 1815, fears of a French invasion permitted the British government to impose severe repressive measures against any activity smacking of pro-French (democratic) attitudes. Retaining the same enemy while altering the terms of ideological repugnance, British observers now began to highlight not just their country's freedoms but the stability of its social structure, which they juxtaposed to the hubristic revolutionary gesture of rebuilding society from the ground up according to abstract notions about "liberty, equality, and fraternity" or (in the words of Thomas Paine), "the Rights of Man." The radical freedom pursued by the French Jacobins was a chimera, warned Edmund Burke in his *Reflections on the Revolution in France* (1790): "Man" did not exist; one could travel the world and never meet him, but only his localized, national avatars. Britannia's admirable liberties were native to herself, "an estate specially belonging to the people of this kingdom without any reference whatever to any other more general or prior right" (119). Burke's was a formula powerfully attractive to many later writers, riding out as they did the century-long process of political democratization taking place in Britain.

The travel writer Frances Trollope, to take one example, seemed to discover the truth of Burke's lesson on her many journeys abroad: as she wrote in *A Visit to Italy* (1842), she felt "more and more, and more again, as I continue my rambles through the world, that the Constitution of ENGLAND when guarded with common prudence from the democratic innovations which have of late years buzzed about it . . . is the only one which appears to be formed in reasonable, honest, and holy conformity to the freedom of man as a human being, and to the necessary restraint inevitable upon his becoming one of a civilized, social compact" (see Buzard 1993: 100). Walter Bagehot's *The English Constitution* (1867), published just as the Second Reform Bill vastly increased the voting population, expanded upon Burke's principle of cultural belonging as inheritance, describing a national collective mentality operating "instinctively, without argument, almost without consciousness" and centered on deference toward established hierarchies (quoted in Herbert 1991: 128–49). Writing at the same time as Bagehot, Matthew Arnold repudiated the Jacobin fantasy of an abstract and universal-rights-bearing humanity in favor of distinct, duty-bearing communities: he maintained in *Culture and Anarchy* that "the deeper I go in my own consciousness, the more simply I abandon myself to it, the more it seems to tell me that I have no rights at all, only duties; and that men get this notion of rights from a process of abstract reasoning, inferring that the obligations they are conscious of towards others, others must be conscious of towards them." (pt. 6, "Our Liberal Practitioners").

According to a chorus of voices besides these, the recommended English or British virtue was, as Thomas Carlyle had written in *Sartor Resartus* (during the first Reform ferment of 1832), "Do the duty which lies nearest thee" (book 2, ch. 9). The specification of that "nearest," the surveying of the territory to be covered by it, was the ideological work of many Victorian writers. In *Bleak House* (1852), for example, Dickens defined a moral community based upon his heroine's model of the "circle of duty" that begins with people personally known and widens to include every unknown person belonging to the nation – but none beyond it. In her last work, *Impressions of Theophrastus Such* (1879), George Eliot's crotchety narrating persona would put forward a similar case. Taking a swipe at the opening lines of Samuel Johnson's "The Vanity of Human Wishes" and their Augustan global perspective, Eliot's Theophrastus asserts that "Affection, intelligence, duty, radiate from a centre, and nature has decided that for us English folk that centre can be neither China nor Peru." More crudely: "I am not bound to feel for a Chinaman as I feel for my fellow-countryman" (147).

The publication of Carlyle's massive study *The French Revolution* in the very first year of Victoria's reign helped guarantee that these older currents of British self-identification by differentiation would persist for decades into the new era. Although Edward Lytton Bulwer declared, in his *England and the English* (1833) – which was addressed to the French diplomat Talleyrand – that "[t]he English of the present day are not the English of twenty years ago" and that "*We no longer hate the French*" (19–20, 38), Carlyle's portrayal of the French cataclysm encouraged Britons to continue regarding their cross-the-channel neighbors as the embodied potential for excesses of violence and vengefulness – and the periodic crises of French nineteenth-century politics (1830, 1848, 1870) seemed to confirm this view. Dickens cribbed from Carlyle extensively in his depiction of bloodthirsty Paris during the Terror, in *A Tale of Two Cities* (1860). The *eminence grise* of the murderous Jacobins in that novel is the silently knitting Mme. Defarge, a combination of Frenchness and femaleness run amok. The more she knits at her list of "enemies of the people," the more she unravels the precious social fabric. How attracted Dickens was to this particular feminization of the foreign threat is suggested by the fact that he supplied a kind of trial run for Mme. Defarge in the villainness Hortense of *Bleak House* (1852). In a novel determined to diagnose and cure Britain's ailing culture, Hortense – Frenchwoman, murderess, mouthpiece of underclass *ressentiment*, and possible lesbian – is the lone foreigner. She displays, as the novel's English heroine, Esther Summerson, sees it, "a lowering energy in her face . . . which seemed to bring visibly before me some woman from the streets of Paris in the reign of terror" (ch. 23). In both works, Dickens poses British against French women, as if the former encapsulated all those virtues of their nation – reasonableness in the face of all-consuming wrath, openness in the face of secrecy and deceit, humility in the face of hubris – that must be defended against Gallic assault.

It is striking that, in the era during which Britain attained unprecedented international clout – an era presided over by a queen who, in 1876, was officially declared an empress – Englishness or Britishness was so routinely allegorized not as some swaggering, militant character but as a vulnerable woman, who must either be defended by some father figure or defend herself by English pluck. In a list of idealized Victorian Englishwomen facing threats on English soil, Esther Summerson joins other Dickensian creations, early and late, from Nell of *The Old Curiosity Shop* (1841), to the title character of *Little Dorrit* (1857), to the patently allegorical Rosa Bud in *The Mystery of Edwin Drood* (1870). Dickens's works repeatedly plead for the proper exercise of a paternal authority – of a sort suggested perhaps by the rather chivalrous narrator's persona – that will nurture, contain, and protect the young Englishwoman who is so liable to be menaced by such monstrous, orientalized scoundrels as Quilp from *The Old Curiosity Shop*, the Blandois of *Little Dorrit*, and the opium-crazed Jasper in *The Mystery of Edwin Drood*. All these villains function as human conduits for suspect influences from around the world. Quilp makes his living from "pursuits . . . diversified and numerous": "He collected the rents of whole colonies of filthy streets and alleys by the waterside, advanced money to the seamen and petty officers of merchant vessels, had a share in the ventures of divers mates of East Indiamen, smoked his smuggled cigars under the very nose of the Custom House, and made appointments on 'Change with men in glazed hats and round jackets pretty well every day" (ch. 4). The antagonist not only works in, but *is*, a port of entry, and his efforts to apprehend Nell are made on behalf of all those contaminating elements he invites into Britain. Novels such as Charlotte Brontë's *Villette* (1853), or those by Dickens's friend Wilkie Collins, most notably *The Woman in White* (1859–60) and *The Moonstone* (1868), also offer versions of British womanhood subject to the alien grasp.

If the ideal figuration of a national character thus depended upon the threat of foreign influences, then it is not surprising that the motif of imperiled Englishness made itself felt with particular intensity in writings concerned with English people abroad. Commentators on the so-called Grand Tour had long debated whether a young Englishman's exposure to foreign customs would benefit or harm the country to which he returned. There was a certain amount of wishful thinking in Edward Gibbon's assertion that he had come back from his eighteenth-century European tour "a better Englishman than I went out" (see Buzard 1993: 99); and for every Gibbon there arose a dissenting voice to warn that exposure to the outside world, unless properly managed and limited, might lead the young tourist astray, encouraging him to ape outlandish manners rather than to perfect English ones. Such a concern took on a markedly more anxious tenor when the traveler was female, as she was much more likely to be in the nineteenth century. A whole subset of travel literature beginning in the immediate post-Napoleonic years consisted of fictions based on a "family abroad plot," which aired worries about national cultural security in stories about the misadventures of British families touring the Continent (see Buzard 1993: 130–52). The engine of mischief in such fictions, usually the fashion-crazed and socially ambitious wife, is primed by the adolescent daughter, who attracts the suspect attentions of penniless Continental noblemen and can be saved from marrying them only by a reassertion of paternal control. Failing that, the young Englishwoman loses her virginity, her happiness, and her identity to the nefarious adventurer. Some variety of authorial peroration typically ensues: in his early variant *The English in Italy* (1825), Lord Normanby says the fate of the once "petulant and vivacious" and now contrite Matilda should furnish

> a striking, and, it is to be hoped, not a useless example to the British fair, who learn, in the enthusiasm for foreign climes and habits, to contemn the domestic virtues of their country, – who mistake the mere charms of novelty for sources of lasting happiness, and who blush not to forfeit the name of English women, in yielding up their hearts and hands to the fickle keeping of a stranger. (quoted in Buzard 1993: 148)

Such unions were in fact rare – though Murray's 1858 *Handbook for Travellers in Southern Italy* took the prospect seriously enough to include a "Caution to English Ladies" which reminded them that "Englishwomen by marriage with a foreigner forfeit their nationality, and are precluded from seeking redress from British consuls or tribunals" (see Buzard 1993: 148–9). Though featured mainly in a variety of now unread novels and magazine pieces, the family-abroad plot could on occasion percolate upward into the work of celebrated authors. In its treatment of two sisters, one easily swayed by foreign fashions, the other steadfastly English and humble, Dickens's *Little Dorrit* borrows from the pattern laid down by such forgotten works as Normanby's; and it may be that the bad-marriage plots of George Eliot's *Middlemarch* (1871–2) and *Daniel Deronda* (1876) testify to the pattern by reversing it, since each involves the cruel wasting of an Englishwoman's youth and vitality at the hands of a morally compromised Englishman, and each holds out a young *foreigner*, met on the Continent, as a figure of redemption.

In these plots, the ultimate target of the foreign suitor is, of course, the English real estate behind the traveling woman. The paterfamilias in one of these tales, learning that his daughter has fallen into the clutches of a dissolute French count, goes so far as to father an heir in order to safeguard that "inheritance derived to us from our forefathers, and to be transmitted to our posterity" of which Edmund Burke had spoken. "[T]o think," this father tells a friend,

> that this fine estate would pass away at my death to a foreign swindler, was more than I could endure . . . The woods, the river, the very ground beneath appeared to reproach me, and I fancied that the fine old trees, as their branches waved aloft, cast a darker shade around, and groaned as though the axe were ready at work to hew them down to supply the wants of a gamester and a stranger. (see Buzard 1993: 142)

Here is the powerful ideological suggestion that the natural setting itself endorses the particular dynasty that occupies it: just as the soil of Ithaca nourishes the tree in which Odysseus carves his dynastic marriage bed, the English ground is full of spirits capable of sanctioning the uses to which it is put, and the users. The notion of a distinctively English spirit of place, or *genius loci*, would appear in numerous nineteenth- and early twentieth-century texts, notably Rudyard Kipling's *Puck of Pook's Hill* (1906).

It is not accidental that the era that began with Britons' renewed access to the Continent after 1815, and that proceeded to make the Continent accessible to more and more segments of the population, should have fostered the rise of modern tourist institutions, which were seen as creating pockets of security around the British tourist as the tourist moved about in foreign fields. The first half of the nineteenth century saw the rise of Thomas Cook, that Emperor of Tourists, as well as of the systematic, helpful, and protective guidebooks of Karl Baedeker and John Murray III – to say nothing of the improvements in transport, accommodation, and finance that facilitated freedom of movement and minimized entanglements with indigenous populations. In Cook's invention of the "package tour" is powerfully encoded the idea of a British collective body able to travel untouched and at will through alien territories. The Consular Act of 1825, which unified and professionalized the system of British consulates around the world, offered a similar guarantee. It was in these comparatively close-to-home developments that some of the foundations were laid for later imperial imaginings. Tourism was noted for having invented safe "little Englands" abroad well before the Empire's hill stations, clubs, and cantonments gained the notice of a broad domestic public. Evident in much of this planning, as in the family-abroad plots just discussed, is a foreshadowing of empire's growing fixation upon the necessity of sequestering the British woman from the contaminating touch of the colonized man. British representations of empire often revolved around the dread of interracial rape, which reached fever pitch in writings following the so-called "Indian Mutiny" of 1857, during which many such rapes were alleged to have occurred (Brantlinger ch. 7). The prospect of the white woman's violation exercised a lasting hold over the British literary imagination of empire: immediately following the events of 1857, it helped to foment a British retributive violence of appalling and perhaps even self-traumatizing brutality (see Herbert 2008); and it forms the central element of E. M. Forster's *A Passage to India* (1924) and of Paul Scott's late novelistic meditation on race and empire, *The Raj Quartet* (1966–75).

After the great convulsion of 1857, the British presence in India had once and for all to be formalized and the boundary between rulers and subjects clarified. Parliament dissolved the East India Company and assigned rule over India to a new secretary of state. A new phase of imperialism began, one aspect of which was the more determined solicitation of women to emigrate to the colonies, where with their soldier or administrator husbands they would form the nucleus of a hyperconscious, miniature British culture in foreign parts. In an earlier phase of colonialism, many unaccompanied European men had routinely taken mistresses and even wives from the local population; the arrival of missionaries after 1813 in the districts under East India Company control had cast a shadow on this practice. But after 1857 the planned presence of resident European wives was supposed to extirpate it altogether, since miscegenation was now increasingly regarded, for racialist reasons among others, as dangerous to the preservation of the British national character and its ruling temper. For these wives, "the tasks of homemaker and mother carried even greater implications for preserving 'civilization' when carried out in the outposts of the empire" than they would do at home (Strobel 17). With their children routinely sent back to England to be educated – foreclosing excessive fraternization with "native" children and servants – imperial wives and mothers could devote themselves to their other function as gatekeepers of transplanted Britishness, and the society over which they presided "mirrored in more rigid form the practices found in Britain" itself (Strobel 9). "Transported to distant parts of the empire," British home furnishings and art images (such as English landscapes) took on a new function as markers of a British social space that held other, "local constructions of place" at bay (Helsinger 13). Kipling was the first writer to gain an audience in Britain for depicting this imperial hothouse culture, in stories of the 1880s such as those collected in *Plain Tales from the Hills* (1888).

The insistent maintenance of Britishness that informed these garrison communities was also to be felt in the fictional mode of the "Imperial Gothic," for which Empire is "a barricade against a new barbarian invasion" – and an extremely porous barricade at that (Brantlinger 230). Concentrated in the last two decades of the century, but foreshadowed in earlier novels by Charlotte Brontë, Dickens, and Collins, among others, Imperial Gothic depicts a Britain alarmingly open to penetration by alien, even demonic forces that insinuate themselves into the fiber of British being. These are the nightmare products – in H. Rider Haggard's *She* (1887), in Bram Stoker's

Dracula (1897), in Arthur Conan Doyle's Sherlock Holmes tales – of that process known as "reverse colonization," by which people and cultural influences from colonized portions of the globe start to make themselves felt as unavoidable presences in the colonial metropolis itself (see Arata; Duncan). The secret addiction of the English cathedral choirmaster, in *Edwin Drood*, is the sinister by-product of empire, the coming-home-to-roost of the Opium Wars that had "opened" China and gained Hong Kong for Britain. This novel entertains the possibility that not just the dismal East End dockland slums, but the quintessentially English cathedral town, could be the scene of that drug-induced madness and criminality to which, official opinion held, "primitive savages" were prone.

In Haggard's sensational novel Ayesha, the dreaded "She-Who-Must-Be-Obeyed" who rules an unknown civilization in the African interior, has designs on the throne of her English counterpart: as the narrator puts it, "the terrible *She* had determined to go to England, and it made me shudder to think what would be the result of her arrival . . . In the end, I had little doubt, she would assume absolute rule over the British dominions, and probably over the whole earth, and though I was sure she would speedily make ours the most glorious and prosperous empire that the world has ever seen, it must be at the cost of a terrible sacrifice of life" (ch. 22). Somewhere midway through this passage the distorting mirror of Ayesha's possible empire becomes a clear one, for it was under Victoria that those events feared by Haggard's narrator did indeed happen. In another bizarre mimicry of Britain's own empire, the vampire Dracula is poised to establish in England "a new and ever widening circle of semi-demons to batten on the helpless" (see Arata 629). Examples such as these suggest that, however much Victorians liked to consider their empire as "final and conclusive proof of Great Britain's providential destiny" (Colley 368), their "complacency" was shadowed by many expressions of anxiety about their nation's susceptibility to infiltration by the angry spirits empire had awakened half a world away.

Corresponding to the troubling suspicion that Britain's identity was something based offshore – a notion already present within British epic poetry of the 1840s (see Tucker ch. 8) – was the recognition that cohabitation within the physical territory of Great Britain failed to convey any meaningful sense of community, or even seemed a mockery of true community. This was so, not simply because any achieved British identity stood liable, under the right kind of political or circumstantial pressures, to devolution back into the more parochial identities of Scots, Welsh, and English, or because no ideologically meaningful United Kingdom identity had ever affectively unified Britain and Ireland. We cannot lose sight of the anomalous condition of nineteenth-century Britons as living, "not in a nation-state, but in a multinational empire," of or the "awkwardness of [the] amalgam": "the United Kingdom of Great Britain and Ireland" is a title "awkwardly combining a recognition of difference with an assertion of unity" (Reynolds 26, 205). Yet beyond the inherent instability of the available identity categories, in the middle decades of the century, the idea that

Britain might lie open to all sorts of malignant infiltration from abroad was adapted to govern representations of the poor and working classes in Britain itself. These segments of the population were described as having been newly discovered by middle-class writers during the economic crises of the 1840s, and their haunts were regularly depicted as unknown or uncharted lands full of menacing savages. Investigators pondered what Carlyle called, in *Past and Present* (1843), the "Condition-of-England Question," and their findings were summarized most famously in a phrase appearing in Benjamin Disraeli's 1845 novel *Sibyl*: Britain was "[t]wo nations; between whom there is no intercourse and no sympathy; who are as ignorant of each other's habits, thoughts, and feelings, as if they were dwellers in different zones, or inhabitants of different planets; who are formed by a different breeding, are fed by different food, are ordered by different manners, and are not governed by the same laws" (book 2, ch. 5). This depressing prospect was given most alarming expression in Henry Mayhew's monumental *London Labour and the London Poor* (published in several editions from 1851), which considered the lower orders of British society as parasitic nomads both physiologically and morally distinct from the settled reading classes.

It was middle-class fear of "invasion" by this subordinate British nation that gave rise to numerous compensatory ideas of the meaningful national whole that could reunite the polarized classes. Disraeli and his conservative "Young England" move-ment of the 1840s sought the "community of purpose that constitutes society," without which "men may be drawn into contiguity, but . . . still continue virtually isolated" (book 2, ch. 5), in a romanticized vision of aristocratic charity and peasant deference; they were derided by reformers like Dickens for their pains. Elizabeth Gaskell, in novels of class conflict like *Mary Barton* (1848) and *North and South* (1855), campaigned for clear channels of communication between employers and employed, the establishment of which would enable all to see "that the interests of one were the interests of all" (*Mary Barton* ch. 37). The fulcrum of arguments like Gaskell's was typically the necessity for British firms to repel foreign competition; workers were to accept reductions in wages, for example, because they recognized this necessity. Yet the moral rhetoric on which such writers relied was Christian-universal: British factory owners and hands were to acknowledge each other as brothers in Christ, but this was a category which, like unrestrained capitalism itself, honored no national boundaries. Where was the Christian concern for the well-being of those German or Belgian brothers in Christ whose wages British competition drove down? Gaskell was a Uni-tarian – her husband was a well-known minister in Manchester – but the community she invoked was, implicitly at least, as specifically national as the one invoked by the national Anglican church.

One of Gaskell's devices in *Mary Barton* for encouraging a single national conscious-ness is recurrent allusion to an English literary canon tacitly understood as the common inheritance of all classes. Motivated by a kind of ethnographic interest, the obviously middle-class narrator lards her text with exotic samples of Manchester workers' songs and speech, but she also consistently draws from a national literary culture (both elite and popular) from which admirable autodidacts among her working-class characters draw as well. Similar pursuits of common linguistic, mythological, or racial legacies for England or Britain are to be found throughout Victorian culture. Widespread interest in English popular legends and songs dates at least from the publication of Bishop Percy's *Reliques of Ancient English Poetry* (1765), but it was mainly in the nineteenth century that the collection and study of materials that had come (in 1846) to be labeled "Folk-Lore" attained a quasi-scientific authority, under the auspices of the Folk-Lore Society (founded in 1878). Its members collaborated, and quarreled, with geographers and physical anthropologists in the massive and ultimately self-destructing project for an Ethnographic Survey of the United Kingdom, attempted by the British Association for the Advancement of Science between 1892 and 1899. After a period of renewed political unrest and urban exposés in the 1880s and 1890s, this scientific grand illusion seems to have been motivated at least in part by the urge to reestablish British identity upon the bedrock of comprehensively understood British racial and cultural characteristics. The concept of a shared national literary canon found especially popular embodiment in Francis Turner Palgrave's *Golden Treasury of English Songs and Lyrics* (1861) and in the institutionalization of the study of "English" (literature, not language) as an academic discipline in the later decades of the century.

In the field of language, Richard Chenevix Trench invested the historical study of English with a religio-national significance in his influential lecture series *English Past and Present* (1855). What is "the love of our own language," Trench asked, "but the love of our country expressing itself in one particular direction?" (Lecture 1). The care of the national language was a task made more urgent by the trials Britain was then undergoing in the international arena. Trench opened his lectures by alluding to the ongoing Crimean war, saying that

> [i]t is one of the compensations, indeed the greatest of all, for the wastefulness, the woe, the cruel losses of war, that it causes a people to know itself a people; and leads one to esteem and prize most that which he has in common with his fellow countrymen, and not now any longer those things which separate and divide him from them. (Lecture 1)

Language was foremost among those common English possessions now worthy of new appreciation. Trench helped set in motion the campaign to produce a *New English Dictionary*, which began publication in 1884 and concluded (as the *OED*'s first edition) in 1928. In a related set of developments, as Meredith Martin has recently shown, "Poets and prosodists grappled with, argued over, and attempted to standardize, alter, or disrupt concepts of 'English meter' throughout the nineteenth and early twentieth centuries: the same era during which English meter became irrevocably associated with English national culture" (2).

Reflection on the Victorian definitions of nation and class shows how partial was the reach of the Great Exhibition that opened its doors on May 1, 1851, how much it identified the interests of one rising class with those of the nation as a whole. What the Exhibition represented was the ascendancy of a middle-class economic and cultural platform over the previously dominant interests of the landed classes. It took aim at, and was assailed by, the same protectionist forces that had been attacked since before Victoria's reign by the Anti-Corn Law League, a group devoted to the repeal of the system of tariffs designed to protect the landed interest by propping up the price of domestic wheat. The contest over these tariffs had been decided when, in 1846, Robert Peel, the Tory Prime Minister, switched from supporting protectionist measures to opposing them, mainly because the disastrous potato blight in Ireland had necessitated the importation of huge amounts of grain. Five years later, the midcentury festival in Hyde Park offered the panoramic vista of worldwide free trade – though, as we have seen, that vista itself remained protectively framed by the category of the nation.

Considering how much ink was spilt on the topic of what the Exhibition would indicate about the condition of Britain, and what it would do in making the lower classes feel part of the national glory, it is interesting to note that the people interviewed in Mayhew's *London Labour and the London Poor* were evidently little touched by the Exhibition mania. In the period preceding and during the Exhibition, Mayhew repeatedly discovered how little purchase the whole affair had on the minds of his interlocutors, whom it is clear he regularly asked about it. Whatever recognition they accorded the event tended to be narrowly self-interested, as in the comment of a London milk-seller: "I don't understand about this Great Exhibition, but no doubt, more new milk will be sold when it's opened, and that's all I cares about" (vol. 1, "Of Milk Selling . . ."). With none of the appropriate reverence but with a pragmatism their social superiors ought to have admired them for, Mayhew's voices of labor and poverty debated only "whether the Great Exhibition would be 'any good' to them, or not" (vol. 1, "Of Street Piemen"). The happening that went by the grandiose official title of the Great Exhibition of the Works of Industry of All Nations (quite a mouthful in itself) was widely referred to by the "other Britons" by the terser label of "The Great Eggs-and-Bacon."

This is to say nothing of those far poorer, "forgotten" people Mayhew also studied, those desperate mendicants and river-scavenging "mud larks" who, just emerging into official consciousness, still lay wholly outside the mainstream cultural order. It was, in great measure, on behalf of such people as these that Dickens began writing *Bleak House* in the fall of 1851, as if in answer to his own call, in *Household Words*, for a second exhibition "for the great display of England's sins and negligences, to be, by steady contemplation of all eyes, and steady union of all hearts, set right" (January 4, 1851, 338). The audacious and expansive masterpiece he produced turned away from the vaunted universalism of the Exhibition in favor of a comprehensive indictment of contemporary Britain. It seemed determined to "depict England in terms almost exactly the opposite of those implicit in the idea of the Exhibition" (N. Page 27), to constitute itself an "anti-Exhibition" in novel form. In so doing, it may have illustrated in particularly bold relief a propensity of the Victorian novel generally. For this was the newly dominant literary genre in which Dickens, William Makepeace Thackeray, Anthony Trollope, George Eliot, and others supplied "a slowly built up picture [of the world] with England – socially, politically, morally charted in immensely fine detail – at the center and a series of overseas territories connected to it at the peripheries" (Said 74). Devoting the great preponderance of its attention to an unprecedentedly detailed portrait of English life and a small quantity of it to the colonies which, largely unrepresented, stood at the margins waiting to receive troublesome characters or resolve troublesome plots, the novel in effect aligned its formal boundaries with those of the imperial nation. This new orientation may have proven appealing, not because it expressed a swaggering confidence about Britain's ability to put the rest of the world in its place, but because it shored up the British nation, in fiction, against the worldwide network of dependencies in which that nation was entangled.

See also 1851, 1870; SEXUALITIES; SPECTACLE; SKIN, HISTORIOGRAPHY PARAPETS

REFERENCES

Arata, S. (1990) "The Occidental Tourist: *Dracula* and the Anxiety of Reverse Colonization." *Victorian Studies* 33, 621–45.

Brantlinger, P. (1988) *Rule of Darkness: British Literature and Imperialism, 1830–1914*. Ithaca and London: Cornell University Press.

Bulwer, E. L. (1970) *England and the English*, ed. S. Meacham. Chicago and London: University of Chicago Press.

Burke, E. (1982) *Reflections on the Revolution in France*, ed. C. C. O'Brien. Harmondsworth: Penguin.

Buzard, J. (1993) *The Beaten Track: European Tourism, Literature, and the Ways to "Culture," 1800–1918*. Oxford: Clarendon/Oxford University Press.

——(2005) *Disorienting Fiction: The Autoethnographic Work of Nineteenth-Century British Novels*. Princeton: Princeton University Press.

Colley, L. (1992) *Britons: Forging the Nation, 1707–1837*. New Haven and London: Yale University Press.

Corbett, M. J. (2003) *Allegories of Union in Irish and English Writing, 1750–1870*. Cambridge: Cambridge University Press.

Crawford, R. (1992) *Devolving English Literature*. Oxford: Clarendon Press.

Dodds, J. W. (1952) *The Age of Paradox: A Biography of England, 1841–1851*. New York and Toronto: Rinehart.

Duncan, I. (1995) "*The Moonstone*, the Victorian Novel, and Imperialist Panic." *Modern Language Quarterly* 55, 297–319.

Eliot, G. (1994) *Impressions of Theophrastus Such*, ed. N. Henry. Iowa City: University of Iowa Press.

ffrench, Y. (1950) *The Great Exhibition: 1851*. London: Harvill.

Helsinger, E. K. (1997) *Rural Scenes and National Representation: Britain, 1815–1850*. Princeton: Princeton University Press.

Herbert, C. (1991) *Culture and Anomie: Ethnographic Imagination in the Nineteenth Century*. Chicago: University of Chicago Press.

——(2008) *War of No Pity: The Indian Mutiny and Victorian Trauma*. Princeton: Princeton University Press.

Jameson, F. (1990) "Modernism and Imperialism." In T. Eagleton, F. Jameson, and E. W. Said, *Nationalism, Colonialism, and Literature*. Minneapolis: University of Minnesota Press.

Koenigsberger, K. (2007) *The Novel and the Menag-erie: Totality, Englishness, and Empire*. Columbus: Ohio State University Press.

Martin, A. E. (2012) *Alter-Nations: Nationalisms, Terror, and the State in Nineteenth-Century Britain and Ireland*. Columbus: Ohio State University Press.

Martin, M. (2012) *The Rise and Fall of Meter: Poetry and English National Culture, 1860–1930*. Princeton: Princeton University Press.

Miller, A. H. (1995) *Novels Behind Glass: Commodity Culture and Victorian Narrative*. Cambridge: Cambridge University Press.

Morse, D. (1993) *High Victorian Culture*. New York: New York University Press.

Page, N. (1990) *Bleak House: A Novel of Connections*. Boston: Twayne.

Parrinder, P. (2006) *Nation and Novel: The English Novel from Its Origins to the Present Day*. Oxford and New York: Oxford University Press.

Poovey, M. (1995) *Making a Social Body: British Cultural Formation, 1830–1864*. Chicago and London: University of Chicago Press.

Reynolds, M. (2001) *The Realms of Verse, 1830–1870: English Poetry in a Time of Nation-Building*. Oxford: Oxford University Press.

Said, E. W. (1993) *Culture and Imperialism*. New York: Knopf.

Strobel, M. (1991) *European Women and the Second British Empire*. Bloomington and Indianapolis: Indiana University Press.

Tucker, H. F. (2008) *Epic: Britain's Heroic Muse 1790–1910*. New York and Oxford: Oxford University Press.

Further Reading

Anderson, B. (1991) *Imagined Communities: Reflections on the Origin and Spread of Nationalism*, 2nd edn. London: Verso.

Dentith, S. (2006) *Epic and Empire in Nineteenth-Century Britain*. Cambridge: Cambridge University Press.

Hobsbawm, E. (1990) *Nations and Nationalism Since 1780: Programme, Myth, Reality*. Cambridge: Cambridge University Press.

Ragussis, M. (1995) *Figures of Conversion: "The Jewish Question" and English National Identity*. Durham: Duke University Press.

32

On the Neo-Victorian, Now and Then

Ann Heilmann and Mark Llewellyn

Are the Victorians the ultimate undead? It seems fitting that a literary period almost framed by the two pivotal texts in the invention of the modern vampire – John William Polidori's *The Vampyre* (1819) and Bram Stoker's *Dracula* (1897) – and strongly marked by a later strain of the Romantic Gothic, should itself prove to have such a revenant influence. Although the modernists tried to stake the Victorian heart through literary experimentation that veered from antithetical to outright agnostic in relation to its nineteenth-century inheritance, still the Victorian lives on. Like Dracula's seamless navigation of the London streets by day, the Victorian afterlife of the architecture of our everyday experience and the omnipresence of nineteenth-century phrases and narratives, ideas, ideals, and phobias speak of something fundamental and visceral.

We are, of course, not Victorian. The post-Victorian age, however, was pre-empted by the Victorians themselves. They had the benefit – granted by themselves but also bestowed by later critics (Hewitt 395–7) – of coming into existence before Victoria ascended the throne in 1837 and, through their Edwardian offshoot, lingering on to the outbreak of World War I in 1914. It is no mean feat to pre-date your own terminological framework and continue into another's. Victoria's 64-year reign is often conflated with the long nineteenth century; and it is this long nineteenth century, with its roots in the revolutionary 1790s and its final expiration point in the postwar 1920s, which dominates the vocabulary of nostalgia, heritage, and a more slippery sense of Victorian "cultural memory" (see Joyce's use of Austen and Forster, and Sadoff's of Austen, as demarcation points for neo-Victorianism). Victoria and her

A New Companion to Victorian Literature and Culture, First Edition. Edited by Herbert F. Tucker.
© 2014 John Wiley & Sons, Ltd. Published 2014 by John Wiley & Sons, Ltd.

descendent influences were also helped by her staunchest critics. Resistance against Victorian aesthetic, political, cultural, and economic values seems futile in the face of the way those values keep returning from the grave of reputational damage like specters. This is illustrated in our own time by the political discourse of successive UK governments drawing on a sentimental and inaccurate notion of Victorian social stability to justify deeply unpopular policy decisions, from 1980s Thatcherite "Victorian Values" and John Major's "Back to Basics" campaign in the 1990s to the 2010 Coalition's resurrection of the Victorian differentiation between "deserving" and "undeserving" poor, or the ongoing legacy of nineteenth-century views on education (Birch).

If we are haunted by the Victorians, so were the modernists. Even when lampooning the Victorian ancestry from which they descended, they could not help finding something inescapable in its influence. The anti-rationalism of Virginia Woolf's *To the Lighthouse* (1927) mocks, through Mr Ramsay's persistent desire to maintain chronological sequence in thought as well as in time ("But after Q? What comes next?," ch. 6), a manifestly Victorian obsession with linear and hierarchical classification systems. Yet this cliché of Victorian staidness and respectability finds a witty counterpoint in the exuberant celebration of the nineteenth century in *Flush* (1933). Woolf's bottom-up choice of a (historical) cocker spaniel as the subject of her mock-biography, rather than his more illustrious owner Elizabeth Barrett Browning, offers an ironic commentary on Lytton Strachey's *Queen Victoria* (1921), which for all its caustic critique nevertheless perpetuates a focus on "eminent Victorians" (the title of Strachey's earlier 1918 group biography). *Flush* repeatedly signals Woolf's disappointment in her generation's failure to acknowledge the multi-faceted nature of the Victorians: while satirizing the notion of the all-enduring impact of Victorian literature, she extends the feminist recovery project of *A Room of One's Own* (1929) by acknowledging the "vivid" class politics of Barrett Browning's *Aurora Leigh* (1856) and then pointing to the class-inflected oversights in *modernist* biography (Woolf's notes 5 and 6). It is not, she seems to suggest, another version of "eminent" Victorians the world needs, but rather a recognition of the "other" Victorians, the class whose labor buttressed and maintained the Victorian empire. "The life of Lily Wilson [the Brownings' maid] . . . cries aloud for the services of a biographer. No human figure in the Browning letters, save the principals, more excites our curiosity and baffles it" (note 6). It was not until 1990 that Woolf's appeal found a response, in Margaret Forster's novel *Lady's Maid*. Attention to class has since become a distinct trait of neo-Victorian fiction, from Sarah Waters's *Tipping the Velvet* (1998), *Affinity* (1999), and *Fingersmith* (2003) to Kate Pullinger's exploration of the Egyptian experiences of Lucie Duff Gordon's maid Sallie Naldrett in *The Mistress of Nothing* (2009).

Admittedly, Woolf did not heed her own advice. Like Strachey's biographies, *Freshwater: A Comedy* (written 1923, performed 1935), set on the Isle of Wight, comically deflates the "Greats," parodying the Poet Laureate Alfred Tennyson, the photographer Julia Margaret Cameron, the painter George Frederick Watts, and

Queen Victoria herself. In lampooning Tennyson's poetical voice and verbosity, Woolf places emphasis on the intoned seriousness of such self-characterization while also, through the figure of Watts's child-wife the actress Ellen Terry, invoking a youthful curiosity and skepticism about the "real" people before her. Woolf's preoccupation with the Victorians originated partly from a wish to trace her own family roots (Cameron was her great-aunt) in spite rather than because of any modernist resistance to what that legacy entailed. For all their parody, both *Freshwater* and *Flush* provide a more human version of individuals than we find in the *Dictionary of National Biography* (1885–91) that was edited by Woolf's father, Sir Leslie Stephen. Where Stephen classified, Woolf characterized.

Indeed, if anybody is to be credited for our inability to escape the Victorians other than the Victorians themselves, it is the modernists. Even that most modernist of poems, T. S. Eliot's *The Waste Land* (1922), in its individualism and quotational fragmentation owes much to Robert Browning's use of monologue to depict characters dramatic and tragi-comic in the face of their own obtuseness and abstraction. For an era so determined to be post-Victorian (just as we too are doggedly insistent on our post-modernism), the wealth of demystifying anecdote about nineteenth-century precursors and ludic debunking of Victorian reputations was matched by an equally persistent desire to name, and so gain leverage upon, what modernism most opposed. Thus the first use of the term "neo-Victorian" is found in Arnold Bennett's *These Twain* in 1916 (ch. 8); the Edwardian Bennett was of course an ambivalent post-Victorian figure, as Woolf's modernist manifesto "Mr Bennett and Mrs Brown" (1923) attests. And it was Ezra Pound (renowned for the modernist catchphrase "Make It New") who coined the term "Victoriana" in 1918 (Mitchell 1).

Modernist angst about Victorian forebears slips between homage and hostility. Strachey's opening comment in *Eminent Victorians* that "[t]he history of the Victorian Age will never be written: we know too much about it" (vii) should not be read as defeatism. That this disclaimer is followed by the assertion that "I have attempted, through the medium of biography, to present some Victorian visions to the modern eye" (vii) is revealing: "some visions" relativizes the project of writing "*the* history" (our emphasis); what Strachey and other modernists were illuminating is the impossibility of producing anything other than multiple rather than singular or definitive stories and visions of the Victorian period.

This state of affairs has not changed in the last hundred years. What has changed is the valence we have come to attach to it. Plurality of vision is vital to neo-Victorianism: a term that, in its broadest sense, denotes post-Victorian culture's creative return to, or engagement with, the Victorian. Neo-Victorianism operates through many different genres, most commonly but by no means exclusively fiction and film. Although in our own work, drawing on Linda Hutcheon's concept of "historiographic metafiction" (105–23), we advocate restricting the definition of neo-Victorianism to embrace works that self-consciously play at a metatextual or metahistorical level with the Victorians (Heilmann and Llewellyn 2010: 4), in practice the term is more generally applied to a great variety of contemporary cultural modes. What become notable here are the blurred demarcation lines between popular and "high" cultures of neo-Victorianism: while steampunk (see Bowser and Croxall) pertains to the former, and A. S. Byatt's Booker-Prize-winning *Possession: A Romance* (1990), with its complex web of literary quotation and pastiche, courts the latter, TV and film adaptations of Victorian classics and neo-Victorian bestsellers like Waters's novels bridge the categories. Another slippage is that between the nineteenth century and the Victorian: to what extent is a historical novel set predominantly in the pre-Victorian period (Barbara Chase-Riboud's *Hottentot Venus*, 2003) or the early twentieth century (Adhaf Soueif's *The Map of Love*, 1999), to be considered neo-"Victorian"? And how geographically specific is the denominator "Victorian" in its neo-historical format? Can European texts which play with nation-specific histories, or North American neo-slave narratives, though set in the nineteenth century, be included in the category? These questions reflect ongoing debates in neo-Victorian studies (Ho; Heilmann and Llewellyn 2013).

For our purposes here, the concept and genre will be tightly defined in terms of the texts and acts that continue to re-vision and re-engage with the Victorian past in self-analytic ways. Yet we must acknowledge that neo-Victorianism, as a broader cultural motif blurring the boundaries between historical fiction and nineteenth-century fact and drawing inspiration from mediated versions of Victoriana, is very much an evolving framework. Frequently such mediations draw not on nineteenth-century sources but on critical interpretations of the period, with one adaptation often speaking to (and from) another adaptation, rather than solely the original text (see Mike Newell's 2012 and the BBC's 2011 *Great Expectations*).

Adaptations of Victorian texts have long provided an accessible means of engagement with nineteenth-century fiction and culture. Among the first radio broadcasts with a period angle was an adaptation of *A Christmas Carol* which, following a first broadcast in 1925, was repeated regularly thereafter (Heilmann and Llewellyn 2010: 215–16). From black-and-white David Lean adaptations of Dickens in the 1940s through to big budget serializations by the BBC and others since the late 1960s, the Victorians have served as a steady source of inspiration for film makers and screenwriters. That the canon used for adaptation remained for a considerable time rather exclusive has been redressed in recent years by, to take just one example, the TV versions of Elizabeth Gaskell's *Cranford* (1851) and Flora Thompson's *Lark Rise to Candleford* (1945) that segued seamlessly in Sunday night viewing schedules at year's end 2007–8. Theater too has, since the post-Angry Young Man days of the 1950s and 1960s, shown a marked fascination for the potential of Victorian adaptation and Victorian modes of understanding the dramatic arts through forms of adaptive practice (Poore). Beyond adaptation, though, theater and poetry have been relatively underplayed in neo-Victorianism, albeit with notable exceptions like Anthony Thwaite's *Victorian Voices* (1980) and Ruth Padel's *Darwin: A Life in Poems* (2009). These more conventional types of adaptation have been complemented by new and alternative forms of fiction, such as the cult classics of Alan Moore, whose graphic novels, including *From Hell* (1991–6) and *The League of Extraordinary Gentlemen* (1999–), have entered the neo-Victorian subversive mainstream. Connected to Moore's opus is the steampunk movement, which kits out modern technology with a fancy-dress version of Victorian lacquering. There is also a flourishing trade in board games and narrative-based computer games that draw on the Victorians for inspiration, text, and plot.

How much do we need to know about the Victorians to gain a satisfactory sense of the intertextual contexts of their explication? This concern has been embedded in neo-Victorian practice from an early stage. Marghanita Laski's under-appreciated *The Victorian Chaise-Longue* (1953), one of the key post-war re-engagements with the Victorian, subtly draws on Charlotte Perkins Gilman's first-wave-feminist Gothic "The Yellow Wallpaper" (1892) to raise important questions about epistemological nuances involved in acts of cultural appropriation. In Laski's novella Melanie, a 1950s wife and young mother who is recovering from tuberculosis (not the hysteria and postnatal rebellion of Gilman's narrator), follows her doctor's advice to take a rest on the Victorian chaise-longue whose purchase mysteriously coincided with the onset of her illness, only to find herself transported back to her 1860s alter ego, Milly. The text responds to Gilman's story by exploring the claustrophobic domestic confinement of women by medical dictate, the Victorian rest-cure treatment which precipitates the narrator's mental breakdown in the original text being replaced in Laski's narrative by the imposition of locked windows in an unventilated sickroom, a metaphorical and literal act of suffocation. At the start of her time-travel predicament, before she realizes the gravity of her entrapment in a new physicality, Melanie begins to find the strange world of Victorian gossip and everyday life an experience more alien than she has formerly imagined. As she sits talking to two female guests who have called for tea in Milly's Victorian home, she ponders how very uninteresting and humdrum the heritage of the lived past (as opposed to its representation in historical narrative) is when one is part of it:

> Their conversation should have been significant, but it was only boring. It was obvious to Melanie that it was not from this drone of timeless platitudes that the one clue would shine in unmistakable illumination . . . They should say something I can remember afterwards, she thought in almost amusement, almost annoyance. Instead of talking about these silly women and the weather and the bazaar, they should speak of Queen Victoria and Florence Nightingale and – But what *should* they be talking about? she asked herself. What *did* happen in 1864? Not the Exhibition, of course, and the Crimea must be over. Is the Prince Consort dead? Who is the Prime Minister? . . . It is I who should know these things . . . I know what the Victorian age was like, of course I do, except that being here, it isn't like that at all. It's just like now. (57)

In highlighting the ambiguities around what we know of the Victorians, and how little that really amounts to, Laski offsets nostalgia for the period with the "bits" of history we do know through the documented, the eventful, and the key-dates approach to historical knowledge. To know the Victorians, to "know what the Victorian age was like," do we have to have an understanding of what happened in 1864 as well as 1851?

Laski's text is also interesting for its emphasis – ordinarily absent from Woolf and the modernists – on the physical legacies of Victorian culture, the materialist and object-centered understanding of their influence. The central item in Laski's book is the chaise-longue, which provides both the literal and the metaphorical seat of knowledge and understanding in the text. In this we might perceive the beginnings of a material turn in engagements with the Victorian past. It was after the mid-1940s that private estates and country houses, which had struggled financially since the nineteenth century, began to come in large numbers into public ownership, largely through the auspices of the National Trust (itself a late-Victorian institution established in 1894). But this transference of so many grand estates into public ownership as an act of high-cultural preservation ran parallel to widespread concerns about the increasing dilapidation of social housing for the post-war masses (Poore 34–8, 169–73).

The physical presence of the nineteenth century in the very fabric of the post-war United Kingdom induced renewed attentiveness to the textual and archival remains of the Victorians too. Part of this arose from the traumas of war itself: in returning to a landscape scarred by modernity and its fighting machines, the post-war generation was caught between the insecurities of the present and nostalgia for a pre-war period (wrongly yet widely) associated with stability and general affluence. New biographies of key Victorian figures (often male) coincided with the birth of Victorian studies as a discipline (the journal *Victorian Studies* began publishing in 1956) and was accompanied by a new public sense of the need to preserve the national architectural heritage (the Victorian Society was founded in 1958 with the aim to save and restore Victorian and Edwardian buildings). The BBC's *Listener* magazine even identified as neo-Victorian the poet John Betjeman and others who were battling for legal rights to protect historic buildings of the nineteenth century: "The neo-Victorian Age is upon us. The Law Courts have become a shrine for the Betjemanites" (June 11, 1959, 1031–2). Campaigns to revitalize public interest in the Victorians and their legacy were thus matched by their newly recovered appeal within literary, artistic, and other cultural circles. This included, of course, thinking about how the Victorian literary heritage did and did not speak to a twentieth-century audience. But it also gave a refreshed impetus to the idea that even previously silenced Victorian voices could now find expression, or could at least be channeled afresh to speak to a contemporary readership newly receptive to such ideas in the late 1950s and 1960s.

Predating this reinvigorated taste for the Victorian age, the modernist writer Jean Rhys's *Wide Sargasso Sea* (1966) was a landmark work in initiating a new consciousness about the possibilities of re-visioning nineteenth-century cultural *Ur*-texts. Rhys's prequel to Charlotte Brontë's *Jane Eyre* (1847) was not so much about deposing the

Victorian classic as about articulating perspectives that were textually marginalized and yet imaginatively central to the original text. In giving a voice to Rochester's first wife, the silenced Creole Bertha Mason, Rhys was able to harness key issues that are elided in *Jane Eyre*, by adding to rather than undermining Brontë's narrative. A critique of first-wave feminism's neglect of the ethnically "Other" woman at a time of emerging second-wave feminist activism, the novel presents a challenge to both Victorian and contemporary racial politics and brings into play significant postcolonial viewpoints, but it does not seek to obliterate the context of an earlier narrative form and its contextual limitations. In effect, Rhys's text served as a model for later writers in thinking about ways of reading – and rewriting – Victorian texts: to fill spaces, to interject interpretation, to insert clues but not to resolve the mystery itself. In his provocatively titled *The Real David Copperfield* (1933) Robert Graves had earlier tackled Dickens's work in a similar manner, albeit with different results. Graves's novel offers a condensed version of Dickens's text, placed into a more modern, and more explicit, dynamic of sex/gender relations in the context of class aspiration and betrayal: a reflection of interwar social and sexual transformation, the adaptation served as a corrective to the Victorian novel.

While Rhys and Graves took a single text as a point of entry, other authors sought to respond more broadly to Victorian themes and narrative modes. Like *Wide Sargasso Sea*, John Fowles's *The French Lieutenant's Woman* (1969) was concerned with questions of gender, the double sexual standard, and the hypocrisy of Victorian social codes. A cornerstone of neo-Victorian fiction, Fowles's work tapped into the wider cultural rediscovery of late-Victorian and Edwardian narratives. The novel followed on closely from the BBC's 1967 TV serialization of John Galsworthy's *The Forsyte Saga* (1922). Interplay of intergenerational dynamics within a single dynasty made more general social and political points for a society newly emerging from the liberation of the early 1960s. (Galsworthy himself, like Bennett, was an early adopter of the term "neo-Victorian," in his 1929 Preface to *Modern Comedy*.) The *Lady Chatterley* trial in 1960, the arrival of the Beatles in the same year, and the conspicuous factoid that, as Philip Larkin would later put it, "sexual intercourse began / In nineteen sixty-three" ("Annus Mirabilis"), provided contexts for revisiting earlier psychological dramas of domestic turmoil through a reassessment of Victorian social realism, just as they acted as a spur to more contemporary approaches in the theater and the TV work of writers like Arnold Wesker and Harold Pinter. Indeed, audiences saw both worlds colliding in Pinter's screenplays of *The French Lieutenant's Woman* (1981) and L. P. Hartley's novel about a cross-class relationship in 1900, *The Go-Between*, published the same year as Laski's novella and filmed in 1970.

The novelty of *The French Lieutenant's Woman* consisted in Fowles's juxtaposition of Victorian and neo-Victorian voices through playful use of the figure of the unreliable omniscient narrator, a technique which has since been adopted by other writers in the genre (see Michel Faber's *The Crimson Petal and the White*, 2002). Fowles's adaptation of William Makepeace Thackeray's trope, in *Vanity Fair* (1847–8), of the showmaster manipulating puppets to bedazzle and at the same time enlighten his audience includes the knowing wink towards the fictionality of his characters' lives at a moment of high tension: "Had they but been able to see into the future! For Ernestina was to outlive all her generation. She was born in 1846. And she died on the day that Hitler invaded Poland" (28). Like Thackeray, Fowles is engaged in constructing a fictional world with believable characters while simultaneously revealing them as figments of his imagination, thus calling into question the classic realist form itself.

Fowles's play with narrative convention is also indebted to George Eliot, whose mock-resistance in *Middlemarch* (1871–2), itself an historical novel, to her authorial role as interlocutor between characters and readers arises when her narrator protests at having "so much to do" in keeping the narrative on track that no time can be spared for an old-fashioned "armchair . . . chat" with readers on "that tempting range of relevancies called the universe" (ch. 15). It is no coincidence that this same chapter's opening section is concerned with literature as history and that the narrator's sense of belatedness is echoed in neo-Victorian fiction. Eliot's "belated historians" are the writers but also the readers of the historical text. In this sense, Eliotian historical fiction is an important precursor to Fowles's in problematizing the fictional fabric of the realist web and the questions it poses about the historian-novelist's role. What emerges from these instances is a recognition of the proximity of "Victorian" to "postmodern" narrative techniques in contemporary writers' concern with inheritance, influence, and literary history. For just as Fowles embeds the illusory origins of his characters in a reading (and a knowledge of his readers' prior reading) of Victorian novels, so Eliot harks back to Fielding's fiction in her narrator's authorial statement. To know the truth about history, Eliot seems to suggest, one must understand all the other matters that are of concern to the writer in the making of it. Part of these other matters is the "belatedness" of fiction writing itself, the debts owed and the allegiances inherited from authors that have gone before. This play with allusion is also present in *The French Lieutenant's Woman* in the introduction of a London servant called Sam, who is, pointedly, not cast as a replica of the Dickensian character:

> Of course to us any Cockney servant called Sam evokes immediately the immortal Weller, and it was certainly from that background that this Sam had emerged. But thirty years had passed since *Pickwick Papers* first coruscated into the world. Sam's love of the equine was not really very deep. He was more like some modern working-class man who thinks a keen knowledge of cars a sign of his social progress. He even knew of Sam Weller, not from the book, but from a stage version of it; and knew the times had changed. (42–3)

The French Lieutenant's Woman demonstrates the complex and complementary ways in which a Victorian fictional past and a conception of the Victorian in the 1960s present can be mediated. While teasing out and interrogating the boundaries between fiction and factual representation, Fowles also toys with his readerly and writerly ambitions for the fiction itself. Such playfulness carries echoes of Woolf but is of a different order, engaging as it does with Roland Barthes's important distinction, in *The Pleasure of the Text* (1973), between the readerly text (*"texte lisible"*), where pleasure is derived from a reading that does not impact on the reader's subjectivity, and the writerly text (*"texte scriptible"*), where pleasure (*"jouissance,"* v) resides in a writing process that explodes conventions of genre and subjectivity (see Ungar). Both modes are important for neo-Victorian engagements with precursor texts.

The allusiveness of much neo-Victorian fiction (and the trait which we contend distinguishes it from historical fiction set in the Victorian period) serves partly to test our loyalty to and understanding of a heritage we associate with linearity and stability. The technique is deployed in other narratives that have entered the neo-Victorian canon, in particular the work of Byatt, which pays homage to the language of the Victorians. Aspects of this strategy can be found in her recent (rather neo-Edwardian than neo-Victorian) novel *The Children's Book* (2009); but it is in *Possession* that the experimentation with pastiche, reader/writer relationships, and tangible and intangible Victorian lineages has greatest hold. Byatt's novel resembles Fowles's in its play with our expectation of the narrative tying up of loose ends that are promptly undone in the final chapter, which reveals to us what the characters never discover, while leaving the afterlife of the contemporary relationship open to speculation. *Possession's* rewriting of literary lives is a common feature of neo-Victorian fiction. Factual writers and their fictional creations take center stage in many texts catering to what Cora Kaplan calls our "biographilia" (37–84). Recent examples include re-imaginings of Henry James (David Lodge's *Author! Author!* and Colm Toibin's *The Master*, both 2004) and adaptations of his best-known text, "The Turn of the Screw" (A. N. Wilson's *A Jealous Ghost*, 2005, and John Harding's *Florence & Giles*, 2010). The work and life of Dickens has also received neo-Victorian attention (Peter Carey's *Jack Maggs*, 1997; Gaynor Arnold's *Girl in a Blue Dress*, 2008; Matthew Pearl's *The Last Dickens*, 2009; Ronald Frame's *Havisham*, 2012).

While *The French Lieutenant's Woman* and *Possession* inaugurated a trend of self-consciously neo-Victorian works, cultural criticism during the late twentieth century placed nostalgia at the heart of neo-Victorianism. Robert Hewison's *The Heritage Industry* (1987) was among a number of critical studies in the late 1980s to interrogate the cultural fascination with all things Victorian, including the United Kingdom's Heritage Act (1983). Hewison's point was that immortalizing the past had the effect of publicly and intellectually stymieing contemporary creative culture. The heritagization of cultural forms and narratives thus became a site of tension, and Byatt's romanticized homage cannot but be read as a rejoinder to the claims of Hewison while at the same time endorsing his anxieties about the slipperiness of institutionally authorized versions of collective memory.

The Irish author Brian Moore's *The Great Victorian Collection* (1975) offers a powerful commentary on such encounters by satirizing the burgeoning heritage industry and its claim to authenticity in reproduction, as found in theme parks. Moore's novel is a Victorian version of Walt Disney World's Magic Kingdom turned nightmare, as his hapless Canadian protagonist, Associate Professor of History Anthony Maloney, wakes in a Californian motel to discover in the parking lot a great exhibition of Victorian artifacts – or what Robert Graves and Alan Hodge in *The Long Weekend* (1940: 352) termed "the neo-Victorian knick-knack collecting habit." At first believed to be a hoax, the exhibition is subsequently authenticated as containing "original" rather than counterfeited artifacts, a discovery which prompts a quasi-religious cult around Maloney and his powers to conjure up historical "reality," including the memorable headline "FURTHER EXAMINATION BY EXPERTS REVEALS GREAT VICTO-RIAN COLLECTION TO BE A 'SECULAR MIRACLE' " (86). Moore's parody of our desire for authenticity and modern secular society's sanctification of the Victorians made an important point at a time when Victorian influences seemed in decline as a result of 1960s liberation from "Victorian values" of prudery, sexual repression, and patriarchal rule; in reality the post-sixties backlash led to a reaffirmation of nineteenth-century modes of living and being. Indeed, Moore's concept of secular gods carries a certain loaded reality: in a post-secular age, the Victorians' struggles with faith, science, and modernity not only represented a model of the angst faced by twentieth-century generations but even more importantly reinforced awareness that modern people lived in a world shaped in the Victorians' image. If not the gods of the twentieth century, the Victorians were nevertheless the creators of the whole fabric in which contemporary society operated.

Drawing too close connections between the Victorians and the present, however, can lead to a form of madness. In Moore's novel, Maloney kills himself rather than face the impossibility of either reviving the past from his imaginings or protecting the now windswept and gradually decaying objects of his collection. The novel ends with an extract from Maloney's psychiatrist Dr Spector's "report in the *Journal of Parapsychology*, Vol. XX, No. V," in which that auspiciously named observer com-ments that

> Later, as is often the case in such matters, fewer and fewer people seemed to believe in the veracity of Maloney's account of the circumstances of the Collection's creation. Nevertheless, as our researches have shown, there seems no reason to doubt that this Collection, a duality which exactly reproduces the originals it commemorates, will continue to exist as a minor marvel in Carmel-by-the-Sea, California. The extent to which it will outlive the man who created it, or its interest to succeeding generations, is, of course, beyond the range of our predictions. (202–3)

From a contemporary UK perspective, with a heritage landscape that now includes Dickens World in a Kent warehouse and a nation that has just experienced the 2012 Dickens bicentenary alongside Olympics and Diamond Jubilee celebrations, it is a fair probability that those "succeeding generations" will continue to seek com-memorations wherever possible.

Yet such commemorative acts are also forms of exclusion. Memory – individual or cultural – is selectively made. Kate Mitchell highlights that acts of memorialization and commemoration are invariably ambiguous, not least for the reasons explored by Fowles and Byatt in terms of the always already fragmented evidence for historical "afterimages." If we draw on neo-Victorian fictions as "memory texts" (3), we have to be alert to the danger of imposing a neo-Victorian claim to authenticity and realism at a perilous boundary between historicism and fiction. When memory elects certain affinities with the past and consciously advances them in acts of commemoration, it inevitably omits other affinities. The roots of this problem lie in the unresolved question of where neo-Victorianism stands in relation to Victorian studies, heritage studies, contemporary literary studies, cultural studies, and historical studies. Rewriting too, of course, constitutes a form of commemoration that reinscribes narrative normativity for those readers who may not recognize instances of deviation or divergence from the original text. To know and understand a rewriting, we must have knowledge of the original; to read the palimpsest, we must be aware that there are texts beneath the surface of the work we are studying.

Byatt's palimpsestic fiction is a case in point since it privileges the literary for its own sake. Later writers, especially Patricia Duncker (*James Miranda Barry*, 1999), Michele Roberts (*In the Red Kitchen*, 1990), and Sarah Waters, have followed a different line in interrogating Victorian assumptions and our preconceptions about them. Grounded in historical research, and owing not a little to the fact that writers like Waters are of a generation that has studied literature at university through the lens of critical theory, many texts exploit the permeability of narratives that are part of the mainstream knowledge of Victorian literary culture while at the same time drawing on more subversive or counter-cultural work that has entered the Victorian archive. Frequently such novels problematize the (im)possibility of writing historical fiction by deploying the metatextual techniques of literature and history. By calling into question issues of "legitimate" storytelling, and probing the ownership of voice and document in relation to narrative authority and intradiegetic authorial permission, each part of Waters's trilogy of textual encounters with the Victorian is premised on the idea of re-enchantment. In making explicit the narrative trick or twist, Waters offers us liberty to accept that all narratives are both fact and fiction, truth and lies.

Such texts illuminate the problem identified in Woolf's earlier neo-Victorian work: that we know the Victorians as much through the documentation of the period, including its literature, as through other means. Neo-Victorian writers and their publishers thus engage in a dual process of fictionalization. Fictional works can be publicized as "authentic copies": "the novel Dickens would have written were he publishing today" constitutes blurb code for a Victorian historical romp or picaresque. At the same time, the claim to an "authentic" recreation of the Victorian is suspect even within the parameters of realism. That this makes the authors of Victorian fiction fair game for reinvention proves more problematic, and blurs the boundaries between an ethics of revision and an ethics of re-encounter. Fiction remodeled and facts redesigned do not share an identical *modus operandi*.

This standoff between the factual and the fictional lies, ultimately, at the core of neo-Victorianism. Embedding in literary texts the documentary "evidence" with which to access the past, while composing them with contemporary concerns and cultural contexts in mind, the neo-Victorian writer simultaneously summons up those who are truly dead because they once just as truly lived, and asserts an individual perspective on the historical phantoms thus resurrected in imagination. Such tensions have existed since the Victorian period itself, and have always included the clash between historicism and literary or cultural interpretation. The historian Miles Taylor argues that

> [W]ithin two decades of the death of Victoria a chasm had opened up between Victorian and post-Victorian sensibilities, which went well beyond the death of one monarch and the accession of her son. Eighty or so years later we still live with the consequences of this remarkable transformation. What we know and understand as the Victorian age is not an exhibit left in a glass case in 1901. On the contrary, the Victorians have been made and remade throughout the twentieth century, as successive generations have used the Victorian past to locate themselves in the present. (1–2)

The "transformation," remarkable or otherwise, inheres in the longevity of a legacy that did not end with the demise of Victoria herself but instead has continually reinvented itself – or, rather, has continually been reinvented. In acknowledging that "[t]he Victorians are more ubiquitous than ever" (9), Taylor identifies our need to believe in them and our need to believe in what they mean to us. If the "Victorians invented many things – including themselves," then this "act of creation" (3) also ensured their constant resurrection. Viewing the Victorians, seeing their shadow even if only in outline, is something that dominates our sense of the present; it is what Simon Joyce calls "the disease of looking backwards" (2). The symptoms, rather than lay us low, encourage us to rebel through reinvention. But they do prompt us to reflect on the fact that we are also a Victorian invention.

Yet obsession with the Victorian possibilities of reinvention (even, one might argue, in criticism) is double-edged. In *Victoriana* Kaplan talks of "the pleasures and dangers evoked by imitation or reference to the narrative forms, individual histories and systems of belief of nineteenth-century Britain" (6). These "pleasures and dangers" reflect the monstrous attraction and repulsion still exerted by the Victorian living dead in our contemporary world. Monsters are, after all, the representation of our own anxieties, the projections of both desire and fear. Given the Victorian period's fascination with its own forms of death, mourning, and rebirth through religious or indeed archaeological resurrection, the spectral return of that past has come to dominate our own version of the lives we lead now. Neo-Victorianism, as Rosario Arias and Patricia Pulham suggest, invokes the Victorian "as a form of revenant, a ghostly visitor from the past that infiltrates our present" (xv–xvi). Victoriana are all around us: partly this is a matter of choice, expressed in modes of commemoration that we initiate through imaginative acts or celebrate and critique through scholarly discourses like this chapter and this book. But there is also the larger landscape, among whose features are the fabric of UK and Commonwealth cities, the influence of bureaucratic modes of regulation and global markets, principles of politics, civic values, and ethics, the ambivalence aroused by science and technology. In some of these we see the Victorians' own concern to make things that would last, that would defeat the constraints of chronology, but in others we see our more recent forebears and our twentieth-century history stepping forward to preserve something older, more concrete than the present yet less tangible than the fabric of the buildings themselves. Such dynamics become more complex when we attempt to extend encounters onto a global scale (Heilmann and Llewellyn 2013), but postcolonial critique in neo-Victorianism is an increasing area of analysis (Ho) alongside a variety of approaches that include postmodernism (Gutleben; Kucich and Sadoff; Munford and Young), gender (King), Gothic, spectrality, and ventriloquism (Arias and Pulham; Kohlke and Gutleben 2012; Davies), science and religion (Glendenning), trauma studies (Kohlke and Gutleben 2010), visual material culture (Boehm-Schnitker and Gruss), family relationships (Kohlke and Gutleben 2011), and childhood studies (Morey and Nelson). What the textual illustrations we have used in this essay and also the broader neo-Victorian examples all around us aim to achieve is to highlight the multiplex ways in which we might view our ongoing encounter with the Victorians in the temporal mirror. Not only do we see what we want to see, but we are complicit in making the mirror image trick us in the process. Indeed, as with the vampire of whom Jonathan Harker cannot catch sight in a looking glass that only and ever reflects his own image, it is most likely the case that what we glimpse in the Victorian mirror is our own longing to recapture the past. Victoria herself, like Dracula, isn't there.

See also 1897; Passing On; Spectacle; Historiography

References and Further Reading

Arias, R., and P. Pulham (eds) (2010) *Haunting and Spectrality in Neo-Victorian Fiction: Possessing the Past*. Basingstoke: Palgrave Macmillan.

Barthes, R. (1975) *The Pleasure of the Text*, trans. R. Miller. Oxford: Blackwell.

Birch, D. (2008) *Our Victorian Education*. Oxford: Blackwell.

Boehm-Schnitker, N., and S. Gruss (eds) (2011) *Spectacles and Things: Visual and Material and/in Neo-Victorianism*, special issue of *Neo-Victorian Studies*, 4: 2.

Bowser, R. A., and B. Croxall (eds) (2010) *Steampunk, Science and (Neo)Victorian Technologies*, special issue of *Neo-Victorian Studies*, 3: 1.

Davies, H. (2012) *Gender and Ventriloquism in Victorian and Neo-Victorian Fiction: Passionate Puppets*. Basingstoke: Palgrave Macmillan.

Fowles, J. (2004) *The French Lieutenant's Woman*. London: Vintage [1969].

Glendenning, J. (2013) *Science and Religion in Neo-Victorian Novels*. London: Routledge.

Graves, R., and A. Hodge (1940) *The Long Weekend: A Social History of Great Britain 1918–1939*. London: Faber and Faber.

Gutleben, C. (2001) *Nostalgic Postmodernism: The Victorian Tradition and the Contemporary British Novel*. Amsterdam: Rodopi.

Heilmann, A., and M. Llewellyn (2010) *Neo-Victorianism: The Victorians in the Twenty-First Century, 1999–2009*. Basingstoke: Palgrave Macmillan.

——(2013) "The Victorians Now: Global Reflections on Neo-Victorianism." *Critical Quarterly* 55: 1, 24–42.

Hewison, R. (1987) *The Heritage Industry: Britain in a Climate of Decline*. London: Methuen.

Hewitt, M. (2006) "Why the Notion of Victorian Britain *Does* Make Sense." *Victorian Studies* 48: 3, 395–438.

Ho, E. (2012) *Neo-Victorianism and the Memory of Empire*. London: Continuum.

Hutcheon, L. (1989) *The Poetics of Postmodernism*. London: Routledge.

Joyce, S. (2007) *The Victorians in the Rearview Mirror*. Athens: Ohio University Press.

Kaplan, C. (2007) *Victoriana: Histories, Fictions, Criticism*. Edinburgh: Edinburgh University Press.

King, J. (2005) *The Victorian Woman Question in Contemporary Fiction*. Basingstoke: Palgrave Macmillan.

Kohlke, M.-L., and C. Gutleben (eds) (2010) *Neo-Victorian Tropes of Trauma*. Amsterdam: Rodopi.

——(eds) (2011) *Neo-Victorian Families*. Amsterdam: Rodopi.

——(eds) (2012) *Neo-Victorian Gothic*. Amsterdam: Rodopi.

Kucich, J., and D. F. Sadoff (eds) (2000) *Victorian Afterlife: Postmodern Culture Rewrites the Nineteenth Century*. Minneapolis: University of Minnesota Press.

Laski, M. (1999) *The Victorian Chaise-Longue*. London: Persephone [1953].

Mitchell, K. (2010) *History and Cultural Memory in Neo-Victorian Fiction: Victorian Afterimages*. Basingstoke: Palgrave Macmillan.

Moore, B. (1988) *The Great Victorian Collection*. London: Palladin [1975].

Morey, A., and C. Nelson (eds) (2012) *The Child in Neo-Victorian Arts and Discourse*, special issue of *Neo-Victorian Studies*, 5: 1.

Munford, R., and P. Young (eds) (2009) *Engaging the Victorians*, special issue of *LIT: Literature Interpretation Theory*, 20: 1 & 2.

Poore, B. (2012) *Heritage, Nostalgia and Modern British Theatre: Staging the Victorians*. Basingstoke: Palgrave Macmillan.

Sadoff, D. F. (2010) *Victorian Vogue: British Novels on Screen*. Minneapolis: University of Minnesota Press.

Strachey, L. (1929) *Eminent Victorians*. London: Chatto and Windus [1918].

Ungar, S. (1998) "Barthes, Roland." In *Encyclopedia of Contemporary French Culture*, ed. A. Hughes, and K. Reader. London: Routledge.

Taylor, M., and M. Woolf (eds) (2004) *The Victorians Since 1901: Histories, Representations and Revisions*. Manchester: Manchester University Press.

Index of Works Cited

A New Companion to Victorian Literature and Culture, First Edition. Edited by Herbert F. Tucker.
© 2014 John Wiley & Sons, Ltd. Published 2014 by John Wiley & Sons, Ltd.

General Subject Index

Page references in **bold**/*italics* indicate an entire chapter.

A New Companion to Victorian Literature and Culture, First Edition. Edited by Herbert F. Tucker.
© 2014 John Wiley & Sons, Ltd. Published 2014 by John Wiley & Sons, Ltd.